also by america's test kitchen

The Complete Plant-Based Cookbook

Meat Illustrated

Cooking for One

How Can It Be Gluten Free Cookbook Collection

The Complete Summer Cookbook

Bowls

Vegetables Illustrated

The Side Dish Bible

Foolproof Fish

100 Techniques

Easy Everyday Keto

Everything Chocolate

The Perfect Pie

How to Cocktail

Spiced

The Ultimate Burger

The New Essentials Cookbook

Dinner Illustrated

America's Test Kitchen Menu Cookbook

Cook's Illustrated Revolutionary Recipes

Tasting Italy: A Culinary Journey

Cooking at Home with Bridget and Julia

The Complete Mediterranean Cookbook

The Complete Diabetes Cookbook

The Complete Slow Cooker

The Complete Make-Ahead Cookbook

The Complete Vegetarian Cookbook

The Complete Cooking for Two Cookbook

Just Add Sauce

How to Braise Everything

How to Roast Everything

Nutritious Delicious

What Good Cooks Know

Cook's Science

The Science of Good Cooking

The Perfect Cake

The Perfect Cookie

Bread Illustrated

Master of the Grill

Kitchen Smarts

Kitchen Hacks

100 Recipes: The Absolute Best Ways to Make the True Essentials

The New Family Cookbook

The America's Test Kitchen Cooking School Cookbook

The Cook's Illustrated Baking Book

The Cook's Illustrated Cookbook

The Complete America's Test Kitchen TV Show Cookbook 2001–2021

The America's Test Kitchen Family Baking Book

America's Test Kitchen Twentieth Anniversary TV Show Cookbook

The Best of America's Test Kitchen (2007–2021 Editions)

Toaster Oven Perfection

Mediterranean Instant Pot

Cook It in Your Dutch Oven

Vegan for Everybody

Sous Vide for Everybody

Air Fryer Perfection

Multicooker Perfection

Food Processor Perfection

Pressure Cooker Perfection

Instant Pot Ace Blender Cookbook

Naturally Sweet

Foolproof Preserving

Paleo Perfected

The Best Mexican Recipes

Slow Cooker Revolution Volume 2: The Easy-Prep Edition

Slow Cooker Revolution

The America's Test Kitchen D.I.Y. Cookbook

THE COOK'S ILLUSTRATED ALL-TIME BEST SERIES

All-Time Best Brunch

All-Time Best Dinners for Two

All-Time Best Sunday Suppers

All-Time Best Holiday Entertaining

All-Time Best Appetizers

All-Time Best Soups

COOK'S COUNTRY TITLES

Big Flavors from Italian America

One-Pan Wonders

Cook It in Cast Iron

Cook's Country Eats Local

The Complete Cook's Country TV Show Cookbook

FOR A FULL LISTING OF ALL OUR BOOKS

CooksIllustrated.com

AmericasTestKitchen.com

praise for america's test kitchen titles

"The book's depth, breadth, and practicality makes it a must-have for seafood lovers."
PUBLISHERS WEEKLY (STARRED REVIEW) ON *FOOLPROOF FISH*

"Another flawless entry in the America's Test Kitchen canon, *Bowls* guides readers of all culinary skill levels in composing one-bowl meals from a variety of cuisines."
BUZZFEED BOOKS ON *BOWLS*

"If there's room in the budget for one multicooker/Instant Pot cookbook, make it this one."
BOOKLIST ON *MULTICOOKER PERFECTION*

"This book upgrades slow cooking for discriminating, 21st-century palates—that is indeed revolutionary."
THE DALLAS MORNING NEWS ON *SLOW COOKER REVOLUTION*

"This book begins with a detailed buying guide, a critical summary of available sizes and attachments, and a list of clever food processor techniques. Easy and versatile dishes follow . . . Both new and veteran food processor owners will love this practical guide."
LIBRARY JOURNAL ON *FOOD PROCESSOR PERFECTION*

Selected as the Cookbook Award Winner of 2019 in the Health and Special Diet Category
INTERNATIONAL ASSOCIATION OF CULINARY PROFESSIONALS (IACP) ON *THE COMPLETE DIABETES COOKBOOK*

"*The Perfect Cookie*. . . is, in a word, perfect. This is an important and substantial cookbook. . . . If you love cookies, but have been a tad shy to bake on your own, all your fears will be dissipated. This is one book you can use for years with magnificently happy results."
THE HUFFINGTON POST ON *THE PERFECT COOKIE*

"The book offers an impressive education for curious cake makers, new and experienced alike. A summation of 25 years of cake making at ATK, there are cakes for every taste."
THE WALL STREET JOURNAL ON *THE PERFECT CAKE*

"The sum total of exhaustive experimentation . . . anyone interested in gluten-free cookery simply shouldn't be without it."
NIGELLA LAWSON ON *THE HOW CAN IT BE GLUTEN-FREE COOKBOOK*

"If you're a home cook who loves long introductions that tell you why a dish works followed by lots of step-by-step hand holding, then you'll love *Vegetables Illustrated*."
THE WALL STREET JOURNAL ON *VEGETABLES ILLUSTRATED*

"True to its name, this smart and endlessly enlightening cookbook is about as definitive as it's possible to get in the modern vegetarian realm."
MEN'S JOURNAL ON *THE COMPLETE VEGETARIAN COOKBOOK*

"A one-volume kitchen seminar, addressing in one smart chapter after another the sometimes surprising whys behind a cook's best practices. . . . You get the myth, the theory, the science, and the proof, all rigorously interrogated as only America's Test Kitchen can do."
NPR ON *THE SCIENCE OF GOOD COOKING*

"The 21st-century *Fannie Farmer Cookbook* or *The Joy of Cooking*. If you had to have one cookbook and that's all you could have, this one would do it."
CBS SAN FRANCISCO ON *THE NEW FAMILY COOKBOOK*

"Some 2,500 photos walk readers through 600 painstakingly tested recipes, leaving little room for error."
ASSOCIATED PRESS ON *THE AMERICA'S TEST KITCHEN COOKING SCHOOL COOKBOOK*

"The go-to gift book for newlyweds, small families, or empty nesters."
ORLANDO SENTINEL ON *THE COMPLETE COOKING FOR TWO COOKBOOK*

"Some books impress by the sheer audacity of their ambition. Backed by the magazine's famed mission to test every recipe relentlessly until it is the best it can be, this nearly 900-page volume lands with an authoritative wallop."
CHICAGO TRIBUNE ON *THE COOK'S ILLUSTRATED COOKBOOK*

"It might become your 'cooking school,' the only book you'll need to make you a proficient cook, recipes included. . . . You can master the 100 techniques with the easy-to-understand instructions, then apply the skill with the recipes that follow."
THE LITCHFIELD COUNTY TIMES ON *100 TECHNIQUES*

the complete
ONE POT

400 Meals

SKILLET · SHEET PAN

INSTANT POT® · DUTCH OVEN + More

AMERICA'S TEST KITCHEN

Library of Congress Cataloging-in-Publication Data has been applied for.

ISBN 978-1-948703-34-5

America's Test Kitchen
21 Drydock Avenue, Boston, MA 02210

Manufactured in the United States of America

10 9 8 7 6 5 4 3 2 1

Distributed by Penguin Random House Publisher Services
Tel: 800.733.3000

Pictured on front cover **Turkey Meatballs with Coconut Rice, Bell Peppers, and Peas (page 105)**

Pictured on back cover **Clockwise from top left: Spiced Wild Rice and Coconut Soup (page 48), Coffee-Chili–Rubbed Steaks with Sweet Potatoes and Scallions (page 145), Prime Rib and Roasted Vegetables (page 180), Pork Pad Thai (page 334), Bouillabaisse (page 252), Hands-Off Spaghetti and Meatballs (page 316)**

Editorial Director, Books **Adam Kowit**

Executive Food Editor **Dan Zuccarello**

Deputy Food Editor **Stephanie Pixley**

Executive Managing Editor **Debra Hudak**

Senior Editors **Leah Colins, Joseph Gitter, Nicole Konstantinakos, Sara Mayer, and Russell Selander**

Associate Editors **Camila Chaparro and Lawman Johnson**

Test Cook **Sarah Ewald**

Assistant Editors **Tess Berger and Kelly Cormier**

Editorial Assistant **Emily Rahravan**

Design Director **Lindsey Timko Chandler**

Deputy Art Director **Allison Boales**

Photography Director **Julie Bozzo Cote**

Photography Producer **Meredith Mulcahy**

Senior Staff Photographers **Steve Klise and Daniel J. van Ackere**

Staff Photographer **Kevin White**

Additional Photography **Joseph Keller and Carl Tremblay**

Food Styling **Tara Busa, Catrine Kelty, Steve Klise, Chantal Lambeth, Ashley Moore, Marie Piraino, Elle Simone Scott, Kendra Smith, and Sally Staub**

Photoshoot Kitchen Team

    Photo Team and Special Events Managers **Allison Berkey**

    Lead Test Cook **Eric Haessler**

    Assistant Test Cooks **Hannah Fenton, Jacqueline Gochenouer, Gina McCreadie, and Christa West**

Senior Manager, Publishing Operations **Taylor Argenzio**

Imaging Manager **Lauren Robbins**

Production and Imaging Specialists **Tricia Neumyer, Dennis Noble, and Amanda Yong**

Copy Editor **Deri Reed**

Proofreader **Pat Jalbert-Levine**

Indexer **Elizabeth Parson**

Chief Creative Officer **Jack Bishop**

Executive Editorial Directors **Julia Collin Davison and Bridget Lancaster**

CONTENTS

WELCOME TO
AMERICA'S TEST KITCHEN

This book has been tested, written, and edited by the folks at America's Test Kitchen, where curious cooks become confident cooks. Located in Boston's Seaport District in the historic Innovation and Design Building, it features 15,000 square feet of kitchen space including multiple photography and video studios. It is the home of *Cook's Illustrated* magazine and *Cook's Country* magazine and is the workday destination for more than 60 test cooks, editors, and cookware specialists. Our mission is to empower and inspire confidence, community, and creativity in the kitchen.

We start the process of testing a recipe with a complete lack of preconceptions, which means that we accept no claim, no technique, and no recipe at face value. We simply assemble as many variations as possible, test a half-dozen of the most promising, and taste the results blind. We then construct our own recipe and continue to test it, varying ingredients, techniques, and cooking times until we reach a consensus. As we like to say in the test kitchen, "We make the mistakes so you don't have to." The result, we hope, is the best version of a particular recipe, but we realize that only you can be the final judge of our success (or failure). We use the same rigorous approach when we test equipment and taste ingredients.

All of this would not be possible without a belief that good cooking, much like good music, is based on a foundation of objective technique. Some people like spicy foods and others don't, but there is a right way to sauté, there is a best way to cook a pot roast, and there are measurable scientific principles involved in producing perfectly beaten, stable egg whites. Our ultimate goal is to investigate the fundamental principles of cooking to give you the techniques, tools, and ingredients you need to become a better cook. It is as simple as that.

To see what goes on behind the scenes at America's Test Kitchen, check out our social media channels for kitchen snapshots, exclusive content, video tips, and much more. You can watch us work (in our actual test kitchen) by tuning in to *America's Test Kitchen* or *Cook's Country* on public television or on our websites. Download our award-winning podcast *Proof*, which goes beyond recipes to solve food mysteries (AmericasTestKitchen.com/proof), or listen to test kitchen experts on public radio (SplendidTable.org) to hear insights that illuminate the truth about real home cooking. Want to hone your cooking skills or finally learn how to bake—with an America's Test Kitchen test cook? Enroll in one of our online cooking classes. And you can engage the next generation of home cooks with kid-tested recipes from America's Test Kitchen Kids.

Our community of home recipe testers provides valuable feedback on recipes under development by ensuring that they are foolproof. You can help us investigate the how and why behind successful recipes from your home kitchen. (Sign up at AmericasTestKitchen.com/recipe_testing.)

However you choose to visit us, we welcome you into our kitchen, where you can stand by our side as we test our way to the best recipes in America.

f facebook.com/AmericasTestKitchen
twitter.com/TestKitchen
youtube.com/AmericasTestKitchen
instagram.com/TestKitchen
pinterest.com/TestKitchen

AmericasTestKitchen.com
CooksIllustrated.com
CooksCountry.com
OnlineCookingSchool.com
AmericasTestKitchen.com/kids

GETTING STARTED

INTRODUCTION

Everyone can appreciate the appeal of a streamlined meal made using a single pot or pan. Practically speaking, using just one pot means quicker cleanup and a simpler, often faster route to dinner. Among the oldest cooking styles, one-pot recipes embody comfort, a communal meal shared together. We've long relished exploring the potential of such dishes, refining our techniques and welcoming a multitude of flavors to the table, and it's all on display here.

Soups and stews are just the start. When we want a dinner featuring the traditional main and sides, we trade the bubbling pot for a sheet pan or roasting pan, or enlist a skillet to pull double duty, turning out food in stages. Because our love of pasta and noodles runs deep, there's a whole chapter of options where they cook directly in their sauce. Another chapter makes the one-pot promise a reality for desserts—and not only do the recipes require just one baking vessel, but many need only one bowl. The collection also flips the lid on several one-pot cooking assumptions.

- **One-pot cooking isn't always slow.** Over 100 of the 400+ recipes can be made in 45 minutes or less.

- **The recipes don't need to serve an army.** While we include hundreds of recipes serving four or more, we've heard from fans seeking recipes with smaller serving sizes but all the same one-pot benefits. In response, we've included scaled-down flavor variations designed to serve two throughout the book.

- **You don't need to sacrifice flavor or texture.** Some one-pot recipes turn out lackluster meals for the sake of simplicity. This book shows how, with just a bit more attention to detail, you can build one-pot dishes with all the flavor and satisfying texture you'd expect from any good recipe.

In every instance, we select the right pot for the recipe to ensure great results, and you can browse recipes by their cooking vessel at the start of each chapter. We also adapted some of our favorite recipes to be especially flexible in our Cook Three Ways features, with choose-your-own pan options and ingredient substitutions.

POTS AND PLANS
SECRETS TO SUCCESSFUL ONE-POT COOKING

Creating a good one-pot meal is a bit like putting together the pieces of a puzzle. A successful recipe requires strategic positioning, careful timing, and the right ingredients to create a foolproof, balanced meal.

One-pot recipes should turn out a complete meal, whether it's a protein and a side, a hearty stew, a pasta dish, or a vegetarian meal. But unlike recipes where you can pull out an extra pan to make the side, turning out a full meal in one pot requires extra care and attention to ensure everything is completely cooked—and still hot—when the meal hits the table.

Good one-pot recipes aren't as simple as dumping all the ingredients in the pot at the same time and walking away. While that method is theoretically easy, it's a surefire way to end up with an unappealing mix of overcooked and undercooked ingredients.

Instead, we looked for outside-the-box ways to get the most out of our favorite everyday pots and pans, such as skillets and sheet pans, as well as some of our specialty pots and pans, such as slow cookers and electric pressure cookers. Along the way, we uncovered plenty of secrets for successful one-pot recipes, from staggering cook times and stacking ingredients to using accessories and selecting flavor-boosting ingredients.

Using our arsenal of foolproof recipes and the following tips, anyone can become a one-pot-cooking pro.

1 Arrange Elements for Even Cooking

2 Stack Ingredients

3 Transfer to the Oven

4 Scale Recipes Up or Down

5 Cook Ingredients in Stages

6 Build Flavor in Layers

1 ARRANGE ELEMENTS FOR EVEN COOKING

Because each cooking vessel has its own unique size and shape, the placement of ingredients is essential for even cooking.

- **Don't overcrowd the pot (or pan)**
Unless the dish is a stew or a braise that's cooked in liquid, each ingredient needs enough space around it to cook through—especially when browning is important. If cooking happens on a large pan such as a sheet pan, leave enough space around everything for air to circulate. When using smaller pots and pans such as a skillet, staggering the cook times (see page 12) can help prevent overcrowding.

- **Pay attention to which area of the pan is the hottest** On the stovetop, placing longer-cooking ingredients closer to the heat source—typically in the center of a skillet—can help them to cook through more quickly. We use this method when making Teriyaki Stir-Fried Beef with Green Beans and Shiitakes (page 149). Pushing the vegetables to the side before adding the beef to the center of the skillet gave the meat direct access to the heat, allowing it to cook through without overcooking the vegetables. In the oven, placing elements that need more cooking around the edges of the pan can better expose them to the oven's heat, while the center

of the pan will be more protected. To make Chicken Kebabs with Potatoes and Green Beans (page 97), we kept the hearty potatoes on the outside of the sheet pan where they could brown and crisp, but placed the green beans in the center to prevent overcooking.

- **Surround proteins in liquid in the slow cooker or pressure cooker**
These unique cooking environments use heat, moisture, and steam to cook food from all sides. To make Chicken with Spiced Freekeh, Cilantro, and Preserved Lemon (page 112) in the Instant Pot, we nestled the chicken into a mixture of broth and freekeh to cook the chicken through.

OUR FAVORITE SHEET PAN

The sheet pan is the unsung hero of kitchen equipment; there is no limit to what this pan can do, so long as it has a few critical features. Our favorite is the **Nordic Ware Baker's Half Sheet**. This pan measures 18 by 13 inches, boasts a sturdy rim, and has a light-colored surface for ideal browning.

For our Coffee-Chili–Rubbed Steaks with Sweet Potatoes and Scallions (page 145), we used half of the pan to cook the steaks and the other half to cook sweet potato wedges, giving everything enough space to cook without steaming. We later placed scallions on top of the sweet potatoes to avoid overcrowding.

2 STACK INGREDIENTS

When arranging one pot meals, placing the ingredients in a single layer isn't your only option; they can also be stacked one on top of the other. Beyond saving space (which is sometimes necessary), stacking ingredients can aid in even cooking.

- **Use vegetables to prop up proteins** The elevation creates a buffer against the pan's direct heat and helps dry air circulate around meat, allowing it to cook and brown more evenly. To make Roasted Pork Chops and Vegetables with Parsley Vinaigrette (page 188), we placed the chops on top of the hearty vegetables (potatoes, carrots, and fennel) so that the meat cooked from both above and below, allowing it to stay juicy without one side overcooking.

- **Make extra tiers** Dutch ovens, slow cookers, and electric pressure cookers have high sides with enough space to accommodate a vessel within a vessel (see page 15). To make Smothered Pork Chops with Broccoli (page 190), we used a steamer basket to elevate the broccoli above the pork chops. A little creative thinking can also make extra space without the need for accessories. When using the Dutch oven, we some-times invert the lid to create a second cooking surface, as we do in our Chicken Stew with Cheddar Biscuits (page 69).

- **Season with drippings** If the top layer of food is a protein such as chicken or beef, it can exude flavorful juices and drippings to season the side below. A roasting pan rack offers an easy way to prop up proteins with ample space below for other food. In meals such as Prime Rib and Roasted Vegetables (page 180), the meat's juices drip onto the vegetables.

- **Boost food on the pan's edge** For our Shrimp Skewers with Cheesy Grits (page 261), we balanced the skewers on the edge of the casserole dish so the shrimp could cook above the grits.

OUR FAVORITE CASSEROLE DISH

A 13 by 9-inch baking dish is the tote bag of kitchenware. It's inexpensive, functional, and great for transporting goods. In the test kitchen, we put 13 by 9-inch baking dishes under the broiler when we want extra browning. For dishes that require broiling, our favorite casserole dish is the **Mrs. Anderson's Baking Lasagna Pan with Handle**. This dish has looped handles that are easy to grab and excellent capacity at 14.25 cups—neither too generous nor too restrictive.

OUR FAVORITE SKILLETS

Slick and inexpensive, nonstick skillets are a must-have for one-pan cooking. Our winner, the **OXO Good Grips Non-Stick 12" Open Frypan**, has a metal utensil–safe surface and an ovensafe handle. A good traditional skillet will last a lifetime if you treat it right. Our winning 12-inch skillet, the **All-Clad D3 Stainless 12" Fry Pan with Lid**, has three layers of cladding, with aluminum sandwiched by steel, for deep, uniform browning. Many of our recipes require some time with the pan covered. If your skillet did not come with a lid, we recommend purchasing a 12-inch oven-safe lid with a heat-resistant handle. A good cast-iron skillet is one of the few pieces of kitchen gear that improves after years of heavy use. As you cook in it, a cast-iron pan gradually takes on a natural, slick patina that releases food easily. Our preferred traditional 12-inch cast-iron skillet is the **Lodge Classic Cast Iron Skillet**. It browns foods deeply, has a preseasoned interior, and it can withstand heavy use without a scratch.

In our Pan-Roasted Chicken Breasts with Root Vegetables (page 107), we placed browned chicken on top of vegetables tossed in the fat from browning the chicken. Once in the oven, the elevated chicken cooked gently while the root vegetables roasted against the hot surface of the pan and the drippings from the chicken coated and flavored the vegetables.

3 TRANSFER TO THE OVEN

While the stovetop is exceptional for browning and searing, the all-encompassing heat of the oven helps food cook evenly, so we often combine the two cooking methods in one-pot meals.

- **Make safety a priority** Make sure the pot or pan you're using (and the lid, if the recipe calls for it) is ovensafe.

- **Pay attention to rack position when the pot goes into the oven** Placing the pot near the bottom of the oven will lead to more browning on the under-side of food; the top of the oven will lend more browning on the top (if the pan is uncovered). In our Chicken Tagine with Fennel, Chickpeas, and Apricots (page 123), we used the upper-middle rack when transferring the uncovered skillet to the oven so that the chicken would brown nicely.

- **Start on the stovetop to develop flavorful fond in the pot** The advance cooking can also help jump-start ingredients that need a little more time. Once the remaining elements have been added to the pot, the whole thing can go into the oven where the flavors have a chance to meld. We use this technique in stews or braised dishes such as Lamb Stew with Green Beans, Tomatoes, and Basil (page 66), where we first brown the meat on the stovetop in a Dutch oven and then let the whole stew cook together in the oven.

- **Use your roasting pan for more than just roasts** We found that we could use the wide pan on the stovetop in a similar fashion to a Dutch oven or a skillet, as we do for our Baked Ziti for a crowd (page 319), before transferring to the oven to finish cooking.

OUR FAVORITE DUTCH OVEN

A heavyweight Dutch oven is a piece you'll have for years, and during our extensive tests our preferences were clear: Look for a heavy enameled cast-iron pot with a tight-fitting lid. Our favorite, the **Le Creuset 7¼ Quart Round Dutch Oven**, is substantial enough to hold and evenly distribute heat without being unbearably heavy. The light-colored interior combined with low, straight sides gives good visibility and makes it easy to monitor browning and thermometer position. And although it's expensive, it is also resistant to damage, making it a worthwhile investment. For a less expensive option, our best buy favorite is the **Cuisinart Chef's Classic Enameled Cast Iron Covered Casserole**.

The filling for Chicken Pot Pie with Spring Vegetables (page 134) requires some time on the stovetop before the whole pot moves to the oven to finish cooking the pot pie filling and the crust (elevated on an inverted Dutch oven lid) at the same time.

4 SCALE RECIPES UP OR DOWN

In this book, we have meals that serve two and we have meals that serve 12. No matter what the dish is, choosing the right cooking vessel to match the serving size is crucial for turning out perfectly cooked meals. If the pan is too small it can lead to overcrowding, which will ultimately result in an unevenly cooked dish. And using a massive pan to cook a meal for two is not only inconvenient, it can also change the cook time.

- **Use a smaller pot for a smaller serving size** A Dutch oven is our go-to for family-sized Classic Ground Beef Chili (page 80), but a version for two barely covers the bottom of the pot, so we switched to a saucepan. The same applies for just about any recipe. We love our workhorse 12-inch skillet, but recipes for two work better in 8- or 10-inch skillets. And lasagna in a 13 by 9-inch casserole dish is typical, but our Easiest-Ever Tomato and Cheese Lasagna for Two (page 324) wouldn't have any layers in a pan that large; a loaf pan produced better results.

- **Remove or swap some ingredients to scale down** Eliminate or find substitutions for ingredients that require extensive preparation or that will yield more than you need when scaling down. For our Cod Baked in Foil with Leeks and Carrots (page 240), we created a for-two version by replacing the leeks and carrots with zucchini and tomatoes, which were simpler to prepare and didn't leave us with leftover vegetables to use up. The result? Cod Baked in Foil with Zucchini and Tomatoes for Two (page 241).

- **Make big-batch meals in the roasting pan** A roasting pan can accommodate much larger quantities than smaller pots and pans, so it's a great option when scaling up meals. To make a big batch of Baked Ziti (page 319) that could serve a crowd, we switched from a Dutch oven to a roasting pan.

- **Change the amount or the cut of meat to avoid waste** Reducing the amount of meat can be as simple as using a smaller amount of the same cut, but sometimes it requires switching to a new cut altogether. When making Spiced Pork Loin with Butternut Squash and Brussels Sprouts (page 206) to serve four to six, a three-pound pork loin roast worked well, but that much meat for two would be wasteful (unless you want leftovers), so instead we switched to a more manageable pork tenderloin. And although we needed two porterhouse steaks to serve four in our Tuscan-Style Steak with Garlicky Spinach (page 147), just one was enough to make a version for two.

OUR FAVORITE ROASTING PAN

Handsome, heavy-duty, and ready to take on everything from herb-flecked chicken breasts to a showstopping holiday roast, the roasting pan is a true kitchen icon. After roasting mountains of potatoes and a barrage of hefty roasts, we determined that our ideal pans are made of stainless steel and aluminum for even heating. Lightweight pans with roomy handles make maneuvering a breeze, even when using oven mitts. The **Calphalon Contemporary Stainless Roasting Pan with Rack** is our favorite, and we guarantee you'll pull out this versatile vessel more than once a year.

OUR FAVORITE LARGE SAUCEPAN

Well-designed saucepans sear, simmer, and steam at a steady, controlled pace; handle comfortably, even when full; and boast tight-fitting lids and stay-cool handles that eliminate the need for a potholder. That's why our favorite is the **All-Clad Stainless 4-Qt Sauce Pan** with uniform, steady heating and good visibility inside the saucepan to monitor browning.

To make enough Classic Beef Stew for a crowd (page 63) of 12 to 14 people we used a roasting pan, which easily held a whopping seven pounds of meat.

5 COOK INGREDIENTS IN STAGES

One of the biggest challenges of one-pot cooking is timing everything correctly. Nobody wants to eat cold meat or overcooked vegetables. Precooking ingredients that require more time before adding quicker-cooking elements can be key to avoiding a disappointing dinner.

- **When a good sear is important, cook ingredients in stages** A crowded pan causes food to steam rather than brown. To get perfectly browned meat for our Steak Tips with Spiced Couscous and Spinach (page 141), we first seared the steak tips and then set them aside to finish cooking the couscous and spinach.

- **Let quicker-cooking ingredients trade off time in the pan while longer-cooking ingredients run the full course** To make Herbed Leg of Lamb with Fingerling Potatoes and Asparagus (page 221), which features a full roast plus hearty potatoes and asparagus, we started the roast and the potatoes together in the oven; after pulling out the roast to rest, we added the asparagus to the potatoes, which were partially cooked, so that everything finished together.

- **Add the quickest-cooking ingredients off heat** In our Chicken and Rice with Carrots and Peas (page 96), the frozen peas needed only a few minutes to warm through (any longer and they turn mushy), so they went in at the end of cooking off heat.

OUR FAVORITE SLOW COOKER

Though new models are always popping up on the market, we have a strong preference for slow cookers that have clear glass lids (so we can keep an eye on the food's progress), are intuitive to use, and bring the food to a safe cooking temperature quickly. Most slow cookers can be programmed to cook for a desired amount of time before switching to a "keep warm" setting, making them convenient for busy home cooks. Our top pick, the **KitchenAid 6-Quart Slow Cooker with Solid Glass Lid**, is just the right size (not too large, not too small). It features built-in internal sensor monitors that adjust the cooking temperature automatically, keeping the contents from boiling and ensuring uniform cooking.

Quinoa and shrimp have very different cook times; to cook them both to perfection in our Shrimp with Spiced Quinoa and Corn Salad (page 256) we first cooked the quinoa for a few hours in the slow cooker and then added the shrimp for the last 30 minutes.

6 BUILD FLAVOR IN LAYERS

Recipes often reuse a pot for the sake of ease, but it actually has a much bigger benefit: building flavor. The many stages of cooking (along with some carefully selected ingredients) build layers of complex flavors that tie the dish together.

- **Use the fat** Flavorful fond builds up in the bottom of pots and pans when browning proteins. Using the rendered fat left in a pot after browning meat to cook other elements of the dish adds complexity and gives sauces body.

- **Bloom aromatic ingredients** Blooming ingredients such as spices, whether right in the pot or in the microwave, releases their oils and can infuse an entire dish with their flavors.

- **Finish with a sauce** While making a sauce on the side as the dish cooks certainly works well, some of our recipes take advantage of the leftover juices in the pot. Reducing the liquid creates a sauce that pairs perfectly with the flavors of the dish.

- **Wipe out the pot or pan when you want flavors to remain distinct** To make Chicken and Arugula Salad with Warm Fig Dressing (page 101) we cooked the chicken before reusing the skillet to make a warm salad dressing; to ensure the chicken flavor didn't overwhelm the flavors of the dressing we wiped out the skillet first.

OUR FAVORITE ELECTRIC PRESSURE COOKER

Electric pressure cookers promise fast, convenient, approachable meals. In our tests, we looked for an electric pressure cooker that sealed well to trap in moisture and had easy-to-use controls. Our winner is the **Instant Pot Duo Evo Plus 9-in-1 Electric Pressure Cooker, 8-QT**. It sears and sautés evenly and its stainless steel cooking pot makes it easy to monitor browning. We love its clear, intuitive digital interface, lid that seals automatically, pressure release switch rather than a valve, and silicone handles on its cooking pot, which prevent the pot from moving around inside the base and make it easy to lift out after cooking. This multi-use pot also has options to slow cook and sous vide.

Our Braised Pork with Broccoli Rabe and Sage (page 208) has multiple layers of flavor. We first browned the pork in the Instant Pot and then used the fat left behind to make a complex cooking liquid, which we reduced at the end to turn into a potent sauce.

USING VESSELS WITHIN VESSELS
Creating a smaller cooking area within one pot can help control the heat, add elevation for more even cooking, or keep ingredients separate. Large cooking vessels can contain accessories such as trivets, soufflé dishes, or baking dishes, and foil slings can make it easier to lift and lower food into the pot.

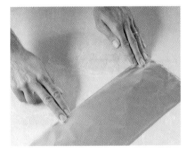

Making a foil sling Fold sheet of aluminum foil into 16 by 6-inch rectangle by folding either in half or in thirds, depending on width of foil.

Using a foil sling for a dish Rest dish in center of sling. Using sling, lower dish into pot (and onto trivet, if required). Allow narrow edges of sling to rest along sides of insert.

ON THE SIDE

Every recipe in this book turns out a complete meal, but sometimes you want a little extra on the side. If you're cooking a recipe that will be feeding a group on the high end of the serving-size range, sometimes an extra side is a must. And leftovers can easily transform into a second meal with the help of an additional side.

SIMPLE SIDES

Easy Green Salad

Serves 4
Total Time 10 minutes

- ½ garlic clove, peeled
- 8 ounces (8 cups) lettuce, torn into bite-size pieces if necessary
- Extra-virgin olive oil
- Vinegar

Rub inside of salad bowl with garlic. Add lettuce. Holding your thumb over mouth of olive oil bottle to control flow, slowly drizzle lettuce with small amount of oil. Toss greens very gently. Continue to drizzle with oil and toss gently until greens are lightly coated and just glistening. Sprinkle with small amounts of vinegar, salt, and pepper to taste while tossing. Serve.

Simple Rice Pilaf

Serves 4 to 6
Total Time 45 minutes

Be sure to rinse the rice until the water runs clear. A nonstick saucepan is crucial to prevent the wet rice from sticking to the pan; for the most evenly cooked rice, use a wide-bottomed saucepan with a tight-fitting lid. Basmati, jasmine, or Texmati rice can be substituted for the long-grain rice.

- 3 tablespoons unsalted butter or vegetable oil
- 1 small onion, chopped fine
- 1 teaspoon table salt
- 1½ cups long-grain white rice, rinsed
- 2½ cups boiling water

1. Melt butter in large nonstick saucepan over medium heat. Add onion and salt and cook until softened, 5 to 7 minutes.

2. Stir in rice and cook until edges begin to turn translucent, about 3 minutes. Stir in boiling water and return to boil. Reduce heat to low, cover, and gently simmer until water is completely absorbed, 16 to 18 minutes.

3. Off heat, uncover and lay clean dish towel over saucepan; cover and let sit for 10 minutes. Fluff rice with fork, season with salt and pepper to taste, and serve.

Simple Rice Pilaf

Buttered Egg Noodles

Serves 8
Total Time 30 minutes

Egg noodles are available in a variety of sizes; be sure to use wide noodles here.

- 1 pound wide egg noodles
- 1 tablespoon table salt
- 4 tablespoons unsalted butter

Bring 4 quarts water to boil in large pot. Add noodles and salt and cook until tender, 6 to 8 minutes. Drain noodles and return to pot. Stir in butter, season with salt and pepper to taste, and serve.

Sautéed Summer Squash Ribbons

Serves 4

Total Time 30 minutes

We like a mix of summer squash and zucchini, but you can use just one or the other. Steeping the minced garlic in lemon juice mellows the garlic's bite; do not skip this step. To avoid overcooking the squash, start checking for doneness at the lower end of the cooking time.

- 1 small garlic clove, minced
- 1 teaspoon grated lemon zest plus 1 tablespoon juice, divided
- 4 (6- to 8-ounce) yellow squash or zucchini, trimmed
- 2 tablespoons plus 1 teaspoon extra-virgin olive oil, divided
- ½ teaspoon kosher salt
- ⅛ teaspoon pepper
- 1½ tablespoons chopped fresh parsley

1. Combine garlic and lemon juice in large bowl and set aside for at least 10 minutes. Using vegetable peeler, shave each squash lengthwise into ribbons. Shave off 3 ribbons from 1 side, then turn squash 90 degrees and shave off 3 more ribbons. Continue to turn and shave ribbons until you reach seeds; discard core.

2. Whisk 2 tablespoons oil, salt, pepper, and lemon zest into lemon juice mixture.

3. Heat remaining 1 teaspoon oil in 12-inch nonstick skillet over medium-high heat until just smoking. Add squash and cook, tossing occasionally with tongs, until squash has softened and is translucent, 3 to 4 minutes. Transfer squash to bowl with dressing, add parsley, and toss to coat. Season with salt and pepper to taste. Transfer to serving platter and serve immediately.

Easy Mashed Potatoes

Serves 4

Total Time 45 minutes

We prefer Yukon Gold potatoes here, but russet potatoes will work in a pinch.

- 2 pounds Yukon Gold potatoes, peeled and sliced ½ inch thick
- ¾ teaspoon table salt, plus salt for cooking potatoes
- ¾ cup half-and-half
- 6 tablespoons unsalted butter
- ½ teaspoon pepper

1. Place potatoes and 1 tablespoon salt in large saucepan, add water to cover by 1 inch, and bring to boil over high heat. Reduce heat to medium and simmer until potatoes are tender and paring knife can be easily slipped in and out of potatoes, 18 to 22 minutes.

2. Meanwhile, combine half-and-half and butter in 2-cup liquid measuring cup and microwave, covered, until butter is melted and mixture is warm to touch, about 2 minutes.

3. Drain potatoes and return them to saucepan. Cook over low heat, stirring, until potatoes are thoroughly dried, about 30 seconds. Remove from heat and, using potato masher, mash potatoes until smooth and no lumps remain. Stir in half-and-half mixture, ¾ teaspoon salt, and pepper until fully incorporated. Season with salt and pepper to taste. Serve.

Garlic-Parmesan Mashed Potatoes for Two

Serves 2

Total Time 40 minutes

- 1 pound Yukon Gold potatoes, peeled and sliced ½ inch thick
- ¼ teaspoon garlic powder
- 2 tablespoons unsalted butter, cut into 2 pieces
- ½ teaspoon garlic, minced to paste, divided
- 1 ounce Parmesan cheese, grated (½ cup)
- ½ teaspoon table salt
- ¼ teaspoon pepper
- ⅓ cup warm whole milk

1. Place potatoes in medium saucepan, add water to cover by 1 inch, and bring to simmer over medium-high heat. Adjust heat to maintain gentle simmer and cook until paring knife can be easily slipped in and out of potatoes, 18 to 22 minutes. Drain potatoes.

2. Combine garlic powder and ¼ teaspoon water in small bowl. Melt butter in now-empty saucepan over medium-low heat. Stir in ⅜ teaspoon garlic paste and garlic powder mixture; cook, stirring constantly, until fragrant and golden, about 1 minute. Transfer butter mixture to medium bowl and thoroughly stir in Parmesan, salt, pepper, and remaining ⅛ teaspoon garlic paste.

3. Place again-empty saucepan over low heat; set ricer or food mill over saucepan. Working in batches, transfer potatoes to hopper and process. Using rubber spatula, stir in butter mixture until incorporated. Stir in warm milk until incorporated. Season with salt and pepper to taste; serve immediately.

Boiled Red Potatoes with Butter and Herbs

Serves 4
Total Time 35 minutes

We prefer to use small red potatoes, measuring 1 to 2 inches in diameter, in this recipe. If using larger potatoes, halve or quarter the potatoes and adjust the cooking time as needed.

- 2 pounds small red potatoes, unpeeled
- 2 tablespoons unsalted butter
- 1 tablespoon minced fresh chives, tarragon, or parsley

Cover potatoes by 1 inch water in large saucepan and bring to boil over high heat. Reduce to simmer and cook until potatoes are tender, 20 to 25 minutes. Drain potatoes well, then toss gently with butter in large bowl until butter melts. Season with salt and pepper to taste, sprinkle with chives, and serve.

Cauliflower Rice

Serves 4 to 6
Total Time 35 minutes

- 1 head cauliflower (2 pounds), cut into 1-inch florets (6 cups)
- 1 tablespoon extra-virgin olive oil
- 1 shallot, minced
- ½ cup chicken or vegetable broth
- ¾ teaspoon table salt
- 2 tablespoons minced fresh parsley

1. Working in 2 batches, pulse cauliflower florets in food processor until finely ground into ¼- to ⅛-inch pieces, 6 to 8 pulses, scraping down sides of bowl as needed; transfer to bowl.

2. Heat oil in large saucepan over medium-low heat until shimmering. Add shallot and cook until softened, about 3 minutes. Stir in cauliflower, broth, and salt. Cover and cook, stirring occasionally, until cauliflower is tender, 12 to 15 minutes.

3. Uncover and continue to cook, stirring occasionally, until cauliflower rice is almost completely dry, about 3 minutes. Off heat, stir in parsley and season with salt and pepper to taste. Serve.

Sautéed Summer Squash Ribbons

Easy Mashed Potatoes

Quinoa Pilaf

Easy Baked Polenta

Quinoa Pilaf

Serves 4 to 6
Total Time 50 minutes

If you buy unwashed quinoa (or if you are unsure whether it's been washed), be sure to rinse it before cooking to remove its bitter protective coating (called saponin).

    1½ cups prewashed white quinoa
     2 tablespoons unsalted butter or extra-virgin olive oil
     1 small onion, chopped fine
     ¾ teaspoon table salt
    1¾ cups water
     3 tablespoons chopped fresh cilantro, parsley, chives, mint, or tarragon
     1 tablespoon lemon juice

1. Toast quinoa in medium saucepan over medium-high heat, stirring frequently, until quinoa is fragrant and makes continuous popping sound, 5 to 7 minutes; transfer to bowl.
2. Add butter to now-empty pan and melt over medium-low heat. Add onion and salt and cook until onion is softened and light golden, 5 to 7 minutes. Stir in water and toasted quinoa, increase heat to medium-high, and bring to simmer. Cover, reduce heat to low, and simmer until grains are just tender and liquid is absorbed, 18 to 20 minutes, stirring once halfway through cooking.
3. Remove pan from heat and let sit, covered, for 10 minutes. Fluff with fork, stir in herbs and lemon juice, and serve.

Easy Baked Polenta

Serves 6 to 8
Total Time 1¼ hours

You can use medium-grind cornmeal or polenta here.

     8 cups water
     2 cups medium-grind polenta
     2 teaspoons table salt
     ⅛ teaspoon pepper
     4 ounces Parmesan cheese, grated (2 cups)
     4 tablespoons unsalted butter, cut into 6 pieces

1. Adjust oven rack to middle position and heat oven to 375 degrees. Combine water, polenta, salt, and pepper in 13 by 9-inch baking dish. Transfer dish to oven and bake, uncovered, until water is absorbed and polenta has thickened, about 60 minutes.
2. Remove baking dish from oven. Whisk in Parmesan and butter until polenta is smooth and creamy. Serve.

MASTER RECIPE FOR GRAINS

To cook the grains listed below, bring water to boil in large pot. Stir in grain and table salt and cook until tender, following timing below. Drain well. All of these grains can be cooked, cooled, and refrigerated in airtight container for up to 3 days. If serving immediately, season with salt and pepper to taste.

GRAIN	DRY AMOUNT (CUPS)	WATER (QUARTS)	SALT (TEASPOON)	COOKED YIELD (CUPS)	COOKING TIME (MINUTES)
Buckwheat	¾	2	½	2	10 to 12
	1½	4	1	4	
Medium- or coarse-grind bulgur	¾	2	½	2	5
	1½	4	1	4	
Pearl barley	¾	2	½	2	20 to 40
	1½	4	1	4	
Farro	¾	2	½	2	15 to 30
	1½	4	1	4	
Freekeh	¾	2	½	2	30 to 45
	1½	4	1	4	
Black rice	¾	2	½	2	20 to 25
	1½	4	1	4	
Long-grain brown rice	¾	2	½	2	25 to 30
	1½	4	1	4	
Long-grain white rice	¾	2	½	2	10 to 15
	1½	4	1	4	
Wild rice	¾	2	½	2	35 to 40
	1½	4	1	4	
Oat berries	¾	2	½	1½	30 to 40
	1½	4	1	3	
Wheat berries	¾	4	½	1½	60 to 70
	1½	4	1	3	

SOUPS

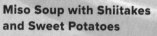
Miso Soup with Shiitakes and Sweet Potatoes

* All slow cooker recipes work in a 4- to 7-quart traditional slow cooker unless noted.
** All Instant Pot recipes work in a 6- to 8-quart Instant Pot or other electric pressure cooker.

Weeknight Chicken Noodle Soup

DUTCH OVEN

Serves 4 to 6
Total Time 45 minutes

Why This Recipe Works A Dutch oven is the ultimate pot for making soup: It has a wide base that's ideal for developing flavor, it accommodates a bounty of ingredients, and its excellent heat retention ensures everything cooks evenly. Most recipes for quick chicken soup call for chunks of chicken and vegetables dumped into store-bought chicken broth and hastily boiled, but this approach typically yields a weak-flavored broth and dry, bland chicken. Our goal was to produce chicken soup with a flavorful broth and tender chicken. Adding tomato paste and thyme to store-bought broth enhanced its body and flavor. Next, we focused on the chicken. Quick-cooking boneless, skinless breasts were the obvious choice, but simply simmering cubes of meat in broth resulted in tough nuggets of chicken. We avoided this problem by poaching whole breasts in the broth and then shredding the meat once cooked. Prepared this way, the chicken remained moist and tender. The addition of egg noodles toward the end of cooking made for a heartier soup. You can substitute boneless skinless chicken thighs for the breasts; increase the cooking time to about 15 minutes (until the chicken registers 175 degrees).

- 1 tablespoon vegetable oil
- 1 onion, chopped fine
- 2 teaspoons tomato paste
- 1 teaspoon minced fresh thyme or ¼ teaspoon dried
- 6 cups chicken broth
- ¼ teaspoon table salt
- 2 carrots, peeled and sliced ¼ inch thick
- 1 celery rib, sliced ¼ inch thick
- 1 pound boneless, skinless chicken breasts, trimmed
- 4 ounces (2 cups) egg noodles
- 2 tablespoons minced fresh parsley

1. Heat oil in Dutch oven over medium heat until shimmering. Add onion and cook until softened and lightly browned, 5 to 7 minutes. Stir in tomato paste and thyme and cook until fragrant, about 30 seconds. Stir in broth and salt, scraping up any browned bits. Stir in carrots and celery and bring to simmer. Nestle chicken into pot. Reduce heat to low, cover, and cook until chicken registers 160 degrees, about 10 minutes.

2. Transfer chicken to cutting board, let cool slightly, then shred into bite-size pieces using 2 forks.

3. Meanwhile, return soup to boil. Stir in noodles and cook until tender, 5 to 8 minutes. Off heat, stir in shredded chicken and let sit until heated through, about 2 minutes. Stir in parsley and season with salt and pepper to taste. Serve.

VARIATION

Weeknight Chicken Noodle Soup for Two

SAUCEPAN

Serves 2
Total Time 45 minutes

You can substitute boneless skinless chicken thighs for the breasts; increase the cooking time to about 15 minutes (until the chicken registers 175 degrees).

- 2 teaspoons vegetable oil
- 1 small onion, chopped fine
- 1 teaspoon tomato paste
- ½ teaspoon minced fresh thyme or ⅛ teaspoon dried
- 3 cups chicken broth
- ⅛ teaspoon table salt
- 1 carrot, peeled and sliced ¼ inch thick
- 1 small celery rib, sliced ¼ inch thick
- 8 ounces boneless, skinless chicken breasts, trimmed
- 2 ounces (1 cup) egg noodles
- 1 tablespoon minced fresh parsley

1. Heat oil in large saucepan over medium heat until shimmering. Add onion and cook until softened and lightly browned, 5 to 7 minutes. Stir in tomato paste and thyme and cook until fragrant, about 30 seconds. Stir in broth and salt, scraping up any browned bits. Stir in carrot and celery and bring to simmer. Nestle chicken into saucepan. Reduce heat to low, cover, and cook until chicken registers 160 degrees, about 10 minutes.

2. Transfer chicken to cutting board, let cool slightly, then shred into bite-size pieces using 2 forks.

3. Meanwhile, return soup to boil. Stir in noodles and cook until tender, 5 to 8 minutes. Off heat, stir in shredded chicken and let sit until heated through, about 2 minutes. Stir in parsley and season with salt and pepper to taste. Serve.

Tortilla Soup
DUTCH OVEN

Serves 6 to 8
Total Time 1½ hours

Why This Recipe Works With its spicy, garlicky, tomatoey broth; tender chunks of chicken; and garnishes galore—plus crispy tortilla chips on top—tortilla soup succeeds in pleasing. We wanted a soup loaded with vibrant flavor, a manageable approach, and easy-to-find ingredients. While traditional Mexican recipes start with homemade stock, there's so much flavor in this soup that store-bought broth works just fine. Typically, the vegetables are charred on a comal (griddle) and then pureed and fried. To simplify, we skipped the charring step and got smoky flavor from chipotles, which we pureed with tomatoes, onion, garlic, and jalapeño before frying the mixture in oil. We poached the chicken in store-bought broth, which we infused with onion, garlic, cilantro, and oregano to give our base plenty of flavor. No chicken tortilla soup would be complete without the tortilla chips, which turn crisp-tender from the steaming broth. Store-bought chips (rather than homemade tortilla strips) were a convenient choice, and creamy avocado and cotija cheese provided the ideal garnishes. For a spicier soup, use the greater amount of chipotle.

2	(12-ounce) bone-in split chicken breasts, trimmed
8	cups chicken broth
1	large white onion, quartered, divided
4	garlic cloves, peeled, divided
8–10	sprigs fresh cilantro, plus extra leaves for serving
1	sprig fresh oregano
¾	teaspoon table salt, divided
2	tomatoes, cored and quartered
½	jalapeño chile, seeded
1–2	tablespoons minced canned chipotle chile in adobo sauce
1	tablespoon vegetable oil
4	ounces tortilla chips, crushed into large pieces (4 cups)
1	avocado, halved, pitted, and diced
8	ounces cotija cheese, crumbled (2 cups)
	Lime wedges

Tortilla Soup

1. Bring chicken, broth, 2 onion quarters, 2 garlic cloves, cilantro sprigs, oregano sprig, and ½ teaspoon salt to simmer in Dutch oven over medium-high heat. Reduce heat to low, cover, and cook until chicken registers 160 degrees, about 20 minutes. Transfer chicken to cutting board, let cool slightly, then shred into bite-size pieces using 2 forks; discard skin and bones. Strain broth through fine-mesh strainer into bowl; discard solids.

2. Process tomatoes, jalapeño, chipotle, remaining 2 onion quarters, and remaining 2 garlic cloves in food processor until smooth, scraping down sides of bowl as needed. Heat oil in now-empty Dutch oven over high heat until shimmering. Add tomato-onion puree and remaining ¼ teaspoon salt and cook, stirring frequently, until mixture has darkened in color, about 10 minutes.

3. Stir in strained broth, bring to simmer, and cook until flavors meld, about 15 minutes. Off heat, stir in shredded chicken and let sit until heated through, about 2 minutes. Season with salt and pepper to taste. Serve, passing tortilla chips, avocado, cotija, extra cilantro leaves, and lime wedges.

Spiced Chicken Soup with Squash and Chickpeas

Chicken Soup with Parmesan Dumplings

Spiced Chicken Soup with Squash and Chickpeas

INSTANT POT

Serves 6 to 8
Total Time 1½ hours

Why This Recipe Works A pressure cooker makes quick work of extracting body-building gelatin from bone-in, skin-on chicken breasts for a richly flavored, hands-off broth, which serves as the ideal base for this unique spin on chicken and vegetable soup. Just 20 minutes under high pressure were enough to ensure the meat was moist and tender and that our vegetable of choice—hearty butternut squash—was cooked to silky perfection. Inspired by hararat, a North African blend of spices such as cumin, coriander, and allspice (also known as Libyan five-spice blend, or bzaar), we incorporated a combination of spices that provided a warm earthiness and subtle heat. Canned chickpeas needed only to be warmed through along with the shredded chicken to finish the soup. Chopped cilantro added a healthy dose of herbal freshness. You can substitute 8 (5- to 7-ounce) bone-in chicken thighs for the breasts.

- 2 tablespoons extra-virgin olive oil
- 1 onion, chopped
- 1¾ teaspoons table salt
- 2 tablespoons tomato paste
- 4 garlic cloves, minced
- 1 tablespoon ground coriander
- 1½ teaspoons ground cumin
- 1 teaspoon ground cardamom
- ½ teaspoon ground allspice
- ¼ teaspoon cayenne pepper
- 7 cups water, divided
- 3 (12-ounce) bone-in split chicken breasts, trimmed
- 1½ pounds butternut squash, peeled, seeded, and cut into 1½-inch pieces (4 cups)
- 1 (15-ounce) can chickpeas, rinsed
- ½ cup chopped fresh cilantro

1. Using highest sauté or browning function, heat oil in electric pressure cooker until shimmering. Add onion and salt and cook until onion is softened, about 5 minutes. Stir in tomato paste, garlic, coriander, cumin, cardamom, allspice, and cayenne and cook until fragrant, about 30 seconds. Stir in 5 cups water, scraping up any browned bits. Nestle chicken into pot, then arrange squash evenly around chicken.

2. Lock lid in place and close pressure release valve. Select high pressure cook function and cook for 20 minutes. Turn off pressure cooker and quick-release pressure. Carefully remove lid, allowing steam to escape away from you.

3. Transfer chicken to cutting board, let cool slightly, then shred into bite-size pieces using 2 forks; discard skin and bones.

4. Using spoon, break squash into bite-size pieces. Stir shredded chicken along with any accumulated juices, chickpeas, and remaining 2 cups water into soup and let sit until heated through, about 2 minutes. Stir in cilantro and season with salt and pepper to taste. Serve.

Chicken Soup with Parmesan Dumplings

DUTCH OVEN

Serves 4 to 6
Total Time 2 hours

Why This Recipe Works Passatelli, a rustic Northern Italian specialty, features tender dumplings deeply flavored with Parmesan and served in a light chicken broth. We made the classic recipe heartier with additional vegetables and a bit easier by using store-bought broth. To enrich the broth we browned our chicken thighs—the fond left behind offered a serious flavor boost—and simmered a Parmesan cheese rind in the broth to infuse it with cheesy, umami flavor. The dumplings are undoubtedly the star of this soup, so we knew we needed to get the texture and flavor just right. Traditional recipes call for bread crumbs, but store-bought bread crumbs were too fine and homemade bread crumbs were too coarse. Panko bread crumbs had just the right consistency. Grated Parmesan and egg whites helped keep the dumplings light and tender. We shaped the dumplings into balls by hand before poaching them in the chicken broth. When first mixed, the dough was too sticky to handle, but a 15-minute rest in the refrigerator allowed the bread crumbs to hydrate more evenly and chilled the dough so that it was firm enough to hold its shape. Fennel, carrots, and escarole complemented the shredded chicken and the flavorful dumplings. To ensure that the dumplings remain intact during cooking, roll them until the surfaces are smooth and no cracks remain.

1½ pounds bone-in chicken thighs, trimmed
1 teaspoon table salt, divided
½ teaspoon pepper, divided
1 teaspoon vegetable oil
1 fennel bulb, 1 tablespoon fronds minced, stalks discarded, bulb halved, cored, and cut into ½-inch pieces, divided
1 onion, chopped fine
2 carrots, peeled and cut into ¾-inch pieces
½ cup dry white wine

8 cups chicken broth
1 Parmesan cheese rind, plus 3 ounces Parmesan, grated (1½ cups), divided
¾ cup panko bread crumbs
2 large egg whites
1 tablespoon water
¼ teaspoon grated lemon zest
Pinch ground nutmeg
½ small head escarole (6 ounces), trimmed and cut into ½-inch pieces

1. Pat chicken dry with paper towels and sprinkle with ½ teaspoon salt and ¼ teaspoon pepper. Heat oil in Dutch oven over medium-high heat until just smoking. Add chicken, skin side down, and cook until well browned, 6 to 8 minutes; transfer to plate.

2. Pour off all but 1 teaspoon fat from pot and reserve 1 tablespoon fat for dumplings. Add fennel bulb, onion, carrots, and remaining ½ teaspoon salt to fat left in pot and cook over medium heat until softened and lightly browned, 5 to 7 minutes. Stir in wine, scraping up any browned bits, and cook until almost completely evaporated, about 2 minutes. Stir in broth and Parmesan rind and bring to simmer. Return chicken and any accumulated juices to pot. Reduce heat to low, cover, and cook until chicken registers 175 degrees, about 30 minutes.

3. Off heat, discard Parmesan rind. Transfer chicken to cutting board, let cool slightly, then shred into bite-size pieces using 2 forks; discard skin and bones. Cover broth to keep warm.

4. Meanwhile, mix grated Parmesan, panko, egg whites, water, lemon zest, nutmeg, remaining ¼ teaspoon pepper, and reserved fat in bowl until thoroughly combined. Refrigerate dough for 15 minutes. Pinch off and roll 1-teaspoon-size pieces of mixture into balls and arrange on large plate (you should have about 28 dumplings).

5. Return broth to simmer over medium-high heat. Add escarole and shredded chicken and return to simmer. Add dumplings and cook, adjusting heat to maintain gentle simmer, until dumplings float to surface and are cooked through, 3 to 5 minutes. Stir in fennel fronds and season with salt and pepper to taste. Serve.

SHREDDING MEAT

To shred chicken, turkey, beef, or pork into bite-size pieces, hold fork in each hand, with tines facing down. Insert tines into cooked meat and gently pull forks away from each other.

CHICKEN AND VEGETABLE SOUP

The key to a stellar chicken soup is a great broth with unadulterated chicken flavor. Building a broth with that much flavor required a two-hour simmer, and bone-in chicken parts cut into pieces were a potent starting point—the resulting broth was clear and refined, and the long simmering time eked out every last bit of flavor from the chicken bones. In our classic Dutch oven soup, browning the chicken parts first added even more flavor to the broth. With the ultimate broth accomplished, finishing the soup was a breeze. For tender, flavorful bites of chicken we included chicken breasts, which we gently poached in the broth—along with carrots and celery—before shredding and returning to the soup. To make this recipe in a pressure cooker and in a slow cooker, we reduced the amount of liquid from 10 to 9 cups to account for little to no evaporation. Since browning the chicken isn't possible in the slow cooker, we relied on a combination of glutamate-rich tomato paste and soy sauce to mimic the deep flavor of browned chicken. The pressure cooker did an exceptional job extracting flavor from the chicken, allowing us to cook the broth for just one hour. You will need a Dutch oven, electric pressure cooker, or slow cooker that holds at least 6 quarts for this recipe. The strained broth can be refrigerated for up to 4 days or frozen for up to 1 month; thaw frozen broth completely before proceeding with recipe.

CLASSIC

DUTCH OVEN

Serves 6 to 8

Total Time 4 hours (3½ hours for the broth, plus 35 minutes to finish the soup)

- 3 pounds whole chicken legs, backs, and/or wings, hacked into 2-inch pieces
- 1 tablespoon vegetable oil
- 1 onion, chopped
- 1 tablespoon tomato paste
- 10 cups water, plus extra as needed
- 1 tablespoon table salt
- 4 sprigs fresh thyme or ½ teaspoon dried
- 2 bay leaves
- 1 pound boneless, skinless chicken breasts, trimmed
- 4 carrots, peeled and cut into ½-inch pieces (2 cups)
- 3 celery ribs, cut into ½-inch pieces (1½ cups)

1. Pat chicken pieces dry with paper towels. Heat oil in large Dutch oven over medium-high heat until just smoking. Brown half of chicken pieces on all sides, 5 to 7 minutes; transfer to bowl. Repeat with remaining chicken pieces; transfer to bowl.

2. Add onion and tomato paste to fat left in pot and cook over medium heat until onion is softened, about 5 minutes. Return chicken pieces and any accumulated juices to pot. Partially cover, reduce heat to medium-low, and cook until chicken releases additional juices, 15 to 20 minutes.

3. Add water, salt, thyme sprigs, and bay leaves and bring to boil. Reduce heat to low, cover, and simmer until broth is flavorful, about 2 hours.

4. Using slotted spoon, discard chicken pieces. Strain broth through fine-mesh strainer into large container; discard solids. Let broth settle for 5 minutes, then skim excess fat from surface using wide, shallow spoon. (You should have 9 cups broth; add extra water as needed to equal 9 cups.)

5. Return broth to now-empty pot and bring to simmer over medium heat. Add chicken breasts, carrots, and celery, partially cover, and cook until chicken registers 165 degrees and vegetables are tender, 15 to 20 minutes.

6. Transfer chicken to cutting board, let cool slightly, then shred into bite-size pieces using 2 forks. Off heat, stir shredded chicken into soup and let sit until heated through, about 2 minutes. Season with salt and pepper to taste. Serve.

MAKE IT YOUR WAY →

> **Use What You've Got** Use boneless, skinless chicken thighs instead of the chicken breasts. Swap in hearty vegetables (celery root, parsnips, turnips) for the carrots and celery. Use other fresh herbs (cilantro, basil, dill, mint).

PRESSURE COOK IT

INSTANT POT

Serves 6 to 8
Total Time 2½ hours (2 hours for the broth, plus 35 minutes to finish the soup)

- 1 tablespoon vegetable oil
- 1 onion, chopped
- 1 tablespoon tomato paste
- 3 pounds whole chicken legs, backs, and/or wings, hacked into 2-inch pieces
- 9 cups water
- 1 tablespoon table salt
- 4 sprigs fresh thyme or ½ teaspoon dried
- 2 bay leaves
- 1 pound boneless, skinless chicken breasts, trimmed
- 4 carrots, peeled and cut into ½-inch pieces (2 cups)
- 3 celery ribs, cut into ½-inch pieces (1½ cups)

1. Using highest sauté or browning function, heat oil in electric pressure cooker until shimmering. Add onion and tomato paste and cook until onion is softened and fond begins to form on bottom of pot, about 5 minutes. Stir in chicken pieces, water, salt, thyme sprigs, and bay leaves.

2. Lock lid in place and close pressure release valve. Select high pressure cook function and cook for 1 hour. Turn off pressure cooker and let pressure release naturally for 15 minutes. Quick-release any remaining pressure, then carefully remove lid, allowing steam to escape away from you.

3. Using slotted spoon, discard chicken pieces. Strain broth through fine-mesh strainer into large container; discard solids. Let broth settle for 5 minutes, then skim excess fat from surface using wide, shallow spoon. (You should have 9 cups broth; add extra water as needed to equal 9 cups.)

4. Return broth to now-empty pressure cooker and bring to simmer using highest sauté or browning function. Add chicken breasts, carrots, and celery, partially cover, and cook until chicken registers 165 degrees and vegetables are tender, 15 to 20 minutes.

5. Transfer chicken to cutting board, let cool slightly, then shred into bite-size pieces using 2 forks. Stir shredded chicken into soup and let sit until heated through, about 2 minutes. Season with salt and pepper to taste. Serve.

SLOW COOK IT

SLOW COOKER

Serves 6 to 8
Cook Time 7 to 8 hours on low or 4 to 5 hours on high for the broth, plus 3 to 4 hours on low to finish the soup

- 1 onion, chopped
- 5 teaspoons vegetable oil, divided
- 1 tablespoon tomato paste
- 3 pounds whole chicken legs, backs, and/or wings, hacked into 2-inch pieces
- 9 cups water
- 1 tablespoon soy sauce
- 2 teaspoons table salt
- 4 sprigs fresh thyme or ½ teaspoon dried
- 2 bay leaves
- 4 carrots, peeled and cut into ½-inch pieces (2 cups)
- 3 celery ribs, cut into ½-inch pieces (1½ cups)
- 1 pound boneless, skinless chicken breasts, trimmed

1. Microwave onion, 1 tablespoon oil, and tomato paste in bowl, stirring occasionally, until onion is softened, about 5 minutes; transfer to slow cooker. Stir in chicken pieces, water, soy sauce, salt, thyme sprigs, and bay leaves. Cover and cook until broth is flavorful, 7 to 8 hours on low or 4 to 5 hours on high.

2. Using slotted spoon, discard chicken pieces. Strain broth through fine-mesh strainer into large container; discard solids. Let broth settle for 5 minutes, then skim excess fat from surface using wide, shallow spoon. (You should have 9 cups broth; add extra water as needed to equal 9 cups.)

3. Microwave carrots, celery, and remaining 2 teaspoons oil in bowl, stirring occasionally, until vegetables are softened, 5 to 7 minutes. Return broth to now-empty slow cooker. Add chicken breasts and vegetables. Cover and cook until chicken registers at least 165 degrees and vegetables are tender, 3 to 4 hours on low.

4. Transfer chicken to cutting board, let cool slightly, then shred into bite-size pieces using 2 forks. Stir shredded chicken into soup and let sit until heated through, about 2 minutes. Season with salt and pepper to taste. Serve.

> **Bulk It Up** Stir baby greens, thinly sliced mushrooms, diced fresh tomatoes, frozen corn or peas, canned beans, cooked noodles, cooked rice, and/or cooked grains into the soup with the shredded chicken.

> **Add an Upgrade** Add minced chipotles, miso paste, Parmesan rinds, and/or citrus zest in place of—or in addition to—the thyme. Drizzle on chili oil, harissa, or pesto. Sprinkle on grated hard cheese (Parmesan or Asiago).

Thai Curry and Coconut Soup with Chicken

SAUCEPAN

Serves 6

Total Time 45 minutes

Why This Recipe Works For a fast soup with bold curry flavor, we opted for store-bought Thai curry paste rather than homemade, which can be a time-consuming and ingredient-intensive endeavor. Using both chicken broth and coconut milk gave us a rich base for our soup, which we enhanced with pungent fish sauce, lemongrass, shallots, and cilantro. Savory, umami-rich mushrooms balanced the sweetness of the broth, and thinly sliced chicken cooked quickly in the liquid. Next up was our key flavor-boosting ingredient: red curry paste. Adding just a dollop whisked with fish sauce and tart lime juice at the very end of cooking allowed all the vibrant flavors of the soup to come through. Garnishing with cilantro, Thai chiles, and scallions lent a burst of freshness and heat. Although we prefer the deeper, richer flavor of regular coconut milk, light coconut milk can be substituted. If fresh Thai chiles are unavailable, substitute one serrano or one-half jalapeño.

1 tablespoon vegetable oil

3 stalks lemongrass, trimmed to bottom 6 inches and minced

3 large shallots, chopped coarse

8 sprigs fresh cilantro, chopped, plus extra whole leaves for serving

4 cups chicken broth

2 (14-ounce) cans coconut milk, divided

3 tablespoons fish sauce, divided, plus extra for seasoning

1 tablespoon sugar

8 ounces white mushrooms, trimmed and sliced thin

1 pound boneless, skinless chicken breasts, trimmed, halved lengthwise, and sliced ¼ inch thick

3 tablespoons lime juice (2 limes), plus lime wedges for serving

2 teaspoons Thai red curry paste

2 Thai chiles, stemmed, seeded, and sliced thin

2 scallions, sliced thin on bias

1. Heat oil in large saucepan over medium heat until shimmering. Add lemongrass, shallots, and cilantro sprigs and cook, stirring often, until just softened but not browned, 2 to 5 minutes. Stir in broth, 1 can coconut milk, and 1 tablespoon fish sauce and bring to simmer. Reduce heat to low, cover, and cook until flavors meld, about 10 minutes.

2. Strain broth through fine-mesh strainer into large bowl or container; discard solids. Return broth to now-empty saucepan. Stir in remaining 1 can coconut milk and sugar and bring to simmer over medium-high heat. Stir in mushrooms and cook until just tender, 2 to 3 minutes. Stir in chicken and cook until no longer pink, 1 to 3 minutes.

3. Remove soup from heat. Whisk lime juice, curry paste, and remaining 2 tablespoons fish sauce together in bowl to dissolve curry, then stir mixture into soup. Season with extra fish sauce to taste. Sprinkle individual portions with extra cilantro leaves, chiles, and scallions before serving with lime wedges.

PREPARING LEMONGRASS

First peel and discard tough, outer layers. Then mince or grate pale lower stalk (freeze it first for easy grating) or bruise it by pounding it and leave it whole to infuse stocks and soups.

INGREDIENT SPOTLIGHT

COCONUT MILK

Coconut milk is not the thin liquid found inside the coconut itself; that's coconut water. Coconut milk is made by steeping equal parts shredded coconut meat and either warm milk or water. The meat is pressed or mashed to release as much liquid as possible, and the mixture is strained; the result is coconut milk. To find our favorite, we selected seven varieties of full-fat canned coconut milk. Panels of 21 tasters sampled each plain and in soup. Not surprisingly, texture proved very important in our tastings. Our least favorite samples were thin and watery or separated quickly. Tasters much preferred samples that were creamy and full-bodied. As for flavor, products lost points if the coconut flavor was too mild or had an "artificial," "sunscreen-y" aroma and taste. Our favorites had fresh coconut flavor and a smooth, creamy texture. The winner of our tasting, **Aroy-D Coconut Milk**, had a "velvety," "luxurious texture" and boasted "clean" and "balanced" flavor.

Greek Chicken and Rice Soup

SAUCEPAN
Serves 6 to 8
Total Time 1¼ hours

Why This Recipe Works The rich, soft texture and bright, citrusy flavor of avgolemono, a traditional Greek soup, centers around four simple pantry staples: chicken broth, rice, eggs, and lemons. To transform this soup from starter to main course, we added tender chicken that is poached to perfection by sitting off the heat in hot broth. We flavored the broth with a spice bundle of citrusy coriander seeds and lemon zest along with fresh dill, whole peppercorns, and a smashed garlic clove that gave it savory depth and enhanced the soup's lemon flavor. Giving the rice a head start before adding the chicken ensured it had adequate time to cook through. Next we turned our attention to the eggs that give this soup its name. Although the eggs lend a luxuriously rich texture to this soup, they can also curdle if cooked improperly. Processing the eggs, yolks, and a portion of the cooked rice in a blender and then stirring this puree into the hot broth helped to heat the eggs gently so they wouldn't overcook and gave our lemony chicken and rice soup a velvety consistency.

1½ pounds boneless, skinless chicken breasts, trimmed
1¾ teaspoons table salt
12 (3-inch) strips lemon zest plus 6 tablespoons juice, divided, plus extra juice for seasoning (3 lemons)
2 sprigs fresh dill, plus 2 teaspoons chopped, divided
2 teaspoons coriander seeds
1 teaspoon black peppercorns
1 garlic clove, peeled and smashed
8 cups chicken broth
1 cup long-grain rice
2 large eggs plus 2 large yolks

1. Cut each chicken breast in half lengthwise. Toss with salt in bowl and let sit at room temperature for at least 15 minutes or up to 30 minutes. Cut 8-inch square of triple-thickness cheesecloth. Place lemon zest, dill sprigs, coriander seeds, peppercorns, and garlic in center of cheesecloth and tie into bundle with kitchen twine.

2. Bring broth, rice, and spice bundle to simmer in large saucepan over high heat. Reduce heat to low, cover, and cook for 5 minutes. Turn off heat, add chicken, cover, and let sit for 15 minutes.

3. Discard spice bundle. Transfer chicken to cutting board, let cool slightly, then shred into bite-size pieces using 2 forks. Using ladle, transfer 1 cup cooked rice to blender (leave any liquid in pot). Add lemon juice and eggs and yolks to blender and process until smooth, about 1 minute.

Turkey Meatball Soup with Kale

4. Stir shredded chicken and any accumulated juices into pot. Return soup to simmer over high heat. Off heat, stir in egg mixture until fully incorporated. Stir in chopped dill and season with salt, pepper, and extra lemon juice to taste. Serve.

Turkey Meatball Soup with Kale

INSTANT POT
Serves 6 to 8
Total Time 1 hour

Why This Recipe Works This Spanish-style meatball soup boasts a sunset-colored broth and lean turkey meatballs kept moist and tender thanks to a panade (a paste made from bread and milk) and sharp Manchego cheese. We started with a traditional Spanish base of onion, bell pepper, and garlic and then added some smoked paprika. Once we deglazed the pot with white wine, we poured in chicken broth, added chopped fresh kale, and dropped in the meatballs. After 3 minutes under pressure, we finished the soup with a sprinkling of parsley and extra Manchego. Be sure to use ground turkey, not ground turkey breast (also labeled 99 percent fat-free), in this recipe. Serve with crusty bread or Garlic Toasts (page 45).

1 slice hearty white sandwich bread, torn into
  1-inch pieces
¼ cup whole milk
1 ounce Manchego cheese, grated (½ cup), plus extra
  for serving
5 tablespoons minced fresh parsley, divided
½ teaspoon table salt
1 pound ground turkey
1 tablespoon extra-virgin olive oil
1 onion, chopped
1 red bell pepper, stemmed, seeded, and cut into
  ¾-inch pieces
4 garlic cloves, minced
2 teaspoons smoked paprika
½ cup dry white wine
8 cups chicken broth
8 ounces kale, stemmed and chopped

1. Using fork, mash bread and milk into paste in large
bowl. Stir in Manchego, 3 tablespoons parsley, and salt until
combined. Add turkey and knead mixture with your hands
until well combined. Pinch off and roll 2-teaspoon-size pieces
of mixture into balls and arrange on large plate (you should
have about 35 meatballs; meatballs can be refrigerated for up
to 24 hours); set aside.

2. Using highest sauté or browning function, heat oil in
electric pressure cooker until shimmering. Add onion and
bell pepper and cook until softened and lightly browned, 5 to
7 minutes. Stir in garlic and paprika and cook until fragrant,
about 30 seconds. Stir in wine, scraping up any browned bits,
and cook until almost completely evaporated, about 5 minutes.
Stir in broth and kale, then gently submerge meatballs.

3. Lock lid in place and close pressure release valve. Select
high pressure cook function and cook for 3 minutes. Turn off
pressure cooker and quick-release pressure. Carefully remove
lid, allowing steam to escape away from you.

4. Stir in remaining 2 tablespoons parsley and season
with salt and pepper to taste. Serve, passing extra Manchego
separately.

STEMMING KALE

Grab end of stem in 1 hand.
Pinch thumb and index
finger of your other hand on
either side of stem as you
strip leaves from bottom to
top of stem.

Beef and Vegetable Soup

DUTCH OVEN

Serves 4
Total Time 45 minutes

Why This Recipe Works One of the best parts of one-pot
cooking is the ability to get a hearty meal on the table in
record time, and this meat and vegetable soup fits the bill. To
make a meaty, satisfying soup that's ready in just 45 minutes,
we found that ground beef was a great alternative to beef
cubes. Not only does ground beef cook quickly, it's easy to
find and is relatively inexpensive compared to other cuts of
meat. A wide-bottomed Dutch oven was the perfect vessel for
quickly browning the beef, and the addition of beef broth
contributed even more rich, meaty flavor. Cutting the carrots,
potatoes, and green beans into small pieces reduced their
cooking time and meant we didn't need to resort to using
frozen ones, while canned diced tomatoes added bright tomato
flavor to our soup. We kept the seasoning simple with some
oregano, salt, and pepper. Stirring in parsley at the end of
cooking ensured its texture remained fresh and provided a
burst of herbal flavor.

1 pound 90 percent lean ground beef
1 onion, chopped
2 carrots, peeled and cut into ½-inch pieces
1 tablespoon minced fresh oregano or 1 teaspoon dried
1 teaspoon table salt
½ teaspoon pepper
4 cups beef broth
1 (14.5-ounce) can diced tomatoes
8 ounces Yukon Gold potatoes, peeled and cut into
  ½-inch pieces
6 ounces green beans, trimmed and cut on bias into
  1-inch lengths
2 tablespoons chopped fresh parsley

1. Cook beef, onion, carrots, oregano, salt, and pepper
in Dutch oven over medium-high heat, breaking up beef with
spoon until no longer pink, about 6 minutes. Add broth,
tomatoes and their juice, and potatoes and bring to simmer.
Reduce heat to low, cover, and cook until potatoes are almost
tender, about 10 minutes.

2. Stir in green beans and simmer, uncovered, until vegetables
are tender and soup has thickened slightly, 10 to 12 minutes.
Stir in parsley and season with salt and pepper to taste. Serve.

Mexican Beef and Vegetable Soup

DUTCH OVEN
Serves 6 to 8
Total Time 1¾ hours

Why This Recipe Works Mexico's version of beef and vegetable soup, caldo de res, is rich with spices, tender chunks of meat, and vegetables. But many traditional recipes require a long cooking time. To streamline, we eliminated bone-in cuts and focused on quicker-cooking boneless cuts. Flavorful, tender, and juicy boneless short ribs proved to be the ideal choice. We browned the meat and then set it aside while we sautéed onion and garlic. Sautéing some oregano and cumin with our aromatics helped bring out their flavors. After adding the broth (a combination of beef broth and chicken broth gave us the best flavor), we returned the beef to the pot and simmered everything. For the vegetables, we liked fresh corn (leaving it on the cob lent noticeable flavor to the broth) and zucchini, but we found that canned tomatoes provided more reliable flavor than fresh. We also added carrots and red potatoes, which contributed an earthiness that enriched the overall flavor of the soup. Staggering the addition of the vegetables to the broth ensured that they each cooked to perfection.

- 1 pound boneless short ribs, trimmed and cut into 1-inch pieces
- ¼ teaspoon table salt
- ⅛ teaspoon pepper
- 1 tablespoon vegetable oil
- 1 onion, chopped
- 5 garlic cloves, minced
- 1 tablespoon minced fresh oregano or 1 teaspoon dried
- ½ teaspoon ground cumin
- 4 cups beef broth
- 2 cups chicken broth
- 1 (14.5-ounce) can diced tomatoes, drained
- 2 bay leaves
- 2 carrots, peeled and cut into ½-inch pieces
- 10 ounces red potatoes, unpeeled, cut into 1-inch pieces
- 1 zucchini, cut into ½-inch pieces
- 2 ears corn, husks and silk removed, cut into 1-inch rounds
- 2 tablespoons minced fresh cilantro
  Sliced radishes
  Lime wedges

1. Pat beef dry with paper towels and sprinkle with salt and pepper. Heat oil in Dutch oven over medium-high heat until just smoking. Brown beef on all sides, 5 to 7 minutes; transfer to bowl.

Beef and Vegetable Soup

Mexican Beef and Vegetable Soup

2. Add onion to fat left in pot and cook over medium heat until softened, about 5 minutes. Stir in garlic, oregano, and cumin and cook until fragrant, about 30 seconds. Stir in beef broth, chicken broth, tomatoes, and bay leaves, scraping up any browned bits, and bring to simmer. Stir in beef along with any accumulated juices, reduce heat to low, cover, and simmer for 30 minutes.

3. Stir in carrots and potatoes and simmer, uncovered, until beef and vegetables are just tender, 20 to 25 minutes. Stir in zucchini and corn and simmer until corn is tender, 5 to 10 minutes. Discard bay leaves. Stir in cilantro and season with salt and pepper to taste. Garnish with radishes and serve with lime wedges.

Beef and Barley Soup
SLOW COOKER
Serves 6 to 8
Cook Time 9 to 11 hours on low or 6 to 8 hours on high

Why This Recipe Works The slow cooker is a hands-off, practical choice for one-pot cooking, but it can be challenging to pack in flavor without the ability to brown and sauté in it. To avoid the need for extra pots and pans, we turned to our favorite slow cooker sidekick: the microwave. Softening the onions in the microwave with tomato paste, vegetable oil, thyme, salt, and pepper made a world of difference in the soup's flavor and allowed us to skip the tedious process of browning the meat. To simplify things further we used trimmed beef blade steaks, which we shredded after they had become meltingly tender in the slow cooker—no need to cut the meat into pieces to start. The addition of soy sauce to the broth base contributed a surprising amount of savory, meaty flavor. Since pearl barley can absorb two to three times its volume in cooking liquid, we needed to be judicious in the quantity we added to the soup: A modest ½ cup lent a pleasing velvety texture without overfilling the slow cooker with swollen grains. Rather than using a portion of the canned tomatoes in our version for two, we opted to take an earthier route by incorporating mushrooms for deep umami flavor. Do not substitute hulled, hull-less, quick-cooking, or presteamed barley (read the ingredient list on the package to determine this).

- 2 onions, chopped fine
- ¼ cup tomato paste
- 2 tablespoons vegetable oil
- 1 tablespoon minced fresh thyme or 1 teaspoon dried
- ½ teaspoon table salt
- ½ teaspoon pepper

Beef and Barley Soup

- 1 (28-ounce) can diced tomatoes
- 4 cups beef broth
- 2 carrots, peeled and chopped
- ⅓ cup soy sauce
- ½ cup pearl barley, rinsed
- 2 bay leaves
- 2 pounds beef blade steaks, ¾ to 1 inch thick, trimmed
- 2 tablespoons minced fresh parsley
- 2 teaspoons red wine vinegar

1. Microwave onions, tomato paste, oil, thyme, salt, and pepper in bowl, stirring occasionally, until onions are softened, about 5 minutes; transfer to slow cooker.

2. Stir in tomatoes and their juice, broth, carrots, soy sauce, barley, and bay leaves. Nestle steaks into slow cooker. Cover and cook until steaks are tender, 9 to 11 hours on low or 6 to 8 hours on high.

3. Discard bay leaves. Transfer steaks to cutting board, let cool slightly, then shred into bite-size pieces using 2 forks; discard fat and gristle. Stir beef into soup and let sit until heated through, about 2 minutes. Stir in parsley and vinegar and season with salt and pepper to taste. Serve.

Beef and Barley Soup with Wild Mushrooms for Two
SLOW COOKER
Serves 2
Cook Time 9 to 11 hours on low or 6 to 8 hours on high

Do not substitute hulled, hull-less, quick-cooking, or presteamed barley (read the ingredient list on the package to determine this).

- 1 onion, chopped fine
- 2 tablespoons tomato paste
- 1 tablespoon vegetable oil
- 1½ teaspoons minced fresh thyme or ½ teaspoon dried
- 1 teaspoon rinsed and minced dried porcini mushrooms
- ½ teaspoon table salt
- ¼ teaspoon pepper
- 3 cups beef broth
- 6 ounces cremini, oyster, and/or white mushrooms, cut into 1-inch pieces
- 1 tablespoon soy sauce
- ¼ cup pearl barley, rinsed
- 1 bay leaf
- 8 ounces beef blade steaks, ¾ to 1 inch thick, trimmed
- 1 tablespoon minced fresh parsley
- 1 teaspoon red wine vinegar

1. Microwave onion, tomato paste, oil, thyme, porcini mushrooms, salt, and pepper in bowl, stirring occasionally, until onions are softened, about 5 minutes; transfer to slow cooker.

2. Stir in broth, cremini mushrooms, soy sauce, barley, and bay leaf. Nestle steaks into slow cooker. Cover and cook until steaks are tender, 9 to 11 hours on low or 6 to 8 hours on high.

3. Discard bay leaf. Transfer steaks to cutting board, let cool slightly, then shred into bite-size pieces using 2 forks; discard fat and gristle. Stir beef into soup and let sit until heated through, about 2 minutes. Stir in parsley and vinegar and season with salt and pepper to taste. Serve.

TRIMMING BLADE STEAKS

To trim blade steaks, halve each steak lengthwise, leaving the gristle on one half. Then simply cut the gristle away.

Beef Pho
INSTANT POT
Serves 6 to 8
Total Time 2¾ hours (2 hours for the broth, plus 45 minutes to finish the soup)

Why This Recipe Works With its richly perfumed broth and its mix of raw/cooked and hot/cold ingredients, beef pho is a delicious study in contrasts. Although it sounds complicated, it's surprisingly one-pot friendly with a few adjustments. Arguably the most important element is the fragrant broth produced by simmering beef bones with aromatics such as ginger, onions, cinnamon, and star anise. Making the broth traditionally requires a simmer of up to six hours, but using a pressure cooker allowed us to extract all of the beefy flavor from the bones in less time. For a broth with more depth and beefy richness, we browned the bones in the microwave before cooking; we also added the trimmings from the steaks we were slicing for the finished soup. To give our deeply aromatic broth the clean, clear look that is a hallmark of pho, we strained and defatted it after cooking. The rest of the soup components were simple: We soaked the quick-cooking rice noodles right in the broth so they would absorb its flavor. We thinly sliced the steaks (freezing them briefly made them firm enough to slice easily) and ladled the hot broth over the slices, which cooked them just enough. A few traditional garnishes of bean sprouts, cilantro, and fish sauce completed the bowl. The finished broth in step 5 should taste overseasoned; the addition of noodles will temper the flavor of the broth.

- 3 pounds beef bones
- 2 onions, quartered through root end, divided
- 3 quarts water, divided
- 2 tablespoons fish sauce, plus extra for serving
- 1 (4-inch) piece ginger, peeled and sliced into thin rounds
- 1 cinnamon stick
- 6 star anise pods
- 6 whole cloves
- 2 tablespoons sugar
- 1 tablespoon table salt
- 1 teaspoon black peppercorns
- 1 (1-pound) boneless strip steak, 1½ to 1¾ inches thick, trimmed, trimmings reserved
- 1 pound (¼-inch-wide) flat rice noodles
  Bean sprouts
  Fresh cilantro springs, Thai or Italian basil sprigs, and/or mint sprigs
  Lime wedges
  Sriracha
  Hoisin sauce

Beef Pho

Pork Ramen

1. Arrange beef bones on paper towel–lined plate and microwave (in batches if microwave is small) until well browned, 8 to 10 minutes. Add bones and 6 onion quarters to electric pressure cooker. Slice remaining 2 onion quarters as thin as possible and set aside for serving. Add 2 quarts water, fish sauce, ginger, cinnamon stick, star anise, cloves, sugar, salt, peppercorns, and reserved steak trimmings to pot.

2. Lock lid in place and close pressure release valve. Select high pressure cook function and cook for 1½ hours. Turn off pressure cooker and let pressure release naturally for 15 minutes. Quick-release any remaining pressure, then carefully remove lid, allowing steam to escape away from you.

3. Set fine-mesh strainer over large bowl or container and line with triple layer of cheesecloth. Discard bones. Strain broth through prepared strainer and let settle for 5 minutes; discard solids. Using wide, shallow spoon, skim excess fat from surface of broth. (Broth can be refrigerated for up to 4 days or frozen for up to 1 month; thaw frozen broth completely before proceeding with recipe.)

4. Meanwhile, cut steak crosswise into 1½-inch-wide strips and place strips on large plate; freeze until very firm, 35 to 45 minutes. Once firm, stand each piece on 1 cut side on cutting board and, using sharp knife, shave beef against grain as thin as possible. (Slices needn't be perfectly intact.) Return steak to plate and refrigerate until ready to serve.

5. Bring broth and remaining 1 quart water to boil in now-empty pressure cooker using highest sauté or browning function. Season with salt to taste. Turn off pressure cooker, add noodles, and let sit, stirring occasionally, until noodles are soft and pliable but not fully tender.

6. Divide noodles between individual serving bowls. Shingle steak evenly over noodles and pile onion on top of steak. Ladle hot broth into each bowl. Serve immediately, passing bean sprouts, cilantro sprigs, lime wedges, sriracha, hoisin, and extra fish sauce separately.

INGREDIENT SPOTLIGHT

RICE NOODLES
Dried rice noodles come in dozens of varieties, but the styles that you're likely to find at the supermarket are rice sticks, which are straight and flat with great chew, and rice vermicelli, which are round strands. We prefer vermicelli made from 100 percent rice flour to those that include a secondary starch such as cornstarch; however, if you can find only noodles that contain cornstarch, just cook them a bit longer.

Pork Ramen

SLOW COOKER

Serves 4 to 6
Cook Time 5 to 6 hours on high or 8 to 9 hours on low, plus 20 minutes on high

Why This Recipe Works To build a savory pork-infused broth that would transform store-bought ramen noodles into a truly delicious meal, we turned to our slow cooker. Packaged ramen noodles were a good starting point, but we discarded the packet of seasoning. Slowly simmering a pork butt roast (a well-marbled cut from the shoulder of the pig) in a mixture of chicken broth and umami-rich white miso gave the broth meaty flavor. Cooking the pork to 195 degrees resulted in a tender yet sliceable roast. Garlic, scallions, ginger, and shiitakes stirred into the broth before cooking layered in aromatic complexity and earthy depth, and steeping a sheet of kombu in the broth while the pork rested further amped up its savoriness. A final drizzle of sesame oil and chili oil added nuttiness and heat. Kombu is a type of kelp that adds savory depth to this ramen; it can be found in most well-stocked grocery stores and Asian markets. You can substitute 1¾ pounds of fresh ramen noodles for the dried. This recipe makes more pork than you will need for the ramen, but cooking the full amount is essential to the broth's flavor. You will need a 5- to 7-quart traditional slow cooker for this recipe. Serve with Soy-Marinated Eggs, if desired.

- 8 cups chicken broth
- ½ cup white miso
- 4 ounces shiitake mushrooms, stemmed and sliced thin
- 4 scallions, white and green parts separated, green parts sliced thin on bias
- 6 garlic cloves, smashed and peeled
- 1 (1½-inch) piece ginger, peeled and sliced into ½-inch-thick rounds
- 1 (2½-pound) boneless pork butt roast, trimmed
- ½ teaspoon pepper
- 1 (4-inch) square piece kombu (optional)
- 6 (3-ounce) packages ramen noodles, seasoning packets discarded
  Toasted sesame oil
  Chili oil

1. Whisk broth and miso together in slow cooker. Add mushrooms, scallion whites, garlic, and ginger. Sprinkle pork with pepper and transfer to slow cooker. Cover and cook until pork is tender and registers 195 degrees, 5 to 6 hours on high or 8 to 9 hours on low. Transfer pork to cutting board and let rest for 20 minutes.

2. Meanwhile, add kombu, if using, to broth mixture in slow cooker and cook, covered, on high for 10 minutes. Using slotted spoon, remove and discard scallion whites, garlic, ginger, and kombu, leaving mushrooms in slow cooker.

3. Add noodles to slow cooker, cover and cook on high until tender, about 8 minutes. Divide mushrooms and noodles evenly among serving bowls. Slice pork in half lengthwise, then slice crosswise ¼ inch thick. Ladle broth into bowls and top with 3 or 4 slices of pork and scallion greens. Serve, passing sesame oil and chili oil separately.

Soy-Marinated Eggs

Makes 4 eggs

You can use this method for one to eight large eggs without altering the timing. Do not marinate the eggs for longer than 4 hours in step 3 or they will become too salty. The soy marinade can be reused to marinate up to three batches of soft-cooked eggs; it can be refrigerated for up to one week and frozen for up to one month.

- 1 cup soy sauce
- ¼ cup mirin
- 2 scallions, sliced thin
- 2 tablespoons grated fresh ginger
- 2 tablespoons sugar
- 2 garlic cloves, minced
- 4 large eggs

1. Bring soy sauce, mirin, scallions, ginger, sugar, and garlic to simmer in small saucepan over medium-high heat, stirring occasionally to dissolve sugar. Off heat, stir in 1 cup cold water; set aside.

2. Bring 3 quarts water to boil in large saucepan over high heat. Fill large bowl halfway with ice and water. Using wire skimmer or slotted spoon, gently lower eggs into boiling water and cook for 7 minutes. Transfer eggs to prepared ice bath and let cool for 5 minutes. Peel eggs.

3. Combine soy sauce mixture and eggs in large zipper-lock bag and place bag in medium bowl. Press out as much air as possible from bag so eggs are fully submerged in liquid, then seal bag. Refrigerate for 4 hours. Remove eggs from marinade using slotted spoon. (Eggs, separated from marinade, can be refrigerated for up to 2 days.)

Meatball and Escarole Soup

SLOW COOKER

Serves 6 to 8
Cook Time 4 to 6 hours on low or 3 to 5 hours on high, plus 15 to 20 minutes on high

Why This Recipe Works Soup with hearty beans, delicate meatballs, and wilted greens is an Italian classic, and making it in a slow cooker helped us cook both the beans and meatballs to just the right texture. We started with canned beans (dried beans were undercooked when the meatballs were ready) and store-bought broth, to which we added onion, garlic, and red pepper flakes. To ensure moist, tender meatballs, we mixed the ground pork with a panade (a combination of bread and milk) as well as some Parmesan for flavor and richness. Microwaving the meatballs before adding them to the slow cooker jump-started the cooking and helped them retain their shape while they slowly finished cooking alongside the beans. Escarole, stirred in toward the end, rounded out our soup perfectly with some freshness and color. Serve with crusty bread or Garlic Toasts (page 45).

- 1 onion, chopped fine
- 1 tablespoon extra-virgin olive oil, plus extra for serving
- ¼ teaspoon table salt
- ¼ teaspoon red pepper flakes
- 4 garlic cloves, minced, divided
- 6 cups chicken broth
- 1 (15-ounce) can cannellini beans, rinsed
- 1 slice hearty white sandwich bread, torn into 1-inch pieces
- ¼ cup whole milk
- 1 ounce Parmesan cheese, grated (½ cup)
- 3 tablespoons minced fresh parsley
- 1½ teaspoons minced fresh oregano or ½ teaspoon dried
- ½ teaspoon pepper
- 1 pound ground pork
- 1 head escarole (1 pound), trimmed and sliced 1 inch thick

1. Microwave onion, oil, salt, pepper flakes, and half of garlic in bowl, stirring occasionally, until onions are softened, about 5 minutes; transfer to slow cooker. Stir in broth and beans.

2. Using fork, mash bread and milk together into paste in large bowl. Stir in Parmesan, parsley, oregano, remaining garlic, and pepper until combined. Add pork and knead mixture with your hands until well combined. Pinch off and roll tablespoon-size pieces of mixture into balls and arrange on large plate (you should have about 24 meatballs; meatballs can be refrigerated for up to 24 hours).

3. Microwave meatballs until firm and no longer pink, about 5 minutes. Gently place meatballs into slow cooker, along with any accumulated juices. Cover and cook until meatballs are tender, 4 to 6 hours on low or 3 to 5 hours on high.

4. Stir escarole into soup, 1 handful at a time (slow cooker will be quite full, but escarole will wilt down). Cover and cook on high until tender, 15 to 20 minutes. Season with salt and pepper to taste. Serve, passing extra oil separately.

Spicy Lamb and Lentil Soup

DUTCH OVEN

Serves 6 to 8
Total Time 2¼ hours

Why This Recipe Works Harira is a spiced, intensely flavored Moroccan soup of lentils, tomatoes, chickpeas, and often chicken or lamb. Our version of this North African specialty uses an inexpensive cut of lamb: shoulder chops. After searing the lamb and setting it aside, we built the stock with onion, a blend of warm spices, and chicken broth. We added the lamb back to the pot along with the lentils and allowed them to simmer in the oven for hands-off, even cooking. Once the lamb was cooked, we removed the pieces to cool before shredding them. We then added the tomatoes and chickpeas for a brief simmer on the stovetop before stirring the shredded meat back in and finishing with plenty of harissa, which contributed spice, heat, and depth. You can use our homemade Harissa (page 39) or any store-bought variety here. If you can't find lamb shoulder chops, you can substitute an equal amount of lamb shoulder roast trimmed of all visible fat.

- 1 pound boneless lamb shoulder chops, trimmed and cut into 2-inch pieces
- ¼ teaspoon table salt
- ⅛ teaspoon plus ¼ teaspoon pepper, divided
- 1 tablespoon extra-virgin olive oil
- 1 onion, chopped fine
- 1 teaspoon grated fresh ginger
- 1 teaspoon ground cumin
- ½ teaspoon paprika
- ¼ teaspoon ground cinnamon
- ¼ teaspoon cayenne pepper
  Pinch saffron threads, crumbled
- 1 tablespoon all-purpose flour
- 10 cups chicken broth
- 1 cup dried brown or green lentils, picked over and rinsed
- 1 pound plum tomatoes, cored and cut into ¾-inch pieces

1 (15-ounce) can chickpeas, rinsed
⅓ cup minced fresh cilantro
¾ cup harissa, divided

1. Adjust oven rack to lower-middle position and heat oven to 325 degrees. Sprinkle lamb with salt and ⅛ teaspoon pepper. Heat oil in Dutch oven over medium-high heat until just smoking. Brown lamb on all sides, about 8 minutes; transfer to plate. Pour off all but 2 tablespoons fat from pot.

2. Add onion to fat left in pot and cook over medium heat until softened, about 5 minutes. Stir in ginger, cumin, paprika, cinnamon, cayenne, saffron, and remaining ¼ teaspoon pepper and cook until fragrant, about 30 seconds. Stir in flour and cook for 1 minute. Gradually whisk in broth, scraping up any browned bits and smoothing out any lumps. Return lamb along with any accumulated juices to pot, bring to simmer, and cook for 10 minutes. Stir in lentils. Cover, place pot in oven, and cook until fork slips easily in and out of lamb and lentils are tender, about 50 minutes.

3. Remove pot from oven. Transfer lamb to cutting board, let cool slightly, then shred into bite-size pieces using 2 forks; discard fat.

4. Meanwhile, stir tomatoes and chickpeas into soup and simmer over medium-high heat until flavors meld, about 10 minutes. Stir in shredded lamb and let sit until heated through, about 2 minutes. Stir in cilantro and ¼ cup harissa and season with salt and pepper to taste. Serve, passing extra harissa separately.

New England Clam Chowder

Harissa

Makes 1 cup
If you can't find Aleppo pepper, you can substitute 1½ teaspoons paprika and 1½ teaspoons finely chopped red pepper flakes.

¾ cup extra-virgin olive oil
12 garlic cloves, minced
¼ cup paprika
2 tablespoons ground coriander
2 tablespoons ground dried Aleppo pepper
2 teaspoons ground cumin
1½ teaspoons caraway seeds
1 teaspoon table salt

Combine all ingredients in bowl and microwave until bubbling and very fragrant, about 1 minute, stirring halfway through microwaving. Let cool completely before serving. (Harissa can be refrigerated for up to 4 days. Bring to room temperature before serving.)

New England Clam Chowder
DUTCH OVEN
Serves 6 to 8
Total Time 45 minutes

Why This Recipe Works Homemade clam chowder is often one of two things: time-consuming and fantastic or quick and forgettable. We wanted to find a middle ground, eliminating laborious prep work without sacrificing flavor. We started by sautéing strips of bacon, saving the slices for garnishing and leaving the fat in the pot for our flavor base. To put the spotlight on the clams, we created a makeshift stock of clam juice and water. We skipped steaming and shucking by turning to chopped canned clams, which imparted fresh clam flavor with little effort. The result? A chowder that was thick, rich, and bursting with clam flavor in under an hour. To make a version for two, we traded the large quantity of potatoes for parsnips and added convenient frozen corn.

4 slices thick-cut bacon, cut into ¼-inch pieces
1 large onion, chopped fine
1 teaspoon minced fresh thyme or ¼ teaspoon dried
2 tablespoons all-purpose flour
4 (6½-ounce) cans minced clams, drained with juice reserved
2 (8-ounce) bottles clam juice
1 cup water
1½ pounds red potatoes, unpeeled, cut into ½-inch pieces
2 bay leaves
1 cup heavy cream
2 tablespoons minced fresh parsley

1. Cook bacon in Dutch oven over medium heat until rendered and crisp, 5 to 7 minutes. Stir in onion and cook until softened, about 5 minutes. Stir in thyme and cook until fragrant, about 30 seconds. Stir in flour and cook for 1 minute. Slowly whisk in reserved clam juice, bottled clam juice, and water, scraping up any browned bits and smoothing out any lumps.

2. Stir in potatoes and bay leaves, bring to simmer, and cook until tender, about 10 minutes. Stir in cream and clams and cook until heated through, about 3 minutes. Off heat, stir in parsley and season with salt and pepper to taste. Serve.

VARIATION

New England Clam Chowder with Parsnips and Corn for Two
SAUCEPAN
Serves 2
Total Time 45 minutes
Other root vegetables such as celery root, turnips, and red potatoes can be used in place of the parsnips.

2 slices bacon, cut into ¼-inch pieces
1 small onion, chopped fine
½ teaspoon minced fresh thyme or ⅛ teaspoon dried
1½ tablespoons all-purpose flour
2 (6½-ounce) cans minced clams, drained with juice reserved
1 (8-ounce) bottle clam juice
4 ounces parsnips, peeled, cut into ½-inch pieces
½ cup heavy cream
½ cup frozen corn, thawed

1. Cook bacon in large saucepan over medium heat until rendered and crisp, 5 to 7 minutes. Stir in onion and cook until softened, about 5 minutes. Stir in thyme and cook until fragrant, about 30 seconds. Stir in flour and cook for 1 minute. Slowly whisk in reserved clam juice and bottled clam juice, scraping up any browned bits and smoothing out any lumps.

2. Stir in parsnips, bring to simmer, and cook until tender, about 10 minutes. Stir in cream, corn, and clams and cook until heated through, about 3 minutes. Off heat, season with salt and pepper to taste. Serve.

Hearty Seafood and Saffron Soup
SLOW COOKER
Serves 4 to 6
Cook Time 6 to 7 hours on low or 4 to 5 hours on high, plus 20 to 30 minutes on high

Why This Recipe Works The slow cooker provides the ideal gentle cooking environment for this tomato-based spiced seafood soup. We started by using the microwave to make a sofrito of onion, bell pepper, and garlic, to which we added tomato paste, paprika, saffron, and red pepper flakes for a rich foundation. Clam juice added briny flavor and a little wine added depth; some water achieved the right consistency. Slowly simmered with bay leaves, our tomatoes and liquid turned fragrant. Adding the seafood at the end ensured that it cooked perfectly. Finished with a picada—a flavorful mixture of bread crumbs, chopped almonds, and olive oil—and a drizzle of olive oil, this soup tasted rich and hearty. Haddock and striped bass are good substitutes for the cod. If desired, you can omit the squid and increase the cod to 1½ pounds. Serve with crusty bread or Garlic Toasts (page 45).

1 onion, chopped fine
1 red bell pepper, stemmed, seeded, and chopped fine
6 garlic cloves, minced
2 tablespoons extra-virgin olive oil, divided, plus extra for serving
2 tablespoons tomato paste
1 tablespoon paprika
¾ teaspoon table salt, divided
¼ teaspoon saffron threads, crumbled
⅛ teaspoon red pepper flakes
1 (28-ounce) can diced tomatoes
2 cups water
1 (8-ounce) bottle clam juice
¼ cup dry white wine
2 bay leaves
1 pound skinless cod fillets, 1 to 1½ inches thick, cut into 1-inch pieces
8 ounces small squid bodies, sliced crosswise into ½-inch-thick rings
⅛ teaspoon pepper
2 tablespoons minced fresh parsley
1 recipe Picada (optional; page 75)

1. Microwave onion, bell pepper, garlic, oil, tomato paste, paprika, ½ teaspoon salt, saffron, and pepper flakes in bowl, stirring occasionally, until vegetables are softened, about 5 minutes; transfer to slow cooker. Stir in tomatoes and their juice, water, clam juice, wine, and bay leaves. Cover and cook until flavors meld, 6 to 7 hours on low or 4 to 5 hours on high.

2. Sprinkle cod and squid with remaining ¼ teaspoon salt and pepper and stir into soup. Cover and cook on high until cod flakes apart when gently prodded with paring knife, 20 to 30 minutes.

3. Discard bay leaves. Gently stir in parsley and season with salt and pepper to taste. Serve, passing extra oil separately and picada, if using.

Cioppino
DUTCH OVEN
Serves 4 to 6
Total Time 1½ hours

Why This Recipe Works Cioppino, a soup featuring an assortment of fish and shellfish simmered in a brightly flavored broth, makes for an elegant one-pot meal. For our version, we used white wine to steam the clams and mussels, removing them as they opened, and saved the briny liquid to add to our broth of aromatics, tomatoes, water, and clam juice. We gently poached halibut and then set it aside to avoid overcooking. After simmering the cooked shellfish in the broth with parsley, we divided the halibut into bowls and ladled the broth and shellfish on top. Swordfish is a good substitute for the halibut. Discard clams or mussels with unpleasant odors, cracked shells, or shells that won't close. If littlenecks are not available, substitute Manila or mahogany clams, or use 2 pounds of mussels. For a spicier dish, use the greater amount of pepper flakes. Serve with crusty bread or Garlic Toasts (page 45).

1	pound littleneck clams, scrubbed
1¼	cups dry white wine
4	tablespoons unsalted butter
1	pound mussels, scrubbed and debearded
¼	cup extra-virgin olive oil, plus extra for serving
2	large onions, chopped fine
½	teaspoon table salt
½	teaspoon pepper
¼	cup water
4	garlic cloves, minced
2	bay leaves
1	tablespoon minced fresh oregano or 1 teaspoon dried
⅛–¼	teaspoon red pepper flakes

Cioppino

1	(28-ounce) can whole peeled tomatoes, drained with juice reserved, chopped coarse
1	(8-ounce) bottle clam juice
1	(1½ pound) skinless halibut fillet, ¾ to 1 inch thick, cut into 6 pieces
¼	cup chopped fresh parsley

1. Bring clams, wine, and butter to boil in covered Dutch oven over high heat. Steam until clams just open, 5 to 8 minutes, transferring them to large bowl as they open. Once all clams have been transferred to bowl, add mussels to liquid left in pot, cover, and cook over high heat until mussels have opened, 2 to 4 minutes, transferring them to bowl with clams as they open. Pour cooking liquid from pot into bowl with clams and mussels, avoiding any grit that has settled on the bottom of the pot. Discard any unopened clams or mussels.

2. Wipe pot clean with paper towels. Heat oil in now-empty pot over medium heat until shimmering. Add onions, salt, and pepper and cook, stirring frequently, until beginning to brown, 7 to 9 minutes. Add water and cook, stirring frequently, until onions are soft, 2 to 4 minutes. Stir in garlic, bay leaves, oregano, and pepper flakes and cook for 1 minute. Stir in tomatoes and reserved juice and clam juice and bring to simmer. Reduce heat to low, cover, and cook for 5 minutes.

3. Submerge halibut in broth, cover, and gently simmer until fish is cooked through, 12 to 15 minutes. Off heat, transfer halibut to plate using slotted spoon, and cover with aluminum foil to keep warm.

4. Stir clams, mussels, and reserved broth into pot and bring to simmer over high heat. Stir in parsley and season with salt and pepper to taste. Divide halibut among serving bowls. Ladle broth, clams, and mussels over halibut. Drizzle with extra oil and serve immediately.

Creamy Carrot Soup with Warm Spices
INSTANT POT
Serves 6 to 8
Total Time 1 hour

Why This Recipe Works Pantry-friendly carrots and onions plus a few delicately balanced aromatics cook for a mere 3 minutes under pressure to produce this rich, satisfying soup. In many carrot soup recipes, the sweet, earthy flavor of the carrots is muted by the addition of other vegetables, fruits, or dairy, so we kept these extras to a minimum to allow the carrot flavor to remain prominent. Inspired by the flavors of the eastern Mediterranean, we added a combination of fresh ginger, ground coriander, fennel, and cinnamon. A touch of baking soda helped break down the carrots, and after a quick spin in the blender we had a satiny-smooth and creamy soup without adding cream. To finish, we topped individual portions with a bit of tart Greek yogurt, a drizzle of pomegranate molasses to underscore the natural sweetness of the carrots, some toasted hazelnuts, and fresh herbs.

- 2 tablespoons extra-virgin olive oil
- 2 onions, chopped
- 1 teaspoon table salt
- 1 tablespoon grated fresh ginger
- 1 tablespoon ground coriander
- 1 tablespoon ground fennel
- 1 teaspoon ground cinnamon
- 4 cups vegetable or chicken broth
- 2 cups water
- 2 pounds carrots, peeled and cut into 2-inch pieces
- ½ teaspoon baking soda
- 2 tablespoons pomegranate molasses
- ½ cup plain Greek yogurt
- ½ cup hazelnuts, toasted, skinned, and chopped
- ½ cup chopped fresh cilantro or mint

Creamy Carrot Soup with Warm Spices

Fresh Corn Chowder

1. Using highest sauté or browning function, heat oil in electric pressure cooker until shimmering. Add onions and salt and cook until onions are softened, 3 to 5 minutes. Stir in ginger, coriander, fennel, and cinnamon and cook until fragrant, about 30 seconds. Stir in broth, water, carrots, and baking soda.

2. Lock lid in place and close pressure release valve. Select high pressure cook function and cook for 3 minutes. Turn off pressure cooker and quick-release pressure. Carefully remove lid, allowing steam to escape away from you.

3. Working in batches, process soup in blender until smooth, 1 to 2 minutes. Return processed soup to pressure cooker and bring to simmer using highest sauté or browning function. Season with salt and pepper to taste. Drizzle individual portions with pomegranate molasses and top with yogurt, hazelnuts, and cilantro before serving.

Fresh Corn Chowder

DUTCH OVEN
Serves 6 to 8
Total Time 1 hour

Why This Recipe Works Great corn chowder captures the clear, sweet flavor of farm-fresh corn, but making a thick, lush chowder that showcases corn's flavor rather than obscures it is no easy feat. We started by cooking chopped bacon in a Dutch oven and used the rendered fat to sauté onion and garlic; this gave us a richly flavored base for our chowder that balanced the corn's sweetness without overpowering it. Water diluted the flavor of the chowder, so instead we used chicken broth as our liquid. Next, we turned our attention to the chowder's star ingredient: corn. For maximum corn flavor, we first added grated corn and corn milk—the liquid which comes from scraping the cobs with the back of a butter knife—before stirring in whole kernels toward the end. To enhance our chowder's creamy consistency, we used a combination of whole milk and heavy cream, which added just the right amount of richness. To thicken the soup slightly, we added a few tablespoons of flour. This soup tastes best with sweet corn from the height of the season; do not substitute frozen corn.

10 ears corn, husks and silk removed
4 slices bacon, chopped fine
1 onion, chopped fine
2 garlic cloves, minced
1 teaspoon minced fresh thyme or ¼ teaspoon dried
3 tablespoons all-purpose flour
3 cups chicken broth
2 cups whole milk
12 ounces red potatoes, unpeeled, cut into ¼-inch pieces
2 bay leaves
1 cup heavy cream
2 tablespoons minced fresh parsley

1. Working with 1 ear of corn at a time, stand 4 ears on end inside large bowl and cut kernels from cob using paring knife. Grate remaining 6 ears over large holes of box grater into separate bowl. Using back of butter knife, scrape remaining pulp from all cobs into bowl with grated corn.

2. Cook bacon in Dutch oven over medium heat until rendered and crisp, 5 to 7 minutes. Stir in onion and cook until softened, 5 to 7 minutes. Stir in garlic and thyme and cook until fragrant, about 30 seconds. Stir in flour and cook for 1 minute. Slowly whisk in broth and milk, scraping up any browned bits and smoothing out any lumps. Stir in potatoes, bay leaves, and grated corn and pulp mixture. Bring to simmer and cook until potatoes are almost tender, about 15 minutes.

3. Stir in remaining corn kernels and cream. Continue to simmer until corn kernels are tender yet still slightly crunchy, about 5 minutes. Discard bay leaves. Stir in parsley and season with salt and pepper to taste. Serve.

PREPARING CORN FOR CHOWDER

1. Stand corn upright inside large bowl and carefully cut kernels from cobs using paring knife.

2. Grate ears of corn over large holes of box grater to release both starch and more intense corn flavor.

3. Before discarding cobs, scrape remaining pulp from each using back of butter knife.

Tuscan Tomato and Bread Soup

Tuscan Tomato and Bread Soup

SAUCEPAN
Serves 4
Total Time 40 minutes

Why This Recipe Works A Tuscan classic, pappa al pomodoro is a hearty, thrifty soup—a perfect example of how simple pantry ingredients can be transformed with astounding results. The traditional preparation for this soup, which calls for day-old bread to be stirred into tomato sauce and doused in olive oil, is delicious but it's also inconsistent. The bread should break down in the warm broth to thicken the soup, but if the bread is too crusty or too distinctly flavored it can quickly change the consistency or overpower the tomato flavor. By using hearty white sandwich bread, a grocery staple, and building a savory tomato soup around it, we ensured the same results every time. Canned crushed tomatoes provided both a heavy tomato presence and consistent texture without requiring hours of stovetop cooking. Blooming sliced garlic in a generous amount of extra-virgin olive oil infused the soup with traditional flavors, boosted its savoriness, and eliminated any canned tomato flavor. A finishing sprinkle of Parmesan, a splash of nice olive oil, and a light scattering of chopped basil brought the dish home.

¼ cup extra-virgin olive oil, plus extra for serving
3 garlic cloves, sliced thin
¼ teaspoon red pepper flakes
1 (28-ounce) can crushed tomatoes
4 ounces hearty white sandwich bread, cut into ½-inch pieces (3 cups)
2 cups chicken broth
1 sprig fresh basil plus 2 tablespoons chopped, divided
½ teaspoon table salt
¼ teaspoon pepper
Grated Parmesan cheese

1. Cook oil, garlic, and pepper flakes in large saucepan over medium heat until garlic is lightly browned, about 4 minutes. Stir in tomatoes, bread, broth, basil sprig, salt, and pepper and bring to simmer. Reduce heat to medium-low, cover, and cook until bread has softened completely and soup has thickened slightly, about 15 minutes, stirring occasionally.

2. Off heat, discard basil sprig. Whisk soup until bread has fully broken down and soup has thickened further, about 1 minute. Sprinkle individual portions with Parmesan and chopped basil and drizzle with extra oil before serving.

NOTES FROM THE TEST KITCHEN

STORING AND REHEATING SOUPS AND STEWS

As tempting as it might seem, don't transfer hot soups and stews straight to the refrigerator. This will increase the fridge's internal temperature, which is dangerous for all the other food stored there. To drop the temperature to a fridge-safe 75 degrees, let the pot cool on the counter for an hour. If you don't have an hour, you can divide the contents of the pot into storage containers to allow the heat to dissipate more quickly, or you can cool it rapidly by using a frozen bottle of water to stir the contents of the pot.

To reheat soups and stews, simmer gently on the stovetop in a sturdy, heavy-bottomed pot. A spin in the microwave in a covered dish works, too. For soups or stews with pasta (which turns mushy) or dairy (which curdles as it freezes), make and freeze the dish without the pasta or dairy. After the thawed soup or stew has been heated through, stir in the uncooked pasta and simmer until just tender, or stir in the dairy and heat gently until hot (do not boil).

Summary Vegetable Soup

Summer Vegetable Soup

DUTCH OVEN
Serves 6 to 8
Total Time 1 hour

Why This Recipe Works Soupe au pistou is a Provençal soup chock-full of fresh vegetables, creamy white beans, and fragrant herbs—a celebration of fresh produce in one pot. Virtually any vegetable can go in the soup, but we liked a combination of leeks, green beans, and zucchini. Many recipes use water for the liquid, but supplementing the water with vegetable broth gave our soup a more rounded base. Canned beans cooked quickly, and adding the liquid to the pot lent extra body and flavor. This soup is traditionally served with a dollop of pistou or pesto. You can use our homemade Classic Basil Pesto or any fresh store-bought variety here. If you cannot find haricots verts (thin green beans), substitute regular green beans and cook them for an extra minute or two. Serve with crusty bread or Garlic Toasts.

- 1 tablespoon extra-virgin olive oil
- 1 leek, white and light green parts only, halved lengthwise, sliced ½ inch thick, and washed thoroughly
- 1 celery rib, cut into ½-inch pieces
- 1 carrot, peeled and sliced ¼ inch thick
- ½ teaspoon table salt
- 2 garlic cloves, minced
- 3 cups vegetable broth
- 3 cups water
- ½ cup orecchiette, small shells, or other short pasta
- 8 ounces haricots verts or green beans, trimmed and cut into ½-inch lengths
- 1 (15-ounce) can cannellini or navy beans
- 1 small zucchini, halved lengthwise, seeded, and cut into ¼-inch pieces
- 1 large tomato, cored, seeded, and cut into ¼-inch pieces
- ¾ cup basil pesto

1. Heat oil in Dutch oven over medium heat until shimmering. Add leek, celery, carrot, and salt and cook until vegetables are softened, 8 to 10 minutes. Stir in garlic and cook until fragrant, about 30 seconds. Stir in broth and water and bring to simmer.

2. Stir in pasta and simmer until slightly softened, about 5 minutes. Stir in haricots verts and simmer until bright green but still crunchy, 3 to 5 minutes. Stir in beans and their liquid, zucchini, and tomato and simmer until pasta and vegetables are tender, about 3 minutes. Season with salt and pepper to taste. Dollop individual portions with pesto and serve.

Classic Basil Pesto

Makes about ¾ cup

- 3 garlic cloves, unpeeled
- ¼ cup pine nuts
- 2 cups fresh basil leaves
- 2 tablespoons fresh parsley leaves
- 8 tablespoons extra-virgin olive oil
- ¼ cup grated Parmesan cheese, plus extra for serving

1. Toast garlic in 8-inch skillet over medium heat, shaking skillet occasionally, until softened and spotty brown, about 8 minutes. When garlic is cool enough to handle, discard skins and chop coarse. Meanwhile, toast pine nuts in now-empty skillet over medium heat, stirring often, until golden and fragrant, 4 to 5 minutes.

2. Place basil and parsley in 1-gallon zipper-lock bag. Pound bag with flat side of meat pounder or with rolling pin until all leaves are bruised.

3. Process garlic, pine nuts, and herbs in food processor until finely chopped, about 1 minute, scraping down sides of bowl as needed. With processor running, slowly add oil until incorporated. Transfer pesto to bowl, stir in Parmesan, and season with salt and pepper to taste. (Pesto can be refrigerated for up to 3 days or frozen for up to 3 months. To prevent browning, press plastic wrap flush to surface or top with thin layer of olive oil. Bring to room temperature before using.)

Garlic Toasts

Makes 8 slices
Be sure to use a high-quality crusty bread, such as a baguette; do not use sliced sandwich bread.

- 8 (1-inch-thick) slices rustic bread
- 1 large garlic clove, peeled
- 3 tablespoons extra-virgin olive oil

Adjust oven rack 6 inches from broiler element and heat broiler. Spread bread evenly in rimmed baking sheet and broil, flipping as needed, until well toasted on both sides, about 4 minutes. Briefly rub 1 side of each toast with garlic, drizzle with oil, and season with salt and pepper to taste. Serve.

BUYING BROTH

Homemade broths taste amazing, but they're not always practical. The reality is that the majority of home cooks rely on supermarket broth for most recipes. When selecting store-bought broth, it's important to choose wisely since what you use can have a big impact on the flavor of your final dish. We prefer chicken broth to beef broth and vegetable broth for its stronger, cleaner flavor, though all have their place in our recipes.

Chicken Broth We like chicken broths with short ingredient lists that include a relatively high percentage of meat-based protein and flavor-boosting vegetables such as carrots, celery, and onions. We also like a lower sodium content—less than 700 milligrams per serving. Our favorite is **Swanson Chicken Stock**.

Vegetable Broth We've found that many of the top brands of vegetable broth have a hefty amount of salt and overpowering vegetable flavor. Our favorite, **Orrington Farms Vegan Chicken Flavored Broth Base & Seasoning**, didn't suffer from the off-flavors that plagued more vegetable-heavy products.

Beef Broth We've found the best beef broths have concentrated beef stock and flavor-enhancing ingredients such as tomato paste and yeast extract near the top of their ingredient lists. Our favorite brand is **Better Than Bouillon Roasted Beef Base**.

Clam Juice Bottled clam juice conveniently brings a bright and mineral-y flavor to seafood dishes. Our favorite, **Bar Harbor Clam Juice**, comes from the shores of clam country in Maine.

Miso Soup with Shiitakes and Sweet Potatoes

SLOW COOKER

Serves 6

Cook Time 4 to 5 hours on low or 3 to 4 hours on high

Why This Recipe Works A great miso soup is all about the rich, flavorful broth, and we knew that our trusty slow cooker was the perfect cooking vessel in which to build up a base packed with flavor. We started by combining a hearty amount of shiitake mushrooms with scallions, ginger, garlic, sesame oil, and red pepper flakes, and we microwaved the mixture until the mushrooms had softened. We then added this mixture to our slow cooker to serve as a flavorful, umami-rich backbone for the broth once combined with water, soy sauce, and miso. Before adding the miso to the slow cooker, we found it best to thin the thick paste with a small amount of water to ensure that it would be fully incorporated into the soup. For extra protein we bumped up the amount of tofu, which is traditional in miso soup, and selected the extra-firm variety, as it held its shape best during cooking. For an interesting twist we added sweet potatoes, which contributed an earthy sweetness, and stirred in watercress for a fresh, peppery finish. Do not substitute soft or silken tofu, as these varieties will break down while cooking.

- 12 ounces shiitake mushrooms, stemmed and sliced thin
- 2 scallions, sliced thin
- 1 (2-inch) piece ginger, peeled and sliced into ¼-inch-thick rounds
- 4 garlic cloves, minced
- 2 teaspoons toasted sesame oil
- ¼ teaspoon table salt
- ⅛ teaspoon red pepper flakes
- 6 cups water, divided
- ½ cup white miso
- 14 ounces extra-firm tofu, cut into ½-inch cubes
- 12 ounces sweet potatoes, peeled and cut into ½-inch pieces
- 1 tablespoon soy sauce, plus extra for seasoning
- 3 ounces (3 cups) watercress, cut into 2-inch pieces

1. Microwave mushrooms, scallions, ginger, garlic, oil, salt, and pepper flakes in bowl, stirring occasionally, until mushrooms are softened, about 5 minutes; transfer to slow cooker.

2. Whisk 1 cup water and miso in now-empty bowl until miso is fully dissolved. Stir miso mixture, tofu, potatoes, soy sauce, and remaining 5 cups water into slow cooker. Cover and cook until potatoes are tender, 4 to 5 hours on low or 3 to 4 hours on high.

3. Discard ginger. Stir in watercress and let sit until slightly wilted, about 3 minutes. Season with salt, pepper, and extra soy sauce to taste. Serve.

Kimchi and Tofu Soup

SAUCEPAN

Serves 4 to 6
Total Time 45 minutes

Why This Recipe Works This spicy Korean soup is typically served sizzling and hot tableside in an earthenware bowl, leading to the name "Hot Pot" that is often seen on Korean restaurant menus across America. We wanted a version of this soup we could make at home, without the traditional earthenware serving vessel, so we built the soup in a large saucepan. This warming soup gets its tang and heat from cabbage kimchi and gochujang, a Korean chile-soybean paste. For supple, tender bites of tofu, we used silken tofu and kept the pieces large to start. As the soup cooks and is stirred, the tofu breaks up into bite-size pieces. You can find gochujang in most well-stocked grocery stores and Asian markets. If enoki mushrooms are unavailable, substitute thinly sliced white button mushrooms. Do not drain the kimchi before measuring it; the pickling liquid is quite flavorful. For a spicier soup, use the larger amount of gochujang. Be sure to cut the tofu into large 2-inch pieces; they will break down as the soup cooks. Serve with rice (see page 21).

- 1 tablespoon vegetable oil
- 6 scallions, white parts sliced thin and green parts cut into 1-inch pieces, divided
- 4 garlic cloves, minced
- 2 teaspoons grated fresh ginger
- 1–3 tablespoons gochujang
- 6 cups vegetable broth
- 28 ounces silken tofu, cut into rough 2-inch pieces
- 1 cup cabbage kimchi, chopped coarse
- 8 ounces daikon radish, trimmed and cut into ½-inch pieces
- 2 tablespoons soy sauce
- 2 ounces enoki mushrooms, trimmed

Cook oil, scallion whites, garlic, ginger, and gochujang in large saucepan over medium-high heat until fragrant, about 2 minutes. Stir in broth, tofu, kimchi, radish, and soy sauce. Bring to simmer and cook, stirring occasionally, until flavors meld, about 15 minutes. Stir in scallion greens and season with salt and pepper to taste. Top individual portions with mushrooms before serving.

Miso Soup with Shiitakes and Sweet Potatoes

Kimchi and Tofu Soup

Portuguese Potato, Sausage, and Greens Soup

DUTCH OVEN
Serves 6 to 8
Total Time 1¼ hours

Why This Recipe Works Everything about caldo verde lends itself to one-pot cooking. The classic Portuguese soup of smoky sausage, potatoes, and sturdy greens is hearty without being fussy or time-consuming. After cooking spicy chorizo in a Dutch oven, we used the leftover fat in the pot to soften our aromatics. This soup's broth is usually made with just water, but for deeper flavor we supplemented the water with some chicken broth. Staggering the addition of the main ingredients ensured everything cooked just right. First we added sturdy Yukon Gold potatoes, followed by collard greens; once the collards had a chance to wilt we returned the cooked chorizo back to the pot. Mashing some of the cooked potatoes helped thicken the soup to the proper consistency. We prefer collard greens here for their delicate sweetness and meaty bite, but kale can be substituted. Portuguese linguiça or Polish kielbasa can be substituted for the Spanish-style chorizo. Serve with crusty bread or Garlic Toasts (page 45).

¼ cup extra-virgin olive oil, divided, plus extra for serving
12 ounces Spanish-style chorizo sausage, cut into ½-inch pieces
1 onion, chopped fine
4 garlic cloves, minced
1¼ teaspoons table salt
¼ teaspoon red pepper flakes
2 pounds Yukon Gold potatoes, peeled and cut into ¾-inch pieces
4 cups chicken broth
4 cups water
1 pound collard greens, stemmed and cut into 1-inch pieces
2 teaspoons white wine vinegar

1. Heat 1 tablespoon oil in Dutch oven over medium-high heat until shimmering. Add chorizo and cook, stirring occasionally, until lightly browned, 4 to 5 minutes. Using slotted spoon, transfer chorizo to bowl; set aside.

2. Add onion, garlic, salt, and pepper flakes to fat left in pot and cook over medium heat until onion is softened, about 5 minutes. Stir in potatoes, broth, and water, bring to simmer, and cook until potatoes are just tender, 8 to 10 minutes.

3. Stir in collard greens, return to simmer, and cook for 10 minutes. Stir in chorizo and simmer until greens are tender,

8 to 10 minutes. Off heat, stir in remaining 3 tablespoons oil and vinegar. Mash portion of potatoes against side of pot to thicken soup as desired. Season with salt and pepper to taste. Drizzle individual portions with extra oil before serving.

Spiced Wild Rice and Coconut Soup

INSTANT POT
Serves 6 to 8
Total Time 1¼ hours

Why This Recipe Works Wild rice can be tricky to cook properly, but the pressure cooker turns this grain tender with just the right amount of chew in this earthy soup that pairs vibrant turmeric with bold garam masala. Along with the spices, we added tomato paste, a serrano chile, and ginger to a combination of vegetable broth and rich coconut milk. We tried putting everything in the pot all at once, but the flavors dulled while cooking, so we reserved half of the coconut milk and some ginger to stir in after cooking. For fresh texture, we stirred in Swiss chard until just wilted, letting it maintain its pleasant bite. Some chopped tomato added just the right amount of sweetness and acidity and a sprinkle of cilantro provided a bright finish. Do not use quick-cooking or presteamed wild rice (read the ingredient list on the package to determine this) in this recipe.

2 tablespoons vegetable oil
2 onions, chopped fine
8 ounces Swiss chard, stems chopped fine, leaves cut into 1½-inch pieces, divided
¾ teaspoon table salt
6 garlic cloves, minced
2 tablespoons grated fresh ginger, divided
1 serrano chile, stemmed, seeded, and minced
1 tablespoon tomato paste
2 teaspoons ground turmeric
1½ teaspoons garam masala
4 cups vegetable or chicken broth
2 (14-ounce) cans coconut milk, divided
1 cup wild rice, picked over and rinsed
1 tomato, cored and chopped
¼ cup chopped fresh cilantro
Lime wedges

1. Using highest sauté or browning function, heat oil in electric pressure cooker until shimmering. Add onions, chard stems, and salt and cook until softened, 3 to 5 minutes. Stir in garlic, 4 teaspoons ginger, serrano, tomato paste, turmeric, and garam masala and cook until fragrant, about 1 minute.

Stir in broth and 1 can coconut milk, scraping up any browned bits, then stir in rice.

2. Lock lid in place and close pressure release valve. Select high pressure cook function and cook for 30 minutes. Turn off pressure cooker and quick-release pressure. Carefully remove lid, allowing steam to escape away from you.

3. Stir remaining can coconut milk and chard leaves into soup and cook, using highest sauté or browning function, until chard leaves are wilted, about 5 minutes. Turn off pressure cooker. Stir in remaining 2 teaspoons ginger and tomato and let sit until heated through, about 2 minutes. Stir in cilantro and season with salt and pepper to taste. Serve with lime wedges.

VARIATION

Curried Wild Rice and Coconut Soup for Two
INSTANT POT

Serves 2

Total Time 1¼ hours

Do not use quick-cooking or presteamed wild rice (read the ingredient list on the package to determine this) in this recipe.

    1 tablespoon vegetable oil
    1 onion, chopped fine
    3 garlic cloves, minced
    1 tablespoon grated fresh ginger
    2 teaspoons Thai red curry paste
    2 cups vegetable or chicken broth
    1 (14-ounce) can coconut milk, divided
    1 tablespoon fish sauce, plus extra for seasoning
    ½ cup wild rice, picked over and rinsed
    1½ tablespoons lime juice, plus lime wedges for serving
    1½ teaspoons sugar
    6 ounces white mushrooms, trimmed and sliced thin
    2 tablespoons chopped fresh cilantro

1. Using highest sauté or browning function, heat oil in electric pressure cooker until shimmering. Add onion and cook until softened, 3 to 5 minutes. Stir in garlic, ginger, and curry paste and cook until fragrant, about 30 seconds. Stir in broth, half of coconut milk, and fish sauce, scraping up any browned bits, then stir in rice.

2. Lock lid in place and close pressure valve. Select high pressure cook function and cook for 30 minutes. Turn off pressure cooker and quick-release pressure. Carefully remove lid, allowing steam to escape away from you.

3. Stir remaining coconut milk, lime juice, and sugar into soup. Stir in mushrooms and cook using highest sauté or browning function until mushrooms are just tender, 3 to 5 minutes. Turn off pressure cooker. Stir in cilantro and season with extra fish sauce and salt and pepper to taste. Serve with lime wedges.

Spiced Wild Rice and Coconut Soup

Easy Tortellini Minestrone
DUTCH OVEN

Serves 4 to 6

Total Time 45 minutes

Why This Recipe Works Minestrone soup should be loaded with fresh-tasting vegetables, creamy beans, and fresh herbs in a rich tomato-based broth. We hoped to streamline minestrone's ingredient list and create a simple weeknight one-pot meal—and we got our start with a convenience product that packed a potent flavor punch: V8 juice. Bacon infused the soup with an underlying richness, and softening our onion and carrots in the leftover fat imbued them with meaty flavor. After adding some garlic and fresh oregano we stirred in a combination of chicken broth and V8 juice to create our deep, tomatoey broth. To make our soup more substantial we added some tortellini and zucchini during the last few minutes of cooking. A final dollop of basil pesto lent bright herbal flavor. Be sure to use fresh tortellini in this soup; frozen or dried tortellini will require different cooking times and additional cooking liquid. Any canned small white beans will work well in this recipe. You can use our homemade Classic Basil Pesto (page 45) or any fresh store-bought variety here.

Tomato, Bulgur, and Red Pepper Soup

2 slices bacon, chopped fine
1 onion, chopped fine
2 carrots, peeled and cut into ½-inch pieces
3 garlic cloves, minced
1 tablespoon minced fresh oregano or 1 teaspoon dried
3½ cups chicken broth
2½ cups V8 juice
1 (15-ounce) can cannellini beans, rinsed
1 (9-ounce) package fresh cheese tortellini
1 zucchini, halved lengthwise, seeded, and cut into ½-inch pieces
½ cup basil pesto

1. Cook bacon in Dutch oven over medium heat until rendered and crisp, 5 to 7 minutes. Stir in onion and carrots and cook until softened, about 5 minutes. Stir in garlic and oregano and cook until fragrant, about 30 seconds.

2. Stir in broth, V8, and beans, scraping up any browned bits. Bring to simmer and cook until beans are heated through and flavors meld, about 10 minutes. Stir in tortellini and zucchini and simmer until tender, 5 to 7 minutes. Season with salt and pepper to taste. Dollop individual portions with pesto before serving.

Tomato, Bulgur, and Red Pepper Soup
DUTCH OVEN
Serves 6 to 8
Total Time 1 hour

Why This Recipe Works There are countless versions of tomato and red pepper soup throughout Turkey, but all are full-flavored and hearty. We started our soup with onion and red bell peppers, softening them before creating a solid flavor backbone with garlic, tomato paste, white wine, dried mint, smoked paprika, and red pepper flakes. For additional smokiness, canned fire-roasted tomatoes did the trick. To add some heft to our soup we added bulgur, a common and versatile ingredient in Turkish and other Mediterranean cuisines. When stirred into a soup, bulgur absorbs the surrounding flavors and releases starch to create a silky texture. Since bulgur is so quick-cooking, we stirred it in toward the end, giving it just enough time to become tender. A sprinkle of fresh mint gave the soup a final punch of flavor.

2 tablespoons extra-virgin olive oil
1 onion, chopped
2 red bell peppers, stemmed, seeded, and chopped
¾ teaspoon table salt
¼ teaspoon pepper
3 garlic cloves, minced
1 teaspoon dried mint, crumbled
½ teaspoon smoked paprika
⅛ teaspoon red pepper flakes
1 tablespoon tomato paste
½ cup dry white wine
1 (28-ounce) can diced fire-roasted tomatoes
4 cups chicken or vegetable broth
2 cups water
¾ cup medium-grind bulgur, rinsed
⅓ cup chopped fresh mint

1. Heat oil in Dutch oven over medium heat until shimmering. Add onion, bell peppers, salt, and pepper and cook until softened and lightly browned, 6 to 8 minutes. Stir in garlic, dried mint, smoked paprika, and pepper flakes and cook until fragrant, about 30 seconds. Stir in tomato paste and cook for 1 minute.

2. Stir in wine, scraping up any browned bits, and cook until reduced by half, about 1 minute. Add tomatoes and their juice and cook, stirring occasionally, until tomatoes soften and begin to break apart, about 10 minutes.

3. Stir in broth, water, and bulgur and bring to simmer. Reduce heat to low, cover, and cook gently until bulgur is tender, about 20 minutes. Season with salt and pepper to taste. Serve, sprinkling individual portions with fresh mint.

Farro and Leek Soup

INSTANT POT
Serves 6 to 8
Total Time 1 hour

Why This Recipe Works Farro is a staple of central Italy, where it predates common wheat. We were intrigued by classic minestra di farro, a hearty soup in which farro's nuttiness shines. To ensure perfectly cooked farro we used our pressure cooker, which turned the tough grains tender in a matter of minutes. Coarsely ground farro is the traditional choice, but since whole farro is easier to find stateside we were happy to discover that it's a cinch to grind your own; a blender cracked a portion of the grains, freeing just enough starch to give our soup rich body. Pancetta delivered a meaty boost and a full pound of leeks gave this soup a pungent sweetness (rounded out by carrots and celery); we loved that the pressure cooker softened even the dark green parts of the leeks in the short time it took the farro to cook through. A sprinkling of parsley and some freshly grated Parmesan finished this simple, satisfying soup. Do not use quick-cooking, presteamed, or pearled farro (read the ingredient list on the package to determine this) in this recipe. Bacon can be used in place of the pancetta.

- 1 cup whole farro
- 1 tablespoon extra-virgin olive oil, plus extra for drizzling
- 3 ounces pancetta, chopped fine
- 1 pound leeks, ends trimmed, chopped, and washed thoroughly
- 2 carrots, peeled and chopped
- 1 celery rib, chopped
- 8 cups chicken broth, plus extra as needed
- ½ cup minced fresh parsley
  Grated Parmesan cheese

1. Pulse farro in blender until about half of grains are broken into smaller pieces, about 6 pulses; set aside.

2. Using highest sauté or browning function, heat oil in electric pressure cooker until shimmering. Add pancetta and cook until lightly browned, 3 to 5 minutes. Stir in leeks, carrots, and celery and cook until softened, about 5 minutes. Stir in broth, scraping up any browned bits, then stir in farro.

3. Lock lid in place and close pressure release valve. Select high pressure cook function and cook for 8 minutes. Turn off pressure cooker and quick-release pressure. Carefully remove lid, allowing steam to escape away from you.

4. Adjust consistency with extra hot broth as needed. Stir in parsley and season with salt and pepper to taste. Drizzle individual portions with extra oil and top with Parmesan before serving.

Red Lentil Soup with North African Spices

Red Lentil Soup with North African Spices

SAUCEPAN
Serves 4 to 6
Total Time 45 minutes

Why This Recipe Works Small red lentils are one of our favorite legumes; they break down quickly into a creamy, thick puree—perfect for a smooth and satisfying soup. Their mild flavor does require a bit of embellishment, so we started by sautéing onion in olive oil and used the warm mixture to bloom some fragrant North African spices: coriander, cumin, ginger, pepper, cinnamon, and cayenne. Tomato paste and garlic completed the base before the addition of the lentils, and a mix of broth and water gave the soup a full, rounded character. After only 15 minutes of cooking, the lentils were soft enough to be pureed with a whisk. A generous dose of lemon juice brought the flavors into focus, and a drizzle of olive oil and a sprinkle of fresh cilantro completed the transformation of commonplace ingredients into an inspired yet comforting soup. Do not substitute brown or green lentils for the red lentils. Serve with Harissa (page 39).

2. Stir in broth, water, and lentils and bring to vigorous simmer. Cook, stirring occasionally, until lentils are soft and about half are broken down, about 15 minutes.

3. Whisk soup vigorously until broken down to coarse puree, about 30 seconds. Adjust consistency with extra hot broth as needed. Stir in lemon juice and season with salt and extra lemon juice to taste. Sprinkle individual portions with cilantro and drizzle with extra oil before serving.

Lentil and Chorizo Soup
INSTANT POT
Serves 6 to 8
Total Time 1 hour

Why This Recipe Works To create a one-pot meal that featured whole lentils suspended in a creamy, but not too thick, broth, we turned to our pressure cooker for reliably well-cooked lentils. Inspired by the Spanish combination of earthy lentils and smoked paprika–scented chorizo sausage, we set out to find the ideal balance of flavors. Tasters agreed that 8 ounces of chorizo was the right amount to render just enough meaty flavor and richness into our soup. To save prep time, we cooked the vegetables in large pieces with the lentils under pressure, pureed them quickly in the food processor, and returned them to the soup to achieve a velvety broth. We prefer French green lentils, or lentilles du Puy, for this recipe, but it will work with any type of lentil except red or yellow. If Spanish-style chorizo is not available, Portuguese linguiça or Polish kielbasa can be substituted. Red wine vinegar can be substituted for the sherry vinegar.

1 tablespoon extra-virgin olive oil, plus extra for drizzling
8 ounces Spanish-style chorizo sausage, quartered lengthwise and sliced thin
4 garlic cloves, minced
1½ teaspoons smoked paprika
5 cups water
1 pound (2¼ cups) French green lentils, picked over and rinsed
4 cups chicken broth
1 tablespoon sherry vinegar, plus extra for seasoning
2 bay leaves
1 teaspoon table salt
1 large onion, peeled
2 carrots, peeled and halved crosswise
½ cup slivered almonds, toasted
½ cup minced fresh parsley

Lentil and Chorizo Soup

2 tablespoons extra-virgin olive oil, plus extra for serving
1 large onion, chopped fine
1 teaspoon table salt
¾ teaspoon ground coriander
½ teaspoon ground cumin
¼ teaspoon ground ginger
¼ teaspoon pepper
⅛ teaspoon ground cinnamon
Pinch cayenne pepper
1 tablespoon tomato paste
1 garlic clove, minced
4 cups chicken or vegetable broth, plus extra as needed
2 cups water
10½ ounces (1½ cups) red lentils, picked over and rinsed
2 tablespoons lemon juice, plus extra for seasoning
¼ cup chopped fresh cilantro

1. Heat oil in large saucepan over medium heat until shimmering. Add onion and salt and cook until softened, about 5 minutes. Stir in coriander, cumin, ginger, pepper, cinnamon, and cayenne and cook until fragrant, about 2 minutes. Stir in tomato paste and garlic and cook for 1 minute.

1. Using highest sauté or browning function, heat oil in electric pressure cooker until shimmering. Add chorizo and cook until lightly browned, 3 to 5 minutes. Stir in garlic and paprika and cook until fragrant, about 30 seconds. Stir in water, scraping up any browned bits, then stir in lentils, broth, vinegar, bay leaves, and salt. Nestle onion and carrots into pot.

2. Lock lid in place and close pressure release valve. Select high pressure cook function and cook for 14 minutes. Turn off pressure cooker and quick-release pressure. Carefully remove lid, allowing steam to escape away from you.

3. Discard bay leaves. Using slotted spoon, transfer onion and carrots to food processor and process until smooth, about 1 minute, scraping down sides of bowl as needed. Stir vegetable mixture into lentils and season with salt, pepper, and extra vinegar to taste. Drizzle individual portions with extra oil, and sprinkle with almonds and parsley before serving.

White Bean Soup with Pancetta and Rosemary

DUTCH OVEN
Serves 6 to 8
Total Time 45 minutes

Why This Recipe Works One of our favorite bean soups is Tuscan white bean soup, which boasts creamy, tender beans and hearty vegetables in a light, velvety broth. We hoped to avoid the lengthy process of soaking dried beans before cooking to make this soup more approachable, and indeed when we tried canned beans we were pleasantly surprised to find that including the liquid from the can added extra body to the broth. We felt that our broth could use some meaty flavor, but traditional white bean soups don't have large pieces of meat. To add extra depth we crisped up chopped pancetta in our Dutch oven. Not only did it lend rich flavor, but the pieces were small enough to take a back seat to the beans. For an herbal note we opted for rosemary, which livened up the soup with its fragrance and flavor. Bacon can be used in place of the pancetta. Any canned small white beans will work well here. Serve with crusty bread or Garlic Toasts (page 45).

2 tablespoons extra-virgin olive oil, plus extra for serving
6 ounces pancetta, chopped
1 onion, chopped fine
1 celery rib, minced
1 carrot, peeled and chopped fine
8 garlic cloves, minced
½ teaspoon minced fresh rosemary
 Pinch red pepper flakes
4 cups chicken or vegetable broth
4 (15-ounce) cans cannellini beans
 Grated Parmesan cheese

1. Heat oil in Dutch oven over medium heat until shimmering. Add pancetta and cook until rendered and crisp, 5 to 7 minutes. Stir in onion, celery, and carrot and cook until softened, about 5 minutes. Stir in garlic, rosemary, and pepper flakes and cook until fragrant, about 30 seconds.

2. Stir in broth and beans and their liquid, scraping up any browned bits. Bring to simmer and cook until flavors meld, about 10 minutes. Season with salt and pepper to taste. Drizzle individual portions with extra oil and sprinkle with Parmesan before serving.

VARIATION

White Bean Soup with Sun-Dried Tomatoes and Kale for Two

SAUCEPAN
Serves 2
Total Time 45 minutes

Any canned small white beans will work well here. Serve with crusty bread or Garlic Toasts (page 45).

2 teaspoons extra-virgin olive oil, plus extra for serving
2 slices bacon, chopped fine
¼ cup finely chopped onion
2 tablespoons minced, oil-packed sun-dried tomatoes
1 garlic clove, minced
¼ teaspoon dried oregano
 Pinch red pepper flakes
2 cups chicken or vegetable broth
1 cup water
1 (15-ounce) can cannellini beans
2 ounces (2 cups) baby kale
 Parmesan cheese

1. Heat oil in large saucepan over medium heat until shimmering. Add bacon and cook until rendered and crisp, about 3 minutes. Stir in onion and cook until softened, about 3 minutes. Stir in tomatoes, garlic, oregano, and pepper flakes and cook until fragrant, about 30 seconds.

2. Stir in broth, water, and beans and their liquid, scraping up any browned bits. Bring to simmer and cook until flavors meld, about 10 minutes. Off heat, stir in kale until wilted. Season with salt and pepper to taste. Drizzle individual portions with extra oil and sprinkle with Parmesan before serving.

Black Bean Soup

SLOW COOKER

Serves 6 to 8

Cook Time 8 to 10 hours on low or 5 to 7 hours on high

Why This Recipe Works Black bean soup is one of our all-time favorite recipes thanks to its combination of sweet, spicy, and smoky flavors. The hands-off, gentle heat of the slow cooker was the ideal environment for softening dried black beans to tender perfection. To guarantee our soup would have plenty of robust flavor even after hours in the slow cooker, we added chili powder to our microwaved aromatics, tossed in a smoked ham hock (which we later shredded), and included chopped celery and carrot. We found that with the slow cooker we could skip soaking the beans; instead we added a pinch of baking soda for faster, even cooking. As for texture, we tried thickeners such as flour, but they muted the flavor of the soup. Mashing some of the cooked beans and stirring them back into the finished soup worked best, providing excellent body and intensifying the flavors as well. To add a touch of brightness, we stirred in minced fresh cilantro. Serve with finely chopped red onion, sour cream, and hot sauce.

- 2 onions, chopped fine
- 3 celery ribs, cut into ½-inch pieces
- 6 garlic cloves, minced
- 2 tablespoons vegetable oil
- 2 tablespoons chili powder
- 4 cups chicken broth
- 2 cups water
- 1 pound (2½ cups) dried black beans, picked over and rinsed
- 1 (12-ounce) smoked ham hock, rinsed
- 2 carrots, peeled and cut into ½-inch pieces
- ⅛ teaspoon baking soda
- 2 bay leaves
- 2 tablespoons minced fresh cilantro

1. Microwave onions, celery, garlic, oil, and chili powder in bowl, stirring occasionally, until onions are softened, about 5 minutes; transfer to slow cooker. Stir in broth, water, beans, ham hock, carrots, baking soda, and bay leaves. Cover and cook until beans are tender, 8 to 10 hours on low or 5 to 7 hours on high.

2. Transfer ham hock to cutting board, let cool slightly, then shred into bite-size pieces using 2 forks; discard fat, skin, and bones. Discard bay leaves.

3. Mash portion of beans with potato masher to thicken soup as desired. Stir in shredded ham and let sit until heated through, about 5 minutes. Stir in cilantro and season with salt and pepper to taste. Serve.

15-Bean Soup with Sausage and Spinach

SLOW COOKER

Serves 6

Cook Time 8 to 10 hours on low or 5 to 7 hours on high

Why This Recipe Works Grocery store 15-bean soup mix promises a hearty soup in record time with meaty undertones, a bright flavor, and an appealingly chunky texture, but the packaged version never quite lives up to expectation. Using the mix as our starting point, we set out to create a 15-bean soup that would deliver on big flavor with the help of our slow cooker. Our first step was to ditch the flavoring packets that come with these soup mixes—their dried seasonings and bits of vegetables offered up zero flavor but a lot of sodium. Instead, a combination of onion, garlic, thyme, and red pepper flakes provided a nice balance of oniony aromatics and herbs, and fresh white mushrooms rounded out the flavor of our soup. For heartiness we added chicken sausage, which held up during the long cooking time and added extra flavor. We stirred in spinach at the end of cooking and allowed it to wilt slightly, adding a fresh, bright element.

- 8 ounces hot or sweet Italian chicken sausage, casings removed, broken into 1-inch pieces
- 1 onion, chopped fine
- 6 garlic cloves, minced
- 1 tablespoon minced fresh thyme or ¾ teaspoon dried
- ¼ teaspoon red pepper flakes
- ¼ teaspoon table salt
- 8 cups chicken broth
- 8 ounces (1¼ cups) 15-bean soup mix, seasoning packet discarded, beans picked over and rinsed
- 8 ounces white mushrooms, trimmed and quartered
- ⅛ teaspoon baking soda
- 2 bay leaves
- 4 ounces (4 cups) baby spinach

1. Microwave sausage, onion, garlic, thyme, pepper flakes, and salt in bowl, stirring occasionally, until onion is softened, about 5 minutes; transfer to slow cooker. Stir in broth, beans, mushrooms, baking soda, and bay leaves. Cover and cook until beans are tender, 8 to 10 hours on low or 5 to 7 hours on high.

2. Discard bay leaves. Stir in spinach, one handful at a time, and let sit until wilted, about 5 minutes. Season with salt and pepper to taste. Serve.

Italian Pasta and Bean Soup

DUTCH OVEN

Serves 8 to 10
Total Time 1 hour

Why This Recipe Works The Italian classic pasta e fagioli delivers on outstanding flavor and perfect al dente texture—without taking all day to make. We started by cooking some pancetta in a Dutch oven and cooked our vegetables in the rendered fat before adding a few minced anchovies for salty, savory flavor. Canned tomatoes and beans offered an easy way to speed up this soup. Adding the tomatoes and beans together allowed them to absorb flavor from each other, and a combination of chicken broth and water added richness without turning our pasta and bean soup into chicken soup. A Parmesan rind gave our soup depth by imparting a subtle cheese flavor throughout (the rind can be replaced with a 2-inch chunk of cheese). Finally, parsley lent a necessary bright note to our soup. Bacon can be used in place of the pancetta.

- 1 tablespoon extra-virgin olive oil, plus extra for serving
- 3 ounces pancetta, chopped fine
- 1 onion, chopped fine
- 1 celery rib, chopped fine
- 4 garlic cloves, minced
- 1 tablespoon minced fresh oregano or 1 teaspoon dried
- ¼ teaspoon red pepper flakes
- 3 anchovy fillets, rinsed and minced
- 4 cups chicken broth
- 2 cups water
- 1 (28-ounce) can diced tomatoes
- 2 (15-ounce) cans cannellini beans, rinsed
- 1 Parmesan cheese rind, plus grated Parmesan for serving
- 1 teaspoon table salt
- 1 cup orzo, ditalini, or other short pasta
- ¼ cup minced fresh parsley

1. Heat oil in Dutch oven over medium heat until shimmering. Add pancetta and cook until rendered, 3 to 5 minutes. Stir in onion and celery and cook until softened, about 5 minutes. Stir in garlic, oregano, pepper flakes, and anchovies and cook until fragrant, about 30 seconds.

2. Stir in broth and water, scraping up any browned bits. Stir in tomatoes and their juice, beans, Parmesan rind, and salt. Bring to simmer and cook until flavors meld, about 10 minutes.

3. Bring soup to boil over medium-high heat. Stir in orzo and cook until al dente, about 8 minutes. Discard Parmesan rind. Stir in parsley and season with salt and pepper to taste. Drizzle individual portions with extra oil and sprinkle with Parmesan before serving.

15-Bean Soup with Sausage and Spinach

Italian Pasta and Bean Soup

STEWS AND CHILIS

White Chicken Chili

* All slow cooker recipes work in a 4- to 7-quart traditional slow cooker unless noted.

** All Instant Pot recipes work in a 6- to 8-quart Instant Pot or other electric pressure cooker.

Daube Provençal

Greek Beef Stew

Daube Provençal

DUTCH OVEN

Serves 6 to 8
Total Time 4 hours

Why This Recipe Works Daube Provençal, also known as daube niçoise, has all the elements of the best beef stews, with a distinctly French flair: tender pieces of beef, a luxurious sauce, and complex flavors. To translate the flavors of Provence into a one-pot meal, we used briny niçoise olives, bright tomatoes, floral orange zest, and the regional flavors of fresh thyme and bay. Anchovies added complexity without a fishy taste, and salt pork contributed rich body. A whole bottle of wine lent bold flavor. With so much liquid in the pot, we found that only partially covering the Dutch oven before transferring it to the oven allowed for enough evaporation to thicken the stew as the meat cooked. Cabernet Sauvignon is our favorite wine for this recipe, but Côtes du Rhône and Zinfandel also work. Because they are added just before serving, use canned whole tomatoes and dice them—uncooked, they are more tender than canned diced tomatoes.

- 1 cup water
- ¾ ounce dried porcini mushrooms, rinsed
- 4 pounds boneless beef chuck-eye roast, pulled apart at seams, trimmed, and cut into 1½-inch pieces
- 1 teaspoon table salt
- 1 teaspoon pepper
- 3 tablespoons extra-virgin olive oil, divided
- 5 ounces salt pork, rind removed
- 1 pound carrots, peeled and sliced 1 inch thick
- 2 onions, halved and sliced thin
- 2 tablespoons tomato paste
- 4 garlic cloves, sliced thin
- ⅓ cup all-purpose flour
- 1 (750-ml) bottle dry red wine
- 1 cup chicken broth, plus extra as needed
- 4 (3-inch) strips orange zest, sliced thin lengthwise
- 3 anchovy fillets, rinsed and minced
- 5 sprigs fresh thyme, tied together with kitchen twine
- 2 bay leaves
- 1 (14.5-ounce) can whole peeled tomatoes, drained and chopped
- 1 cup pitted niçoise or kalamata olives
- 2 tablespoons minced fresh parsley

1. Microwave water and mushrooms in covered bowl until steaming, about 1 minute. Drain mushrooms in fine-mesh strainer lined with coffee filter, reserving ¼ cup liquid, and chop mushrooms. Set mushrooms and reserved liquid aside.

2. Adjust oven rack to lower-middle position and heat oven to 325 degrees. Pat beef dry with paper towels and sprinkle with salt and pepper. Heat 2 tablespoons oil in Dutch oven over medium-high heat until shimmering. Brown half of beef on all sides, 8 to 10 minutes; transfer to large bowl. Repeat with remaining 1 tablespoon oil and remaining beef; transfer to bowl.

3. Reduce heat to medium and add salt pork, carrots, onions, tomato paste, and garlic to fat left in pot. Cook, stirring occasionally, until light brown, about 2 minutes. Stir in flour and cook for 1 minute. Slowly whisk in wine, scraping up any browned bits and smoothing out any lumps. Stir in broth, 1 cup water, and beef with any accumulated juices and bring to simmer.

4. Stir in mushrooms and their liquid, orange zest, anchovies, thyme bundle, and bay leaves, arranging beef so it is completely covered by liquid; partially cover pot and place in oven. Cook until beef is tender, 2 ½ to 3 hours.

5. Discard salt pork, thyme bundle, and bay leaves. Using wide, shallow spoon, skim excess fat from surface of stew. Stir in tomatoes and olives and let sit until heated through, about 2 minutes. Adjust consistency with extra hot broth as needed. Stir in parsley and season with salt and pepper to taste. Serve.

Greek Beef Stew

DUTCH OVEN

Serves 4 to 6
Total Time 3 hours

Why This Recipe Works With ultratender beef, a wine-and-spice-infused tomato sauce, and a sweet underpinning of braised pearl onions, stifado (which basically means "stew" in Greek) offers an easy, intriguing take on beef stew. For sweet, creamy onions with complex, caramelized flavor, we began by sautéing frozen pearl onions with a pinch of sugar to jump-start the development of flavorful browning. To avoid overwhelming the sauce with a potpourri of spices, we added a cinnamon stick (rather than ground cinnamon, which can be easy to overdo), a balanced amount of earthy cumin, and ⅛ teaspoon of fragrant allspice. As for the beef, we started with a well-marbled chuck-eye roast and skipped the tedious step of browning it in batches, opting instead to simply stir the uncooked beef into the stew and place the pot in a 300-degree oven without a lid. Exposed to the heat of the oven, the broth-wine mixture reduced, intensified, and thickened into a full-bodied sauce while the beef developed deep, flavorful browning. One 14.4-ounce bag of frozen pearl onions contains about 3 ½ cups. Do not thaw the onions before cooking. Serve with pita bread.

2½ pounds boneless beef chuck-eye roast, pulled apart at seams, trimmed, and cut into 1-inch pieces
  2 teaspoons kosher salt, divided
½ teaspoon pepper
3½ cups frozen pearl onions
  2 tablespoons extra-virgin olive oil
½ teaspoon sugar
  2 tablespoons tomato paste
  3 garlic cloves, minced
  1 teaspoon ground cumin
⅛ teaspoon ground allspice
  2 tomatoes, cored and chopped
2¼ cups chicken broth
¾ cup dry white wine
  1 cinnamon stick
  2 bay leaves
¼ cup chopped fresh parsley
    Crumbled feta cheese

1. Adjust oven rack to middle position and heat oven to 300 degrees. Sprinkle beef with 1 ½ teaspoons salt and pepper; set aside.

2. Cook onions, oil, sugar, and remaining ½ teaspoon salt in large Dutch oven over medium-high heat until onions are softened and deeply browned, 10 to 12 minutes. Add tomato paste, garlic, cumin, and allspice and cook until fragrant, about 1 minute. Add tomatoes and cook until tomatoes break down and mixture is darkened and thick, about 5 minutes.

3. Add broth, wine, cinnamon stick, bay leaves, and beef to pot, scraping up any browned bits. Increase heat to high and bring to simmer. Transfer to oven and cook, uncovered, for 1 hour.

4. Remove pot from oven and stir to redistribute beef. Return pot to oven and continue to cook, uncovered, until meat is tender, 1 ½ to 2 hours longer.

5. Discard cinnamon stick and bay leaves. Using wide, shallow spoon, skim excess fat from surface of stew. Stir in parsley. Serve, sprinkled with feta cheese.

REMOVING FAT FROM SOUPS AND STEWS

Let cooking liquid settle, then use wide, shallow spoon to skim fat off surface. Be sure to hold spoon parallel to surface of liquid; you want to collect as little broth as possible.

Easy Beef Stew with Mushrooms and Bacon

INSTANT POT
Serves 4
Total Time 1 hour

Why This Recipe Works For a beef stew that we could make on a weeknight—one that was mostly hands-off but would still produce tender meat and a luxurious gravy—we started with beefy boneless short ribs and employed our pressure cooker; its moist heat is perfect for making stews since it effortlessly tenderizes tough cuts of meat. We found we could skip the time-consuming step of browning the beef and still build flavor by sautéing bacon and using the fat to cook tomato paste and thyme. Stirring the cooked bacon back into the stew, along with umami-rich mushrooms and soy sauce, contributed savory depth. Flour thickened the stew, and frozen pearl onions lent subtle sweetness.

- 4 slices bacon, chopped
- ¼ cup tomato paste
- 1 teaspoon minced fresh thyme or ¼ teaspoon dried
- ¼ cup all-purpose flour
- 1½ cups beef broth, plus extra as needed
- 2 tablespoons soy sauce
- 1½ pounds boneless beef short ribs, trimmed and cut into 1-inch pieces
- 1½ pounds cremini mushrooms, trimmed and quartered
- 1 cup frozen pearl onions, thawed
- 2 tablespoons minced fresh parsley

1. Using highest sauté or browning function, cook bacon in electric pressure cooker until rendered and crisp, 5 to 7 minutes. Using slotted spoon, transfer bacon to paper towel–lined plate; set aside.

2. Add tomato paste and thyme to fat left in pressure cooker and cook until fragrant, about 30 seconds. Stir in flour and cook for 1 minute. Slowly whisk in broth and soy sauce, scraping up any browned bits and smoothing out any lumps. Stir beef, mushrooms, and onions into pressure cooker.

3. Lock lid in place and close pressure release valve. Select high pressure cook function and cook for 30 minutes. Turn off pressure cooker and quick-release pressure. Carefully remove lid, allowing steam to escape away from you.

4. Using wide, shallow spoon, skim excess fat from surface of stew. Adjust consistency with extra hot broth as needed. Stir in parsley and reserved bacon. Season with salt and pepper to taste. Serve.

Beef Goulash

DUTCH OVEN
Serves 6 to 8
Total Time 3 hours

Why This Recipe Works While Americanized versions typically feature ultralong ingredient lists, traditional Hungarian goulash is the simplest of stews, calling for little more than beef, onions, and a whole lot of paprika. Tasters preferred traditional sweet paprika to hot or smoked because of its floral, fruity qualities, but when we used enough to pack a flavor punch, the spice contributed a gritty, dusty texture. Consulting a few Hungarian restaurants, we discovered they used "paprika cream," a smooth product made from a blend of paprika and red bell peppers. Since paprika cream is hard to find, we created our own by pureeing a drained jar of roasted red peppers with tomato paste, vinegar, and the paprika; this gave our stew the bold flavor and smooth texture we were after. A Dutch oven easily accommodated the large quantities of meat, onions, and carrots. When we seared the meat it competed with the paprika's flavor, so instead we softened the onions first and then stirred in the paprika mixture and the raw meat and moved the whole pot to the oven to slowly cook. Paprika is vital to this recipe, so it's best to use a fresh container. Don't substitute smoked or hot paprika for the sweet paprika. Serve with sour cream and Buttered Egg Noodles (page 17).

- 4 pounds boneless beef chuck-eye roast, pulled apart at seams, trimmed, and cut into 1½-inch pieces
- 2 teaspoons table salt, divided
- 1 (12-ounce) jar roasted red peppers, rinsed
- ⅓ cup sweet paprika
- 2 tablespoons tomato paste
- 1 tablespoon distilled white vinegar, divided
- 3 pounds onions, chopped fine
- 2 tablespoons vegetable oil
- 4 carrots, peeled and sliced 1 inch thick
- 1 bay leaf
- 1 cup beef broth, plus extra as needed

1. Adjust oven rack to lower-middle position and heat oven to 325 degrees. Sprinkle beef with 1 teaspoon salt. Process red peppers, paprika, tomato paste, and 2 teaspoons vinegar in food processor until smooth, 1 to 2 minutes, scraping down sides of bowl as needed.

Beef Goulash

1. Pull apart roast at its major seams (delineated by lines of fat and silverskin). Use knife as necessary.

2. With knife, trim off excess fat and silverskin. Cut meat into pieces, according to recipe.

2. Combine onions, oil, and remaining 1 teaspoon salt in Dutch oven. Cover and cook over medium heat, stirring occasionally, until onions soften but have not yet begun to brown, 8 to 10 minutes. (If onions begin to brown, reduce heat to medium-low and stir in 1 tablespoon water.)

3. Stir in pepper mixture and cook, uncovered, until onions begin to stick to bottom of pot, about 2 minutes. Stir in beef, carrots, and bay leaf and use rubber spatula to scrape down sides of pot. Cover, transfer pot to oven, and cook until beef is almost tender and surface of liquid is ½ inch below top of meat, 2 to 2½ hours, stirring every 30 minutes.

4. Stir in broth until surface of liquid measures ¼ inch from top of meat (beef should not be fully submerged). Cover and continue to cook until beef is tender, about 30 minutes.

5. Remove pot from oven and discard bay leaf. Using wide, shallow spoon, skim excess fat from surface of stew. Adjust consistency with extra hot broth as needed. Stir in remaining 1 teaspoon vinegar and season with salt and pepper to taste. Serve.

INGREDIENT SPOTLIGHT

SWEET AND SMOKED PAPRIKA

Paprika is a generic term for a spice made from grinding dried red chile pods (and sometimes the seeds and stems as well) to a fine powder. Whether paprika is labeled sweet or smoked is determined by the variety (or varieties) of pepper used and how the peppers are cultivated and processed.

Sweet Paprika Sweet paprika is made from a combination of mild red peppers. Our favorite, **The Spice House Hungarian Sweet Paprika**, is available only through mail-order, but we think its earthy, fruity flavors and toasty aroma make it worthwhile.

Smoked Paprika Smoked paprika is produced by drying peppers (either sweet or hot) over smoldering oak embers for a deep, musky flavor; it is best used to season hearty meats or to add a smoky aroma to boldly flavored dishes. Our favorite smoked paprika is **Simply Organic Smoked Paprika,** which has a smoke that "lingered" "without being overpowering."

CLASSIC BEEF STEW

Great beef stew showcases fall-apart meat and tender vegetables draped in a rich brown gravy. We wanted a recipe that we could scale up or down to feed any number of people. We started our classic recipe with a Dutch oven before creating versions that could feed a crowd using an unconventional cooking vessel—a roasting pan—or that could feed two using an ovensafe saucepan. We chose chuck-eye roast for its great flavor and plentiful collagen, which melted into tender gelatin while cooking slowly in the oven. For our version for two, boneless beef short ribs were a better option as they were easier to find in the right portion size without sacrificing rich, beefy flavor. Browning the meat ensured that it got a thorough sear and didn't steam, boosting the savory flavor of the gravy. But for our big batch version, we skipped the arduous step of browning a large amount of meat and let the oven do the work for us; roasting the stew, uncovered, with the beef partially submerged, gave us flavorful browning without the work. Along with traditional stew components such as onions, garlic, red wine, and broth (we preferred chicken broth over beef for its subtle flavor), we added tomato paste, which is rich in glutamates—compounds that give meat its savory taste and contribute considerable flavor. Potatoes, carrots, and peas rounded out our soul-warming beef stew. Cabernet Sauvignon is our favorite wine for this recipe, but Côtes du Rhône and Zinfandel also work.

CLASSIC

DUTCH OVEN
Serves 6 to 8
Total Time 3 hours

- 4 pounds boneless beef chuck-eye roast, pulled apart at seams, trimmed, and cut into 1½-inch pieces
- 2½ teaspoons table salt, divided
- 1 teaspoon pepper
- ¼ cup vegetable oil, divided
- 2 onions, chopped fine
- 3 garlic cloves, minced
- 1 tablespoon tomato paste
- 1 tablespoon minced fresh thyme or 1 teaspoon dried
- ¼ cup all-purpose flour
- 1 cup dry red wine
- 2½ cups chicken broth, plus extra as needed
- 1 pound carrots, peeled and sliced 1 inch thick
- 2 bay leaves
- 1½ pounds red potatoes, unpeeled, cut into 1-inch pieces
- 1 cup frozen peas
- ¼ cup chopped fresh parsley

1. Adjust oven rack to lower-middle position and heat oven to 325 degrees. Pat beef dry with paper towels and sprinkle with 1 teaspoon salt and pepper. Heat 2 tablespoons oil in Dutch oven over medium-high heat until just smoking. Brown half of beef on all sides, 8 to 10 minutes; transfer to large bowl. Repeat with 1 tablespoon oil and remaining beef; transfer to bowl.

2. Add onions, remaining 1 tablespoon oil, and remaining 1½ teaspoons salt and cook over medium heat until softened, about 5 minutes. Stir in garlic, tomato paste, and thyme and cook until fragrant, about 30 seconds. Stir in flour and cook for 1 minute. Slowly whisk in wine, scraping up any browned bits and smoothing out any lumps.

3. Stir in broth, carrots, bay leaves, and beef with any accumulated juices and bring to simmer. Cover, transfer pot to oven, and cook for 1 hour.

4. Stir in potatoes and continue to cook, covered, until meat is just tender, 1½ to 2 hours.

5. Remove pot from oven and discard bay leaves. Stir in peas and let sit until heated through, about 2 minutes. Adjust consistency with extra hot broth as needed. Stir in parsley and season with salt and pepper to taste. Serve.

MAKE IT YOUR WAY →

> **Use What You've Got** Substitute boneless short ribs for the chuck roast. Use beer or white wine for the red wine. Use butternut squash, fennel, parsnips, or turnips for the potatoes and carrots. Use frozen corn, green beans, or lima beans for the peas. Add fresh cilantro, basil, or dill.

COOK IT FOR A CROWD

ROASTING PAN
Serves 12 to 14
Total Time 5¼ hours

- ¼ cup vegetable oil
- 2 pounds onions, chopped fine
- 1 tablespoon table salt, divided
- 6 garlic cloves, minced
- 2 tablespoons tomato paste
- 2 tablespoons minced fresh thyme or 2 teaspoons dried
- ½ cup all-purpose flour
- 2 cups dry red wine
- 4 cups chicken broth, plus extra as needed
- 4 bay leaves
- 7 pounds boneless beef chuck-eye roast, pulled apart at seams, trimmed, and cut into 1½-inch pieces
- 2 teaspoons pepper
- 3 pounds red potatoes, unpeeled, cut into 1-inch pieces
- 2 pounds carrots, peeled and sliced 1 inch thick
- 2 cups frozen peas
- ⅓ cup chopped fresh parsley

1. Adjust oven rack to lower-middle position and heat oven to 325 degrees. Heat oil in 16 by 12-inch roasting pan over medium heat (over 2 burners, if possible) until shimmering. Add onions and 1½ teaspoons salt and cook until softened and lightly browned, 8 to 10 minutes.

2. Stir in garlic, tomato paste, and thyme and cook until fragrant, about 30 seconds. Stir in flour and cook for 1 minute. Slowly whisk in wine, scraping up any browned bits and smoothing out any lumps. Slowly whisk in broth and bay leaves and bring to simmer. Remove pan from heat.

3. Sprinkle beef with remaining 1½ teaspoons salt and pepper and nestle into stew in single layer so pieces are three-quarters submerged (beef should not be fully submerged). Transfer pan to oven and cook for 2 to 2½ hours.

4. Stir in potatoes and carrots and continue to cook until beef and vegetables are tender, about 2 hours longer, stirring halfway through cooking.

5. Remove pan from oven and discard bay leaves. Stir in peas and let sit until heated through, about 5 minutes. Adjust consistency with extra hot broth as needed. Stir in parsley and season with salt and pepper to taste. Serve.

> **Bulk it Up** Stir hearty greens, cabbage, and/or mushrooms into stew during last 30 minutes of cooking. Add roasted red peppers, dried fruit (apricots, figs, raisins), and/or olives during last 5 minutes of cooking.

COOK IT FOR TWO

SAUCEPAN
Serves 2
Total Time 3 hours
Look for lean short ribs cut from the chuck. If in doubt, ask your butcher for the cut by its technical designation: NAMP 130A. You will need an ovensafe large saucepan with a tight-fitting lid for this recipe.

- 1 pound boneless beef short ribs, trimmed and cut into 1½-inch pieces
- ½ teaspoon table salt
- ¼ teaspoon pepper
- 1 tablespoon vegetable oil
- ½ onion, chopped fine
- 1 teaspoon tomato paste
- 1½ teaspoons minced fresh thyme or ½ teaspoon dried
- 1 tablespoon all-purpose flour
- ¼ cup dry red wine
- 1½ cups chicken broth, plus extra as needed
- 2 carrots, peeled and sliced 1 inch thick
- 1 bay leaf
- 1 red potato, unpeeled, cut into 1-inch pieces
- ¼ cup frozen peas
- 1 tablespoon chopped fresh parsley

1. Adjust oven rack to lower-middle position and heat oven to 325 degrees. Pat beef dry with paper towels and sprinkle with salt and pepper. Heat oil in large saucepan over medium-high heat until just smoking. Brown beef on all sides, 8 to 10 minutes; transfer to bowl.

2. Add onion to fat left in saucepan and cook over medium heat until softened, about 5 minutes. Stir in tomato paste and thyme and cook until fragrant, about 30 seconds. Stir in flour and cook for 1 minute. Slowly whisk in wine, scraping up any browned bits and smoothing out any lumps.

3. Stir in broth, carrots, bay leaf, and beef with any accumulated juices and bring to simmer. Cover, transfer saucepan to oven, and cook for 1 hour.

4. Stir in potato and continue to cook, covered, until beef and vegetables are tender, 1 to 1½ hours.

5. Discard bay leaf. Stir in peas and let sit until heated through, about 2 minutes. Adjust consistency with extra hot broth as needed. Stir in parsley and season with salt and pepper to taste. Serve.

> **Add an Upgrade** Add spice blends (chili powder, garam masala, ras el hanout), minced anchovies, rinsed and minced porcini mushrooms, and/or strips of citrus zest in place of—or in addition to—the thyme.

Pork Stew with Sausage, Potatoes, and Cabbage

DUTCH OVEN
Serves 6 to 8
Total Time 2½ hours

Why This Recipe Works In the realm of stews, pork is often overlooked in favor of other proteins or overpowered by more assertive ingredients, but this robust stew puts pork at the forefront. We took inspiration from a classic French dish, potée, a stew that uses multiple parts of the pig, at least one of which is always smoked, to yield deep, meaty flavor. For our version, we chose a mix of pork butt for its tasty, succulent meat; collagen-rich smoked ham hocks for smokiness and a silky consistency; and kielbasa for a firm bite and additional smoky flavor. We built a flavorful backbone with onion, garlic, and herbes de Provence, and a combination of water and chicken broth for the liquid kept our stew flavorful but not heavy. Cooking the pork butt and ham hocks in the oven gave them plenty of time to turn tender. We added potatoes, carrots, and cabbage halfway through cooking the pork and ham hocks to prevent the vegetables from becoming mushy. We removed the ham hocks to shred the meat, which we added back to the stew. A final sprinkling of parsley rounded out the flavors and contributed freshness. Pork butt roast is often labeled Boston butt in the supermarket.

- 2 tablespoons vegetable oil
- 1 onion, chopped
- ½ teaspoon table salt
- ¼ teaspoon pepper
- 3 garlic cloves, minced
- 2 teaspoons herbes de Provence
- 3 pounds boneless pork butt roast, pulled apart at seams, trimmed, and cut into 1½-inch pieces
- 1¼ pounds smoked ham hocks, rinsed
- 5 cups water
- 4 cups chicken broth, plus extra as needed
- 1 pound Yukon Gold potatoes, unpeeled, cut into ¾-inch pieces
- 4 carrots, peeled and cut into ½-inch pieces
- 12 ounces kielbasa sausage, halved lengthwise and sliced ½ inch thick
- ½ head savoy cabbage, cored and shredded (8 cups)
- ¼ cup minced fresh parsley

1. Adjust oven rack to lower-middle position and heat oven to 325 degrees. Heat oil in Dutch oven over medium heat until shimmering. Add onion, salt, and pepper and cook until softened and lightly browned, 5 to 7 minutes. Stir in garlic and herbes de Provence and cook until fragrant, about 30 seconds. Add pork, ham hocks, water, and broth and bring to simmer. Cover, transfer pot to oven, and cook until pork is tender, 1 to 1½ hours.

2. Remove pot from oven. Transfer ham hocks to cutting board, let cool slightly, then shred meat from hocks into bite-size pieces using 2 forks; discard skin, fat, and bones. Meanwhile, stir potatoes and carrots into stew, return covered pot to oven, and cook until vegetables are almost tender, 20 to 25 minutes.

3. Remove pot from oven and stir in shredded ham, kielbasa, and cabbage. Return covered pot to oven and cook until kielbasa is heated through and cabbage is wilted and tender, 15 to 20 minutes. Adjust consistency with extra hot broth as needed. Stir in parsley and season with salt and pepper to taste. Serve.

Chipotle Pork and Hominy Stew

INSTANT POT
Serves 6 to 8
Total Time 1½ hours

Why This Recipe Works Inspired by New Mexican posole, this fragrant stew combines toothsome hominy and tender chunks of pork in a mildly spicy base. Cooking the pork butt roast and hominy in the oven can take hours, so we used the pressure cooker to make a faster version that would maintain the stew's characteristically complex flavor. Plenty of onion plus jalapeños and garlic offered bold aromatics, while a bit of chipotle chile in adobo brought smoky depth and spice. In the insulated heat of the pressure cooker, the pork cooked up ultratender. We also found that adding the canned hominy before cooking allowed it to absorb lots of flavor from the porky broth, and the fluffy, chewy corn kernels released some starch, which nicely thickened the stew. Chopped cilantro, stirred in at the end, added fresh flavor. To make a version for two, we swapped the large pork butt roast for country-style ribs. A full can of hominy was too overwhelming, so instead we used a portion of a can of white beans. Pork butt roast is often labeled Boston butt in the supermarket.

- 1 tablespoon vegetable oil
- 2 onions, chopped fine
- 2 jalapeño chiles, stemmed, seeded, and minced
- 1½ teaspoons table salt
- ¾ teaspoon pepper
- 4 garlic cloves, minced
- 2 teaspoons minced canned chipotle chile in adobo sauce

2 teaspoons minced fresh oregano or
½ teaspoon dried
⅓ cup all-purpose flour
1 cup dry white wine
3½ pounds boneless pork butt roast, pulled apart at
seams, trimmed, and cut into 1-inch pieces
2 cups chicken broth, plus extra as needed
2 (15-ounce) cans white or yellow hominy, rinsed
8 ounces carrots, peeled and sliced 1 inch thick
2 bay leaves
¼ cup chopped fresh cilantro
Lime wedges

1. Using highest sauté or browning function, heat oil in electric pressure cooker until shimmering. Add onions, jalapeños, salt, and pepper and cook until softened and lightly browned, 5 to 7 minutes. Stir in garlic, chipotle, and oregano and cook until fragrant, about 30 seconds. Stir in flour and cook for 1 minute. Slowly whisk in wine, scraping up any browned bits and smoothing out any lumps. Stir in pork, broth, hominy, carrots, and bay leaves.

2. Lock lid in place and close pressure release valve. Select high pressure cook function and cook for 25 minutes. Turn off pressure cooker and quick-release pressure. Carefully remove lid, allowing steam to escape away from you.

3. Discard bay leaves. Using wide, shallow spoon, skim excess fat from surface of stew. Adjust consistency with extra hot broth as needed. Stir in cilantro and season with salt and pepper to taste. Serve with lime wedges.

Chipotle Pork and Hominy Stew

VARIATION

Chipotle Pork and Bean Stew for Two
INSTANT POT
Serves 2
Total Time 1¼ hours
Any canned small white beans will work well here.

2 teaspoons vegetable oil
1 small onion, chopped fine
1 jalapeño chile, stemmed, seeded, and minced
½ teaspoon table salt
¼ teaspoon pepper
2 garlic cloves, minced
½ teaspoon minced canned chipotle chile in adobo sauce
1 teaspoon minced fresh oregano or ¼ teaspoon dried
1 tablespoon all-purpose flour
⅓ cup dry white wine
1 pound boneless country-style pork ribs, trimmed and
cut into 1-inch pieces
⅔ cup chicken broth, plus extra as needed
¾ cup canned cannellini beans, rinsed
1 carrot, peeled and sliced 1 inch thick
1 bay leaf
2 tablespoons chopped fresh cilantro
Lime wedges

1. Using highest sauté or browning function, heat oil in electric pressure cooker until shimmering. Add onion, jalapeño, salt, and pepper and cook until softened and lightly browned, about 5 minutes. Stir in garlic, chipotle, and oregano and cook until fragrant, about 30 seconds. Stir in flour and cook for 1 minute. Slowly whisk in wine, scraping up any browned bits and smoothing out any lumps. Stir in pork, broth, beans, carrot, and bay leaf.

2. Lock lid in place and close pressure release valve. Select high pressure cook function and cook for 25 minutes. Turn off pressure cooker and quick-release pressure. Carefully remove lid, allowing steam to escape away from you.

3. Discard bay leaf. Using wide, shallow spoon, skim excess fat from surface of stew. Adjust consistency with extra hot broth as needed. Stir in cilantro and season with salt and pepper to taste. Serve with lime wedges.

Spicy Pork and Black Bean Stew
SLOW COOKER

Serves 6 to 8
Cook Time 9 to 10 hours on low or 6 to 7 hours on high

Why This Recipe Works The Brazilian dish known as feijoada is an ultrasatisfying stew featuring creamy black beans in a full-bodied, smoke-and-pork-infused broth all piled high with chorizo and juicy ribs. To ensure our stew would have creamy beans instilled with deep pork flavor, we used the slow cooker for a long, slow simmer. A bit of baking soda added to the beans helped them cook evenly and achieve a tender, not mealy, texture. Adding a ham hock provided body and smokiness that more than made up for any flavor lost by not browning the meat on the stovetop. And finally, we found that raising the ribs out of the cooking liquid by stacking them on top of the other ingredients kept them from overcooking and becoming mushy, ensuring a perfect result every time. If Spanish-style chorizo is not available, Portuguese linguiça or Polish kielbasa can be substituted. You will need a 5- to 7-quart slow cooker for this recipe.

- 5 cups water, plus extra as needed
- 1 pound (2½ cups) dried black beans, picked over and rinsed
- 4 garlic cloves, peeled and smashed
- 2 bay leaves
- 1 teaspoon table salt, divided
- ½ teaspoon pepper, divided
- ⅛ teaspoon baking soda
- 1 pound Spanish-style chorizo sausage, halved crosswise
- 1 (12-ounce) smoked ham hock, rinsed
- 1 onion, halved
- 1 (2½- to 3-pound) rack St. Louis–style spareribs, trimmed and cut into 3 pieces
  Orange wedges

1. Combine water, beans, garlic, bay leaves, ½ teaspoon salt, ¼ teaspoon pepper, and baking soda in slow cooker. Nestle chorizo, ham hock, and onion into bean mixture. Sprinkle ribs with remaining ½ teaspoon salt and remaining ¼ teaspoon pepper. Place ribs on top of bean mixture, taking care to submerge as little of ribs as possible and overlapping as necessary. Cover and cook until beans and ribs are tender, 9 to 10 hours on low or 6 to 7 hours on high.

2. Transfer ribs, ham hock, and chorizo to cutting board and tent with aluminum foil. Discard onion and bay leaves. Transfer 1 cup of beans to bowl and mash with potato masher or fork until smooth; stir mashed beans back into stew in slow cooker.

3. Shred meat from ham hock into bite-size pieces; discard skin, fat, and bones. Stir ham into stew. Adjust consistency with extra hot water as needed. Slice chorizo ½ inch thick. Slice ribs between bones. Transfer meat to serving platter and serve with stew, passing orange wedges separately.

Lamb Stew with Green Beans, Tomatoes, and Basil
DUTCH OVEN

Serves 6
Total Time 3 hours

Why This Recipe Works Lamb has an appealing grassy flavor that makes it a great alternative to beef for a rich stew featuring tender chunks of meat. We knew that selecting the right cut would be essential so we started there, and were happy to discover that boneless lamb shoulder gave us the same bold flavor as pricier lamb leg. A shoulder roast is also ideal for braising, becoming meltingly tender as it cooks. Onions, garlic, tomatoes, and rosemary provided a solid flavor base for the stewing liquid, and a little flour ensured that our stew would develop the spoon-coating consistency we desired. A combination of water and white wine worked well and kept the flavor of the lamb in the foreground. To keep the potatoes and green beans from breaking down completely, we added them halfway through cooking. A final sprinkling of basil just before serving added pleasant freshness. If you can't find boneless lamb shoulder, substitute 4½ pounds bone-in lamb shoulder chops, 1 to 1½ inches thick, trimmed and cut off the bone into 1½-inch pieces.

- 3 pounds boneless lamb shoulder roast, pulled apart at seams, trimmed, and cut into 1½-inch pieces
- 1½ teaspoons table salt, divided
- ½ teaspoon pepper
- 3 tablespoons vegetable oil, divided
- 3 onions, chopped
- 3 garlic cloves, minced
- 1 tablespoon minced fresh rosemary or 1 teaspoon dried
- ¼ cup all-purpose flour
- ½ cup dry white wine
- 1¾ cups water, divided, plus extra as needed
- 1 (14.5-ounce) can diced tomatoes
- 2 pounds Yukon Gold potatoes, peeled and cut into ½-inch pieces
- 12 ounces green beans, trimmed and halved
- ¼ cup chopped fresh basil

**Lamb Stew with Green Beans,
Tomatoes, and Basil**

1. Adjust oven rack to lower-middle position and heat oven to 325 degrees. Pat lamb dry with paper towels and sprinkle with ¾ teaspoon salt and pepper. Heat 1 tablespoon oil in Dutch oven over medium-high heat until just smoking. Brown half of lamb on all sides, 8 to 10 minutes; transfer to large bowl. Repeat with 1 tablespoon oil and remaining lamb; transfer to bowl.

2. Add onions, remaining 1 tablespoon oil, and remaining ¾ teaspoon salt to fat left in pot and cook over medium heat until softened, 5 to 7 minutes. Stir in garlic and rosemary and cook until fragrant, about 30 seconds. Stir in flour and cook for 1 minute.

3. Slowly whisk in wine and 1 cup water, scraping up any browned bits and smoothing out any lumps. Stir in remaining ¾ cup water, tomatoes and their juice, and lamb and any accumulated juices and bring to simmer. Cover, transfer pot to oven, and cook for 1 hour.

4. Remove pot from oven. Stir in potatoes and sprinkle green beans over top. Return covered pot to oven and cook until lamb and vegetables are tender, about 1 hour. Adjust consistency with extra hot water as needed. Stir in basil and season with salt and pepper to taste. Serve.

Spiced Lamb Stew with White Beans
INSTANT POT
Serves 6 to 8
Total Time 1¼ hours, plus 8 hours brining

Why This Recipe Works Inspired by loubia, a dish of stewed white beans that is well loved in Morocco, we set out to create a hearty, satisfying stew with a warm-spiced tomatoey base, tender lamb, and perfectly cooked beans. We used thrifty lamb shoulder chops here for their easy availability and forgiving cook time (other cuts were tough by the time the beans were ready). We chose dried beans over canned for their superior flavor and texture, and brined them for 8 hours so they cooked up soft but still intact. The pressure cooker produced evenly cooked beans and melt-in-your-mouth tender pieces of lamb that finished at the same time.

1½ tablespoons table salt for brining
1 pound (2½ cups) dried great Northern beans, picked over and rinsed
2 (12-ounce) lamb shoulder chops (blade or round bone), ¾ to 1 inch thick, trimmed and halved
½ teaspoon table salt
2 tablespoons extra-virgin olive oil, plus extra for serving
1 onion, chopped fine
2 red bell peppers, stemmed, seeded, and cut into 1-inch pieces
2 tablespoons tomato paste
3 garlic cloves, minced
2 teaspoons paprika
2 teaspoons ground cumin
1½ teaspoons ground ginger
¼ teaspoon cayenne pepper
½ cup dry white wine
2 cups chicken broth, plus extra as needed
2 tablespoons chopped fresh parsley

1. Dissolve 1½ tablespoons salt in 2 quarts cold water in large container. Add beans and soak at room temperature for at least 8 hours or up to 24 hours. Drain and rinse well.

2. Pat lamb dry with paper towels and sprinkle with ½ teaspoon salt. Using highest sauté or browning function, heat oil in pressure cooker until just smoking. Brown lamb on both sides, 8 to 10 minutes; transfer to plate.

3. Add onion and bell peppers to fat left in pot and cook, using highest sauté or browning function, until softened, about 5 minutes. Stir in tomato paste, garlic, paprika, cumin, ginger, and cayenne and cook until fragrant, about 30 seconds. Stir in wine, scraping up any browned bits, then stir in broth and beans.

4. Nestle lamb and any accumulated juices into beans. Lock lid in place and close pressure release valve. Select high pressure cook function and cook for 3 minutes. Turn off pressure cooker and let pressure release naturally for 15 minutes. Quick-release any remaining pressure, then carefully remove lid, allowing steam to escape away from you.

5. Transfer lamb to cutting board, let cool slightly, then shred into bite-size pieces using 2 forks; discard fat and bones. Stir lamb and parsley into stew and season with salt and pepper to taste. Adjust consistency with extra hot broth as needed. Drizzle individual portions with extra oil before serving.

INGREDIENT SPOTLIGHT

DRIED BEANS

Canned beans are undeniably convenient, but there are instances when dried beans are central to the success of a recipe. Here's what to know about them.

Buying When shopping for beans, it's essential to select "fresh" dried beans. Buy those that are uniform in size and have a smooth exterior. When dried beans are fully hydrated and cooked, they should be plump, with taut skins, and have creamy insides; spent beans will have wrinkled skin and a dry, almost gritty texture.

Storing Uncooked beans should be stored in a cool, dry place in a sealed plastic or glass container. Beans are less susceptible than rice and grains to pests and spoilage, but it's still best to use them within a month or two.

Sorting and Rinsing Prior to cooking, you should pick over dried beans for any small stones or debris and then rinse the beans to wash away any dust or impurities. The easiest way to check for small stones is to spread the beans on a large plate or rimmed baking sheet.

Soaking We typically recommend salt-soaking beans for traditional stovetop recipes and pressure cooker recipes to soften their skins and encourage even cooking, but we find the low, slow cooking of the slow cooker allows us to skip this step without any negative results.

Easy Chicken Stew
INSTANT POT
Serves 4
Total Time 1 hour

Why This Recipe Works Great chicken stew combines the pure flavor of a rich broth with tender pieces of chicken and chunks of vegetables; to make chicken stew even better, we wanted to use a pressure cooker to turn out dinner in just one hour. To ensure that each element remained distinct we added our ingredients in stages, starting with aromatics sautéed with tomato paste for deeper flavor. Next, we stirred in boneless chicken thighs, red potatoes, and carrots and pressure cooked the stew for just two minutes to cook all three perfectly. We shredded the chicken and stirred it back in with peas and parsley. For a version to serve two, we swapped out the carrots and peas in favor of a Mediterranean-inspired flavor profile featuring fennel, olives, and lemon zest. Do not substitute boneless, skinless chicken breasts for the thighs in this recipe.

  3 tablespoons vegetable oil
  1 onion, chopped fine
1½ teaspoons table salt
  ¾ teaspoon pepper
  5 garlic cloves, minced
  1 tablespoon tomato paste
1½ teaspoons minced fresh thyme or ½ teaspoon dried
  ¼ cup all-purpose flour
  ¾ cup dry white wine
  2 pounds boneless, skinless chicken thighs, trimmed
  3 cups chicken broth, plus extra as needed
  1 pound red potatoes, unpeeled, cut into ½-inch pieces
  4 carrots, peeled and sliced ½ inch thick
  2 bay leaves
  ¾ cup frozen peas
  2 tablespoons fresh minced parsley

1. Using highest sauté or browning function, heat oil in electric pressure cooker until shimmering. Add onion, salt, and pepper and cook until softened and lightly browned, about 5 minutes. Stir in garlic, tomato paste, and thyme and cook until fragrant, about 30 seconds. Stir in flour and cook for 1 minute. Slowly whisk in wine, scraping up any browned bits and smoothing out any lumps.

2. Stir in chicken, broth, potatoes, carrots, and bay leaves. Lock lid in place and close pressure release valve. Select high pressure cook function and cook for 2 minutes.

3. Turn off pressure cooker and quick-release pressure. Carefully remove lid, allowing steam to escape away from you. Transfer chicken to cutting board, let cool slightly, then shred into bite-size pieces using 2 forks. Discard bay leaves.

4. Stir shredded chicken and any accumulated juices and peas into stew and let sit until heated through, about 2 minutes. Adjust consistency with extra hot broth as needed. Stir in parsley and season with salt and pepper to taste. Serve.

VARIATION

Easy Chicken Stew with Fennel and Olives for Two

INSTANT POT

Serves 2

Total Time 1 hour

Do not substitute boneless, skinless chicken breasts for the thighs in this recipe. If your fennel bulb doesn't have fronds, you can substitute an equal amount of fresh basil, parsley, or tarragon.

- 1 tablespoon extra-virgin olive oil
- 1 small fennel bulb, 1 tablespoon fronds minced, stalks discarded, bulb halved, cored, and cut into ½-inch pieces
- ¾ teaspoon table salt
- ½ teaspoon pepper
- 2 garlic cloves, minced
- 1 teaspoon tomato paste
- ¾ teaspoon ground coriander
- 4 teaspoons all-purpose flour
- ¼ cup dry white wine
- 12 ounces boneless, skinless chicken thighs, trimmed
- ½ cup chicken broth, plus extra as needed
- ½ cup water
- 1 red potato, unpeeled, cut into ½-inch pieces
- 3 (2-inch) strips lemon zest
- 2 tablespoons pitted kalamata olives, chopped

1. Using highest sauté or browning function, heat oil in electric pressure cooker until shimmering. Add fennel pieces, salt, and pepper and cook until softened and lightly browned, about 5 minutes. Stir in garlic, tomato paste, and coriander and cook until fragrant, about 30 seconds. Stir in flour and cook for 30 seconds. Slowly whisk in wine, scraping up any browned bits and smoothing out any lumps.

2. Stir in chicken, broth, water, potato, and lemon zest. Lock lid in place and close pressure release valve. Select high pressure cook function and cook for 6 minutes.

3. Turn off pressure cooker and quick-release pressure. Carefully remove lid, allowing steam to escape away from you. Transfer chicken to cutting board, let cool slightly, then shred into bite-size pieces using 2 forks. Discard lemon zest.

4. Stir shredded chicken and any accumulated juices into stew and let sit until heated through, about 2 minutes. Adjust consistency with extra hot broth as needed. Stir in fennel fronds and olives and season with salt and pepper to taste. Serve.

Chicken Stew with Cheddar Biscuits

Chicken Stew with Cheddar Biscuits

DUTCH OVEN

Serves 6 to 8

Total Time 1¾ hours

Why This Recipe Works Chicken and biscuits are a match made in comfort-food heaven, but this duo usually requires an arsenal of pots and pans so we knew streamlining this hearty dish into a one-pot meal would be a challenge. After many attempts, we found our answer in an unconventional approach: inverting the Dutch oven lid and baking the savory, cheddar-cheese-infused biscuits above the stew. This allowed our biscuits to bake without turning soggy. The result? Tender chicken stew and flaky biscuits together in one pot. Swiss chard, sweet potatoes, and turnips rounded out our stew.

Biscuits
- 2 cups (10 ounces) all-purpose flour
- 2 ounces sharp cheddar cheese, shredded (½ cup)
- 2 teaspoons sugar
- 2 teaspoons baking powder
- ½ teaspoon table salt
- 1½ cups heavy cream

Chicken Stew with Winter Vegetables

Chicken and Sausage Gumbo

Filling

- 4 (12-ounce) bone-in split chicken breasts, trimmed
- 1 teaspoon table salt, divided
- ½ teaspoon pepper
- 2 tablespoons vegetable oil, divided
- 1 onion, chopped fine
- 10 ounces Swiss chard, stems chopped, leaves cut into 1-inch pieces, divided
- 3 garlic cloves, minced
- ¼ cup all-purpose flour
- 2 cups chicken broth, plus extra as needed
- 12 ounces sweet potatoes, peeled and cut into ½-inch pieces
- 8 ounces turnips, peeled and cut into ½-inch pieces
- ½ cup heavy cream
- 2 tablespoons dry sherry
- ¼ cup minced fresh parsley

1. For the biscuits Adjust oven rack to lowest position and heat oven to 425 degrees. Whisk flour, cheddar, sugar, baking powder, and salt together in bowl. Stir in cream and mix until dough forms. Turn dough out onto lightly floured counter and knead dough briefly until smooth, about 30 seconds. Flatten dough into 7-inch circle and cut into 8 wedges. Cover with plastic wrap and set aside.

2. For the filling Pat chicken dry with paper towels and sprinkle with ½ teaspoon salt and pepper. Heat 1 tablespoon oil in Dutch oven over medium-high heat until just smoking. Add chicken, skin side down, and cook until well browned, 6 to 8 minutes; transfer to plate.

3. Add remaining 1 tablespoon oil, onion, chard stems, and remaining ½ teaspoon salt to now-empty pot and cook over medium heat until onion is softened, about 5 minutes. Stir in garlic and cook until fragrant, about 30 seconds. Stir in flour and cook for 1 minute. Slowly whisk in broth, scraping up any browned bits and smoothing out any lumps.

4. Stir in sweet potatoes and turnips and bring to simmer. Nestle chicken, skin side up, into pot and add any accumulated juices. Place lid upside down on pot and cover with trimmed piece of parchment paper. Lay biscuits on lid with wide ends flush to edge of lid. Bake until biscuits are golden brown and chicken registers 160 degrees, 25 to 30 minutes, rotating pot halfway through baking.

5. Remove pot from oven and reduce oven temperature to 300 degrees. Transfer biscuits to wire rack and let cool. Transfer chicken to cutting board, let cool slightly, then shred into bite-size pieces using 2 forks; discard skin and bones.

6. Meanwhile, stir chard leaves into pot and continue to cook in oven, uncovered and stirring occasionally, until filling is thickened and vegetables are tender, 10 to 15 minutes.

7. Remove pot from oven. Stir in shredded chicken, cream, and sherry, cover, and let sit until heated through, about 5 minutes. Adjust consistency with extra hot broth as needed. Stir in parsley and season with salt and pepper to taste. Serve with biscuits.

Chicken Stew with Winter Vegetables
DUTCH OVEN
Serves 6
Total Time 2 hours

Why This Recipe Works Hearty winter vegetables such as potatoes, parsnips, and celery root are often overlooked in favor of bright summer produce, but here they're the stars of a comforting soup ready-made for a blustery winter day. Browning the meaty boneless chicken thighs on the stovetop added rich flavor, and the rendered fat aided in browning and melding the flavors of the aromatics: onions, garlic, and fresh thyme. Some flour ensured a smooth, thick texture, and after the addition of white wine and chicken broth we introduced our rustic mix of vegetables: red potatoes, celery root, and parsnips—along with some carrots for earthy sweetness—all cut into chunks. Chicken stew is at its best when it's gently simmered, so after returning the browned chicken to the pot we transferred it to the oven to cook undisturbed for an hour. All our stew needed was a sprinkling of fresh parsley before serving. Do not substitute boneless, skinless chicken breasts for the thighs in this recipe. Turnips or rutabagas can be substituted for the carrots, celery root, or parsnips, if desired.

3 pounds boneless, skinless chicken thighs, trimmed and cut into 1-inch pieces
1 teaspoon table salt, divided
½ teaspoon pepper
3 tablespoons vegetable oil, divided
2 onions, chopped fine
4 garlic cloves, minced
1 teaspoon minced fresh thyme or ¼ teaspoon dried
¼ cup all-purpose flour
3½ cups chicken broth, plus extra as needed
½ cup dry white wine
8 ounces red potatoes, unpeeled, cut into ¾-inch pieces
8 ounces celery root, peeled and cut into ¾-inch pieces
8 ounces parsnips, peeled and sliced ½ inch thick
3 carrots, peeled and sliced ½ inch thick
2 bay leaves
¼ cup minced fresh parsley

1. Adjust oven rack to lower-middle position and heat oven to 325 degrees. Pat chicken dry with paper towels and sprinkle with ¾ teaspoon salt and pepper. Heat 1 tablespoon oil in Dutch oven over medium-high heat until just smoking. Brown half of chicken on all sides, 8 to 10 minutes; transfer to large bowl. Repeat with 1 tablespoon oil and remaining chicken; transfer to bowl.

2. Add onions, remaining 1 tablespoon oil, and remaining ¼ teaspoon salt to fat left in pot and cook over medium heat until softened, about 5 minutes. Stir in garlic and thyme and cook until fragrant, about 30 seconds. Stir in flour and cook for 1 minute. Slowly whisk in broth and wine, scraping up any browned bits and smoothing out any lumps.

3. Stir in potatoes, celery root, parsnips, carrots, bay leaves, and chicken with any accumulated juices and bring to simmer. Cover, transfer pot to oven, and cook until chicken is very tender, about 1 hour.

4. Remove pot from oven and discard bay leaves. Adjust consistency with extra hot broth as needed. Stir in parsley and season with salt and pepper to taste. Serve.

Chicken and Sausage Gumbo
SLOW COOKER
Serves 4 to 6
Cook Time 4 to 6 hours on low

Why This Recipe Works There are two requirements for exceptional gumbo: long-simmered flavor and a dark roux (flour toasted in hot oil). The slow cooker was the perfect choice to accomplish the long simmering time without having to keep an eye on the stove all day, but how could we make gumbo in a slow cooker if it doesn't get hot enough to make the roux? By starting with the microwave. After 6 minutes in the microwave with regular stirring, our roux was properly browned. Next we added the essential flavorings of onions, bell pepper, celery, garlic, and Creole seasoning to the roux and continued to microwave the mixture until the vegetables were softened. We transferred our gumbo base to the slow cooker where it gently simmered with the chicken, spicy andouille sausage, and frozen okra. The test kitchen's favorite Creole seasoning is Tony Chachere's Original Creole Seasoning. If andouille is not available, Portuguese linguiça or Polish kielbasa can be substituted. Serve with rice (see page 21). Make sure to use a microwave-safe measuring cup or bowl. We recommend placing it on a dry dish towel when you remove it from the microwave since it's best to avoid placing very hot tempered glass directly onto a cold surface.

¾ cup all-purpose flour
½ cup vegetable oil
2 onions, chopped
1 green bell pepper, stemmed, seeded, and chopped
1 celery rib, chopped fine
4 garlic cloves, minced
1 tablespoon Creole seasoning
4 cups chicken broth, plus extra as needed
12 ounces andouille sausage, sliced ½ inch thick
10 ounces frozen cut okra
2 bay leaves
1½ pounds boneless, skinless chicken thighs, trimmed
4 scallions, white and green parts separated and sliced thin
Hot sauce

1. Whisk flour and oil together in large bowl. Microwave and stir in 45-second increments until mixture is color of peanut butter, about 3 minutes. Continue microwaving and stirring in 15-second increments until mixture is color of ground cinnamon, about 3 minutes.

2. Stir onions, bell pepper, celery, garlic, and Creole seasoning into roux and microwave, stirring occasionally, until vegetables are softened, 5 to 7 minutes; transfer to slow cooker. Stir in broth until combined, then stir in andouille, okra, and bay leaves. Nestle chicken into slow cooker. Cover and cook until chicken is tender, 4 to 6 hours on low.

3. Transfer chicken to cutting board, let cool slightly, then shred into bite-size pieces using 2 forks.

4. Discard bay leaves. Using wide, shallow spoon, skim any excess fat from surface of gumbo. Stir in chicken and scallion whites and let sit until heated through, about 2 minutes. Adjust consistency with extra hot broth as needed. Season with salt and pepper to taste. Sprinkle individual portions with scallion greens and serve, passing hot sauce separately.

Chicken Bouillabaisse
INSTANT POT
Serves 4 to 6
Total Time 1 hour

Why This Recipe Works Although French bouillabaisse is classically made with fish, swapping in chicken made this dish perfect for the pressure cooker and more weeknight-friendly. The ingredients that give bouillabaisse its robust flavor—such as garlic, fennel, and saffron—could withstand high pressure, making for an intensely fragrant broth. Browning the chicken and the aromatics helped boost savory flavor. A small amount of licorice-flavored liqueur provided the traditional anise note, while canned tomatoes lent welcome acidity and brightness. Do not substitute bone-in chicken breasts for the thighs in this recipe. Serve with crusty bread or Garlic Toasts (page 45).

8 (5- to 7-ounce) bone-in chicken thighs, trimmed
½ teaspoon table salt
½ teaspoon pepper
2 tablespoons extra-virgin olive oil, divided
1 small fennel bulb, stalks discarded, bulb halved, cored, and sliced thin
4 garlic cloves, minced
1 tablespoon tomato paste
¼ teaspoon saffron threads, crumbled
¼ teaspoon cayenne pepper
1 tablespoon all-purpose flour
¼ cup dry white wine
¼ cup pastis or Pernod
3 cups chicken broth, plus extra as needed
1 (14.5-ounce) can diced tomatoes, drained
12 ounces Yukon Gold potatoes, unpeeled, cut into ¾-inch pieces
1 (3-inch) strip orange zest
1 tablespoon chopped fresh tarragon or parsley

1. Pat chicken dry with paper towels and sprinkle with salt and pepper. Using highest sauté or browning function, heat 1 tablespoon oil in electric pressure cooker until just smoking. Add half of chicken, skin side down, and cook until well browned, 6 to 8 minutes; transfer to plate. Repeat with remaining 1 tablespoon oil and remaining chicken; transfer to plate.

2. Add fennel to fat left in pressure cooker and cook using highest sauté or browning function until softened, 3 to 5 minutes. Stir in garlic, tomato paste, saffron, and cayenne and cook until fragrant, about 30 seconds. Stir in flour and cook for 1 minute. Slowly whisk in wine and pastis, scraping up any browned bits and smoothing out any lumps. Stir in broth, tomatoes, potatoes, and orange zest. Nestle chicken, skin side up, into pot, and add any accumulated juices.

3. Lock lid in place and close pressure release valve. Select high pressure cook function and cook for 3 minutes. Turn off pressure cooker and quick-release pressure. Carefully remove lid, allowing steam to escape away from you.

4. Transfer chicken to plate and discard skin, if desired. Discard orange zest. Let cooking liquid settle, then skim excess fat from surface using wide, shallow spoon. Adjust consistency with extra hot broth as needed. Stir in tarragon and season with salt and pepper to taste. Divide stew between individual shallow bowls and top with chicken. Serve.

Fisherman's Stew

SLOW COOKER

Serves 4 to 6

Cook Time 5 to 7 hours on low or 3 to 5 hours on high, plus 30 minutes on high

Why This Recipe Works To make a fish stew featuring tender and moist cod and shrimp, a full-flavored broth, spicy chorizo, and hearty potatoes, we turned to the slow cooker to perfectly cook each component. We started by softening the onion, chorizo, and garlic in the microwave before combining them with the potatoes and a broth of white wine, clam juice, and diced tomatoes in the slow cooker. We let the gentle heat of the slow cooker work its magic until the potatoes were tender and the broth was richly flavored. Finally, we added the seafood and cooked it in the flavorful broth for 30 minutes. All the stew needed before serving was a sprinkle of parsley for bright freshness. If Spanish-style chorizo is not available, Portuguese linguiça or Polish kielbasa can be substituted. Haddock and striped bass are good substitutes for the cod. For a richer stew, serve with Garlic Aioli and crusty bread or Garlic Toasts (page 45).

Fisherman's Stew

- 1 onion, chopped
- 8 ounces Spanish-style chorizo sausage, cut into ¼-inch pieces
- 4 garlic cloves, minced
- 1 pound red potatoes, unpeeled, cut into ½-inch pieces
- 2 (8-ounce) bottles clam juice
- 1 (14.5-ounce) can diced tomatoes, drained
- ¼ cup dry white wine
- 1½ pounds skinless cod fillets, 1 to 1½ inches thick, cut into 2- to 3-inch pieces
- 8 ounces large shrimp (26 to 30 per pound), peeled, deveined, and tails removed
- ¼ teaspoon table salt
- ¼ teaspoon pepper
- 2 tablespoons minced fresh parsley

1. Microwave onion, chorizo, and garlic in bowl, stirring occasionally, until onion is softened, about 5 minutes; transfer to slow cooker. Stir in potatoes, clam juice, tomatoes, and wine. Cover and cook until flavors meld and potatoes are tender, 5 to 7 hours on low or 3 to 5 hours on high.

2. Sprinkle cod and shrimp with salt and pepper, then nestle into stew. Cover and cook on high until shrimp are opaque throughout and cod flakes apart when gently prodded with paring knife, about 30 minutes. Adjust consistency with hot water as needed. Season with salt and pepper to taste. Sprinkle with parsley and serve.

Garlic Aioli

Makes about 1¼ cups

Using a combination of vegetable oil and extra-virgin olive oil is crucial to the flavor of the aioli.

- 2 large egg yolks
- 2 teaspoons Dijon mustard
- 2 teaspoons lemon juice
- 1 garlic clove, minced
- ¾ cup vegetable oil
- 1 tablespoon water
- ½ teaspoon table salt
- ¼ teaspoon pepper
- ¼ cup extra-virgin olive oil

Process egg yolks, mustard, lemon juice, and garlic in food processor until combined, about 10 seconds. With processor running, slowly drizzle in vegetable oil, about 1 minute. Transfer mixture to medium bowl and whisk in water, salt, and pepper. Whisking constantly, slowly drizzle in olive oil. (Aioli can be refrigerated for up to 4 days.)

Sicilian Fish Stew

Spanish Shellfish Stew

Sicilian Fish Stew

INSTANT POT

Serves 4

Total Time 45 minutes

Why This Recipe Works In Sicily, fish stew is a celebration of local flavors with its balance of sweet, sour, and salty notes. The heat of the pressure cooker works exceptionally well here for cooking tender fish and breaking down tomatoes to a stewy consistency. We chose swordfish because its meaty texture and distinct flavor could stand up to a symphony of bold flavors. For the base, we created a quick stock using aromatic onions, garlic, thyme, and red pepper flakes simmered with white wine, chopped tomatoes, and clam juice, and mixed in golden raisins and capers for sweet and briny bursts of flavor. After just 1 minute under pressure, the swordfish emerged tender and succulent. To finish our stew, we put together a bright topping of orange zest, mint, and garlic, and stirred in toasted pine nuts for crunch. Halibut is a good substitute for the swordfish. Serve with crusty bread or Garlic Toasts (page 45).

2 tablespoons extra-virgin olive oil
2 onions, chopped fine
1 teaspoon table salt
½ teaspoon pepper
1 teaspoon minced fresh thyme or ¼ teaspoon dried
Pinch red pepper flakes
4 garlic cloves, minced, divided
1 (28-ounce) can whole peeled tomatoes, drained with juice reserved, chopped coarse
1 (8-ounce) bottle clam juice
¼ cup dry white wine
¼ cup golden raisins
2 tablespoons capers, rinsed
1½ pounds skinless swordfish steak, 1 to 1½ inches thick, cut into 1-inch pieces
¼ cup pine nuts, toasted
¼ cup minced fresh mint
1 teaspoon grated orange zest

1. Using highest sauté or browning function, heat oil in electric pressure cooker until shimmering. Add onions, salt, and pepper and cook until softened, about 5 minutes. Stir in thyme, pepper flakes, and three-quarters of garlic and cook until fragrant, about 30 seconds. Stir in tomatoes and reserved juice, clam juice, wine, raisins, and capers. Nestle swordfish into pot and spoon some cooking liquid over top.

2. Lock lid in place and close pressure release valve. Select high pressure cook function and cook for 1 minute. Turn off pressure cooker and quick-release pressure. Carefully remove lid, allowing steam to escape away from you.

3. Combine pine nuts, mint, orange zest, and remaining garlic in bowl. Adjust consistency with hot water as needed. Season stew with salt and pepper to taste. Sprinkle individual portions with pine nut mixture before serving.

Spanish Shellfish Stew

DUTCH OVEN

Serves 4 to 6
Total Time 1 hour

Why This Recipe Works Chock-full of shrimp, clams, mussels, and scallops; seasoned with saffron and paprika; and thickened with a picada (a mixture of ground almonds, bread crumbs, and olive oil), this stew is bursting with an appealing array of flavors and textures. We began with a Spanish sofrito of onion, red bell pepper, and garlic to which we added paprika, saffron, red pepper flakes, and bay leaves. The juice from canned tomatoes and dry white wine formed a lively broth, and a little brandy lent depth of flavor. Shells contain significant flavor, so we enriched the broth by steeping the shrimp shells in wine while we prepared the other ingredients. Since each of the shellfish was a different size, we knew we'd have to stagger the cooking; the clams went into the stew first, followed by the mussels and scallops, and finally the shrimp. Stirring in the picada at the end adds richness and thickens the stew; do not omit it. Buy shrimp with their shells on and reserve the shells when cleaning the shrimp; they add important flavor to the cooking liquid in step 1. Use a Dutch oven that holds 6 quarts or more for this recipe. Serve with crusty bread or Garlic Toasts (page 45).

  3 tablespoons extra-virgin olive oil, divided
  8 ounces medium-large shrimp (31 to 40 per pound), peeled and deveined, shells reserved
1½ cups dry white wine or dry vermouth
  1 onion, chopped fine
  1 red bell pepper, stemmed, seeded, and chopped fine
  3 garlic cloves, minced
  1 teaspoon paprika
  ¼ teaspoon saffron threads, crumbled
  ⅛ teaspoon red pepper flakes
  2 bay leaves
  1 (28-ounce) can whole peeled tomatoes, drained with juice reserved, chopped
  2 tablespoons brandy (optional)
1½ pounds littleneck clams, scrubbed
  8 ounces mussels, scrubbed and debearded

 12 ounces large sea scallops, tendons removed
  1 recipe Picada
  1 tablespoon minced fresh parsley
    Lemon wedges

1. Heat 1 tablespoon oil in large Dutch oven medium heat until shimmering. Add shrimp shells and cook, stirring frequently, until spotty brown, 2 to 4 minutes. Off heat, stir in wine, scraping up any browned bits. Transfer to bowl, cover, and let steep until ready to use.

2. Heat remaining 2 tablespoons oil in now-empty Dutch oven over medium-high heat until shimmering. Add onion and bell pepper and cook until softened and lightly browned, 5 to 7 minutes. Stir in garlic, paprika, saffron, pepper flakes, and bay leaves and cook until fragrant, about 30 seconds. Stir in tomatoes and reserved juice and brandy, if using, scraping up any browned bits, and cook until slightly thickened, 5 to 7 minutes.

3. Strain wine mixture through fine-mesh strainer into Dutch oven, pressing on solids to extract as much liquid as possible, and return to simmer; discard solids.

4. Nestle clams into pot, cover, and cook for 4 minutes. Nestle mussels and scallops into pot, cover, and continue to simmer until most clams have opened, about 3 minutes. Arrange shrimp evenly over stew, cover, and continue to cook until shrimp are opaque throughout, scallops are firm and opaque in center, and clams and mussels have opened, about 2 minutes.

5. Off heat, discard bay leaves and any clams and mussels that refuse to open. Stir in picada and parsley and season with salt and pepper to taste. Serve in wide, shallow bowls with lemon wedges.

Picada

Makes about ⅔ cup

  ½ cup panko bread crumbs
  ¼ cup slivered almonds, chopped fine
  1 tablespoon extra-virgin olive oil

Toss panko and almonds with oil in bowl until evenly coated. Microwave, stirring frequently, until light golden brown, 1 to 3 minutes; set aside to cool. (Picada can be stored in airtight container for up to 2 days.)

Spanish Shellfish Stew for Two
SAUCEPAN
Serves 2
Total Time 1 hour

Be sure to buy shrimp with their shells on and reserve the shells when cleaning the shrimp; they add important flavor to the cooking liquid in step 1. Serve with crusty bread or Garlic Toasts (page 45).

  5 teaspoons extra-virgin olive oil, divided
  4 ounces medium-large shrimp (31 to 40 per pound), peeled and deveined, shells reserved
  ¾ cup dry white wine or dry vermouth
  1 small onion, chopped fine
  ½ red bell pepper, chopped fine
  1 garlic clove, minced
  ½ teaspoon paprika
  ⅛ teaspoon saffron threads, crumbled
  ⅛ teaspoon red pepper flakes
  1 (14-ounce) can whole peeled tomatoes, drained with juice reserved, chopped
  1 tablespoon brandy (optional)
 12 ounces littleneck clams, scrubbed
  6 ounces large sea scallops, tendons removed
  ½ recipe Picada (page 75)
  1 tablespoon minced fresh parsley
     Lemon wedges

1. Heat 2 teaspoons oil in large saucepan oven medium heat until shimmering. Add shrimp shells and cook, stirring frequently, until spotty brown, about 2 minutes. Off heat, stir in wine, scraping up any browned bits. Transfer to bowl, cover, and let steep until ready to use.

2. Heat remaining 1 tablespoon oil in now-empty saucepan over medium-high heat until shimmering. Add onion and bell pepper and cook until softened and lightly browned, about 5 minutes. Stir in garlic, paprika, saffron, and pepper flakes and cook until fragrant, about 30 seconds. Stir in tomatoes and reserved juice and brandy, if using, scraping up any browned bits, and cook until slightly thickened, 5 to 7 minutes.

3. Strain wine mixture through fine-mesh strainer into saucepan, pressing on solids to extract as much liquid as possible, and return to simmer; discard solids.

4. Nestle clams into saucepan, cover, and cook for 4 minutes. Nestle scallops into saucepan, cover, and continue to simmer until most clams have opened, about 3 minutes. Arrange shrimp evenly over stew, cover, and continue to cook until shrimp are opaque throughout, scallops are firm and opaque in center, and clams have opened, about 2 minutes.

5. Off heat, discard any clams that refuse to open. Stir in picada and parsley and season with salt and pepper to taste. Serve in wide, shallow bowls with lemon wedges.

Hearty Ten-Vegetable Stew
DUTCH OVEN
Serves 6 to 8
Total Time 2¼ hours

Why This Recipe Works Vegetable stew should be the simplest of one-pot meals—just nestle bright, fresh vegetables in a pot and let everything meld together. But vegetables are full of moisture and natural sugars, which means that the stew can turn out both watery and sweet. To produce a stew with deep, robust, and savory flavor, we needed to carefully choose our vegetables and broth. Mushrooms cooked until well browned added meatiness, a good dose of both sautéed onion and garlic brought a distinct savory character, wine brightened up the flavor with its acidity, and herbs lent an earthy quality and fullness to the stew. Adding ten types of vegetables in stages ensured each was perfectly cooked. Kale greens or curly-leaf spinach, stemmed and sliced ½ inch thick, can be substituted for the chard leaves (omit the stems); the kale may require up to 5 minutes of additional simmering time in step 4 to become tender.

   2 tablespoons extra-virgin olive oil, divided
   1 pound white mushrooms, trimmed and sliced thin
   ½ teaspoon table salt
   8 ounces Swiss chard, stems chopped fine, leaves sliced ½ inch thick, divided
   2 onions, chopped fine
   1 celery rib, cut into ½-inch pieces
   1 carrot, peeled and cut into 1-inch pieces
   1 red bell pepper, stemmed, seeded, and cut into ½-inch pieces
   6 garlic cloves, minced
   1 tablespoon tomato paste
   2 teaspoons minced fresh thyme or ½ teaspoon dried
   2 tablespoons all-purpose flour
   ½ cup dry white wine
   3 cups vegetable or chicken broth, plus extra as needed
  2½ cups water
   8 ounces red potatoes, unpeeled, cut into 1-inch pieces
   2 parsnips, peeled and cut into 1-inch pieces
   8 ounces celery root, peeled and cut into 1-inch pieces
   2 bay leaves
   1 zucchini, halved lengthwise, seeded, and cut into ½-inch pieces

Hearty Ten-Vegetable Stew

Quinoa and Vegetable Stew
DUTCH OVEN

Serves 6 to 8
Total Time 1 hour

Why This Recipe Works Drawing inspiration from South American quinoa stew, we spiced our version with paprika, garlic, cumin, and coriander, plus onion and red bell pepper, for a flavor-packed base. Tomatoes, red potatoes, sweet corn, and frozen peas provided a colorful mix of vegetables. We added the quinoa after the potatoes had softened, cooking it until it released starch to help give the stew body. Finally, we added garnishes: queso fresco, avocado, and cilantro. We like the convenience of prewashed quinoa; rinsing removes the quinoa's bitter protective coating (called saponin). If you buy unwashed quinoa, rinse it and then spread it out on a clean dish towel to dry for 15 minutes. Do not omit the garnishes, as they are important to the flavor of the stew.

2 tablespoons extra-virgin olive oil
1 onion, chopped
1 red bell pepper, stemmed, seeded, and cut into ½-inch pieces
5 garlic cloves, minced
1 tablespoon paprika
2 teaspoons ground coriander
1½ teaspoons ground cumin
6 cups vegetable or chicken broth, plus extra as needed
1 pound red potatoes, unpeeled, cut into ½-inch pieces
1 cup prewashed white quinoa
1 cup fresh or frozen corn
2 tomatoes, cored and chopped coarse
1 cup frozen peas
8 ounces queso fresco or feta cheese, crumbled (2 cups)
1 avocado, halved, pitted, and diced
½ cup minced fresh cilantro

1. Heat oil in Dutch oven over medium heat until shimmering. Add onion and bell pepper and cook until softened, 5 to 7 minutes. Stir in garlic, paprika, coriander, and cumin and cook until fragrant, about 30 seconds. Stir in broth and potatoes and bring to simmer. Reduce heat to medium-low and simmer gently for 10 minutes.

2. Stir in quinoa and simmer for 8 minutes. Stir in corn and simmer until potatoes and quinoa are just tender, 5 to 7 minutes. Stir in tomatoes and peas and simmer until heated through, about 2 minutes. Adjust consistency with extra hot broth as needed. Season with salt and pepper to taste. Sprinkle individual portions with queso fresco, avocado, and cilantro before serving.

¼ cup minced fresh parsley
1 tablespoon lemon juice

1. Heat 1 tablespoon oil in Dutch oven over medium heat until shimmering. Add mushrooms and salt, cover, and cook until mushrooms have released their liquid, about 5 minutes. Uncover and continue to cook until mushrooms are dry and browned, 5 to 10 minutes.

2. Stir in remaining 1 tablespoon oil, chard stems, onions, celery, carrot, and bell pepper and cook until vegetables are well browned, 7 to 10 minutes. Stir in garlic, tomato paste, and thyme and cook until fragrant, about 30 seconds. Stir in flour and cook for 1 minute. Stir in wine, scraping up any browned bits, and cook until nearly evaporated, about 1 minute.

3. Stir in broth, water, potatoes, parsnips, celery root, and bay leaves and bring to simmer. Reduce heat to medium-low, partially cover, and cook until stew is thickened and vegetables are tender, about 1 hour.

4. Stir in zucchini and chard leaves and simmer, uncovered, until just tender, 5 to 10 minutes. Off heat, discard bay leaves. Adjust consistency with extra hot broth as needed. Stir in parsley and lemon juice and season with salt and pepper to taste. Serve.

Wheat Berry and Wild Mushroom Stew

SLOW COOKER

Serves 6 to 8
Cook Time 8 to 10 hours on low or 5 to 7 hours on high

Why This Recipe Works Earthy mushrooms and sweet, nutty wheat berries promise a vegetarian stew with great flavor. Wheat berries are among the sturdiest of grains, which meant they could be left unattended in the slow cooker without worry; they were hearty enough to maintain their chewy texture even after 10 hours in the pot. Using two types of mushrooms—cremini and dried porcini—ensured that our stew had tender bites of mushroom and intense umami flavor. To give the stew a boost, we stirred in some Madeira, adding an extra splash of the fortified wine at the end of cooking for brightness. A healthy pile of baby spinach stirred in during the last few minutes of cooking provided color and freshness. If using quick-cooking or presteamed wheat berries (the ingredient list on the package specifies the type), you will need to decrease the cooking time in step 1. The wheat berries will retain a chewy texture once fully cooked. The amount of spinach may seem like a lot at first, but it wilts down substantially.

- 2 pounds cremini mushrooms, trimmed and sliced thin
- ½ ounce dried porcini mushrooms, rinsed and minced
- 3 garlic cloves, minced
- 3 tablespoons extra-virgin olive oil, divided, plus extra for drizzling
- 2 teaspoons minced fresh thyme or ½ teaspoon dried
- ½ teaspoon table salt
- 6 cups vegetable or chicken broth, plus extra as needed
- 1½ cups wheat berries
- ½ cup dry Madeira or sherry, divided
- 6 ounces (6 cups) baby spinach
  Grated Parmesan cheese

1. Microwave cremini mushrooms, porcini mushrooms, garlic, 1 tablespoon oil, thyme, and salt in bowl, stirring occasionally, until mushrooms are softened, about 5 minutes; transfer to slow cooker. Stir in broth, wheat berries, and 6 tablespoons Madeira. Cover and cook until wheat berries are tender, 8 to 10 hours on low or 5 to 7 hours on high.

2. Stir in spinach, 1 handful at a time, and let sit until wilted, about 5 minutes. Adjust consistency with extra hot broth as needed. Stir in remaining 2 tablespoons oil and remaining 2 tablespoons Madeira and season with salt and pepper to taste. Drizzle individual portions with extra oil and sprinkle with Parmesan before serving.

Hearty Tuscan White Bean Stew

INSTANT POT

Serves 6 to 8
Total Time 1 hour, plus 8 hours brining

Why This Recipe Works This simple, hearty bean stew hails from Tuscany and showcases one of the region's favorite ingredients—cannellini beans—with pancetta, aromatic vegetables, and hearty greens. Determined to avoid tough, exploded beans in our stew, we soaked the beans overnight in salted water, which softened the skins to prevent them from bursting; once soaked, we used the pressure cooker to cook the beans to a perfect tender, creamy consistency. To assemble the soup, we sautéed pancetta (the Italian bacon) to give the stew smoky, meaty notes. Cooking the vegetables in the rendered pancetta fat infused the soup with hearty, savory flavor. Next we added in the beans, kale, and tomatoes along with a bay leaf and a sprig of fresh rosemary, which added deep herbal flavor. A drizzle of olive oil before serving added extra richness. We prefer the color and texture of Lacinato kale in this stew, but you can substitute curly kale or 6 ounces of bagged, chopped kale.

- 1½ tablespoons table salt for brining
- 1 pound (2½ cups) dried cannellini beans, picked over and rinsed
- 1 tablespoon extra-virgin olive oil, plus extra for drizzling
- 4 ounces pancetta, cut into ¼-inch pieces
- 1 onion, chopped fine
- 2 celery ribs, cut into ½-inch pieces
- 2 carrots, peeled and cut into ½-inch pieces
- 8 garlic cloves, smashed and peeled
- 3 cups chicken broth, plus extra as needed
- 8 ounces kale, stemmed and cut into 1-inch pieces
- 1 (14.5-ounce) can diced tomatoes
- 2 bay leaves
- 1 sprig fresh rosemary

1. Dissolve 1½ tablespoons salt in 2 quarts cold water in large container. Add beans and soak at room temperature for at least 8 hours or up to 24 hours. Drain and rinse well.

2. Using highest sauté or browning function, heat oil in electric pressure cooker until just smoking. Add pancetta and cook, stirring often, until rendered and crisp, about 5 minutes. Stir in onion, celery, and carrots and cook until softened, about 5 minutes. Stir in garlic and cook until fragrant, about 30 seconds. Stir in broth, scraping up any browned bits.

3. Stir in beans, kale, tomatoes and their juice, bay leaves, and rosemary sprig. Lock lid in place and close pressure release valve. Select high pressure cook function and cook for 3 minutes.

4. Turn off pressure cooker and let pressure release naturally for 15 minutes. Quick-release any remaining pressure, then carefully remove lid, allowing steam to escape away from you. Discard bay leaves and rosemary sprig. Adjust consistency with extra hot broth as needed. Season stew with salt and pepper to taste. Drizzle individual portions with extra oil before serving.

Vegetable and Chickpea Stew

Hearty White Bean Stew with Sausage and Mustard Greens for Two

INSTANT POT

Serves 2

Total Time 45 minutes

You can substitute Lacinato or curly kale for the mustard greens, if desired. Any canned small white beans will work well here.

1	tablespoon extra-virgin olive oil, plus extra for drizzling
8	ounces hot or sweet Italian pork sausage, casings removed
1	small onion, chopped fine
1	celery rib, cut into ½-inch pieces
3	garlic cloves, smashed and peeled
2	teaspoons chopped fresh oregano or ½ teaspoon dried
1½	cups chicken broth, plus extra as needed
1	(15-ounce) can cannellini beans, rinsed
4	ounces mustard greens, stemmed and cut into 1-inch pieces
¼	cup pitted kalamata olives, chopped
½	teaspoon grated lemon zest plus 1 tablespoon lemon juice

1. Using highest sauté or browning function, heat oil in electric pressure cooker until just smoking. Add sausage and cook, breaking up meat with wooden spoon, until beginning to brown, about 5 minutes. Stir in onion and celery and cook until softened, about 5 minutes. Stir in garlic and oregano and cook until fragrant, about 30 seconds.

2. Stir in broth, scraping up any browned bits, then stir in beans and mustard greens. Lock lid in place and close pressure release valve. Select high pressure cook function and cook for 5 minutes. Turn off pressure cooker and quick-release pressure. Carefully remove lid, allowing steam to escape away from you.

3. Adjust consistency with extra hot broth as needed. Stir in olives and lemon zest and juice. Season with salt and pepper to taste. Drizzle individual portions with extra oil before serving.

Vegetable and Chickpea Stew

INSTANT POT

Serves 6 to 8

Total Time 1 hour

Why This Recipe Works In this Lebanese-inspired stew, bold spices are an exciting contrast to a bounty of vegetables. We wanted to cut down on the lengthy list of spices included in many Lebanese recipes, so we turned to baharat, a potent Middle Eastern spice blend. To further streamline this stew, we used a pressure cooker, which makes quick work of cooking the chickpeas and vegetables. Using the sauté function, we browned bell peppers and onion to develop depth. The baharat was next, followed by a little garlic and tomato paste. After cooking it all under pressure, we simmered the delicate zucchini in the stew to ensure that it remained green and tender, and also added convenient canned chickpeas to warm through. A little olive oil drizzled on just before serving provided richness, while chopped mint added freshness. If you can't find baharat, you can substitute 1½ teaspoons ground nutmeg, 1½ teaspoons paprika, ½ teaspoon ground coriander, ½ teaspoon ground cinnamon, and ½ teaspoon ground cumin.

- ¼ cup extra-virgin olive oil, plus extra for drizzling
- 2 red bell peppers, stemmed, seeded, and cut into 1-inch pieces
- 1 onion, chopped fine
- ½ teaspoon table salt
- ½ teaspoon pepper
- 1½ tablespoons baharat
- 4 garlic cloves, minced
- 1 tablespoon tomato paste
- 4 cups vegetable or chicken broth, plus extra as needed
- 1 (28-ounce) can whole peeled tomatoes, drained with juice reserved, chopped
- 1 pound Yukon Gold potatoes, peeled and cut into ½-inch pieces
- 2 zucchini, quartered lengthwise and sliced 1 inch thick
- 1 (15-ounce) can chickpeas, rinsed
- ⅓ cup chopped fresh mint

1. Using highest sauté or browning function, heat oil in electric pressure cooker until shimmering. Add bell peppers, onion, salt, and pepper and cook until vegetables are softened and lightly browned, 5 to 7 minutes. Stir in baharat, garlic, and tomato paste and cook until fragrant, about 1 minute. Stir in broth and tomatoes and reserved juice, scraping up any browned bits, then stir in potatoes.

2. Lock lid in place and close pressure release valve. Select high pressure cook function and cook for 9 minutes. Turn off pressure cooker and quick-release pressure. Carefully remove lid, allowing steam to escape away from you.

3. Stir zucchini and chickpeas into stew and cook, using highest sauté or browning function, until zucchini is tender, 10 to 15 minutes. Turn off pressure cooker. Adjust consistency with extra hot broth as needed. Season with salt and pepper to taste. Drizzle individual portions with extra oil and sprinkle with mint before serving.

Classic Ground Beef Chili

INGREDIENT SPOTLIGHT

CHILI POWDER
To determine our favorite chili powder, we tasted seven widely available brands. Our top picks stuck with classic flavorings: cumin, oregano, and garlic. We also liked the addition of paprika, which gave complexity. In the end, **Morton & Bassett Chili Powder** was the winner for its deep, roasty flavor; subtle sweetness; and just the right amount of heat.

Classic Ground Beef Chili
DUTCH OVEN
Serves 4 to 6
Total Time 1½ hours

Why This Recipe Works Good ground beef chili should come together easily and relatively quickly, but it shouldn't taste as if it did. The flavors should be rich and balanced, the texture thick and hearty. To create deeply flavorful chili, we started by developing a fond (browned bits of beef) on the bottom of a Dutch oven. After building this flavor base, we bloomed the dried spices in hot oil to bring out their lively personalities. We pureed half the beans with canned tomatoes to thicken the chili without having to simmer it all day, adding the remaining beans later on to give our chili heft and texture. For a spicier chili, use the greater amount of chipotle. Serve with your favorite chili garnishes.

- 1 (28-ounce) can whole peeled tomatoes
- 2 (15-ounce) cans kidney beans, rinsed, divided
- 1 tablespoon vegetable oil
- 1½ pounds 85 percent lean ground beef
- 1 onion, chopped fine

1½ teaspoons table salt
1 teaspoon pepper
3 tablespoons chili powder
1–2 tablespoons minced canned chipotle chile in adobo sauce
1 tablespoon ground coriander
1 tablespoon garlic powder
2 teaspoons ground cumin
2 teaspoons dried oregano
2 cups water, plus extra as needed

1. Process tomatoes and their juice and half of beans in food processor until smooth, about 30 seconds; set aside.

2. Heat oil in Dutch oven over medium-high heat until just smoking. Add beef, onion, salt, and pepper and cook, breaking up meat with wooden spoon, until any liquid has evaporated and fond begins to form on bottom of pot, 12 to 14 minutes. Add chili powder, chipotle, coriander, garlic powder, cumin, and oregano and cook, stirring frequently, until fragrant, about 2 minutes.

3. Stir in water, scraping up any browned bits. Stir in tomato mixture and remaining beans and bring to simmer. Reduce heat to medium-low, cover partially, and cook until thickened and flavors meld, about 45 minutes. (If chili begins to stick to bottom of pot or looks too thick, stir in extra water as needed.) Season with salt and pepper to taste. Serve.

VARIATION

Classic Ground Beef Chili for Two

SAUCEPAN

Serves 2

Total Time 1 hour

Any canned bean will work well here. For a spicier chili, use the greater amount of chipotle. Serve with your favorite chili garnishes.

1 (14-ounce) can whole peeled tomatoes
1 (15-ounce) can kidney beans, rinsed, divided
1 tablespoon vegetable oil
12 ounces 85 percent lean ground beef
1 small onion, chopped fine
¼ teaspoon table salt
⅛ teaspoon pepper
2 tablespoons chili powder
1–2 teaspoons minced canned chipotle chile in adobo sauce
1 teaspoon ground coriander
1 teaspoon garlic powder
1 teaspoon ground cumin
¼ teaspoon dried oregano
1 cup water, plus extra as needed

1. Process tomatoes and their juice and half of beans in food processor until smooth, about 30 seconds; set aside.

2. Heat oil in large saucepan over medium-high heat until just smoking. Add beef, onion, salt, and pepper and cook, breaking up meat with wooden spoon, until any liquid has evaporated and fond begins to form on bottom of pot, 6 to 8 minutes. Add chili powder, chipotle, coriander, garlic powder, cumin, and oregano and cook, stirring frequently, until fragrant, about 2 minutes.

3. Stir in water, scraping up any browned bits. Stir in tomato mixture and remaining beans and bring to simmer. Reduce heat to medium-low, cover partially, and cook until thickened and flavors meld, about 30 minutes. (If chili begins to stick to bottom of saucepan or looks too thick, stir in extra water as needed.) Season with salt and pepper to taste. Serve.

Golden Northern Cornbread

Serves 8 to 10

If stone-ground cornmeal is unavailable, any fine- or medium-ground cornmeal will work; do not use coarse-ground cornmeal.

1 cup (5 ounces) stone-ground cornmeal
1 cup (5 ounces) all-purpose flour
4 teaspoons sugar
2 teaspoons baking powder
½ teaspoon baking soda
½ teaspoon table salt
2 large eggs
⅔ cup buttermilk
⅔ cup whole milk
2 tablespoons unsalted butter, melted and cooled

1. Adjust oven rack to middle position and heat oven to 425 degrees. Grease 9-inch square baking pan. Whisk cornmeal, flour, sugar, baking powder, baking soda, and salt together in large bowl, then make well in center of bowl.

2. Crack eggs into well and stir gently with wooden spoon. Add buttermilk and milk and quickly stir until batter is almost combined. Stir in melted butter until batter is just combined.

3. Pour batter into prepared pan and smooth top. Bake until top is golden brown and lightly cracked and edges have pulled away from sides of pan, about 25 minutes, rotating pan halfway through baking. Let cornbread cool in pan for 5 to 10 minutes before serving.

Beef and Three-Bean Chili

INSTANT POT
Serves 4 to 6
Total Time 1 hour

Why This Recipe Works A pressure cooker can produce chili with bold, long-simmered flavor with a minimum of hands-on time. A combination of chili powder, cumin, and garlic was all we needed to give this chili great flavor. We used crushed tomatoes plus chicken broth for a base with the proper consistency. Browning the beef is standard in chili recipes, but we found that the browned meat overcooked easily in the intense heat of the pressure cooker, so we mixed it with a panade (a mixture of bread and milk) to help it stay moist, and sautéed the meat just until it lost its pink color. We prefer a combination of all three beans here, but a single variety will also work. Serve with your favorite chili garnishes.

- 1 slice hearty white sandwich bread, torn into 1-inch pieces
- 2 tablespoons whole milk
- ¾ teaspoon table salt, divided
- ½ teaspoon pepper
- 1½ pounds 85 percent lean ground beef
- 2 tablespoons vegetable oil
- 1 onion, chopped fine
- 2 tablespoons chili powder
- 2 teaspoons ground cumin
- 4 garlic cloves, minced
- 1 cup chicken broth, plus extra as needed
- 3 (15-ounce) cans black, kidney, and/or pinto beans, rinsed
- 1 (28-ounce) can crushed tomatoes

1. Using fork, mash bread, milk, ½ teaspoon salt, and pepper together into paste in large bowl. Add beef and knead mixture with your hands until well combined.

2. Using highest sauté or browning function, heat oil in electric pressure cooker until shimmering. Add onion and remaining ¼ teaspoon salt and cook until softened, about 5 minutes. Stir in chili powder, cumin, and garlic and cook until fragrant, about 30 seconds. Add beef mixture and cook, breaking up meat with wooden spoon, until no longer pink, about 4 minutes. Stir in broth, scraping up any browned bits, then stir in beans and tomatoes.

3. Lock lid in place and close pressure release valve. Select high pressure cook function and cook for 10 minutes. Turn off pressure cooker and quick-release pressure. Carefully remove lid, allowing steam to escape away from you. Adjust consistency with extra hot broth as needed. Season with salt and pepper to taste. Serve.

Hearty Beef and Vegetable Chili

DUTCH OVEN
Serves 6 to 8
Total Time 3¼ hours

Why This Recipe Works Most chili recipes are either meat-based or vegetarian, but this chili offers the best of both worlds with satisfying chunks of beef and hearty vegetables. We started with beef chuck-eye, a cut of meat that transforms from tough to meltingly tender after simmering; browning it first contributed rich flavor. Garlic, cumin, chipotle, and chili powder gave our stew depth and heat, balanced by sweet potatoes and red bell pepper. Using a mild beer as the liquid added complexity. We added some of the potatoes at the outset to break down and thicken the stew, and we stirred in the beans with the tomatoes so that they absorbed flavor without falling apart. Once our meat was tender, we added the rest of our potatoes and bell pepper. For a spicier chili, use the greater amount of chipotle. Serve with your favorite chili garnishes.

- 3½ pounds boneless beef chuck-eye roast, pulled apart at seams, trimmed, and cut into 1-inch pieces
- 1¾ teaspoons table salt, divided
- ½ teaspoon pepper
- 3 tablespoons vegetable oil, divided
- 1 onion, chopped
- 1½ pounds sweet potatoes, peeled and cut into ½-inch pieces, divided
- 3 garlic cloves, minced
- 1 tablespoon ground cumin
- 1–2 tablespoons minced canned chipotle chile in adobo sauce
- 2 teaspoons chili powder
- 1 (28-ounce) can diced tomatoes
- 1½ cups mild lager, such as Budweiser
- 2 (15-ounce) cans black beans, rinsed
- 1 red bell pepper, stemmed, seeded, and cut into ½-inch pieces
- 4 scallions, sliced thin

1. Adjust oven rack to lower-middle position and heat oven to 325 degrees. Pat beef dry with paper towels and sprinkle with ¾ teaspoon salt and pepper. Heat 1 tablespoon oil in Dutch oven over medium heat until shimmering. Brown half of beef on all sides, 8 to 10 minutes; transfer to large bowl. Repeat with 1 tablespoon oil and remaining beef; transfer to bowl.

2. Add onion, ¾ cup sweet potatoes, and remaining 1 tablespoon oil to fat left in pot and cook over medium heat until just beginning to brown, 5 to 7 minutes. Stir in garlic, cumin, chipotle, chili powder, and remaining 1 teaspoon salt and cook until fragrant, about 30 seconds. Stir in tomatoes and their juice and beer, scraping up any browned bits, and bring to simmer. Stir in beans and beef with any accumulated juices, scraping up any browned bits.

3. Cover, transfer pot to oven, and cook, stirring occasionally, until sweet potatoes are broken down and beef is just tender, 1½ to 2 hours. Stir in remaining sweet potatoes and bell pepper and continue to cook, covered, until meat and sweet potatoes are tender, about 20 minutes.

4. Remove pot from oven, uncover, and let chili sit until thickened slightly, about 15 minutes. Adjust consistency with hot water as needed. Season with salt and pepper to taste. Sprinkle individual portions with scallions before serving.

Chili con Carne

INSTANT POT
Serves 6 to 8
Total Time 1½ hours

Why This Recipe Works Texans are famous for a style of chili where beef is the undeniable star of the show. Chili con carne features hefty chunks of meat—and little else—simmered in a rich, chile-infused sauce. Beef chuck-eye roast boasted beefy flavor, and the pressure cooker turned the meat meltingly tender in a fraction of the time traditional recipes require. For a sauce with body, we opted for a nontraditional thickener: corn tortillas. Grinding them in the food processor ensured they seamlessly blended into the chili, thickening it without obscuring the beefy flavor. The pressure cooker intensified the flavors of chili powder and smoky canned chipotles in adobo, so much so that we found we could easily forgo dried or fresh chiles. For a spicier chili, use the greater amount of chipotle. Serve with your favorite chili garnishes.

- 4 (6-inch) corn tortillas, chopped coarse
- 3½ pounds boneless beef chuck-eye roast, pulled apart at seams, trimmed, and cut into 1-inch pieces
- 1 teaspoon table salt
- ½ teaspoon pepper
- 3 tablespoons vegetable oil, divided
- 1 onion, chopped
- 1 jalapeño chile, stemmed, seeded, and minced
- 2 tablespoons chili powder
- 2 tablespoons ground cumin
- 5 garlic cloves, minced
- 1–2 tablespoons minced canned chipotle chile in adobo sauce
- 1½ cups chicken broth, plus extra as needed
- 1 (28-ounce) can crushed tomatoes
  Lime wedges

Chili con Carne

1. Process tortilla pieces in food processor to fine crumbs, about 30 seconds; set aside. Pat beef dry with paper towels and sprinkle with salt and pepper. Using highest sauté or browning function, heat 2 tablespoons oil in electric pressure cooker until just smoking. Brown half of beef on all sides, 8 to 10 minutes; transfer to large bowl. Repeat with remaining 1 tablespoon oil and beef; transfer to bowl.

2. Add onion and jalapeño to fat left in pressure cooker and cook, using highest sauté or browning function, until softened and lightly browned, about 5 minutes. Stir in chili powder, cumin, garlic, and chipotle and cook until fragrant, about 1 minute. Stir in broth, scraping up any browned bits, then stir in tomatoes and beef with any accumulated juices. Sprinkle tortilla crumbs over top.

3. Lock lid in place and close pressure release valve. Select high pressure cook function and cook for 27 minutes. Turn off pressure cooker and quick-release pressure. Carefully remove lid, allowing steam to escape away from you.

4. Stir chili to combine and adjust consistency with extra hot broth as needed. Season with salt and pepper to taste. Serve with lime wedges.

New Mexican Red Pork Chili

SLOW COOKER

Serves 6 to 8

Cook Time 9 to 10 hours on low or 6 to 7 hours on high

Why This Recipe Works Inspired by the New Mexican stew carne adovada, this chili features meltingly tender chunks of pork in an intense, richly flavored red chile sauce. The slow cooker was the obvious vessel of choice for this easy, long simmering chili, and pork butt was the ideal cut of meat; with plenty of fat marbled throughout, it resulted in supremely tender chunks of pork that didn't dry out. For the sauce, chili powder, oregano, and chipotle chiles provided a solid layer of warmth and depth, while fresh coffee brought a balance of robust, bittersweet flavors. Since the flavor of dried chiles is sometimes described as raisiny, we went to the source, adding raisins before serving to achieve fruity nuance. Stirring in fresh cilantro, lime zest, and lime juice at the end helped brighten this earthy dish. Pork butt roast is often labeled Boston butt in the supermarket. For a spicier chili, use the greater amount of chipotle. You will need a 5- to 7- quart slow cooker for this recipe. Serve with your favorite chili garnishes.

- 2 onions, chopped fine
- ¼ cup chili powder
- 6 garlic cloves, minced
- 2 tablespoons vegetable oil
- 2 tablespoons tomato paste
- 2 tablespoons all-purpose flour
- 1 teaspoon table salt
- ¾ teaspoon dried oregano
- 1–2 tablespoons minced canned chipotle chile in adobo sauce
- 4 pounds boneless pork butt roast, pulled apart at seams, trimmed, and cut into 1½-inch pieces
- 2 cups chicken broth, plus extra as needed
- ½ cup brewed coffee
- 1 tablespoon packed brown sugar, plus extra for seasoning
- 2 bay leaves
- ½ cup raisins
- ¼ cup minced fresh cilantro
- 1 teaspoon grated lime zest plus 1 tablespoon juice, plus extra juice for seasoning

1. Combine onions, chili powder, garlic, oil, tomato paste, flour, salt, oregano, and chipotle in bowl. Microwave, stirring occasionally, until onions are softened, about 5 minutes; transfer to slow cooker. Stir in pork, broth, coffee, sugar, and bay leaves. Cover and cook until pork is tender, 9 to 10 hours on low or 6 to 7 hours on high.

2. Discard bay leaves. Stir raisins into chili and let sit until heated through, about 5 minutes. Stir in cilantro and lime zest and juice. Adjust consistency with extra hot broth as needed. Season with salt, pepper, extra sugar, and extra lime juice to taste. Serve.

Classic Turkey Chili

DUTCH OVEN

Serves 4 to 6

Total Time 2½ hours

Why This Recipe Works Making good turkey chili isn't as easy as replacing ground beef with ground turkey. As we quickly found out, a simple swap resulted in overcooked meat floating in the chili. To combat this, we sautéed half of the ground poultry, breaking it up into small pieces, to distribute the flavor while it simmered. For improved texture and moister meat, we pinched the remaining ground turkey into small pieces and stirred them into the chili toward the end of the simmering time. Some of the meat dissolved into the sauce, giving it a meaty flavor, while the rest retained its texture. Be sure to use ground turkey, not ground turkey breast (also labeled 99 percent fat-free). For a spicier chili, use the greater amount of pepper flakes. Serve with your favorite chili garnishes.

- 1 tablespoon vegetable oil
- 2 onions, chopped fine
- 1 red bell pepper, stemmed, seeded, and cut into ½-inch pieces
- 6 garlic cloves, minced
- ¼ cup chili powder
- 1 tablespoon ground cumin
- 2 teaspoons ground coriander
- 1–2 teaspoons red pepper flakes
- 1 tablespoon minced fresh oregano or 1 teaspoon dried
- ½ teaspoon cayenne pepper
- 1½ pounds 93 percent lean ground turkey, divided
- 2 (15-ounce) cans kidney beans, rinsed
- 1 (28-ounce) can diced tomatoes
- 1 (28-ounce) can crushed tomatoes
- 2 cups chicken broth, plus extra as needed

1. Heat oil in Dutch oven over medium heat until shimmering. Add onions, bell pepper, garlic, chili powder, cumin, coriander, pepper flakes, oregano, and cayenne and cook, stirring often, until vegetables are softened, about 10 minutes.

2. Add 1 pound turkey, increase heat to medium-high, and cook, breaking up meat with wooden spoon, until no longer pink, about 4 minutes. Stir in beans, diced tomatoes and their juice, crushed tomatoes, and broth and bring to simmer. Reduce heat to medium-low and cook, uncovered, until chili has begun to thicken, about 1 hour.

3. Pat remaining 8 ounces turkey together into ball, then pinch off teaspoon-size pieces of meat and stir into chili. Continue to simmer, stirring occasionally, until turkey is tender and chili is slightly thickened, about 40 minutes. (If chili begins to stick to bottom of pot or looks too thick, stir in extra broth as needed.) Season with salt and pepper to taste and serve.

White Chicken Chili

DUTCH OVEN
Serves 6 to 8
Total Time 1½ hours

Why This Recipe Works Beef chili may be more commonly known, but its counterpart, white chicken chili, allows the chiles, herbs, and spices to take center stage. We put our food processor to work to quickly chop the chiles, onions, and garlic; for the chiles, a combination of poblano, Anaheim, and jalapeño provided flavor and heat. Next, we thickened the base of the chili by pureeing a portion of the beans and broth. To ensure the chicken breasts stayed moist after browning, we poached them in the chili itself. If you can't find Anaheim chiles, add another jalapeño and poblano. Any canned small white beans will work well here. For a spicier chili, reserve all or a portion of the jalapeño ribs and seeds and add them to the processor in step 1. Serve with your favorite chili garnishes.

- 3 poblano chiles, stemmed, seeded, and chopped coarse, divided
- 3 Anaheim chiles, stemmed, seeded, and chopped coarse, divided
- 2 onions, chopped coarse, divided
- 6 garlic cloves, chopped, divided
- 2 (15-ounce) cans cannellini beans, rinsed, divided
- 3 cups chicken broth, divided, plus extra as needed
- 3 pounds bone-in split chicken breasts, trimmed
- ¾ teaspoon table salt, divided
- ¼ teaspoon pepper
- 1 tablespoon vegetable oil, plus extra as needed
- 3 jalapeño chiles, stemmed, seeded, and minced, divided
- 1 tablespoon ground cumin
- 1½ teaspoons ground coriander
- ¼ cup minced fresh cilantro
- 4 scallions, sliced thin
- 3 tablespoons lime juice (2 limes)

New Mexican Red Pork Chili

White Chicken Chili

Black Bean Chili

1. Working in 2 batches, pulse half of poblanos, half of Anaheims, onions, and half of garlic in food processor until consistency of chunky salsa, 10 to 12 pulses, scraping down sides of bowl as needed; transfer to bowl. Process 1 cup beans and 1 cup broth in now-empty processor until smooth, about 30 seconds.

2. Pat chicken dry with paper towels and sprinkle with ½ teaspoon salt and pepper. Heat oil in Dutch oven over medium-high heat until just smoking. Brown chicken on all sides, about 8 minutes; transfer to plate.

3. Pour off all but 1 tablespoon fat from pot (add extra oil as needed to equal 1 tablespoon). Add chile mixture, half of jalapeños, cumin, coriander, and remaining ¼ teaspoon salt to fat left in pot. Cover partially and cook over medium heat, stirring occasionally, until vegetables are softened, about 10 minutes. Stir in pureed bean mixture and remaining 2 cups broth. Return chicken and any accumulated juices to pot and bring to simmer. Reduce heat to medium-low, cover partially, and cook, stirring occasionally, until chicken registers 160 degrees, 15 to 20 minutes, flipping chicken halfway through cooking.

4. Transfer chicken to cutting board, let cool slightly, then shred into bite-size pieces using 2 forks; discard skin and bones.

5. Meanwhile, stir remaining beans into chili and simmer, uncovered, until beans are heated through and chili has thickened slightly, about 10 minutes. Off heat, stir in shredded chicken and let sit until heated through, about 2 minutes. Adjust consistency with extra hot broth as needed. Stir in cilantro, scallions, lime juice, and remaining jalapeño. Season with salt and pepper to taste. Serve.

VARIATION

White Chicken Chili for Two
SAUCEPAN
Serves 2
Total Time 1 hour
Any canned small white beans will work well here. For a spicier chili, reserve all or a portion of the jalapeño ribs and seeds and add them to the processor in step 1. Serve with your favorite chili garnishes.

    2 poblano chiles, stemmed, seeded,
         and chopped coarse
    1 small onion, chopped coarse
    1 jalapeño chile, stemmed, seeded, and chopped coarse
    2 garlic cloves, chopped
    1 (15-ounce) can cannellini beans, rinsed, divided
    2 cups chicken broth, divided, plus extra as needed
    1 (12-ounce) bone-in chicken breast, trimmed
    ¼ teaspoon table salt
    ¼ teaspoon pepper
    1 tablespoon vegetable oil
    1 teaspoon ground cumin
    1 teaspoon ground coriander
    3 tablespoons chopped fresh cilantro
    1 tablespoon lime juice

1. Pulse poblanos, onion, jalapeño, and garlic in food processor until consistency of chunky salsa, 10 to 12 pulses, scraping down sides of bowl as needed; transfer to bowl. Process half of beans and ½ cup broth in now-empty processor until smooth, about 30 seconds.

2. Pat chicken dry with paper towels and sprinkle with salt and pepper. Heat oil in large saucepan over medium-high heat until just smoking. Brown chicken on all sides, about 8 minutes; transfer to plate.

3. Add chile mixture, cumin, and coriander to fat left in saucepan and cook until vegetables are softened, 5 to 7 minutes. Stir in pureed bean mixture and remaining 1½ cups broth. Return chicken and any accumulated juices to pot and bring to simmer. Reduce heat to medium-low, cover partially, and cook, stirring occasionally, until chicken registers 160 degrees, 15 to 20 minutes, flipping chicken halfway through cooking.

4. Transfer chicken to cutting board, let cool slightly, then shred into bite-size pieces using 2 forks; discard skin and bones.

5. Meanwhile, stir remaining beans into chili and simmer, uncovered, until beans are heated through and chili has thickened slightly, about 5 minutes. Off heat, stir in shredded chicken and let sit until heated through, about 2 minutes. Adjust consistency with extra hot broth as needed. Stir in cilantro and lime juice and season with salt and pepper to taste. Serve.

Black Bean Chili

INSTANT POT
Serves 4 to 6
Total Time 1¼ hours, plus 8 hours brining

Why This Recipe Works Black bean chili should be all about the beans—they should be creamy, tender, and well seasoned. We wanted a hearty bean chili that was as rich, savory, and deeply satisfying as any meat chili out there, and we knew we wanted to use the pressure cooker to ensure perfectly cooked beans. Tasters preferred the texture of dried beans over canned, and soaking the beans in salted water helped them hold their shape and cook evenly. Creating big flavor in bean chili can be tricky since beans lack the depth of flavor that meat has, but using the sauté function to brown a hefty amount of aromatics and bloom spices worked well to give the chili depth. We also added white mushrooms and red bell peppers for body. A cup of broth and a can of crushed tomatoes provided enough liquid for our beans to cook evenly while still resulting in a thick, hearty final stew. Served with a spritz of lime and a sprinkle of minced cilantro, this rich chili was so satisfying that no one missed the meat. For a spicier chili, use the greater amount of chipotle. Serve with your favorite chili garnishes.

1½ tablespoons table salt for brining
1 pound (2½ cups) dried black beans, picked over and rinsed
3 tablespoons vegetable oil
1 onion, chopped fine
9 garlic cloves, minced
2 tablespoons ground cumin
1½ tablespoons chili powder
1–3 teaspoons minced canned chipotle chile in adobo sauce
1 (28-ounce) can crushed tomatoes
1 cup vegetable or chicken broth, plus extra as needed
1 pound white mushrooms, trimmed and halved if small or quartered if large
2 red bell peppers, stemmed, seeded, and cut into ½-inch pieces
2 bay leaves
½ cup minced fresh cilantro
Lime wedges

1. Dissolve 1½ tablespoons salt in 2 quarts cold water in large container. Add beans and soak at room temperature for at least 8 hours or up to 24 hours. Drain and rinse well.

2. Using highest sauté or browning function, heat oil in electric pressure cooker until shimmering. Add onion and cook until softened, 3 to 5 minutes. Stir in garlic, cumin, chili powder, and chipotle and cook until fragrant, about 1 minute. Stir in tomatoes and broth, scraping up any browned bits, then stir in beans, mushrooms, bell peppers, and bay leaves.

3. Lock lid in place and close pressure release valve. Select high pressure cook function and cook for 40 minutes. Turn off pressure cooker and quick-release pressure. Carefully remove lid, allowing steam to escape away from you.

4. Discard bay leaves. Adjust consistency with extra hot broth as needed. Stir in cilantro and season with salt and pepper to taste. Serve with lime wedges.

INGREDIENT SPOTLIGHT

DRIED BLACK BEANS
Canned beans may be convenient, but their flavor and texture never match those of dried. We tested three brands of dried black beans, including one mail-order heirloom variety, by sampling them plain (cooked with onions, salt, and a bay leaf) and cooked in Cuban-style black beans and rice. Surprisingly, the heirloom variety became blown out and mushy, while the beans from the two national supermarket brands emerged from the pot perfectly intact and creamy. Tasters appreciated the superior flavor of the fresher heirloom beans (which are sold within one year of harvest), but in the end, we had to concede that the supermarket beans cooked perfectly in every test. Our favorite was **Goya Dried Black Beans**, which offered "nutty," "buttery" bean flavor and a reliably uniform texture.

POULTRY

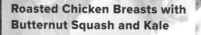

Roasted Chicken Breasts with
Butternut Squash and Kale

* All slow cooker recipes work in a 4- to 7-quart traditional slow cooker unless noted.

** All Instant Pot recipes work in a 6- to 8-quart Instant Pot or other electric pressure cooker.

Sautéed Chicken with
Cherry Tomatoes,
Olives, and Feta

Chicken Fricassee with Apples

Sautéed Chicken with Cherry Tomatoes, Olives, and Feta

SKILLET

Serves 4
Total Time 45 minutes

Why This Recipe Works Quick sautéed chicken breasts are a blank canvas for bright flavors. Using the same pan that we used to cook the chicken to also prepare a warm relish that is part sauce, part side takes advantage of all the flavorful brown bits already in the pan, and this approach can be varied to accommodate other vegetables (as with our variation that is scaled down to serve two). Dredging the prepped and seasoned chicken in flour preserved moisture, maximized browning, and minimized sticking. After cooking the chicken, we assembled the relish. Halving and cooking the tomatoes released some of their liquid. Olives provided a salty contrast to the sweet tomatoes. Feta cheese contributed a bit of creaminess and tang, and mint leaves added color and freshness.

½ cup all-purpose flour
4 (6- to 8-ounce) boneless, skinless chicken breasts, trimmed
⅛ teaspoon table salt
⅛ teaspoon pepper
3 tablespoons extra-virgin olive oil, divided
2 garlic cloves, minced
12 ounces cherry tomatoes, halved
⅓ cup pitted kalamata olives, chopped
2 tablespoons water
1 ounce feta cheese, crumbled (¼ cup)
¼ cup shredded fresh mint

1. Spread flour in shallow dish. Pound thicker end of chicken breasts between 2 sheets of plastic wrap to uniform ½-inch thickness. Pat chicken dry with paper towels and sprinkle with salt and pepper. Working with 1 breast at a time, lightly dredge chicken in flour, shaking off excess.

2. Heat 2 tablespoons oil in 12-inch nonstick skillet over medium-high heat until shimmering. Cook chicken until well browned and registers 160 degrees, 6 to 8 minutes per side. Transfer chicken to serving platter, tent with aluminum foil, and let rest while making relish.

3. Cook remaining 1 tablespoon oil and garlic in now-empty skillet over medium heat until fragrant, about 30 seconds. Stir in tomatoes, olives, and water, scraping up any browned bits, and cook until tomatoes are just softened, about 2 minutes. Stir in any accumulated chicken juices and season with salt and pepper to taste. Spoon relish over chicken and sprinkle with feta and mint. Serve.

VARIATION

Sautéed Chicken with Cherry Tomatoes, Toasted Corn, and Avocado for Two

SKILLET

Serves 2

Total Time 45 minutes

Serve with lime wedges.

⅓ cup all-purpose flour

2 (6- to 8-ounce) boneless, skinless chicken breasts, trimmed

⅛ teaspoon table salt
    Pinch pepper

2 tablespoons extra-virgin olive oil, divided

½ cup frozen corn, thawed

1 garlic clove, minced

6 ounces cherry tomatoes, halved

1 tablespoon water

½ avocado, diced

2 tablespoons minced fresh cilantro

1. Spread flour in shallow dish. Pound thicker end of chicken breasts between 2 sheets of plastic wrap to uniform ½-inch thickness. Pat chicken dry with paper towels and sprinkle with salt and pepper. Working with 1 breast at a time, lightly dredge chicken in flour, shaking off excess.

2. Heat 1 tablespoon oil in 10-inch nonstick skillet over medium-high heat until shimmering. Cook chicken until well browned and registers 160 degrees, 6 to 8 minutes per side. Transfer chicken to serving platter, tent with aluminum foil, and let rest while making relish.

3. Heat remaining 1 tablespoon oil in now-empty skillet over medium heat until shimmering. Add corn and cook, without stirring, until well browned, about 4 minutes. Stir in garlic and cook until fragrant, about 30 seconds. Stir in tomatoes and water, scraping up any browned bits, and cook until tomatoes are just softened, about 2 minutes. Stir in any accumulated chicken juices and season with salt and pepper to taste. Spoon relish over chicken and sprinkle with avocado and cilantro. Serve.

POUNDING CHICKEN BREASTS

To create chicken breasts of even thickness, simply pound the thicker ends of the breasts until they are all of uniform thickness. Though some breasts will still be larger in size, at least they will cook at the same rate.

Chicken Fricassee with Apples

SKILLET

Serves 4

Total Time 1 hour

Why This Recipe Works Chicken fricassee is an old-fashioned country dish of stewed chicken in a creamy sauce. For our version, we dredged the chicken breasts lightly in flour before sautéing, which not only protected the chicken's exterior from becoming tough while cooking but also thickened the sauce and gave it body. Apple cider and chicken broth created a savory yet fruit-forward balance while cream and cider vinegar finished the dish with richness and brightness. Adding vibrant apples to the mix created a complex and delicate sweetness that enhanced the savory chicken. Fuji, Gala, and Braeburn apples remained sweet once cooked (unlike Granny Smith apples, which tasted sour) and contributed the best apple flavor. Browning the apples in butter—and adding them back to the skillet to warm through once the chicken was cooked—gave them beautiful color without overcooking them and added caramelized flavor to the sauce. Additionally, searing the apples set their pectin and helped them retain their shape. Note that the apples are not peeled; their red skins contribute visual contrast to this otherwise pale dish. Cut each apple into 16 wedges; each wedge will be approximately ½ inch thick.

¼ cup all-purpose flour

4 (6- to 8-ounce) boneless, skinless chicken breasts, trimmed

⅛ teaspoon plus ¼ teaspoon table salt, divided

⅛ teaspoon plus ¼ teaspoon pepper, divided

3 tablespoons unsalted butter, divided

2 Fuji, Gala, or Braeburn apples, cored and each cut into sixteen ½-inch-thick wedges

1 onion, chopped

2 teaspoons minced fresh thyme

½ cup apple cider

½ cup chicken broth

½ cup heavy cream

2 teaspoons cider vinegar

1 tablespoon minced fresh chives

1. Spread flour in shallow dish. Pound thicker end of chicken breasts between 2 sheets of plastic wrap to uniform ½-inch thickness. Pat chicken dry with paper towels and sprinkle with ⅛ teaspoon salt and ⅛ teaspoon pepper. Working with 1 breast at a time, lightly dredge chicken in flour, shaking off excess.

2. Melt 2 tablespoons butter in 12-inch nonstick skillet over medium heat. Cook apples, cut sides down, until browned, about 5 minutes per side, moving and redistributing apples as needed for even browning. Transfer to plate; set aside.

3. Melt remaining 1 tablespoon butter in now-empty skillet over medium heat. Add chicken and cook until lightly browned, about 2 minutes per side; transfer to separate plate.

4. Add onion, thyme, remaining ¼ teaspoon salt, and remaining ¼ teaspoon pepper to now-empty skillet and cook over medium heat until softened and lightly browned, 5 to 7 minutes. Stir in cider and broth, scraping up any browned bits, and bring mixture to simmer. Return chicken and any accumulated juices to skillet. Reduce heat to medium-low, cover, and cook until chicken registers 160 degrees, 8 to 12 minutes.

5. Transfer chicken to serving platter and tent with aluminum foil. Add cream and apples to skillet. Increase heat to medium-high and bring to boil. Cook until sauce has thickened slightly, about 2 minutes. Stir in vinegar and any accumulated chicken juices. Season with salt and pepper to taste. Spoon sauce and apples over chicken and sprinkle with chives. Serve.

Crispy Parmesan Chicken with Warm Fennel, Radicchio, and Arugula Salad

SKILLET
Serves 4
Total Time 1 hour

Why This Recipe Works With its crisp coating and juicy, tender meat, Parmesan chicken is a surefire crowd-pleaser and a guaranteed win for any weeknight dinner. Pasta is a classic pairing, but we were more interested in a fresh side that would brighten up our savory breaded chicken and wouldn't require the use of another pan. After the chicken cutlets had finished cooking through, we took advantage of the preheated skillet to soften thinly sliced fennel and halved cherry tomatoes. We tossed the cooked vegetables in a simple vinaigrette of minced shallot, Dijon mustard, white wine vinegar, and extra-virgin olive oil. Raw radicchio and baby arugula added crunch and a light bitterness that paired well with the sweetness of the fennel and contrasted perfectly with the rich, juicy chicken. Use the large holes of a box grater to shred the Parmesan. The skillet will initially be crowded but the cutlets will shrink as they cook.

4 (6- to 8-ounce) boneless, skinless chicken breasts, trimmed
2 large eggs
1¼ teaspoons table salt, divided
½ teaspoon pepper
1 cup panko bread crumbs
3 ounces Parmesan cheese, shredded (1 cup)
½ cup vegetable oil for frying, divided
1 tablespoon white wine vinegar
1 small shallot, minced
½ teaspoon Dijon mustard
¼ cup extra-virgin olive oil, divided
1 fennel bulb, stalks discarded, bulb halved, cored, and sliced thin
12 ounces cherry tomatoes, halved
½ head radicchio (5 ounces), cored and sliced thin
2 ounces (2 cups) baby arugula

1. Remove any tenderloins from breasts and reserve for another use. Cut each breast horizontally into 2 thin cutlets, then cover with plastic wrap and pound to even ¼-inch thickness.

2. Beat eggs, 1 teaspoon salt, and pepper together in shallow dish. Combine panko and Parmesan in second shallow dish. Working with 1 cutlet at a time, dredge in egg mixture, allowing excess to drip off, then coat all sides with panko mixture, pressing gently so crumbs adhere.

3. Adjust oven rack to middle position and heat oven to 200 degrees. Heat ¼ cup vegetable oil and small pinch panko mixture in 12-inch nonstick skillet over medium-high heat. When panko has turned golden brown, place 4 cutlets in skillet. Cook, without moving cutlets, until bottoms are deep golden brown, 2 to 3 minutes. Using tongs, carefully flip cutlets and cook on second side until deep golden brown, 2 to 3 minutes.

4. Transfer cutlets to paper towel–lined platter, season with salt to taste, and keep warm in oven. Wipe skillet clean with paper towels. Repeat with remaining ¼ cup vegetable oil and remaining 4 cutlets; transfer to platter and keep warm in oven. Wipe skillet clean with paper towels.

5. Whisk vinegar, shallot, mustard, and remaining ¼ teaspoon salt together in large bowl. Whisking constantly, slowly drizzle in 3 tablespoons olive oil until emulsified.

6. Heat remaining 1 tablespoon olive oil in now-empty skillet over medium heat until shimmering. Add fennel and cook until softened and just beginning to brown, 5 to 7 minutes; transfer to bowl with vinaigrette. Add tomatoes, radicchio, and arugula and gently toss to combine. Season with salt and pepper to taste and serve with chicken.

Prosciutto-Wrapped Chicken with Asparagus

SKILLET
Serves 4
Total Time 45 minutes

Why This Recipe Works Wrapping chicken breasts in salty, flavorful prosciutto served a double purpose in this dish by seasoning the lean breasts while protecting the surface from drying out. Cooking the wrapped chicken on the stovetop gave flavorful browning to the prosciutto. After transferring the chicken to a cutting board and topping it with creamy fontina, we arranged asparagus in the skillet and then placed the cheese-topped chicken on top before transferring the whole thing to the oven. The asparagus cooked through perfectly underneath the chicken and the cheese on top melted to gooey perfection. Before serving we made a quick vinaigrette for the asparagus packed with bright but nutty flavor thanks to toasted pecans, Dijon mustard, and shallot. Look for asparagus spears that are between ¼ and ½ inch near the base. You will need a 12-inch ovensafe skillet for this recipe.

- 4 (6- to 8-ounce) boneless, skinless chicken breasts, trimmed
- ½ teaspoon pepper, divided
- 8 thin slices prosciutto (4 ounces), divided
- 5 tablespoons extra-virgin olive oil, divided
- 4 thin slices fontina cheese (4 ounces), divided
- 2 pounds asparagus, trimmed
- 2½ tablespoons white wine vinegar
- 2 tablespoons toasted chopped pecans
- 1½ teaspoons Dijon mustard
- 1 small shallot, sliced thin
- 1 teaspoon minced fresh thyme
  Pinch table salt

1. Adjust oven rack to middle position and heat oven to 350 degrees. Pound thicker end of chicken breasts between 2 sheets of plastic wrap to uniform ½-inch thickness. Pat chicken dry with paper towels and sprinkle with pepper. Slightly overlap 2 prosciutto slices on cutting board, lay chicken breast in center, and fold prosciutto over chicken. Repeat with remaining prosciutto and chicken.

2. Heat 1 tablespoon oil in 12-inch ovensafe skillet over medium-high heat until just smoking. Cook chicken until prosciutto is lightly browned, about 2 minutes per side. Transfer to cutting board and top with fontina.

3. Add half of asparagus to now-empty skillet with tips pointed in 1 direction and add remaining asparagus with tips pointed in opposite direction. Using tongs, toss asparagus

Crispy Parmesan Chicken with Warm Fennel, Radicchio, and Arugula Salad

Prosciutto-Wrapped Chicken with Asparagus

with 1 tablespoon oil, then redistribute spears in even layer. Arrange chicken breasts on top of asparagus and bake until chicken registers 160 degrees and asparagus is tender and bright green, about 12 minutes.

4. Using potholders, remove skillet from oven. Whisk remaining 3 tablespoons oil, vinegar, pecans, mustard, shallot, thyme, and salt in bowl until thoroughly combined. Being careful of hot skillet handle, transfer chicken to cutting board and let rest for 5 minutes. Toss asparagus with half of dressing. Serve chicken with asparagus, passing remaining dressing separately.

Chicken Baked in Foil with Fennel and Sun-Dried Tomatoes

SHEET PAN

Serves 4

Total Time 1 hour, plus 1 hour chilling

Why This Recipe Works Baking food in foil packets (or en papillote) promises an easy one-dish meal since the foil traps steam to gently cook everything and contains the mess for minimal cleanup. To ensure that our quick-cooking chicken breasts were seasoned throughout, we sprinkled them all over with salt before assembling the packets and then refrigerated the packets for at least an hour. Leaving headroom at the top of the packets allowed maximum steam circulation for even cooking, and checking the temperature of the chicken through the foil let us monitor its progress. Layering the heartier potatoes under the chicken insulated the delicate meat from the hot pan. Two convenient pantry products—olives and sun-dried tomatoes—lent bold flavor as did a final boost of balsamic vinegar and fresh basil.

Chicken Baked in Foil with Fennel and Sun-Dried Tomatoes

  5 tablespoons extra-virgin olive oil
  6 garlic cloves, sliced thin
  1 teaspoon minced fresh thyme
  ¼ teaspoon red pepper flakes
 12 ounces Yukon Gold potatoes, unpeeled, sliced crosswise ¼ inch thick
  1 fennel bulb, stalks discarded, bulb halved, cored, and cut into ½-inch-thick wedges, layers separated
  ½ large red onion, sliced ½ inch thick, layers separated
  ¼ cup oil-packed sun-dried tomatoes, rinsed, patted dry, and chopped fine
  ¼ cup pitted kalamata olives, chopped fine
  ¾ teaspoon table salt, divided
  4 (6- to 8-ounce) boneless, skinless chicken breasts, trimmed
  ¼ teaspoon pepper
  2 tablespoons balsamic vinegar
  2 tablespoons minced fresh basil

1. Spray centers of four 20 by 12-inch sheets of aluminum foil with vegetable oil spray. Microwave oil, garlic, thyme, and pepper flakes in large bowl until garlic begins to brown, about 1 minute. Add potatoes, fennel, onion, tomatoes, olives, and ½ teaspoon salt to bowl with garlic oil and toss to combine.

2. Pound thicker end of chicken breasts between 2 sheets of plastic wrap to uniform ½-inch thickness. Pat chicken dry with paper towels and sprinkle with remaining ¼ teaspoon salt and pepper. Position 1 piece of prepared foil with long side parallel to edge of counter. In center of foil, arrange one-quarter of potato slices in 2 rows perpendicular to edge of counter. Lay 1 chicken breast on top of potato slices. Place one-quarter of vegetables around chicken. Repeat with remaining prepared foil, remaining potato slices, remaining chicken, and remaining vegetables. Drizzle any remaining oil mixture from bowl over chicken.

3. Bring short sides of foil together and crimp to seal tightly. Crimp remaining open ends of packets, leaving as much headroom as possible inside packets. Refrigerate for at least 1 hour or up to 24 hours.

4. Adjust oven rack to lowest position and heat oven to 475 degrees. Place packets on rimmed baking sheet and bake until chicken registers 160 degrees, 18 to 23 minutes. (To check temperature, poke thermometer through foil of 1 packet and into chicken.) Let chicken rest in packets for 3 minutes.

5. Transfer chicken packets to individual serving plates, open carefully (steam will escape), and slide contents onto plates. Drizzle vinegar over chicken and vegetables and sprinkle with basil. Serve.

Unstuffed Ham & Cheese Chicken with Roasted Broccoli

SHEET PAN
Serves 4
Total Time 45 minutes

Why This Recipe Works Most chicken cordon bleu recipes call for pounding the chicken breasts before stuffing them with ham and cheese, rolling them up, coating them with bread crumbs, and baking or frying the lot—not exactly weeknight-friendly dining. For an easier path to cordon bleu heaven, we arranged chicken breasts on a sheet pan and topped them with slices of ham and shredded Gruyère for an inside-out approach. Brushing the chicken with mustard added a tangy sharpness and also provided the "glue" to help the ham and cheese stay in place. For the crunchy, golden bread-crumb topping, we used crushed Ritz crackers, which stayed crisp and offered a rich, buttery flavor. Broccoli wedges roasted right alongside the chicken and completed the meal. After 20 minutes in a hot oven, our streamlined chicken cordon bleu delivered all the rich flavors and appealing textures of authentic versions. Swiss cheese can be substituted for the Gruyère.

4	(6- to 8-ounce) boneless, skinless chicken breasts, trimmed
2	tablespoons Dijon mustard
4	ounces deli ham (4 slices), divided
4	ounces Gruyère cheese, shredded (1 cup), divided
15	Ritz crackers, coarsely crushed (¾ cup)
1	head broccoli (about 1½ pounds)
2	tablespoons extra-virgin olive oil
½	teaspoon sugar
¼	teaspoon table salt
⅛	teaspoon pepper
	Lemon wedges

1. Adjust oven rack to lower-middle position and heat oven to 475 degrees. Spray rimmed baking sheet with vegetable oil spray.

2. Pound thicker end of chicken breasts between 2 sheets of plastic wrap to uniform ½-inch thickness. Pat chicken dry with paper towels. Spread mustard over top of chicken, then top each breast with 1 slice ham and ¼ cup Gruyère. Sprinkle cracker crumbs over cheese and press on crumbs to adhere. Arrange chicken breasts side by side (and alternating thicker end to thinner end) on one side of prepared sheet.

3. Cut broccoli at juncture of florets and stems; remove outer peel from stalk. Cut stalk into ½-inch-thick planks, 2 to 3 inches long. Cut crowns into 4 wedges if 3 to 4 inches in diameter or 6 wedges if 4 to 5 inches in diameter. Toss broccoli with oil, sugar, salt, and pepper. Lay broccoli, cut side down, on opposite side of sheet from chicken. Roast until chicken registers 160 degrees and broccoli is well browned and tender, 20 to 25 minutes, rotating sheet halfway through roasting. Serve with lemon wedges.

CUTTING BROCCOLI INTO WEDGES

1. Cut broccoli stalks from crowns horizontally across base of broccoli crowns.

2. Cut broccoli crowns into either four or six wedges, depending on size of crowns.

3. Trim or peel tough outer skin from stalks, then cut stalks into ½-inch-thick planks 2 to 3 inches long.

Chicken and Rice with Carrots and Peas

SKILLET
Serves 4
Total Time 1 hour

Why This Recipe Works To serve up superior chicken and rice, we opted out of convenience items such as canned soup and instant rice—common choices for this simple dish—in favor of fresher (but no less convenient) ingredients. We prepared the quick-cooking chicken breasts first, seasoning them simply with salt and pepper and searing them on one side for some flavorful browning. Wanting to avoid the mushy texture and bland taste of instant rice, we selected long-grain rice, which was tender and flavorful after cooking; sautéing the rice in the aromatics helped keep the grains distinct yet creamy when we poured in the chicken broth. We finished cooking the chicken right in the rice, removing it from the skillet as soon as it cooked through and letting the rice continue to simmer gently as it absorbed the flavorful liquid. A scattering of peas offered bright bursts of color and freshness, while a squeeze of lemon juice and a sprinkle of parsley perked everything up. Be sure to use chicken breasts that are roughly the same size to ensure even cooking. You will need a 12-inch skillet with a tight-fitting lid for this recipe. The skillet will be fairly full once you add the browned chicken in step 3, so you may want to consider using a straight-sided skillet or sauté pan if you have one. Fresh basil, chives, tarragon, or cilantro can be substituted for the parsley.

- 4 (6- to 8-ounce) boneless, skinless chicken breasts, trimmed
- 1 teaspoon table salt, divided
- ¼ teaspoon pepper
- 2 tablespoons vegetable oil
- 1 onion, chopped fine
- 1½ cups long-grain white rice
- 3 garlic cloves, minced
  Pinch red pepper flakes
- 4 carrots, peeled and sliced on bias ½ inch thick
- 3½ cups chicken broth
- 1 cup frozen peas
- 2 tablespoons lemon juice
- 1 tablespoon minced fresh parsley

Chicken and Rice with Carrots and Peas

1. Pat chicken dry with paper towels and sprinkle with ½ teaspoon salt and pepper. Heat oil in 12-inch skillet over medium-high heat until just smoking. Add chicken and cook until golden brown on 1 side, 4 to 6 minutes; transfer to plate.

2. Add onion and remaining ½ teaspoon salt to fat left in skillet and cook until softened, about 5 minutes. Stir in rice, garlic, and pepper flakes and cook until fragrant, about 30 seconds. Stir in carrots, then stir in broth, scraping up any browned bits.

3. Nestle chicken, browned side up, into skillet, along with any accumulated juices. Bring to simmer, then reduce heat to medium-low, cover, and simmer gently until chicken registers 160 degrees, about 10 minutes.

4. Transfer chicken to cutting board, tent loosely with aluminum foil, and let rest while finishing rice. Stir rice mixture to recombine, then cover and cook until liquid is absorbed and rice is tender, 5 to 10 minutes.

5. Off heat, sprinkle with peas, cover, and let warm through, about 2 minutes. Sprinkle with lemon juice and gently fluff rice mixture with fork. Slice chicken into ½-inch-thick slices and arrange on top of rice. Sprinkle with parsley and serve.

Chicken Kebabs with Potatoes and Green Beans

SHEET PAN

Serves 4
Total Time 1½ hours, plus ½ hour chilling

Why This Recipe Works Kebabs aren't only for grilling. With just a bit of staggered cooking and a unique arrangement, we created a complete meal featuring chicken, vegetables, and starch all on a sheet pan. Marinating the chicken in yogurt and Thai red curry paste seasoned it, kept it juicy, and helped brown the exterior. Creating a layer of potatoes around the perimeter of the baking sheet (the best place for browning) jump-started their cooking and ensured that they were cooked through at the same time as the kebabs. Next, we added green beans to the center of the sheet and broiled them for quick cooking and flavorful browning. Rather than add the chicken directly to the sheet pan (which would cause it to steam), we used the skewers to prop the chicken pieces on top of the potatoes; this placed them closer to the broiler element where they developed an appealing charred exterior. A quick stir-together sauce of more yogurt and a touch more red curry paste finished things off. Look for small red potatoes measuring 1 to 2 inches in diameter. You will need four 12-inch metal skewers for this recipe.

Chicken
- ½ cup plain Greek yogurt
- 2 tablespoons red curry paste
- 1 tablespoon vegetable oil
- 1 teaspoon table salt
- ½ teaspoon pepper
- 4 (6- to 8-ounce) boneless, skinless chicken breasts, trimmed and cut into 2-inch chunks

Sauce
- ½ cup plain Greek yogurt
- ¼ cup chopped fresh cilantro
- 1 tablespoon lime juice
- 1 tablespoon water
- 1 teaspoon red curry paste
- ¼ teaspoon table salt
- ⅛ teaspoon pepper

Vegetables
- 1½ pounds small red potatoes, unpeeled, halved
- ¼ cup vegetable oil, divided
- ¾ teaspoon table salt, divided
- ½ teaspoon pepper, divided
- 1 pound green beans, trimmed

1. For the chicken Whisk yogurt, curry paste, oil, salt, and pepper together in medium bowl. Add chicken and toss to combine. Refrigerate for at least 30 minutes or up to 1 hour. Thread chicken onto four 12-inch metal skewers; set aside.

2. For the sauce Whisk all ingredients together in bowl.

3. For the vegetables Adjust oven rack to middle position and heat oven to 475 degrees. Line rimmed baking sheet with aluminum foil. Toss potatoes, 2 tablespoons oil, ½ teaspoon salt, and ¼ teaspoon pepper together on prepared sheet. Arrange potatoes cut side down around outside of sheet. Roast until bottoms begin to brown, about 15 minutes.

4. Remove sheet from oven and heat broiler. Toss green beans with remaining 2 tablespoons oil, remaining ¼ teaspoon salt, and remaining ¼ teaspoon pepper. Place green beans in center of sheet. Place kebabs around perimeter of sheet on top of potatoes. Return sheet to oven and broil until chicken is lightly charred on top, about 8 minutes. Flip kebabs and continue to broil until lightly charred on second side and chicken registers 160 degrees, 6 to 8 minutes. Serve kebabs with vegetables and sauce.

Three-Cup Chicken

SKILLET

Serves 4
Total Time 45 minutes

Why This Recipe Works Legend has it that the recipe for three-cup chicken is right in the name: one cup each of soy sauce, sesame oil, and rice wine to make a sauce for tender pieces of chicken. But few modern recipes follow this formula since a full cup of oil makes the dish greasy, and 1 cup each of soy sauce and rice wine take too long to reduce. Instead, we scaled the volume of the liquids, using just ⅓ cup each of soy sauce and Shaoxing wine and cutting down the oil to 3 tablespoons of vegetable oil and 1 tablespoon of sesame oil, which we added at the end. Some traditional recipes call for butchering a whole chicken, but for ease we started with bone-less, skinless chicken thighs marinated in the soy sauce and rice wine along with a touch of brown sugar. Ginger and a hefty amount of garlic created a potent backbone, while scallions, Thai basil, and toasted sesame oil balanced the flavors. Stir-fries cook quickly, so have everything prepped before you begin cooking. We developed this recipe for a 12-inch nonstick skillet, but a 14-inch flat-bottomed wok can be used instead. We prefer the flavor of Thai basil in this recipe, but you can substitute sweet Italian basil, if desired. For a spicier dish, use the larger amount of red pepper flakes.

Three-Cup Chicken

- ⅓ cup soy sauce
- ⅓ cup Shaoxing wine or dry sherry
- 1 tablespoon packed brown sugar
- 1½ pounds boneless, skinless chicken thighs, trimmed and cut into 2-inch pieces
- 3 tablespoons vegetable oil
- 1 (2-inch) piece ginger, peeled, halved lengthwise, and sliced into thin half-rounds
- 12 garlic cloves, peeled and halved lengthwise
- ½–¾ teaspoon red pepper flakes
- 6 scallions, white and green parts separated and sliced thin on bias
- 1 tablespoon water
- 1 teaspoon cornstarch
- 1 cup fresh Thai basil leaves, large leaves halved lengthwise
- 1 tablespoon toasted sesame oil

1. Whisk soy sauce, wine, and sugar together in medium bowl. Add chicken and toss to coat; set aside.

2. Heat vegetable oil, ginger, garlic, and pepper flakes in 12-inch nonstick skillet over medium-low heat. Cook, stirring frequently, until garlic is golden brown and beginning to soften, 8 to 10 minutes.

3. Add chicken and marinade to skillet, increase heat to medium-high, and bring to simmer. Reduce heat to medium-low and simmer for 10 minutes, stirring occasionally. Stir in scallion whites and continue to cook until chicken registers about 200 degrees, 8 to 10 minutes.

4. Whisk water and cornstarch together in small bowl, then stir into sauce. Simmer until sauce is slightly thickened, about 1 minute. Off heat, stir in basil, sesame oil, and scallion greens. Transfer to platter and serve.

VARIATION

Three-Cup Chicken for Two
SKILLET
Serves 2
Total Time 45 minutes
We prefer the flavor of Thai basil in this recipe, but you can substitute sweet Italian basil, if desired. For a spicier dish, use the larger amount of red pepper flakes.

- 3 tablespoons soy sauce
- 3 tablespoons Shaoxing wine or dry sherry
- 1½ teaspoons packed brown sugar
- 12 ounces boneless, skinless chicken thighs, trimmed and cut into 2-inch pieces
- 1½ tablespoons vegetable oil

Stir-Fried Chicken with Bok Choy and Crispy Noodle Cake

1 (1-inch) piece ginger, peeled, halved lengthwise, and sliced into thin half-rounds

6 garlic cloves, peeled and halved lengthwise

¼–½ teaspoon red pepper flakes

3 scallions, white and green parts separated and sliced thin on bias

1½ teaspoons water

½ teaspoon cornstarch

½ cup Thai basil leaves, large leaves halved lengthwise

1½ teaspoons toasted sesame oil

1. Whisk soy sauce, wine, and sugar together in medium bowl. Add chicken and toss to coat; set aside.

2. Heat vegetable oil, ginger, garlic, and pepper flakes in 10-inch nonstick skillet over medium-low heat. Cook, stirring frequently, until garlic is golden brown and beginning to soften, 8 to 10 minutes.

3. Add chicken and marinade to skillet, increase heat to medium-high, and bring to simmer. Reduce heat to medium-low and simmer for 10 minutes, stirring occasionally. Stir in scallion whites and continue to cook until chicken registers about 200 degrees, 8 to 10 minutes.

4. Whisk water and cornstarch together in small bowl, then stir into sauce; simmer until sauce is slightly thickened, about 1 minute. Remove skillet from heat. Stir in basil, sesame oil, and scallion greens. Transfer to platter and serve.

Stir-Fried Chicken with Bok Choy and Crispy Noodle Cake

SKILLET

Serves 4

Total Time 1¼ hours

Why This Recipe Works Quick to cook yet complex in flavor, stir-fries are a superb weeknight dinner. A pan-fried noodle cake—crispy and crunchy on the outside and tender and chewy inside—offered a fun change of pace from the usual white rice. To brighten up the chicken, we gave it a quick soak in a simple marinade, and a savory stir-fry sauce with soy sauce and oyster sauce tied everything together. We had the most success with fresh Chinese noodles, which made for a cohesive cake. A nonstick skillet was crucial, as it kept the cake from sticking and falling apart; it also allowed us to use less oil so the cake wasn't greasy. Stir-fries cook quickly, so have everything prepped before you begin cooking. To make slicing the chicken easier, freeze it for 15 minutes. Fresh Chinese noodles are often found in the produce section of larger supermarkets.

Sauce

¼ cup chicken broth

2 tablespoons soy sauce

1 tablespoon Shaoxing wine or dry sherry

1 tablespoon oyster sauce

1 teaspoon sugar

1 teaspoon cornstarch

¼ teaspoon red pepper flakes

Noodle Cake

1 (9-ounce) package fresh Chinese noodles

1 teaspoon table salt

2 scallions, sliced thin

¼ cup vegetable oil, divided

Chicken Stir-Fry

2 teaspoons water

⅛ teaspoon baking soda

1 pound boneless, skinless chicken breasts, trimmed and sliced thin

2 tablespoons toasted sesame oil

1 tablespoon soy sauce

1 tablespoon Shaoxing wine or dry sherry

1 tablespoon cornstarch

3 tablespoons plus 1 teaspoon vegetable oil, divided

1 tablespoon grated fresh ginger

1 garlic clove, minced

1 pound bok choy, stalks sliced ¼ inch thick on bias, greens sliced ½ inch thick, divided

1 small red bell pepper, stemmed, seeded, and cut into ¼-inch-wide strips

1. For the sauce Whisk all ingredients together in small bowl; set aside.

2. For the noodle cake Bring 6 quarts water to boil in large pot. Add noodles and salt and cook, stirring often, until almost tender, 2 to 3 minutes. Drain noodles, then toss with scallions.

3. Heat 2 tablespoons oil in 12-inch nonstick skillet over medium heat until shimmering. Spread noodles evenly across bottom of skillet and press with spatula to flatten. Cook until bottom of cake is crispy and golden brown, 5 to 8 minutes.

4. Slide noodle cake onto large plate. Add remaining 2 tablespoons oil to skillet and swirl to coat. Invert noodle cake onto second plate and slide, browned side up, back into skillet. Cook until golden brown on second side, 5 to 8 minutes.

5. Slide noodle cake onto cutting board and let sit for at least 5 minutes before slicing into wedges. (Noodle cake can be transferred to paper towel–lined platter and kept warm in 200 degree oven for up to 20 minutes.) Wipe skillet clean with paper towels.

Massaman Chicken Curry with Potatoes and Peanuts

6. For the chicken stir-fry While noodles boil, combine water and baking soda in medium bowl. Add chicken and toss to coat; let sit for 5 minutes. Add sesame oil, soy sauce, Shaoxing wine, and cornstarch and toss until well combined. Combine 1 tablespoon vegetable oil, ginger, and garlic in bowl; set aside.

7. Heat 2 teaspoons vegetable oil in now-empty skillet over medium-high heat until just smoking. Add half of chicken and increase heat to high. Cook, tossing slowly but constantly, until no longer pink, 2 to 6 minutes. Transfer chicken to clean, dry large bowl and cover with aluminum foil. Repeat with 2 teaspoons vegetable oil and remaining chicken; transfer to bowl.

8. Heat remaining 1 tablespoon vegetable oil in again-empty skillet over high heat until just smoking. Add bok choy stalks and bell pepper and cook, tossing slowly but constantly, until lightly browned, 2 to 3 minutes.

9. Push vegetables to sides of skillet and reduce heat to medium. Add ginger mixture to center and cook, mashing mixture into skillet, until fragrant, about 30 seconds. Stir mixture into vegetables. Add bok choy greens and cook until beginning to wilt, about 30 seconds.

10. Add chicken with any accumulated juices. Whisk sauce to recombine, then add to skillet. Increase heat to high and cook, tossing constantly, until sauce is thickened, about 30 seconds. Transfer to serving platter and serve with noodle cake.

Massaman Chicken Curry with Potatoes and Peanuts

SKILLET

Serves 4 to 6
Total Time 1¼ hours

Why This Recipe Works This savory-sweet massaman curry is a Thai dish that's spiced but not spicy. To the traditional shallots, ginger, and garlic we added dried New Mexican chiles, five-spice powder, and ground cumin for ample complexity and depth of flavor. Blending the chiles, shallots, and garlic into a smooth paste yielded incredibly robust flavors. We sautéed the paste to intensify the flavors before stirring in coconut milk and chicken broth to make a rich curry with enough body to cling to the chicken and potatoes. Then it was just a matter of simmering the potatoes, onion, chicken, and peanuts until they were tender. A final garnish of lime zest and cilantro added a splash of color and brightness. The ingredients for the curry paste can be doubled to make extra for future use. Serve with rice (see page 21).

Massaman Curry Paste
1½ ounces (about 6) dried New Mexican chiles, stemmed, seeded, and torn into ½-inch pieces (1½ cups)
4 shallots, chopped
½ cup chopped fresh ginger
¼ cup water
7 garlic cloves, chopped
1½ tablespoons lime juice
1½ tablespoons vegetable oil
1 tablespoon fish sauce
1 teaspoon five-spice powder
½ teaspoon ground cumin
½ teaspoon pepper

Curry
1 teaspoon vegetable oil
1 (14-ounce) can coconut milk
1¼ cups chicken broth
1 pound Yukon Gold potatoes, unpeeled, cut into ¾-inch pieces
1 onion, chopped
⅓ cup dry-roasted peanuts
¾ teaspoon table salt
1 pound boneless, skinless chicken thighs, trimmed and cut into 1-inch pieces
2 teaspoons grated lime zest
¼ cup chopped fresh cilantro

1. For the curry paste Process all ingredients in blender until smooth paste forms, about 4 minutes, scraping down sides of blender jar as needed. (Curry paste can be refrigerated for up to 1 week or frozen for up to 2 months; if frozen, thaw completely before using.)

2. For the curry Heat oil in Dutch oven over medium heat until shimmering. Add curry paste and cook, stirring frequently, until paste is fragrant and darkens in color, about 3 minutes. Stir in coconut milk, broth, potatoes, onion, peanuts, and salt, scraping up any browned bits. Bring to simmer and cook until potatoes are just tender, 12 to 14 minutes.

3. Stir in chicken, return to simmer, and cook until chicken is tender, 10 to 12 minutes. Off heat, stir in lime zest. Serve, passing cilantro separately.

Chicken and Arugula Salad with Warm Fig Dressing

SKILLET

Serves 4
Total Time 45 minutes

Why This Recipe Works A warm salad dressing pulls the elements of this simple dinner together to create a cohesive, flavorful dish. Drawing inspiration from the foods of the Mediterranean, we started with beautiful, deep purple figs. Fresh figs have a subtle floral sweetness, which we wanted to enhance by seasoning our dressing with warm spices. After trying a variety of spices, we settled on coriander for its light citrus note to complement the figs. We browned the chicken for deep flavor, and used a skillet to bloom our spices and warm the figs along with some chickpeas. We shredded our chicken before tossing everything together. Toasted almonds were the ideal topping, adding plenty of crunch—a perfect contrast to the soft figs.

1½ pounds boneless, skinless chicken breasts, trimmed
¾   teaspoon table salt, divided
½   teaspoon pepper, divided
1   tablespoon plus ⅓ cup extra-virgin olive oil, divided
1   large shallot, halved and sliced thin
2   teaspoons ground coriander
3   tablespoons red wine vinegar
2   teaspoons honey
1   (15-ounce) can chickpeas, rinsed
12 figs, stemmed and quartered
5   ounces (5 cups) baby arugula
⅓   cup fresh tarragon or basil leaves, torn if large
½   cup sliced almonds, toasted

Chicken and Arugula Salad with Warm Fig Dressing

1. Pound thicker end of chicken breasts between 2 sheets of plastic wrap to uniform ½-inch thickness. Pat chicken dry with paper towels and sprinkle with ¼ teaspoon salt and ¼ teaspoon pepper. Heat 1 tablespoon oil in 12-inch nonstick skillet over medium-high heat until just smoking. Cook chicken until browned and registers 160 degrees, 5 to 7 minutes per side.

2. Transfer chicken to cutting board, let cool slightly, then shred into bite-size pieces using 2 forks. Wipe skillet clean with paper towels.

3. Heat remaining ⅓ cup oil in now-empty skillet over medium heat until shimmering. Add shallot and cook until softened, about 2 minutes. Stir in coriander and cook until fragrant, about 30 seconds. Off heat, whisk in vinegar, honey, remaining ½ teaspoon salt, and remaining ¼ teaspoon pepper. Stir in chickpeas and figs and let sit until heated through, about 2 minutes.

4. Toss shredded chicken, arugula, tarragon, and chickpea mixture together in serving bowl. Sprinkle with almonds and serve.

Chicken Sausages with Braised Red Cabbage and Potatoes

DUTCH OVEN

Serves 4 to 6
Total Time 1¼ hours

Why This Recipe Works This fresh take on sausage and cabbage captures the flavor of an all-day braise in under an hour and a half. The Dutch oven offered ample surface area to brown the sausage and potatoes as well as enough space to braise the cabbage. Chicken sausage, browned for a quick flavor boost, kept things easy, and braising red cabbage in cider with grated apple, bay leaves, and thyme offered complexity and kept its texture intact. The bright acidity from a splash of cider vinegar rounded things out. To give the potatoes a jump-start, we cooked them quickly in the microwave before browning them in the Dutch oven for a crisp exterior. Chicken sausage is available in a variety of flavors; feel free to use any flavor that you think will work well in this dish. Turkey sausage can be substituted for the chicken sausage. Look for small red potatoes measuring 1 to 2 inches in diameter; if your potatoes are larger, be sure to quarter them.

1½ pounds small red potatoes, unpeeled, halved
¼ cup vegetable oil, divided
¾ teaspoon table salt, divided
¼ teaspoon pepper
1½ pounds raw chicken sausage
1 onion, halved and sliced thin
1 head red cabbage (2 pounds), cored and shredded
1½ cups apple cider
1 Granny Smith apple, peeled and grated
2 bay leaves
1½ teaspoons minced fresh thyme or ½ teaspoon dried
2 tablespoons cider vinegar
2 tablespoons minced fresh chives

1. Toss potatoes with 1 tablespoon oil, ¼ teaspoon salt, and pepper in bowl. Cover and microwave, stirring occasionally, until potatoes are tender, about 5 minutes; drain well.

2. Meanwhile, heat 1 tablespoon oil in Dutch oven over medium heat until shimmering. Brown sausage on all sides, about 5 minutes; transfer to plate.

Chicken Sausages with Braised Red Cabbage and Potatoes

3. Add onion and remaining ½ teaspoon salt to fat left in pot and cook over medium heat until onion is softened, about 5 minutes. Stir in cabbage, cider, apple, bay leaves, and thyme. Nestle sausage into vegetables and add any accumulated juices. Cover and cook until cabbage is very tender and sausage registers at least 160 degrees, 20 to 25 minutes.

4. Uncover and simmer until liquid is almost evaporated, 2 to 3 minutes. Transfer sausage to serving platter and discard bay leaves. Stir vinegar into vegetables and season with salt and pepper to taste. Transfer vegetables to platter with sausage and tent with aluminum foil.

5. Wipe pot clean with paper towels. Add remaining 2 tablespoons oil to now-empty pot and heat over medium heat until shimmering. Add potatoes cut side down and cook until browned, 2 to 5 minutes. Transfer to platter with sausage and cabbage, sprinkle with chives, and serve.

SHREDDING CABBAGE

1. Cut cabbage into quarters, then trim and discard core.

2. Separate cabbage into small stacks of leaves that flatten when pressed.

3. Use chef's knife to cut each stack of cabbage leaves into thin shreds.

Braised Chicken Sausages with White Beans and Spinach

INSTANT POT

Serves 4
Total Time 45 minutes

Why This Recipe Works For this hearty, wintry braise, a simple combination of sausage, beans, and rosemary is transformed into a rich, warming ragout by the heat of the pressure cooker. We started with delicately flavored cannellini beans and Italian chicken sausage, which was full of spices such as fennel and caraway and provided ample flavor to the dish. We combined broth, wine, minced garlic, and rosemary for a flavorful cooking liquid that seasoned the beans as they cooked. Diced tomatoes added a pop of color and acidity. Once the sausages were cooked and the beans were tender, we moved the sausages to a platter to rest. Stirring some baby spinach into the beans before serving allowed it to wilt slightly. Chicken sausage is available in a variety of flavors; feel free to use any flavor that you think will work well in this dish. Turkey sausage can be substituted for the chicken sausage. Any canned small white beans will work well here.

1 tablespoon extra-virgin olive oil, plus extra for serving
1½ pounds raw hot or sweet Italian chicken sausage
2 shallots, peeled, halved, and sliced thin
3 garlic cloves, minced
½ cup dry white wine
½ cup chicken broth
2 (15-ounce) cans cannellini beans, rinsed
1 (14.5-ounce) can diced tomatoes, drained
1 sprig fresh rosemary
¼ teaspoon pepper
4 ounces (4 cups) baby spinach
2 ounces Parmesan cheese, shaved

1. Using highest sauté or browning function, heat oil in electric pressure cooker until just smoking. Brown sausages on all sides, 6 to 8 minutes, transfer to plate.

2. Add shallots to fat let in pressure cooker and cook until softened, about 1 minute. Stir in garlic and cook until fragrant, about 30 seconds. Stir in wine, scraping up any browned bits. Stir in broth, beans, tomatoes, rosemary sprig, and pepper. Nestle sausages into pot and add any accumulated juices.

3. Lock lid in place and close pressure release valve. Select high pressure cook function and cook for 4 minutes. Turn off pressure cooker and quick-release pressure. Carefully remove lid, allowing steam to escape away from you.

4. Transfer sausages to serving platter, tent with aluminum foil, and let rest while finishing beans. Stir spinach into beans, 1 handful at a time, and let sit until spinach is slightly wilted, about 1 minute. Season with salt and pepper to taste. Transfer bean mixture to platter with sausages. Sprinkle with Parmesan and drizzle with extra oil. Serve.

INGREDIENT SPOTLIGHT

CANNELLINI BEANS

We tasted five nationally distributed supermarket brands of canned cannellini beans—plain, in dip, and in soup—rating their flavor, texture, and overall appeal. Tasters' favorite canned beans were **Goya Cannellini**, which were "well seasoned," "big and meaty," and "very satisfying," with both "earthy sweetness" and "savory flavor." Their texture was consistently "ultracreamy and smooth," with a "nice firm bite."

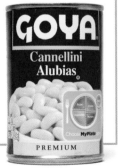

Braised Chicken Sausages with Chickpeas and Kale for Two

INSTANT POT

Serves 2

Total Time 45 minutes

Chicken sausage is available in a variety of flavors; feel free to use any flavor that you think will work well in this dish. Turkey sausage can be substituted for the chicken sausage. Any canned small white beans will work well here.

- 2 teaspoons extra-virgin olive oil
- 12 ounces raw hot or sweet Italian chicken sausage
- 1 shallot, peeled, halved, and sliced thin
- 1 garlic clove, minced
- ¼ cup dry white wine
- ½ cup chicken broth
- 1 (15-ounce) can chickpeas, rinsed
- ⅛ teaspoon pepper
- 2 ounces (2 cups) baby kale
- 2 teaspoons minced fresh dill
- ¼ teaspoon lemon zest plus 2 teaspoons juice

1. Using highest sauté or browning function, heat oil in electric pressure cooker until just smoking. Brown sausages on all sides, 6 to 8 minutes, transfer to plate.

2. Add shallot to fat left in pressure cooker and cook until softened, about 1 minute. Stir in garlic and cook until fragrant, about 30 seconds. Stir in wine, scraping up any browned bits. Stir in broth, chickpeas, and pepper. Nestle sausages into pot and add any accumulated juices.

3. Lock lid in place and close pressure release valve. Select high pressure cook function and cook for 4 minutes. Turn off pressure cooker and quick-release pressure. Carefully remove lid, allowing steam to escape away from you.

4. Transfer sausages to plate, tent with aluminum foil, and let rest while finishing beans. Stir kale into beans, 1 handful at a time, and let sit until kale is slightly wilted, about 1 minute. Stir in dill and lemon zest and juice and season with salt and pepper to taste. Serve sausages with chickpea mixture.

Italian Braised Chicken Sausages with Potatoes and Peppers

SLOW COOKER

Serves 4

Cook Time 3 to 4 hours on low

Why This Recipe Works The gentle, moist heat of the slow cooker perfectly cooks sausage and a trio of vegetables to create this satisfying meal. We started with chicken sausages and chose to pair them with creamy red potatoes, bell peppers, and onion. We microwaved the vegetables with tomato paste, garlic, oregano, and red pepper flakes, which served two purposes: This step infused the potatoes, peppers, and onion with plenty of flavor and also gave them a head start so that they would finish cooking at the same time as the sausages. Fresh basil stirred in right before serving brightened up this dish. Chicken sausage is available in a variety of flavors; feel free to use any flavor that you think will work well in this dish. Turkey sausage can be substituted for the chicken sausage. You will need a 5- to 7-quart oval slow cooker for this recipe.

- 12 ounces red potatoes, unpeeled, quartered and sliced ¼ inch thick
- 3 red or green bell peppers, stemmed, seeded, and cut into ¼-inch-wide strips
- 1 onion, halved and sliced ½ inch thick
- ¼ cup tomato paste
- 2 tablespoons water
- 3 garlic cloves, minced
- 2 teaspoons minced fresh oregano or ½ teaspoon dried
- ¼ teaspoon red pepper flakes
- ¼ cup chicken broth
- 1½ pounds raw chicken sausage
- 2 tablespoons chopped fresh basil

1. Microwave potatoes, bell peppers, onion, tomato paste, water, garlic, oregano, and pepper flakes in covered bowl, stirring occasionally, until vegetables are almost tender, about 15 minutes; transfer to slow cooker. Stir in broth. Nestle sausage into slow cooker, cover, and cook until sausage and vegetables are tender, 3 to 4 hours on low.

2. Transfer sausage to serving platter. Stir basil into vegetable mixture and season with salt and pepper to taste. Transfer vegetable mixture to platter with sausage. Serve.

Turkey Meatballs with Coconut Rice, Bell Peppers, and Peas

Turkey Meatballs with Coconut Rice, Bell Peppers, and Peas

SKILLET
Serves 4
Total Time 1½ hours

Why This Recipe Works Boldly flavored turkey meatballs cook up perfectly juicy and tender nestled in a skillet of creamy coconut rice. We packed the meatballs with cilantro, scallions, and ginger for fresh brightness and then added chili-garlic sauce and fish sauce for heat and savory depth. We bound the mixture together and kept the meatballs moist with an egg and some panko bread crumbs. After browning the meatballs, we sautéed red bell pepper in the leftover fat, and then we added rice and cooked it until it was translucent around the edges (a step that added nutty flavor and prevented future clumping). To cook the rice, we swapped out one-third of the water for coconut milk—just enough for a noticeable coconut sweetness but not so much that the finished dish was stodgy. The meatballs and rice finished cooking together in the covered skillet, and we rounded out the meal with the addition of thawed frozen peas. We finished the dish with more fresh herbs, a squeeze of lime, and some chopped peanuts for a welcome crunch. Be sure to use ground turkey, not ground turkey breast (also labeled 99 percent fat-free), in this recipe. We like the flavor of jasmine rice here, though any long-grain white rice will work. You will need a 12-inch nonstick skillet with a tight-fitting lid for this recipe.

- 1 pound ground turkey
- ½ cup panko bread crumbs
- 6 scallions, sliced thin, divided
- ½ cup chopped fresh cilantro, divided
- 1 large egg, lightly beaten
- 2 tablespoons Asian chili-garlic sauce, plus extra for serving
- 2 tablespoons fish sauce, divided
- 1 tablespoon grated fresh ginger
- 1 teaspoon table salt, divided
- 2 tablespoons vegetable oil
- 2 red bell peppers, stemmed, seeded, and sliced into ¼-inch-thick strips (2 cups)
- 1 cup long-grain white rice, rinsed
- 1½ cups water
- ⅔ cup canned coconut milk
- ½ cup frozen peas, thawed
- ¼ cup dry-roasted peanuts, chopped coarse
  Lime wedges

1. Using your hands, mix turkey, panko, two-thirds of scallions, ¼ cup cilantro, egg, chili-garlic sauce, 1 tablespoon fish sauce, ginger, and ½ teaspoon salt in bowl until thoroughly combined. Using wet hands, pinch off and roll 2-tablespoon-size pieces of mixture into balls and arrange on large plate (you should have about 20 meatballs); refrigerate for 15 minutes.

2. Heat oil in 12-inch nonstick skillet over medium-high heat until shimmering. Brown meatballs on all sides, 5 to 7 minutes; return to plate.

3. Add bell peppers to fat left in skillet and cook until beginning to brown, about 2 minutes. Add rice and cook, stirring frequently, until edges of rice begin to turn translucent, about 1 minute. Stir in water, coconut milk, remaining 1 tablespoon fish sauce, and remaining ½ teaspoon salt and bring to boil. Return meatballs to skillet and add any accumulated juices. Cover, reduce heat to low, and cook for 20 minutes.

4. Remove skillet from heat and let sit, covered, for 10 minutes. Gently stir peas into rice and let sit until heated through, about 2 minutes. Sprinkle with peanuts, remaining one-third of scallions, and remaining ¼ cup cilantro. Serve with lime wedges and extra chili-garlic sauce.

Crispy Skillet Turkey Burgers with Tomato-Feta Salad

Crispy Skillet Turkey Burgers with Tomato-Feta Salad

SKILLET

Serves 4

Total Time 45 minutes

Why This Recipe Works A little bit of cheese goes a long way in helping these turkey burgers stay moist. Mixing Monterey Jack into the lean turkey meat created juicy pockets of fat, which yielded a more desirable interior texture, and the cheese crisped around the edges of the burger, creating a crunchy crust. We found that adding panko bread crumbs and a little bit of mayonnaise kept the burgers from becoming too dense. For toppings, we particularly liked the tanginess of onions to cut through the richness of the burger. An easy salad of bright, juicy cherry tomatoes, tangy feta, and aromatic oregano provided the perfect complement to our crispy, hearty burgers, and a spoonful of lemon-oregano mayonnaise over the burger tied the whole dish together. Be sure to use ground turkey, not ground turkey breast (also labeled 99 percent fat-free), in this recipe.

3 tablespoons extra-virgin olive oil, divided
1 tablespoon minced fresh oregano, divided
1 garlic clove, minced
¾ teaspoon grated lemon zest plus 2 tablespoons juice, divided
1 teaspoon pepper, divided
¾ teaspoon table salt, divided
12 ounces cherry tomatoes, halved
1 small red onion, halved and sliced, divided
7 tablespoons mayonnaise, divided
1 pound ground turkey
1 cup panko bread crumbs
2 ounces Monterey Jack cheese, shredded (½ cup)
2 ounces feta cheese, crumbled (½ cup)
4 hamburger buns
1 cup baby arugula

1. Whisk 2 tablespoons oil, 1½ teaspoons oregano, garlic, ½ teaspoon lemon zest, 1 tablespoon lemon juice, ¼ teaspoon pepper, and ¼ teaspoon salt together in medium bowl. Add tomatoes and half of onion and toss to coat; set aside.

2. Whisk 3 tablespoons mayonnaise, remaining 1½ teaspoons oregano, remaining ¼ teaspoon lemon zest, remaining 1 tablespoon lemon juice, and ¼ teaspoon pepper together in small bowl; set aside.

3. Using your hands, mix turkey, panko, Monterey Jack, remaining ½ teaspoon pepper, remaining ½ teaspoon salt, and remaining ¼ cup mayonnaise in bowl until thoroughly

---

NOTES FROM THE TEST KITCHEN

BUYING GROUND TURKEY

In most supermarkets, you'll find three different types of ground turkey: ground white meat, ground dark meat, and a blend of the two (simply labeled ground turkey). Packages usually state the fat percentage, though it is not always displayed prominently; typically, the darker the meat, the higher the fat content. The juiciest and most flavorful ground turkey we tried was made with only dark meat, which has 15 to 20 percent fat (80 to 85 percent lean). If you want a lighter version, opt for the 7 percent fat (93 percent lean) blended choice. Just steer clear of the all-white-meat ground turkey, also labeled 99 percent fat-free—taste tests using this ultra-lean meat yielded results that tasters called dry and devoid of flavor.

combined. Divide burger mixture into 4 lightly packed balls, then gently flatten into ¾-inch-thick patties. Heat remaining 1 tablespoon oil in 12-inch nonstick skillet over medium heat until shimmering. Add patties and cook until well browned and meat registers 160 degrees, about 5 minutes per side.

4. Add feta to tomato mixture and gently toss to combine. Season with salt and pepper to taste. Place burgers on bun bottoms, spread with layer of lemon-oregano mayo, and top with remaining onion and arugula. Serve with tomato-feta salad.

Pan-Roasted Chicken Breasts with Root Vegetables

SKILLET
Serves 4
Total Time 1¼ hours

Why This Recipe Works For this version of classic roast chicken and vegetables, we knew we could use our skillet to get a great seared crust on juicy, bone-in chicken breasts, but could we cook the vegetables in sync? To start, we seared our chicken to crisp the skin to golden brown perfection. After the initial sear, we took the chicken out of the skillet and filled the pan with potatoes, parsnips, carrots, and shallots, all cut into bite-size pieces. We then put the chicken back in the pan on top of the vegetables and moved the whole thing to the oven. Elevating the chicken on top of the vegetables allowed the meat to gently cook while the root vegetables roasted against the hot surface of the pan, which helped them to cook quickly and evenly. Once the chicken was done, we removed it and let it rest while we finished cooking the vegetables. A simple sprinkling of chives was all that was needed to finish our dish. Use small red potatoes measuring 1 to 2 inches in diameter; if your potatoes are larger, cut them into 1-inch pieces to ensure that they cook through properly. You will need a 12-inch oven-safe skillet for this recipe.

4 (12-ounce) bone-in split chicken breasts, trimmed
1 teaspoon table salt, divided
¾ teaspoon pepper, divided
1 tablespoon vegetable oil
1 pound small red potatoes, unpeeled, quartered
8 ounces parsnips, peeled, halved lengthwise, and cut into 1-inch pieces
4 carrots, peeled, halved lengthwise, and cut into 1-inch pieces
4 shallots, peeled and quartered
1 teaspoon minced fresh rosemary or ¼ teaspoon dried
1 tablespoon minced fresh chives

Pan-Roasted Chicken Breasts with Root Vegetables

1. Adjust oven rack to middle position and heat oven to 450 degrees. Pound thicker end of chicken breasts between 2 sheets of plastic wrap to ¾- to 1-inch thickness. Pat chicken dry with paper towels and sprinkle with ½ teaspoon salt and ½ teaspoon pepper. Heat oil in 12-inch ovensafe skillet over medium-high heat until just smoking. Place chicken skin side down in skillet and cook until well browned on first side, 5 to 7 minutes. Flip chicken and continue to cook until lightly browned on second side, about 3 minutes; transfer to plate.

2. Add potatoes, parsnips, carrots, shallots, rosemary, remaining ½ teaspoon salt, and remaining ¼ teaspoon pepper to fat left in skillet and toss to coat. Place chicken skin side up on top of vegetables, transfer skillet to oven, and roast until chicken registers 160 degrees, 20 to 25 minutes.

3. Using potholders, remove skillet from oven. Transfer chicken to serving platter, tent with aluminum foil, and let rest while finishing vegetables.

4. Being careful of hot skillet handle, stir vegetables, return skillet to oven, and roast until vegetables are tender, about 15 minutes. Stir in chives and season with salt and pepper to taste. Serve chicken with vegetables.

Pan-Roasted Chicken Breasts with Sweet Potatoes and Fennel for Two

SKILLET

Serves 2

Total Time 1¼ hours

You will need a 10-inch ovensafe skillet for this recipe.

2 (12-ounce) bone-in split chicken breasts, trimmed
½ teaspoon table salt, divided
¼ teaspoon pepper
2 teaspoons vegetable oil
12 ounces sweet potatoes, peeled and cut into 1-inch pieces
1 small fennel bulb (8 ounces), stalks discarded, bulb halved and cut into ½-inch wedges through core
2 shallots, peeled and quartered
1 teaspoon minced fresh thyme or ¼ teaspoon dried
2 teaspoons minced fresh tarragon

1. Adjust oven rack to middle position and heat oven to 450 degrees. Pound thicker end of chicken breasts between 2 sheets of plastic wrap to ¾- to 1-inch thickness. Pat chicken dry with paper towels and sprinkle with ¼ teaspoon salt and pepper. Heat oil in 10-inch ovensafe skillet over medium-high heat until just smoking. Place chicken skin side down in skillet and cook until well browned on first side, 5 to 7 minutes. Flip chicken and continue to cook until lightly browned on second side, about 3 minutes; transfer to plate.

2. Add potatoes, fennel, shallots, thyme, and remaining ¼ teaspoon salt to fat left in skillet; toss to coat. Place chicken skin side up on top of vegetables, transfer skillet to oven, and roast until chicken registers 160 degrees, 20 to 25 minutes.

3. Using potholders, remove skillet from oven. Transfer chicken to serving platter, tent with aluminum foil, and let rest while finishing vegetables.

4. Being careful of hot skillet handle, stir vegetables, return skillet to oven, and roast until vegetables are tender, about 15 minutes. Stir in tarragon and season with salt and pepper to taste. Serve chicken with vegetables.

TRIMMING SPLIT CHICKEN BREASTS

Using kitchen shears, trim off rib section from each breast, following vertical line of fat from tapered end of breast up to socket where wing was attached.

Roasted Chicken Parts with Brussels Sprouts and Shallots

SHEET PAN

Serves 4

Total Time 1¼ hours

Why This Recipe Works For a meal packed with well-browned, herb-flecked chicken and vegetables that roasted at the same rate, we arranged our ingredients on a sheet pan with their cooking times in mind. After tossing the root vegetables with fresh thyme and rosemary, we arranged halved Brussels sprouts in the center of the pan. To ensure that the chicken breasts stayed moist while the meatier thighs and drumsticks cooked through, we placed the breasts in the center of the pan atop the sprouts and the thighs and drumsticks around the perimeter where they would take on (and benefit from) more direct contact with the oven's intense heat. Brushing the parts with herb butter added richness and browning. Roasted together in a hot oven, everything emerged browned and perfectly cooked. Use Brussels sprouts no bigger than golf balls, as larger ones are often tough and woody.

1½ pounds Brussels sprouts, trimmed and halved
12 ounces shallots, peeled and halved
6 garlic cloves, peeled
4 teaspoons minced fresh thyme, divided
1 tablespoon vegetable oil, divided
2 teaspoons minced fresh rosemary, divided
1 teaspoon sugar
1½ teaspoons table salt, divided
1 teaspoon pepper, divided
2 tablespoons unsalted butter, melted
3½ pounds bone-in chicken pieces (2 split breasts cut in half, 2 drumsticks, and 2 thighs), trimmed

1. Adjust oven rack to upper-middle position and heat oven to 475 degrees. Toss Brussels sprouts and shallots with garlic, 2 teaspoons thyme, oil, 1 teaspoon rosemary, sugar, ¾ teaspoon salt, and ¼ teaspoon pepper. Combine butter, remaining 2 teaspoons thyme, remaining 1 teaspoon rosemary, ¼ teaspoon salt, and ¼ teaspoon pepper in bowl; set aside.

2. Pat chicken dry with paper towels and sprinkle with remaining ½ teaspoon salt and remaining ½ teaspoon pepper. Place vegetables in single layer on rimmed baking sheet, arranging Brussels sprouts in center. Place chicken skin side up on top of vegetables, arranging breast pieces in center and leg and thigh pieces around perimeter of sheet.

3. Brush chicken with herb butter and roast until breasts register 160 degrees and thighs/drumsticks register 175 degrees, 35 to 40 minutes, rotating sheet halfway through roasting. Transfer chicken to serving platter and let rest for 5 minutes. Toss vegetables with pan juices and transfer to dish with chicken. Serve.

Roasted Chicken Breasts with Ratatouille

SHEET PAN
Serves 4
Total Time 1 hour

Why This Recipe Works The pairing of roasted chicken and ratatouille captures the simple flavors of summer, but preparation for the ratatouille alone can require multiple pans and cooking stages. Seeking an easier method, we turned to a sheet pan. Not only would its large surface area accommodate both the chicken and the vegetables, but exposing the vegetables to dry heat would prevent them from becoming soggy. Bone-in chicken breasts gave us juicy, tender meat without being too fussy or producing too much grease. To get golden skin, we preheated the baking sheet, oiled it to prevent sticking, and placed the chicken, skin side down, on the pan to sear. We chopped eggplant and zucchini into bite-size pieces, tossed them with canned tomatoes, and seasoned the trio with garlic and plenty of thyme before scattering the vegetables opposite the chicken. Halfway through roasting, we flipped the chicken, stirred the vegetables, and added lemon wedges. Minutes later, our chicken was ready, the ratatouille was tender and moist but not wet, and we even had juicy roasted lemon wedges to squeeze over everything.

- 1 (14.5-ounce) can diced tomatoes, drained
- 12 ounces eggplant, cut into ½-inch pieces
- 2 small zucchini (6 ounces each), cut into ½-inch pieces
- 3 tablespoons extra-virgin olive oil, divided
- 1 tablespoon minced fresh thyme or 1 teaspoon dried, divided
- 2 garlic cloves, minced
- 1 teaspoon table salt, divided
- ¾ teaspoon pepper, divided
- 4 (12-ounce) bone-in split chicken breasts, trimmed
- 1 lemon, quartered
- 2 tablespoons minced fresh parsley

Roasted Chicken Breasts with Ratatouille

1. Adjust oven rack to upper-middle position, place rimmed baking sheet on rack, and heat oven to 450 degrees. Toss tomatoes, eggplant, and zucchini with 2 tablespoons oil, 1 teaspoon thyme, garlic, ½ teaspoon salt, and ¼ teaspoon pepper. Pat chicken dry with paper towels and sprinkle with remaining 2 teaspoons thyme, remaining ½ teaspoon salt, and remaining ½ teaspoon pepper.

2. Brush remaining 1 tablespoon oil evenly over hot sheet. Place chicken skin side down on 1 side of sheet and spread vegetables in single layer on other side. Roast until chicken releases from sheet and vegetables begin to wilt, about 10 minutes.

3. Flip chicken skin side up and stir vegetables. Place lemon quarters cut side down on sheet. Continue to roast, stirring vegetables occasionally, until chicken registers 160 degrees and vegetables are tender, 10 to 15 minutes.

4. Remove sheet from oven, tent with aluminum foil, and let rest for 5 minutes. Transfer chicken to serving platter. Toss vegetables with pan juices, season with salt and pepper to taste, and transfer to platter with chicken. Sprinkle parsley over vegetables and serve with roasted lemon wedges.

Lemon–Goat Cheese Stuffed Chicken Breasts with Carrots

SHEET PAN

Serves 4
Total Time 1 hour

Why This Recipe Works It's hard to beat a juicy chicken breast stuffed with a cheesy filling, but the process of stuffing the filling in is typically too much hassle for a weeknight. We wanted an easier version of stuffed chicken, without the fuss of butterflying, pounding, rolling, and tying the chicken. Boneless, skinless chicken breasts were a nonstarter; they required too much knife work. Bone-in, skin-on chicken breasts, on the other hand, proved to be the right choice. To create a pocket for a dollop of our creamy filling of goat cheese, lemon zest, and herbs, all we needed to do was gently separate the skin from the meat. Cranking the oven up to 475 degrees guaranteed that the chicken baked up golden and crispy. Carrots, sliced thin and tossed in brown sugar to enhance their sweetness, roasted right alongside the chicken to complete the meal.

    4   ounces goat cheese, softened
    3   tablespoons extra-virgin olive oil, divided
    2   teaspoons minced fresh thyme
    1   garlic clove, minced
    1   teaspoon grated lemon zest
    1   teaspoon table salt, divided
    1   teaspoon pepper, divided
    4   (12-ounce) bone-in split chicken breasts, trimmed
  1½   pounds carrots, peeled and sliced ½ inch thick on bias
    1   tablespoon packed brown sugar

1. Adjust oven rack to middle position and heat oven to 475 degrees. Combine goat cheese, 1 tablespoon oil, thyme, garlic, lemon zest, ¼ teaspoon salt, and ¼ teaspoon pepper in bowl.

2. Pat chicken dry with paper towels. Using your fingers, carefully loosen center portion of skin covering each breast. Place about 1½ tablespoons cheese mixture under skin, directly on meat in center of each breast half. Gently press on skin to spread out cheese mixture. Brush chicken skin with 1 tablespoon oil, then sprinkle chicken with ½ teaspoon salt and ½ teaspoon pepper.

3. Place chicken skin side up on 1 side of rimmed baking sheet. Toss carrots with sugar, remaining 1 tablespoon oil, remaining ¼ teaspoon salt, and remaining ¼ teaspoon pepper. Spread carrots in single layer on other side of sheet. Roast until chicken registers 160 degrees, 35 to 40 minutes, rotating sheet halfway through roasting.

4. Transfer chicken to serving platter, tent with aluminum foil, and let rest for 5 minutes. Toss carrots with pan juices, season with salt and pepper to taste, and transfer to platter with chicken. Serve.

STUFFING BONE-IN CHICKEN BREASTS

1. Using your fingers, carefully loosen center portion of skin covering each breast, making pocket for filling.

2. Using spoon, place cheese mixture underneath loosened skin, over center of each chicken breast. Gently press on skin to spread out filling.

Roasted Chicken Breasts with Butternut Squash and Kale

SHEET PAN

Serves 4
Total Time 1 hour

Why This Recipe Works To get the chicken and vegetables in this autumnal meal to cook at the same rate, we used bone-in split chicken breasts, which contain less fat than a whole chicken and don't run the risk of smothering the vegetables underneath, which would cause them to steam. Halving the breasts assisted in even cooking. We selected a colorful mix of hearty vegetables to pair with our chicken: butternut squash, kale, and shallots. A sprinkling of dried cranberries added a sweet-tart element and textural appeal, and a simple sage marinade worked to season both the chicken and vegetables. Because we used only breast meat, we were able to drastically shorten the cooking time (compared to a whole chicken) to just 25 minutes, plenty of time to achieve crispy chicken skin, tender—but not mushy—squash, and fully cooked and lightly crisped kale. We topped our chicken with a drizzle of light, creamy yogurt sauce accented with orange zest and garlic to bring the whole dish into harmony. Both curly and Lacinato kale will work in this recipe.

Roasted Chicken Breasts with Butternut Squash and Kale

2. Vigorously squeeze and massage kale with hands in large bowl until leaves are uniformly darkened and slightly wilted, about 1 minute. Add squash, shallots, cranberries, whole garlic cloves, and ¼ cup oil mixture and toss to combine. Whisk paprika into remaining oil mixture, then add chicken and toss to coat.

3. Spread vegetables in single layer on rimmed baking sheet, then place chicken skin side up on top of vegetables. Roast until chicken registers 160 degrees, 25 to 35 minutes, rotating sheet halfway through roasting.

4. Transfer chicken to serving platter, tent with aluminum foil, and let rest for 5 minutes. Toss vegetables with pan juices, season with salt and pepper to taste, and transfer to platter with chicken. Drizzle ¼ cup yogurt sauce over chicken and serve, passing remaining yogurt sauce separately.

Crispy Chicken with Spiced Carrot, Orange, and Chickpea Salad

SKILLET
Serves 4
Total Time 45 minutes

Why This Recipe Works All of the prep work for the spicy-sweet side salad in this recipe happens on the countertop, simplifying this spin on chicken and vegetables. For super-crispy chicken breasts, we pounded them to an even thickness and started them in a cold skillet with the skin side down to give the fat under the skin time to render. The quick, earthy salad of carrots, chickpeas, feta, and oranges is balanced by a tart lemon-harissa dressing. Harissa is a traditional North African condiment made from a blend of hot chile peppers and can be found in the international aisle of most well-stocked supermarkets; spiciness will vary greatly by brand. If you can't find harissa, you can make your own (see page 39). You will need a 12-inch skillet with a tight-fitting lid for this recipe. Use a coarse grater to shred the carrots.

½ cup extra-virgin olive oil
2 tablespoons minced fresh sage
2 teaspoons honey
1 teaspoon table salt
½ teaspoon pepper
¾ cup plain whole milk yogurt
1 tablespoon water
7 garlic cloves, peeled (6 whole, 1 minced) and divided
1 teaspoon grated orange zest
8 ounces kale, stemmed and cut into 2-inch pieces
2 pounds butternut squash, peeled, seeded, and cut into 1-inch pieces (6 cups)
8 shallots, peeled and halved
½ cup dried cranberries
2 teaspoons paprika
4 (12-ounce) bone-in split chicken breasts, trimmed and halved crosswise

1. Adjust oven rack to upper-middle position and heat oven to 475 degrees. Whisk oil, sage, honey, salt, and pepper in large bowl until well combined. In separate bowl, whisk yogurt, water, minced garlic, orange zest, and 1 tablespoon oil mixture together; set yogurt sauce aside for serving.

4 (12-ounce) bone-in split chicken breasts, trimmed
1 teaspoon table salt, divided
½ teaspoon pepper
2 oranges
2 tablespoons harissa
1 tablespoon lemon juice
1 pound carrots, peeled and shredded
1 (15-ounce) can chickpeas, rinsed
3 ounces feta cheese, cut into ½-inch pieces (¾ cup)
2 tablespoons minced fresh mint
2 tablespoons extra-virgin olive oil

Chicken with Spiced Freekeh,
Cilantro, and Preserved Lemon

Chicken with Spiced Freekeh, Cilantro, and Preserved Lemon

INSTANT POT

Serves 4
Total Time 1 hour

Why This Recipe Works Smoky, earthy freekeh shines in this pressure cooker chicken dinner. Cooking the grain under pressure together with the chicken—as well as chicken broth bolstered with spices—upped the savoriness. Cilantro added freshness, sesame seeds lent texture, and preserved lemon brought intense brightness. You can find freekeh in the grain aisle or natural foods section of most well-stocked supermarkets; it is sometimes spelled frikeh or farik. Do not substitute whole freekeh in this dish, as it requires a different cooking method and will not work in this recipe. We think the fragrant and floral notes of preserved lemon are an important addition to this dish, but if you can't find it you can substitute 1 tablespoon lemon zest. Serve with yogurt.

  2 tablespoons extra-virgin olive oil,
     plus extra for drizzling
  1 onion, chopped fine
  4 garlic cloves, minced
  2 teaspoons smoked paprika
  ¼ teaspoon ground cardamom
  ¼ teaspoon red pepper flakes
  2¼ cups chicken broth
  1½ cups cracked freekeh, rinsed
  4 (12-ounce) bone-in split chicken breasts,
     trimmed and halved crosswise
  ½ teaspoon table salt
  ¼ teaspoon pepper
  ¼ cup chopped fresh cilantro
  2 tablespoons sesame seeds, toasted
  ½ preserved lemon, pulp and white pith removed,
     rind rinsed and minced (2 tablespoons)

1. Pound thicker end of chicken breasts between 2 sheets of plastic wrap to ¾- to 1-inch thickness. Pat chicken dry with paper towels and sprinkle with ½ teaspoon salt and pepper. Place chicken skin side down in cold 12-inch nonstick skillet. Cover skillet and place over medium heat. Cook chicken, without moving, until skin is light golden brown, about 15 minutes.

2. Meanwhile, cut away peel and pith from oranges. Holding fruit over bowl, use paring knife to slice between membranes to release segments. Cut segments in half crosswise and let drain in fine-mesh strainer set over large bowl, reserving juice. Whisk harissa, lemon juice, and remaining ½ teaspoon salt into reserved juice. Add orange segments and carrots and toss to combine; set aside.

3. Increase heat to medium-high and continue to cook chicken, covered, until skin is deep golden brown and crispy and breasts register 160 degrees, 10 to 15 minutes, rotating skillet halfway through cooking. Transfer chicken skin side up to serving platter, tent with aluminum foil, and let rest for 5 minutes.

4. Drain salad in fine-mesh strainer and return to now-empty bowl. Stir in chickpeas, feta, mint, and oil and season with salt and pepper to taste. Serve with chicken.

1. Using highest sauté or browning function, heat oil in electric pressure cooker until shimmering. Add onion and cook until softened, 3 to 5 minutes. Stir in garlic, paprika, cardamom, and pepper flakes and cook until fragrant, about 30 seconds. Stir in broth and freekeh. Sprinkle chicken with salt and pepper. Nestle skin side up into freekeh mixture. Lock lid in place and close pressure release valve. Select high pressure cook function and cook for 5 minutes.

2. Turn off pressure cooker and quick-release pressure. Carefully remove lid, allowing steam to escape away from you. Transfer chicken to serving platter and discard skin, if desired. Tent with aluminum foil and let rest while finishing freekeh.

3. Gently fluff freekeh with fork. Lay clean dish towel over pot, replace lid, and let sit for 5 minutes. Season with salt and pepper to taste. Transfer freekeh to serving platter with chicken and sprinkle with cilantro, sesame seeds, and preserved lemon. Drizzle with extra oil and serve.

Lemon-Oregano Chicken with Warm Tabbouleh Salad

SLOW COOKER

Serves 4
Cook Time 2 to 3 hours on low

Why This Recipe Works Most grains require much more time than quick-cooking chicken breasts do to become tender enough to eat, but using the slow cooker allowed us to time everything just right. The result was perfectly tender chicken and bulgur, which is one of the few hearty grains that can cook in the slow cooker without breaking down and becoming gummy. Rubbing the chicken with an aromatic mixture of garlic, oregano, and lemon zest seasoned not only the chicken but also the bulgur as it cooked. We drained the bulgur at the end of cooking to remove excess liquid. Looking to enhance the bright, fresh flavors of the chicken, we turned the bulgur into a vibrant tabbouleh salad by seasoning it with olive oil, lemon juice, parsley, and tomatoes. A quick, tangy yogurt sauce with even more herbs and lemon was the perfect finishing touch. When shopping, don't confuse bulgur with cracked wheat, which needs a much longer cooking time and will not work in this recipe. You will need a 5- to 7-quart oval slow cooker for this recipe. Check the chicken's temperature after 2 hours of cooking and continue to monitor until it registers 160 degrees.

- 1 cup medium-grind bulgur, rinsed
- 1 cup chicken broth
- 1 teaspoon table salt, divided
- 3 tablespoons extra-virgin olive oil, divided
- 4 teaspoons minced fresh oregano, divided
- 1¼ teaspoons grated lemon zest, divided, plus 3 tablespoons juice
- 1 garlic clove, minced
- ¼ teaspoon pepper
- 4 (12-ounce) bone-in split chicken breasts, skin removed, trimmed
- ½ cup plain Greek yogurt
- ½ cup minced fresh parsley, divided
- 3 tablespoons water
- 8 ounces cherry tomatoes, quartered

Lemon-Oregano Chicken with Warm Tabbouleh Salad

1. Lightly coat slow cooker with vegetable oil spray. Combine bulgur, broth, and ¼ teaspoon salt in slow cooker. Microwave 1 tablespoon oil, 1 tablespoon oregano, 1 teaspoon lemon zest, garlic, ½ teaspoon salt, and pepper in bowl until fragrant, about 30 seconds; let cool slightly. Rub chicken with oregano mixture, then arrange skinned side up in even layer in prepared slow cooker. Cover and cook until chicken registers 160 degrees, 2 to 3 hours on low.

2. Whisk yogurt, 1 tablespoon parsley, water, remaining 1 teaspoon oregano, remaining ¼ teaspoon lemon zest, and remaining ¼ teaspoon salt together in bowl. Season with salt and pepper to taste.

3. Transfer chicken to serving platter, brushing any bulgur that sticks to breasts back into slow cooker. Drain bulgur mixture, if necessary, and return to now-empty slow cooker. Add tomatoes, lemon juice, remaining 7 tablespoons parsley, and remaining 2 tablespoons oil and fluff with fork to combine. Season with salt and pepper to taste. Serve chicken with tabbouleh and yogurt sauce.

Pulled Chicken Sandwiches with Sweet and Tangy Coleslaw

DUTCH OVEN
Serves 6 to 8
Total Time 1½ hours

Why This Recipe Works Slow-cooked on a grill, pulled chicken has incredible smoky flavor. The time and effort required means that this dish is often reserved for entertaining, so we wanted an indoor version with the texture and flavor of outdoor slow-smoked pulled chicken in a fraction of the time. We started by braising boneless, skinless chicken thighs in chicken broth, salt, sugar, molasses, gelatin, and liquid smoke, which replicated the smoky flavor of the grill. The gelatin and broth helped mimic the unctuous texture and intense chicken flavor of whole chicken parts. For richness, we skipped trimming the fat from the thighs and added the rendered fat back to the finished chicken. Finally, we mixed the shredded meat with some of the barbecue sauce and cooked it briefly to drive off excess moisture. Do not trim the fat from the chicken thighs; it contributes to the flavor and texture of the pulled chicken. If you don't have 3 tablespoons of fat to add back to the pot in step 3, add melted butter to make up the difference. We like mild molasses in this recipe; do not use blackstrap.

Coleslaw
- 2 tablespoons cider vinegar
- 2 tablespoons extra-virgin olive oil
- 2 tablespoons sugar
- 4 cups shredded red or green cabbage

Sauce
- 1½ cups ketchup
- ¼ cup molasses
- 2 tablespoons Worcestershire sauce
- 1 tablespoon hot sauce
- ½ teaspoon table salt
- ½ teaspoon pepper

Chicken
- 1 cup chicken broth
- 2 tablespoons molasses
- 1 tablespoon sugar
- 1 tablespoon liquid smoke, divided
- 1 teaspoon unflavored gelatin
- 1 teaspoon table salt
- 2 pounds boneless, skinless chicken thighs, halved crosswise
  Hot sauce
- 6–8 hamburger buns

1. For the coleslaw Whisk vinegar, oil, and sugar in large bowl until sugar has dissolved; add cabbage and toss to combine; set aside for serving.

2. For the sauce Whisk all ingredients together in bowl; set aside.

3. For the chicken Bring broth, molasses, sugar, 2 teaspoons liquid smoke, gelatin, and salt to boil in large Dutch oven over high heat, stirring to dissolve sugar. Add chicken and return to simmer. Reduce heat to medium-low, cover, and cook, stirring occasionally, until chicken is easily shredded with fork, about 25 minutes.

4. Transfer chicken to medium bowl and set aside. Strain cooking liquid through fine-mesh strainer into fat separator (do not wash pot). Let liquid settle for 5 minutes; skim fat from surface using wide, shallow spoon. Set aside fat and defatted liquid.

5. Using tongs, squeeze chicken until shredded into bite-size pieces. Transfer chicken, 1 cup sauce, ½ cup reserved defatted liquid, 3 tablespoons reserved fat, and remaining 1 teaspoon liquid smoke to now-empty pot. Cook mixture over medium heat, stirring frequently, until liquid has been absorbed and exterior of meat appears dry, about 5 minutes. Season with salt, pepper, and hot sauce to taste.

6. Toss coleslaw to recombine and season with salt and pepper to taste. Serve chicken on buns, topped with coleslaw, passing remaining sauce separately.

Shredded Chicken Tacos

DUTCH OVEN
Serves 4
Total Time 45 minutes

Why This Recipe Works Braising in a Dutch oven is often a long, slow cooking process, but this technique is also well suited for quick weeknight-friendly dinners such as this flavor-packed chicken taco filling. We built a well-balanced braising base with smoky chipotle in adobo, aromatic garlic and cilantro, bright orange juice, and savory Worcestershire sauce. Nestling chicken breasts right into the pot imbued both the braising liquid and the chicken with bold flavor; covering the pot during the brief cook time ensured that the chicken cooked evenly. Once the chicken was done, we reduced the braising liquid into an easy sauce right in the Dutch oven. A little mustard thickened the sauce and provided a sharp counterpoint to the sweet orange juice. Finally, we shredded and sauced the chicken and spooned it into warm tortillas. Serve with shredded cheese, shredded lettuce, chopped tomatoes, diced avocado, and sour cream. For more information on warming tortillas, see page 116.

Shredded Chicken Tacos

3. Meanwhile, increase heat to medium-high and cook liquid left in pot until reduced to ¼ cup, about 5 minutes. Off heat, whisk in mustard. Add chicken and remaining ¼ cup cilantro and toss to combine. Season with salt and pepper to taste. Serve with tortillas and lime wedges.

Easy Tomatillo Chicken Soft Tacos
SLOW COOKER
Serves 6
Cook Time 4 to 6 hours on low

Why This Recipe Works The slow cooker offers a hands-off, easy cooking method for these simple chicken tacos. Cooking the chicken for our taco filling in store-bought tomatillo salsa flavored it in a big way without the time-consuming prep necessary for fresh tomatillos. Fresh poblano chiles lent a little heat to the sauce and created a more complex flavor profile than salsa alone, and a small amount of oregano enhanced and deepened the flavors even further. We found that boneless chicken thighs worked best here; they required little prep and after 4 to 6 hours in the slow cooker they were meltingly tender and easily shredded. Finishing with a little lime juice and cilantro added fresh flavor. Jarred tomatillo salsa is also called salsa verde. We don't discard any of the cooking liquid, as it helps season the chicken and keep the filling moist; a slotted spoon works best for serving the filling. Serve with lime wedges, diced avocado, queso fresco, and/or sour cream. For more information on warming tortillas, see page 116.

3 tablespoons unsalted butter
4 garlic cloves, minced
2 teaspoons minced canned chipotle chile in
    adobo sauce
¾ cup chopped fresh cilantro, divided
½ cup orange juice
1 tablespoon Worcestershire sauce
1½ pounds boneless, skinless chicken breasts, trimmed
1 teaspoon yellow mustard
    Salt and pepper
12 (6-inch) flour tortillas, warmed
    Lime wedges

1. Melt butter in Dutch oven over medium-high heat. Add garlic and chipotle and cook until fragrant, about 30 seconds. Stir in ½ cup cilantro, orange juice, and Worcestershire and bring to simmer. Nestle chicken into pot. Reduce heat to medium-low, cover, and cook until chicken registers 160 degrees, about 15 minutes, flipping chicken halfway through cooking.

2. Transfer chicken to cutting board, let cool slightly, then shred into bite-size pieces using 2 forks.

1 cup jarred tomatillo or tomato salsa
2 poblano chiles, stemmed, seeded, and chopped
¼ teaspoon table salt
¼ teaspoon pepper
1 teaspoon minced fresh oregano or ¼ teaspoon dried
3 pounds boneless, skinless chicken thighs, trimmed
¼ cup minced fresh cilantro
2 tablespoons lime juice
18 (6-inch) flour tortillas, warmed

1. Combine salsa, poblanos, salt, pepper, and oregano in slow cooker. Nestle chicken into slow cooker, cover, and cook until tender, 4 to 6 hours on low.

2. Using tongs, break chicken into bite-size pieces. Stir in cilantro and lime juice and season with salt and pepper to taste. Serve with tortillas.

Easy Tomatillo Chicken Soft Tacos for Two

SLOW COOKER

Serves 2

Cook Time 4 to 6 hours on low

We don't discard any of the cooking liquid, as it helps season the chicken and keep the filling moist; a slotted spoon works best for serving the filling. Serve with lime wedges, diced avocado, queso fresco, and/or sour cream.

- ½ cup jarred tomatillo or tomato salsa
- 1 poblano chile, stemmed, seeded, and chopped
- ⅛ teaspoon table salt
- ⅛ teaspoon pepper
- ½ teaspoon minced fresh oregano or ⅛ teaspoon dried
- 1 pound boneless, skinless chicken thighs, trimmed
- 2 tablespoons minced fresh cilantro
- 1 tablespoon lime juice
- 6 (6-inch) flour tortillas, warmed

1. Combine salsa, poblano, salt, pepper, and oregano in slow cooker. Nestle chicken into slow cooker, cover, and cook until tender, 4 to 6 hours on low.

2. Using tongs, break chicken into bite-size pieces. Stir in cilantro and lime juice and season with salt and pepper to taste. Serve with tortillas.

NOTES FROM THE TEST KITCHEN

WARMING TORTILLAS

Warming tortillas to soften them is crucial. If your tortillas are dry, pat each with a little water before warming them. Wrap warmed tortillas in aluminum foil or a clean dish towel to keep them warm and soft.

On the Stovetop Work with one tortilla at a time. For a gas stove, place the tortilla over a medium flame until slightly charred, about 30 seconds per side. For an electric stove, toast the tortilla in a skillet over medium-high heat until it is softened and speckled with brown spots, 20 to 30 seconds per side. Transfer the toasted tortillas to a plate and cover with a dish towel to keep them warm.

In the Oven Wrap up to six tortillas in aluminum foil and place them in a 350-degree oven for about 5 minutes. To keep the tortillas warm, simply leave them wrapped in foil until ready to use.

Teriyaki Chicken Thighs with Sesame Vegetables

SHEET PAN

Serves 4

Total Time 1¼ hours

Why This Recipe Works We wanted a fresh take on teriyaki that would yield crispy chicken in a sweet, sticky sauce. Sheet-pan roasting proved ideal: We could crisp the chicken before applying a glaze while simultaneously preparing a vegetable "stir-fry" in the same pan. We browned chicken thighs in the oven, slashing the skin and placing them on a wire rack to allow the rendered fat to drain away. We tossed sliced bell pepper and mushrooms with garlic and ginger and spread them alongside the chicken to roast. Snap peas went in 10 minutes later so they wouldn't overcook. Briefly broiling everything crisped the thighs' skin further. As for the teriyaki sauce, a few pantry items did the trick, and we thickened it in the microwave before brushing it on our chicken. Depending on your wire rack, you may need to place parchment paper underneath the vegetables to prevent them from falling through.

- 8 (5- to 7-ounce) bone-in chicken thighs, trimmed
- 2 tablespoons vegetable oil, divided
- 1 red bell pepper, stemmed, seeded, and cut into ¼-inch-wide strips
- 8 ounces shiitake mushrooms, stemmed and sliced thin
- 3 garlic cloves, minced, divided
- 1 tablespoon grated fresh ginger, divided
- 8 ounces snap peas, strings removed
- 5 tablespoons mirin
- 5 tablespoons soy sauce
- ¼ cup water
- 3 tablespoons sugar
- 2 teaspoons cornstarch
- ⅛ teaspoon red pepper flakes
- 1 tablespoon toasted sesame oil
- 1 tablespoon toasted sesame seeds
- ½ teaspoon table salt

1. Adjust 1 oven rack to lower-middle position and second rack 8 inches from broiler element. Heat oven to 450 degrees. Set wire rack in rimmed baking sheet lined with aluminum foil. Make 3 diagonal slashes through skin of each thigh with sharp knife (do not cut into meat). Brush chicken with 1 tablespoon vegetable oil. Lay chicken skin side up on half of prepared rack and roast for 20 minutes.

2. Toss bell pepper and mushrooms with remaining 1 tablespoon vegetable oil, half of garlic, and 1½ teaspoons ginger. Spread vegetables over empty side of rack. Rotate rack and continue to roast for 10 minutes. Sprinkle snap peas over vegetables and continue to roast until chicken registers 165 degrees and vegetables start to brown, about 10 minutes.

3. Remove sheet from oven and heat broiler. Place sheet on upper rack and broil until chicken and vegetables are well browned and chicken registers 175 degrees, 3 to 5 minutes. Meanwhile, combine mirin, soy sauce, water, sugar, cornstarch, pepper flakes, remaining garlic, and remaining 1½ teaspoons ginger in bowl and microwave, whisking occasionally, until thickened, 3 to 5 minutes.

4. Remove sheet from oven, brush chicken with 3 tablespoons sauce, and let rest for 5 minutes. Transfer vegetables to clean bowl, toss with sesame oil, sesame seeds, and salt. Serve vegetables and chicken with remaining sauce.

Chicken Leg Quarters with Cauliflower and Shallots

SHEET PAN
Serves 4
Total Time 1 hour

Why This Recipe Works A sadly underutilized cut, chicken leg quarters take to roasting like a duck to water, growing tender as they cook while the skin crisps up beautifully. For our one-pan supper, we paired them with cauliflower, which also shines when roasted. Deeply slashing the chicken helped the seasonings (garlic, lemon zest, sage) to penetrate the meat and the fat to render for crispier skin. Arranging the chicken around the pan's edges exposed it to the oven's heat and protected the cauliflower from drying out; the chicken's juices helped soften the cauliflower. Toward the end of cooking, we scattered grape tomatoes over the cauliflower for color and juicy bursts of acidity, and then used the broiler to impart pleasant charring. Some leg quarters are sold with the backbone attached; removing it before cooking makes the chicken easier to serve. If you substitute cherry tomatoes for grape tomatoes, halve them before adding to the pan.

1 head cauliflower (2 pounds), cored and cut into
   8 wedges through stem
6 shallots, peeled and halved
¼ cup extra-virgin olive oil, divided
2 tablespoons chopped fresh sage or 2 teaspoons
   dried, divided
1 teaspoon table salt, divided
1 teaspoon pepper, divided
4 (10-ounce) chicken leg quarters, trimmed
2 garlic cloves, minced

Chicken Leg Quarters with Cauliflower and Shallots

1 teaspoon grated lemon zest, plus lemon wedges
   for serving
8 ounces grape tomatoes
1 tablespoon chopped fresh parsley

1. Adjust 1 oven rack to lower-middle position and second rack 6 inches from broiler element. Heat oven to 475 degrees. Gently toss cauliflower and shallots with 2 tablespoons oil, 1 tablespoon sage, ½ teaspoon salt, and ½ teaspoon pepper on rimmed baking sheet. Arrange cauliflower pieces cut side down in single layer in center of sheet.

2. Pat chicken dry with paper towels. Make 4 diagonal slashes through skin and meat of each leg quarter with sharp knife (each slash should reach bone). Sprinkle chicken with remaining ½ teaspoon salt and remaining ½ teaspoon pepper. Place each piece of chicken skin side up in 1 corner of sheet; rest chicken directly on sheet, not on vegetables.

3. Whisk garlic, lemon zest, remaining 2 tablespoons oil, and remaining 1 tablespoon sage together in bowl. Brush skin side of chicken with seasoned oil mixture. Transfer sheet to lower rack and roast until chicken registers 175 degrees, cauliflower is browned, and shallots are tender, 25 to 30 minutes, rotating sheet halfway through roasting.

4. Remove sheet from oven and heat broiler. Scatter tomatoes over vegetables. Place sheet on upper rack and broil until chicken skin is browned and crisp and tomatoes have begun to wilt, 3 to 5 minutes.

5. Remove sheet from oven and let rest for 5 minutes. Sprinkle with parsley and serve with lemon wedges.

Peruvian Roast Chicken Leg Quarters with Swiss Chard and Sweet Potatoes

ROASTING PAN

Serves 6

Total Time 1¾ hours, plus 1 hour marinating

Why This Recipe Works One of the world's great roast chickens, pollo a la brasa, boasts a bronzed exterior seasoned with a paste of garlic, spices, lime juice, chile, and mint. Lacking the spit traditionally used to roast the bird whole, we used leg quarters instead. They fit neatly in a roasting pan and yielded bronzed skin coated in a bold, flavorful paste. We smeared the paste over and under the skin before letting the chicken rest to allow the flavors to meld. We used our roasting pan to brown sweet potatoes before arranging the chicken on top and roasting both, allowing the chicken drippings to baste the potatoes. We then removed the chicken and potatoes to rest while we cooked Swiss chard in the rich juices left behind. Some leg quarters are sold with the backbone attached; removing it before cooking makes the chicken easier to serve. You can substitute 1 tablespoon of minced serrano chile for the habanero, if desired. Wear gloves when handling the chile.

¼ cup fresh mint leaves
10 garlic cloves (5 chopped, 5 sliced), divided
¼ cup extra-virgin olive oil, divided
1 tablespoon ground cumin
1 tablespoon honey
2 teaspoons smoked paprika
2 teaspoons dried oregano
2 teaspoons grated lime zest plus ¼ cup juice (2 limes), plus lime wedges for serving
2 teaspoons pepper
1¾ teaspoons table salt, divided
1 teaspoon minced habanero chile
6 (10-ounce) chicken leg quarters, trimmed
3 pounds sweet potatoes, peeled, ends trimmed, and sliced into 1-inch-thick rounds
4 pounds Swiss chard, stemmed and cut into 1-inch pieces
2 tablespoons minced fresh cilantro

Peruvian Roast Chicken Leg Quarters with Swiss Chard and Sweet Potatoes

1. Adjust oven rack to middle position and heat oven to 425 degrees. Process mint, chopped garlic, 1 tablespoon oil, cumin, honey, paprika, oregano, lime zest and juice, pepper, 1 teaspoon salt, and habanero in blender until smooth, 20 seconds.

2. Using your fingers, gently loosen skin covering thighs and drumsticks and spread half of paste directly on meat. Spread remaining half of paste over exterior of chicken. Place chicken in 1-gallon zipper-lock bag and refrigerate for at least 1 hour or up to 24 hours.

3. Toss potatoes with 1 tablespoon oil and ½ teaspoon salt. Heat remaining 2 tablespoons oil in 16 by 12-inch roasting pan over medium-high heat (over 2 burners, if possible) until shimmering. Add potatoes cut side down and cook until well browned on first side, 6 to 8 minutes.

4. Off heat, flip potatoes and lay chicken skin side up on top. Roast until chicken registers 175 degrees and potatoes are tender, 40 to 50 minutes, rotating pan halfway through roasting.

5. Remove pan from oven. Transfer potatoes and chicken to serving platter, tent with aluminum foil, and let rest for 5 minutes. Being careful of hot pan handles, pour off all but ¼ cup liquid left in pan. Add sliced garlic and cook over high heat (over 2 burners, if possible) until fragrant, about

30 seconds. Add chard and remaining ¼ teaspoon salt and cook, stirring constantly, until chard is wilted and tender, about 8 minutes; transfer to serving bowl.

6. Sprinkle cilantro over chicken and potatoes and serve with chard and lime wedges.

Chicken Thighs with Lentils and Butternut Squash

INSTANT POT
Serves 4
Total Time 1¼ hours

Why This Recipe Works Inspired by the vibrant spices featured in North African fare, this dish of rich, tender chicken paired with stewed lentils and butternut squash all cooks to perfection thanks to the heat of the pressure cooker, which renders the lentils and squash tender much more quickly than stovetop cooking or roasting. We started by blooming a mixture of warm, floral spices to infuse the lentils as they cooked. Next we stirred in the lentils, broth, and butternut squash, and nestled the chicken in before cooking under pressure until the squash softened and melted into the lentils, its sweetness tempering the vegetal legumes. We made a quick salad from parsley leaves and shallot with a lemon vinaigrette. The brightness of the leafy green herbs and the subtle sharpness of the shallot tied the whole dish together and provided a nice contrast to the soft, earthy lentils. We prefer French green lentils, or lentilles du Puy, for this recipe, but it will work with any type of lentil except red or yellow.

    2   large shallots, halved and sliced thin, divided
    5   teaspoons extra-virgin olive oil, divided
    ½   teaspoon grated lemon zest plus 2 teaspoons juice
    1   teaspoon table salt, divided
    8   (5- to 7-ounce) bone-in chicken thighs, trimmed
    ¼   teaspoon pepper
    2   garlic cloves, minced
    1½ teaspoons caraway seeds
    1   teaspoon ground coriander
    1   teaspoon ground cumin
    ½   teaspoon paprika
    ⅛   teaspoon cayenne pepper
    2   cups chicken broth
    1   cup French green lentils, picked over and rinsed
    2   pounds butternut squash, peeled, seeded, and cut into 1½-inch pieces (6 cups)
    1   cup fresh parsley or cilantro leaves

1. Combine half of shallots, 1 tablespoon oil, lemon zest and juice, and ¼ teaspoon salt in bowl; set aside. Pat chicken dry with paper towels and sprinkle with ½ teaspoon salt and pepper. Using highest sauté or browning function, heat remaining 2 teaspoons oil in electric pressure cooker until just smoking. Place chicken skin side down in pot and cook until well browned on first side, about 5 minutes; transfer to plate.

2. Add remaining shallot and remaining ¼ teaspoon salt to fat left in pressure cooker and cook, using highest sauté or browning function, until shallot is softened, about 2 minutes. Stir in garlic, caraway, coriander, cumin, paprika, and cayenne and cook until fragrant, about 30 seconds. Stir in broth, scraping up any browned bits, then stir in lentils.

3. Nestle chicken skin side up into lentils and add any accumulated juices. Arrange squash on top. Lock lid in place and close pressure release valve. Select high pressure cook function and cook for 16 minutes.

4. Turn off pressure cooker and quick-release pressure. Carefully remove lid, allowing steam to escape away from you. Transfer chicken to plate and discard skin, if desired. Season lentil mixture with salt and pepper to taste. Add parsley to shallot mixture and toss to combine. Serve chicken with lentil mixture, topping individual portions with shallot-parsley salad.

PREPARING BUTTERNUT SQUASH

1. Lop ends off squash and use chef's knife to cut it into 2 pieces where bulb meets neck.

2. Use vegetable peeler to peel away skin and fibrous yellow flesh down to bright orange flesh.

3. Halve bulb end, then scoop out and discard seeds and pulp. Cut or slice into pieces as directed in recipe.

BRAISED CHICKEN THIGHS WITH TOMATOES AND MUSHROOMS

We were inspired by Italian cacciatore to create a dish of long-simmered chicken paired with rustic ingredients and earthy flavors. Umami-rich portobello mushrooms and tomato paste heightened the meaty notes, and garlic and thyme lent a flavorful backbone. Cooking bone-in chicken thighs (chicken leg quarters or drumsticks also work well for this recipe) in a combination of red wine, broth, and diced tomatoes yielded moist, well-seasoned chicken. A Dutch oven is the classic choice for braised dishes, as its ability to conduct and retain heat results in perfectly tender meat with robust flavors. But we found that we could shave off some of the long braising time using the heat of the pressure cooker. Or turn this dish into a low-and-slow hands-off meal with the slow cooker. Browning the chicken in the Dutch oven and pressure cooker versions rendered some of the fat, which we used to cook the aromatics, mushrooms, and onions for deep, meaty flavor. Since browning is impossible in the slow cooker, we instead microwaved these ingredients to release some of their flavor.

CLASSIC

DUTCH OVEN
Serves 4
Total Time 2 hours

- 8 (5- to 7-ounce) bone-in chicken thighs, trimmed
- 1 teaspoon table salt, divided
- ¼ teaspoon pepper
- 1 tablespoon extra-virgin olive oil
- 1 pound portobello mushroom caps, gills removed, caps halved and sliced ½ inch thick
- 1 onion, chopped
- 2 tablespoons tomato paste
- 1½ tablespoons all-purpose flour
- 4 garlic cloves, minced
- 2 teaspoons minced fresh thyme or ½ teaspoon dried
- 1½ cups dry red wine
- ½ cup chicken broth
- 1 (14.5-ounce) can diced tomatoes, drained
- 2 tablespoons chopped fresh parsley

1. Adjust oven rack to lower-middle position and heat oven to 300 degrees. Pat chicken dry with paper towels and sprinkle with ½ teaspoon salt and pepper. Heat oil in Dutch oven over medium-high heat until just smoking. Cook half of chicken skin side down until well browned, about 5 minutes; transfer chicken skin side up to plate. Repeat with remaining chicken; transfer to plate.

2. Pour off all but 1 tablespoon fat from pot. Add mushrooms, onion, and remaining ½ teaspoon salt to fat left in pot. Partially cover and cook until mushrooms are softened and have released their liquid, about 5 minutes. Stir in tomato paste, flour, garlic, and thyme and cook until fragrant, about 1 minute. Slowly whisk in wine, scraping up any browned bits and smoothing out any lumps.

3. Stir in broth and tomatoes and bring to simmer. Nestle thighs into pot and add any accumulated juices. Cover, transfer pot to oven, and cook until chicken registers at least 195 degrees, about 1 hour.

4. Remove pot from oven and transfer chicken to serving platter. Discard skin, if desired. Stir parsley into sauce and season with salt and pepper to taste. Spoon sauce over chicken and serve.

MAKE IT YOUR WAY
→

> **Use What You've Got** Substitute chicken leg quarters or chicken drumsticks for chicken thighs. Substitute white wine for red wine, vegetable broth for chicken broth, fire-roasted tomatoes for traditional tomatoes, and/or fresh herbs (basil, dill, cilantro) for parsley.

PRESSURE COOK IT

INSTANT POT
Serves 4
Total Time 1¼ hours

- 8 (5- to 7-ounce) bone-in chicken thighs, trimmed
- 1 teaspoon table salt, divided
- ½ teaspoon pepper
- 2 teaspoons extra-virgin olive oil
- 1 pound portobello mushroom caps, gills removed, caps halved and sliced ½ inch thick
- 1 onion, chopped
- 2 tablespoons tomato paste
- 1 tablespoon all-purpose flour
- 4 garlic cloves, minced
- 1 tablespoon minced fresh thyme or 1 teaspoon dried
- ½ cup dry red wine
- ½ cup chicken broth
- 1 (14.5-ounce) can diced tomatoes, drained
- 2 tablespoons chopped fresh parsley

1. Pat chicken dry with paper towels and sprinkle with ½ teaspoon salt and pepper. Using highest sauté or browning function, heat oil in electric pressure cooker until just smoking. Cook half of chicken skin side down until well browned, about 5 minutes; transfer to plate.

2. Add mushrooms, onion, and remaining ½ teaspoon salt to fat left in pressure cooker. Partially cover and cook, using highest sauté or browning function, until mushrooms are softened and have released their liquid, about 5 minutes. Stir in tomato paste, flour, garlic, and thyme and cook until fragrant, about 1 minute. Slowly whisk in wine, scraping up any browned bits and smoothing out any lumps.

3. Stir in broth and tomatoes. Nestle browned thighs and remaining uncooked thighs into pressure cooker and add any accumulated juices. Lock lid in place and close pressure release valve. Select high pressure cook function; cook for 9 minutes.

4. Turn off pressure cooker and quick-release pressure. Carefully remove lid, allowing steam to escape away from you. Transfer chicken to serving platter. Discard skin, if desired. Tent with aluminum foil and let rest while finishing sauce.

5. Using highest sauté or browning function, bring sauce to simmer and cook until thickened slightly, about 8 minutes. Turn off pressure cooker. Stir in parsley and season with salt and pepper to taste. Spoon sauce over chicken and serve.

> **Bulk it Up** Include chopped bacon, and/or chopped pancetta with onion. Add diced hearty vegetables (butternut squash, celery root, fennel, parsnips). Stir thawed frozen vegetables into sauce before parsley and let sit until heated through, about 2 minutes.

SLOW COOK IT

SLOW COOKER
Serves 4
Cook Time 4 to 6 hours on low

- 1 pound portobello mushroom caps, gills removed, caps halved and sliced ½ inch thick
- 1 onion, chopped
- ¼ cup tomato paste
- 2 tablespoons all-purpose flour
- 4 garlic cloves, minced
- 1 tablespoon extra-virgin olive oil
- 2 teaspoons minced fresh thyme or ½ teaspoon dried
- 1 teaspoon table salt, divided
- ¼ cup dry red wine
- ½ cup chicken broth
- 1 (14.5-ounce) can diced tomatoes, drained
- 8 (5- to 7-ounce) bone-in chicken thighs, skin removed, trimmed
- ½ teaspoon pepper
- 2 tablespoons minced fresh parsley

1. Microwave mushrooms, onion, tomato paste, flour, garlic, oil, thyme, and ½ teaspoon salt in bowl, stirring occasionally, until vegetables are softened and mushrooms release their liquid, 6 to 8 minutes; transfer to slow cooker. Slowly whisk in wine, smoothing out any lumps. Stir in broth and tomatoes. Sprinkle chicken with remaining ½ teaspoon salt and pepper and nestle into slow cooker. Cover and cook until chicken is tender, 4 to 6 hours on low.

2. Transfer chicken to serving platter. Stir parsley into sauce and season with salt and pepper to taste. Spoon sauce over chicken and serve.

> **Add an Upgrade** Add spice blends (chili powder, garam masala, ras el hanout, herbes de Provence), minced anchovies, and/or strips citrus zest in place of—or in addition to—thyme. Finish with extra-virgin olive oil, harissa, pesto, olives, or grated Parmesan or Asiago.

Lemony Chicken Thighs with Fingerling Potatoes and Olives

Lemony Chicken Thighs with Fingerling Potatoes and Olives

INSTANT POT

Serves 4

Total Time 1 hour

Why This Recipe Works In this simple dish, the pressure cooker turns out tender, juicy chicken thighs and delicate fingerling potatoes that absorb the appealing aromas of garlic, lemon, and olives. After browning the chicken thighs, we toasted some garlic cloves and added chicken broth and sliced lemon before returning the browned chicken to the pot and layering potatoes on top. After cooking it all under pressure, we especially loved the supple texture of the lemon slices, which melted into the sauce. Olives, fresh parsley, and a drizzle of olive oil were the perfect finish. Look for potatoes that are approximately 1 inch in diameter. Slice the lemon as thinly as possible; this allows the pieces to melt into the sauce.

8 (5- to 7-ounce) bone-in chicken thighs, trimmed
½ teaspoon table salt
¼ teaspoon pepper
2 teaspoons extra-virgin olive oil, plus extra for drizzling
4 garlic cloves, peeled and smashed
½ cup chicken broth
1 small lemon (½ quartered and sliced thin, ½ quartered for serving), divided
1½ pounds fingerling potatoes, unpeeled
¼ cup pitted brine-cured green or black olives, halved
2 tablespoons coarsely chopped fresh parsley

1. Pat chicken dry with paper towels and sprinkle with salt and pepper. Using highest sauté or browning function, heat oil in electric pressure cooker until just smoking. Place half of chicken skin side down in pot and cook until well browned on first side, about 5 minutes; transfer to plate. Repeat with remaining chicken; transfer to plate.

2. Add garlic to fat left in pressure cooker and cook, using highest sauté or browning function, until golden and fragrant, about 2 minutes. Stir in broth and sliced lemon, scraping up any browned bits. Return chicken skin side up to pressure cooker and add any accumulated juices. Arrange potatoes on top. Lock lid in place and close pressure release valve. Select high pressure cook function and cook for 10 minutes.

3. Turn off pressure cooker and quick-release pressure. Carefully remove lid, allowing steam to escape away from you. Transfer chicken to serving platter. Stir olives and parsley into potatoes and season with salt and pepper to taste. Serve chicken with potatoes and remaining lemon.

Chicken Tagine with Fennel, Chickpeas, and Apricots

Chicken Tagine with Fennel, Chickpeas, and Apricots

SKILLET
Serves 4
Total Time 1¾ hours

Why This Recipe Works While traditional spice blends for Moroccan tagines can contain upwards of 30 spices, we found just a few everyday spices were necessary to re-create the authentic notes of Moroccan chicken tagine in a simple skillet supper. We used skin-on chicken thighs and started by browning the meat. Next we browned fennel in the rendered fat and bloomed a blend of spicy, earthy, and warm ground spices and a whole cinnamon stick, which cooked with the dish and infused the whole thing with flavor. We added a few broad ribbons of lemon zest as well to give the tagine a rich citrus back note. Brine-cured olives provided the meatiness and piquant flavor of hard-to-find Moroccan ones, and some dried apricots, which plumped among the chickpeas and broth, created well-rounded sweetness for this well-spiced dish. Chopped parsley, stirred in right before serving, was the perfect finishing touch to freshen the flavors. You will need a 12-inch ovensafe skillet for this recipe.

- 2 tablespoons extra-virgin olive oil, divided, plus extra as needed
- 5 garlic cloves, minced
- 1½ teaspoons paprika
- ½ teaspoon ground turmeric
- ½ teaspoon ground cumin
- ¼ teaspoon ground ginger
- ¼ teaspoon cayenne pepper
- 2 (15-ounce) cans chickpeas, rinsed, divided
- 8 (5- to 7-ounce) bone-in chicken thighs, trimmed
- ¾ teaspoon table salt, divided
- ½ teaspoon pepper
- 1 large fennel bulb, stalks discarded, bulb halved and cut into ½-inch-thick wedges through core
- 3 (2-inch) strips lemon zest, plus lemon wedges for serving
- 1 cinnamon stick
- ½ cup dry white wine
- 1 cup chicken broth
- 1 cup pitted large brine-cured green or black olives, halved
- ½ cup dried apricots, halved
- 2 tablespoons chopped fresh parsley

1. Adjust oven rack to upper-middle position and heat oven to 350 degrees. Combine 1 tablespoon oil, garlic, paprika, turmeric, cumin, ginger, and cayenne in bowl; set aside. Place ½ cup chickpeas in second bowl and mash to coarse paste with potato masher.

2. Pat chicken dry with paper towels and sprinkle with ½ teaspoon salt and pepper. Heat remaining 1 tablespoon oil in 12-inch ovensafe skillet over medium-high heat until just smoking. Cook chicken skin side down until skin is crisped and well browned, 8 to 10 minutes; transfer chicken skin side up to plate.

3. Pour off all but 2 tablespoons fat from skillet. Heat fat left in skillet over medium heat until shimmering. Arrange fennel cut side down in skillet and sprinkle with remaining ¼ teaspoon salt. Cover and cook until lightly browned, 3 to 5 minutes per side. Push fennel to sides of skillet. Add spice mixture, lemon zest, and cinnamon stick to center and cook, mashing spice mixture into skillet, until fragrant, about 30 seconds. Stir spice mixture into fennel. Stir in wine, scraping up any browned bits, and cook until almost evaporated, about 2 minutes.

4. Stir in broth, olives, apricots, mashed chickpeas, and whole chickpeas and bring to simmer. Nestle chicken skin side up into skillet, keeping skin above liquid. Roast until fennel is tender and chicken registers 185 degrees, 35 to 40 minutes. Using pot holders, remove skillet from oven. Discard lemon zest and cinnamon stick. Season with salt and pepper to taste. Sprinkle with parsley and serve with lemon wedges.

Chicken and Rice with Caramelized Onions, Cardamom, and Raisins

DUTCH OVEN
Serves 6
Total Time 2 hours

Why This Recipe Works Inspired by the warming, complex spices used in traditional chicken biryani, we set out to make chicken and rice with Indian flair. After browning chicken thighs to boost their flavor, we created a darkly sweet base by caramelizing sliced onions with brown sugar. To that we added a bold, colorful array of spices—fresh ginger, cardamom, cumin, and saffron—and bloomed their flavors before adding our cooking liquid: chicken broth. Once the browned chicken had a chance to simmer in this richly flavored liquid, we stirred in the rice and moved the whole production to the oven to finish cooking in its gentle, even heat. After about 20 minutes and a few periodic stirs, the grains had taken on a golden hue and tender texture. We shredded the chicken for easier eating and stirred in some raisins and minced cilantro for bursts of sweetness and freshness. To keep the dish from becoming greasy, it is important to remove excess fat and most of the skin from the chicken thighs, leaving just enough skin to protect the meat. Be sure to stir the rice gently when cooking in step 3; aggressive stirring will make it gluey.

2½ pounds bone-in chicken thighs, trimmed
1 teaspoon table salt, divided
½ teaspoon pepper
1 tablespoon extra-virgin olive oil
3 onions, halved and sliced thin
1 teaspoon packed brown sugar
4 garlic cloves, minced
2 teaspoons grated fresh ginger
½ teaspoon ground cardamom
½ teaspoon ground cumin
⅛ teaspoon saffron threads, crumbled
1 teaspoon minced fresh thyme or ¼ teaspoon dried
2½ cups chicken broth
2 cups long-grain white rice, rinsed
⅓ cup raisins
3 tablespoons minced fresh cilantro
½ teaspoon grated lemon zest plus 4 teaspoons juice

1. Adjust oven rack to middle position and heat oven to 350 degrees. Pat chicken dry with paper towels and sprinkle with ½ teaspoon salt and pepper. Heat oil in Dutch oven over medium-high heat until just smoking. Cook half of chicken skin side down until well browned, about 5 minutes; transfer chicken skin side up to plate. Repeat with remaining chicken; transfer to plate.

2. Pour off all but 2 tablespoons fat from pot. Add onions, sugar, and remaining ½ teaspoon salt and cook over medium heat, stirring often, until onions are deep golden brown, 25 to 35 minutes. Stir in garlic, ginger, cardamom, cumin, saffron, and thyme and cook until fragrant, about 30 seconds. Stir in broth, scraping up any browned bits. Nestle chicken skin side up into pot and add any accumulated juices. Bring to simmer, then reduce heat to low, cover, and cook for 20 minutes.

3. Gently stir in rice. Cover, transfer pot to oven, and cook, stirring occasionally, until chicken registers 175 degrees, rice is tender, and liquid has been absorbed, 20 to 30 minutes.

4. Remove pot from oven and transfer chicken to cutting board; cover pot and set aside. Let chicken cool slightly, then shred into bite-size pieces using 2 forks; discard skin and bones. Gently stir shredded chicken, raisins, cilantro, and lemon zest and juice into rice, and season with salt and pepper to taste. Cover and let sit until chicken is heated through, about 5 minutes. Serve.

Chicken with Spiced Couscous and Carrots

SKILLET
Serves 4
Total Time 1 hour

Why This Recipe Works Potent harissa serves as the flavor backbone in this spiced skillet dish. Couscous cooks in a fraction of the time required for most grains and rice, so we centered the dish on this starch. Other ingredients common to North African cuisine, creamy chickpeas and sweet carrots, accompany the rich, savory, bronzed-skin chicken thighs. And of course, the deeply complex harissa easily flavors it all without us having to turn to a litany of spices, garlic, and oil. Searing the thighs first developed plenty of flavorful fond in the pan; after this step, we quickly braised them while the couscous cooked in the same pan. Finishing with lemon juice and fresh parsley brightened up this savory dish, which we served with more of the bold spice paste. Harissa is a traditional North African condiment made from a blend of hot chile peppers and can be found in the international aisle of most well-stocked supermarkets; spiciness will vary greatly by brand. If you can't find harissa, you can make your own (see page 39). You will need a 12-inch ovensafe skillet with a tight-fitting lid for this recipe. The couscous mixture will appear dry in step 3; do not add extra liquid as the chicken will release juices as it cooks.

8 (5- to 7-ounce) bone-in chicken thighs, trimmed
1½ teaspoons table salt, divided
1 teaspoon pepper, divided
1 tablespoon vegetable oil
1 pound carrots, peeled and cut into 2-inch lengths, thin pieces halved lengthwise, thick pieces quartered lengthwise
1 onion, chopped
1 (15-ounce) can chickpeas, rinsed
¾ cup water
2 tablespoons harissa, plus extra for serving
1 cup couscous
⅓ cup minced fresh parsley
2 tablespoons lemon juice

1. Adjust oven rack to middle position and heat oven to 450 degrees. Pat chicken dry with paper towels and sprinkle with ½ teaspoon salt and ½ teaspoon pepper. Heat oil in 12-inch ovensafe skillet over medium-high heat until just smoking. Cook chicken skin side down until well browned, about 5 minutes; transfer chicken skin side up to plate.

2. Pour off all but 1 tablespoon fat from skillet. Add carrots, onion, remaining 1 teaspoon salt, and remaining ½ teaspoon pepper and cook over medium heat until onion is softened, about 5 minutes. Stir in chickpeas, water, and harissa, scraping up any browned bits, and bring to boil.

3. Stir in couscous, scraping down any that sticks to sides of skillet. Nestle chicken skin side up into skillet and add any accumulated juices. Cover, transfer skillet to oven, and bake until chicken registers 175 degrees, 15 to 20 minutes.

4. Using pot holders, remove skillet from oven and transfer chicken to serving platter. Being careful of hot skillet handle, add parsley and lemon juice to couscous mixture and fluff with fork to combine. Season with salt and pepper to taste. Serve, passing extra harissa separately.

Arroz Con Pollo
DUTCH OVEN
Serves 6
Total Time 2 hours

Why This Recipe Works For a streamlined arroz con pollo full of classic flavors, we briefly marinated bone-in chicken thighs in a mixture of vinegar, salt, pepper, and oregano and then stewed the meat with tomato sauce, olives, capers, and rice until it became fall-off-the-bone tender. We started the chicken skin-on to take advantage of the flavorful rendered fat but removed the skin after cooking. Using spoons rather than forks to pull apart the cooked meat gave us appealing chunks instead of shreds. To keep the dish from becoming greasy, it is important to remove excess fat and most of the skin from the chicken thighs, leaving just enough skin to protect the meat. Long-grain rice can be substituted for the medium-grain rice; however, you will need to increase the amount of water to ¾ cup.

- 6 garlic cloves, minced
- 5 teaspoons distilled white vinegar, divided
- 1½ teaspoons minced fresh oregano or ¼ teaspoon dried
- 1¾ teaspoons table salt, divided
- ½ teaspoon pepper
- 4 pounds bone-in chicken thighs, trimmed
- 2 tablespoons extra-virgin olive oil, divided
- 1 onion, chopped fine
- 1 small green bell pepper, stemmed, seeded, and chopped fine
- ¼ teaspoon red pepper flakes
- ¼ cup minced fresh cilantro, divided
- 1¾ cups chicken broth

Arroz Con Pollo

- 1 (8-ounce) can tomato sauce
- ¼ cup water, plus extra as needed
- 3 cups medium-grain white rice
- ½ cup pitted brine-cured green olives, halved
- 1 tablespoon capers, rinsed
- ½ cup jarred whole pimentos, cut into 2 by ¼-inch strips
  Lemon wedges

1. Adjust oven rack to middle position and heat oven to 350 degrees. Combine garlic, 1 tablespoon vinegar, oregano, 1 teaspoon salt, and pepper in large bowl. Add chicken and toss to coat. Cover and let sit at room temperature for 15 minutes.

2. Meanwhile, heat 1 tablespoon oil in Dutch oven over medium heat until shimmering. Add onion and bell pepper and cook until softened, about 5 minutes. Stir in pepper flakes and cook until fragrant, about 30 seconds. Stir in 2 tablespoons cilantro.

3. Push vegetables to sides of pot and increase heat to medium-high. Add chicken skin side down to center of pot and cook on both sides, 2 to 4 minutes per side, reducing heat if chicken begins to brown. Stir in broth, tomato sauce, and water and bring to simmer. Cover, reduce heat to medium-low, and cook for 20 minutes.

3. Place chicken breast side up on top of potatoes and transfer skillet to oven. Roast until breast registers 160 degrees and thighs register 175 degrees, 1 to 1¼ hours. Using potholders, remove skillet from oven. Transfer chicken to carving board and let rest while finishing potatoes.

4. Being careful of hot skillet handle, cover skillet, return potatoes to oven, and roast until tender, about 20 minutes. Carve chicken and serve with potatoes and lemon wedges.

Herbed Chicken with Warm Spring Vegetable Salad

SLOW COOKER

Serves 4

Cook Time 4 to 5 hours on low, plus 20 minutes on high

Why This Recipe Works A slow cooker might not be the first vessel that comes to mind when preparing a whole chicken, but we were surprised to find that it could turn out a tender, juicy bird. A simple aromatic mixture of oil, shallot, garlic, and thyme rubbed under the skin added a layer of flavor to the meat. Cooking the chicken breast side down in the slow cooker kept the breast meat moist during cooking. For a springtime spin on chicken and vegetables, we opted for radishes and snap peas. First we scattered seasoned radish halves around the chicken; while the chicken rested, we stirred sugar snap peas into the slow cooker with the braised radishes and cooked on high until the snap peas were crisp-tender. A creamy dill dressing was the perfect flavorful accompaniment to our spring vegetable salad. Check the chicken's temperature after 4 hours of cooking and continue to monitor until the breast registers 160 degrees and the thighs register 175 degrees. You will need a 5- to 7-quart oval slow cooker for this recipe.

- ¼ cup extra-virgin olive oil, divided
- 1 shallot, minced
- 4 garlic cloves, minced, divided
- 2 teaspoons minced fresh thyme or ½ teaspoon dried
- 1 teaspoon table salt, divided
- ½ teaspoon pepper, divided
- 1 (4-pound) whole chicken, giblets discarded
- 1 pound radishes, trimmed and halved
- 1 pound sugar snap peas, strings removed
- ¼ cup plain whole-milk yogurt
- ¼ cup mayonnaise
- 2 tablespoons minced fresh dill
- 1 tablespoon red wine vinegar
- 1 teaspoon sugar
  Lemon wedges

1. Microwave 3 tablespoons oil, shallot, three-quarters of garlic, thyme, ½ teaspoon salt, and ¼ teaspoon pepper in bowl until fragrant, about 30 seconds; let cool slightly.

2. Using your fingers, gently loosen skin covering breast and thighs of chicken. Place half of oil mixture under skin, directly on meat in center of each side of breast and on thighs. Gently press skin to distribute oil mixture over meat. Rub entire exterior surface of chicken with remaining oil mixture. Place chicken breast side down into slow cooker.

3. Toss radishes with remaining 1 tablespoon oil, ¼ teaspoon salt, and remaining ¼ teaspoon pepper in clean bowl, then arrange around chicken. Cover and cook until breast registers 160 degrees and thighs register 175 degrees, 4 to 5 hours on low.

4. Transfer chicken to carving board and let rest while finishing vegetables. Stir snap peas into slow cooker, cover, and cook on high until crisp-tender, about 20 minutes.

5. Whisk yogurt, mayonnaise, dill, vinegar, sugar, remaining ¼ teaspoon salt, and remaining garlic together in large bowl. Using slotted spoon, transfer vegetables to bowl with dressing and toss to coat; discard cooking liquid. Season with salt and pepper to taste. Carve chicken, discarding skin if desired. Serve with radish salad and lemon wedges.

Roast Chicken with Warm Bread Salad

SKILLET

Serves 4

Total Time 1½ hours, plus 24 hours salting

Why This Recipe Works San Francisco's famed Zuni Café serves a perfect roast chicken over a chewy-crisp, warm bread-and-greens salad that has a cultlike following. We pay homage to the dish with this simplified take, which is much more streamlined but still hits all the right notes: salty, savory, sweet, fresh, and bright. To preserve the soft texture of the arugula and highlight the way its pepperiness offsets the moist chicken and rich bread, we served the salad on the side. Salting and refrigerating the chicken drew moisture from the flesh, forming a brine that was eventually reabsorbed, seasoning the meat and keeping it juicy. We tossed pieces of crusty bread with some vegetable oil and chicken broth to help it crisp up to make flavorful, savory croutons for the salad. Roasting the chicken on top of the croutons added a deep meatiness to them thanks to the flavorful drippings. This recipe was developed using Diamond Crystal Kosher Salt. If you have Morton Kosher Salt, which is denser, use only ½ teaspoon in the chicken cavity. If using kosher chicken, do not salt in step 2, but sprinkle with salt in step 4. For the bread, we prefer a round rustic loaf with a chewy, open crumb and a sturdy crust.

- 1 (4-pound) whole chicken, giblets discarded
- 1 tablespoon plus ½ teaspoon kosher salt, divided
- 4 (1-inch-thick) slices crusty bread (8 ounces), bottom crust removed, cut into ¾- to 1-inch pieces (5 cups)
- ¼ cup chicken broth
- 6 tablespoons plus 2 teaspoons extra-virgin olive oil, divided
- ½ teaspoon pepper, divided
- 2 tablespoons champagne vinegar
- 1 teaspoon Dijon mustard
- 3 scallions, sliced thin
- 2 tablespoons dried currants
- 5 ounces (5 cups) baby arugula

1. With chicken breast side down, use kitchen shears to cut through bones on either side of backbone and discard backbone. Do not trim any excess fat or skin. Flip chicken over and press on breastbone to flatten.

2. Using your fingers, gently loosen center portion of skin covering each side of breast and legs. Rub ½ teaspoon salt under skin of each side of breast, ½ teaspoon salt under skin of each leg, and 1 teaspoon salt into bird's cavity. Tuck wingtips behind back and turn legs so drumsticks face inward toward breasts. Place chicken on large plate and refrigerate, uncovered, for 24 hours.

3. Adjust oven rack to middle position and heat oven to 475 degrees. Spray 12-inch ovensafe skillet with vegetable oil spray. Toss bread with broth and 2 tablespoons oil until pieces are evenly moistened. Arrange bread in skillet in single layer, with majority of crusted pieces near center, crust side up.

4. Pat chicken dry with paper towels and place skin side up on top of bread, centered over crusted pieces. Brush 2 teaspoons oil over chicken skin and sprinkle with ¼ teaspoon salt and ¼ teaspoon pepper. Roast chicken until skin is deep golden brown and thickest part of breast registers 160 degrees and thighs register 175 degrees, 45 to 50 minutes, rotating skillet halfway through roasting. (Bread should be mix of softened, golden-brown, and crunchy pieces.)

5. While chicken roasts, whisk vinegar, mustard, remaining ¼ teaspoon salt, and remaining ¼ teaspoon pepper together in large bowl. While whisking constantly, slowly drizzle in remaining ¼ cup oil until combined. Stir in scallions and currants and set aside.

6. Transfer chicken to carving board and let rest for 15 minutes. Carve chicken and whisk any accumulated juices into vinaigrette. Add bread and arugula to vinaigrette and toss to coat. Transfer salad to serving platter and serve with chicken.

Herbed Chicken with Warm Spring Vegetable Salad

Roast Chicken with Warm Bread Salad

Spice-Rubbed Roasted Turkey Breast with Green Beans

Roast Turkey Breast with Herb Stuffing and Cranberry Sauce

Spice-Rubbed Roasted Turkey Breast with Green Beans

SKILLET

Serves 6 to 8

Total Time 2½ hours, plus 24 hours salting

Why This Recipe Works Turkey isn't just for Thanksgiving, so for this non-holiday meal we kicked up the meat's mild flavor with a unique, bold spice rub and introduced an easy, fresh side. We applied our rub of five-spice powder, cumin, garlic powder, cayenne, cardamom, and salt directly to the meat before refrigerating the breast for 24 hours. This added immense flavor and the salt helped the meat stay moist during roasting. Brushing the skin with melted butter at the start of roasting and cranking the oven to 500 degrees at the end of roasting guaranteed a crisp exterior. Using a skillet to roast the breast allowed us to contain the drippings, which we used to sauté our vegetable: a helping of crisp, verdant green beans. If using a self-basting turkey (such as a frozen Butterball) or kosher turkey, do not add salt to the rub in step 2. You will need a 12-inch ovensafe skillet for this recipe.

- 1 (6- to 7-pound) bone-in whole turkey breast
- 4 teaspoons kosher salt, divided
- 2 teaspoons five-spice powder
- 1½ teaspoons ground cumin
- 1 teaspoon garlic powder
- ¼ teaspoon cayenne pepper
- ¼ teaspoon ground cardamom
- 2 tablespoons unsalted butter, melted
- 1 large shallot, sliced thin
- 2 pounds green beans, trimmed

1. Using kitchen shears, cut through ribs following vertical line of fat where breast meets back, from tapered end of breast to wing joint. Using your hands, bend back away from breast to pop shoulder joint out of socket. With paring knife, cut through joint between bones to separate back from breast; discard back. Trim excess fat from breast.

2. Place turkey breast side up on cutting board. Combine 2 teaspoons salt, five-spice powder, cumin, garlic powder, cayenne, and cardamom in bowl. Using your fingers, gently loosen and separate turkey skin from each side of breast. Peel skin back, leaving it attached at top and center of breast. Rub 2 teaspoons spice mixture onto each side of breast, then lay skin back in place. Rub remaining spice mixture into underside of bird's cavity. Refrigerate turkey, uncovered, for 24 hours.

3. Adjust oven rack to middle position and heat oven to 325 degrees. Pat turkey dry with paper towels. Arrange turkey breast skin side up in 12-inch ovensafe skillet, tucking ribs under breast and arranging so narrow end of breast is not touching skillet. Brush melted butter evenly over turkey and sprinkle with 1 teaspoon salt. Roast until breast registers 130 degrees, 1 to 1¼ hours.

4. Using potholder, remove skillet from oven and increase temperature to 500 degrees. When oven reaches 500 degrees, return turkey to oven and roast until skin is deeply browned and breast registers 160 degrees, 15 to 30 minutes. Using spatula, loosen turkey from skillet and transfer to carving board. Let rest for 30 minutes.

5. Meanwhile, being careful of hot skillet handle, pour off all but 1 tablespoon fat from skillet. Add shallot and cook over medium heat until softened, about 1 minute. Add green beans, ¼ cup water, and remaining 1 teaspoon salt and toss to combine. Reduce heat to medium-low, cover, and cook until green beans are just tender, 12 to 15 minutes.

6. Uncover, increase heat to medium, and cook until water evaporates and beans are tender, 3 to 5 minutes. Season with salt and pepper to taste. Carve turkey and serve with green beans.

Roast Turkey Breast with Herb Stuffing and Cranberry Sauce

ROASTING PAN
Serves 6 to 8
Total Time 1¾ hours, plus 3 hours brining

Why This Recipe Works To get the flavors of a holiday dinner without the extensive holiday cleanup, we cooked turkey breast and stuffing in one pan. To start, we sautéed fresh herbs and aromatics right in the roasting pan before placing an herb butter–rubbed turkey breast on top. For the stuffing, we sprinkled bread cubes around the breast so they could toast in the oven and absorb the turkey's juices. Starting at a high temperature allowed the turkey's fat to render for supercrisp skin; we later lowered the heat to allow the bird to cook through gently. A tangy-sweet cranberry sauce comes together quickly in the microwave. If using a self-basting turkey breast (such as a frozen Butterball) or kosher turkey, do not brine in step 1.

½ cup table salt for brining
1 (6- to 7-pound) bone-in whole turkey breast
5 tablespoons unsalted butter, softened, divided
2 tablespoons minced fresh sage, divided
2 tablespoons minced fresh thyme, divided
1½ teaspoons table salt, divided

¾ teaspoon pepper, divided
1 onion, chopped fine
2 celery ribs, minced
1 pound hearty white sandwich bread, cut into ½-inch pieces
12 ounces (3 cups) frozen cranberries, thawed
1 cup sugar
¼ cup water
1 cup chicken broth, plus extra as needed
1 tablespoon minced fresh parsley

1. Using kitchen shears, cut through ribs following vertical line of fat where breast meets back, from tapered end of breast to wing joint. Using your hands, bend back away from breast to pop shoulder joint out of socket. With paring knife, cut through joint between bones to separate back from breast; discard back. Trim excess fat from breast. Dissolve ½ cup salt in 4 quarts cold water in large container. Submerge turkey in brine, cover, and refrigerate for at least 3 hours or up to 6 hours. Remove turkey from brine and pat dry with paper towels.

2. Adjust oven rack to middle position and heat oven to 425 degrees. Place turkey breast side up on cutting board. Mash 3 tablespoons butter, 1 tablespoon sage, 1 tablespoon thyme, 1 teaspoon salt, and ½ teaspoon pepper together in bowl. Using your fingers, gently loosen and separate turkey skin from each side of breast. Peel skin back, leaving it attached at top and center of breast. Spread one-quarter of butter mixture onto each side of breast, then lay skin back in place. Spread remaining butter mixture evenly over skin.

3. Melt remaining 2 tablespoons butter in 16 by 12-inch roasting pan over medium heat (over 2 burners, if possible). Add onion, celery, ¼ teaspoon salt, and remaining ¼ teaspoon pepper and cook until vegetables are softened, about 5 minutes. Stir in remaining 1 tablespoon sage and remaining 1 tablespoon thyme and cook until fragrant, about 30 seconds. Off heat, place turkey skin side up on top of vegetables, tucking ribs under breast, and arrange bread around turkey. Roast turkey for 30 minutes.

4. Reduce oven temperature to 325 degrees and continue to roast turkey until breast registers 160 degrees, about 1 hour.

5. Meanwhile, combine cranberries, sugar, water, and remaining ¼ teaspoon salt in bowl and microwave, stirring occasionally, until cranberries are broken down and juicy, about 10 minutes. Coarsely mash cranberries with fork; set aside for serving.

6. Remove pan from oven. Transfer turkey to carving board and let rest for 30 minutes. Stir broth and parsley into stuffing left in pan, cover with aluminum foil, and let sit for 10 minutes; add extra broth if stuffing is dry. Carve turkey and serve with stuffing and cranberry sauce.

Easy Chicken Enchiladas

CASSEROLE DISH

Serves 4 to 6
Total Time 1 hour

Why This Recipe Works From making the sauce and cooking the filling to rolling the tortillas, preparing enchiladas can be a time-consuming, labor-intensive endeavor. We set out to streamline this dish so we could serve boldly flavored enchiladas any night of the week. Although canned enchilada sauce is passable, we decided to create our own alternative, fresh-tasting sauce, combining canned tomato sauce with chili powder, cumin, sugar, salt, and pepper. Smooth-melting Monterey Jack cheese bound the filling together. After spreading some of the sauce over the bottom of our casserole dish, we filled our corn tortillas (warmed to make them more pliable) and arranged them in the dish. After we spread on the remaining sauce and sprinkled on some extra cheese for a bubbly topping, our nearly effortless enchiladas were ready for baking to meaty, cheesy perfection. An average-size rotisserie chicken should yield between 3 and 4 cups of shredded meat. You can also use a double batch of our recipe for Easy Poached Chicken (page 133).

 1 (15-ounce) can tomato sauce
 ½ cup water
 3 tablespoons chili powder
 2 teaspoons ground cumin
 2 teaspoons sugar
 ¾ teaspoon garlic powder
 ¼ teaspoon pepper
 8 ounces Monterey Jack cheese, shredded
   (2 cups), divided
 3 cups shredded cooked chicken
 3 tablespoons minced fresh cilantro, divided
 12 (6-inch) corn tortillas
 2 tablespoons vegetable oil
   Lime wedges

1. Adjust oven rack to middle position and heat oven to 450 degrees. Whisk tomato sauce, water, chili powder, cumin, sugar, garlic powder, and pepper together in bowl. In separate bowl, combine 1 cup Monterey Jack, chicken, 2 tablespoons cilantro, and ½ cup tomato sauce mixture.

2. Spread ½ cup sauce over bottom of 13 by 9-inch baking dish. Brush both sides of tortillas with oil. Stack tortillas, wrap in damp dish towel, and place on plate; microwave until warm and pliable, about 1 minute.

3. Working with 1 warm tortilla at a time, spread ⅓ cup chicken filling across center. Roll tortilla tightly around filling and place seam side down in baking dish; arrange enchiladas in 2 columns across width of dish. Pour remaining sauce over top to cover completely and sprinkle remaining 1 cup Monterey Jack down center of enchiladas.

4. Cover dish tightly with greased aluminum foil and bake until enchiladas are heated through and cheese is melted, about 20 minutes. Remove dish from oven and let cool for 10 minutes. Sprinkle with remaining 1 tablespoon cilantro and serve with lime wedges.

VARIATION

Easy Chicken Enchiladas for Two

CASSEROLE DISH

Serves 2
Total Time 1 hour

An average-size rotisserie chicken should yield between 3 and 4 cups of shredded meat. You can also use our recipe for Easy Poached Chicken (page 133).

 1 (8-ounce) can tomato sauce
 ⅓ cup water
 1 tablespoon chili powder
 1 teaspoon ground cumin
 1 teaspoon sugar
 ¼ teaspoon garlic powder
 ⅛ teaspoon pepper
 4 ounces Monterey Jack cheese, shredded
   (1 cup), divided
 1½ cups shredded cooked chicken
 2 tablespoons minced fresh cilantro, divided
 6 (6-inch) corn tortillas
 1½ tablespoons vegetable oil
   Lime wedges

1. Adjust oven rack to middle position and heat oven to 450 degrees. Whisk tomato sauce, water, chili powder, cumin, sugar, garlic powder, and pepper together in bowl. In separate bowl, combine ½ cup Monterey Jack, chicken, 1 tablespoon cilantro, and ¼ cup tomato sauce mixture.

2. Spread ¼ cup sauce over bottom of 8-inch square baking dish. Brush both sides of tortillas with oil. Stack tortillas, wrap in damp dish towel, and place on plate; microwave until warm and pliable, about 1 minute.

3. Working with 1 warm tortilla at a time, spread ⅓ cup chicken filling across center. Roll tortilla tightly around filling and place seam side down in baking dish in single row. Pour remaining sauce over top to cover completely and sprinkle remaining ½ cup Monterey Jack down center of enchiladas.

4. Cover dish tightly with greased aluminum foil and bake until enchiladas are heated through and cheese is melted, about 20 minutes. Remove dish from oven and let cool for 10 minutes. Sprinkle with remaining 1 tablespoon cilantro and serve with lime wedges.

Easy Chicken, Spinach, and Artichoke Pot Pie

CASSEROLE DISH
Serves 4
Total Time 1 hour

Why This Recipe Works In this spin on chicken pot pie inspired by spinach and artichoke dip, thawed frozen spinach mixed with jarred artichokes and Boursin cheese provides a flavorful, creamy base. Shredded carrots and capers introduced contrasting texture and briny zing. For a lush sauce, we used broth, cream, and, for thickening, Wondra flour. We tossed the chicken with lemon zest for brightness, and placed it atop the vegetables to keep the meat from drying out. A buttery sheet of puff pastry made the perfect top. While we prefer the flavor and texture of jarred whole baby artichoke hearts in this recipe, you can substitute 6 ounces frozen artichoke hearts, thawed and patted dry, for the jarred. You can substitute an equal amount of all-purpose flour for the Wondra flour, if necessary; however, the sauce will have a pasty, slightly gritty texture. To thaw frozen puff pastry, let it sit either in the refrigerator for 24 hours or on the counter for 30 minutes to 1 hour.

- 1¼ pounds frozen spinach, thawed and squeezed dry
- 1 (5.2-ounce) package Boursin Garlic & Fine Herbs cheese
- 1 cup jarred whole artichoke hearts packed in water, halved
- 2 carrots, peeled and shredded
- ¾ cup chicken broth
- ½ cup heavy cream
- ¼ cup capers, rinsed
- 1 tablespoon Wondra flour
- 12 ounces boneless, skinless chicken breasts, trimmed and sliced thin
- 1 teaspoon grated lemon zest
- ⅛ teaspoon table salt
- ⅛ teaspoon pepper
- 1 (9½- by 9-inch) sheet puff pastry, thawed
- 1 large egg, lightly beaten with 2 tablespoons water

Easy Chicken, Spinach, and Artichoke Pot Pie

Easy Poached Chicken

Makes about 2 cups
This recipe can be easily halved or doubled; do not alter amount of water.

- 12 ounces boneless, skinless chicken breasts, trimmed
- ¼ teaspoon table salt
- 1 tablespoon vegetable oil

Pat chicken dry with paper towels and sprinkle with salt. Heat oil in 12-inch skillet over medium-high heat until just smoking. Brown chicken on first side, 6 to 8 minutes. Flip chicken, add ½ cup water, and cover. Reduce heat to medium-low and continue to cook until chicken registers 160 degrees, 5 to 7 minutes. Transfer chicken to cutting board, let cool slightly, then shred into bite-size pieces using 2 forks. Makes about 2 cups.

1. Adjust oven rack to middle position and heat oven to 425 degrees. Grease 8-inch square baking dish. Combine spinach, Boursin, artichokes, carrots, broth, cream, capers, and Wondra together in bowl, then transfer to prepared dish.

2. Toss chicken with lemon zest, salt, and pepper and spread in even layer over spinach mixture. Cut puff pastry into 8-inch square and place over top of chicken. Cut four 2-inch slits in center of dough, then brush dough with egg mixture.

3. Bake until crust is golden brown and filling is bubbling, 30 to 35 minutes, rotating dish halfway through baking. Remove pot pie from oven and let cool for 10 minutes before serving.

Chicken Pot Pie with Spring Vegetables

DUTCH OVEN
Serves 6
Total Time 1½ hours

Why This Recipe Works The delights of classic chicken pot pie are many, from the burnished, flaky crust to the luscious, savory filling. But putting it together can be a chore: Between making pie dough (which often requires pulling out a food processor), poaching chicken in one pot and building a gravy in another, and then transferring the filling and crust to a pie plate to bake, this comfort food requires a major time commitment, not to mention a battery of pots and pans. We wanted an easier way and found our trusty Dutch oven to be just the ticket to get us there. Boneless, skinless chicken thighs, cut into pieces, were easy to work with and stayed moist through cooking. We simply stirred bite-size pieces of chicken right into the gravy and turned to two powerhouse ingredients—tomato paste and soy sauce—to boost savoriness without being distinguishable in their own right. To give our pot pie fresh spring flavor we swapped in leeks for onions and stirred in some fresh asparagus, peas, and tarragon after pulling the pot from the oven. With our one-pot filling perfected, we turned to the crust. Instead of labor-intensive homemade pastry, we decided to use buttery store-bought puff pastry and wove it into a simple but stunning lattice. Baking the delicate lattice top separate from the filling ensured it held its shape. We simply turned the lid of the Dutch oven upside down to act as a baking sheet before covering the pot and baked the pastry on top. A simple egg wash turned the crust a deep golden. Once we slid the baked crust onto the filling, our simplified centerpiece was complete. To thaw frozen puff pastry, let it sit either in the refrigerator for 24 hours or on the counter for 30 minutes to 1 hour. We prefer to place the baked pastry on top of the filling in the pot just before serving for an impressive presentation; however, you can also cut the pastry into wedges and place them over individual portions of the filling.

MAKING A LATTICE TOP

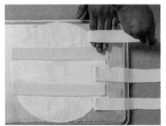 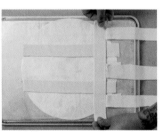  

1. Space 5 pastry strips parallel and evenly across parchment circle. Fold back first, third, and fifth strips almost completely.

2. Lay pastry strip perpendicular to second and fourth strips, keeping it snug to folded edges of pastry, then unfold strips.

3. Repeat laying remaining 4 pastry strips evenly across parchment circle, alternating between folding back second and fourth strips and first, third, and fifth strips to create lattice pattern.

4. Using pizza cutter, trim edges of pastry following outline of parchment circle.

1 (9½ by 9-inch) sheet puff pastry, thawed
4 tablespoons unsalted butter
1 pound leeks, white and light green parts only, halved lengthwise, cut into ½-inch pieces, and washed thoroughly
4 carrots, peeled and cut into ½-inch pieces
1 teaspoon table salt
4 garlic cloves, minced
2 teaspoons tomato paste
½ cup all-purpose flour
3 cups chicken broth, plus extra as needed
¼ cup heavy cream
1 teaspoon soy sauce
2 bay leaves
2 pounds boneless, skinless chicken thighs, trimmed and cut into 1-inch pieces
1 large egg, lightly beaten
1 pound asparagus, trimmed and cut on bias into 1-inch lengths
1 cup frozen peas
2 tablespoons chopped fresh tarragon or parsley
1 tablespoon grated lemon zest plus 2 teaspoons juice

1. Cut sheet of parchment paper to match outline of Dutch oven lid and place on large plate or upturned rimmed baking sheet. Roll puff pastry sheet into 15 by 11-inch rectangle on lightly floured counter. Using pizza cutter or sharp knife, cut pastry widthwise into ten 1½-inch-wide strips.

2. Space 5 pastry strips parallel and evenly across parchment circle. Fold back first, third, and fifth strips almost completely. Lay additional pastry strip perpendicular to second and fourth strips, keeping it snug to folded edges of pastry, then unfold strips. Repeat laying remaining 4 pastry strips evenly across parchment circle, alternating between folding back second and fourth strips and first, third, and fifth strips to create lattice pattern. Using pizza cutter, trim edges of pastry following outline of parchment circle. Cover loosely with plastic wrap and refrigerate while preparing filling.

3. Adjust oven rack to lower-middle position and heat oven to 400 degrees. Melt butter in Dutch oven over medium heat. Add leeks, carrots, and 1 teaspoon salt and cook until vegetables are softened, 5 to 7 minutes. Stir in garlic and tomato paste and cook until fragrant, about 1 minute. Stir in flour and cook for 1 minute.

Chicken Pot Pie with Spring Vegetables

4. Slowly stir in broth, scraping up any browned bits and smoothing out any lumps. Stir in cream, soy sauce, and bay leaves. Bring to simmer and cook until mixture is thickened, about 3 minutes. Stir in chicken and return to simmer.

5. Off heat, cover pot with inverted lid and carefully place parchment with pastry on lid. Brush pastry with egg and sprinkle with salt. Transfer pot to oven and bake until pastry is puffed and golden brown, 25 to 30 minutes, rotating pot halfway through baking.

6. Remove pot from oven. Transfer parchment with pastry to wire rack; discard parchment. Remove lid and discard bay leaves. Stir asparagus into filling and cook over medium heat until crisp-tender, 3 to 5 minutes. Off heat, stir in peas and let sit until heated through, about 5 minutes. Adjust filling consistency with extra hot broth as needed. Stir in tarragon and lemon zest and juice. Season with salt and pepper to taste. Set pastry on top of filling and serve.

BEEF

Boneless Rib Roast with
Yorkshire Pudding

* All slow cooker recipes work in a 4- to 7-quart traditional slow cooker unless noted.

** All Instant Pot recipes work in a 6- to 8-quart Instant Pot or other electric pressure cooker.

Steak Tips with Spicy Cauliflower

SKILLET
Serves 4
Total Time 45 minutes

Why This Recipe Works Steak tips make for an incredibly easy weeknight meal. They're relatively quick-cooking compared to larger cuts of meat, they provide satisfying beefy flavor, and they're versatile enough to pair with a wide range of side dishes. For a flavor-packed side that didn't require much effort, we started by making a relish of roasted red peppers, hot cherry peppers, parsley, and capers. Using a covered skillet allowed us to cook 1-inch pieces of cauliflower until tender in only about 10 minutes. We then tossed the warm cauliflower with the relish to help it better absorb the flavors. Searing the steak tips in the same hot skillet was the final step in putting together this fuss-free but flavorful meal. We prefer steak tips cooked to medium-rare, but if you prefer them more or less done, see our guidelines on page 141.

- ½ cup jarred roasted red peppers, patted dry and chopped
- 5 tablespoons extra-virgin olive oil, divided
- ¼ cup finely chopped jarred hot cherry peppers
- 2 tablespoons chopped fresh parsley
- 1 tablespoon capers, rinsed and minced
- ¾ teaspoon table salt, divided
- ⅛ teaspoon plus ¼ teaspoon pepper, divided
- 1 large head cauliflower (3 pounds), cored and cut into 1-inch pieces
- 2 pounds sirloin steak tips, trimmed and cut into 2-inch pieces

1. Combine red peppers, 3 tablespoons oil, cherry peppers, parsley, capers, ¼ teaspoon salt, and ⅛ teaspoon pepper in large bowl; set aside.

2. Heat 1 tablespoon oil in 12-inch skillet over medium-high heat until shimmering. Add cauliflower, cover, and cook, stirring occasionally, until browned and tender, about 10 minutes. Add cauliflower to relish and toss to combine. Season with salt and pepper to taste.

3. Pat steak tips dry with paper towels and sprinkle with remaining ½ teaspoon salt and remaining ¼ teaspoon pepper. Heat remaining 1 tablespoon oil in now-empty skillet over medium-high heat until just smoking. Add steak tips and cook until browned on all sides and meat registers 120 to 125 degrees (for medium-rare), 6 to 10 minutes. Serve steak tips with cauliflower.

Steak Tips with Wilted Spinach, Goat Cheese, and Pear Salad

SKILLET
Serves 4
Total Time 40 minutes

Why This Recipe Works After searing steak tips, we took advantage of the fond left in the skillet to build a warm dressing for a wilted salad imbued with complex meaty flavor. To make the dressing, we added a bit of oil to the pan and sautéed shallot, garlic, and pistachios. For a salad that would give us wilted but not swampy greens, we used baby spinach, which was tender and sweet, and tossed it with our warm dressing to soften the spinach leaves just slightly. A ripe pear was just the thing to liven up this simple salad with sweet crunch, while crumbled goat cheese added a pleasantly tart creaminess. Substituting Gorgonzola, apple, pecans, and balsamic vinegar in our scaled-down variation for two retained the tart-sweet flavor balance with more pantry-friendly ingredients. We prefer steak tips cooked to medium-rare, but if you prefer them more or less done, see our guidelines on page 141.

- 2 pounds sirloin steak tips, trimmed and cut into 2-inch pieces
- ¾ teaspoon table salt, divided
- ¼ teaspoon plus ⅛ teaspoon pepper, divided
- 3 tablespoons extra-virgin olive oil, divided
- 6 ounces (6 cups) baby spinach
- 1 ripe but firm pear, halved, cored, and sliced thin
- 3 tablespoons chopped pistachios
- 1 shallot, halved and sliced thin
- 1 garlic clove, minced
- 1 teaspoon minced fresh thyme or ¼ teaspoon dried
- ½ teaspoon grated lemon zest plus 2 tablespoons juice
- 2 ounces goat cheese, crumbled (½ cup)

1. Pat steak tips dry with paper towels and sprinkle with ½ teaspoon salt and ¼ teaspoon pepper. Heat 1 tablespoon oil in 12-inch skillet over medium-high heat until just smoking. Add steak tips and cook until browned on all sides and meat registers 120 to 125 degrees (for medium-rare), 6 to 10 minutes. Transfer steak tips to serving platter and let rest while finishing salad.

2. Combine spinach and pear in large bowl. Add pistachios, shallot, garlic, thyme, remaining 2 tablespoons oil, remaining ¼ teaspoon salt, and remaining ⅛ teaspoon pepper to now-empty skillet and cook over medium heat until pistachios are toasted and shallot is softened, about 2 minutes. Stir in lemon zest and juice and any accumulated meat juices. Immediately pour warm dressing over spinach and toss gently to wilt. Season with salt and pepper to taste. Sprinkle with goat cheese. Serve with steak tips.

VARIATION

Steak Tips with Wilted Spinach, Gorgonzola, and Apple Salad for Two

SKILLET

Serves 2

Total Time 40 minutes

We prefer steak tips cooked to medium-rare, but if you prefer them more or less done, see our guidelines on page 141.

- 1 pound sirloin steak tips, trimmed and cut into 2-inch pieces
- ¼ teaspoon plus ⅛ teaspoon table salt, divided
- ⅛ teaspoon plus pinch pepper, divided
- 5 teaspoons extra-virgin olive oil, divided
- 3 ounces (3 cups) baby spinach
- ½ red apple, cored and sliced thin
- 2 tablespoons chopped pecans
- 1 shallot, sliced thin
- 1 garlic clove, minced
- ½ teaspoon minced fresh thyme or ⅛ teaspoon dried
- 1½ tablespoons balsamic vinegar
- 1 ounce Gorgonzola cheese, crumbled (¼ cup)

1. Pat steak tips dry with paper towels and sprinkle with ¼ teaspoon salt and ⅛ teaspoon pepper. Heat 2 teaspoons oil in 10-inch skillet over medium-high heat until just smoking. Add steak tips and cook until browned on all sides and meat registers 120 to 125 degrees (for medium-rare), 6 to 10 minutes. Transfer steak tips to serving platter and let rest while finishing salad.

2. Combine spinach and apple in large bowl. Add pecans, shallot, garlic, thyme, remaining 1 tablespoon oil, remaining ⅛ teaspoon salt, and remaining pinch pepper to now-empty skillet and cook over medium heat until pecans are toasted and shallot is softened, about 2 minutes. Stir in vinegar and any accumulated meat juices. Immediately pour warm dressing over spinach and toss gently to wilt. Season with salt and pepper to taste. Sprinkle with Gorgonzola. Serve with steak tips.

Steak Tips with Spicy Cauliflower

NOTES FROM THE TEST KITCHEN

BUYING STEAK TIPS

Steak tips come from various muscles in the sirloin and round. After tasting 50 pounds of steak tips, tasters had a clear favorite: sirloin steak tips, also known as flap meat, which can be sold as whole steaks, cubes, and strips. Flap meat has a rich, deep, beefy flavor and a distinctive longitudinal grain. A whole piece of flap meat weighs about 2½ pounds. One piece can range in thickness from ½ inch to 1½ inches.

We found that it's best to buy flap meat in steak form rather than in cubes or strips, which are often cut from nearby muscles in the hip and butt that are neither as tasty nor as tender.

Steak Tips with Horseradish Potato Salad

Steak Tips with Spiced Couscous and Spinach

Steak Tips with Horseradish Potato Salad

DUTCH OVEN

Serves 4
Total Time 45 minutes

Why This Recipe Works Using a Dutch oven two ways allowed us to make a one-pot steak and potato meal. First we used its large capacity to cook potatoes for potato salad; starting them in an inch of cold, salted water and bringing them to a simmer ensured even cooking. We then seared our steak tips (which we marinated in Worcestershire, salt, and garlic powder for deep, savory flavor), taking advantage of the Dutch oven's wide bottom. For a light but creamy potato salad dressing we used both sour cream and mayonnaise. Celery and celery leaves added dimension, and horseradish nicely accented the meat and the potatoes. Small red potatoes measuring 1 to 2 inches in diameter can be substituted for the fingerling potatoes. If celery leaves are not available, increase the parsley to ½ cup. The strength of prepared horseradish can vary greatly; start with 1 tablespoon and add more according to taste. We prefer steak tips cooked to medium-rare, but if you prefer them more or less done, see our guidelines on page 141.

- 2 teaspoons Worcestershire sauce
- 1¼ teaspoons table salt, plus salt for cooking potatoes, divided
- 1 teaspoon garlic powder
- 2 pounds sirloin steak tips, trimmed and cut into 2-inch pieces
- 1½ pounds fingerling potatoes, unpeeled, halved lengthwise
- 3 tablespoons white wine vinegar, divided
- ½ teaspoon pepper, divided
- 1 tablespoon vegetable oil
- ¼ cup mayonnaise
- ¼ cup sour cream
- 2 celery ribs, minced, plus ½ cup celery leaves, divided
- ¼ cup finely chopped red onion
- 1–3 tablespoons prepared horseradish
- ¼ cup fresh parsley leaves

1. Combine Worcestershire, ¾ teaspoon salt, and garlic powder in medium bowl. Add steak tips and toss until evenly coated; set aside.

2. Place potatoes and 1 teaspoon salt in Dutch oven and cover with cold water by 1 inch. Bring to simmer over medium-high heat and cook until potatoes are tender, 10 to 15 minutes.

3. Drain potatoes and spread into single layer on rimmed baking sheet. Drizzle with 2 tablespoons vinegar and gently toss to coat. Refrigerate potatoes until slightly cooled, about 15 minutes.

4. Meanwhile, wipe pot clean with paper towels. Pat steak tips dry with paper towels and sprinkle with ¼ teaspoon pepper. Heat oil in now-empty pot over medium-high heat until just smoking. Add steak tips and cook until well browned on all sides and meat registers 120 to 125 degrees (for medium-rare), 6 to 10 minutes. Transfer steak tips to serving platter and let rest while finishing salad.

5. Whisk mayonnaise, sour cream, minced celery, onion, horseradish, remaining ½ teaspoon salt, remaining ¼ teaspoon pepper, and remaining 1 tablespoon vinegar together in large bowl. Add potatoes, celery leaves, and parsley and gently toss to combine. Serve with steak tips.

Steak Tips with Spiced Couscous and Spinach

DUTCH OVEN

Serves 4
Total Time 45 minutes

Why This Recipe Works Inspired by the warm spices and dried fruit common in Moroccan dishes, we paired spiced steak tips with a side dish of tender couscous, hearty chickpeas, and flavorful golden raisins. A simple spice rub of cumin, cinnamon, salt, and pepper thoroughly seasoned the steak tips, which we seared in a hot Dutch oven for flavorful browning. Cooking the couscous, chickpeas, and raisins in the same pot we used to sear the steak tips gave our side dish a savory, meaty backbone. Stirring baby spinach in at the end allowed it to wilt slightly before serving. We prefer steak tips cooked to medium-rare, but if you prefer them more or less done, see our guidelines at right.

    2 teaspoons ground cumin
    2 teaspoons table salt
 1½ teaspoons ground cinnamon
    ¼ teaspoon pepper
    2 pounds sirloin steak tips, trimmed and cut into
       2-inch pieces
    1 tablespoon vegetable oil
 1¼ cups water
    1 (15-ounce) can chickpeas, rinsed
    ¾ cup couscous
    ½ cup golden raisins
    2 ounces (2 cups) baby spinach, chopped

1. Combine cumin, salt, cinnamon, and pepper in bowl. Pat steak tips dry with paper towels and sprinkle with 1 tablespoon spice mixture. Heat oil in Dutch oven over medium-high heat until just smoking. Add steak tips and cook until browned on all sides and meat registers 120 to 125 degrees (for medium-rare), 6 to 10 minutes. Transfer steak tips to plate, tent with aluminum foil, and let rest while preparing couscous.

2. Combine water, chickpeas, couscous, raisins, and remaining spice mixture in now-empty pot and bring to boil over medium-high heat. Remove from heat, cover, and let sit until couscous is tender, about 5 minutes. Fold in spinach, one handful at a time. Serve with steak tips.

NOTES FROM THE TEST KITCHEN

TAKING THE TEMPERATURE OF MEAT
Since the temperature of beef, lamb, and pork will continue to rise as the meat rests—an effect called carryover cooking—they should be removed from the oven or pan when they are 5 to 10 degrees below the desired serving temperature. The following temperatures should be used to determine when to stop the cooking process.

FOR THIS INGREDIENT	COOK TO THIS TEMPERATURE
Beef/Lamb	
Rare	115 to 120 degrees (120 to 125 degrees after resting)
Medium-Rare	120 to 125 degrees (125 to 130 degrees after resting)
Medium	130 to 135 degrees (135 to 140 degrees after resting)
Medium-Well	140 to 145 degrees (145 to 150 degrees after resting)
Well-Done	150 to 155 degrees (155 to 160 degrees after resting)
Pork	
Chops and Tenderloin	145 degrees (150 degrees after resting)
Loin Roasts	140 degrees (145 degrees after resting)

Steak Tips with Tomatillo Salsa and Refried Black Beans

SKILLET

Serves 4

Total Time 45 minutes

Why This Recipe Works Tomatillo salsa, also called salsa verde, offers bright, tangy flavors that balance the richness of steak tips in this satisfying skillet dinner. This salsa is a staple of Mexican cooking that's easy to make at home; we pulsed the husked tomatillos in a food processor to break them down before transferring the pieces to a strainer to drain off some of the excess liquid (reserving some for later). Once we combined them with jalapeños, cilantro, and garlic, we had a salsa that was thick enough to cling. Next we browned steak tips in a skillet and then set them aside to rest while finishing the meal. For our riff on refried beans, we used black beans instead of the traditional pinto beans and infused them with plenty of flavor—by using the fond left in the skillet from searing the steak and by incorporating tomatillo flavor from the reserved salsa liquid. Mashing the beans produced just the right texture. We prefer steak tips cooked to medium-rare, but if you prefer them more or less done, see our guidelines on page 141.

- 1 pound tomatillos, husks and stems removed, rinsed well, dried, and halved
- 2 jalapeño chiles, stemmed, seeded, and minced, divided
- ½ cup minced fresh cilantro, divided
- 2 garlic cloves, minced, divided
- 2 pounds sirloin steak tips, trimmed and cut into 2-inch pieces
- ½ teaspoon table salt
- ¼ teaspoon pepper
- 2 tablespoons vegetable oil, divided
- 1 onion, chopped fine
- 1 teaspoon ground cumin
- 2 (15-ounce) cans black beans, rinsed

1. Pulse tomatillos in food processor until coarsely chopped, about 8 pulses. Transfer to fine-mesh strainer set over bowl and let drain for 5 minutes; reserve ¾ cup liquid. Combine half of jalapeños, ¼ cup cilantro, half of garlic, drained tomatillos, and ¼ cup reserved tomatillo liquid in bowl. Season with salt and pepper to taste; set aside for serving.

2. Pat steak tips dry with paper towels and sprinkle with salt and pepper. Heat 1 tablespoon oil in 12-inch skillet over medium-high heat until just smoking. Add steak tips and cook until browned on all sides and meat registers 120 to 125 degrees (for medium-rare), 6 to 10 minutes.

3. Transfer steak tips to plate, tent with aluminum foil, and let rest while preparing beans. Heat remaining 1 tablespoon oil in now-empty skillet over medium heat until shimmering. Add onion and cook until softened, about 5 minutes. Stir in cumin, remaining jalapeño, and remaining garlic and cook until fragrant, about 30 seconds. Stir in beans and remaining ½ cup reserved tomatillo liquid. Using potato masher, coarsely mash beans. Cook, stirring occasionally, until thickened, about 3 minutes. Stir in remaining ¼ cup cilantro and season with salt and pepper to taste. Serve steak with beans and salsa.

Spice-Rubbed Flank Steak with Toasted Corn and Black Bean Salad

SKILLET

Serves 4

Total Time 1 hour, plus 1 hour salting

Why This Recipe Works The big, beefy flavor of flank steak is well suited to the grill; to bring this cut indoors we needed a method with equally flavorful results. A bold spice rub greatly enhanced the flavor of the steak—a combination of chili powder, cumin, coriander, cinnamon, and red pepper flakes added just the right amount of heat and complexity. To cook our whole flank steak we used a skillet, which allowed our spiced steak to develop a deliciously browned crust on the stovetop before being transferred to the oven to roast. A bright black bean and corn salad complemented the beef. To bring out the corn's sweet flavor, we reused our skillet to brown it while the steak rested. We prefer to use fresh corn here; however, 2 cups frozen thawed corn can be substituted, if necessary. For a spicier salad, use the larger amount of chipotle. We prefer this steak cooked to medium-rare, but if you prefer it more or less done, see our guidelines on page 141. You will need a 12-inch ovensafe skillet for this recipe.

- 1½ teaspoons chili powder
- 1½ teaspoons ground cumin
- 1½ teaspoons packed dark brown sugar
- ¾ teaspoon ground coriander
- 1 teaspoon kosher salt
- ½ teaspoon pepper
  Pinch ground cinnamon
  Pinch red pepper flakes
- 1 (2-pound) flank steak, trimmed
- 3 tablespoons plus 1 teaspoon vegetable oil, divided
- 2 tablespoons lime juice
- 2 scallions, sliced thin

Spice-Rubbed Flank Steak with Toasted Corn and Black Bean Salad

1–2 teaspoons minced canned chipotle chile in adobo sauce
1 (15-ounce) can black beans, rinsed
1 red bell pepper, stemmed, seeded, and chopped fine
¼ cup minced fresh cilantro
3 ears corn, kernels cut from cobs

1. Combine chili powder, cumin, sugar, coriander, salt, pepper, cinnamon, and pepper flakes in bowl. Rub steak with spice mixture, cover with plastic wrap, and refrigerate for at least 1 hour or up to 24 hours.

2. Adjust oven rack to middle position and heat oven to 450 degrees. Whisk 2 tablespoons oil, lime juice, scallions, and chipotle together in large bowl. Stir in beans, bell pepper, and cilantro; set aside.

3. Pat steak dry with paper towels. Heat 1 tablespoon oil in 12-inch ovensafe skillet over medium-high heat until just smoking. Place steak in skillet and cook until well browned on first side, 3 to 4 minutes. Flip steak, transfer skillet to oven, and roast until steak is browned on second side and registers 120 to 125 degrees (for medium-rare), 4 to 5 minutes.

4. Using potholder, remove skillet from oven. Being careful of hot skillet handle, transfer steak to cutting board, tent with aluminum foil, and let rest while preparing salad.

5. Wipe skillet clean with paper towels. Heat remaining 1 teaspoon oil in now-empty skillet over medium heat until shimmering. Add corn and cook, without stirring, until well browned, 5 to 7 minutes. Stir corn into bean salad and season with salt and pepper to taste. Slice steak thin against grain and serve with corn-bean salad.

Strip Steaks with Mushrooms, Asparagus, and Potatoes

SKILLET

Serves 4
Total Time 45 minutes

Why This Recipe Works A unique approach to layering is key to cooking each component perfectly in this skillet dinner. To start, we used the skillet to provide intense heat for a perfect sear on our strip steaks. Adding the potatoes and mushrooms to the steak juices left in the skillet amped up their flavor, and partially cooking them on the stove cooked off enough of their moisture so that they browned in the oven. We layered asparagus on top of the other vegetables and topped the asparagus with the steaks, which allowed all the components to finish cooking at the same time. A creamy horseradish sauce helped unify all the elements of our savory bistro dinner. We prefer these steaks cooked to medium-rare, but if you prefer them more or less done, see our guidelines on page 141. The strength of prepared horseradish can vary greatly; start with 1 tablespoon and add more according to taste. You will need a 12-inch ovensafe skillet for this recipe. You can use a 12-inch nonstick skillet, but make sure it's ovensafe to 400 degrees.

½ cup sour cream
1–2 tablespoons prepared horseradish
2 tablespoons water
2¼ teaspoons table salt, divided
1 teaspoon pepper, divided
2 (1-pound) boneless strip steaks, 1½ to 1¾ inches thick, trimmed and halved crosswise
3 tablespoons unsalted butter, divided, plus 1 tablespoon melted
1 pound Yukon Gold potatoes, unpeeled, cut into ¾-inch pieces
12 ounces cremini mushrooms, trimmed and quartered
1 shallot, halved and sliced thin
3 garlic cloves, sliced thin
1 tablespoon chopped fresh thyme
1 pound asparagus, trimmed

Hibachi-Style Steaks with Zucchini and Shiitakes

Hibachi-Style Steaks with Zucchini and Shiitakes

SKILLET
Serves 4
Total Time 45 minutes

Why This Recipe Works We wanted to deliver all the savory-sweet appeal of a hibachi steakhouse dinner at home. Home kitchens lack the powerful heat and wide space of the flattop, so instead we created a steakhouse-worthy meal in a skillet: juicy strip steaks with shiitakes, onions, and zucchini. We avoided overcrowding—and encouraged browning—by cooking the steak and vegetables separately. As a bonus, cooking the vegetables second gave them a superflavorful start thanks to the steak drippings in the still-hot skillet. We finished the sliced steaks and perfectly browned vegetables with a rich, savory soy-garlic butter. White pepper lends a unique flavor to the stir-fry; black pepper is not a good substitute. We prefer these steaks cooked to medium-rare, but if you prefer them more or less done, see our guidelines on page 141. If using a nonstick skillet, heat the oil in the skillet over medium-high heat until just smoking before adding the steaks in step 2.

- 3 tablespoons unsalted butter, melted
- 2 tablespoons soy sauce
- 2 garlic cloves, minced
- 2 (1-pound) boneless strip or rib-eye steaks, 1½ to 1¾ inches thick, trimmed
- 1¼ teaspoons white pepper, divided
- 1 teaspoon table salt, divided
- 1 tablespoon vegetable oil
- 2 zucchini (8 ounces each), halved lengthwise and sliced ¾ inch thick
- 2 onions, cut into ¾-inch pieces
- 6 ounces shiitake mushrooms, stemmed and halved if small or quartered if large
- 2 tablespoons mirin

1. Combine melted butter, soy sauce, and garlic in bowl; set aside. Pat steaks dry with paper towels and sprinkle with 1 teaspoon white pepper and ¾ teaspoon salt.

2. Heat 12-inch skillet over medium-high heat for 5 minutes. Add oil to skillet and swirl to coat. Add steaks and cook, flipping every 2 minutes, until well browned and meat registers 120 to 125 degrees (for medium-rare), 10 to 13 minutes. Transfer steaks to carving board, tent with aluminum foil, and let rest while preparing vegetables.

3. Add zucchini, onions, mushrooms, remaining ¼ teaspoon white pepper, and remaining ¼ teaspoon salt to fat left in skillet and stir to combine. Pat vegetables into even layer

1. Adjust oven rack to middle position and heat oven to 400 degrees. Combine sour cream, horseradish, water, ¼ teaspoon salt, and ¼ teaspoon pepper in bowl; set aside.

2. Heat 12-inch skillet over medium-high heat for 5 minutes. Pat steaks dry with paper towels and sprinkle with ¾ teaspoon salt and ¼ teaspoon pepper. Melt 1 tablespoon butter in preheated skillet. Add steaks and cook until well browned on both sides, about 3 minutes per side. Transfer steaks to plate; set aside.

3. Melt 2 tablespoons butter in now-empty skillet over medium-high heat. Stir in potatoes, mushrooms, 1 teaspoon salt, and remaining ½ teaspoon pepper. Cook, stirring occasionally, until vegetables are lightly browned, about 10 minutes. Add shallot, garlic, and thyme and cook until shallot is just softened, about 2 minutes.

4. Off heat, place asparagus in single layer on top of vegetables in skillet. Drizzle asparagus with melted butter and sprinkle with remaining ¼ teaspoon salt. Place steaks on top of asparagus.

5. Transfer skillet to oven and roast until steaks register 120 to 125 degrees (for medium-rare), 10 to 15 minutes. Tent skillet with aluminum foil and let steaks rest for 5 minutes. Serve with horseradish sauce.

and cook over medium-high heat, without stirring, until beginning to brown, about 3 minutes. Stir and continue to cook for 2 minutes. Add mirin and 2 tablespoons soy-garlic butter to skillet and continue to cook until liquid has evaporated and vegetables are well browned, about 2 minutes.

4. Transfer vegetables to serving platter. Slice steaks ¼ inch thick and transfer to platter with vegetables. Drizzle steaks with remaining soy-garlic butter. Serve.

Coffee-Chili–Rubbed Steaks with Sweet Potatoes and Scallions

SHEET PAN
Serves 4
Total Time 1¼ hours

Why This Recipe Works While we usually depend on a ripping-hot skillet to turn out steaks with a strong crust, we saw potential in our sheet pan to give us similar results for a complete meal using a more hands-off approach. A pleasantly bitter coffee rub accentuated the meat's savoriness; chili powder added heat, and brown sugar guaranteed some appealing caramelization. We sliced sweet potatoes into wedges and let them soften in the pan as it heated up, then added the steaks 25 minutes in and scattered scallions over the potatoes. Since the pan had preheated while cooking the sweet potatoes, it provided the sizzle we love (and the sear that comes with it) when we added the steaks. Our steaks reached a juicy medium-rare in only 12 minutes. To give our dish a final flourish, we served our steaks with quick-pickled radishes. Don't be afraid to use all of the coffee rub on the steak—it aids in browning in addition to adding flavor. The scallions should be left whole; trim off only the small roots. We prefer these steaks cooked to medium-rare, but if you prefer them more or less done, see our guidelines on page 141.

- 10 radishes, trimmed and sliced thin
- 1 tablespoon lime juice, plus lime wedges for serving
- 1 tablespoon table salt, divided
- 2¼ teaspoons pepper, divided
- 1½ pounds sweet potatoes, unpeeled, cut lengthwise into 1-inch wedges
- 2 tablespoons extra-virgin olive oil, divided
- 16 scallions, trimmed
- 2 tablespoons packed dark brown sugar
- 1 tablespoon finely ground coffee
- 1 tablespoon chili powder
- 2 (1-pound) boneless strip or rib-eye steaks, 1½ to 1¾ inches thick, trimmed

Coffee-Chili–Rubbed Steaks with Sweet Potatoes and Scallions

1. Adjust oven rack to lower-middle position and heat oven to 450 degrees. Toss radishes with lime juice and ¼ teaspoon salt in bowl; cover and refrigerate until ready to serve.

2. Toss potatoes with 1½ tablespoons oil, 1 teaspoon salt, and 1 teaspoon pepper in bowl. Place potatoes skin side down on half of rimmed baking sheet. Roast until potatoes begin to soften, about 25 minutes.

3. Meanwhile, toss scallions with remaining ½ tablespoon oil, ¼ teaspoon salt, and ¼ teaspoon pepper in now-empty bowl. Combine sugar, coffee, chili powder, remaining 1½ teaspoons salt, and remaining 1 teaspoon pepper in small bowl. Pat steaks dry with paper towels and rub with spice mixture.

4. Lay scallions on top of potatoes. Place steaks on empty side of sheet. Roast until steaks register 120 to 125 degrees (for medium-rare) and potatoes are fully tender, 12 to 15 minutes, rotating sheet halfway through roasting.

5. Remove sheet from oven. Transfer steaks bottom side up to cutting board, tent with aluminum foil, and let rest for 5 minutes. Leave vegetables on sheet and tent with foil. Slice steaks ¼ inch thick and serve with vegetables, pickled radishes, and lime wedges.

Seared Steaks with Crispy Potatoes and Herb Sauce

Seared Steaks with Crispy Potatoes and Herb Sauce

SKILLET

Serves 4
Total Time 50 minutes

Why This Recipe Works The true star of this simple meat-and-potatoes skillet meal is the potent herb sauce that coats everything. Inspired by the bright, garlicky flavors of Argentinean chimichurri, we created a bold parsley sauce by stirring fresh parsley with olive oil, red onion, and red wine vinegar. Adding four garlic cloves promised plenty of kick, and red pepper flakes delivered a bit of pleasant heat. With our sauce ready, we seared beefy, well-marbled strip steaks in a hot skillet until well browned. Cooking the steaks to medium-rare kept the meat moist and tender. For a perfectly crisp side of potatoes that used the same pan, we cut red potatoes into wedges and jump-started their cooking in the microwave. Using the meaty juices left behind in the skillet, we imparted some flavorful browning onto the wedges, giving them an appealing golden hue and crisp bite. Feel free to use a single herb or a combination of herbs for the sauce. We prefer these steaks cooked to medium-rare, but if you prefer them more or less done, see our guidelines on page 141.

- 1 cup minced fresh parsley, basil, and/or cilantro
- ¾ cup extra-virgin olive oil, divided
- ¼ cup finely chopped red onion
- ¼ cup red wine vinegar
- 4 garlic cloves, minced
- 1¾ teaspoons table salt, divided
- ¼ teaspoon red pepper flakes
- 1½ pounds red potatoes, unpeeled, cut into 1-inch wedges
- ½ teaspoon pepper, divided
- 2 (1-pound) boneless strip or rib-eye steaks, 1½ to 1¾ inches thick, trimmed

1. Combine parsley, ½ cup oil, onion, vinegar, garlic, 1 teaspoon salt, and pepper flakes in bowl; set aside for serving.

2. Toss potatoes with 1 tablespoon oil, ¼ teaspoon salt, and ¼ teaspoon pepper in bowl. Cover and microwave, stirring occasionally, until potatoes begin to soften, 5 to 7 minutes; drain well.

3. Heat 1 tablespoon oil in 12-inch nonstick skillet over medium-high heat until just smoking. Pat steaks dry with paper towels and sprinkle with remaining ½ teaspoon salt and remaining ¼ teaspoon pepper. Place steaks in skillet and cook, without moving, until well browned on first side, 3 to 5 minutes. Flip steaks, reduce heat to medium, and continue

Tuscan-Style Steak with Garlicky Spinach

to cook until meat registers 120 to 125 degrees (for medium-rare), 5 to 7 minutes. Transfer steaks to cutting board, tent with aluminum foil, and let rest while finishing potatoes.

4. Heat remaining 2 tablespoons oil in now-empty skillet over medium heat until shimmering. Add potatoes and cook, stirring occasionally, until well browned, about 10 minutes. Slice steaks ¼ inch thick and serve with potatoes, passing parsley sauce separately.

VARIATION

Seared Steak with Crispy Potatoes and Herb Sauce for Two

SKILLET

Serves 2

Total Time 50 minutes

Feel free to use a single herb or a combination of herbs for the sauce. We prefer this steak cooked to medium-rare, but if you prefer it more or less done, see our guidelines on page 141.

- 6 tablespoons extra-virgin olive oil, divided
- ¼ cup minced fresh parsley, basil, and/or cilantro
- 1 small shallot, minced
- 1 tablespoon red wine vinegar
- 1 garlic clove, minced
- ½ teaspoon plus ⅛ teaspoon table salt, divided
- ⅛ teaspoon red pepper flakes
- 12 ounces red potatoes, unpeeled, cut into 1-inch wedges
- ¼ teaspoon pepper, divided
- 1 (1-pound) boneless strip or rib-eye steak, 1½ to 1¾ inches thick, trimmed

1. Combine ¼ cup oil, parsley, shallot, vinegar, garlic, ¼ teaspoon salt, and pepper flakes in bowl; set aside for serving.

2. Toss potatoes with 1 teaspoon oil, ⅛ teaspoon salt, and ⅛ teaspoon pepper in bowl. Cover and microwave, stirring occasionally, until potatoes begin to soften, 5 to 7 minutes; drain well.

3. Heat 2 teaspoons oil in 10-inch nonstick skillet over medium-high heat until just smoking. Pat steak dry with paper towels and sprinkle with remaining ¼ teaspoon salt and remaining ⅛ teaspoon pepper. Place steak in skillet and cook, without moving, until well browned on first side, 3 to 5 minutes. Flip steak, reduce heat to medium, and continue to cook until meat registers 120 to 125 degrees (for medium-rare), 5 to 7 minutes. Transfer steak to cutting board, tent with aluminum foil, and let rest while finishing potatoes.

4. Heat remaining 1 tablespoon oil in now-empty skillet over medium heat until shimmering. Add potatoes and cook, stirring occasionally, until well browned, about 10 minutes. Slice steak ¼ inch thick and serve with potatoes, passing parsley sauce separately.

Tuscan-Style Steak with Garlicky Spinach

SKILLET

Serves 4

Total Time 45 minutes

Why This Recipe Works To put the spotlight on the juicy, perfectly cooked porterhouse steaks in this recipe we kept the seasonings to a minimum. We perfumed the meat with subtle garlic flavor by rubbing the steaks with a garlic clove before browning them in a skillet. Since a porterhouse can feel like a meal in itself, we kept the rest simple, adding a side of garlicky spinach to complete the meal. Parcooking the spinach in the microwave helped rid it of excess liquid. We then cooked the spinach in the same skillet with even more garlic (sliced rather than minced to keep it from burning). If you don't have a microwave-safe bowl large enough to accommodate the entire amount of spinach, cook it in a smaller bowl in two batches; reduce the amount of water to 2 tablespoons per batch and the cooking time for each batch to 1 to 2 minutes. We prefer these steaks cooked to medium-rare, but if you prefer them more or less done, see our guidelines on page 141.

- 24 ounces (24 cups) baby spinach
- ¼ cup water
- 2 (1¾-pound) porterhouse or T-bone steaks, 1 to 1½ inches thick, trimmed
- 5 garlic cloves (1 halved, 4 sliced thin), divided
- ½ teaspoon table salt
- ¼ teaspoon pepper
- ¼ cup extra-virgin olive oil, divided
- ¼ teaspoon red pepper flakes
  Lemon wedges

1. Working in batches if necessary, microwave spinach and water in covered bowl, stirring occasionally, until spinach is beginning to wilt and has decreased in volume by half, about 4 minutes. Remove bowl from microwave and keep covered for 1 minute. Carefully uncover spinach, allowing steam to escape away from you, and transfer to colander. Squeeze spinach between tongs to release excess liquid; set aside.

2. Pat steaks dry with paper towels, rub halved garlic clove over bone and meat on each side, and sprinkle with salt and pepper. Heat 1 tablespoon oil in 12-inch skillet over medium-high heat until just smoking. Place steaks in skillet and cook, without moving, until well browned on first side, 5 to 7 minutes. Flip steaks, reduce heat to medium, and continue to cook until meat registers 120 to 125 degrees (for medium-rare), 5 to 12 minutes. Transfer steaks to carving board, tent with aluminum foil, and let rest for 5 to 10 minutes.

3. Cook 1 tablespoon oil, pepper flakes, and sliced garlic in now-empty skillet over medium heat until fragrant, about 2 minutes. Add spinach and cook until heated through, about 2 minutes. Season with salt and pepper to taste.

4. Cut strip and tenderloin pieces off bones, then slice each piece ¼ inch thick. Transfer steaks to serving platter and drizzle with remaining 2 tablespoons oil. Serve with spinach and lemon wedges.

VARIATION

Tuscan-Style Steak with Garlicky Spinach for Two
SKILLET
Serves 2
Total Time 45 minutes
We prefer these steaks cooked to medium-rare, but if you prefer them more or less done, see our guidelines on page 141.

12 ounces (12 cups) baby spinach
2 tablespoons water
1 (1¾-pound) porterhouse or T-bone steak,
   1 to 1½ inches thick, trimmed
3 garlic cloves (1 halved, 2 sliced thin), divided
¼ teaspoon table salt
⅛ teaspoon pepper
2 tablespoons plus 1 teaspoon extra-virgin olive
   oil, divided
⅛ teaspoon red pepper flakes
   Lemon wedges

1. Microwave spinach and water in covered bowl, stirring occasionally, until spinach is beginning to wilt and has decreased in volume by half, 1 to 2 minutes. Remove bowl from microwave and keep covered for 1 minute. Carefully uncover spinach, allowing steam to escape away from you, and transfer to colander. Squeeze spinach between tongs to release excess liquid; set aside.

2. Pat steak dry with paper towels, rub halved garlic clove over bone and meat on each side, and sprinkle with salt and pepper. Heat 2 teaspoons oil in 10-inch skillet over medium-high heat until just smoking. Place steak in skillet and cook, without moving, until well browned on first side, 5 to 7 minutes. Flip steak, reduce heat to medium, and continue to cook until meat registers 120 to 125 degrees (for medium-rare), 5 to 12 minutes. Transfer steak to carving board, tent with aluminum foil, and let rest for 5 to 10 minutes.

3. Cook 2 teaspoons oil, pepper flakes, and sliced garlic in now-empty skillet over medium heat until fragrant, about 2 minutes. Add spinach and cook until heated through, about 2 minutes. Season with salt and pepper to taste.

4. Cut strip and tenderloin pieces off bone, then slice each piece ¼ inch thick. Transfer steak to serving platter and drizzle with remaining 1 tablespoon oil. Serve with spinach and lemon wedges.

SLICING T-BONE AND PORTERHOUSE STEAKS

1. Cut along bone to remove smaller tenderloin section from bone.

2. Turn steak around and cut large strip section.

3. Slice each section crosswise ¼ inch thick.

INGREDIENT SPOTLIGHT

PORTERHOUSE VERSUS T-BONE STEAKS
A porterhouse steak is really just a huge T-bone steak—usually large enough to serve two people. Because of its size (it's typically cut thicker than the T-bone), you'll often see it served sliced up for portioning purposes. The T-bone is cut from the front of the short loin, which captures the tapered part of the tenderloin; the tenderloin portion of the porterhouse is larger than it is on the T-bone, because it's cut farther back. This larger tenderloin portion gives the porterhouse a higher price tag. In fact, there are rules to this prized cut: The USDA requires a steak's tenderloin portion to measure 1¼ inches or greater from bone to edge for it to be classified "porterhouse."

Teriyaki Stir-Fried Beef with
Green Beans and Shiitakes

1 (1½-pound) flank steak, trimmed
1 tablespoon water
¼ teaspoon baking soda
3 garlic cloves, minced
1 tablespoon grated fresh ginger
3 tablespoons vegetable oil, divided
½ cup chicken broth
3 tablespoons soy sauce, divided
2 tablespoons sugar
1 tablespoon mirin
1¾ teaspoons cornstarch, divided
¼ teaspoon red pepper flakes
8 ounces shiitake mushrooms, stemmed and cut into
   1-inch pieces
12 ounces green beans, trimmed and halved
4 scallions, cut into 1½-inch pieces, white parts
   quartered lengthwise

1. Cut steak with grain into 2½- to 3-inch-wide strips
and place on large plate; freeze until firm, about 15 minutes.
Cut strips crosswise against grain into ⅛-inch-thick slices.
Combine water and baking soda in medium bowl. Add beef
and toss to coat; let sit for 5 minutes.

2. Combine garlic, ginger, and 1 tablespoon oil in small
bowl; set aside. Whisk broth, 2 tablespoons soy sauce, sugar,
mirin, 1 teaspoon cornstarch, and pepper flakes in second
small bowl until sugar has dissolved; set aside. Add remaining
1 tablespoon soy sauce and remaining ¾ teaspoon cornstarch
to beef and toss until well combined.

3. Heat 2 teaspoons oil in 12-inch nonstick skillet over
medium-high heat until just smoking. Add half of beef and
increase heat to high. Cook, tossing beef slowly but constantly, until no longer pink, 2 to 6 minutes; transfer to clean
medium bowl. Repeat with 2 teaspoons oil and remaining
beef; transfer to bowl with first batch of beef.

4. Heat remaining 2 teaspoons oil in now-empty skillet
over high heat until just smoking. Add mushrooms and green
beans and cook, tossing slowly but constantly, until spotty
brown, 2 to 6 minutes. Add 2 tablespoons water (water will
sputter), cover, and cook until green beans are crisp-tender,
2 to 3 minutes.

5. Push vegetables to one side of skillet and reduce heat
to medium. Add garlic mixture to clearing and cook, mashing
mixture into skillet, until fragrant, about 30 seconds. Stir
garlic mixture into vegetables.

6. Whisk broth mixture to recombine, then add to skillet
along with beef and any accumulated juices and scallions.
Increase heat to high and cook, tossing constantly, until sauce
has thickened, about 30 seconds. Serve.

Teriyaki Stir-Fried Beef with Green Beans and Shiitakes

SKILLET
Serves 4
Total Time 50 minutes

Why This Recipe Works Versatile stir-fries are ready-made
skillet dinners, but because they cook so quickly it's important
to time everything just right. We started by slicing flank steak
thin and coating it in a mixture of baking soda and water,
which upped the pH of the meat and helped it stay tender.
Coating the meat in a mixture of soy sauce and cornstarch
heightened its savory flavor, and searing in batches ensured
optimal browning. Green beans and meaty shiitakes, browned
first and steamed to finish, provided contrast. Mashing fresh
ginger and garlic in the center of the pan unlocked more flavor
before we tossed everything with a gently spicy sauce. Stir-fries
cook quickly, so have everything prepped before you begin cooking. We developed this recipe for a 12-inch nonstick skillet
with a tight-fitting lid, but a 14-inch flat-bottomed wok can
be used instead. Serve with rice (see page 21).

Teriyaki Stir-Fried Beef with Green Beans and Shiitakes for Two

SKILLET

Serves 2

Total Time 45 minutes

Stir-fries cook quickly, so have everything prepped before you begin cooking. We developed this recipe for a 12-inch nonstick skillet with a tight-fitting lid, but a 14-inch flat-bottomed wok can be used instead. Serve with rice (see page 21).

 1 (12-ounce) flank steak, trimmed
1½ teaspoons water
 ⅛ teaspoon baking soda
 2 garlic cloves, minced
1½ teaspoons grated fresh ginger
 2 tablespoons vegetable oil, divided
 ¼ cup chicken broth
 5 teaspoons soy sauce, divided
 1 tablespoon sugar
1½ teaspoons mirin
 ¾ teaspoon cornstarch, divided
 ⅛ teaspoon red pepper flakes
 4 ounces shiitake mushrooms, stemmed and cut into 1-inch pieces
 6 ounces green beans, trimmed and halved
 2 scallions, cut into 1½-inch pieces, white parts quartered lengthwise

1. Cut steak with grain into 2½- to 3-inch-wide strips and place on large plate; freeze until firm, about 15 minutes. Cut strips crosswise against grain into ⅛-inch-thick slices. Combine water and baking soda in medium bowl. Add beef and toss to coat; let sit for 5 minutes.

2. Combine garlic, ginger, and 2 teaspoons oil in small bowl; set aside. Whisk broth, 1 tablespoon soy sauce, sugar, mirin, ½ teaspoon cornstarch, and pepper flakes in second small bowl until sugar has dissolved; set aside. Add remaining 2 teaspoons soy sauce and remaining ¼ teaspoon cornstarch to beef and toss until well combined.

3. Heat 2 teaspoons oil in 12-inch nonstick skillet over medium-high heat until just smoking. Add beef and increase heat to high. Cook, tossing beef slowly but constantly, until no longer pink, 2 to 6 minutes; transfer to clean medium bowl.

4. Heat remaining 2 teaspoons oil in now-empty skillet over high heat until just smoking. Add mushrooms and green beans and cook, tossing slowly but constantly, until spotty brown, 2 to 6 minutes. Add 2 tablespoons water (water will sputter), cover, and cook until green beans are crisp-tender, 2 to 3 minutes.

5. Push vegetables to one side of skillet and reduce heat to medium. Add garlic mixture to clearing and cook, mashing mixture into skillet, until fragrant, about 30 seconds. Stir garlic mixture into vegetables.

6. Whisk broth mixture to recombine, then add to skillet along with beef and any accumulated juices and scallions. Increase heat to high and cook, tossing constantly, until sauce has thickened, about 30 seconds. Serve.

Stir-Fried Thai-Style Beef with Chiles and Shallots

SKILLET

Serves 4

Total Time 50 minutes

Why This Recipe Works Two sources bring the heat to this sophisticated Thai stir-fry: a generous amount of sliced Thai chiles, plus sriracha, an easily controllable heat source. Tossing flank steak with baking soda and water ensured it would stay tender while cooking. We then made a marinade for the beef with briny fish sauce, spicy white pepper, and citrusy coriander. After searing the meat in a skillet, we set it aside and cooked shallots and garlic in the same pan. More fish sauce, as well as brown sugar, rice vinegar, and sriracha, all went in the skillet before we added the meat back in and tossed it all to bring the flavors together. Fresh mint and cilantro, a few crunchy chopped peanuts, and a squeeze of bright lime juice finished the dish. White pepper lends a unique flavor to the stir-fry; black pepper is not a good substitute. If fresh Thai chiles are unavailable, substitute one serrano or one-half jalapeño. Stir-fries cook quickly, so have everything prepped before you begin cooking. We developed this recipe for a 12-inch nonstick skillet, but a 14-inch flat-bottomed wok can be used instead. Serve with rice (see page 21).

 1 (1½-pound) flank steak, trimmed
 3 tablespoons water, divided
 ¼ teaspoon baking soda
 2 tablespoons plus 1 teaspoon vegetable oil, divided
 3 garlic cloves, minced
 3 Thai chiles, stemmed, seeded, and sliced thin
 3 tablespoons fish sauce, divided
 2 tablespoons unseasoned rice vinegar
 1 tablespoon packed light brown sugar
 1 tablespoon sriracha
 ¾ teaspoon ground coriander
 ¾ teaspoon cornstarch

Stir-Fried Thai-Style Beef with Chiles and Shallots

⅛ teaspoon ground white pepper

3 shallots, peeled, quartered, and layers separated

½ cup coarsely chopped fresh mint, divided

½ cup fresh cilantro leaves, divided

⅓ cup dry-roasted peanuts, chopped

Lime wedges

1. Cut steak with grain into 2½- to 3-inch-wide strips and place on large plate; freeze until firm, about 15 minutes. Cut strips crosswise against grain into ⅛-inch-thick slices. Combine 1 tablespoon water and baking soda in medium bowl. Add beef and toss to coat; let sit for 5 minutes.

2. Combine 1 teaspoon oil, garlic, and Thai chiles in small bowl; set aside. Whisk 2 tablespoons fish sauce, vinegar, sugar, sriracha, and remaining 2 tablespoons water in third small bowl until sugar has dissolved; set aside. Add remaining 1 tablespoon fish sauce, coriander, cornstarch, and pepper to beef and toss until well combined.

3. Heat 2 teaspoons oil in 12-inch nonstick skillet over medium-high heat until just smoking. Add half of beef and increase heat to high. Cook, tossing beef slowly but constantly, until no longer pink, 2 to 6 minutes; transfer to clean medium bowl. Repeat with 2 teaspoons oil and remaining beef; transfer to bowl with first batch of beef.

4. Heat remaining 2 teaspoons oil in now-empty skillet over high heat until just smoking. Add shallots and cook, tossing slowly but constantly, until beginning to soften, 3 to 5 minutes. Push shallots to one side of skillet and reduce heat to medium. Add garlic mixture to clearing and cook, mashing mixture into skillet, until fragrant, about 30 seconds. Stir garlic mixture into vegetables.

5. Add fish sauce mixture to skillet and increase heat to high. Cook until slightly reduced and thickened, about 30 seconds. Return beef and any accumulated juices to skillet and toss to combine. Off heat, stir in ¼ cup mint and ¼ cup cilantro. Sprinkle with peanuts, remaining ¼ cup mint, and remaining ¼ cup cilantro. Serve with lime wedges.

CUTTING UP FLANK STEAK FOR STIR-FRY

1. Cut steak with grain into 2½- to 3-inch-wide strips. To make slicing flank steak easier, freeze it until firm, about 15 minutes.

2. Cut strips crosswise against grain into ⅛-inch-thick slices.

Steak Fajitas

SHEET PAN
Serves 4
Total Time 45 minutes

Why This Recipe Works Restaurant fajitas are a sizzling spectacle served up in a skillet, but to make a recipe at home that served more than one or two people we needed more space than a skillet could provide. Instead, we turned to a baking sheet, which could easily accommodate a good-sized flank steak along with plenty of peppers and onion to serve four. Since we couldn't sear the meat on a baking sheet, we relied on a potent, dark-colored spice rub to make up for the missing flavor and color. A mixture of chili powder, brown sugar, salt, and pepper did the trick. After tossing strips of bell peppers, rings of red onion, and slices of garlic in vegetable oil, salt, and pepper, we spread them out on the baking sheet and slid it into the oven on the lower-middle rack to ensure that the vegetables browned rather than steamed. We then pushed the vegetables to one side of the baking sheet and added the rubbed steak, cut into three equal pieces, to the other side. Cooked to medium instead of medium-rare, the steak was less chewy when sliced and dropped into a tortilla. We tossed the browned, tender vegetables with a little lime juice to brighten their flavors and sprinkled both the vegetables and sliced steak with chopped cilantro for a burst of freshness. We prefer to cook this steak to medium so that it is less chewy and therefore easier to eat; if you prefer it more or less done, see our guidelines on page 141. Feel free to use a mix of bell peppers for a more colorful presentation. Serve with Pico de Gallo, avocado or guacamole, sour cream, your favorite hot sauce, and/or lime wedges.

  3 green, red, orange, and/or yellow bell peppers, stemmed, seeded, and cut into ½-inch-wide strips
  1 large red onion, cut into ½-inch-thick rounds
  3 garlic cloves, sliced thin
  1 tablespoon vegetable oil
  1 tablespoon table salt, divided
  2 teaspoons pepper, divided
1½ tablespoons chili powder
  1 teaspoon packed brown sugar
  1 (1½-pound) flank steak, trimmed
12–18 (6-inch) flour tortillas
  1 tablespoon lime juice
  2 tablespoons chopped fresh cilantro

1. Adjust oven rack to lower-middle position and heat oven to 475 degrees. Toss bell peppers, onion, garlic, oil, 1 teaspoon salt, and 1 teaspoon pepper together on rimmed baking sheet and spread into even layer. Roast until vegetables are lightly browned around edges, about 10 minutes.

2. Meanwhile, combine chili powder, sugar, remaining 2 teaspoons salt, and remaining 1 teaspoon pepper in bowl. Cut steak lengthwise with grain into 3 equal pieces. Pat steaks dry with paper towels, then sprinkle with spice mixture. Wrap tortillas in aluminum foil; set aside.

3. Remove sheet from oven. Using rubber spatula, push vegetables to 1 half of sheet. Place steaks on other half of sheet, leaving space between steaks. Roast until vegetables are spotty brown and meat registers 130 to 135 degrees (for medium), about 8 minutes.

4. Remove sheet from oven, transfer steaks to cutting board, and let rest, uncovered, for 5 minutes. Place tortilla packet in oven until warm, about 5 minutes. Transfer vegetables to serving platter and toss with lime juice.

5. Slice steaks thin against grain and transfer to platter with vegetables. Sprinkle with cilantro. Serve steak and vegetables with warm tortillas.

Pico de Gallo

Makes about 1½ cups
To make this sauce spicier, include the jalapeño ribs and seeds.

  3 tomatoes, cored and chopped
  ¼ teaspoon table salt
  ¼ cup finely chopped red onion
  ¼ cup chopped fresh cilantro
  1 jalapeño chile, stemmed, seeded, and minced
  1 tablespoon lime juice
  1 garlic clove, minced

Toss tomatoes with salt in bowl. Transfer to colander and let drain for 30 minutes. Combine drained tomatoes, onion, cilantro, jalapeño, lime juice, and garlic in bowl. Season with salt and pepper to taste.

Shredded Beef Lettuce Wraps with Pickled Cucumber and Bean Sprouts

SLOW COOKER
Serves 4 to 6
Cook Time 7 to 9 hours on low or 4 to 6 hours on high

Why This Recipe Works The constant, gentle heat of the slow cooker turns short ribs meltingly tender and shreddable, so we wanted a recipe that would highlight the supple meat. We looked to the flavors of Korean BBQ for inspiration and created a base of fruity hoisin sauce, fresh ginger, and garlic. Instead of adding extra liquid (typically broth or water) to our base as we do for most braises, we allowed the meat's natural juices to meld with the glaze base to build a flavor-rich sauce. The addition of rice vinegar, more hoisin, and sesame oil after cooking brightened the flavor of the dish, while scallions added freshness. Quick-pickled cucumber and bean sprouts lent welcome crunch and were an ideal contrast to the tender meat. We prefer to serve the short rib and pickles wrapped in lettuce leaves to be eaten like a taco, but they are also delicious served over rice.

Beef
- ½ cup hoisin sauce, divided
- 4 teaspoons grated fresh ginger
- 4 garlic cloves, minced
- ¼ teaspoon red pepper flakes
- 2 pounds boneless beef short ribs, trimmed and cut into 1½-inch pieces
- 1 tablespoon rice vinegar
- 2 teaspoons toasted sesame oil
- 2 scallions, sliced thin

Pickles
- 1 cup unseasoned rice vinegar
- 2 tablespoons sugar
- 1½ teaspoons table salt
- 4 ounces (2 cups) bean sprouts
- 1 cucumber, peeled, quartered lengthwise, seeded, and sliced thin on bias

- 2 heads Bibb lettuce (8 ounces each), leaves separated

1. For the beef Combine 6 tablespoons hoisin, ginger, garlic, and pepper flakes in slow cooker. Stir in beef, cover, and cook until tender, 7 to 9 hours on low or 4 to 6 hours on high.

Steak Fajitas

Shredded Beef Lettuce Wraps with Pickled Cucumber and Bean Sprouts

Wild Mushroom Burgers with Bistro Salad

Meatball Subs with Roasted Broccoli

Wild Mushroom Burgers with Bistro Salad

SKILLET
Serves 4
Total Time 1 hour

Why This Recipe Works With their earthy flavor and satisfying texture, wild mushrooms make an intensely savory, meaty topping for these decadent beef burgers. Starting our patties with 85 percent lean beef guaranteed juicy meat, and pressing a small indentation into the shaped patties prevented them from puffing up while cooking. For perfectly cooked mushrooms, we cooked them covered until they released their moisture. Next, we uncovered the mushrooms and cooked them until golden brown and tender, which fortified their umami-rich flavor without making them chewy. Aromatics provided another layer of flavor and parsley leaves added freshness. Once it was piled on the patties, the mushroom topping intensified the meatiness of the burgers. We finished by spreading tangy goat cheese over the bun tops, which provided a pleasing contrast to the rich flavor of the mushrooms. To pair with these luxuriously beefy burgers, we wanted a lighter side. Inspired by bistro salad, we made a quick dressing with red wine vinegar, Dijon mustard, and shallot for bright, sharp flavors and mayonnaise for a little creaminess. We drizzled the dressing over a combination of frisée and romaine, which provided crunchy texture and a slight bitterness. Although we prefer a mix of wild mushrooms, you can use 12 ounces of just one type if you'd like. We prefer these burgers cooked to medium-rare, but if you prefer them more or less done, see our guidelines on page 141.

Burgers

- 1¾ pounds 85 percent lean ground beef
- 3 tablespoons unsalted butter, divided
- 1 onion, chopped
- 12 ounces chanterelle, shiitake, and oyster mushrooms, trimmed and cut into 1-inch pieces
- ¾ teaspoon table salt, divided
- 2 garlic cloves, minced
- 1 teaspoon minced fresh thyme or ¼ teaspoon dried
- ¼ cup dry white wine
- ½ teaspoon pepper
- 1 tablespoon vegetable oil
- ⅓ cup fresh parsley leaves
- 4 ounces goat cheese, room temperature
- 4 hamburger buns, toasted if desired

Salad

- 1 tablespoon red wine vinegar
- 1½ teaspoons minced shallot
- ½ teaspoon mayonnaise
- ½ teaspoon Dijon mustard
- ⅛ teaspoon table salt
- ⅛ teaspoon pepper
- 3 tablespoons extra-virgin olive oil
- 1 head frisée (6 ounces), trimmed and cut into 1-inch pieces
- 1 romaine lettuce heart (6 ounces), trimmed and cut into 1-inch pieces

1. For the burgers Divide ground beef into 4 lightly packed balls, then gently flatten into ¾-inch-thick patties. Using your fingertips, press center of each patty down until about ½ inch thick, creating slight indentation; set aside.

2. Melt 2 tablespoons butter in 12-inch skillet over medium heat. Add onion and cook until softened, about 5 minutes. Stir in mushrooms and ¼ teaspoon salt, cover, and cook until mushrooms have released their moisture, about 3 minutes. Add remaining 1 tablespoon butter and cook, uncovered, until mushrooms are deep golden brown and tender, 5 to 7 minutes. Stir in garlic and thyme and cook until fragrant, about 30 seconds. Stir in wine and cook, scraping up any browned bits, until liquid is nearly evaporated, about 30 seconds; transfer to bowl and cover to keep warm.

3. Sprinkle patties with remaining ½ teaspoon salt and pepper. Heat oil in now-empty skillet over medium heat until just smoking. Transfer patties to skillet indentation side up and cook until well browned on first side, 2 to 4 minutes. Flip patties and continue to cook until browned on second side and meat registers 120 to 125 degrees (for medium-rare), 3 to 5 minutes. Transfer burgers to platter and let rest while preparing salad.

4. For the salad Whisk vinegar, shallot, mayonnaise, mustard, salt, and pepper together in large bowl. While whisking constantly, slowly drizzle in oil until combined. Add frisée and romaine and toss to coat. Season with salt and pepper to taste.

5. Stir parsley into mushroom mixture and season with salt and pepper to taste. Spread goat cheese on bun tops. Serve burgers on buns, topped with mushroom mixture, passing salad separately.

Meatball Subs with Roasted Broccoli
SHEET PAN
Serves 4
Total Time 1 hour

Why This Recipe Works Saucy meatball subs with melted cheese are a deli staple, but for home cooks making the key components of these sandwiches—the meatballs and sauce—can be a chore that leaves a massive mess in the kitchen. To keep things simple our entire recipe happens on a sheet pan in the oven and avoids the usual stovetop splatter. Panko bread crumbs and egg helped bind the meatballs and kept them tender, and dropping the rolled meatballs right from the mixing bowl onto the sheet pan eliminated extra dishes. For our side dish, we wanted something light to balance out these filling sandwiches. Broccoli tossed with a little oil and sugar for sweetness roasted right alongside the meatballs to satisfy our need for something green. And rather than making our own sauce, we turned to convenient jarred pasta sauce. Assembling the subs on the sheet pan and putting the completed sandwiches back in the oven for just a few minutes allowed the cheese and sauce to warm through. We developed this recipe using jarred marinara sauce, but you can also use our Quick Marinara Sauce (page 317). Toasting the rolls prevents them from becoming soggy before serving.

- ¾ cup panko bread crumbs
- 2 large eggs, lightly beaten
- 1 teaspoon garlic powder
- 1¼ teaspoons table salt, divided
- ¾ teaspoon pepper, divided
- 1¼ pounds 85 percent lean ground beef
- 1 head broccoli (about 1½ pounds)
- 2 tablespoons extra-virgin olive oil, plus extra for drizzling
- ½ teaspoon sugar
- 4 (6-inch) Italian sub rolls, split lengthwise and toasted
- 1⅓ cups jarred marinara sauce
- 4 thin slices deli provolone cheese (4 ounces)
- 2 teaspoons lemon juice

1. Adjust oven rack to middle position and heat oven to 475 degrees. Grease aluminum foil–lined rimmed baking sheet.

2. Using fork, mash panko and eggs together into paste in large bowl. Stir in garlic powder, 1 teaspoon salt, and ½ teaspoon pepper. Add ground beef and knead mixture with your hands until well combined. Pinch off and roll 2-inch pieces of mixture into balls and arrange on 1 half of prepared sheet (you should have 12 meatballs).

3. Cut broccoli at juncture of florets and stems; remove outer peel from stalk. Cut stalk into ½-inch-thick planks, 2 to 3 inches long. Cut crowns into 4 wedges if 3 to 4 inches in diameter or 6 wedges if 4 to 5 inches in diameter. Toss broccoli with oil, sugar, remaining ¼ teaspoon salt, and remaining ¼ teaspoon pepper. Lay broccoli cut side down on opposite side of sheet from meatballs. Roast until meatballs are cooked through, about 20 minutes.

4. Transfer meatballs to plate and return sheet to oven. Continue to roast broccoli until tender, about 5 minutes. Transfer broccoli to serving platter. Discard foil.

5. Place rolls on now-empty sheet and lay 3 meatballs inside each roll. Top meatballs on each sandwich with ⅓ cup marinara sauce and 1 slice provolone. Bake until cheese is melted and sauce is heated through, about 5 minutes. Drizzle broccoli with lemon juice and extra oil. Serve with meatball subs.

INGREDIENT SPOTLIGHT

JARRED PASTA SAUCE

Tomato sauce is a staple of Italian American cooking, and though we usually prefer to make our own from canned or fresh tomatoes, some nights call for a quick jarred sauce. To find a winner, we tasted 10 jarred pasta sauces plain and tossed with spaghetti. We focused on sauces labeled as marinara, traditional, or tomato basil and eliminated any containing wine, cheese, vegetables, meat, or cream. In the end, **Rao's Homemade Marinara Sauce**

won the tasting. This sauce had "vibrant tomato flavor," "bright" acidity, and "gentle aromatic undertones" of garlic and basil. Its hearty dose of olive oil lent a "buttery," "creamy" richness to pasta. Tasters also loved its "balanced," "natural" sweetness, which reminded many tasters of "homemade."

Zucchini Noodles with Pesto Meatballs

SHEET PAN
Serves 4
Total Time 45 minutes

Why This Recipe Works This simplified sheet-pan spin on spaghetti and meatballs delivers classic flavors without ever using the stovetop. To start, we passed up the traditional pasta noodles in favor of spiralized zucchini, which didn't require boiling. Roasting the noodles removed excess moisture and concentrated their flavor. Rather than a traditional marinara, we chose a richly flavored simple basil pesto that paired well with the flavor of the zucchini and then topped it with cherry tomatoes as a nod to the classic. A panade of panko bread crumbs and milk helped keep the meatballs tender, and for even more pesto flavor we added some to the meatballs, infusing them with herbal notes. A sprinkling of nutty Parmesan offered a rich finishing touch. We prefer to spiralize our own zucchini; you can substitute 1 pound of store-bought spiralized zucchini, though they tend to be drier and less flavorful. Avoid buying large zucchini, which have thicker skins and more seeds. You can use our Classic Basil Pesto (page 45) or any fresh store-bought variety here.

¾ cup panko bread crumbs
¾ cup milk
½ cup basil pesto, divided
1 teaspoon table salt, divided
¼ teaspoon red pepper flakes
1 pound 85 percent lean ground beef
3 zucchini (8 ounces each), ends trimmed
2 teaspoons extra-virgin olive oil
¼ teaspoon pepper
4 ounces cherry tomatoes, quartered
¼ cup grated Parmesan cheese

1. Adjust oven rack to middle position and heat oven to 375 degrees. Using fork, mash panko and milk into paste in large bowl. Stir in 5 tablespoons pesto, ¾ teaspoon salt, and pepper flakes until combined. Add ground beef and knead mixture with your hands until well combined. Pinch off and roll mixture into 1½-inch meatballs (you should have 12 meatballs); set aside.

2. Using spiralizer, cut zucchini into ⅛-inch-thick noodles, then cut noodles into 12-inch lengths. Toss zucchini with oil, pepper, and remaining ¼ teaspoon salt on rimmed baking sheet and spread into even layer. Roast for 5 minutes, then push zucchini to sides of sheet and arrange meatballs in center. Roast until zucchini is tender and meatballs are cooked through, 10 to 15 minutes.

3. Remove zucchini and meatballs from oven. Transfer zucchini to colander and shake to remove any excess liquid. Toss zucchini with remaining 3 tablespoons pesto in bowl, then divide among individual serving bowls. Top with meatballs, tomatoes, and Parmesan. Serve.

Glazed Meatloaf with Potatoes and Brussels Sprouts

SHEET PAN
Serves 4
Total Time 1½ hours

Why This Recipe Works In the test kitchen we've found that we often prefer a free-form meatloaf made on a sheet pan since we can coat the sides with all of the flavorful glaze. The bonus of this cooking method is that there's ample space on the sheet pan to roast side dishes at the same time. For a totally hands-off one-pan meal of meatloaf, roasted potatoes, and Brussels sprouts, we started by choosing straightforward meatloaf ingredients that didn't require precooking. A panade of crushed saltines and milk kept the ground beef moist in the oven. Soy sauce and grated Parmesan cheese added savory depth while fresh thyme, granulated garlic, and red pepper flakes added pep. Two eggs held the meatloaf together, and a coating of ketchup turned into an intensely sweet and tangy glaze that nicely complemented the meat. Hearty small red potatoes and Brussels sprouts were the perfect vegetables to roast alongside the meatloaf; they only got better the longer they cooked in the 400-degree oven, turning creamy inside and deeply browned and crisp on the bottom. To brighten up the vegetables' deep roasted flavor, we gave them a quick toss in a lemon-parsley oil just before serving. There are about 35 saltines in one sleeve of crackers. Use small red potatoes measuring 1 to 2 inches in diameter; if your potatoes are larger, cut them into 1-inch pieces to ensure that they cook through properly. Use Brussels sprouts no bigger than golf balls, as larger ones are often tough and woody.

Zucchini Noodles with Pesto Meatballs

Glazed Meatloaf with Potatoes and Brussels Sprouts

35 square saltines
2 ounces Parmesan cheese, grated (1 cup)
2 large eggs
¼ cup milk
¼ cup soy sauce
1½ tablespoons minced fresh thyme,
   or 1½ teaspoons dried
1½ teaspoons granulated garlic
¼ teaspoon red pepper flakes
¾ teaspoon table salt, divided
½ teaspoon pepper, divided
2 pounds 85 percent lean ground beef
½ cup ketchup
1 pound small red potatoes, unpeeled, halved
1 pound Brussels sprouts, trimmed and halved
3 tablespoons extra-virgin olive oil, divided
1 tablespoon chopped fresh parsley
½ teaspoon grated lemon zest

1. Adjust oven rack to lower-middle position and heat oven to 400 degrees. Spray rimmed baking sheet with vegetable oil spray.

2. Transfer saltines to 1-gallon zipper-lock bag, seal bag, and crush fine with rolling pin. Combine Parmesan, eggs, milk, soy sauce, thyme, granulated garlic, pepper flakes, ¼ teaspoon salt, ¼ teaspoon pepper, and saltine crumbs in large bowl. Mix until all crumbs are moistened and mixture forms paste. Add beef and mix with your hands to thoroughly combine.

3. Transfer meatloaf mixture to center of prepared sheet. Using your wet hands, shape into 9 by 5-inch rectangle; top should be flat and meatloaf should be an even 1½ inches thick. Brush top and sides of meatloaf with ketchup.

4. Toss potatoes, Brussels sprouts, 2 tablespoons oil, remaining ½ teaspoon salt, and remaining ¼ teaspoon pepper together in bowl. Place vegetables cut side down on sheet around meatloaf. Bake until meatloaf registers 160 degrees and vegetables are tender and browned on bottoms, 40 to 45 minutes, rotating sheet halfway through baking.

5. Remove sheet from oven. Transfer meatloaf to cutting board; let rest for 10 minutes. Stir parsley, lemon zest, and remaining 1 tablespoon oil in medium bowl until combined. Transfer vegetables to parsley mixture and toss until evenly coated. Slice meatloaf and serve with vegetables.

VARIATION

Glazed Meatloaf with Carrots and Turnips for Two
SHEET PAN
Serves 2
Total Time 1¼ hours

10 square saltines
¼ cup grated Parmesan cheese
1 large egg
2 tablespoons water
2 teaspoons soy sauce
¾ teaspoon minced fresh thyme or ⅛ teaspoon dried
½ teaspoon granulated garlic
¼ teaspoon pepper, divided
12 ounces 85 percent lean ground beef
3 tablespoons ketchup
2 carrots, peeled and cut into 2½-inch lengths,
   halved or quartered lengthwise to create
   ½-inch-diameter pieces
6 ounces turnips, peeled and cut into 1-inch pieces
¼ teaspoon table salt
4 teaspoons extra-virgin olive oil, divided
¼ teaspoon grated lemon zest

1. Adjust oven rack to lower-middle position and heat oven to 400 degrees. Spray rimmed baking sheet with vegetable oil spray.

2. Transfer saltines to 1-gallon zipper-lock bag, seal bag, and crush fine with rolling pin. Combine Parmesan, egg, water, soy sauce, thyme, granulated garlic, ⅛ teaspoon pepper, and saltine crumbs in large bowl. Mix until all crumbs are moistened and mixture forms paste. Add beef and mix with your hands to thoroughly combine.

3. Transfer meatloaf mixture to center of prepared sheet. Using your wet hands, shape into 7 by 3½-inch rectangle; top should be flat and meatloaf should be an even 1½ inches thick. Brush top and sides of meatloaf with ketchup.

4. Toss carrots, turnips, salt, 2 teaspoons oil, and remaining ⅛ teaspoon pepper together in bowl. Place vegetables cut side down on sheet around meatloaf. Bake until meatloaf registers 160 degrees and vegetables are tender and browned on bottoms, 25 to 35 minutes, rotating sheet halfway through baking.

5. Remove sheet from oven. Transfer meatloaf to cutting board; let rest for 10 minutes. Stir lemon zest and remaining 2 teaspoons oil in medium bowl until combined. Transfer vegetables to zest mixture and toss until evenly coated. Slice meatloaf and serve with vegetables.

Braised Blade Steaks with Mushrooms, Vidalias, and Steamed Asparagus

DUTCH OVEN

Serves 4

Total Time 3¼ hours

Why This Recipe Works Braising large pieces of meat typically takes up an entire Dutch oven, so we were pleased to find that we could cook a vegetable side dish at the same time using a steamer basket to make a second tier in the pot. Tough blade steaks turned meltingly tender when braised and produced a sauce full of beefy flavor. Along with them we braised earthy mushrooms (two kinds for textural contrast) and sweet Vidalia onions. Dry sherry added complexity. Toward the end of the braising time we added asparagus, which we steamed right over the meat and tossed with a lemon-chive compound butter; more lemon and chives balanced our rich sauce. Use asparagus spears between ¼ and ½ inch in diameter at base. Any sweet onion, such as Walla Walla, can be substituted for the Vidalia onion. Serve with Buttered Egg Noodles (page 17). You will need a collapsible steamer basket for this recipe.

- 4 (6- to 8-ounce) beef blade steaks, ¾ to 1 inch thick, trimmed
- 1 teaspoon table salt, divided
- ¼ teaspoon pepper
- 2 tablespoons vegetable oil, divided
- 2 Vidalia onions, halved and sliced thin
- 12 ounces cremini mushrooms, trimmed and sliced thin
- 12 ounces portobello mushroom caps, halved and sliced thin
- 1 tablespoon minced fresh thyme or 1 teaspoon dried
- 1½ teaspoons paprika
- 2 tablespoons all-purpose flour
- ¾ cup dry sherry
- ¾ cup chicken broth
- 1 pound thin asparagus, trimmed
- 1 tablespoon unsalted butter, softened
- 1 tablespoon grated lemon zest plus 2 tablespoons juice, divided
- 3 tablespoons minced fresh chives, divided

1. Adjust oven rack to lower-middle position and heat oven to 325 degrees. Pat steaks dry with paper towels and sprinkle with ½ teaspoon salt and pepper. Heat 1 tablespoon oil in Dutch oven over medium-high heat until just smoking. Brown steaks on both sides, 8 to 10 minutes; transfer to plate.

2. Add 1 tablespoon oil, onions, and remaining ½ teaspoon salt to now-empty pot and cook over medium heat, stirring often, until onions are softened, 8 to 10 minutes. Stir

Braised Blade Steaks with Mushrooms, Vidalias, and Steamed Asparagus

in cremini and portobello mushrooms, cover, and cook until mushrooms begin to release their liquid, about 5 minutes.

3. Uncover and cook, stirring often, until mushrooms and onions begin to brown, 10 to 12 minutes. Stir in thyme and paprika and cook until fragrant, about 30 seconds. Stir in flour and cook for 1 minute. Stir in sherry, scraping up browned bits and smoothing out any lumps. Stir in broth and mushroom mixture and bring to simmer. Nestle steaks and any accumulated juices into pot and bring to simmer. Cover, transfer pot to oven, and cook until steaks are very tender, about 2 hours.

4. Remove pot from oven, uncover, and place steamer basket on top of steaks. Add asparagus to steamer, cover pot, and continue to cook in oven until asparagus is tender, 10 to 15 minutes. Meanwhile, mash softened butter, lemon zest, and 1 tablespoon chives together with fork in large bowl.

5. Remove pot from oven and remove basket of asparagus from pot. Transfer asparagus to bowl with butter mixture and toss until butter is melted. Transfer steaks to serving platter, tent with aluminum foil, and let rest while finishing sauce. Strain braising liquid through fine-mesh strainer into fat separator; spoon strained vegetables over steaks. Combine defatted braising liquid, lemon juice, and remaining 2 tablespoons chives in separate bowl. Season with salt and pepper to taste. Serve steaks with asparagus, passing sauce separately.

Braised Steaks with Garlicky Smashed Potatoes

SLOW COOKER

Serves 4

Cook Time 8 to 10 hours on low or 5 to 7 hours on high

Why This Recipe Works The gentle braising environment of the slow cooker has one major pitfall: Fitting both a main dish and a side in the pot can feel like a jigsaw puzzle where one misplaced piece results in unevenly cooked food. The key to success in this steak-and-potatoes meal turned out to be a steamer basket. Placing the potatoes in the basket on top of the steaks elevated them above the braising liquid and allowed them to steam gently, ensuring they cooked through before we smashed them with garlic, half-and-half, and melted butter. Below the potatoes, blade steaks braised in a mix of onions, garlic, and tomato paste until they were nearly fall-apart tender. For a sauce, we simply defatted the braising liquid and served it with the rich steak and creamy potatoes. Use small red potatoes measuring 1 to 2 inches in diameter; if your potatoes are larger, cut them into 1-inch pieces to ensure that they cook through properly. You will need a 5- to 7-quart oval slow cooker and collapsible steamer basket for this recipe.

- 2 onions, chopped fine
- 2 tablespoons tomato paste
- 3 garlic cloves, peeled
- 1 tablespoon vegetable oil
- 1 teaspoon minced fresh thyme or ¼ teaspoon dried
- 4 (6- to 8-ounce) beef blade steaks, ¾ to 1 inch thick, trimmed
- ½ teaspoon table salt
- ¼ teaspoon pepper
- 1½ pounds small red potatoes, unpeeled
- ¾ cup warm half-and-half, plus extra as needed
- 3 tablespoons unsalted butter, melted

1. Microwave onions, tomato paste, garlic, oil, and thyme in bowl, stirring occasionally, until onions are softened, about 5 minutes; transfer to slow cooker.

2. Sprinkle steaks with salt and pepper and nestle into slow cooker. Place steamer basket on top of steaks and arrange potatoes in basket. Cover and cook until beef is tender, 8 to 10 hours on low or 5 to 7 hours on high.

3. Transfer potatoes to large bowl. Transfer steaks to serving dish and tent with aluminum foil. Strain sauce into fat separator and let sit for 5 minutes. Transfer garlic cloves to small bowl and discard remaining solids.

4. Using fork, smash garlic to paste. Break potatoes into large chunks with rubber spatula. Fold in garlic paste, half-and-half, and melted butter until incorporated and only small chunks of potato remain. Adjust potatoes' consistency with extra warm half-and-half as needed and season with salt and pepper to taste. Pour defatted sauce over steaks. Serve with potatoes.

VARIATION

Braised Steaks with Herbed Smashed Potatoes for Two

SLOW COOKER

Serves 2

Cook Time 8 to 10 hours on low or 5 to 7 hours on high

Use small red potatoes measuring 1 to 2 inches in diameter; if your potatoes are larger, cut them into 1-inch pieces to ensure that they cook through properly. Feel free to use a combination of herbs here. You will need an oval slow cooker and collapsible steamer basket for this recipe.

- 1 onion, chopped fine
- 1 tablespoon tomato paste
- 1 tablespoon vegetable oil
- ½ teaspoon minced fresh thyme or ⅛ teaspoon dried
- 2 (6- to 8-ounce) beef blade steaks, ¾ to 1 inch thick, trimmed
- ¼ teaspoon table salt
- ⅛ teaspoon pepper
- 12 ounces small red potatoes, unpeeled
- 6 tablespoons warm half-and-half, plus extra as needed
- 2 tablespoons unsalted butter, melted
- 2 tablespoons minced fresh chives, basil, parsley, and/or tarragon

1. Microwave onion, tomato paste, oil, and thyme in bowl, stirring occasionally, until onion is softened, about 5 minutes; transfer to slow cooker.

2. Sprinkle steaks with salt and pepper and nestle into slow cooker. Place steamer basket on top of steaks and arrange potatoes in basket. Cover and cook until beef is tender, 8 to 10 hours on low or 5 to 7 hours on high.

3. Transfer potatoes to large bowl. Transfer steaks to serving dish and tent with aluminum foil. Strain sauce into fat separator and let sit for 5 minutes; discard solids.

4. Break potatoes into large chunks with rubber spatula. Fold in half-and-half, melted butter, and chives until incorporated and only small chunks of potato remain. Adjust potatoes' consistency with extra warm half-and-half as needed and season with salt and pepper to taste. Pour defatted sauce over steaks. Serve with potatoes.

Cuban Braised Shredded Beef

Cuban Braised Shredded Beef

DUTCH OVEN

Serves 4 to 6

Total Time 3 hours

Why This Recipe Works A comforting Cuban dish of braised and shredded beef, sliced peppers and onions, chopped green olives, and a brothy sauce, ropa vieja is as hearty as it is rustic. Traditionally, the dish requires making a beef stock and then using the meat and some of the liquid to make a separate sauté with onion, pepper, and spices. To turn it into a one-pot meal, we combined the two methods using a Dutch oven to braise, which meant that all of the beef's juices ended up in the final dish. We eschewed traditional flank steak in favor of brisket, which contains the right mix of beefy flavor and collagen to guarantee tender, flavorful, juicy shreds. We cut the brisket ahead of time into 2-inch-wide strips, which sped up cooking and made shredding a breeze. To mimic the meatiness that commonly comes from an MSG-spiked seasoning blend, we chose to sear the meat before braising, and we added glutamate-rich anchovies to the mix. We found that slowly caramelizing the onion and pepper strips mimicked the deep flavor of a traditional sofrito without requiring an extra step. The final addition of briny chopped green olives and a splash of white wine vinegar brought all the flavors into sharp focus. We prefer the leaner flat cut brisket for this recipe, but the point cut can also be used. Serve with rice (see page 21).

- 1 (2-pound) beef brisket, flat cut, 1½ to 2½ inches thick, fat trimmed to ¼ inch
- ½ teaspoon table salt
- ½ teaspoon pepper
- 5 tablespoons vegetable oil, divided
- 2 onions, halved and sliced thin
- 2 red bell peppers, stemmed, seeded, and sliced into ¼-inch-wide strips
- 2 anchovy fillets, rinsed, patted dry, and minced
- 4 garlic cloves, minced
- 2 teaspoons ground cumin
- 1½ teaspoons dried oregano
- ½ cup dry white wine
- 2 cups chicken broth
- 1 (8-ounce) can tomato sauce
- 2 bay leaves
- ¾ cup pitted green olives, chopped coarse
- ¾ teaspoon white wine vinegar, plus extra for seasoning

1. Adjust oven rack to middle position and heat oven to 300 degrees. Cut brisket against grain into 2-inch-wide strips. Cut any strips longer than 5 inches in half crosswise. Sprinkle beef with salt and pepper.

2. Heat ¼ cup oil in Dutch oven over medium-high heat until just smoking. Brown beef on all sides, 7 to 10 minutes; transfer to large plate. Add onions and bell peppers to fat left in pot and cook until softened and pot bottom develops fond, 10 to 15 minutes; transfer to bowl and set aside.

3. Add remaining 1 tablespoon oil, anchovies, garlic, cumin, and oregano to now-empty pot and cook over medium heat until fragrant, about 30 seconds. Stir in wine, scraping up any browned bits, and cook until mostly evaporated, about 1 minute. Stir in broth, tomato sauce, and bay leaves. Return beef and any accumulated juices to pot and bring to simmer. Cover, transfer pot to oven and cook until beef is just tender, 2 to 2¼ hours, flipping meat halfway through cooking.

4. Transfer beef to cutting board, let cool slightly, then shred into ¼-inch-thick pieces using 2 forks.

5. Meanwhile, add olives and reserved vegetables to pot. Bring to simmer over medium-high heat and cook until thickened and measures 4 cups, 5 to 7 minutes. Discard bay leaves. Stir in beef and vinegar and season with salt, pepper, and extra vinegar to taste. Serve.

Wine-Braised Short Ribs with Potatoes

Braised Beef Short Ribs with Daikon and Shiitakes

Wine-Braised Short Ribs with Potatoes

INSTANT POT
Serves 4
Total Time 2¼ hours

Why This Recipe Works Braising in a pressure cooker is an ideal method for bone-in short ribs—the meat turns meltingly tender, the sauce makes itself, and there's minimal hands-on prep work. Served with red potatoes in a smoothly acidic, complex sauce, we had an easy but elegant meal. We started by browning the short ribs to create a flavorful base for the braising liquid. To the fond in the pot we added onion, garlic, oregano, red wine, whole peeled tomatoes, and a bit of tomato paste. After an hour under pressure, the short ribs were perfectly cooked. As the ribs rested, we defatted the braising liquid and then used it to cook our potatoes in just 4 minutes under pressure. A sprinkle of fresh parsley was the perfect finish. English-style short ribs contain a single rib bone. Buy ribs that are 4 to 5 inches long and have at least 1 inch of meat on top of the bone, avoiding ones that have little meat and large bones. Use small red potatoes measuring 1 to 2 inches in diameter; if your potatoes are larger, cut them into 1-inch pieces to ensure that they cook through properly.

3 pounds bone-in English-style beef short ribs, trimmed
1¼ teaspoons table salt, divided
½ teaspoon pepper
1 tablespoon extra-virgin olive oil
1 onion, chopped fine
6 garlic cloves, minced
2 tablespoons tomato paste
1 tablespoon minced fresh oregano or 1 teaspoon dried
1 (14.5-ounce) can whole peeled tomatoes, drained with ¼ cup juice reserved, chopped coarse
½ cup dry red wine
1 pound small red potatoes, unpeeled, halved
2 tablespoons minced fresh parsley

1. Pat short ribs dry with paper towels and sprinkle with 1 teaspoon salt and pepper. Using highest sauté or browning function, heat oil in electric pressure cooker until just smoking. Brown half of short ribs on all sides, 6 to 8 minutes; transfer to plate. Repeat with remaining short ribs; transfer to plate.

2. Add onion and remaining ¼ teaspoon salt to fat left in pressure cooker and cook, using highest sauté function, until onion is softened, about 3 minutes. Stir in garlic, tomato paste, and oregano and cook until fragrant, about 30 seconds.

Stir in tomatoes and reserved juice and wine, scraping up any browned bits. Nestle short ribs meat side down into pot and add any accumulated juices. Lock lid in place and close pressure release valve. Select high pressure cook function and cook for 60 minutes.

3. Turn off pressure cooker and let pressure release naturally for 15 minutes. Quick-release any remaining pressure, then carefully remove lid, allowing steam to escape away from you. Transfer short ribs to serving platter, tent with aluminum foil, and let rest while preparing potatoes.

4. Strain braising liquid through fine-mesh strainer into fat separator; transfer solids to now-empty pot. Let braising liquid settle for 5 minutes, then pour 1½ cups defatted liquid and any accumulated juices into pot with solids; discard remaining liquid. Add potatoes. Lock lid in place and close pressure release valve. Select high pressure cook function and cook for 4 minutes. Turn off pressure cooker and quick-release pressure. Carefully remove lid, allowing steam to escape away from you.

5. Using slotted spoon, transfer potatoes to platter with short ribs. Season sauce with salt and pepper to taste. Spoon sauce over short ribs and potatoes and sprinkle with parsley. Serve.

Braised Beef Short Ribs with Daikon and Shiitakes

DUTCH OVEN
Serves 6
Total Time 3 hours

Why This Recipe Works This Korean special-occasion dish features tender braised beef short ribs coated in a luxurious sauce. To start, we used the blender to make the base of our flavorful, slightly sweet sauce. We pureed an Asian pear (a traditional component) with sugar, rice vinegar, and soy sauce until smooth. After sautéing the aromatics—scallions, garlic, and ginger—in a Dutch oven, we deglazed the pan with sake, added the short ribs, and let them simmer. Defatting the sauce after a couple hours of braising ensured that the sauce was rich but not greasy. Daikon radish and chestnuts added indulgent flavor. English-style short ribs contain a single rib bone. Buy ribs that are 4 to 5 inches long and have at least 1 inch of meat on top of the bone, avoiding ones that have little meat and large bones. If you can't find red dates (sometimes sold as jujubes), substitute Medjool dates. Use a large Dutch oven with a capacity of 6 quarts or more for this recipe.

2 cups water
1 ounce dried shiitake mushrooms, rinsed
1 Asian pear, peeled, halved, cored, and cut into 1-inch pieces
½ cup soy sauce
¼ cup sugar
1 tablespoon unseasoned rice vinegar
1 tablespoon vegetable oil
6 scallions, white parts sliced thin, green parts cut into 1-inch pieces, divided
6 garlic cloves, minced
1 tablespoon grated fresh ginger
1 cup sake or dry vermouth
5 pounds bone-in English-style beef short ribs, trimmed
1 pound daikon radish, peeled and cut into 1-inch pieces
1 cup (6 ounces) peeled cooked chestnuts, broken into large pieces (optional)
8 large dried red dates, pitted and halved

1. Adjust oven rack to lower-middle position and heat oven to 325 degrees. Microwave water and mushrooms in covered bowl until steaming, about 1 minute. Let sit until softened, about 10 minutes. Drain mushrooms in fine-mesh strainer, reserve soaking liquid, and quarter mushrooms.

2. Process pear, soy sauce, sugar, and vinegar in blender until smooth, about 30 seconds, scraping down sides of blender jar as needed.

3. Heat oil in large Dutch oven over medium heat until shimmering. Add scallion whites, garlic, and ginger and cook until fragrant, about 1 minute. Stir in sake and cook until reduced by half, about 2 minutes. Stir in pear mixture and reserved mushroom liquid. Nestle ribs bone side up into pot (ribs will overlap) and bring to simmer. Cover, transfer pot to oven, and cook for 2 hours.

4. Remove pot from oven. Using slotted spoon, transfer ribs to bowl and cover with aluminum foil to keep warm. Strain braising liquid through fine-mesh strainer into fat separator; discard solids. Let liquid settle for 5 minutes, then return defatted liquid to now-empty pot. Stir in radish; chestnuts, if using; and reserved mushrooms. Return short ribs meat side up to pot and bring to simmer over medium-high heat. Cover partially, return pot to oven, and cook until meat and vegetables are tender, 30 minutes to 1 hour. Using wide, shallow spoon, skim excess fat from surface of sauce. Stir in dates and sprinkle with scallion greens. Serve.

CLASSIC POT ROAST

Pot roast is a one-pot Sunday supper classic, and it's easy to see why. Fall-apart meat and tender vegetables coated in a flavor-packed sauce made from the delicious juices left in the pot make for a comforting, satisfying meal. This hands-off roast is surprisingly versatile, lending itself well to being cooked in a Dutch oven, electric pressure cooker, or slow cooker with a wide range of vegetable and mix-in options. For our classic recipe, we stuck with the traditional carrots and potatoes. We started with a chuck-eye roast, a well-marbled cut that's ideal for braising. A combination of beef broth and red wine created the perfect balance of deep, savory flavor for the braising liquid. In the Dutch oven, we supplemented the mixture with some water since some of the liquid would cook off in the oven. The carrots and potatoes could withstand the full cook time in the faster pressure cooker and the gentler slow cooker, but when we added the vegetables to the Dutch oven at the outset of cooking they became mushy; adding them halfway through easily solved the problem. Reducing the liquid left after cooking in both the Dutch oven and pressure cooker gave us a luxurious sauce; since this wasn't possible in the slow cooker, we added one tablespoon of flour to help thicken the sauce. If your carrots are very thick, slice them in half lengthwise first to ensure even cooking.

CLASSIC

DUTCH OVEN
Serves 6 to 8
Total Time 4¼ hours

- 1 (3½- to 4-pound) boneless beef chuck-eye roast, trimmed and halved
- 1 teaspoon table salt
- 1 teaspoon pepper
- 3 tablespoons vegetable oil, divided
- 1 onion, chopped
- 4 garlic cloves, minced
- 1 tablespoon tomato paste
- 1½ teaspoons minced fresh thyme or ½ teaspoon dried
- 2 cups beef broth
- 1 cup water
- ½ cup dry red wine
- 2 bay leaves
- 2 pounds carrots, peeled and cut into 3-inch lengths
- 2 pounds red potatoes, cut into 1½-inch pieces

1. Adjust oven rack to lower-middle position and heat oven to 300 degrees. Pat beef dry with paper towels; tie each piece crosswise with kitchen twine at 1½-inch intervals. Sprinkle with salt and pepper. Heat 2 tablespoons oil in Dutch oven over medium-high heat until just smoking. Brown roasts on all sides, 8 to 10 minutes; transfer to plate.

2. Add remaining 1 tablespoon oil and onion to fat left in pot; cook over medium heat until softened, about 5 minutes. Stir in garlic, tomato paste, and thyme; cook until fragrant, about 30 seconds. Stir in broth, water, wine, and bay leaves, scraping up any browned bits. Return roasts to pot along with any accumulated juices. Cover, transfer pot to oven, and cook for 2 hours, flipping roasts halfway through cooking.

3. Nestle carrots and potatoes into pot. Cook, covered, until vegetables and beef are tender and fork slips easily in and out of meat, 1 hour to 1½ hours.

4. Remove pot from oven. Transfer roasts to carving board, tent with aluminum foil, and let rest while finishing sauce. Transfer vegetables to large bowl and cover to keep warm.

5. Strain braising liquid through fine-mesh strainer into fat separator; discard solids. Return defatted liquid to pot, bring to simmer and cook for 5 minutes.

6. Discard twine and slice roasts ½ inch thick against grain. Serve with vegetables, passing sauce separately.

MAKE IT YOUR WAY →

> **Use What You've Got** Substitute beer or white wine for the red wine. Substitute hearty vegetables (butternut squash, celery root, fennel, parsnips, Yukon Gold potatoes, turnips) for the red potatoes and carrots.

PRESSURE COOK IT

INSTANT POT

Serves 6 to 8

Total Time 2½ hours

If using a 6-quart pressure cooker, reduce beef, potatoes, and carrots by half and proceed with recipe as directed.

- 1 (3½- to 4-pound) boneless beef chuck-eye roast, trimmed and halved
- 1 teaspoon table salt
- 1 teaspoon pepper
- 3 tablespoons vegetable oil, divided
- 1 onion, chopped
- 4 garlic cloves, minced
- 1 tablespoon tomato paste
- 1½ teaspoons minced fresh thyme or ½ teaspoon dried
- 2 cups beef broth
- ½ cup dry red wine
- 2 bay leaves
- 2 pounds carrots, peeled and cut into 3-inch lengths
- 2 pounds red potatoes, cut into 1½-inch pieces

1. Pat beef dry with paper towels; tie each piece crosswise with kitchen twine at 1½-inch intervals. Sprinkle with salt and pepper. Using highest sauté or browning function, heat 2 tablespoons oil in electric pressure cooker until just smoking. Brown roasts on all sides, 8 to 10 minutes; transfer to plate.

2. Add remaining 1 tablespoon oil and onion to fat left in pressure cooker; cook, using highest sauté or browning function, until vegetables are softened, 3 to 5 minutes. Stir in garlic, tomato paste, and thyme; cook until fragrant, about 30 seconds. Stir in broth, wine, and bay leaves, scraping up any browned bits. Return roasts to pot along with any accumulated juices. Nestle carrots and potatoes into pot.

3. Lock lid in place and close pressure release valve. Select high pressure cook function and cook for 40 minutes. Turn off pressure cooker and let pressure release naturally for 15 minutes. Quick-release remaining pressure; carefully remove lid.

4. Transfer roasts to carving board; let rest while finishing sauce. Transfer vegetables to large bowl and cover to keep warm.

5. Strain braising liquid through fine-mesh strainer into fat separator; discard solids. Return defatted liquid to pressure cooker, bring to simmer, using highest sauté or browning function, and cook for 5 minutes.

6. Discard twine and slice roasts ½ inch thick against grain. Serve with vegetables, passing sauce separately.

SLOW COOK IT

SLOW COOKER

Serves 6 to 8

Cook Time 10 to 11 hours on low or 7 to 8 hours on high

If using a 4-quart slow cooker, reduce beef, potatoes, and carrots by half and proceed with recipe as directed.

- 1 onion, chopped
- 2 tablespoons vegetable oil, divided
- 4 garlic cloves, minced
- 1½ tablespoons tomato paste
- 1 tablespoon all-purpose flour
- 1½ teaspoons minced fresh thyme or ½ teaspoon dried
- 2 cups beef broth
- ½ cup dry red wine
- 2 bay leaves
- 1 (3½- to 4-pound) boneless beef chuck-eye roast, trimmed and halved
- 1 teaspoon table salt
- 1 teaspoon pepper
- 2 pounds carrots, peeled and cut into 3-inch lengths
- 2 pounds red potatoes, cut into 1½-inch pieces

1. Microwave onion, oil, garlic, tomato paste, flour, and thyme in bowl, stirring occasionally, until vegetables are softened, about 5 minutes; transfer to slow cooker. Stir in broth, wine, and bay leaves.

2. Tie each piece of beef crosswise with kitchen twine at 1½-inch intervals. Sprinkle with salt and pepper. Nestle roasts into slow cooker and arrange carrots and potatoes on top. Cover and cook until beef is tender, 10 to 11 hours on low or 7 to 8 hours on high.

3. Transfer roasts to carving board, tent with aluminum foil, and let rest for 10 minutes. Transfer vegetables to large bowl and cover to keep warm. Strain braising liquid through fine-mesh strainer into fat separator; discard solids.

4. Discard twine and slice roasts ½ inch thick against grain. Serve with vegetables, passing sauce separately.

> **Bulk it Up** Add canned beans, frozen vegetables, roasted red peppers, dried fruit, and/or olives to the strained braising liquid and simmer for 5 minutes.

> **Add an Upgrade** Add spice blends (herbes de Provence, garam masala, ras el hanout), rinsed and minced porcini mushrooms, and/or strips of citrus zest in place of—or in addition to—thyme.

Braised Short Ribs with
Fennel and Pickled Grapes

Braised Short Ribs with Fennel and Pickled Grapes

INSTANT POT

Serves 4
Total Time 1¾ hours

Why This Recipe Works This pressure cooker meal brings together tender braised boneless beef short ribs and aromatic fennel topped with the unique sweet-tart punch of quick-pickled grapes. We browned our short ribs in the pressure cooker, and then we built the braising liquid with chicken broth, fennel, onion, garlic, fennel seeds, and rosemary. We cooked everything under pressure for 35 minutes, which resulted in short ribs with a fall-apart texture. We strained the vegetables and defatted the sauce, pouring some of it over the beef and vegetables. If boneless short ribs are unavailable, you can substitute an equal amount of boneless beef chuck-eye roast. Don't core the fennel before cutting it into wedges; the core helps hold the wedges together during cooking.

2 pounds boneless beef short ribs, trimmed and cut into 2-inch pieces
1 teaspoon table salt, divided
1 tablespoon extra-virgin olive oil
1 fennel bulb, 2 tablespoons fronds chopped, stalks discarded, bulb halved and sliced into 1-inch-thick wedges
1 onion, halved and sliced ½ inch thick
4 garlic cloves, minced
2 teaspoons fennel seeds
½ cup chicken broth
1 sprig fresh rosemary
¼ cup red wine vinegar
1 tablespoon sugar
4 ounces seedless red grapes, halved (½ cup)

1. Pat short ribs dry with paper towels and sprinkle with ½ teaspoon salt. Using highest sauté or browning function, heat oil in electric pressure cooker until just smoking. Brown short ribs on all sides, 6 to 8 minutes; transfer to plate.

2. Add fennel wedges, onion, and ¼ teaspoon salt to fat left in pressure cooker and cook, using highest sauté or browning function, until vegetables are softened and lightly browned, about 5 minutes. Stir in garlic and fennel seeds and cook until fragrant, about 30 seconds. Stir in broth and rosemary sprig, scraping up any browned bits. Nestle short ribs into vegetable mixture and add any accumulated juices. Lock lid in place and close pressure release valve. Select high pressure cook function and cook for 35 minutes.

NOTES FROM THE TEST KITCHEN

BUYING BONELESS SHORT RIBS

Flavorful, easy-to-prep boneless short ribs aren't actually cut from the rib section of the cow, as their name implies. When buying, look for lean short ribs cut from the chuck, or shoulder, of the animal. If in doubt, ask your butcher for the cut by its technical designation: NAMP 130A. If boneless short ribs are unavailable, you can substitute an equal amount of boneless beef chuck-eye roast.

And what about bone-in short ribs? We don't recommend them as a substitute for boneless short ribs since they are cut from a different part of the cow—the plate, or front belly.

3. Meanwhile, microwave vinegar, sugar, and remaining ¼ teaspoon salt in bowl until simmering, about 1 minute. Add grapes and let sit, stirring occasionally, for 20 minutes. Drain grapes and return to now-empty bowl. (Drained grapes can be refrigerated for up to 1 week.)

4. Turn off pressure cooker and let pressure release naturally for 15 minutes. Quick-release any remaining pressure, then carefully remove lid, allowing steam to escape away from you. Transfer short ribs to serving platter, tent with aluminum foil, and let rest while finishing sauce.

5. Strain braising liquid through fine-mesh strainer into fat separator. Discard rosemary sprig and transfer vegetables to platter with short ribs using slotted spoon. Let braising liquid settle for 5 minutes, then pour ¾ cup defatted liquid over short ribs and vegetables; discard remaining liquid. Sprinkle with grapes and fennel fronds. Serve.

VARIATION

Braised Short Ribs with Tomatoes, Olives, and Orange for Two

INSTANT POT

Serves 2

Total Time 1¾ hours

If boneless short ribs are unavailable, you can substitute an equal amount of boneless beef chuck-eye roast.

- 1 pound boneless beef short ribs, trimmed and cut into 2-inch pieces
- ½ teaspoon table salt, divided
- 1 tablespoon extra-virgin olive oil
- 1 onion, quartered through root end
- 1 tablespoon minced fresh thyme or 1 teaspoon dried
- 2 garlic cloves, minced
- 2 teaspoons tomato paste
- 1 (14.5-ounce) can whole peeled tomatoes, drained with juice reserved, halved
- ¼ cup chicken broth
- ¼ cup pitted kalamata olives, chopped
- 1½ tablespoons chopped fresh parsley, divided
- 2 teaspoons grated orange zest

1. Pat short ribs dry with paper towels and sprinkle with ¼ teaspoon salt. Using highest sauté or browning function, heat oil in electric pressure cooker until just smoking. Brown short ribs on all sides, 6 to 8 minutes; transfer to plate.

2. Add onion and ¼ teaspoon salt to fat left in pressure cooker and cook, using highest sauté or browning function, until softened and lightly browned, about 5 minutes. Stir in thyme, garlic, and tomato paste and cook until fragrant, about 30 seconds. Stir in tomatoes and reserved juice and broth,

scraping up any browned bits. Nestle short ribs into vegetable mixture and add any accumulated juices. Lock lid in place and close pressure release valve. Select high pressure cook function and cook for 35 minutes.

3. Turn off pressure cooker and let pressure release naturally for 15 minutes. Quick-release any remaining pressure, then carefully remove lid, allowing steam to escape away from you. Transfer short ribs to serving platter, tent with aluminum foil, and let rest while finishing sauce.

4. Combine olives, parsley, and orange zest in bowl. Using slotted spoon, transfer vegetables to platter with short ribs. Strain braising liquid through fine-mesh strainer into fat separator. Let braising liquid settle for 5 minutes, then pour ¼ cup defatted liquid over short ribs and vegetables; discard remaining liquid. Sprinkle with olive mixture and serve.

Osso Buco with Sweet and Spicy Peperonata

INSTANT POT

Serves 6

Total Time 2¼ hours

Why This Recipe Works Osso buco—a famous Italian dish of tender braised veal shanks and vegetables topped with a bright, piquant gremolata (a mix of garlic, citrus peel, and parsley)—is the kind of meal that's typically reserved for restaurant dinners or special-occasion cooking. To create a simplified at-home spin on this dish that minimized prep and cleanup, we transferred the braising, which usually happens in a Dutch oven, to the pressure cooker. Veal shanks are perfectly suited to this appliance: They become remarkably moist and supple thanks to the pressure cooker's ability to draw out their plentiful collagen and transform it into gelatin. To serve six people, we used good-size shanks and tied them around the equator to keep the meat attached to the bones. Browning the shanks in batches built savory fond and prevented overcrowding in the pressure cooker, and deglazing with wine enhanced the flavor of the meat. While a finishing dollop of gremolata usually does the work of offsetting the veal's richness, we decided on a different Italian specialty: sweet and spicy peperonata, a classic condiment of stewed bell peppers, onions, and tomatoes, which we accented with capers and caper brine. We tried cooking our peperonata with the veal shanks, but the peppers became too soft and lost their brightness. Instead, we kept the veal cooking liquid very simple—just wine, thyme, and garlic—and cooked our peperonata at the end, while the veal shanks rested.

6 (14- to 16-ounce) veal shanks, 1½ inches thick, trimmed and tied around equator
¾ teaspoon table salt, divided
¼ teaspoon pepper
¼ cup extra-virgin olive oil, divided
3 sprigs fresh thyme
8 garlic cloves, minced, divided
¾ cup dry white wine
4 red or yellow bell peppers, stemmed, seeded, and cut into ¼-inch-wide strips
1 onion, halved and sliced thin
1 (14.5-ounce) can diced tomatoes, drained
¼ cup raisins
2 tablespoons tomato paste
¼ teaspoon red pepper flakes
2 tablespoons capers plus 4 teaspoons caper brine
½ cup chopped fresh basil

1. Pat shanks dry with paper towels and sprinkle with ½ teaspoon salt and pepper. Using highest sauté or browning function, heat 2 tablespoons oil in electric pressure cooker until just smoking. Brown half of shanks on 1 side, 4 to 6 minutes; transfer to plate. Repeat with remaining shanks; transfer to plate.

2. Add thyme sprigs and half of garlic to fat left in pressure cooker and cook until fragrant, about 30 seconds. Stir in wine, scraping up any browned bits. Nestle shanks into pot (shanks will overlap) and add any accumulated juices.

3. Lock lid in place and close pressure release valve. Select high pressure cook function and cook for 1 hour. Turn off pressure cooker and let pressure release naturally for 15 minutes. Quick-release any remaining pressure, then carefully remove lid, allowing steam to escape away from you.

4. Transfer shanks to serving platter and discard twine. Tent with aluminum foil and let rest while cooking peperonata. Discard cooking liquid and wipe pressure cooker clean with paper towels.

5. Using highest sauté or browning function, heat remaining 2 tablespoons oil in now-empty pot until shimmering. Add bell peppers, onion, tomatoes, raisins, tomato paste, pepper flakes, remaining ¼ teaspoon salt, and remaining garlic. Cover partially and cook, stirring occasionally, until vegetables are softened, 10 to 15 minutes. Turn off pressure cooker. Stir in capers and brine and season with salt and pepper to taste. Spoon peperonata over shanks and sprinkle with basil. Serve.

Corned Beef and Cabbage Dinner
SLOW COOKER
Serves 6 to 8
Cook Time 9 to 10 hours on low or 6 to 7 hours on high

Why This Recipe Works In the States, corned beef and cabbage is rarely eaten outside of St. Patrick's Day—and maybe for good reason. When traditionally boiled, the meat often comes out salty and dry, and the vegetables are usually overcooked and bland. We wanted to use the steady, gentle heat of the slow cooker to get moist, tender corned beef and perfectly cooked vegetables. Placement of the ingredients in the slow cooker turned out to be the key to success. We put the meat in first, sprinkled the seasoning (pickling spice) over it, and placed the potatoes and carrots between the meat and the wall of the slow cooker. This arrangement gave us enough room to add the cabbage from the get-go, rather than at the end of cooking. Use small red potatoes measuring 1 to 2 inches in diameter; if your potatoes are larger, cut them into 1-inch pieces to ensure that they cook through properly. Avoid buying a cabbage larger than 1½ pounds; it will be hard to fit into the slow cooker. You will need a 5- to 7- quart oval slow cooker for this recipe.

1 (3- to 4-pound) corned beef brisket, flat cut, fat trimmed to ¼ inch, rinsed
1 tablespoon pickling spice
1½ pounds small red potatoes, unpeeled
1 pound carrots, peeled and halved crosswise
1 head green cabbage (1½ pounds), cored and cut into 6 wedges
4 tablespoons unsalted butter, cut into ½-inch pieces

1. Place brisket in slow cooker and sprinkle with pickling spice. Arrange potatoes and carrots between meat and sides of slow cooker. Arrange cabbage over meat. Add 6 cups water to slow cooker. Cover and cook until beef is tender and fork slips easily in and out of meat, 9 to 10 hours on low or 6 to 7 hours on high.

2. Turn off slow cooker. Transfer brisket to carving board, tent with aluminum foil, and let rest for 20 minutes. Cover slow cooker to keep vegetables warm while beef rests.

3. Slice brisket ½ inch thick against grain and arrange on serving platter. Using slotted spoon, transfer vegetables to dish with beef. Dot vegetables with butter. Serve.

Modern Beef Pot Pie

SKILLET

Serves 4 to 6

Total Time 2 hours

Why This Recipe Works The litany of pots and pans required to make both the filling and the crust for pot pie makes this comforting dish far too fussy for casual cooking. To create a simplified version with a savory beef filling, we knew that browning boneless short ribs (which we liked for their richness) for deeper flavor was a must, so we seared the meat in a skillet and then used the leftover fat to cook the carrots and onion. A little flour helped thicken the filling to a rich consistency. To satisfy our craving for crust without requiring another pan, we pondered easy yet delicious alternatives. Ultimately, we landed on slices of crusty bread brushed with oil and sprinkled with Parmesan cheese. Toasted under the broiler, the cheesy top browned and crisped while the underside of the bread absorbed some of the pot pie's juices. Frozen peas stirred in just before adding the crust and a final sprinkle of parsley lent a little freshness and color to our easy and delicious beef pot pie. You will need a 12-inch broiler-safe skillet with a tight-fitting lid for this recipe.

- 2 pounds boneless beef short ribs, trimmed and cut into ¾-inch pieces
- ½ teaspoon table salt
- ¼ teaspoon pepper
- 3 tablespoons vegetable oil, divided
- 6 carrots, peeled and cut into ½-inch pieces
- 1 onion, chopped fine
- 2 tablespoons tomato paste
- 4 garlic cloves, minced
- 3 tablespoons all-purpose flour
- ½ cup red wine
- 2½ cups beef broth
- 1 cup frozen peas
- 1 (18-inch) baguette, sliced ½ inch thick, ends discarded
- 1 ounce Parmesan cheese, grated (½ cup)
- 2 tablespoons minced fresh parsley

1. Adjust oven rack to middle position and heat oven to 400 degrees. Pat beef dry with paper towels and sprinkle with salt and pepper. Heat 1 tablespoon oil in 12-inch broiler-safe skillet over medium-high heat until just smoking. Brown beef on all sides, 8 to 10 minutes; transfer to bowl.

2. Add carrots and onion to fat left in skillet and cook over medium heat until softened and lightly browned, 5 to 7 minutes. Stir in tomato paste and garlic and cook until fragrant, about 30 seconds. Stir in flour and cook for 1 minute.

Corned Beef and Cabbage Dinner

Modern Beef Pot Pie

3. Stir in wine, scraping up any browned bits, and cook until almost completely evaporated, about 2 minutes. Slowly stir in broth, smoothing out any lumps. Bring to simmer, then stir in beef and any accumulated juices. Cover, transfer skillet to oven, and cook until beef is tender, about 1 hour, stirring once halfway through cooking.

4. Using pot holder, remove skillet from oven. Adjust oven rack 8 inches from broiler element and heat broiler. Being careful of hot skillet handle, stir peas into beef mixture and season with salt and pepper to taste.

5. Brush bread with remaining 2 tablespoons oil and shingle around edge of skillet, leaving center open. Sprinkle Parmesan over bread. Broil until cheese is melted and bread is browned, about 2 minutes. Remove skillet from oven and let casserole cool for 5 minutes. Sprinkle with parsley and serve.

VARIATION

Modern Beef Pot Pie with Mushrooms and Sherry for Two
SKILLET
Serves 2
Total Time 2 hours

You will need a 10-inch broiler-safe skillet with a tight-fitting lid for this recipe.

1	pound boneless beef short ribs, trimmed and cut into ¾-inch pieces
¼	teaspoon table salt
⅛	teaspoon pepper
2	tablespoons vegetable oil, divided
12	ounces cremini mushrooms, trimmed and quartered
1	small onion, chopped fine
1	tablespoon tomato paste
1	teaspoon minced fresh thyme or ¼ teaspoon dried
1½	tablespoons all-purpose flour
¼	cup dry sherry
1¼	cups beef broth
1	(8-inch) baguette, sliced ½ inch thick, ends discarded
1	ounce Gruyère cheese, shredded (¼ cup)
2	tablespoons minced fresh chives

1. Adjust oven rack to middle position and heat oven to 400 degrees. Pat beef dry with paper towels and sprinkle with salt and pepper. Heat 2 teaspoons oil in 10-inch broiler-safe skillet over medium-high heat until just smoking. Brown beef on all sides, 8 to 10 minutes; transfer to bowl.

2. Add mushrooms, onion, and 1 teaspoon oil to fat left in skillet and cook over medium heat until mushrooms have released their liquid and vegetables are softened and lightly browned, about 8 minutes. Stir in tomato paste and thyme and cook until fragrant, about 30 seconds. Stir in flour and cook for 1 minute.

3. Stir in sherry, scraping up any browned bits, and cook until almost completely evaporated, about 2 minutes. Slowly stir in broth, smoothing out any lumps. Bring to simmer, then stir in beef and any accumulated juices. Cover, transfer skillet to oven, and cook until beef is tender, about 1 hour, stirring once halfway through cooking.

4. Using pot holder, remove skillet from oven. Adjust oven rack 8 inches from broiler element and heat broiler. Being careful of hot skillet handle, season filling with salt and pepper to taste.

5. Brush bread with remaining 1 tablespoon oil and shingle around edge of skillet, leaving center open. Sprinkle Gruyère over bread. Broil until cheese is melted and bread is browned, about 2 minutes. Remove skillet from oven and let casserole cool for 5 minutes. Sprinkle with chives and serve.

Shepherd's Pie
DUTCH OVEN
Serves 4 to 6
Total Time 1½ hours

Why This Recipe Works Recipes for shepherd's pie are invariably fussy, calling for different pots for each of the key steps: boiling the potatoes for the topping, cooking the filling, and assembling the pie before transferring it to the oven. To streamline this familiar favorite, we used a Dutch oven for every step to save on cleanup without sacrificing flavor. While some recipes use lamb, we preferred the subtler flavor of beef and used 93 percent lean ground beef to avoid a greasy filling. A little baking soda upped the pH of the lean meat to keep it from drying out. An onion and mushroom gravy, spiked with Worcestershire sauce, complemented the beef filling. For the mashed potatoes, we cut way back on the dairy, which made for a lighter topping—just the right complement to the hearty meat filling underneath. Don't use ground beef that's fattier than 93 percent or the dish will be greasy.

1½	pounds 93 percent lean ground beef
1½	teaspoons table salt, divided, plus salt for cooking potatoes
½	teaspoon pepper, divided
½	teaspoon baking soda
2½	pounds russet potatoes, peeled and cut into 1-inch pieces
4	tablespoons unsalted butter, melted
½	cup milk

1 large egg yolk
  2 teaspoons vegetable oil
  1 onion, chopped
  4 ounces white mushrooms, trimmed and chopped
  1 tablespoon tomato paste
  2 garlic cloves, minced
  2 tablespoons Madeira or ruby port
  2 tablespoons all-purpose flour
1¼ cups beef broth
  2 carrots, peeled and chopped
  2 teaspoons Worcestershire sauce
  2 sprigs fresh thyme
  1 bay leaf

1. Toss beef with 2 tablespoons water, 1 teaspoon salt, ¼ teaspoon pepper, and baking soda in bowl until thoroughly combined. Set aside for 20 minutes.

2. Place potatoes and 1 tablespoon salt in Dutch oven and add water to cover by 1 inch. Bring to boil over high heat, reduce heat to medium-low, and simmer until potatoes are tender and paring knife can be slipped in and out of potatoes with no resistance, 8 to 10 minutes. Drain potatoes and transfer to large bowl. Mash potatoes or press potatoes through ricer set over bowl. Stir in melted butter. Whisk milk and egg yolk together in small bowl, then stir into potatoes. Season with salt and pepper to taste. Cover and set aside.

3. Adjust oven rack to middle position and heat oven to 450 degrees. Wipe pot clean with paper towels. Heat oil in now-empty pot over medium heat until shimmering. Add onion, mushrooms, remaining ½ teaspoon salt, and remaining ¼ teaspoon pepper and cook, stirring occasionally, until vegetables are just starting to soften and dark bits form on bottom of pot, 4 to 6 minutes.

4. Stir in tomato paste and garlic and cook until bottom of pot is dark brown, about 2 minutes. Stir in Madeira and cook, scraping up any browned bits, until evaporated, about 1 minute. Stir in flour and cook for 1 minute. Stir in broth, carrots, Worcestershire, thyme sprigs, and bay leaf and bring to boil, scraping up any browned bits.

5. Reduce heat to medium-low, add beef in 2-inch chunks to broth, and bring to gentle simmer. Cover and cook until beef is cooked through, 10 to 12 minutes, stirring and breaking up meat chunks with 2 forks halfway through cooking. Discard thyme sprigs and bay leaf. Season with salt and pepper to taste.

6. Place mashed potatoes in large zipper-lock bag and snip off 1 corner to create 1-inch opening. Pipe potatoes in even layer over filling, making sure to cover entire surface. Smooth potatoes with back of spoon. Transfer pot to oven and bake until filling is bubbling around edges, about 10 minutes. Let cool for 10 minutes before serving.

Beef Taco Bake

Beef Taco Bake
CASSEROLE DISH
Serves 4 to 6
Total Time 1 hour

Why This Recipe Works This deconstructed taco casserole has melty, meaty, crunchy layers that deliver all of the fun and flavorful toppings of a good taco night in each bite, all baked together in just one casserole dish. Refried beans are a common side for tacos, so we decided to add them to our casserole. We combined the canned refried variety with spicy Ro-tel tomatoes and minced cilantro and spread the creamy mixture into our dish as the first layer. For a rich, cheesy layer, we sprinkled on Colby Jack cheese—a variety that promised even melting and minimal grease. To incorporate that classic taco shell crunch, we broke shells into pieces and scattered them over the cheese. For the meat, we opted for 90 percent lean ground beef to preempt any crunch-diminishing grease. Stirring chopped onion, garlic, chili powder, and oregano into the beef and microwaving the mixture kept the texture crumbly and bloomed the seasonings. We livened the beef layer by stirring in more Ro-tel tomatoes, cider vinegar for tang, and brown sugar for subtle sweetness. After adding the beef mixture to

Reuben Strata

Top Sirloin Roast with Caramelized Potatoes and Carrots

the dish, we topped it off with more cheese and shell pieces before baking. Finished with a sprinkling of fresh sliced scallions, this family-friendly casserole delivered all the taco flavors we love, and cleanup was a snap. If you can't find Ro-tel tomatoes, substitute one 14.5-ounce can diced tomatoes, drained, and one 4-ounce can chopped green chiles, drained. Colby Jack cheese is also known as CoJack; if unavailable, substitute Monterey Jack cheese. Serve with your favorite taco toppings such as shredded lettuce, sour cream, salsa, and avocado.

1 pound 90 percent lean ground beef
1 onion, chopped fine
4 garlic cloves, minced
2 tablespoons chili powder
1½ teaspoons minced fresh oregano or ½ teaspoon dried
½ teaspoon table salt
¼ teaspoon pepper
2 teaspoons apple cider vinegar
1 teaspoon packed brown sugar
2 (10-ounce) cans Ro-tel Diced Tomatoes & Green Chilies, drained
1 (16-ounce) can refried beans
¼ cup minced fresh cilantro
8 ounces Colby Jack cheese, shredded (2 cups), divided
12 taco shells, broken into 1-inch pieces (2 cups), divided
2 scallions, sliced thin

1. Adjust oven rack to middle position and heat oven to 375 degrees. Combine beef, onion, garlic, chili powder, oregano, salt, and pepper in bowl and microwave, stirring occasionally and breaking up meat, until most of beef is cooked (some pink will remain), about 5 minutes. Stir in vinegar, sugar, and half of tomatoes.

2. Combine remaining tomatoes, refried beans, and cilantro in separate bowl and spread evenly into 8-inch square baking dish. Sprinkle with ½ cup cheese and scatter 1 cup broken taco shells over top. Crumble beef mixture into dish and sprinkle with ½ cup cheese. Top with remaining 1 cup broken taco shells and remaining 1 cup cheese.

3. Bake until filling is bubbling and cheese is melted and spotty brown, about 25 minutes. Remove dish from oven and let cool for 10 minutes. Sprinkle with scallions and serve.

Reuben Strata

CASSEROLE DISH

Serves 4 to 6
Total Time 2 hours, plus 1 hour chilling

Why This Recipe Works Reubens are a deli counter classic—layers of rye bread, warm corned beef, and melted Swiss cheese are always a good thing. But making individual sandwiches can be a pain, so instead we took the flavors of a Reuben and turned them into a strata, a brunch-worthy one-pan casserole with flavorful layers. Using seeded rye bread proved very important in giving us a strong rye flavor. We also used a whole pound of corned beef. Layering the two with some Swiss cheese and then bathing everything in a simple custard delivered a creamy texture that really hit home. And of course you can't have a Reuben without sauerkraut, but adding this zingy ingredient before baking muted its flavor. Instead, sprinkling it (along with some extra cheese) on top after baking and then broiling to finish kept its picklelike tang intact.

8 slices seeded rye bread, toasted
1 pound thinly sliced deli corned beef, chopped
8 ounces Swiss cheese, shredded (2 cups), divided
3 large eggs
1½ cups whole milk
1 teaspoon table salt
½ teaspoon pepper
12 ounces sauerkraut, rinsed and squeezed dry
2 tablespoons minced fresh chives

1. Spray 8-inch square broiler-safe baking dish with vegetable oil spray. Arrange half of bread in prepared dish. Sprinkle half of corned beef over bread, then top with ⅔ cup Swiss. Repeat with remaining bread, remaining corned beef, and ⅔ cup Swiss to make second layer.

2. Whisk eggs, milk, salt, and pepper together in bowl, then pour evenly over top. Cover dish tightly with plastic wrap, pressing it flush to surface. Weigh strata down and refrigerate for at least 1 hour or up to 24 hours.

3. Adjust oven rack to upper-middle position and heat oven to 325 degrees. Meanwhile, let strata sit at room temperature for 20 minutes. Unwrap strata and bake until edges and center are puffed and edges have pulled away slightly from sides of dish, about 50 minutes, rotating dish halfway through baking.

4. Remove dish from oven, adjust oven rack 8 inches from broiler element, and heat broiler. Sprinkle sauerkraut over top of strata, then sprinkle with remaining ⅔ cup Swiss. Broil until cheese is melted and golden, about 5 minutes. Remove dish from broiler and let cool for 10 minutes. Sprinkle with chives and serve.

INGREDIENT SPOTLIGHT

SAUERKRAUT
To find out which kraut is king, we tried six nationally available supermarket sauerkrauts plain, with hot dogs, and in pierogi. In the end, we liked **Eden Organic Sauerkraut** best. With a "slight sweetness" and subtle notes of "zing" and "funk," this jarred kraut lent a tanginess that "complemented" but "didn't overpower" the main dish.

Top Sirloin Roast with Caramelized Potatoes and Carrots

ROASTING PAN

Serves 6 to 8
Total Time 2 hours

Why This Recipe Works When most people think of a beef roast, prime rib or tenderloin comes to mind. And while both are tender and flavorful, we wanted a more affordable roast beef dinner option. Boneless top sirloin roast fit the bill because it provides beefy flavor and has enough marbling to stay tender, but not so much that it would require hours of cooking to break down its fat. A roasting pan offered an easy one-pan option for a complete meal: We could use it to sear the meat on the stovetop and then transfer it to the oven. Roasting at a low temperature allowed plenty of time for heat to be conducted through the roast's center for even cooking. Carrots and potatoes were a natural pairing, and zapping them in the microwave ensured that they would finishing cooking at roughly the same time as the roast. We left the pan in a 250-degree oven for 45 minutes before cranking up the heat for some bonus browning on both the roast and vegetables. At that point, we gave the veggies just a little extra time in the oven for more deeply caramelized flavor. Top sirloin roast is also labeled top butt roast, center-cut roast, spoon roast, shell roast, or shell sirloin roast; do not confuse it with a whole top sirloin butt roast or top loin roast. Look for an evenly shaped roast with a ¼-inch fat cap. If your carrots are very thick, slice them in half lengthwise first to ensure even cooking.

Beef en Cocotte with Creamy Mushroom Barley

4. Remove pan from oven and increase oven temperature to 500 degrees. Continue to roast until beef registers 120 to 125 degrees (for medium-rare), 10 to 15 minutes.

5. Transfer beef to carving board, tent with aluminum foil, and let rest for 15 minutes. Meanwhile, continue to roast vegetables until well browned, 10 to 20 minutes. Remove twine from roast, slice ¼ inch thick, and serve with vegetables.

Beef en Cocotte with Creamy Mushroom Barley

DUTCH OVEN

Serves 6
Total Time 2½ hours

Why This Recipe Works En cocotte cooking, which uses a tightly sealed Dutch oven in a low-temperature oven, traps all of the heat and steam to gently cook meat to a succulent texture. We started with an inexpensive top sirloin roast, which we knew would cook up tender and juicy. The ample space in the pot provided an opportunity for a side dish that would cook simultaneously and soak up the beef's delicious juices, so we added nutty barley. While a beef roast would typically reach medium-rare in far less time than that needed to cook barley, we found that the barley provided insulation and brought the beef's cooking time into closer alignment with its own. This dish warranted luxurious flavors, so we incorporated porcini mushrooms, brandy for deglazing, and Parmesan to enrich the creamy barley. To cut the richness, we made a bright salsa verde, the perfect accent to our elegant one-pot supper. To keep the barley from becoming greasy, trim the beef well. Top sirloin roast is also labeled top butt roast, center-cut roast, spoon roast, shell roast, or shell sirloin roast; do not confuse it with a whole top sirloin butt roast or top loin roast. Look for an evenly shaped roast with a ¼-inch fat cap. Do not substitute hulled, hull-less, quick-cooking, or presteamed barley (read the ingredient list on the package to determine this).

Beef
- 1 (3- to 4-pound) boneless top sirloin roast, trimmed
- 1 teaspoon table salt
- ½ teaspoon pepper
- 3 tablespoons vegetable oil, divided
- 8 ounces white mushrooms, trimmed and sliced thin
- 1¼ cups pearl barley, rinsed
- 1 onion, chopped

- 2 pounds carrots, peeled and cut into 2-inch lengths
- 2 pounds red potatoes, unpeeled, cut into 1½-inch pieces
- ¼ cup vegetable oil, divided
- 1 tablespoon minced fresh thyme or 1 teaspoon dried
- 1½ teaspoons table salt, divided
- ¾ teaspoon pepper, divided
- 1 (3- to 4-pound) boneless top sirloin roast, trimmed

1. Adjust oven rack to lower-middle position and heat oven to 250 degrees. Microwave carrots, potatoes, and 3 tablespoons water in covered bowl, stirring occasionally, until vegetables are nearly tender, 15 to 20 minutes. Drain well, then toss with 3 tablespoons oil, thyme, ½ teaspoon salt, and ¼ teaspoon pepper.

2. Pat beef dry with paper towels and tie with kitchen twine at 1½-inch intervals. Sprinkle with remaining 1 teaspoon salt and remaining ½ teaspoon pepper. Heat remaining 1 tablespoon oil in 16 by 12-inch roasting pan over medium-high heat until just smoking. Place beef fat side down in pan and cook until well browned on first side, about 5 minutes.

3. Off heat, flip roast browned side up and spread vegetables around meat. Roast until beef registers 110 degrees, 45 minutes to 1 hour.

½ ounce dried porcini mushrooms, rinsed and minced

3 garlic cloves, minced

1 tablespoon tomato paste

1 teaspoon minced fresh thyme or ¼ teaspoon dried

3 tablespoons brandy

2 cups beef broth

1 cup chicken broth

1 cup water

1 ounce Parmesan cheese, grated (½ cup)

Salsa Verde

5 tablespoons extra-virgin olive oil

¼ cup minced fresh parsley

2 teaspoons sherry vinegar

1 garlic clove, minced

1. For the beef Adjust oven rack to lowest position and heat oven to 250 degrees. Pat beef dry with paper towels and tie with kitchen twine at 1½-inch intervals. Sprinkle with salt and pepper. Heat 2 tablespoons oil in Dutch oven over medium-high heat until just smoking. Brown beef well on all sides, 8 to 10 minutes; transfer to plate.

2. Add remaining 1 tablespoon oil, white mushrooms, barley, onion, and porcini mushrooms to now-empty pot and cook over medium heat until onion is softened, about 5 minutes. Stir in garlic, tomato paste, and thyme and cook until fragrant, about 30 seconds. Off heat, stir in brandy, scraping up any browned bits, and cook using residual heat of pot until almost completely evaporated, about 30 seconds. Return pot to medium-high heat, stir in broths and water, and bring to simmer.

3. Off heat, return browned beef and any accumulated juices to pot. Cover, transfer pot to oven, and cook until beef registers 120 to 125 degrees (for medium-rare), 1 hour to 1 hour 20 minutes.

4. Remove pot from oven. Transfer roast to carving board, tent with aluminum foil, and let rest for 15 minutes. (If barley is underdone, continue to cook over medium heat, adding additional water as needed, until tender.) Stir Parmesan into barley mixture and cook over medium heat until creamy, 1 to 2 minutes. Season with salt and pepper to taste; cover to keep warm.

5. For the salsa verde Whisk all ingredients together in bowl and season with salt and pepper to taste. (Sauce can be refrigerated for up to 2 days. Bring to room temperature and whisk to recombine before serving.)

6. Remove twine from roast and slice ¼ inch thick. Serve beef with barley and sauce.

Chuck Roast in Foil

Chuck Roast in Foil
ROASTING PAN
Serves 4 to 6
Total Time 5½ hours

Why This Recipe Works Traditionally, this lazy cook's pot roast involves simply rubbing a chuck roast with onion soup mix, wrapping it in foil, and cooking it in the oven until tender. While we like the simplicity of this dish, we aren't fans of its artificial, salty taste. Instead, we skipped the packaged mix and started with onion powder, salt, and soy sauce, which enhanced the roast's beefy flavor. Brown sugar added sweetness and depth, while a surprise ingredient—a little espresso powder—provided toasty complexity. Dividing the roast in half allowed us to apply more of the flavorful spice rub to its exterior. Wrapping the meat in foil trapped steam and tenderized the meat, and adding potatoes and carrots to the foil pouch before placing it in a roasting pan gave us a simple, complete meal. You will need an 18-inch-wide roll of heavy-duty aluminum foil for wrapping the roast. Use small red potatoes measuring 1 to 2 inches in diameter; if your potatoes are larger, cut them into 1-inch pieces to ensure that they cook through properly.

Prime Rib and Roasted Vegetables

1 (7-pound) first-cut beef standing rib roast (3 bones), with ½-inch fat cap
2 tablespoons plus 1 teaspoon kosher salt, divided
2½ teaspoons pepper, divided
2 pounds carrots, peeled, cut into 2-inch lengths, halved or quartered lengthwise to create ½-inch-diameter pieces
1 pound parsnips, peeled and sliced ½ inch thick on bias
1 pound Brussels sprouts, trimmed and halved
1 red onion, halved and sliced through root end into ½-inch wedges
2 teaspoons minced fresh thyme

1. Using sharp knife, cut 1-inch crosshatch pattern in roast's fat cap, being careful not to cut into beef. Rub 2 tablespoons salt thoroughly over roast and into slits. Refrigerate, uncovered, for at least 24 hours or up to 4 days.

2. Adjust oven rack to lower-middle position and heat oven to 250 degrees. Set V-rack in large roasting pan and spray with vegetable oil spray. Sprinkle roast with 2 teaspoons pepper and arrange fat side up on prepared V-rack. Roast until beef registers 120 to 125 degrees (for medium-rare), 3 to 3½ hours. Transfer V-rack with roast to carving board and let rest for 1 hour.

3. Meanwhile, increase oven temperature to 425 degrees. Using fork, remove solids in pan, leaving liquid fat behind (there should be about 2 tablespoons; if not, supplement with vegetable oil). Toss carrots, parsnips, Brussels sprouts, onion, thyme, remaining 1 teaspoon salt, and remaining ½ teaspoon pepper with fat in pan. Roast vegetables until tender and browned, 45 to 50 minutes, redistributing halfway through cooking.

4. Remove pan from oven and heat broiler. Carefully nestle V-rack with roast among vegetables in pan. Broil roast until fat cap is evenly browned, rotating pan as necessary, about 5 minutes. Transfer roast to carving board, carve beef from bones, and slice ¾ inch thick. Season vegetables with salt and pepper to taste. Serve beef with vegetables.

Prime Rib and Roasted Vegetables

Prime Rib and Roasted Vegetables

ROASTING PAN

Serves 8 to 10
Total Time 4¾ hours, plus 24 hours salting

Why This Recipe Works Prime rib is a celebration-worthy cut of meat, and we wanted to take advantage of all of the flavorful drippings to cook supremely delicious vegetables to accompany this centerpiece roast. We began by scoring and salting a standing rib roast and refrigerating it for at least 24 hours to ensure tender, well-seasoned beef. Roasting the beef in a roasting pan in a low oven for 3 hours yielded evenly pink and juicy meat. While the meat rested, we reused the roasting pan to cook a mix of root vegetables and Brussels sprouts in the flavorful beef drippings. Adding the meat back to the pan with the browned, tender vegetables for a final stint under the broiler turned the outside of the roast crispy and golden and brought the whole dish together. Look for a roast with an untrimmed fat cap, ideally ½ inch thick. We prefer this roast cooked to medium-rare, but if you prefer it more or less done, see our guidelines on page 141. Use Brussels sprouts no bigger than golf balls, as larger ones are often tough and woody.

CARVING PRIME RIB

1. Using a carving fork to hold the roast in place, cut along the rib bones to sever the meat from the bones.

2. Set the roast cut side down and slice ¾ inch thick.

Roast Beef Tenderloin with Smoky Potatoes and Persillade Relish

ROASTING PAN
Serves 6
Total Time 3 hours

Why This Recipe Works Small red potatoes pair perfectly with a simple roast beef tenderloin in this company-worthy meal. Smoked paprika on the potatoes complemented the roasted meat, while in turn the potatoes gained deep flavor from sharing the roasting pan with the tenderloin. Tying the roast ensured even cooking. This tender meat benefits from a zesty sauce, so we made a simple yet bold persillade relish of parsley, capers, and cornichons. Center-cut beef tenderloin roasts are sometimes sold as Châteaubriand. Ask your butcher to prepare a trimmed center-cut Châteaubriand, as this cut is not usually available without special ordering. We prefer to use extra-small red potatoes measuring less than 1 inch in diameter. Larger potatoes can be used, but it may be necessary to return the potatoes to the oven to finish cooking while the roast is resting in step 5. We prefer this roast cooked to medium-rare, but if you prefer it more or less done, see our guidelines on page 141.

Beef and Potatoes

- 1 (3-pound) center-cut beef tenderloin roast, trimmed
- 3¼ teaspoons kosher salt, divided
- 1¼ teaspoons pepper, divided
- 1 teaspoon baking soda
- 3 tablespoons extra-virgin olive oil, divided
- 3 pounds extra-small red potatoes, unpeeled
- 5 scallions, minced
- 4 garlic cloves, minced
- 1 tablespoon smoked paprika
- ½ cup water

Persillade Relish

- ¾ cup minced fresh parsley
- ½ cup extra-virgin olive oil
- 6 tablespoons minced cornichons plus 1 teaspoon brine
- ¼ cup capers, rinsed and chopped coarse
- 3 garlic cloves, minced
- 1 scallion, minced
- 1 teaspoon sugar
- ½ teaspoon kosher salt
- ¼ teaspoon pepper

1. For the beef and potatoes Pat roast dry with paper towels. Combine 2¼ teaspoons salt, 1 teaspoon pepper, and baking soda in small bowl. Rub salt mixture evenly over roast

Roast Beef Tenderloin with Smoky Potatoes and Persillade Relish

and let sit for 1 hour. Tuck tail end and tie roast with kitchen twine at 1½-inch intervals. Adjust oven rack to middle position and heat oven to 425 degrees.

2. Heat 2 tablespoons oil in large roasting pan over medium-high heat until shimmering. Add potatoes, scallions, garlic, paprika, remaining 1 teaspoon salt, and remaining ¼ teaspoon pepper and cook until scallions are softened, about 1 minute. Off heat, stir in water, scraping up any browned bits. Transfer roasting pan to oven and roast potatoes for 15 minutes.

3. Brush remaining 1 tablespoon oil over surface of roast. Remove pan from oven, stir potato mixture, and lay beef on top. Reduce oven temperature to 300 degrees. Return pan to oven and roast until beef registers 120 to 125 degrees (for medium-rare), 45 to 55 minutes, rotating pan halfway through roasting.

4. For the persillade relish While beef roasts, combine all ingredients in bowl. (Sauce can be refrigerated for up to 2 days. Bring to room temperature and whisk to recombine before serving.)

5. Remove pan from oven. Transfer roast to carving board, tent with aluminum foil, and let rest for 15 minutes. Cover potatoes in pan with foil to keep warm. Remove twine from roast, slice ½ inch thick, and serve with potatoes and relish.

PORK AND LAMB

Pork Loin en Cocotte with Barley, Butternut Squash, and Swiss Chard

* All slow cooker recipes work in a 4- to 7-quart traditional slow cooker unless noted.

** All Instant Pot recipes work in a 6- to 8-quart Instant Pot or other electric pressure cooker.

Pan-Seared Pork Cutlets with Horseradish-Herb Green Beans

SKILLET
Serves 4
Total Time 45 minutes

Why This Recipe Works Simple sautéed pork cutlets and green beans make an easy, fresh weeknight meal, but if you don't pay proper attention to the quick-cooking ingredients, the thin cutlets can turn out dry and rubbery and the green beans mushy and bland. We made our own tender cutlets by gently pounding pieces of pork tenderloin to an even thickness. Using a piping-hot skillet to sear the cutlets yielded golden brown exteriors and moist, juicy interiors. While the pork rested, we sautéed our green beans in the same skillet until they were spotty brown but not cooked through, and then steamed them in the covered pan. We uncovered the skillet to quickly evaporate the water and finish browning the beans until they reached the perfect crisp-tender texture. Horseradish, lemon juice, and parsley brightened up the flavor profile. To finish our dish with zesty flavor, we made a compound butter with garlic and herbs to divide between the green beans and the pork. You will need a 12-inch skillet with a tight-fitting lid for this recipe.

- 4 tablespoons unsalted butter, softened, divided
- 3 garlic cloves, minced
- 2 teaspoons minced fresh thyme
- 2 teaspoons minced fresh chives
- 2 (1-pound) pork tenderloins, trimmed
- ¾ teaspoon table salt, divided
- ¼ teaspoon plus ⅛ teaspoon pepper, divided
- 2 tablespoons vegetable oil, divided
- 1 pound green beans, trimmed and cut into 2-inch lengths
- 1 tablespoon prepared horseradish, drained
- 1 tablespoon minced fresh parsley
  Lemon wedges

1. Combine 3 tablespoons butter, garlic, thyme, and chives in bowl; set aside.

2. Cut each tenderloin on bias into 4 equal pieces. Working with 1 piece at a time, place pork cut side down between 2 sheets of parchment paper or plastic wrap and gently pound to even ½-inch thickness. Pat pork dry with paper towels and sprinkle with ½ teaspoon salt and ¼ teaspoon pepper.

3. Heat 1 tablespoon oil in 12-inch skillet over medium-high heat until just smoking. Brown 4 cutlets, about 2 minutes per side; transfer to serving platter. Repeat with remaining

1 tablespoon oil and remaining 4 cutlets; transfer to platter. Dollop 3 tablespoons herb butter over cutlets, tent with aluminum foil, and let rest while making green beans.

4. Melt remaining 1 tablespoon butter in now-empty skillet over medium heat. Add green beans, remaining ¼ teaspoon salt, and remaining ⅛ teaspoon pepper and cook, stirring occasionally, until spotty brown, 3 to 5 minutes. Add ¼ cup water, cover, and cook until green beans are bright green and still crisp, about 2 minutes. Uncover and continue to cook until water evaporates, 30 to 60 seconds. Stir in horseradish and remaining herb butter and cook until green beans are crisp-tender and beginning to wrinkle, 1 to 3 minutes. Off heat, stir in parsley and season with salt and pepper to taste. Serve cutlets with green beans and lemon wedges.

VARIATION

Pan-Seared Pork Cutlets with Lemon-Caper Green Beans for Two

SKILLET
Serves 2
Total Time 35 minutes

- 3 tablespoons unsalted butter, softened, divided
- 1 tablespoon capers, rinsed and minced
- 1 teaspoon minced fresh chives
- 1 teaspoon Dijon mustard
- 1 teaspoon grated lemon zest, plus lemon wedges for serving
- 1 (1-pound) pork tenderloin, trimmed
- ¼ teaspoon plus ⅛ teaspoon table salt, divided
- ⅛ teaspoon plus pinch pepper, divided
- 1 tablespoon vegetable oil
- 8 ounces green beans, trimmed and cut into 2-inch lengths

1. Combine 2 tablespoons butter, capers, chives, mustard, and lemon zest in bowl; set aside.

2. Cut tenderloin on bias into 4 equal pieces. Working with 1 piece at a time, place pork cut side down between 2 sheets of parchment paper or plastic wrap and gently pound to even ½-inch thickness. Pat pork dry with paper towels and sprinkle with ¼ teaspoon salt and ⅛ teaspoon pepper.

3. Heat oil in 12-inch skillet over medium-high heat until just smoking. Brown cutlets, about 2 minutes per side; transfer to serving platter. Dollop 1½ tablespoons herb butter over cutlets, tent with aluminum foil, and let rest while making green beans.

4. Melt remaining 1 tablespoon butter in now-empty skillet over medium heat. Add green beans, remaining ⅛ teaspoon salt, and remaining pinch pepper and cook, stirring occasionally, until spotty brown, 3 to 5 minutes. Add 2 tablespoons water, cover, and cook until green beans are bright green and still crisp, about 2 minutes. Uncover and continue to cook until water evaporates, 30 to 60 seconds. Stir in remaining herb butter and cook until green beans are crisp-tender and beginning to wrinkle, 1 to 3 minutes. Season with salt and pepper to taste. Serve cutlets with green beans and lemon wedges.

Sesame Pork Cutlets with Wilted Napa Cabbage Salad

SKILLET
Serves 4
Total Time 1 hour

Why This Recipe Works A skillet is the perfect tool for browning, offering the opportunity for pork with a crisp coating, and reusing the same pan to prepare a warm cabbage salad completed the meal. Bread crumb coatings can turn out mushy and soggy, so we updated the traditional flour, egg, and bread crumb formula with an untraditional ingredient: sesame seeds. Using a whopping ⅔ cup of seeds ensured the crust had ample sesame flavor and kept it extra-crisp. Once the pork was finished, we kept it warm in the oven and reused the skillet to make a salad to complement the sesame chops: We browned garlic and ginger in sesame oil and then added cabbage and carrot, cooking them until the cabbage leaves wilted slightly. Matchsticks of pear contributed crunch and a touch of sweetness, a perfect contrast to the savory pork cutlets. We like using Asian pear in this recipe for its bright crispness, but Bosc or Anjou pears will also work. You will need a 12-inch nonstick skillet with a tight-fitting lid for this recipe.

2 (1-pound) pork tenderloins, trimmed
1 teaspoon table salt, divided
½ teaspoon pepper, divided
2 large eggs
1 cup panko bread crumbs
⅔ cup sesame seeds
½ cup vegetable oil for frying, divided
1 tablespoon toasted sesame oil
2 garlic cloves, minced
1 teaspoon grated fresh ginger
1 small head napa cabbage (1½ pounds), cored and shredded
1 carrot, peeled and shredded
1 Asian pear, peeled, halved, cored, and cut into 2-inch matchsticks
¼ cup fresh cilantro leaves
3 tablespoons rice vinegar

Pan-Seared Pork Cutlets with Horseradish-Herb Green Beans

Sesame Pork Cutlets with Wilted Napa Cabbage Salad

1. Cut each tenderloin on bias into 4 equal pieces. Working with 1 piece at a time, place pork cut side down between 2 sheets of parchment paper or plastic wrap and gently pound to even ½-inch thickness. Pat pork dry with paper towels and sprinkle with ½ teaspoon salt and ¼ teaspoon pepper.

2. Beat eggs, remaining ½ teaspoon salt, and remaining ¼ teaspoon pepper in shallow dish. Combine panko and sesame seeds in second shallow dish. Working with 1 cutlet at a time, dredge in egg mixture, allowing excess to drip off, then coat with sesame-panko mixture, pressing gently to adhere; transfer to platter.

3. Heat ¼ cup vegetable oil and small pinch panko mixture in 12-inch nonstick skillet over medium-high heat. When panko has turned golden brown, place 4 cutlets in skillet. Cook, without moving cutlets, until bottoms are deep golden brown, 2 to 3 minutes. Using tongs, carefully flip cutlets and cook on second side until deep golden brown, 2 to 3 minutes.

4. Transfer to paper towel–lined plate. Wipe skillet clean with paper towels. Repeat with remaining ¼ cup vegetable oil and remaining 4 cutlets; transfer to platter. Wipe skillet clean with paper towels.

5. Cook sesame oil, garlic, and ginger in now-empty skillet over medium heat until fragrant, about 30 seconds. Add cabbage and carrot, cover, and cook until just wilted, stirring occasionally, about 5 minutes. Off heat, add pear, cilantro, and rice vinegar and toss to combine. Season with salt and pepper to taste, and serve with pork.

Crunchy Parmesan-Crusted Pork Chops with Glazed Winter Squash

TURNING TENDERLOIN INTO CUTLETS

1. Cut tenderloin into pieces as directed in recipe.

2. Lay each piece between 2 sheets of parchment paper or plastic wrap and pound with meat pounder until roughly ½ inch thick.

Crunchy Parmesan-Crusted Pork Chops with Glazed Winter Squash

SHEET PAN
Serves 4
Total Time 1 hour

Why This Recipe Works Sheet pan meals seem like the ultimate weeknight convenience—just drop everything on the pan and pop it in the oven—but without using the stovetop to brown, turning out pork with a crispy coating can be a challenge. For pork chops with maximum crunch, we used a coating of Parmesan-seasoned panko. Pretoasting the panko in the microwave with some oil proved the key to a perfectly browned crust on our juicy chops, while elevating the pork on a wire rack ensured our crust stayed crunchy. As for our side, we sliced acorn squash into rings for a beautiful scalloped shape and gave them a head start in the microwave, softening them just enough so they would finish roasting at the same time as the pork. A sweet-tart cranberry sauce rounded out our autumnal menu and the microwave helped again here; it easily cooked our cranberries, producing the perfect sauce for our hearty roasted dinner.

2 cups panko bread crumbs, toasted
3 tablespoons extra-virgin olive oil, divided
¼ cup all-purpose flour
2 large eggs
3 tablespoons Dijon mustard
1¾ teaspoons table salt, divided
¾ teaspoon pepper, divided
2 ounces Parmesan cheese, grated (1 cup)
¼ cup minced fresh parsley
4 (6- to 8-ounce) boneless pork chops, ¾ to 1 inch thick, trimmed
1 large acorn squash (2 pounds), sliced into ½-inch-thick rings and seeded
1 cup plus 1 tablespoon sugar, divided
12 ounces (3 cups) fresh or thawed frozen cranberries
¼ cup water
¼ teaspoon five-spice powder

1. Adjust oven rack to middle position and heat oven to 425 degrees. Toss panko with 2 tablespoons oil in bowl until evenly coated. Microwave panko, stirring every 30 seconds, until light golden brown, about 5 minutes; let cool slightly. Spread flour in shallow dish. Whisk eggs, mustard, 1 teaspoon salt, and ½ teaspoon pepper together in second shallow dish. Toss panko, Parmesan, and parsley together in third shallow dish.

2. Set wire rack in aluminum foil–lined rimmed baking sheet and spray with vegetable oil spray. Using sharp knife, cut 2 slits, about 2 inches apart, through fat on edge of each pork chop. Pat chops dry with paper towels. Working with 1 chop at a time, dredge in flour, dip in egg mixture, allowing excess to drip off, then coat with toasted panko mixture, pressing gently to adhere. Lay pork chops on 1 side of prepared wire rack, spaced at least ¼ inch apart.

3. Place squash on large plate, brush with remaining 1 tablespoon oil, and sprinkle with ½ teaspoon salt and remaining ¼ teaspoon pepper. Microwave squash until it begins to soften but still holds its shape, 8 to 10 minutes.

4. Place squash on empty side of rack, slightly overlapping if needed, and sprinkle with 1 tablespoon sugar. Roast pork chops and squash until pork registers 145 degrees and squash is lightly tender, 20 to 30 minutes, rotating sheet halfway through roasting. Remove sheet from oven and let rest for 5 minutes.

5. Meanwhile, combine cranberries, remaining 1 cup sugar, water, five-spice powder, and remaining ¼ teaspoon salt in bowl and microwave, stirring occasionally, until cranberries are broken down and juicy, about 10 minutes. Coarsely mash cranberries with fork and serve with pork chops and squash.

Barbecued Pork Chops with Succotash Salad

SKILLET
Serves 4
Total Time 45 minutes

Why This Recipe Works Think barbecued pork chops only come off a grill? Think again. With the help of a skillet, we produced highly flavorful pork chops indoors. We simmered the pork chops directly in store-bought barbecue sauce for flavor and ease and then served the thick, syrupy sauce over our chops, which gave them a caramelized, almost-grilled flavor. To keep our chops from curling up, we cut two slits through the fat on the edge of the pork chop. For a fresh and complementary side, we took classic succotash and turned it into a salad. We sautéed some corn in the skillet to give it a bit of char; next we added lima beans until warmed through and tossed both with baby spinach, bell pepper, lime juice, and chives for a side salad with bright tang. Because fresh lima beans can be difficult to find, we used frozen lima beans which taste equally fresh and have a shorter cooking time. As for the corn, kernels scraped from fresh ears tasted much sweeter than frozen, and they gave the succotash nice crunch.

4 (6- to 8-ounce) boneless pork chops, ¾ to 1 inch thick, trimmed
1 teaspoon table salt, divided
½ teaspoon pepper, divided
3 tablespoons extra-virgin olive oil, divided
1 cup barbecue sauce
¼ cup water
4 ears corn, kernels cut from cobs
2 cups frozen lima beans
1 red bell pepper, stemmed, seeded, and chopped
4 ounces (4 cups) baby spinach
2 tablespoons lime juice
2 tablespoons minced fresh chives

1. Using sharp knife, cut 2 slits, about 2 inches apart, through fat on edge of each pork chop. Pat chops dry with paper towels and sprinkle with ½ teaspoon salt and ¼ teaspoon pepper. Heat 1 tablespoon oil in 12-inch skillet over medium-high heat until just smoking. Place chops in skillet and cook until well browned on first side, about 6 minutes.

2. Reduce heat to medium. Pour barbecue sauce and water in skillet, flip chops, and cook until pork registers 145 degrees, 8 to 10 minutes. Transfer pork chops to serving platter, tent with aluminum foil, and let rest while preparing salad. Pour sauce from skillet into serving bowl; cover to keep warm. Wipe skillet clean with paper towels.

3. Heat 1 tablespoon oil in now-empty skillet over medium-high heat until shimmering. Add corn and cook, without stirring, for 3 minutes. Stir in lima beans and cook until warmed through, about 2 minutes; transfer to large bowl. Add bell pepper, spinach, lime juice, chives, remaining 1 tablespoon oil, remaining ½ teaspoon salt, and remaining ¼ teaspoon pepper and toss to coat. Serve pork chops with salad and barbecue sauce.

Maple-Glazed Pork Chops with Sweet Potato–Bacon Hash

SKILLET

Serves 4
Total Time 45 minutes

Why This Recipe Works Breakfast meets dinner in this skillet meal that builds up layers of flavor in the pan. Here, we pair succulent, maple-glazed pork chops with a savory, smoky bacon and sweet potato hash. We jump-started the potatoes in the microwave while we cooked our bacon in the skillet. Using some of the rendered fat to brown the pork chops—which we slit to prevent curling—allowed them to absorb bacony flavor. Once the chops had browned, we transferred them to a plate and added the potatoes, along with the crisped bacon bits and some thyme, to the skillet to finish cooking. To finish, we created a flavorful glaze from sweet maple syrup, sharp cider vinegar, and tangy mustard, which we simmered until thickened and used as a glossy coating for our juicy pork chops.

1¼ pounds sweet potatoes, peeled and cut into ¾-inch pieces
6 slices bacon, chopped fine
4 (12-ounce) bone-in pork rib or center-cut chops, 1 to 1½ inches thick, trimmed
½ teaspoon table salt
¼ teaspoon pepper
2 teaspoons minced fresh thyme
½ cup maple syrup
1 tablespoon cider vinegar
2 teaspoons Dijon mustard

1. Microwave potatoes in covered bowl until tender, 4 to 7 minutes. Meanwhile, cook bacon in 12-inch nonstick skillet over medium heat until rendered and crisp, 5 to 7 minutes. Using slotted spoon, transfer bacon to paper towel–lined bowl. Pour off fat, reserving 2 tablespoons.

2. Using sharp knife, cut 2 slits, about 2 inches apart, through fat on edge of each pork chop. Pat chops dry with paper towels and sprinkle with salt and pepper. Heat 1 tablespoon reserved fat in now-empty skillet over medium-high heat until just smoking. Place chops in skillet in pinwheel formation and brown on both sides, 8 to 10 minutes; transfer to plate and tent with aluminum foil.

3. Add remaining 1 tablespoon reserved fat and potatoes to now-empty skillet and cook, turning occasionally, until well browned, 5 to 7 minutes. Stir in thyme and bacon. Season with salt and pepper to taste. Transfer to serving bowl and cover to keep warm.

4. Add maple syrup, vinegar, and mustard to now-empty skillet and cook until thickened, about 2 minutes. Return pork chops to skillet along with any accumulated juices and simmer, turning often, until glaze coats chops and pork registers 145 degrees, about 2 minutes. Serve with potatoes.

Roasted Pork Chops and Vegetables with Parsley Vinaigrette

SHEET PAN

Serves 4
Total Time 1 hour

Why This Recipe Works Pan-searing may be the most common cooking method for bone-in pork chops, but roasting them on a sheet pan in the oven turns out tender, juicy meat and provides extra space to cook a side of root vegetables at the same time. Since pork chops cook relatively quickly, we partially roasted the vegetables—a rustic mix of thick-sliced Yukon Gold potatoes, carrot spears, and fennel wedges—to give them a head start. For a bold hit of flavor, we tossed them with fresh rosemary and peeled whole garlic cloves, which turned deliciously creamy when roasted. Once the vegetables had softened and taken on some color, we added our pork chops, which we'd seasoned with a rub of pepper, salt, paprika, and coriander for a deeply flavored crust. Finally, we whisked together a simple parsley vinaigrette to drizzle over the pork, ensuring our meal would end on an herbal note.

1 pound Yukon Gold potatoes, unpeeled, halved lengthwise, and cut crosswise into ½-inch-thick slices
1 pound carrots, peeled and cut into 3-inch lengths, thick ends quartered lengthwise
1 fennel bulb, stalks discarded, bulb halved, cored, and cut into ½-inch-thick wedges
10 garlic cloves, peeled

3. Arrange pork chops on top of vegetables and continue to roast until pork registers 145 degrees and vegetables are tender, 10 to 15 minutes, rotating sheet halfway through roasting.

4. Remove sheet from oven and let pork chops rest for 5 minutes. Whisk remaining oil, remaining ¼ teaspoon salt, remaining ¼ teaspoon pepper, vinegar, parsley, shallot, and sugar together in bowl. Drizzle vinaigrette over pork and vegetables. Serve.

VARIATION

Roasted Pork Chops and Vegetables with Basil Vinaigrette for Two

SHEET PAN

Serves 2

Total Time 40 minutes

Feel free to use a mix of squash and zucchini for a more colorful presentation.

- 2 (12-ounce) bone-in pork rib or center-cut chops, 1 to 1½ inches thick, trimmed
- ¼ cup extra-virgin olive oil, divided
- ½ teaspoon plus ⅛ teaspoon table salt, divided
- ¼ teaspoon plus ⅛ teaspoon pepper, divided
- 1 pound yellow summer squash or zucchini, quartered lengthwise and cut into 2-inch pieces
- 1 tablespoon chopped fresh basil
- 1 tablespoon balsamic vinegar
- ½ small shallot, minced
  Pinch sugar

1. Adjust oven rack to upper-middle position and heat oven to 450 degrees. Using sharp knife, cut 2 slits, about 2 inches apart, through fat on edge of each pork chop. Pat chops dry with paper towels, rub with 1 teaspoon oil, then sprinkle with ¼ teaspoon salt and ⅛ teaspoon pepper. Arrange pork chops in center of rimmed baking sheet and roast for 5 minutes.

2. Meanwhile, toss squash with 2 teaspoons oil, ¼ teaspoon salt, and ⅛ teaspoon pepper in bowl. Distribute vegetable mixture in even layer around pork chops on sheet and continue to roast until pork register 145 degrees and vegetables are tender, 5 to 10 minutes.

3. Remove sheet from oven and let pork chops rest for 5 minutes. Whisk remaining 3 tablespoons oil, remaining ⅛ teaspoon salt, remaining ⅛ teaspoon pepper, basil, vinegar, shallot, and sugar together in bowl. Drizzle vinaigrette over pork and vegetables. Serve.

Roasted Pork Chops and Vegetables with Parsley Vinaigrette

- 2 teaspoons minced fresh rosemary or ¾ teaspoon dried
- ⅓ cup extra-virgin olive oil, divided
- 2 teaspoons table salt, divided
- 1½ teaspoons pepper, divided
- 1 teaspoon paprika
- 1 teaspoon ground coriander
- 4 (12-ounce) bone-in pork rib or center-cut chops, 1 to 1½ inches thick, trimmed
- 4 teaspoons red wine vinegar
- 2 tablespoons minced fresh parsley
- 1 small shallot, minced
- ⅛ teaspoon sugar

1. Adjust oven rack to upper-middle position and heat oven to 450 degrees. Toss potatoes, carrots, and fennel with garlic, rosemary, 1 tablespoon oil, ¾ teaspoon salt, and ¼ teaspoon pepper in bowl and spread in single layer on rimmed baking sheet. Roast until beginning to soften, about 25 minutes.

2. Combine 1 teaspoon salt, 1 teaspoon pepper, paprika, and coriander in bowl. Using sharp knife, cut 2 slits, about 2 inches apart, through fat on edge of each pork chop. Pat chops dry with paper towels, rub with 1 teaspoon oil, then sprinkle with spice mixture.

Smothered Pork Chops with Broccoli

DUTCH OVEN

Serves 4

Total Time 2¼ hours

Why This Recipe Works Southern-style smothered pork chops are the epitome of simple, satisfying comfort food: You simply season the chops, sear them, and then simmer them in gravy until they're perfectly tender. But adding a side dish to the meal proved challenging until we tried a unique one-pot arrangement. Placing a steamer basket in a Dutch oven created extra space and allowed us to cook a side of broccoli over the pork. Browning blade-cut chops in bacon fat (reserving the crisped bacon for garnish) created a savory foundation for the gravy, which we built right in the pot. Finally, we nestled in our browned chops and transferred the pot to the oven, where the tough cut of pork rendered its fat slowly. After the chops had cooked for an hour, we added the steamer basket and broccoli and put everything back in the oven to finish together. You will need a collapsible steamer basket for this recipe.

Smothered Pork Chops with Broccoli

3 slices bacon, chopped fine

4 (8- to 10-ounce) bone-in blade-cut pork chops, ¾ inch thick, trimmed

¾ teaspoon table salt, divided

¼ teaspoon pepper

¼ cup extra-virgin olive oil, divided

1 onion, halved and sliced thin

4 garlic cloves, minced

1 teaspoon minced fresh thyme or ¼ teaspoon dried

½ teaspoon red pepper flakes

2 tablespoons all-purpose flour

2 tablespoons water

1¾ cups chicken broth

2 bay leaves

1 pound broccoli florets, cut into 1-inch pieces

2 tablespoons minced fresh parsley

1. Adjust oven rack to lower-middle position and heat oven to 300 degrees. Cook bacon in Dutch oven over medium heat until rendered and crisp, 5 to 7 minutes. Using slotted spoon, transfer bacon to paper towel–lined bowl. Pour off all but 2 tablespoons fat left in pot.

2. Using sharp knife, cut 2 slits, about 2 inches apart, through fat on edge of each pork chop. Pat chops dry with paper towels and sprinkle with ½ teaspoon salt and pepper. Heat fat left in pot over medium-high heat until just smoking. Add pork chops (they will overlap slightly) and brown on both sides, 7 to 10 minutes; transfer to plate.

3. Add 2 tablespoons oil, onion, and remaining ¼ teaspoon salt to now-empty pot and cook over medium heat until softened and lightly browned, 5 to 7 minutes. Stir in garlic, thyme, and pepper flakes and cook until fragrant, about 30 seconds. Stir in flour and cook for 1 minute. Stir in water, scraping up any browned bits and smoothing out any lumps. Reduce heat to medium-low and cook, stirring often, until well browned, about 5 minutes.

4. Slowly whisk in broth, scraping up any browned bits. Add bay leaves. Nestle pork chops into pot and add any accumulated juices. Cover, transfer pot to oven, and cook until chops are almost fork-tender, about 1 hour.

5. Remove pot from oven, uncover, and place steamer basket on top of pork chops. Add broccoli to steamer, cover pot, and continue to cook in oven until broccoli is tender, about 20 minutes.

6. Remove pot from oven and remove basket of broccoli from pot. Toss broccoli in bowl with remaining 2 tablespoons oil and season with salt and pepper to taste. Transfer pork chops to serving platter, tent with aluminum foil, and let rest while finishing sauce. Using large spoon, skim excess fat from surface of sauce. Bring sauce to simmer over medium heat and cook until thickened, about 5 minutes. Discard bay leaves and season with salt and pepper to taste. Spoon sauce over chops, sprinkle with bacon and parsley, and serve with broccoli.

Smothered Pork Chops with Leeks and Mustard

INSTANT POT

Serves 4
Total Time 1½ hours

Why This Recipe Works This Provençal take on smothered pork chops uses the pressure cooker to transform a hefty pound and a half of leeks (including their usually tough dark green parts) into a luscious, pungent, meltingly tender topping for our flavorful pork chops. Blade chops—with their combination of light and dark meat, connective tissue, marbled fat, and bone—were ideal for pressure cooking, as the meat became tender and moist. After browning the pork chops in the pressure cooker, we set them aside to cook salty pancetta before adding wine, leeks, and a little flour to make a rich, savory gravy infused with meaty flavor. We added the browned chops back in and cooked the whole thing under pressure until the pork was tender and the leeks had cooked down to a rich consistency. Taking a cue from classic French flavors, we combined the sweet, aromatic leeks with tangy Dijon mustard. Bacon can be substituted for the pancetta.

> 4 (8- to 10-ounce) bone-in blade-cut pork chops, ¾ inch thick, trimmed
> ½ teaspoon table salt
> ½ teaspoon pepper
> 4 teaspoons extra-virgin olive oil, divided
> 2 ounces pancetta, chopped fine
> 1 tablespoon all-purpose flour
> ¾ cup dry white wine
> 1½ pounds leeks, ends trimmed, halved lengthwise, sliced into 3-inch lengths, and washed thoroughly
> 1 tablespoon Dijon mustard
> 2 tablespoons chopped fresh parsley

1. Using sharp knife, cut 2 slits, about 2 inches apart, through fat on edge of each pork chop. Pat chops dry with paper towels and sprinkle with salt and pepper. Using highest sauté or browning function, heat 2 teaspoons oil in electric pressure cooker until just smoking. Brown 2 pork chops on both sides, 6 to 8 minutes; transfer to plate. Repeat with remaining 2 teaspoons oil and remaining chops; transfer to plate.

2. Add pancetta to fat left in pressure cooker and cook, using highest sauté or browning function, until softened and lightly browned, about 2 minutes. Stir in flour and cook for 30 seconds. Stir in wine, scraping up any browned bits and smoothing any lumps. Stir in leeks and cook until softened, about 3 minutes. Nestle pork chops into pot (chops will overlap) and add any accumulated juices. Lock lid in place and close pressure release valve. Select high pressure cook function and cook for 10 minutes.

3. Turn off pressure cooker and let pressure release naturally for 15 minutes. Quick-release any remaining pressure, then carefully remove lid, allowing steam to escape away from you. Transfer pork chops to serving platter, tent with aluminum foil, and let rest while finishing leeks.

4. Using highest sauté or browning function, bring leek mixture to simmer. Stir in mustard and cook until slightly thickened, about 5 minutes. Season with salt and pepper to taste. Spoon leek mixture over pork chops and sprinkle with parsley. Serve.

PREPARING LEEKS

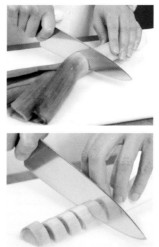

1. Trim and discard root and dark green leaves.

2. Cut trimmed leek in half lengthwise and slice into pieces according to recipe.

3. Rinse cut leeks thoroughly using salad spinner or bowl of water to remove dirt and sand.

Deviled Pork Chops with Scalloped Potatoes

Deviled Pork Chops with Scalloped Potatoes

CASSEROLE DISH

Serves 4
Total Time 1½ hours

Why This Recipe Works Complex and flavorful, deviled pork chops and rich scalloped potatoes create a comfort-food dinner. Scalloped potatoes usually require a casserole dish, so to contain the cooking to just one pan we layered the pork chops on top of the potatoes and baked them both in the oven. We gave the potatoes a head start, microwaving them with chicken broth, rosemary, and onion and garlic powders until beginning to soften. For a lush sauce, we stirred in cream and Wondra flour and then baked the potatoes for 30 minutes; meanwhile we breaded the chops. We boosted the crumb coating with Parmesan cheese to ensure it crisped; we also added Dijon mustard, mayonnaise, and hot sauce, which not only helped the coating cling but offered a spicy flavor boost to the usual egg wash. We placed our deviled pork chops on top of the potatoes and baked everything until the tender potatoes were bathed in their sauce and the pork boasted a golden-brown crust. You can substitute an equal amount of all-purpose flour for the Wondra flour, if necessary; however, the sauce will have a pasty, slightly gritty texture.

Pork Chops with Chile Rice and Peanuts

2 pounds russet potatoes, peeled and sliced ¼ inch thick
¾ cup chicken broth
1½ teaspoons minced fresh rosemary or ½ teaspoon dried
½ teaspoon onion powder
¼ teaspoon garlic powder
1 teaspoon table salt, divided
¾ cup heavy cream
2 tablespoons Wondra flour
½ teaspoon pepper, divided
1 cup panko bread crumbs
1½ ounces Parmesan cheese, grated (¾ cup), divided
1 tablespoon Dijon mustard
1½ teaspoons mayonnaise
1½ teaspoons hot sauce
4 (6- to 8-ounce) boneless pork chops, ¾ to 1 inch thick, trimmed
1 tablespoon minced fresh parsley

1. Adjust oven rack to middle position and heat oven to 400 degrees. Combine potatoes, broth, rosemary, onion powder, garlic powder, and ½ teaspoon salt in large bowl; cover and microwave until edges of potatoes are translucent and pliable, about 8 minutes.

PREVENTING CURLED PORK CHOPS

To prevent pork chops from buckling and curling when cooked, cut 2 small slits, about 2 inches apart, through outer layer of fat on each chop.

2. Stir cream, Wondra, and ¼ teaspoon pepper into hot potato mixture. Transfer mixture to greased 13 by 9-inch baking dish and press into even layer. Cover with aluminum foil and bake until potatoes are nearly tender, about 30 minutes.

3. Meanwhile, microwave panko in bowl, stirring every 30 seconds, until light golden brown, about 5 minutes; let cool slightly. Combine ¼ cup Parmesan and panko in shallow dish. Whisk mustard, mayonnaise, hot sauce, remaining ½ teaspoon salt, and remaining ¼ teaspoon pepper together in small bowl. Cut 2 slits, about 2 inches apart, through fat on edges of each pork chop. Pat chops dry with paper towels. Working with 1 chop at a time, brush 1 side with mustard mixture, then press chop, mustard side down, into panko mixture, pressing gently to adhere. Lay chop, coated side up, on plate.

4. Remove potatoes from oven, uncover, and sprinkle evenly with remaining ½ cup Parmesan. Place pork chops coated side up on top of potatoes in dish. Bake, uncovered, until pork registers 145 degrees, 10 to 15 minutes.

5. Remove dish from oven and let rest about 10 minutes. Sprinkle with parsley and serve.

Pork Chops with Chile Rice and Peanuts

SKILLET
Serves 4
Total Time 1 hour

Why This Recipe Works Honey, lime, chile, and fragrant spices flavor this pork chop and rice dish inspired by the chile-lime peanuts sold by street vendors throughout Mexico. We seared just one side of the pork chops in a skillet to develop some browning without overcooking them. Next we sautéed onion, garlic, seasonings, and tomato paste in some of the fat before adding broth. Simmering both the pork chops and rice in this liquid infused each with flavor, and once the chops were done we removed them and let the rice finish cooking. A quick vinaigrette of cilantro, lime zest, lime juice, oil, and honey delivered a tangy-sweet finish to the dish, and folding chopped peanuts into the rice added even more flavor and satisfying crunch. You will need a 12-inch skillet with a tight-fitting lid for this recipe.

- 4 (6- to 8-ounce) boneless pork chops, ¾ to 1 inch thick, trimmed
- ½ teaspoon plus ⅛ teaspoon table salt, divided
- ¼ teaspoon pepper
- 3 tablespoons extra-virgin olive oil, divided
- 1 onion, chopped fine
- 3 garlic cloves, minced
- 1 tablespoon tomato paste
- 1 tablespoon minced fresh oregano or 1 teaspoon dried
- 1 teaspoon ancho chile powder
- ¼ teaspoon ground coriander
  Pinch cayenne pepper
- 1½ cups long-grain white rice
- 4 cups chicken broth
- ¼ cup minced fresh cilantro, divided
- 1 tablespoon honey
- 2 teaspoons grated lime zest plus 3 tablespoons juice (2 limes)
- ⅓ cup unsalted dry-roasted peanuts, chopped

1. Using sharp knife, cut 2 slits, about 2 inches apart, through fat on edge of each pork chop. Pat chops dry with paper towels and sprinkle with ½ teaspoon salt and pepper. Heat 1 tablespoon oil in 12-inch skillet over medium-high heat until just smoking. Brown chops well on 1 side, about 5 minutes; transfer to plate.

2. Pour off all but 1 tablespoon fat from skillet. Add onion to fat left in skillet and cook over medium heat until softened, about 5 minutes. Stir in garlic, tomato paste, oregano, chile powder, coriander, and cayenne and cook until fragrant, about 30 seconds. Stir in rice to coat with spices, then stir in broth.

3. Nestle pork chops browned side up into skillet and add any accumulated juices. Bring to simmer, then reduce heat to medium-low, cover, and cook until chops register 145 degrees, 6 to 8 minutes.

4. Transfer pork chops to serving platter, tent with aluminum foil, and let rest while finishing rice. Stir rice mixture to recombine, then cover and cook until liquid is absorbed and rice is tender, 10 to 15 minutes. Meanwhile, whisk remaining 2 tablespoons oil, 2 tablespoons cilantro, honey, lime zest and juice, and remaining ⅛ teaspoon salt together in bowl.

5. Off heat, gently fold peanuts and remaining 2 tablespoons cilantro into rice and season with salt and pepper to taste; transfer to platter with chops. Drizzle honey-lime vinaigrette over pork chops and serve.

Stir-Fried Pork, Eggplant, and Onions with Garlic and Black Pepper

SKILLET

Serves 4

Total Time 45 minutes

Why This Recipe Works When developing a stir-fried pork and vegetable recipe, we found that coating pork tenderloin in a simple mixture of fish sauce and soy sauce and cooking it quickly (about two minutes) in a skillet over high heat kept the meat tender and beautifully seasoned. Because our vegetable choices of eggplant and onion cook at different rates, we had to batch-cook them and add the garlic—a whopping 12 cloves—at the end so it cooked long enough to develop its flavor but not long enough to burn. Chicken broth, more fish sauce and soy sauce, lime juice, and a little brown sugar formed a complex, flavorful stir-fry sauce, and cornstarch provided just enough thickening power so that the sauce lightly cloaked the meat and veggies. Stir-fries cook quickly, so have everything prepped before you begin cooking. We developed this recipe for a 12-inch nonstick skillet, but a 14-inch flat-bottomed wok can be used instead.

Stir-Fried Pork, Eggplant, and Onions with Garlic and Black Pepper

2 (12-ounce) pork tenderloins, trimmed
1 tablespoon water
¼ teaspoon baking soda
12 garlic cloves, minced
¼ cup vegetable oil, divided
2 teaspoons pepper
3 tablespoons fish sauce, divided
3 tablespoons soy sauce, divided
2½ tablespoons packed light brown sugar
2 tablespoons chicken broth
2 teaspoons lime juice
1¾ teaspoons cornstarch, divided
1 pound eggplant, cut into ¾-inch pieces
1 large onion, cut into ¼-inch-thick wedges
¼ cup coarsely chopped fresh cilantro

1. Cut each tenderloin in half lengthwise and place on large plate; freeze until firm, about 15 minutes. Cut strips crosswise into ⅛-inch-thick slices. Combine water and baking soda in medium bowl. Add pork and toss to coat; let sit for 5 minutes.

2. Combine garlic, 1 tablespoon oil, and pepper in small bowl; set aside. Whisk 2½ tablespoons fish sauce, 2½ tablespoons soy sauce, sugar, broth, lime juice, and 1 teaspoon cornstarch in second small bowl until sugar has dissolved; set aside. Add remaining 1½ teaspoons fish sauce, remaining 1½ teaspoons soy sauce, and remaining ¾ teaspoon cornstarch to pork and toss until well combined.

3. Heat 2 teaspoons oil in 12-inch nonstick skillet over medium-high heat until just smoking. Add half of pork and increase heat to high. Cook, tossing pork slowly but constantly, until no longer pink, 2 to 6 minutes; transfer to large bowl. Repeat with 2 teaspoons oil and remaining pork; transfer to bowl with first batch of pork.

4. Heat 1 tablespoon oil in now-empty skillet over high heat until just smoking. Add eggplant and cook, tossing slowly but constantly, until spotty brown, about 8 minutes; transfer to bowl with pork. Heat remaining 2 teaspoons oil in again-empty skillet over high heat until just smoking. Add onion and cook, tossing slowly but constantly, until just beginning to brown, about 2 minutes.

5. Push onion to one side of skillet and reduce heat to medium. Add garlic mixture to clearing and cook, mashing mixture into skillet, until fragrant, about 30 seconds. Stir garlic mixture into onion.

6. Whisk fish sauce mixture to recombine, then add to skillet along with pork-eggplant mixture and any accumulated juices. Increase heat to high and cook, tossing constantly, until sauce has thickened, about 30 seconds. Sprinkle with cilantro and serve.

Stir-Fried Pork, Asparagus, and Red Bell Pepper with Gingery Oyster Sauce for Two

SKILLET

Serves 2

Total Time 45 minutes

Stir-fries cook quickly, so have everything prepped before you begin cooking. We developed this recipe for a 12-inch nonstick skillet, but a 14-inch flat-bottomed wok can be used instead.

  1 (12-ounce) pork tenderloin, trimmed
1½ teaspoons water
  ⅛ teaspoon baking soda
  1 tablespoon grated fresh ginger
  2 tablespoons plus 1 teaspoon vegetable oil, divided
  ¼ cup chicken broth
  2 tablespoons oyster sauce
  1 tablespoon Shaoxing wine or dry sherry, divided
  1 teaspoon toasted sesame oil
  1 teaspoon unseasoned rice vinegar
  ¾ teaspoon cornstarch, divided
  1 teaspoon soy sauce
  4 ounces asparagus, trimmed and cut on bias into 2-inch lengths
  1 small red bell pepper, stemmed, seeded, and cut into 2-inch-long matchsticks
  1 scallion, sliced thin on bias

1. Cut tenderloin in half lengthwise and place on large plate; freeze until firm, about 15 minutes. Cut strips crosswise into ⅛-inch-thick slices. Combine water and baking soda in medium bowl. Add pork and toss to coat; let sit for 5 minutes.

2. Combine ginger and 1 tablespoon vegetable oil in small bowl; set aside. Whisk broth, oyster sauce, 2½ teaspoons Shaoxing wine, sesame oil, vinegar, and ½ teaspoon cornstarch in second small bowl; set aside. Add soy sauce, remaining ½ teaspoon Shaoxing wine, and remaining ¼ teaspoon cornstarch to pork and toss until well combined.

3. Heat 2 teaspoons vegetable oil in 12-inch nonstick skillet over medium-high heat until just smoking. Add pork and increase heat to high. Cook, tossing pork slowly but constantly, until no longer pink, 2 to 6 minutes; transfer to clean bowl.

4. Heat remaining 2 teaspoons oil in now-empty skillet over high heat until just smoking. Add asparagus and bell pepper and cook, tossing slowly but constantly, until tender and spotty brown, 2 to 6 minutes.

5. Push vegetables to one side of skillet and reduce heat to medium. Add ginger mixture to clearing and cook, mashing mixture into skillet, until fragrant, about 30 seconds. Stir ginger mixture into vegetables.

6. Whisk broth mixture to recombine, then add to skillet along with pork and any accumulated juices. Increase heat to high and cook, tossing constantly, until sauce has thickened, about 30 seconds. Sprinkle with scallion and serve.

NOTES FROM THE TEST KITCHEN

STORING MEAT SAFELY

Proper storage is the best way to prolong the shelf life of meat and prevent waste.

Refrigerating Meat Raw meat should be refrigerated well wrapped and never on shelves that are above other food. Check regularly that your refrigerator's temperature is between 35 and 40 degrees. Most raw and cooked meat will keep for two to three days in the refrigerator. Raw ground meat and raw poultry will keep for two days. Smoked ham and bacon will keep for up to two weeks.

Freezing Meat The slow process of freezing that occurs in a home freezer (as compared with a commercial freezer) causes large ice crystals to form. The crystals rupture the cell walls of the meat, permitting the release of juices during cooking and resulting in drier meat. To freeze meat, wrap it well in plastic wrap and then place the meat in a zipper-lock bag and squeeze out excess air. Label the bag and use the meat within a few months.

Thawing Meat All meat can be thawed safely on a plate or rimmed baking sheet in the refrigerator (and this is the only safe method for large cuts such as whole chickens). Never thaw meat on the counter, where bacteria will rapidly multiply.

Quick Thaw for Small Cuts Flat cuts such as chicken breasts, pork chops, and steaks will thaw more quickly when left on a metal surface, because metal can transfer ambient heat more quickly than wood or plastic. To thaw frozen wrapped steaks, chops, and ground meat (flattened to 1 inch thick before freezing), place in a skillet (heavy steel and cast-iron skillets work best) in a single layer. Flip the meat every half-hour until thawed. Small cuts can also be sealed in zipper-lock bags and submerged in hot (140-degree) water—this will safely thaw chicken breasts, steaks, and chops in under 15 minutes.

Pulled Pork Tacos with Radish-Apple Slaw

SLOW COOKER

Serves 4 to 6
Cook Time 9 to 11 hours on low or 6 to 8 hours on high

Why This Recipe Works Pulled pork tacos may not seem like a weeknight meal, but employing a slow cooker proved to be an easy, hands-off way to tenderize tough yet richly flavored pork butt over the course of a day, yielding succulent meat in time for dinner. To give our pulled pork an equally rich sauce, we deployed just the right pantry staples—chili powder, cumin, chipotle chiles, canned tomato sauce, and raisins—to produce a quick mole with complex flavor. Blending the sauce gave it the perfect consistency. For a topping with plenty of crunch, we created a slaw featuring tart apples, peppery radishes, and red onion. Avocado added creamy richness, while a dressing spiked with lime brightened things up and cilantro lent a bright, grassy note. Pork butt roast is often labeled Boston butt in the supermarket. For more information on warming tortillas, see page 116.

Pork

- 1 tablespoon extra-virgin olive oil
- 2 tablespoons chili powder
- 2 tablespoons ground cumin
- 1 tablespoon minced canned chipotle chile in adobo sauce
- 3 garlic cloves, lightly crushed and peeled
- 1 (15-ounce) can tomato sauce
- 1 cup raisins
- ¾ teaspoon table salt
- ¾ teaspoon pepper
- 1 (2½- to 3-pound) boneless pork butt roast, trimmed

Radish-Apple Slaw

- ¼ cup extra-virgin olive oil
- 2 tablespoons lime juice
- 1 tablespoon cider vinegar
- 1 teaspoon table salt
- 12 ounces radishes, trimmed and cut into ¼-inch wedges
- 1 Granny Smith apple, cored and cut into 2-inch-long matchsticks
- 1 small red onion, halved and sliced thin
- 2 avocados, halved, pitted, and cut into ½-inch pieces
- 4 ounces cotija cheese, crumbled (1 cup)
- 1 cup fresh cilantro leaves
- 12–18 (6-inch) corn tortillas, warmed

1. For the pork Microwave oil, chili powder, cumin, chipotle, and garlic in small bowl until fragrant, about 1 minute. Combine oil mixture, tomato sauce, raisins, salt, and pepper in slow cooker. Slice pork crosswise into 4 equal pieces and trim excess fat. Nestle pork into slow cooker, cover, and cook until tender, 9 to 11 hours on low or 6 to 8 hours on high.

2. Transfer pork to cutting board, let cool slightly, then shred into bite-size pieces using 2 forks; discard excess fat.

3. Using wide, shallow spoon, skim excess fat from surface of sauce. Process sauce in blender until smooth, about 1 minute. (Adjust sauce consistency with hot water as needed.) Combine 2 cups sauce and pork in now-empty slow cooker and season with salt and pepper to taste.

4. For the radish-apple slaw Whisk oil, lime juice, vinegar, and salt together in large bowl. Add radishes, apple, and onion and toss to coat. Gently fold in avocados, cotija, and cilantro. Season with salt and pepper to taste. Serve pork with tortillas, remaining sauce, and slaw.

VARIATION

Pulled Pork Tacos with Radish-Apple Slaw for Two

SLOW COOKER

Serves 2
Cook Time 5 to 7 hours on low or 3 to 5 hours on high
For more information on warming tortillas, see page 116.

Pork

- 2 teaspoons extra-virgin olive oil
- 2 teaspoons chili powder
- 2 teaspoons ground cumin
- 1 teaspoon minced canned chipotle chile in adobo sauce
- 1 garlic clove, lightly crushed and peeled
- 1 pound boneless country-style pork ribs, trimmed and cut into 2-inch pieces
- 1 (8-ounce) can tomato sauce
- ⅓ cup raisins
- ¼ teaspoon table salt
- ¼ teaspoon pepper

Radish-Apple Slaw

- 2 tablespoons extra-virgin olive oil
- 1 tablespoon lime juice
- 1½ teaspoons cider vinegar
- ½ teaspoon table salt
- 6 ounces radishes, trimmed and cut into ¼-inch wedges
- ½ Granny Smith apple, cored and cut into 2-inch-long matchsticks
- ¼ cup thinly sliced red onion
- 1 avocado, halved, pitted, and cut into ½-inch pieces

2 ounces cotija cheese, crumbled (½ cup)
½ cup fresh cilantro leaves
4–6 (6-inch) corn tortillas, warmed

1. For the pork Microwave oil, chili powder, cumin, chipotle, and garlic in small bowl until fragrant, about 1 minute. Combine pork, oil mixture, tomato sauce, raisins, salt, and pepper in slow cooker. Cover and cook until tender, 5 to 7 hours on low or 3 to 5 hours on high.

2. Transfer pork to cutting board, let cool slightly, then shred into bite-size pieces using 2 forks; discard excess fat.

3. Using wide, shallow spoon, skim excess fat from surface of sauce. Process sauce in blender until smooth, about 1 minute. (Adjust sauce consistency with hot water as needed.) Combine ¾ cup sauce and pork in now-empty slow cooker and season with salt and pepper to taste.

4. For the radish-apple slaw Whisk oil, lime juice, vinegar, and salt together in large bowl. Add radishes, apple, and onion and toss to coat. Gently fold in avocado, cotija, and cilantro. Season with salt and pepper to taste. Serve pork with tortillas, remaining sauce, and slaw.

Vietnamese Pork Banh Mi
SKILLET
Serves 4
Total Time 50 minutes, plus 30 minutes chilling

Why This Recipe Works Banh mi is Vietnamese street food at its best, consisting of a soft-style Vietnamese baguette split in half and loaded with all kinds of meats and vegetables. Variations abound, but in all of them the star is the pickled daikon radish and carrots. For our at-home version, we pickled radishes and carrots in brown sugar, lime juice, and fish sauce for balanced sweet-citrusy-savory flavor. Next we marinated thinly sliced pork in more lime juice, fish sauce, and sugar plus pepper flakes before quickly cooking it in a hot skillet. Sriracha mayo plus a smear of decadent chicken liver pâté and plenty of cucumbers, jalapeño, and cilantro completed the rich, satisfying flavor profile. You can find pâté in the gourmet cheese section of most well-stocked supermarkets. Be sure to use a smooth-textured pâté, not a coarse country pâté. Avoid pickling the radishes and carrots for longer than 1 hour; the radishes will begin to turn limp, gray, and bitter.

Pickles
¼ cup water
1 tablespoon fish sauce
1 tablespoon packed dark brown sugar
½ teaspoon grated lime zest plus ¼ cup juice (2 limes)

Vietnamese Pork Banh Mi

½ teaspoon table salt
8 ounces daikon radish, peeled and cut into 2-inch-long matchsticks
1 small carrot, peeled and cut into 2-inch-long matchsticks

Banh Mi
1 (12-ounce) pork tenderloin, trimmed and halved crosswise
3 tablespoons fish sauce
1 teaspoon grated lime zest plus 2 tablespoons juice, divided
2 tablespoons packed dark brown sugar
½ teaspoon red pepper flakes
1 tablespoon vegetable oil
⅓ cup mayonnaise
4 teaspoons sriracha
6 ounces chicken or duck liver pâté
1 (18-inch) baguette, ends trimmed, cut crosswise into 4 equal lengths, and halved lengthwise
½ English cucumber, halved lengthwise and sliced thin
1 jalapeño chile, stemmed and sliced thin
1 cup fresh cilantro leaves and stems, trimmed and cut into 2-inch lengths

1. For the pickles Bring water, fish sauce, sugar, lime zest and juice, and salt to simmer in 12-inch nonstick skillet; transfer to medium bowl. Stir in radish and carrot and refrigerate for at least 15 minutes or up to 1 hour. Drain vegetables and set aside for serving.

2. For the banh mi Meanwhile, place pork pieces between 2 sheets of parchment paper or plastic wrap and pound to ¼-inch thickness. Whisk fish sauce, lime juice, sugar, and pepper flakes in large bowl until sugar has dissolved. Add pork and toss to coat. Cover and refrigerate for at least 30 minutes or up to 1 hour.

3. Remove pork from marinade and pat dry with paper towels. Heat oil in now-empty skillet over medium-high heat until shimmering. Add pork, reduce heat to medium, and cook until pork is well browned and registers 140 degrees, about 4 minutes per side. Transfer pork to cutting board and let rest for 5 to 10 minutes.

4. Whisk mayonnaise, sriracha, and lime zest together in small bowl. Slice pork ¼ inch thick. Spread pâté evenly over cut sides of baguette, followed by mayonnaise mixture. Layer pickled vegetables, pork, cucumber, jalapeño, and cilantro evenly over bottom halves. Top with baguette tops and serve.

Philadelphia Roast Pork Sandwiches with Broccoli Rabe

Philadelphia Roast Pork Sandwiches with Broccoli Rabe

SHEET PAN

Serves 4
Total Time 1¼ hours

Why This Recipe Works The underdog rival for the title of Philly's best sandwich loads up a hoagie (aka Italian sub) roll with juicy pork, garlicky broccoli rabe, provolone, and vinegary hot peppers for a feast in a bun. Sandwich shops prepare each component separately hours in advance, but for a streamlined home version we roasted the meat, greens, and peppers side by side on a sheet pan. We skipped the standard pork shoulder in favor of smaller, quick-cooking pork tenderloin, seasoning it heavily with rosemary and fennel seeds and roasting it until just cooked through. Shaving it as thinly as possible mimicked the usual shreds of long-cooked pork shoulder. Finally, tossing it with oil and vinegar punched up the flavor and kept it moist. The vegetables roasted alongside the tenderloin: assertive broccoli rabe with lots of garlic and pepper flakes, and sweet red bell pepper to complement the bitter greens. While the meat rested, we used our sheet pan to toast the rolls; slices of provolone melted over the buns provided the extra richness we needed to make these sandwiches perfect.

1 tablespoon minced fresh rosemary
1 tablespoon fennel seeds
¼ teaspoon table salt
¼ teaspoon pepper
1 (1-pound) pork tenderloin, trimmed
6 tablespoons extra-virgin olive oil, divided
1 pound broccoli rabe, trimmed and cut into 1-inch pieces
4 garlic cloves, minced
1 teaspoon red pepper flakes
2 red bell peppers, stemmed, seeded, and sliced thin
4 (6-inch) Italian sub rolls, split lengthwise
6 ounces sliced provolone cheese
2 tablespoons red wine vinegar

1. Adjust oven rack to middle position and heat oven to 450 degrees. Combine rosemary, fennel seeds, salt, and pepper in small bowl. Rub tenderloin with 2 tablespoons oil and sprinkle with rosemary mixture. Place on one side of rimmed baking sheet and roast for 10 minutes.

2. Toss broccoli rabe with 2 tablespoons oil, garlic, and pepper flakes in bowl. In separate bowl, toss bell peppers with 1 tablespoon oil. Remove sheet from oven and flip pork.

Spread broccoli rabe and bell peppers on hot sheet next to pork. Roast until pork registers 145 degrees and broccoli rabe and bell peppers are browned, about 20 minutes.

3. Remove sheet from oven. Transfer pork to cutting board, tent with aluminum foil, and let rest for 5 minutes. Transfer vegetables to bowl and cover with foil to keep warm. Wipe sheet clean with paper towels, lay split rolls open on sheet, and top with provolone. Bake rolls until bread is lightly toasted and cheese is melted, about 5 minutes.

4. Slice pork as thin as possible, transfer to clean bowl, and toss with vinegar and remaining 1 tablespoon oil. Nestle pork, broccoli rabe, and bell peppers into warm rolls and serve.

Skillet Sausage and Cheese Pizza
SKILLET
Serves 4
Total Time 45 minutes

Why This Recipe Works We wanted to come up with an easier, quicker way to make pizza at home. Our idea was to build the pizza in a skillet, give the crust a jump-start with heat from the stovetop, and then transfer it to the oven to cook through—no pizza stone required. We oiled the skillet before adding the dough and turning up the heat; this not only kept the dough from sticking but also encouraged browning. A simple no-cook sauce of canned tomatoes, olive oil, and garlic required nothing more than a quick whir in the food processor. To finish, we topped our pizza with a combination of mozzarella and a little Parmesan as well as some Italian sausage. We prefer to use our homemade Classic Pizza Dough (page 292) here; however, you can substitute 1 pound of store-bought pizza dough. Let the dough sit at room temperature while preparing the remaining ingredients and heating the oven; otherwise, it will be difficult to stretch. Feel free to omit the sausage if you are looking for a simpler cheese pizza. You will need a 12-inch ovensafe skillet for this recipe.

1 (14.5-ounce) can whole peeled tomatoes, drained with juice reserved
5 tablespoons extra-virgin olive oil, divided
½ teaspoon red wine vinegar
½ teaspoon dried oregano
1 small garlic clove, minced
1 pound pizza dough, room temperature
12 ounces sweet or hot Italian pork sausage, casings removed

8 ounces whole-milk mozzarella cheese, shredded (2 cups)
1 ounce Parmesan cheese, grated (½ cup)

1. Adjust oven rack to upper-middle position and heat oven to 500 degrees. Process tomatoes, 1 tablespoon oil, vinegar, oregano, and garlic in food processor until smooth, about 30 seconds. Transfer mixture to 2-cup liquid measuring cup and add reserved tomato juice until sauce measures 1 cup. Season with salt and pepper to taste. (Sauce can be refrigerated for up to 1 week or frozen for up to 1 month.)

2. Grease 12-inch ovensafe skillet with 2 tablespoons oil. Transfer dough to lightly floured counter, divide in half, and gently shape each half into ball. Cover 1 dough ball with plastic wrap. Coat remaining dough ball lightly with flour and gently flatten into 8-inch disk using your fingertips. Using rolling pin, roll dough into 11-inch circle, dusting dough lightly with flour as needed. (If dough springs back during rolling, let rest for 10 minutes before rolling again.)

3. Transfer dough to prepared skillet; reshape as needed. Using back of spoon or ladle, spread ½ cup sauce in thin layer over surface of dough, leaving ½-inch border around edge. Pinch 6 ounces sausage into approximate dime-size pieces and evenly distribute over sauce. Sprinkle 1 cup mozzarella and ¼ cup Parmesan evenly over sausage.

4. Set skillet over medium-high heat and cook until outside edge of dough is set, pizza is lightly puffed, and bottom crust is spotty brown when gently lifted with spatula, 2 to 3 minutes. Transfer pizza to oven and bake until crust is brown and cheese is golden in spots, 7 to 10 minutes. Using potholders, remove skillet from oven and slide pizza onto cutting board. Let pizza cool slightly before slicing and serving. Being careful of hot skillet handle, repeat with remaining 2 tablespoons oil, dough, sauce, 1 cup mozzarella, and ¼ cup Parmesan.

VARIATION

Skillet Fontina, Arugula, and Prosciutto Pizza for Two
SKILLET
Serves 2
Total Time 45 minutes
We prefer to use our homemade Classic Pizza Dough (page 292) here; however, you can substitute 8 ounces of store-bought pizza dough. Let the dough sit at room temperature while preparing the remaining ingredients and heating the oven; otherwise, it will be difficult to stretch. The sauce will yield more than needed for the recipe; extra sauce can be refrigerated for up to 1 week or frozen for up to 1 month. You will need a 12-inch ovensafe skillet for this recipe.

1 (14.5-ounce) can whole peeled tomatoes, drained with juice reserved
¼ cup extra-virgin olive oil, divided
½ teaspoon red wine vinegar
½ teaspoon dried oregano
1 small garlic clove, minced
8 ounces pizza dough, room temperature
4 ounces fontina cheese, shredded (1 cup)
1 cup baby arugula
1 ounce thinly sliced prosciutto, cut into ½-inch strips

1. Adjust oven rack to upper-middle position and heat oven to 500 degrees. Process tomatoes, 1 tablespoon oil, vinegar, oregano, and garlic in food processor until smooth, about 30 seconds. Transfer mixture to 2-cup liquid measuring cup and add reserved tomato juice until sauce measures 1 cup. Season with salt and pepper to taste.

2. Grease 12-inch ovensafe skillet with 2 tablespoons oil. Lightly coat dough ball with flour and gently flatten into 8-inch disk on counter using your fingertips. Using rolling pin, roll dough into 11-inch circle, dusting dough lightly with flour as needed. (If dough springs back during rolling, let rest for 10 minutes before rolling again.)

3. Transfer dough to prepared skillet; reshape as needed. Using back of spoon or ladle, spread ½ cup sauce in thin layer over surface of dough, leaving ½-inch border around edge. Sprinkle fontina evenly over sauce.

4. Set skillet over medium-high heat and cook until outside edge of dough is set, pizza is lightly puffed, and bottom crust is spotty brown when gently lifted with spatula, 2 to 3 minutes. Transfer pizza to oven and bake until crust is brown and cheese is golden in spots, 7 to 10 minutes.

5. Toss arugula with remaining 1 tablespoon oil and season with salt and pepper to taste. Using potholders, remove skillet from oven and slide pizza onto cutting board. Let pizza cool slightly, then top with arugula and prosciutto. Slice and serve.

INGREDIENT SPOTLIGHT

FONTINA
We tasted seven different fontina cheeses to find our favorite. The nutty-sweet, funky, and earthy flavors of authentic Fontina Val d'Aosta appealed to tasters who love other complex cheeses such as Gruyère and Comté, but it's not easy to find in supermarkets. Our favorite supermarket fontina is the more widely available **Boar's Head Fontina Cheese**, a Swedish-style cheese known for having a soft, creamy texture and a buttery, tangy flavor similar to that of gouda.

Pork Sausage with Polenta
SKILLET
Serves 4
Total Time 1¼ hours

Why This Recipe Works To make this Italian American classic using only one skillet, we looked to "instant" polenta—which is already cooked and dried—because it needed only to be whisked into hot liquid to turn into a savory porridge. We started by lightly browning sliced onion, red bell pepper, and fennel. After setting the vegetables aside, we added milk and water to the now-empty skillet and brought the mixture to a boil before whisking in the polenta (along with butter and Parmesan cheese for richness). But the fond left in the pan from browning the vegetables turned the cooking liquid a grayish-brown; to solve this, we switched to a nonstick skillet so that the flavorful browned bits stayed on the vegetables rather than in the pan. We topped the polenta with the partially cooked vegetables, added raw sausages, and slid the skillet into the oven to finish cooking and brown the sausages. You will need a 12-inch ovensafe nonstick skillet for this recipe.

2 tablespoons extra-virgin olive oil
1 red bell pepper, stemmed, seeded, and sliced thin
1 onion, halved and sliced thin
1 fennel bulb, stalks discarded, bulb halved, cored, and sliced thin
3 garlic cloves, minced
1¾ teaspoons table salt, divided
½ teaspoon pepper, divided
¼ teaspoon red pepper flakes
1½ cups whole milk
1½ cups water
¾ cup instant polenta
2 ounces Parmesan cheese, grated (1 cup)
4 tablespoons unsalted butter
1½ pounds hot or sweet Italian sausage
1 tablespoon minced fresh parsley

1. Adjust oven rack to upper-middle position and heat oven to 450 degrees. Heat oil in 12-inch ovensafe nonstick skillet over medium-high heat until shimmering. Add bell pepper, onion, fennel, garlic, ¾ teaspoon salt, ¼ teaspoon pepper, and pepper flakes and cook until vegetables are softened and browned, about 10 minutes, stirring occasionally; transfer to bowl.

2. Add milk, water, remaining 1 teaspoon salt, and remaining ¼ teaspoon pepper to now-empty skillet and bring to boil over high heat. Whisking constantly, slowly add polenta. Reduce heat to low and cook, whisking constantly, until polenta thickens and whisk leaves distinct trail, about 2 minutes.

3. Off heat, whisk in Parmesan and butter until incorporated. Distribute vegetable mixture over polenta, then evenly space sausages on top of vegetables. Bake until sausages are browned and register at least 160 degrees, about 25 minutes. Let rest for 10 minutes. Sprinkle with parsley and serve.

Pork Sausage with White Beans and Mustard Greens

INSTANT POT
Serves 4
Total Time 1 hour

Why This Recipe Works The south of France is known for its rich stews that combine meaty sausage, creamy white beans, and fresh greens. For our slightly less stew-y version, we turned to the pressure cooker to ensure that the beans were perfectly broken down and paired with juicy sausages and wilted greens. We first browned easy-to-find Italian sausage using the pressure cooker's sauté function and then cooked it under pressure with convenient canned navy beans and peppery mustard greens. For a bright, textural finish, we made lemon-scented bread crumbs to sprinkle over the completed dish and topped it with tangy goat cheese. If mustard greens are unavailable, you can substitute kale.

  2 tablespoons extra-virgin olive oil, divided
1½ pounds hot or sweet Italian sausage
  1 onion, chopped fine
  1 tablespoon minced fresh thyme or 1 teaspoon dried
  2 garlic cloves, minced
  ¾ cup chicken broth
  ¼ cup dry white wine
  2 (15-ounce) cans navy beans, rinsed
  1 pound mustard greens, stemmed and cut into
     2-inch pieces
  ½ cup panko bread crumbs
  2 tablespoons chopped fresh parsley
  ½ teaspoon grated lemon zest plus 1 teaspoon juice
  4 ounces goat cheese, crumbled (1 cup)

1. Using highest sauté or browning function, heat 1 tablespoon oil in electric pressure cooker until just smoking. Brown sausages on all sides, 6 to 8 minutes; transfer to plate.

Pork Sausage with White Beans and Mustard Greens

2. Add onion to fat left in pressure cooker and cook, using highest sauté or browning function, until softened, about 5 minutes. Stir in thyme and garlic and cook until fragrant, about 30 seconds. Stir in broth and wine, scraping up any browned bits, then stir in beans. Add mustard greens, then place sausages on top. Lock lid in place and close pressure release valve. Select high pressure cook function and cook for 2 minutes.

3. Meanwhile, toss panko with remaining 1 tablespoon oil in bowl until evenly coated. Microwave, stirring every 30 seconds, until light golden brown, about 5 minutes. Let cool slightly, then stir in parsley and lemon zest; set aside for serving.

4. Turn off pressure cooker and quick-release pressure. Carefully remove lid, allowing steam to escape away from you. Transfer sausages to plate. Stir lemon juice into bean and mustard greens mixture and season with salt and pepper to taste. Serve sausages with bean and mustard greens mixture, sprinkling individual portions with seasoned bread crumbs and goat cheese.

1. Heat oil in large Dutch oven over medium heat until shimmering. Brown bratwurst on all sides, 6 to 8 minutes. Transfer sausages to cutting board and cut each in half crosswise.

2. Arrange potatoes in single layer in now-empty pot. Arrange cabbage wedges in single layer on top of potatoes. Layer corn, carrots, onion, garlic, thyme sprigs, bay leaves, salt, and pepper over cabbage. Pour beer over vegetables and lay browned bratwurst on top.

3. Bring to boil over medium-high heat (wisps of steam will be visible). Cover, reduce heat to medium, and simmer for 15 minutes. Add bell peppers and continue to simmer, covered, until potatoes are tender, about 15 minutes. (Use long skewer to test potatoes for doneness.)

4. Transfer bratwurst and vegetables to serving platter; discard thyme sprigs and bay leaves. Sprinkle 1 cup cooking liquid over bratwurst and vegetables. Serve, passing remaining cooking liquid separately.

Chorizo, Corn, and Tomato Tostadas with Lime Crema

SHEET PAN
Serves 4
Total Time 45 minutes

Why This Recipe Works Tostadas are flat, crisped tortillas that serve as a crunchy base for rich, flavorful toppings. Preparing all the components for tostadas could easily become laborious, so to simplify things we used a sheet pan to brown chorizo and corn and smartly deployed our other ingredients. While the chorizo and corn cooked, we warmed our tostadas—spread with a flavorful black bean–jalapeño mixture—directly on the oven rack below. In addition to using the chiles, we tossed some of their brine with the beans for added flavor, and tossed more of it with coleslaw mix for a quick-pickled cabbage topping. Fresh cherry tomatoes and lime juice added tang; more lime juice went into an easy crema that brought richness. Sprinkled with queso fresco and cilantro, our tostadas were hefty enough for a meal and hit all of our taste buds. Look for tostadas next to the taco kits at most supermarkets; our favorite brand of tostadas is Mission Tostadas Estilo Casero.

  1 (14-ounce) bag green coleslaw mix
  1 tablespoon finely chopped jarred jalapeños,
     plus ¼ cup brine, divided
  ½ cup sour cream
  3 tablespoons lime juice (2 limes), divided

  8 ounces Spanish-style chorizo sausage,
     halved lengthwise and sliced ¼ inch thick
  4 ears corn, kernels cut from cobs
  1 tablespoon vegetable oil
  1 (15-ounce) can black beans, rinsed
  ¼ cup vegetable broth
 12 (6-inch) corn tostadas
  6 ounces cherry tomatoes, quartered
  4 ounces queso fresco or feta cheese, crumbled (1 cup)
  ¼ cup fresh cilantro leaves

1. Adjust oven racks to upper-middle and lower-middle positions, place rimmed baking sheet on upper rack, and heat oven to 450 degrees. Toss coleslaw mix with 3 tablespoons jalapeño brine in bowl and season with salt and pepper to taste; set aside for serving. Whisk sour cream and 2 tablespoons lime juice together in second bowl; set aside for serving.

2. Toss chorizo, corn, and oil in large bowl and spread in single layer on hot sheet. Cook until browned, about 15 minutes.

3. Meanwhile, combine beans, broth, jalapeños, and remaining 1 tablespoon brine in now-empty bowl and microwave until heated through, about 2 minutes. Mash beans with potato masher until spreadable, season with salt and pepper to taste, and spread evenly over tostadas. During final 5 minutes of roasting chorizo, place tostadas directly on lower oven rack to warm through.

4. Remove sheet from oven. Sprinkle tomatoes and remaining 1 tablespoon lime juice over chorizo mixture and toss to combine. Divide mixture evenly among tostadas. Top tostadas with slaw, lime crema, queso fresco, and cilantro. Serve.

Braised Country-Style Ribs with Black-Eyed Peas and Collard Greens

DUTCH OVEN
Serves 6 to 8
Total Time 2 hours

Why This Recipe Works There's a simple Southern side dish in which black-eyed peas, collard greens, and a smoked ham hock are stewed together for hours until the beans are creamy, the greens are velvety soft, and the broth is suffused with the smoky sweetness of the ham. Our goal was to capitalize on the flavors and basic technique of this dish, but expand it into a full-blown stew-like meal with the addition of a heftier cut of meat—and to fit everything in the same pot, we would use a roomy Dutch oven. Ham hocks may be flavorful, but they yield a scant amount of edible meat. Hefty country-style ribs were a much better choice; taken from the backbone of the pig at the juncture of the shoulder and the loin, this cut is very flavorful and resilient because of the relatively high amount of fat and connective tissue between the bones. When we stewed the collards from start to finish with the beans and ribs, they became soggy and took on an unappealing drab green color. While this is common, we prefer a bit more color and bite, so we sliced the greens thin and simmered them at the end of cooking for just a few minutes. The dish was flavorful and porky, but we missed the smokiness provided by ham hocks so we added some bacon. Pickled red onion was a brilliant finish, cutting through the richness and enlivening the dish.

2	pounds boneless country-style pork ribs, trimmed
½	teaspoon table salt, divided
¼	teaspoon pepper, divided
1	teaspoon vegetable oil
4	ounces bacon, sliced crosswise into ¼-inch strips
1	red onion, chopped
1	large celery rib, chopped fine
6	garlic cloves, minced
3½	cups chicken broth
1	cup water
1	pound dried black-eyed peas, picked through and rinsed
2	bay leaves
1	pound collard greens, stemmed and sliced thin
1	recipe Quick Pickled Onions (page 223)

1. Adjust oven rack to lower-middle position and heat oven to 300 degrees. Pat ribs dry with paper towels and sprinkle with salt and pepper. Heat oil in Dutch oven over medium-high heat until just smoking. Brown ribs on all sides, 8 to 10 minutes; transfer to plate.

2. Pour off fat from pot. Add bacon to now-empty pot and cook over medium heat until most of fat has rendered, about 3 minutes. Stir in onion and celery and cook until softened and lightly browned, 5 to 7 minutes. Stir in garlic and cook until fragrant, about 30 seconds. Stir in broth and water, scraping up any browned bits. Stir in black-eyed peas and bay leaves, then nestle ribs into pot and add any accumulated juices. Bring to simmer, cover, and transfer pot to oven. Cook until ribs and black-eyed peas are tender, about 1 hour.

3. Transfer ribs to cutting board, tent with aluminum foil, and let rest while cooking collards. Discard bay leaves. Stir collard greens into pot and cook over medium-high heat until wilted and tender, 4 to 8 minutes. Season with salt and pepper to taste. Serve immediately with ribs, black-eyed peas, and pickled onions.

Chorizo, Corn, and Tomato Tostadas with Lime Crema

Braised Country-Style Ribs with Black-Eyed Peas and Collard Greens

SPICED PORK LOIN WITH BUTTERNUT SQUASH AND BRUSSELS SPROUTS

This impressive yet simple dinner of warmly spiced pork with hearty roasted butternut squash and Brussels sprouts is ideal for a crisp autumn day. A pork loin roast was just right for a family-size meal, but we switched to a smaller tenderloin to make a version for two without a mountain of leftovers. Giving the pork a head start ensured perfectly cooked meat and tender (not mushy) vegetables. Placing the pork fat side down produced not only a satisfying sizzle in our preheated pan, but it also turned out a flavorful crust as well. The classic recipe and the recipe for a crowd work best with a pork roast that is about 7 to 8 inches long and 4 to 5 inches wide. We like to leave a ¼-inch-thick layer of fat on top of the roast; if your roast has a thicker fat cap, trim it back to be about ¼ inch thick. If the pork is enhanced (injected with a salt solution), do not salt in step 1. In the recipe for two, be sure to remove the silver-skin from the tenderloin. You will need a 12-inch ovensafe skillet for the recipe for two. Use Brussels sprouts no bigger than golf balls, as larger ones are often tough and woody.

MAKE IT YOUR WAY
→

CLASSIC

SHEET PAN
Serves 4 to 6
Total Time 1½ hours, plus 1 hour salting

- 2 tablespoons plus ½ teaspoon packed brown sugar, divided
- 1½ tablespoons kosher salt, divided
- 1 (2½- to 3-pound) boneless pork loin roast, trimmed
- 2 teaspoons ground coriander
- 2 teaspoons paprika
- ½ teaspoon pepper, divided
- 2 pounds butternut squash, peeled, seeded, and cut into 1-inch pieces
- 1 pound Brussels sprouts, trimmed and halved
- ¼ cup extra-virgin olive oil, divided
- 3 garlic cloves, minced
- ¼ cup chopped fresh parsley
- 2 tablespoons cider vinegar
- 1½ teaspoons Dijon mustard

1. Combine 2 tablespoons sugar and 1 tablespoon salt in bowl. Rub pork with sugar mixture, wrap in plastic wrap, and refrigerate for at least 1 hour or up to 24 hours.

2. Adjust oven rack to middle position, place rimmed baking sheet on rack, and heat oven to 400 degrees. Combine coriander, paprika, and ¼ teaspoon pepper in bowl. Pat pork dry with paper towels, sprinkle with spice mixture, and tie at 1½-inch intervals with kitchen twine. Arrange pork fat side down in center of hot sheet and roast for 30 minutes.

3. Meanwhile, toss squash and Brussels sprouts with 2 tablespoons oil, garlic, and 1 teaspoon salt in bowl. Arrange squash mixture on sheet, cut sides down, around pork. Roast until pork registers 140 degrees, 15 to 20 minutes.

4. Remove sheet from oven. Transfer roast to carving board, tent with aluminum foil, and let rest while squash mixture finishes cooking. Gently stir squash mixture and continue to roast until tender, 10 to 15 minutes.

5. Whisk parsley, vinegar, mustard, remaining ½ teaspoon sugar, remaining ½ teaspoon salt, remaining ¼ teaspoon pepper, and remaining 2 tablespoons oil together in large bowl. Transfer vegetables to bowl with vinaigrette and toss to combine. Season with salt and pepper to taste. Slice roast ½ inch thick and serve with vegetables.

> **Use What You've Got** Substitute spice blends (herbes de Provence, garam masala, ras el hanout) for the coriander and paprika. Substitute hearty vegetables (celery root, fennel, parsnips, Yukon Gold potatoes, turnips) for the squash and Brussels sprouts. Substitute fresh herbs (basil, chives, dill, tarragon) for the parsley.

COOK IT FOR TWO

SKILLET
Serves 2
Total Time 1 hour

- 1 teaspoon ground coriander
- 1 teaspoon ground paprika
- ¾ teaspoon plus ⅛ teaspoon table salt, divided
- ¼ teaspoon pepper, divided
- 1 (12- to 16-ounce) pork tenderloin, trimmed
- 3 tablespoons extra-virgin olive oil, divided
- 8 ounces Brussels sprouts, trimmed and halved
- 8 ounces butternut squash, peeled, seeded, and cut into 1-inch pieces
- 2 garlic cloves, minced
- 2 tablespoons chopped fresh parsley
- 1 tablespoon cider vinegar
- ¾ teaspoon Dijon mustard
- ¼ teaspoon brown sugar

1. Adjust oven rack to middle position and heat oven to 475 degrees. Combine coriander, paprika, ¼ teaspoon salt, and ⅛ teaspoon pepper in small bowl. Pat tenderloin dry with paper towels and sprinkle with spice mixture.

2. Heat 1 tablespoon oil in 12-inch ovensafe skillet over medium-high heat until just smoking. Brown tenderloin on all sides, 6 to 8 minutes; transfer to plate.

3. Off heat, add Brussels sprouts, squash, garlic, 1 tablespoon oil, and ½ teaspoon salt to now-empty skillet and toss to combine. Place tenderloin on top of vegetables and roast until pork registers 145 degrees, 12 to 15 minutes.

4. Using pot holder, remove skillet from oven. Transfer tenderloin to carving board, tent with aluminum foil, and let rest while Brussels sprouts mixture finishes cooking. Being careful of hot skillet handle, gently stir Brussels sprouts mixture and continue to roast until tender, about 10 minutes.

5. Whisk parsley, vinegar, mustard, sugar, remaining ⅛ teaspoon salt, remaining ⅛ teaspoon pepper, and remaining 1 tablespoon oil together in large bowl. Transfer vegetables to bowl with vinaigrette and toss to combine. Season with salt and pepper to taste. Slice tenderloin ½ inch thick and serve with vegetables.

COOK IT FOR A CROWD

ROASTING PAN
Serves 6 to 8
Total Time 1½ hours plus 1 hour salting

- ¼ cup plus 1 teaspoon packed brown sugar, divided
- 3 tablespoons kosher salt, divided
- 2 (2½- to 3-pound) boneless pork loin roasts, trimmed
- 4 teaspoons ground coriander
- 4 teaspoons paprika
- 1 teaspoon pepper, divided
- 4 pounds butternut squash, peeled, seeded, and cut into 1-inch pieces
- 2 pounds Brussels sprouts, trimmed and halved
- ½ cup extra-virgin olive oil, divided
- 6 garlic cloves, minced
- ½ cup chopped fresh parsley
- ¼ cup cider vinegar
- 1 tablespoon Dijon mustard

1. Combine ¼ cup sugar and 2 tablespoons salt in bowl. Rub pork with sugar mixture, wrap in plastic wrap, and refrigerate for at least 1 hour or up to 24 hours.

2. Adjust oven rack to middle position, place 16 by 12-inch roasting pan on rack, and heat oven to 400 degrees. Combine coriander, paprika, and ½ teaspoon pepper in bowl. Pat pork dry with paper towels, sprinkle with spice mixture, and tie at 1½-inch intervals with kitchen twine. Arrange pork fat side down in center of hot pan, spaced 1 inch apart, and roast for 15 minutes.

3. Meanwhile, toss squash and Brussels sprouts with ¼ cup oil, garlic, and 2 teaspoons salt in bowl. Arrange squash mixture in pan, cut sides down, around pork. Roast until pork registers 140 degrees, 30 to 40 minutes.

4. Remove pan from oven. Transfer roasts to carving board, tent with aluminum foil, and let rest for 15 minutes. While pork rests, gently stir squash mixture and continue to roast until tender, 5 to 10 minutes.

5. Whisk parsley, vinegar, mustard, remaining 1 teaspoon sugar, remaining 1 teaspoon salt, remaining ½ teaspoon pepper, and remaining ¼ cup oil together in small bowl. Drizzle vinaigrette over vegetables and toss to combine. Season with salt and pepper to taste. Slice roast ½ inch thick and serve with vegetables.

> **Bulk it Up** Toss chopped dried fruit (apricots, raisins, cranberries, cherries, figs, prunes) with the squash mixture before roasting.

> **Add an Upgrade** Toss toasted nuts (almonds, pecans, walnuts, pine nuts, pistachios) with the vegetables before serving.

Braised Pork with Broccoli Rabe and Sage

INSTANT POT
Serves 4
Total Time 1¼ hours

Why This Recipe Works Tender, meaty pork, pleasantly bitter broccoli rabe, and a silky, aromatic sauce all come together to make a deliciously cohesive meal in a pressure cooker. We started by browning pieces of juicy, richly flavored pork butt and then combined garlic, white wine, and aromatic sage—as well as just a touch of flour to add body—with the fond in the pot to build the braising liquid. After releasing the pressure, we removed the tender pork; as it rested, we cooked the broccoli rabe in the remaining sauce for just 3 minutes using the sauté function. A half teaspoon of freshly grated orange zest added a final burst of brightness. Pork butt roast is often labeled Boston butt in the supermarket.

- 1½ pounds boneless pork butt roast, trimmed and cut into 2-inch pieces
- ½ teaspoon table salt
- ½ teaspoon pepper
- 1 tablespoon extra-virgin olive oil
- 2 tablespoons minced fresh sage, divided
- 5 garlic cloves, peeled and smashed
- 1 tablespoon all-purpose flour
- ¼ cup chicken broth
- ¼ cup dry white wine
- 1 pound broccoli rabe, trimmed and cut into 1-inch pieces
- ½ teaspoon grated orange zest

1. Pat pork dry with paper towels and sprinkle with salt and pepper. Using highest sauté or browning function, heat oil in electric pressure cooker until just smoking. Brown pork on all sides, 6 to 8 minutes; transfer to plate.

2. Add 1 tablespoon sage, garlic, and flour to fat left in pot and cook, using highest sauté or browning function, until fragrant, about 1 minute. Stir in broth and wine, scraping up any browned bits. Return pork to pot along with any accumulated juices. Lock lid in place and close pressure release valve. Select high pressure cook function and cook for 30 minutes.

3. Turn off pressure cooker and let pressure release naturally for 15 minutes. Quick-release any remaining pressure, then carefully remove lid, allowing steam to escape away from you. Transfer pork to serving dish, tent with aluminum foil, and let rest while preparing broccoli rabe.

4. Whisk sauce until smooth and bring to simmer using highest sauté or browning function. Stir in broccoli rabe and cook, partially covered, until tender and bright green, about 3 minutes. Stir in orange zest and remaining 1 tablespoon sage. Serve pork with broccoli rabe mixture.

Caraway-Crusted Pork Tenderloin with Sauerkraut and Apples

SKILLET
Serves 4
Total Time 1 hour

Why This Recipe Works The caraway crust on this pork tenderloin serves double duty: The seeds add crunchy texture to the tender pork, and the flavor of the aromatic caraway, which toasts as the pork sears in the skillet, thoroughly seasons the meat with bold flavor. For a tart-sweet side dish, we paired apples, cooked in the same skillet until softened, with flavorful sauerkraut. Brown sugar added sweetness to complement the apples and balance the potent sauerkraut. Roasting the pork on top of the mixture melded the flavors further. To ensure that the tenderloins don't curl during cooking, be sure to remove the silverskin from the meat. There's no need to peel the apples; we prefer red-skinned Fujis or Galas to give the dish more color, but any sweet apple will do. You will need a 12-inch ovensafe skillet for this recipe.

- 2 (12- to 16-ounce) pork tenderloins, trimmed
- 1 tablespoon caraway seeds
- 1⅛ teaspoons table salt, divided
- ½ teaspoon plus ⅛ teaspoon pepper, divided
- 2 tablespoons vegetable oil, divided
- 2 apples, cored, halved, and cut into ¼-inch-thick slices
- 1 onion, chopped fine
- 1 pound sauerkraut, rinsed and squeezed dry
- 2 tablespoons packed light brown sugar
- 2 tablespoons minced fresh dill

1. Adjust oven rack to middle position and heat oven to 475 degrees. Pat tenderloins dry with paper towels and sprinkle with caraway seeds, 1 teaspoon salt, and ½ teaspoon pepper, pressing lightly to adhere. Heat 1 tablespoon oil in 12-inch ovensafe skillet over medium-high heat until just smoking. Brown tenderloins on all sides, 5 to 7 minutes; transfer to plate.

Caraway-Crusted Pork Tenderloins with Sauerkraut and Apples

2. Add remaining 1 tablespoon oil, apples, onion, remaining ⅛ teaspoon salt, and remaining ⅛ teaspoon pepper to now-empty skillet and cook over medium heat until softened, about 5 minutes, scraping up any browned bits. Stir in sauerkraut and sugar. Place tenderloins on top of sauerkraut mixture and roast until pork registers 140 degrees, 12 to 15 minutes.

3. Using potholder, remove skillet from oven and transfer tenderloins to carving board, tent with aluminum foil, and let rest for 5 minutes. Slice tenderloins ½ inch thick. Being careful of hot skillet handle, stir dill into sauerkraut mixture and serve with pork.

TRIMMING PORK SILVERSKIN

Silverskin is a swath of connective tissue located between the meat and the fat that covers its surface. To remove, slip a knife under it, angle slightly upward, and use a gentle back-and-forth motion to cut it away.

Pork Tenderloin with Fennel, Tomatoes, Artichokes, and Olives

SHEET PAN

Serves 4

Total Time 1¼ hours

Why This Recipe Works Sweet, herbal fennel supplemented with artichokes, olives, and tomatoes serves as the bed for pork tenderloin in this sheet pan meal inspired by the flavors of Provence. Mild pork lends itself well to bold seasonings, so we used a dry rub, which added both flavor and color to our tenderloins without having to brown them. Herbes de Provence lent a distinct flavor profile. After jump-starting the fennel in the microwave, we roasted the tenderloins on top of the vegetables. While we prefer the flavor and texture of jarred whole baby artichoke hearts in this recipe, you can substitute 12 ounces frozen artichoke hearts, thawed and patted dry, for the jarred. To ensure that the tenderloins don't curl during cooking, be sure to remove the silverskin from the meat.

2 large fennel bulbs, stalks discarded, bulbs halved, cored, and sliced ½ inch thick
2 cups jarred whole baby artichokes packed in water, quartered, rinsed, and patted dry
½ cup pitted kalamata olives, halved
3 tablespoons extra-virgin olive oil
2 (12- to 16-ounce) pork tenderloins, trimmed
2 teaspoons herbes de Provence
½ teaspoon table salt
¼ teaspoon pepper
1 pound cherry tomatoes, halved
1 tablespoon grated lemon zest
2 tablespoons minced fresh parsley

1. Adjust oven rack to lower-middle position and heat oven to 450 degrees. Microwave fennel and 2 tablespoons water in covered bowl until softened, about 5 minutes. Drain fennel, then toss with artichokes, olives, and oil.

2. Pat tenderloins dry with paper towels. Sprinkle with herbes de Provence, salt, and pepper. Spread fennel mixture evenly on rimmed baking sheet, then place tenderloins over top. Roast until pork registers 145 degrees, 25 to 30 minutes, turning tenderloins over halfway through roasting.

3. Remove sheet from oven. Transfer tenderloins to carving board, tent with aluminum foil, and let rest while finishing vegetables. Stir tomatoes and lemon zest into fennel mixture on sheet and return to oven. Roast until fennel is tender and tomatoes have softened, about 10 minutes. Stir in parsley and season with salt and pepper to taste. Slice tenderloins ½ inch thick and serve with vegetables.

Spiced Pork Tenderloin with
Raisin-Almond Couscous

Pork Tenderloin and
Panzanella Salad

Spiced Pork Tenderloin with Raisin-Almond Couscous

SLOW COOKER
Serves 4
Cook Time 1 to 2 hours on low plus 15 minutes on high

Why This Recipe Works The slow cooker makes it easy to turn out succulent, warmly spiced pork tenderloin, and as a bonus we could repurpose the potent cooking liquid to make our side. First we seasoned the pork, but rather than rely on a laundry list of spices we used fragrant garam masala (an Indian spice blend) for complex flavor. Once the pork was cooked, we set it aside to rest and simply stirred couscous into the slow cooker along with some raisins; 15 minutes later we had a richly flavored couscous salad, which we finished with some sliced almonds. An easy fresh parsley vinaigrette united the flavors of the spiced pork and couscous. You will need an oval slow cooker for this recipe. To ensure that the tenderloins don't curl during cooking, be sure to remove the silverskin from the meat. Because they are cooked gently and not browned, the tenderloins will be rosy throughout. Check the tenderloins' temperature after 1 hour of cooking and continue to monitor until they register 145 degrees.

- 1 cup chicken broth
- 4 garlic cloves, minced, divided
- 2 (12- to 16-ounce) pork tenderloins, trimmed
- 2 teaspoons garam masala
- ½ teaspoon table salt
- ¼ teaspoon pepper
- 1 cup couscous
- ½ cup raisins
- ¼ cup sliced almonds, toasted
- ½ cup extra-virgin olive oil
- ½ cup minced fresh parsley
- 2 tablespoons red wine vinegar

1. Combine broth and half of garlic in slow cooker. Sprinkle tenderloins with garam masala, salt, and pepper. Nestle tenderloins into slow cooker, side by side, alternating thicker end to thinner end. Cover and cook until pork registers 145 degrees, 1 to 2 hours on low.

2. Transfer tenderloins to carving board, tent with aluminum foil, and let rest while finishing couscous. Measure out and reserve 1 cup cooking liquid; discard remaining liquid.

Combine reserved liquid, couscous, and raisins in now-empty slow cooker. Cover and cook on high until couscous is tender, about 15 minutes. Fluff couscous with fork, then stir in almonds.

3. Whisk oil, parsley, vinegar, and remaining garlic together in bowl and season with salt and pepper to taste. Slice tenderloins into ½ inch thick slices and serve with couscous and vinaigrette.

VARIATION

Spiced Pork Tenderloin with Cherry-Pepita Couscous for Two

SLOW COOKER

Serves 2

Cook Time 1 to 2 hours on low plus 15 minutes on high

You will need an oval slow cooker for this recipe. To ensure that the tenderloin doesn't curl during cooking, be sure to remove the silverskin from the meat. Because it is cooked gently and not browned, the tenderloin will be rosy throughout. Check the tenderloin's temperature after 1 hour of cooking and continue to monitor until it registers 145 degrees.

¾ cup chicken broth

2 garlic cloves, minced, divided

1 (12- to 16-ounce) pork tenderloin, trimmed

1 teaspoon garam masala

¼ teaspoon table salt

¼ teaspoon pepper

½ cup couscous

¼ cup chopped dried cherries

2 tablespoons pepitas, toasted

¼ cup extra-virgin olive oil

¼ cup minced fresh mint

1 tablespoon red wine vinegar

1. Combine broth and half of garlic in slow cooker. Sprinkle tenderloin with garam masala, salt, and pepper. Nestle tenderloin into slow cooker, cover, and cook until pork registers 145 degrees, 1 to 2 hours on low.

2. Transfer tenderloin to carving board, tent with aluminum foil, and let rest while finishing couscous. Measure out and reserve ½ cup cooking liquid; discard remaining liquid. Combine reserved liquid, couscous, and cherries in now-empty slow cooker. Cover and cook on high until couscous is tender, about 15 minutes. Fluff couscous with fork, then stir in pepitas.

3. Whisk oil, mint, vinegar, and remaining garlic together in bowl and season with salt and pepper to taste. Slice tenderloins ½ inch thick and serve with couscous and vinaigrette.

Pork Tenderloin and Panzanella Salad

SHEET PAN

Serves 4

Total Time 1 hour

Why This Recipe Works We built a meal around the toasted bread salad known as panzanella by adding roasted pork tenderloin and a mix of fresh and roasted vegetables for complexity. First, we placed two pork tenderloins on a rimmed baking sheet and brushed them with a mixture of balsamic vinegar, brown sugar, and whole-grain mustard that complemented the sweet nuances of the pork. A bit of cornstarch added to the mixture ensured that it adhered to the pork. The sheet pan provided ample space, allowing us to surround the tenderloins with pieces of summer squash, red onion, bell pepper, and baguette and roast everything together until the pork was rosy in the center, the vegetables were tender, and the bread was toasted and crunchy. While the pork rested, we tossed the bread and roasted vegetables with fresh cucumber, cherry tomatoes, basil, and a bright balsamic vinaigrette with whole-grain mustard, garlic, capers, and caper brine. Sourdough bread can be used in place of the baguette. To ensure that the tenderloins don't curl during cooking, be sure to remove the silverskin from the meat.

3 tablespoons balsamic vinegar, divided

2 tablespoons whole-grain mustard, divided

1 tablespoon packed brown sugar

1 teaspoon cornstarch

2 (12- to 16-ounce) pork tenderloins, trimmed

1 teaspoon plus ⅛ teaspoon table salt, divided

¾ teaspoon plus ⅛ teaspoon pepper, divided

1 (12-inch) baguette, cut into 1-inch pieces

1 red onion, cut into 1-inch pieces

1 red bell pepper, stemmed, seeded, and cut into ½-inch-wide strips

1 yellow summer squash, quartered lengthwise and cut into 1-inch pieces

½ cup extra-virgin olive oil, divided

1 tablespoon capers, rinsed, plus 1 tablespoon brine

1 garlic clove, minced

½ English cucumber, quartered lengthwise and cut into ½-inch pieces

6 ounces cherry tomatoes, halved

½ cup coarsely chopped fresh basil, divided

1. Adjust oven rack to middle position and heat oven to 450 degrees. Whisk 1 tablespoon vinegar, 1 tablespoon mustard, sugar, and cornstarch in bowl until no lumps of cornstarch remain.

2. Pat tenderloins dry with paper towels and sprinkle with ½ teaspoon salt and ¼ teaspoon pepper. Place tenderloins in center of rimmed baking sheet (it's OK if they are touching) and brush tops and sides with all of vinegar mixture.

3. Toss baguette, onion, bell pepper, squash, ¼ cup oil, ½ teaspoon salt, and ½ teaspoon pepper in large bowl until baguette and vegetables are well coated with oil. Distribute vegetable mixture around tenderloins on sheet. Roast until pork registers 145 degrees, about 20 minutes, stirring vegetable mixture halfway through roasting.

4. Whisk capers and brine, garlic, remaining 2 tablespoons vinegar, remaining 1 tablespoon mustard, remaining ⅛ teaspoon salt, remaining ⅛ teaspoon pepper, and remaining ¼ cup oil together in now-empty bowl.

5. Transfer tenderloins to carving board, tent with aluminum foil, and let rest for 10 minutes. Meanwhile, add cucumber, tomatoes, 6 tablespoons basil, and vegetable mixture to bowl with caper dressing and toss to combine; transfer to serving platter. Slice tenderloins ½ inch thick and arrange over salad. Sprinkle with remaining 2 tablespoons basil and serve.

Pork Loin en Cocotte with Kale, Shallots, and Mustard

Caption: Pork Loin en Cocotte with Kale, Shallots, and Mustard

Caption: Pork Loin en Cocotte with Barley, Butternut Squash, and Swiss Chard

Pork Loin en Cocotte with Kale, Shallots, and Mustard

DUTCH OVEN
Serves 4 to 6
Total Time 1¼ hours, plus 1½ hours brining

Why This Recipe Works The process for cooking en cocotte is simple: Place a browned roast along with a few aromatics in a Dutch oven, cover, and bake in a low oven, where the meat essentially steams in the contained, moist-heat environment. Never ones to mess with simplicity, we decided to give this basic pork loin roast just a touch of modern flair. Introducing kale to the pot seemed like a good start—the pork's juices would flavor the greens as they cooked. Seasoning the pork with herbes de Provence delivered a heady dose of flavors and fragrances all at once. After browning the roast and softening some shallots, we built our cooking liquid, boosting the rendered juices and residual fond with chicken broth. We gave the hearty kale a head start, allowing it to wilt before adding the browned roast. We removed the pork when it reached 140 degrees and let it come to temperature while resting on the cutting board. We used that time to finish the kale, letting the cooking liquid evaporate and infuse the greens with flavor. The addition of butter and mustard created a saucy, rich accompaniment to the juicy herbed pork. This recipe works best with a pork roast that is about 7 to 8 inches long and 4 to 5 inches wide. We like to leave a ¼-inch-thick layer of fat on top of the roast; if your roast has a thicker fat cap, trim it back to be about ¼ inch thick. If the pork is enhanced (injected with a salt solution), do not brine in step 1 but sprinkle with ¾ teaspoon salt in step 2. You can substitute 1 teaspoon each dried thyme, dried rosemary, and dried marjoram for the herbes de Provence in this recipe.

½ cup sugar for brining
½ cup table salt for brining
1 (2½- to 3-pound) boneless pork loin roast, trimmed
1 tablespoon herbes de Provence
½ teaspoon pepper
3 tablespoons vegetable oil, divided
1 pound shallots, peeled and quartered
1 cup chicken broth
1 pound kale, stemmed and cut into 1-inch pieces
1 tablespoon unsalted butter
1 tablespoon whole-grain mustard

1. Dissolve sugar and salt in 2 quarts cold water in large container. Submerge pork in brine, cover, and refrigerate for at least 1½ hours or up to 2 hours.

2. Adjust oven rack to lowest position and heat oven to 250 degrees. Remove pork from brine and pat dry with paper towels. Sprinkle with herbes de Provence and pepper and tie at 1½-inch intervals with kitchen twine. Heat 2 tablespoons oil in Dutch oven over medium-high heat until just smoking. Brown pork on all sides, 8 to 10 minutes; transfer to large plate.

3. Add remaining 1 tablespoon oil and shallots to fat left in pot and cook over medium heat until shallots are softened and lightly browned, 5 to 7 minutes. Stir in broth, scraping up any browned bits, and bring to simmer. Stir in kale, cover, and cook, stirring occasionally, until bright green and wilted, about 5 minutes.

4. Off heat, nestle pork into pot and add any accumulated juices. Cover, transfer pot to oven, and cook until pork registers 140 degrees, 25 to 35 minutes.

5. Remove pot from oven. Transfer pork to carving board, tent with aluminum foil, and let rest for 15 minutes. Meanwhile, simmer kale, uncovered, over medium-high heat until tender and liquid has nearly evaporated, 3 to 5 minutes. Stir in butter and mustard, season with salt and pepper to taste, and cover to keep warm.

6. Remove twine from roast and slice ¼ inch thick. Serve with kale.

Pork Loin en Cocotte with Barley, Butternut Squash, and Swiss Chard

DUTCH OVEN
Serves 4 to 6
Total Time 1¾ hours, plus 1½ hours brining

Why This Recipe Works For a version of pork loin en cocotte with a grain-forward side, we decided to pair the pork with a combination of nutty barley, sweet butternut squash, and tender chard. After seasoning the brined pork with fresh thyme and pepper, we browned it to build flavor. We then nestled it in the Dutch oven with a mixture of pearled barley, chicken broth, and white wine. Once the pot was covered, the low heat and trapped moisture jump-started the barley and kept the pork from overcooking. After removing the cooked pork loin, we transferred the pot to the stovetop to continue cooking the barley while the roast rested. We added cubed butternut squash and Swiss chard stems to soften and cook through before stirring in the quick-cooking chard leaves and some Parmesan cheese for a bit of richness. The barley's starches gave the mixture a creamy, risotto-like texture that complemented the juicy, lean pork. This recipe works best with a pork roast that is about 7 to 8 inches long and 4 to 5 inches wide. We like to leave a ¼-inch-thick layer of fat on top of the roast; if your roast has a thicker fat cap, trim it back to be about ¼ inch thick. If the pork is enhanced (injected with a salt solution), do not brine in step 1 but sprinkle with ¾ teaspoon salt in step 2. Do not substitute hulled, hull-less, quick-cooking, or presteamed barley (read the ingredient list on the package to determine this).

½ cup sugar for brining
½ cup table salt for brining
1 (2½- to 3-pound) boneless pork loin roast, trimmed
2 tablespoons minced fresh thyme, divided
½ teaspoon pepper
3 tablespoons vegetable oil, divided
1 onion, chopped
1 cup pearl barley, rinsed
¼ teaspoon table salt
3 garlic cloves, minced
¼ cup dry white wine
4 cups chicken broth
½ small butternut squash, peeled, seeded, and cut into ½-inch pieces (2½ cups)
8 ounces Swiss chard, stems chopped, leaves cut into 1-inch pieces, divided
1 ounce Parmesan cheese, grated (½ cup)
2 teaspoons cider vinegar

1 pound parsnips, peeled and cut into 2-inch lengths, thick ends quartered lengthwise

2 tablespoons plus 1 teaspoon extra-virgin olive oil, divided

⅛ teaspoon plus ¼ teaspoon table salt, divided

¼ teaspoon pepper, divided

1 tablespoon honey, warmed, divided

4 (6-ounce) lamb loin chops, 1¼ inches thick, trimmed

1 tablespoon Dijon mustard

1 teaspoon minced fresh rosemary

1 garlic clove, minced

1 teaspoon grated lemon zest plus 1 teaspoon juice

1 teaspoon water

1. Adjust oven rack to middle position and heat oven to 450 degrees. Toss parsnips with 1 tablespoon oil, ⅛ teaspoon salt, and ⅛ teaspoon pepper and spread in single layer on rimmed baking sheet. Roast until beginning to soften, about 10 minutes.

2. Combine 1½ teaspoons honey and 2 teaspoons oil in small bowl. Pat lamb chops dry with paper towels, brush with honey-oil mixture, and sprinkle with remaining ¼ teaspoon salt and remaining ⅛ teaspoon pepper. Arrange lamb chops on top of parsnips and continue to roast until chops register 120 to 125 degrees (for medium-rare) and parsnips are tender, 10 to 15 minutes, rotating sheet halfway through roasting.

3. Microwave mustard, rosemary, garlic, lemon zest and juice, water, remaining 2 teaspoons oil, and remaining 1½ teaspoons honey in large bowl until fragrant, about 15 seconds, stirring once halfway through microwaving. Transfer lamb chops to plate and brush with 1 tablespoon mustard mixture. Tent with aluminum foil and let rest while finishing parsnips.

4. Transfer parsnips to bowl with remaining mustard mixture and toss to coat. Season with salt and pepper to taste. Serve lamb with parsnips.

NOTES FROM THE TEST KITCHEN

DOMESTIC VERSUS IMPORTED LAMB

While most of the beef and pork sold in American markets is raised domestically, you can purchase both imported and domestic lamb. Domestic lamb has a larger size and milder flavor, while lamb imported from Australia or New Zealand has a gamier taste. Imported lamb is pasture-fed on mixed grasses, while lamb raised in the United States begins on a diet of grass but finishes with grain. The switch to grain impacts the composition of the animal's fat—and ultimately leads to sweeter-tasting meat.

Lamb Chops with Shaved Zucchini Salad

INSTANT POT

Serves 4

Total Time 1½ hours

Why This Recipe Works When buying lamb chops, many people turn to the tried-and-true (and expensive) rib or loin chops. The oddly shaped, more affordable shoulder chops rarely get a second look, but they should: Their abundant connective tissue and bone (read: flavor) make them ideal for braising in the pressure cooker, where these economical chops transform into the fork-tender, juicy focal point of an easy and impressive meal. Rather than pairing our lamb chops with a braised side, we opted for a salad that contrasted with the rich meat. Tender shaved zucchini—with a lemony dressing, tangy goat cheese, sweet raisins, and fresh mint—was the perfect accompaniment. The success of the salad depends on using small, in-season zucchini and good olive oil. A vegetable peeler makes easy work of slicing the zucchini into ribbons.

4 (8- to 12-ounce) lamb shoulder chops (blade or round bone), about ¾ inch thick, trimmed

¾ teaspoon table salt, divided

¾ teaspoon pepper, divided

2 tablespoons extra-virgin olive oil, divided

1 onion, chopped

5 garlic cloves, minced

½ cup chicken broth

1 bay leaf

4 zucchini (6 ounces each), sliced lengthwise into ribbons

1 teaspoon grated lemon zest plus 1 tablespoon juice

2 ounces goat cheese, crumbled (½ cup)

¼ cup chopped fresh mint

2 tablespoons raisins

1. Pat lamb chops dry with paper towels and sprinkle with ½ teaspoon salt and ½ teaspoon pepper. Using highest sauté or browning function, heat 1½ teaspoons oil in electric pressure cooker until just smoking. Brown half of chops on both sides, 6 to 8 minutes; transfer to plate. Repeat with 1½ teaspoons oil and remaining chops; transfer to plate.

2. Add onion to fat left in pressure cooker and cook, using highest sauté or browning function, until softened, about 5 minutes. Stir in garlic and cook until fragrant, about 30 seconds. Stir in broth and bay leaf, scraping up any browned bits. Return chops to pot along with any accumulated juices (chops will overlap). Lock lid in place and close pressure release valve. Select high pressure cook function and cook for 20 minutes.

3. Turn off pressure cooker and let pressure release naturally for 15 minutes. Quick-release any remaining pressure, then carefully remove lid, allowing steam to escape away from you. Transfer chops to serving platter. Gently toss zucchini with lemon zest and juice, remaining 1 tablespoon oil, remaining ¼ teaspoon salt, and remaining ¼ teaspoon pepper in bowl. Arrange zucchini on serving dish with lamb, and sprinkle with goat cheese, mint, and raisins. Serve.

Herbed Leg of Lamb with Fingerling Potatoes and Asparagus

ROASTING PAN
Serves 6 to 8
Total Time 1¾ hours

Why This Recipe Works A roasted boneless leg of lamb is impressive enough for a holiday celebration, but could we make a non-holiday version that required less prep and cleanup? Starting with a butterflied leg of lamb was a good first step, and pounding it to an even thickness made it even easier to work with. We spread a potent herb paste of parsley, mint, and garlic over the lamb before rolling and tying the roast so it would infuse the lamb from the inside out. After a quick sear on the stovetop right in the roasting pan, we positioned the lamb fat side down on a bed of potatoes before moving it to the oven where the fat slowly rendered, seasoning the potatoes below. We flipped the lamb halfway through cooking to allow the fat to crisp. While the lamb rested, we tossed asparagus in the pan drippings and let the vegetables continue to roast until tender. We prefer the subtler flavor of lamb labeled "domestic" or "American" for this recipe. Look for potatoes that are about 2 inches long and 1 inch in diameter. Small red potatoes measuring 1 to 2 inches in diameter can be substituted for the fingerling potatoes. Make sure to use asparagus spears between ¼ and ½ inch in diameter at base. We prefer this roast cooked to medium-rare, but if you prefer it more or less done, see our guidelines on page 141.

- ½ cup fresh mint leaves
- ½ cup fresh parsley leaves
- 3 tablespoons extra-virgin olive oil, divided
- 3 garlic cloves, peeled
- 1 (3½- to 4-pound) butterflied leg of lamb
- 1¼ teaspoons table salt, divided
- 1¼ teaspoons pepper, divided
- 2 pounds fingerling potatoes, unpeeled
- 2 pounds asparagus, trimmed
- 1 tablespoon grated lemon zest

Lamb Chops with Shaved Zucchini Salad

1. Adjust oven rack to lower-middle position and heat oven to 375 degrees. Process mint, parsley, 1 teaspoon oil, and garlic in food processor until finely chopped, scraping down sides of bowl as needed, about 1 minute; transfer to bowl.

2. Place lamb on cutting board with fat cap facing up. Using sharp knife, trim fat to between ⅛- and ¼-inch thickness. Flip lamb over and trim any pockets of fat and connective tissue. Cover with sheet of plastic wrap and pound to even 1-inch thickness. Rub interior with 2 teaspoons oil and sprinkle with ½ teaspoon salt and ½ teaspoon pepper. Spread 1½ tablespoons herb mixture evenly over lamb, leaving 1-inch border around edge. Roll roast tightly and tie with kitchen twine at 1½-inch intervals. Rub exterior of roast with 1 tablespoon oil and sprinkle with ½ teaspoon salt and ½ teaspoon pepper.

3. Heat remaining 1 tablespoon oil in 16 by 12-inch roasting pan over medium-high heat until just smoking. Brown roast well on all sides, 8 to 10 minutes; transfer to large plate.

4. Off heat, toss potatoes in fat left in pan, then spread into even layer. Place roast fat side down on top of potatoes. Transfer pan to oven and roast until lamb registers 120 to 125 degrees (for medium-rare), 45 minutes to 1 hour, flipping lamb halfway through roasting. Transfer roast to carving board, tent with aluminum foil, and let rest while finishing vegetables.

5. Increase oven temperature to 450 degrees. Push potatoes to one half of pan. Add asparagus to clearing and toss with remaining ¼ teaspoon salt, remaining ¼ teaspoon pepper, and any accumulated pan juices. Spread asparagus into even layer and roast vegetables until asparagus is crisp-tender, 10 to 12 minutes.

6. Transfer asparagus to serving platter. Toss potatoes with lemon zest and remaining herb mixture in pan and season with salt and pepper to taste; transfer to platter with asparagus. Remove twine from roast and slice ½ inch thick. Serve lamb with potatoes and asparagus.

PREPARING BONELESS LEG OF LAMB

1. Place lamb on cutting board with fat cap facing up. Using sharp knife, trim fat cap to ⅛ inch.

2. Flip lamb over and trim any pockets of fat and connective tissue from underside of lamb. Pound roast to even 1-inch thickness.

Lamb Meatballs with Couscous and Pickled Onions

INSTANT POT

Serves 4
Total Time 1 hour

Why This Recipe Works Lamb's robust, grassy flavor offers a refreshing change of pace from the usual pork or beef, but cooking a large cut of lamb isn't always realistic for a weeknight. For a faster lamb option, we used the pressure cooker to cook ground lamb meatballs seasoned with Mediterranean-inspired herbs and spices. We wanted the flavor of tahini (a paste made from toasted sesame seeds) to take center stage, so we made a tahini sauce and mixed it with bread crumbs as a panade, and then spooned more sauce over the finished dish. The meatballs cooked in just 1 minute under pressure; after setting them aside to rest, we stirred couscous into the remaining liquid to cook in the residual heat and absorb the flavors. Roasted red peppers and pickled onions added bright flavor and texture. You can substitute an equal amount of 85 percent lean ground beef for the lamb, if desired.

¼ cup tahini
¼ cup water
1 teaspoon grated lemon zest plus 3 tablespoons juice, divided
1 garlic clove, minced
3 tablespoons panko bread crumbs
1 pound ground lamb
¼ cup chopped fresh mint, divided
1 teaspoon ground cinnamon, divided
1 teaspoon ground cumin, divided
¾ teaspoon table salt, divided
1 tablespoon extra-virgin olive oil
1 onion, chopped fine
⅛ teaspoon cayenne pepper
1 cup chicken broth, plus extra as needed
1 cup couscous
½ cup jarred roasted red peppers, rinsed, patted dry, and chopped
½ cup Quick Pickled Onions (page 223)

1. Whisk tahini, water, 2 tablespoons lemon juice, and garlic together in bowl until smooth (mixture will appear broken at first). Season with salt and pepper to taste. (Sauce can be refrigerated for up to 4 days; bring to room temperature before using.)

2. Using fork, mash ¼ cup sauce and panko together in bowl to form paste. Add ground lamb, 2 tablespoons mint, ½ teaspoon cinnamon, ½ teaspoon cumin, and ½ teaspoon salt and knead with hands until thoroughly combined. Pinch off and roll mixture into twelve 1½-inch meatballs.

3. Using highest sauté or browning function, heat oil in electric pressure cooker until shimmering. Add onion and remaining ¼ teaspoon salt and cook until onion is softened, about 5 minutes. Stir in remaining ½ teaspoon cinnamon, remaining ½ teaspoon cumin, and cayenne and cook until fragrant, about 30 seconds. Stir in broth, scraping up any browned bits. Add meatballs to pot. Lock lid in place and close pressure release valve. Select high pressure cook function and cook for 1 minute.

4. Turn off pressure cooker and quick-release pressure. Carefully remove lid, allowing steam to escape away from you. Using slotted spoon, transfer meatballs to plate, tent with aluminum foil, and let rest while cooking couscous. (You should have about 2 cups cooking liquid remaining in pot; add extra broth as needed to equal 2 cups.)

5. Using highest sauté or browning function, bring liquid in pot to simmer. Stir in couscous, red peppers, and lemon zest and remaining 1 tablespoon juice. Turn off pressure cooker, cover, and let sit for 10 minutes. Fluff couscous gently with fork and transfer to serving dish. Arrange meatballs on top and drizzle with remaining sauce. Sprinkle with pickled onions and remaining 2 tablespoons mint. Serve.

Lamb Meatballs with Couscous and Pickled Onions for Two

INSTANT POT

Serves 2

Total Time 1 hour

You can substitute an equal amount of 85 percent lean ground beef for the lamb, if desired.

  3 tablespoons plain whole-milk yogurt, plus extra for serving
1½ tablespoons panko bread crumbs
  8 ounces ground lamb
  2 tablespoons chopped fresh cilantro, divided
1¼ teaspoons garam masala, divided
  ½ teaspoon table salt, divided
1½ teaspoons extra-virgin olive oil
  ½ onion, chopped fine
  ¾ cup chicken broth, plus extra as needed
  ½ cup couscous
  2 tablespoons dried currants
  2 tablespoons chopped toasted pistachios
  ¼ cup Quick Pickled Onions

1. Using fork, mash yogurt and panko together in bowl to form paste. Add ground lamb, 1 tablespoon cilantro, ¾ teaspoon garam masala, and ¼ teaspoon salt and knead with hands until thoroughly combined. Pinch off and roll mixture into eight 1½-inch meatballs.

2. Using highest sauté or browning function, heat oil in electric pressure cooker until shimmering. Add onion and remaining ¼ teaspoon salt and cook until onion is softened, about 5 minutes. Stir in remaining ½ teaspoon garam masala and cook until fragrant, about 30 seconds. Stir in broth, scraping up any browned bits. Add meatballs to pot. Lock lid in place and close pressure release valve. Select high pressure cook function and cook for 1 minute.

3. Turn off pressure cooker and quick-release pressure. Carefully remove lid, allowing steam to escape away from you. Using slotted spoon, transfer meatballs to plate, tent with aluminum foil, and let rest while cooking couscous. (You should have about 1 cup cooking liquid remaining in pot; add extra broth as needed to equal 1 cup.)

4. Using highest sauté or browning function, bring liquid in pot to simmer. Stir in couscous and currants. Turn off pressure cooker, cover, and let sit for 10 minutes. Fluff couscous gently with fork and transfer to individual plates. Arrange meatballs on top and sprinkle with pistachios. Sprinkle with pickled onions and remaining 1 tablespoon cilantro. Serve with extra yogurt.

Lamb Meatballs with Couscous and Pickled Onions

Quick Pickled Onions

Makes 1 cup

  1 cup red wine vinegar
  ⅓ cup sugar
  ⅛ teaspoon table salt
  1 red onion, halved and sliced thin through root end

Microwave vinegar, sugar, and salt in medium bowl until simmering, 1 to 2 minutes. Stir in onion and let sit, stirring occasionally, for 45 minutes. Drain. (Drained pickled onions can be refrigerated for up to 1 week.)

Lamb Meatballs with Orzo and Tomatoes

Lamb Pita Sandwiches

Lamb Meatballs with Orzo and Tomatoes

DUTCH OVEN

Serves 4

Total Time 1¼ hours

Why This Recipe Works Pasta and meatballs are a classic duo, but for a unique spin on this pairing we used orzo instead of spaghetti, made meatballs with ground lamb, and enhanced the dish with bold mint, oregano, and cinnamon. To cook the meatballs and orzo in the same pot, we first used our Dutch oven to brown the meatballs and then used the fat to cook aromatics and give the orzo a supersavory base. A panade of Greek yogurt and panko kept the meatballs moist and lent tanginess. After toasting the orzo in the pot, we added white wine and broth and cooked the orzo until it was nearly tender before nestling in the meatballs to cook through. Bright cherry tomatoes added freshness and a sprinkling of crumbled feta contributed richness. Depending on the size of your Dutch oven, you may need to brown the meatballs in two batches.

½ cup plain whole-milk Greek yogurt
¼ cup panko bread crumbs
3 tablespoons water
1 large egg
2 tablespoons minced fresh mint plus 2 tablespoons torn leaves, divided
4 garlic cloves, minced, divided
2 teaspoons minced fresh oregano or ½ teaspoon dried
1½ teaspoons table salt, divided
⅛ teaspoon pepper
¾ teaspoon ground cinnamon
1½ pounds ground lamb
2 tablespoons extra-virgin olive oil
1 onion, chopped fine
2 cups orzo
3 cups chicken broth
½ cup dry white wine
8 ounces cherry tomatoes, halved
2 ounces feta cheese, crumbled (½ cup)

1. Mash yogurt, panko, and water together with fork in large bowl to form paste. Stir in egg, minced mint, half of garlic, oregano, 1 teaspoon salt, pepper, and cinnamon until combined. Add ground lamb and knead with your hands until thoroughly combined. Pinch off and roll mixture into 1½-inch meatballs (you should have 18 meatballs).

2. Heat oil in Dutch oven over medium-high heat until just smoking. Brown meatballs on all sides, 8 to 10 minutes; transfer to plate. Pour off all but 2 tablespoons fat from pot.

3. Add onion and remaining ½ teaspoon salt to fat left in pot and cook over medium heat until softened and lightly browned, 5 to 7 minutes. Stir in remaining garlic and cook until fragrant, about 30 seconds. Add orzo and cook, stirring frequently, until lightly browned and golden, about 5 minutes.

4. Stir in broth and wine, scraping up any browned bits. Bring to simmer and cook, stirring occasionally, until most of liquid has been absorbed and orzo is almost tender, 7 to 10 minutes.

5. Reduce heat to medium-low and nestle meatballs into orzo. Cover and cook until orzo is tender and meatballs are fully cooked through, 5 to 10 minutes. Sprinkle with tomatoes, feta, and torn mint. Serve.

Lamb Pita Sandwiches

SKILLET
Serves 4
Total Time 1¼ hours

Why This Recipe Works Classic Greek gyros feature seasoned, marinated lamb; the traditional method for cooking the meat employs an electric vertical rotisserie on which layers of sliced and marinated leg of lamb are stacked. After cooking for hours, the meat is shaved with a long knife, creating pieces with crisp exteriors and moist interiors. To translate the recipe to the home kitchen, we found that ground lamb formed into patties and browned in a skillet came close to reproducing the texture of rotisserie lamb. A panade of pita bread crumbs, lemon juice, and garlic gave our patties a sturdier structure and savory flavor. Tzatziki sauce, with its combination of cucumbers, yogurt, salt, garlic, lemon, and mint, is a common topping. If using pocketless pitas, do not cut off the tops in step 1; instead, use a portion of a fifth pita to create crumbs. The skillet may appear crowded when you begin cooking the patties, but they will shrink slightly as they cook.

  4 (8-inch) pita breads
  ½ onion, chopped coarse
  4 teaspoons lemon juice
  1 tablespoon minced fresh oregano or
    1 teaspoon dried
  2 garlic cloves, minced
  ½ teaspoon table salt
  ¼ teaspoon pepper
  1 pound ground lamb
  2 teaspoons vegetable oil
  1 recipe Tzatziki Sauce
  1 large tomato, sliced thin
  2 cups shredded iceberg lettuce
  2 ounces feta cheese, crumbled (½ cup)

1. Adjust oven rack to middle position and heat oven to 350 degrees. Cut top quarter off each pita bread. Tear quarters into 1-inch pieces. (You should have ¾ cup pita pieces.) Stack pitas and tightly wrap with aluminum foil. Process onion, lemon juice, oregano, garlic, salt, pepper, and pita bread pieces in food processor until smooth paste forms, about 30 seconds. Transfer onion mixture to large bowl. Add ground lamb and gently mix with your hands until thoroughly combined. Divide mixture into 12 equal pieces and roll into balls. Gently flatten balls into round disks about ½ inch thick and 2½ inches in diameter.

2. Place foil-wrapped pitas directly on oven rack and heat for 10 minutes. Meanwhile, heat oil in 12-inch nonstick skillet over medium-high heat until just smoking. Add patties and cook until well browned and crust forms, 3 to 4 minutes. Flip patties, reduce heat to medium, and cook until well browned and crust forms on second side, about 5 minutes. Transfer patties to paper towel–lined plate.

3. Using spoon, spread one-quarter of tzatziki sauce inside each pita. Divide patties evenly among pitas; top each sandwich with tomato slices, ½ cup shredded lettuce, and 2 tablespoons feta. Serve immediately.

Tzatziki Sauce

Makes about 1 cup
Although we prefer the richness of plain whole-milk yogurt for the sauce, low-fat yogurt can be substituted.

  1 cup plain whole-milk yogurt
  ½ cucumber, peeled, seeded, and cut into
    ¼-inch pieces (½ cup)
  1 tablespoon lemon juice
  ¼ teaspoon table salt, divided
  1 tablespoon minced fresh mint or dill
  1 small garlic clove, minced

1. Line fine-mesh strainer set over deep container or bowl with 3 paper coffee filters or triple layer of paper towels. Spoon yogurt into lined strainer, cover, and refrigerate for 30 minutes.

2. Meanwhile, combine cucumber, lemon juice, and ⅛ teaspoon salt in colander set over bowl and let sit for 30 minutes. Discard drained yogurt liquid. Combine yogurt, cucumber, mint, garlic, and remaining ⅛ teaspoon salt in clean bowl. (Sauce can be refrigerated for up to 2 days.)

SEAFOOD

Mediterranean
Shrimp

* All slow cooker recipes work in a 4- to 7-quart traditional slow cooker unless noted.

** All Instant Pot recipes work in a 6- to 8-quart Instant Pot or other electric pressure cooker.

Roasted Salmon with Broccoli,
Red Potatoes, and Mustard Sauce

Pan-Seared Paprika Salmon
with Spicy Green Beans

Roasted Salmon with Broccoli, Red Potatoes, and Mustard Sauce

SHEET PAN

Serves 4
Total Time 1 hour

Why This Recipe Works Salmon, broccoli, and red potatoes all require very different cooking times, but we embraced the challenge of creating a sheet pan meal with all three by using a standard one-pan technique: staggering. The potatoes required the most oven time, but starting them first and adding the broccoli and salmon partway through roasting overcrowded the pan. Instead, we started with both potatoes and broccoli in the pan, roasting them at 500 degrees for 22 minutes—enough time for the broccoli to take on plenty of color and the spuds to soften. We removed the broccoli from the pan and arranged four salmon fillets in its place. Reducing the temperature to 275 degrees allowed the salmon to roast gently while the potatoes finished cooking. In just 11 minutes, the fillets reached a juicy medium-rare and the potatoes boasted tender, creamy interiors beneath their golden-brown crusts. A sauce of chopped chives, whole-grain mustard, and lemon juice gave this simple meal some real pizzazz. Use small red potatoes measuring 1 to 2 inches in diameter; if your potatoes are larger, cut them into 1-inch pieces to ensure that they cook through properly.

¼ cup minced fresh chives
5 tablespoons plus 2 teaspoons extra-virgin olive oil, divided
2 tablespoons whole-grain mustard
2 teaspoons lemon juice, plus lemon wedges for serving
1 teaspoon honey
Pinch plus 1¼ teaspoons table salt, divided
Pinch plus 1 teaspoon pepper, divided
1 pound small red potatoes, unpeeled, halved
1 pound broccoli florets, cut into 2-inch pieces
1 (2-pound) skin-on salmon fillet, 1 to 1½ inches thick, sliced crosswise into 4 equal pieces

1. Adjust oven rack to lowest position and heat oven to 500 degrees. Combine chives, 2 tablespoons oil, mustard, lemon juice, honey, pinch salt, and pinch pepper in bowl; set aside for serving.

2. Brush rimmed baking sheet with 1 tablespoon oil. Toss potatoes with 1 tablespoon oil, ½ teaspoon salt, and ½ teaspoon pepper and arrange cut side down on half of sheet. Toss broccoli with 1 tablespoon oil, ¼ teaspoon salt, and

¼ teaspoon pepper and arrange on empty side of sheet. Roast until potatoes are light golden brown and broccoli is well browned and tender, 22 to 24 minutes, rotating sheet halfway through roasting.

3. Pat salmon dry with paper towels, rub thoroughly with remaining 2 teaspoons oil, and sprinkle with remaining ½ teaspoon salt and remaining ¼ teaspoon pepper.

4. Remove sheet from oven and reduce oven temperature to 275 degrees. Transfer broccoli, browned side up, to serving platter and tent with aluminum foil to keep warm. Place salmon skin side down on now-empty side of sheet and continue to roast until center of salmon is still translucent when checked with tip of paring knife and registers 125 degrees (for medium-rare), 11 to 15 minutes, rotating sheet halfway through roasting.

5. Slide fish spatula along underside of salmon fillets and transfer to platter, leaving skin behind; discard skin. Transfer potatoes to platter with broccoli and salmon. Serve with lemon wedges and mustard sauce.

NOTES FROM THE TEST KITCHEN

BUYING SALMON

Cuts of Salmon Our preference is for thick center-cut fillets, which can be poached, steamed, pan-seared, or roasted. Cut from the head end or center, these fillets are thick enough to sear nicely without overcooking. To ensure uniform pieces of salmon that cook at the same rate, we find it best to buy a whole fillet and cut it into pieces ourselves. Stay away from thin fillets, which are cut from the tail end—one end is very thin and will overcook before the fillet gets a good sear while the other is always much thicker.

Skin-on or Skinless Some recipes benefit from using skin-on salmon; for recipes that call for skinless salmon, you can remove it yourself or ask your fishmonger to do it.

Farmed Versus Wild Farmed salmon is available all year round, raised on confined farms. Wild salmon is available from spring to early fall and caught in open waters. Farmed salmon is thicker and has a lighter color than wild salmon. In season, we often prefer the more pronounced flavor of wild-caught salmon to farmed. High-quality wild salmon is available only from late spring through the end of summer.

Pan-Seared Paprika Salmon with Spicy Green Beans

SKILLET
Serves 4
Total Time 45 minutes

Why This Recipe Works Quick-cooking salmon takes just a few minutes to reach medium-rare in a skillet, and coating the fish with smoked paprika, salt, and pepper promised a well-seasoned and well-browned crust. Using a nonstick skillet guaranteed the fish wouldn't stick. After cooking the salmon, we set it aside and used our skillet to make a side that would complement the smokiness of the fish without taking too long to prepare. Cooking green beans in two steps—first searing them for browning and then steaming them to cook through—turned out crisp-tender beans. Using smashed garlic instead of minced ensured it wouldn't burn, and jarred hot banana pepper rings added a flavor boost. You will need a 12-inch nonstick skillet with a tight-fitting lid for this recipe.

1¼ teaspoons smoked paprika, divided
 1 teaspoon table salt, divided
 ½ teaspoon pepper, divided
 1 (2-pound) skin-on salmon fillet, 1 to 1½ inches thick, sliced crosswise into 4 equal pieces
 2 tablespoons extra-virgin olive oil, divided
 1 pound green beans, trimmed
 6 garlic cloves, smashed
 ½ cup jarred hot banana pepper rings

1. Combine 1 teaspoon paprika, ½ teaspoon salt, and ¼ teaspoon pepper in bowl. Pat salmon dry with paper towels and sprinkle with paprika mixture. Heat 1 tablespoon oil in 12-inch nonstick skillet over medium-high heat until shimmering. Place salmon skin side up in skillet and cook until well browned on first side, 4 to 6 minutes. Flip salmon, reduce heat to medium, and cook until center is still translucent when checked with tip of paring knife and registers 125 degrees (for medium-rare), 3 to 6 minutes. Transfer to serving platter and sprinkle with remaining ¼ teaspoon paprika. Wipe skillet clean with paper towels.

2. Heat remaining 1 tablespoon oil in now-empty skillet over medium-high heat until just smoking. Add green beans, garlic, remaining ½ teaspoon salt, and remaining ¼ teaspoon pepper and cook, stirring often, until green beans and garlic turn spotty brown, about 6 minutes. Add 2 tablespoons water, cover, and reduce heat to medium. Cook until green beans are crisp-tender, about 1 minute. Off heat, stir in pepper rings and season with salt and pepper to taste. Serve salmon with green beans.

Sweet and Sour Salmon with Bok Choy

SKILLET
Serves 4
Total Time 45 minutes

Why This Recipe Works A vibrant sauce of salty, sweet, sour, and bitter flavors livens up this simple pan-seared salmon. Using a nonstick skillet allowed us to cut down on oil; since we were using an already oily fish, this helped prevent a greasy finished dish. Cooking the salmon to 125 degrees promised the perfect doneness after the fillets rested on the serving platter. We used the same skillet to cook tender bok choy by adding a little water and covering the pan to let the bok choy steam. The skillet then served a third purpose as we used it to cook our bright and tangy lime sauce, which needed to simmer for just a few minutes to reach the perfect consistency for drizzling over our salmon and bok choy. You will need a 12-inch nonstick skillet with a tight-fitting lid for this recipe. Serve with rice (see page 21).

⅓ cup packed brown sugar
⅓ cup lime juice (3 limes)
2 tablespoons toasted sesame oil
1 tablespoon fish sauce
2 garlic cloves, minced
1 teaspoon red pepper flakes
1 (2-pound) skin-on salmon fillet, 1 to 1½ inches thick, sliced crosswise into 4 equal pieces
½ teaspoon table salt
¼ teaspoon pepper
2 tablespoons vegetable oil, divided
4 heads baby bok choy (4 ounces each), halved

1. Whisk sugar, lime juice, sesame oil, fish sauce, garlic, and pepper flakes together in bowl; set aside.

2. Pat salmon dry with paper towels and sprinkle with salt and pepper. Heat 1 tablespoon vegetable oil in 12-inch nonstick skillet over medium-high heat until shimmering. Place salmon skin side up in skillet and cook until well browned on first side, 4 to 6 minutes. Flip salmon, reduce heat to medium, and cook until center is still translucent when checked with tip of paring knife and registers 125 degrees (for medium-rare), 3 to 6 minutes. Transfer salmon to serving platter, tent with aluminum foil, and let rest while preparing bok choy and sauce.

3. Wipe skillet clean with paper towels. Heat remaining 1 tablespoon vegetable oil in now-empty skillet over medium heat until shimmering. Add bok choy and 2 tablespoons water and immediately cover. Cook, covered, shaking pan occasionally, for 2 minutes. Remove lid and continue to cook, stirring constantly, until all water has evaporated, stems are crisp-tender, and leaves are wilted, about 2 minutes. Transfer to platter with salmon.

4. Add sugar mixture to again-empty skillet and cook over medium heat until slightly thickened and reduced to ½ cup, 3 to 4 minutes. Drizzle sauce over salmon and bok choy and serve.

VARIATION

Sweet and Sour Salmon with Bok Choy for Two

SKILLET
Serves 2
Total Time 45 minutes

3 tablespoons packed brown sugar
3 tablespoons lime juice (2 limes)
1 tablespoon toasted sesame oil
1½ teaspoons fish sauce
1 garlic clove, minced
¼ teaspoon red pepper flakes
2 (8-ounce) skin-on salmon fillets, 1 to 1½ inches thick
¼ teaspoon table salt
⅛ teaspoon pepper
1 tablespoon vegetable oil, divided
2 heads baby bok choy (4 ounces each), halved

1. Whisk sugar, lime juice, sesame oil, fish sauce, garlic, and pepper flakes together in bowl; set aside.

2. Pat salmon dry with paper towels and sprinkle with salt and pepper. Heat 1½ teaspoons vegetable oil in 10-inch nonstick skillet over medium-high heat until shimmering. Place salmon skin side up in skillet and cook until well browned on first side, 4 to 6 minutes. Flip salmon, reduce heat to medium, and cook until center is still translucent when checked with tip of paring knife and registers 125 degrees (for medium-rare), 3 to 6 minutes. Transfer salmon to serving platter, tent with aluminum foil, and let rest while preparing bok choy and sauce.

3. Wipe skillet clean with paper towels. Heat remaining 1½ teaspoons vegetable oil in now-empty skillet over medium heat until shimmering. Add bok choy and 2 tablespoons water and immediately cover. Cook, covered, shaking pan occasionally, for 2 minutes. Remove lid and continue to cook, stirring constantly, until all water has evaporated, stems are crisp-tender, and leaves are wilted, about 2 minutes. Transfer to platter with salmon.

4. Add sugar mixture to again-empty skillet and cook over medium heat until slightly thickened and reduced to ¼ cup, 1 to 2 minutes. Drizzle sauce over salmon and bok choy and serve.

Glazed Salmon with Black-Eyed Peas, Walnuts, and Pomegranate

SHEET PAN

Serves 4
Total Time 45 minutes

Why This Recipe Works The secret to perfectly cooked sheet pan salmon is simple: a preheated pan. Cranking the oven to 500 degrees ensured that the pan would be sizzling hot to help with browning, while turning down the heat when the salmon went into the oven allowed it to cook through gently. Sweet-tangy pomegranate molasses was a flavor-packed short-cut to a thick, shiny glaze for the rich fish. Canned black-eyed peas (no cooking required) made a great base for a hearty salad with crunchy toasted nuts, fresh scallions, and tart pomegranate seeds, and more pomegranate molasses created a punchy dressing.

- 1 (2-pound) skin-on salmon fillet, 1 to 1½ inches thick, sliced crosswise into 4 equal pieces
- ¼ cup pomegranate molasses, divided
- ¾ teaspoon table salt, divided
- ¼ teaspoon plus ⅛ teaspoon pepper, divided
- 3 tablespoons extra-virgin olive oil
- 2 tablespoons lemon juice
- 2 (15-ounce) cans black-eyed peas, rinsed
- ½ cup pomegranate seeds
- ½ cup walnuts, toasted and chopped
- ½ cup chopped fresh parsley
- 4 scallions, sliced thin

1. Adjust oven rack to lowest position, place rimmed baking sheet on rack, and heat oven to 500 degrees. Pat salmon dry with paper towels, brush with 1 tablespoon pomegranate molasses, and sprinkle with ½ teaspoon salt and ¼ teaspoon pepper.

2. Once oven reaches 500 degrees, reduce oven temperature to 275 degrees. Remove sheet from oven and carefully place salmon skin side down on hot sheet. Roast salmon until center is still translucent when checked with tip of paring knife and registers 125 degrees (for medium-rare), 9 to 13 minutes.

3. Whisk oil, lemon juice, 2 tablespoons pomegranate molasses, remaining ¼ teaspoon salt, and remaining ⅛ teaspoon pepper in large bowl until combined. Add black-eyed peas, pomegranate seeds, walnuts, parsley, and scallions and toss to combine. Season with salt and pepper to taste.

4. Remove sheet from oven and brush salmon with remaining 1 tablespoon pomegranate molasses. Slide fish spatula along underside of salmon fillets and transfer to serving platter, leaving skin behind; discard skin. Serve salmon with black-eyed-pea salad.

Sweet and Sour Salmon with Bok Choy

Glazed Salmon with Black-Eyed Peas, Walnuts, and Pomegranate

Salmon with Lemon-Garlic Mashed Cauliflower

INSTANT POT
Serves 4
Total Time 1 hour

Why This Recipe Works Salmon cooks quickly, so it requires exact timing and careful hands-on attention to get a complete meal just right using most traditional cooking methods. Enter the pressure cooker—with its consistent moisture level and temperature, plus its precise timing, the results are virtually foolproof. Here, a mild, smooth mash of cauliflower forms the perfect base for salmon fillets rubbed with ras el hanout, an aromatic North African blend of warm spices. The pressure cooker allowed us to sync the cooking times of the cauliflower and salmon, so creating a one-pot meal was simply a matter of using a foil sling to separate the two to make cooking and serving as straightforward as possible. We started by blooming a generous amount of garlic, and then we added the cauliflower and a small amount of broth before placing the salmon in the pot. After the salmon cooked under pressure for a mere 2 minutes, we removed it and mashed the cauliflower right in the pot, adding lemon zest at the end for a fragrant, floral punch. This recipe works best with farmed salmon; we do not recommend using wild salmon here, as it is much leaner. The salmon should register about 125 degrees (for medium-rare) after cooking; if it doesn't, partially cover the pot with the lid and continue to cook using the highest sauté function until the desired temperature is achieved. You can find ras el hanout in the spice aisle of most well-stocked supermarkets.

2 tablespoons extra-virgin olive oil
4 garlic cloves, peeled and smashed
½ cup chicken or vegetable broth
¾ teaspoon table salt, divided
1 large head cauliflower (3 pounds), cored and cut into 2-inch florets
1 (2-pound) skin-on salmon fillet, 1 to 1½ inches thick, sliced crosswise into 4 equal pieces
½ teaspoon ras el hanout
½ teaspoon grated lemon zest
3 scallions, sliced thin
1 tablespoon sesame seeds, toasted

1. Using highest sauté or browning function, cook oil and garlic in electric pressure cooker until garlic is fragrant and light golden brown, about 3 minutes. Turn off pressure cooker, then stir in broth and ¼ teaspoon salt. Arrange cauliflower in pot in even layer.

2. Fold sheet of aluminum foil into 16 by 6-inch sling. Sprinkle flesh side of salmon with ras el hanout and remaining ½ teaspoon salt, then arrange skin side down in center of sling. Using sling, lower salmon into pressure cooker on top of cauliflower; allow narrow edges of sling to rest along sides of insert. Lock lid in place and close pressure release valve. Select high pressure cook function and cook for 2 minutes.

3. Turn off pressure cooker and quick-release pressure. Carefully remove lid, allowing steam to escape away from you. Using sling, transfer salmon to large plate. Tent with foil and let rest while finishing cauliflower.

4. Using potato masher, mash cauliflower mixture until no large chunks remain. Using highest sauté or browning function, cook cauliflower, stirring often, until slightly thickened, about 3 minutes. Stir in lemon zest and season with salt and pepper to taste. Serve salmon with cauliflower, sprinkling individual portions with scallions and sesame seeds.

Salmon with Mediterranean Rice Salad

SLOW COOKER
Serves 4
Cook Time 1 to 2 hours on low

Why This Recipe Works While using a slow cooker to cook fish may sound counterintuitive—fish typically cooks through quickly and can require frequent checking—its gentle heat is actually ideal and offers foolproof, walk-away convenience. The biggest challenge with this cooking method was creating a side dish concurrently; space in the slow cooker was limited and we needed something that would cook in the same amount of time as the salmon. Traditional rice would take hours to cook through, but by using convenient instant rice we found that we were able to cook both the rice and the salmon simultaneously. We first added the instant rice and already-boiling water to the bottom of the pot, and then covered the rice with a piece of parchment paper. We placed the salmon on top of the parchment, which gave the fillets plenty of space and guaranteed even cooking; additionally, the steam from the rice below aided in cooking the fish through. Once we had our method down pat, we turned to the flavors. Since we were keeping the salmon simple, our rice needed some bold flavors to round out the meal. We decided on a Greek profile for a vinaigrette using red wine vinegar, honey, garlic, and oregano. Once the rice was cooked, we stirred in cherry tomatoes, whole parsley leaves, feta, and the dressing. Be sure to use instant rice (sometimes labeled minute rice); traditional rice takes much longer to cook and won't work here. You will need a 5- to 7-quart oval slow cooker for this recipe. For an accurate measurement of boiling water, bring a full kettle of water to a boil and then measure out the desired amount. Check the salmon's temperature after 1 hour of cooking and continue to monitor until it registers 135 degrees.

1½ cups instant white rice
⅓ cup extra-virgin olive oil, divided
1 teaspoon table salt, divided
¾ teaspoon pepper, divided
1 (2-pound) skin-on salmon fillet, 1 to 1½ inches thick, sliced crosswise into 4 equal pieces
¼ cup red wine vinegar
1 tablespoon honey
2 teaspoons minced fresh oregano
2 garlic cloves, minced
8 ounces cherry tomatoes, quartered
½ cup fresh parsley leaves
2 ounces feta cheese, crumbled (½ cup)
 Lemon wedges

1. Lightly coat slow cooker with vegetable oil spray. Combine 1⅔ cups boiling water, rice, 1 tablespoon oil, ½ teaspoon salt, and ½ teaspoon pepper in prepared slow cooker. Gently press 16 by 12-inch sheet of parchment paper onto surface of water, folding down edges as needed.

2. Sprinkle salmon with remaining ½ teaspoon salt and remaining ¼ teaspoon pepper and arrange skin side down in even layer on top of parchment. Cover and cook until salmon is opaque throughout when checked with tip of paring knife and registers 135 degrees (for medium), 1 to 2 hours on low.

3. Using 2 metal spatulas, transfer salmon to serving platter; discard parchment and remove any white albumin from salmon. Whisk vinegar, honey, oregano, garlic, and remaining oil together in bowl. Fluff rice with fork, then gently fold in tomatoes, parsley, feta, and ½ cup vinaigrette. Season with salt and pepper to taste. Drizzle remaining vinaigrette over salmon and serve with salad and lemon wedges.

CREATING A PARCHMENT SHIELD

Press 16 by 12-inch sheet of parchment paper firmly onto rice or vegetables, folding down edges as needed.

Salmon with Lemon-Garlic Mashed Cauliflower

Salmon with Mediterranean Rice Salad

SALMON WITH SPICED CHICKPEA, CUCUMBER, AND TOMATO SALAD

Succulent salmon paired with an effortless salad is the ideal weeknight meal, and this versatile dish lends itself well to a variety of cooking methods, flavors, and add-ins. For a recipe that would work in a Dutch oven, slow cooker, or pressure cooker, we needed to take advantage of the deep space of these pots. Using a foil sling for our salmon not only made the fish easy to remove, but it also created an elevated surface which allowed us to cook part of our side below. We bloomed potent garam masala with some oil and added canned chickpeas (other spice blends or canned beans can be substituted). While the salmon cooked, the chickpeas below warmed through and absorbed the flavors of the spices. Mixing a little water with the chickpeas created the perfect steamy environment for the salmon above. Once drained, we combined our warm chickpeas with cool, crunchy cucumbers and tomatoes and a quick dressing of oil, shallot, and lemon juice for a salad with complex flavors and textures. We like the addition of mint for freshness, but other herbs will work as well.

CLASSIC

DUTCH OVEN
Serves 4
Total Time 1 hour

⅓ cup extra-virgin olive oil, divided
1 tablespoon garam masala
2 (15-ounce) cans chickpeas, rinsed
¾ teaspoon table salt, divided
½ teaspoon pepper, divided
1 (1½-pound) skinless salmon fillet, 1 to 1½ inches thick, sliced crosswise into 4 equal pieces
1 shallot, minced
1 teaspoon grated lemon zest plus 2 tablespoons juice
1 English cucumber, halved lengthwise and sliced thin
8 ounces cherry tomatoes, halved
¼ cup coarsely chopped fresh mint

1. Adjust oven rack to lowest position and heat oven to 250 degrees. Cook 1 tablespoon oil and garam masala in Dutch oven over medium heat until fragrant, about 2 minutes. Off heat, stir in chickpeas, ¼ cup water, ¼ teaspoon salt, and ¼ teaspoon pepper and spread into even layer.

2. Fold sheet of aluminum foil into 12 by 9-inch sling. Sprinkle flesh side of salmon with remaining ½ teaspoon salt and remaining ¼ teaspoon pepper, then arrange skinned side down in center of sling. Using sling, lower salmon into pot on top of chickpeas; allow narrow edges of sling to rest along sides of pot. Cover, transfer pot to oven, and cook until center of salmon is still translucent when checked with tip of paring knife and registers 125 degrees (for medium-rare), 25 to 30 minutes.

3. Meanwhile, whisk remaining oil, shallot, and lemon zest and juice together in large bowl. Add cucumber, tomatoes, and mint and gently toss to combine.

4. Remove pot from oven. Using sling, transfer salmon to large plate. Strain chickpeas through fine-mesh strainer; discard cooking liquid. Transfer chickpeas to bowl with vegetables and toss to combine. Season with salt and pepper to taste. Serve salmon with salad.

MAKE IT YOUR WAY

→

> **Use What You've Got** Substitute another spice mix (ras el hanout, chili powder, herbes de Provence) for garam masala. Substitute other canned beans (kidney beans, navy beans, cannellini beans, black beans) for chickpeas. Substitute other fresh herbs (cilantro, basil, dill, parsley, or tarragon) for mint.

SLOW COOK IT

SLOW COOKER

Serves 4

Cook Time 1 to 2 hours on low

You will need a 5- to 7-quart oval slow cooker for this recipe. Check the salmon's temperature after 1 hour of cooking and continue to monitor until it registers 135 degrees.

- ⅓ cup extra-virgin olive oil, divided
- 1 tablespoon garam masala
- 2 (15-ounce) cans chickpeas, rinsed
- ¾ teaspoon table salt, divided
- ½ teaspoon pepper, divided
- 1 (1½-pound) skinless salmon fillet, 1 to 1½ inches thick, sliced crosswise into 4 equal pieces
- 1 shallot, minced
- 1 teaspoon grated lemon zest plus 2 tablespoons juice
- 1 English cucumber, halved lengthwise and sliced thin
- 8 ounces cherry tomatoes, halved
- ¼ cup coarsely chopped fresh mint

1. Microwave 1 tablespoon oil and garam masala in bowl until fragrant, about 30 seconds; transfer to slow cooker. Stir in chickpeas, ¼ cup water, ¼ teaspoon salt, and ¼ teaspoon pepper and spread into even layer.

2. Fold sheet of aluminum foil into 12 by 9-inch sling. Sprinkle flesh side of salmon with remaining ½ teaspoon salt and remaining ¼ teaspoon pepper, then arrange skinned side down in center of sling. Using sling, lower salmon into slow cooker on top of chickpeas; allow narrow edges of sling to rest along sides of insert. Cover and cook until salmon is opaque throughout when checked with tip of paring knife and registers 135 degrees (for medium), 1 to 2 hours on low.

3. Meanwhile, whisk remaining oil, shallot, and lemon zest and juice together in large bowl. Add cucumber, tomatoes, and mint and gently toss to combine.

4. Using sling, transfer salmon to large plate. Strain chickpeas through fine-mesh strainer; discard cooking liquid. Transfer chickpeas to bowl with vegetables and toss to combine. Season with salt and pepper to taste. Serve salmon with salad.

PRESSURE COOK IT

INSTANT POT

Serves 4

Total Time 30 minutes

- ⅓ cup extra-virgin olive oil, divided
- 1 tablespoon garam masala
- 2 (15-ounce) cans chickpeas, rinsed
- ¾ teaspoon table salt, divided
- ½ teaspoon pepper, divided
- 1 (1½-pound) skinless salmon fillet, 1 to 1½ inches thick, sliced crosswise into 4 equal pieces
- 1 shallot, minced
- 1 teaspoon grated lemon zest plus 2 tablespoons juice
- 1 English cucumber, halved lengthwise and sliced thin
- 8 ounces cherry tomatoes, halved
- ¼ cup coarsely chopped fresh mint

1. Using highest sauté or browning function, cook 1 tablespoon oil and garam masala in electric pressure cooker until fragrant, about 1 minute. Turn off pressure cooker and stir in chickpeas, ½ cup water, ¼ teaspoon salt, and ¼ teaspoon pepper.

2. Fold sheet of aluminum foil into 12 by 9-inch sling. Sprinkle flesh side of salmon with remaining ½ teaspoon salt and remaining ¼ teaspoon pepper, then arrange skinned side down in center of sling. Using sling, lower salmon into pressure cooker on top of chickpeas; allow narrow edges of sling to rest along sides of pot.

3. Lock lid in place and close pressure release valve. Select high pressure cook function and cook for 5 minutes. Turn off pressure cooker and quick-release pressure. Carefully remove lid, allowing steam to escape away from you.

4. Meanwhile, whisk remaining oil, shallot, and lemon zest and juice together in large bowl. Add cucumber, tomatoes, and mint and gently toss to combine.

5. Using sling, transfer salmon to large plate. Strain chickpeas through fine-mesh strainer; discard cooking liquid. Transfer chickpeas to bowl with vegetables and toss to combine. Season with salt and pepper to taste. Serve salmon with salad.

> **Bulk it Up** Add baby spinach, baby arugula, quartered baby artichoke hearts, olives, and/or chopped roasted red peppers to dressing in step 3. Sprinkle salad with chopped toasted nuts (almonds, walnuts, pine nuts) and/or crumbled feta or goat cheese before serving.

> **Add an Upgrade** Add red pepper flakes or Aleppo pepper to oil with the garam masala. Brush salmon with pomegranate molasses, pepper jelly, or fig jam before cooking.

Salmon Burgers with Asparagus and Lemon-Herb Sauce

Salmon Tacos with Collards and Radish Slaw

Salmon Burgers with Asparagus and Lemon-Herb Sauce

SHEET PAN

Serves 4

Total Time 45 minutes

Why This Recipe Works Salmon burgers are far more delicate than traditional ground beef burgers, and they're much more prone to falling apart in a skillet or on a grill. For a more foolproof method, we turned to a sheet pan to cook the tender patties, which allowed us to cook a side dish simultaneously. A food processor made quick work of chopping not just the fish but also fresh bread crumbs. The bread and some mayonnaise (plus tangy mustard and briny capers) helped bind the burgers together while letting the salmon still shine through. When it comes to cooking, salmon burgers don't need much of it. Broiling was clearly the best option; the direct heat browned the exterior as much as possible without overcooking the interior. For the side dish, we opted for broiler-friendly asparagus, simply seasoned with salt and pepper. A tart, herbal sauce of bright lemon and creamy mayonnaise, and fresh scallions and parsley was the perfect topping for these rich burgers. For a version for two, we swapped the asparagus for cabbage and made a spicy, tangy, wasabi mayonnaise to spread on top of the burgers. Be sure to use raw salmon here; do not substitute cooked or canned salmon.

6 tablespoons mayonnaise, divided
2 scallions, minced, divided
3 tablespoons chopped fresh parsley, divided
1 tablespoon lemon juice
1 slice hearty white sandwich bread, torn into 1-inch pieces
1 pound skinless salmon fillets, cut into 1-inch pieces
1 tablespoon Dijon mustard
2 teaspoons capers, rinsed and minced
½ teaspoon table salt, divided
⅛ teaspoon plus ¼ teaspoon pepper, divided
1 pound asparagus, trimmed
1 teaspoon extra-virgin olive oil
4 hamburger buns
1 small head Bibb lettuce, leaves separated

1. Whisk ¼ cup mayonnaise, half of scallions, 1 tablespoon parsley, and lemon juice together in bowl. Season with salt and pepper to taste; set aside for serving.

2. Adjust oven rack 4 inches from broiler element and heat broiler. Pulse bread in food processor to fine crumbs, about 4 pulses; transfer to large bowl. Working in 2 batches, pulse salmon in now-empty food processor until coarsely ground, about 4 pulses; transfer to bowl with bread crumbs and toss to combine. Add mustard, capers, remaining 2 tablespoons mayonnaise, remaining scallions, remaining 2 tablespoons parsley, ¼ teaspoon salt, and ⅛ teaspoon pepper and gently fold into salmon mixture until well combined.

3. Line rimmed baking sheet with aluminum foil. Divide salmon mixture into 4 equal portions and gently pack into 1-inch-thick patties, about 3½ inches wide. Place patties on 1 side of prepared sheet. Toss asparagus with oil, remaining ¼ teaspoon salt, and remaining ¼ teaspoon pepper and spread in single layer on empty side of sheet. Broil until burgers are lightly browned on top, 4 to 6 minutes. Flip burgers and asparagus and continue to broil until burgers register 125 degrees (for medium-rare) and asparagus is lightly browned and tender, 3 to 6 minutes.

4. Transfer burgers and asparagus to serving platter; discard foil. Arrange buns cut side up in single layer on now-empty sheet and broil until lightly browned, 30 seconds to 1 minute. Top bun bottoms with lettuce, burgers, lemon-herb sauce, and bun tops. Serve with asparagus.

VARIATION

Salmon Burgers with Charred Cabbage and Wasabi Mayonnaise for Two

SHEET PAN

Serves 2

Total Time 45 minutes

Be sure to use raw salmon here; do not substitute cooked or canned salmon. If wasabi powder is unavailable, you can substitute 1 teaspoon prepared horseradish. Do not substitute green cabbage. Don't core the cabbage before cutting it into wedges; the core helps hold the wedges together during cooking.

    3 tablespoons mayonnaise, divided
    ½ teaspoon wasabi powder
    ½ teaspoon soy sauce
    ½ slice hearty white sandwich bread
    8 ounces skinless salmon, cut into 1-inch pieces
    1 scallion, minced
  1½ teaspoons grated fresh ginger
    ¼ teaspoon plus ⅛ teaspoon table salt, divided
    ¼ teaspoon pepper, divided
    ½ small head savoy cabbage, cut into 1½-inch wedges
    1 tablespoon vegetable oil
    1 teaspoon toasted sesame oil
    ½ teaspoon rice wine vinegar
    2 hamburger buns
    4 leaves Bibb lettuce

1. Whisk 2 tablespoons mayonnaise, wasabi, and soy sauce together in bowl; set aside for serving.

2. Adjust oven rack 4 inches from broiler element and heat broiler. Pulse bread in food processor to fine crumbs, about 4 pulses; transfer to large bowl. Pulse salmon in now-empty food processor until coarsely ground, about 4 pulses; transfer to bowl with bread crumbs and toss to combine. Add remaining 1 tablespoon mayonnaise, scallion, ginger, ¼ teaspoon salt, and ⅛ teaspoon pepper and gently fold into salmon mixture until well combined.

3. Line rimmed baking sheet with aluminum foil. Divide salmon mixture into 2 equal portions and gently pack into 1-inch-thick patties, about 3½ inches wide. Place patties on 1 side of prepared sheet. Brush cut sides of cabbage with vegetable oil and sprinkle with remaining ⅛ teaspoon salt and remaining ⅛ teaspoon pepper. Arrange cabbage cut side down in single layer on empty side of sheet. Broil until burgers are lightly browned on top and cabbage is lightly charred, 3 to 5 minutes. Flip burgers and cabbage and continue to broil until burgers register 125 degrees (for medium-rare), 3 to 5 minutes.

4. Transfer burgers and cabbage to serving platter; discard foil. Arrange buns cut side up in single layer on now-empty sheet and broil until lightly browned, 30 seconds to 1 minute. Drizzle cabbage with sesame oil and vinegar. Top bun bottoms with lettuce, burgers, wasabi mayonnaise, and bun tops. Serve with cabbage.

Salmon Tacos with Collards and Radish Slaw

SKILLET

Serves 4 to 6

Total Time 35 minutes

Why This Recipe Works Rich salmon makes a satisfying, quick-cooking taco filling, and these salmon tacos—flavored with a bold spice rub and topped with crunchy slaw and creamy crema—are sure to be the hit of taco night. Chili powder, salt, and pepper added a kick of heat to the fish, and cooking it in a nonstick skillet over medium-high heat gave us flavorful browning in the few minutes it took for the fish to cook through. For a slaw that would stand up to the salmon, we turned to dark, leafy collards. Though collards are typically cooked, we found that thinly slicing them allowed us to skip this step. Radishes, jícama, and red onion rounded out the slaw, and a bright crema of pureed avocado, lime juice, yogurt, and cilantro lent creaminess for a rich finish. For more information on warming tortillas, see page 116.

Avocado Crema

- ½ avocado, pitted and chopped
- ¼ cup chopped fresh cilantro
- 3 tablespoons water
- 1 tablespoon lime juice
- 1 tablespoon plain low-fat yogurt

Tacos

- ¼ teaspoon grated lime zest plus 2 tablespoons juice
- 1 teaspoon table salt, divided
- 4 ounces collard greens, stemmed and sliced very thin (2 cups)
- 4 ounces jícama, peeled and cut into 2-inch-long matchsticks
- 4 radishes, trimmed and cut into 1-inch-long matchsticks
- ½ small red onion, halved and sliced thin
- ¼ cup fresh cilantro leaves
- 1½ teaspoons chili powder
- ¼ teaspoon pepper
- 1 (2-pound) skinless salmon fillet, 1 to 1½ inches thick, sliced crosswise into 4 equal pieces
- 1 tablespoon vegetable oil
- 12–18 (6-inch) corn tortillas, warmed
  Hot sauce

1. For the avocado crema Process all ingredients in food processor until completely smooth, about 1 minute, scraping down sides of bowl as needed. Season with salt and pepper to taste. Transfer crema to bowl and refrigerate until ready to serve.

2. For the tacos Whisk lime zest and juice and ¼ teaspoon salt together in large bowl. Add collard greens, jícama, radishes, onion, and cilantro and toss to combine; set aside.

3. Combine chili powder, pepper, and remaining ¾ teaspoon salt in small bowl. Pat salmon dry with paper towels and sprinkle evenly with spice mixture. Heat oil in 12-inch nonstick skillet over medium-high heat until shimmering. Place salmon skin side up in skillet and cook until well browned on first side, 4 to 6 minutes. Flip salmon, reduce heat to medium, and cook until center is still translucent when checked with tip of paring knife and registers 125 degrees (for medium-rare), 3 to 6 minutes. Transfer salmon to plate and let cool slightly, about 2 minutes. Using 2 forks, flake fish into 2-inch pieces; discard skin.

4. Divide fish, collard slaw, and avocado crema evenly among tortillas, and drizzle with hot sauce to taste. Serve.

Seared Trout with Brussels Sprouts and Bacon

SKILLET
Serves 4
Total Time 45 minutes

Why This Recipe Works Using the same skillet for each component of this dish does more than just streamline the process and limit cleanup; it also helps build layers of flavor to create a cohesive main course and side. You don't often see hardy Brussels sprouts paired with seafood, but we love the heft they provide to an otherwise delicate dish—and trout, especially when given a crispy skin, has a presence that easily stands up to the sprouts. After cooking the sprouts in the skillet, we moved them to the oven, ensuring they would still be warm when our trout finished cooking. Smoky bacon, a classic with Brussels sprouts, went into the skillet next and tied the dish together; we used the rendered bacon fat in the skillet to sear the trout and then added the cooked bacon to the sprouts. Use Brussels sprouts no bigger than golf balls, as larger ones are often tough and woody. You will need a 12-inch nonstick skillet with a tight-fitting lid for this recipe.

- 1 pound Brussels sprouts, trimmed and halved
- ¼ cup extra-virgin olive oil, plus extra as needed
- 2 garlic cloves, minced
- ½ teaspoon minced fresh thyme or ⅛ teaspoon dried
- 1¼ teaspoons table salt, divided
- ⅛ teaspoon plus ½ teaspoon pepper, divided
- 3 slices bacon, cut into ½-inch pieces
- 1 teaspoon ground coriander
- ½ teaspoon dry mustard
- 4 (6- to 8-ounce) boneless, butterflied whole trout
  Lemon wedges

1. Adjust oven rack to middle position and heat oven to 200 degrees. Arrange Brussels sprouts in single layer, cut sides down, in 12-inch nonstick skillet. Drizzle oil evenly over sprouts. Cover skillet, place over medium-high heat, and cook until sprouts are bright green and cut sides have started to brown, about 5 minutes.

2. Uncover and continue to cook until cut sides of sprouts are deeply and evenly browned and paring knife slides in with little to no resistance, 2 to 3 minutes, adjusting heat and moving sprouts as necessary to prevent them from overbrowning. Stir in garlic, thyme, ¼ teaspoon salt, and ⅛ teaspoon pepper and

Seared Trout with Brussels Sprouts and Bacon

cook until fragrant, about 30 seconds. Transfer sprouts to large heatproof bowl, cover loosely with aluminum foil, and keep warm in oven.

3. Cook bacon in now-empty skillet over medium-high heat until rendered and crisp, about 5 minutes. Using slotted spoon, transfer bacon to paper towel–lined plate. Pour off and reserve 2 tablespoons fat from skillet. (If necessary, add extra oil to equal 2 tablespoons.)

4. Combine coriander, mustard, remaining 1 teaspoon salt, and remaining ½ teaspoon pepper in bowl. Pat trout dry with paper towels and sprinkle with spice mixture. Heat 1 tablespoon reserved fat in again-empty skillet over medium-high heat until shimmering. Place 2 fillets flesh side down in skillet and cook until browned and trout flakes apart when gently prodded with paring knife, about 3 minutes per side. Transfer to serving platter and keep warm in oven. Repeat with remaining 1 tablespoon reserved fat and remaining 2 fillets; transfer to platter.

5. Gently fold bacon into Brussels sprouts and season with salt and pepper to taste. Serve trout with Brussels sprouts and lemon wedges.

Roasted Cod with Artichokes, Olives, and Sun-Dried Tomatoes

CASSEROLE DISH

Serves 4
Total Time 1 hour

Why This Recipe Works A meal from a casserole dish doesn't have to mean bland and old-fashioned, and this roasted cod—inspired by the bold, bright flavors of the Mediterranean—proves it. Using a pantry-friendly combination of tender jarred baby artichokes, sweet sun-dried tomatoes, and briny kalamata olives as our base for the fish kept prep work light and promised to infuse the mild fish with plenty of flavor. We roasted the artichokes first, tossing them with the tomatoes' packing oil to deepen their flavor. We stirred in the sun-dried tomatoes and chopped olives as well as some grated lemon zest before finally nestling in the cod fillets, which we brushed with more of the potent tomato oil. Haddock and striped bass are good substitutes for the cod. Thin tail-end fillets can be folded to achieve proper thickness. While we prefer the flavor and texture of jarred whole baby artichoke hearts in this recipe, you can substitute 18 ounces frozen artichoke hearts, thawed and patted dry, for the jarred.

- 3 cups jarred whole baby artichokes packed in water, quartered, rinsed, and patted dry
- ¾ cup oil-packed sun-dried tomatoes, drained, ¼ cup oil reserved, divided
- ¾ teaspoon table salt, divided
- ½ teaspoon pepper, divided
- 1 teaspoon grated lemon zest plus 1 tablespoon juice, divided
- ½ cup pitted kalamata olives, chopped
- 4 (6- to 8-ounce) skinless cod fillets, 1 to 1½ inches thick
- 2 tablespoons chopped fresh basil

1. Adjust oven rack to middle position and heat oven to 450 degrees. Toss artichokes with 2 tablespoons tomato oil, ¼ teaspoon salt, and ¼ teaspoon pepper in bowl. Spread into 13 by 9-inch baking dish and roast until lightly browned, about 15 minutes.

2. Stir lemon zest, olives, tomatoes, and 1 tablespoon tomato oil into artichokes in dish. Pat cod dry with paper towels, then nestle into artichoke mixture. Brush tops of cod with remaining 1 tablespoon tomato oil and sprinkle with remaining ½ teaspoon salt and remaining ¼ teaspoon pepper. Bake until cod flakes apart when gently prodded with paring knife and registers 140 degrees, 15 to 18 minutes. Drizzle with lemon juice, sprinkle with basil, and serve.

Cod Baked in Foil with Leeks and Carrots

4 tablespoons unsalted butter, softened
1 teaspoon minced fresh thyme
2 garlic cloves, minced, divided
1¼ teaspoons grated lemon zest, divided, plus lemon wedges for serving
1 teaspoon table salt, divided
½ teaspoon pepper, divided
2 tablespoons minced fresh parsley
2 carrots, peeled and cut into 2-inch matchsticks
1 pound leeks, white and light green parts only, halved lengthwise, washed thoroughly, and cut into 2-inch matchsticks
¼ cup dry vermouth or dry white wine
4 (6- to 8-ounce) skinless cod fillets, 1 to 1½ inches thick

1. Adjust oven rack to lower-middle position and heat oven to 450 degrees. Mash butter, thyme, half of garlic, ¼ teaspoon lemon zest, ¼ teaspoon salt, and ⅛ teaspoon pepper in bowl. In separate bowl, combine parsley, remaining garlic, and remaining 1 teaspoon lemon zest; set aside. In third bowl, combine carrots, leeks, ¼ teaspoon salt, and ⅛ teaspoon pepper.

2. Cut eight 12-inch sheets of aluminum foil; arrange 4 flat on counter. Divide vegetable mixture among foil sheets, mounding it in center, and sprinkle with vermouth. Pat cod dry with paper towels, sprinkle with remaining ½ teaspoon salt and remaining ¼ teaspoon pepper, and place on top of vegetables. Spread butter mixture over fish.

3. Place second square of foil on top of cod. Press edges of foil together and fold over several times until packet is well sealed and measures about 7 inches. (Packets can be refrigerated for up to 3 hours; if refrigerated for longer than 30 minutes, increase cooking time to 17 minutes.)
Place packets on rimmed baking sheet, overlapping as needed.

4. Bake packets until cod registers 140 degrees, about 15 minutes. Carefully open foil, allowing steam to escape away from you. Using thin metal spatula, gently slide cod and vegetables, and any accumulated juices, onto plate. Sprinkle with parsley mixture and serve with lemon wedges.

Cod Baked in Foil with Leeks and Carrots

SHEET PAN
Serves 4
Total Time 45 minutes

Why This Recipe Works Cooking cod en papillote, or folded in a pouch, is a French technique that allows the fish to steam and emerge moist and flavorful. The pouch is virtually cleanup-free and can contain vegetables underneath the fish for a complete meal. We made packets of leak-proof foil and placed them on a sheet pan on the oven's lower-middle rack, which concentrated the exuded liquid for deeper flavor. Carrots and leeks, cut into matchsticks, cooked at the same rate as the fish. A flavorful compound butter on top added richness. Haddock and striped bass are good substitutes for the cod. Thin tail-end fillets can be folded to the proper thickness. To test for doneness, use a permanent marker to mark an "X" on the outside of the foil where the fish fillet is the thickest, then insert an instant-read thermometer through the "X" into the fish to measure its internal temperature. Open each packet promptly after baking to prevent overcooking.

TUCKING A COD TAIL

If using any tail-end fillets, simply tuck the thinner end under itself before cooking so that it will cook at the same rate as thicker fillets.

VARIATION

Cod Baked in Foil with Zucchini and Tomatoes for Two

SHEET PAN

Serves 2

Total Time 1 hour

Haddock and striped bass are good substitutes for the cod. Thin tail-end fillets can be folded to the proper thickness. To test for doneness, use a permanent marker to mark an "X" on the outside of the foil where the fish fillet is the thickest, then insert an instant-read thermometer through the "X" into the fish to measure its internal temperature. Open each packet promptly after baking to prevent overcooking.

- 1 large zucchini, trimmed and sliced ¼ inch thick
- ½ teaspoon plus ⅛ teaspoon table salt, divided
- 1 tomato, cored, seeded, and chopped
- 1 tablespoon extra-virgin olive oil
- 1 garlic clove, minced
- ½ teaspoon minced fresh oregano
   Pinch red pepper flakes
- ¼ teaspoon pepper, divided
- 2 teaspoons lemon juice, plus lemon wedges for serving
- 2 (6- to 8-ounce) skinless cod fillets, 1 to 1½ inches thick
- 1 tablespoon chopped fresh basil

1. Toss zucchini with ¼ teaspoon salt in colander and let sit for 30 minutes. Pat zucchini dry with paper towels, pressing firmly on each slice to remove as much liquid as possible. Combine tomato, oil, garlic, oregano, pepper flakes, ⅛ teaspoon salt, and ⅛ teaspoon pepper in bowl.

2. Adjust oven rack to lower-middle position and heat oven to 450 degrees. Cut four 12-inch sheets of aluminum foil; arrange 2 sheets flat on counter. Shingle zucchini in center of each sheet and sprinkle with lemon juice. Pat cod dry with paper towels, sprinkle with remaining ¼ teaspoon salt and remaining ⅛ teaspoon pepper, and place on top of zucchini. Spread tomato mixture over cod.

3. Place second square of foil on top of cod. Press edges of foil together and fold over several times until packet is well sealed and measures about 7 inches. (Packets can be refrigerated for up to 3 hours; if refrigerated for longer than 30 minutes, increase cooking time to 17 minutes.) Place packets on rimmed baking sheet.

4. Bake packets until cod registers 140 degrees, about 15 minutes. Carefully open foil, allowing steam to escape away from you. Using thin metal spatula, gently slide cod and vegetables and any accumulated juices onto platter. Sprinkle with basil and serve with lemon wedges.

ASSEMBLING COD IN FOIL PACKETS

1. Cut eight 12-inch sheets of foil; arrange 4 flat on counter. Place vegetables in center of foil sheets and sprinkle with vermouth.

2. Pat cod dry with paper towels, season with salt and pepper, and place on top of vegetables. Spread butter mixture on top of fish.

3. Place second square of foil on top of fish. Press edges of foil together and fold over several times until packet is well sealed and measures about 7 inches.

Cod with Warm Beet and Arugula Salad

INSTANT POT

Serves 4

Total Time 1 hour

Why This Recipe Works We love the combination of sweet, earthy beets and light, buttery cod, but these two elements usually require very different cooking times—beets can take up to an hour to roast in the oven, while delicate cod cooks through very quickly. By using a pressure cooker and staggering the cook times, we were able to create a meal with both in just under an hour. We gave the beets a jump-start by cooking them for just 3 minutes under pressure—the intense heat of the pressure cooker rendered the nutrient-packed skins of our unpeeled beets utterly undetectable. Next, we created a foil sling on which to suspend our cod atop the beets and cooked both for just 2 minutes under pressure, long enough to finish the beets and fully cook the cod. Arugula, a lemony dressing, and a sprinkling of dukkah—a crunchy, flavor-packed Egyptian condiment—brought it all together. Look for beets

Cod with Warm Beet and Arugula Salad

measuring approximately 2 inches in diameter. Haddock and striped bass are good substitutes for the cod. Thin tail-end fillets can be folded to achieve proper thickness. The cod should register about 135 degrees after cooking; if it doesn't, partially cover the pot with the lid and continue to cook using the highest sauté or browning function until the desired temperature is achieved. We prefer to make our own Dukkah, but any store-bought variety will work.

¼ cup extra-virgin olive oil, divided, plus extra for drizzling
1 shallot, sliced thin
2 garlic cloves, minced
1½ pounds small beets, scrubbed, trimmed, and cut into ½-inch wedges
½ cup chicken or vegetable broth
1 tablespoon dukkah, plus extra for sprinkling
¼ teaspoon table salt
4 (6- to 8-ounce) skinless cod fillets, 1½ inches thick
1 tablespoon lemon juice
2 ounces (2 cups) baby arugula

1. Using highest sauté or browning function, heat 1 table-spoon oil in electric pressure cooker until shimmering. Add shallot and cook until softened, about 2 minutes. Stir in garlic and cook until fragrant, about 30 seconds. Stir in beets and broth. Lock lid in place and close pressure release valve. Select high pressure cook function and cook for 3 minutes. Turn off pressure cooker and quick-release pressure. Carefully remove lid, allowing steam to escape away from you.

2. Fold sheet of aluminum foil into 16 by 6-inch sling. Combine 2 tablespoons oil, dukkah, and salt in bowl, then brush cod with oil mixture. Arrange cod skinned side down in center of sling. Using sling, lower cod into pressure cooker; allow narrow edges of sling to rest along sides of insert. Lock lid in place and close pressure release valve. Select high pressure cook function and cook for 2 minutes.

3. Turn off pressure cooker and quick-release pressure. Carefully remove lid, allowing steam to escape away from you. Using sling, transfer cod to large plate. Tent with foil and let rest while finishing beet salad.

4. Combine lemon juice and remaining 1 tablespoon oil in large bowl. Using slotted spoon, transfer beets to bowl with oil mixture. Add arugula and gently toss to combine. Season with salt and pepper to taste. Serve cod with salad, sprinkling individual portions with extra dukkah and drizzling with extra oil.

Dukkah

Makes about ½ cup
This eastern Mediterranean blend of nuts, seeds, and spices makes for a fragrant and crunchy garnish.

1½ teaspoons coriander seeds, toasted
¾ teaspoon cumin seeds, toasted
½ teaspoon fennel seeds, toasted
2 tablespoons sesame seeds, toasted
3 tablespoons shelled pistachios, toasted and chopped fine
½ teaspoon flake sea salt, such as Maldon
½ teaspoon pepper

Process coriander seeds, cumin seeds, and fennel seeds in spice grinder until finely ground, about 30 seconds. Add sesame seeds and pulse until coarsely ground, about 4 pulses; transfer to small bowl. Stir in pistachios, salt, and pepper. (Dukkah can be refrigerated for up to 3 months.)

Lemon-Herb Cod Fillets with Crispy Garlic Potatoes

SHEET PAN

Serves 4
Total Time 1¼ hours

Why This Recipe Works Easy but elegant, this unconventional sheet pan take on classic roasted cod and potatoes uses thinly sliced russet potatoes as a bed to shield the cod from the direct heat of the pan, ensuring moist, flaky fish and well-browned potatoes. We tossed the potatoes with melted butter, garlic, and thyme for plenty of flavor and shingled them in four individual portions for an attractive presentation. After shaping our potato rectangles, we gave them a head start of 30 minutes, then laid a cod fillet on top of each. To highlight the fish's clean flavor, we topped each fillet with a few small pieces of butter, a sprig of fresh thyme, and a couple thin slices of lemon. We slid our pan back into the oven where the dry heat melted the butter, basting the fish and drawing the herbal and citrus flavors through the fillets and down over the potatoes. Haddock and striped bass are good substitutes for the cod. Thin tail-end fillets can be folded to achieve proper thickness.

1½ pounds russet potatoes, unpeeled, sliced into ¼-inch-thick rounds
  2 tablespoons unsalted butter, melted, plus 3 tablespoons cut into ¼-inch pieces, divided
  3 garlic cloves, minced
  1 teaspoon minced fresh thyme, plus 4 sprigs, divided
  1 teaspoon table salt, divided
  ½ teaspoon pepper, divided
  4 (6- to 8-ounce) skinless cod fillets, 1 to 1½ inches thick
  1 lemon, thinly sliced

1. Adjust oven rack to lower-middle position and heat oven to 425 degrees. Toss potatoes with melted butter, garlic, minced thyme, ½ teaspoon salt, and ¼ teaspoon pepper in bowl. Shingle potatoes into four 6 by 4-inch rectangular piles on rimmed baking sheet. Roast until spotty brown and just tender, 30 to 35 minutes, rotating sheet halfway through roasting.

2. Pat cod dry with paper towels and sprinkle with remaining ½ teaspoon salt and remaining ¼ teaspoon pepper. Lay 1 cod fillet skinned side down on top of each potato pile and top with butter pieces, thyme sprigs, and lemon slices. Bake until cod flakes apart when gently prodded with paring knife and registers 140 degrees, about 15 minutes.

3. Remove sheet from oven. Slide spatula underneath potatoes and cod and gently transfer to individual plates. Serve.

Lemon-Herb Cod Fillets with Crispy Garlic Potatoes

Halibut with Red Potatoes, Corn, and Andouille

SHEET PAN

Serves 4
Total Time 1 hour

Why This Recipe Works The best thing about roasting halibut on a sheet pan is that it concentrates the mild fish's sweetness in mere minutes, and this dish keeps things efficient even while incorporating multiple sides by staggering the cook times. Inspired by the spicy, rich flavors of Lowcountry shrimp boils, we paired our roasted halibut with smoky andouille sausage, sweet corn, and tender red potatoes. We managed to keep the meal mostly hands-off without letting anything over-cook by first roasting the halved potatoes, corn, and andouille in a 500-degree oven. Once the corn's kernels were nicely plumped, we removed the cobs, lowered the temperature to 425 degrees, and made room on the sheet pan for the halibut fillets; the hot pan helped brown the fish as it cooked through. We gave the corn and halibut a rich, authentic finish by slathering them with a citrusy Old Bay compound butter. Striped bass and swordfish are good substitutes for the halibut. To ensure that your fish cooks evenly, purchase fillets that are similarly shaped and uniformly thick. Use small red potatoes measuring 1 to 2 inches in diameter; if your potatoes are larger, cut them into 1-inch pieces to ensure that they cook through properly. If andouille is not available, Portuguese linguiça or Polish kielbasa can be substituted.

    4 tablespoons unsalted butter, softened
    2 teaspoons Old Bay seasoning
    1 teaspoon lemon juice
    3 tablespoons vegetable oil, divided
 1½ pounds small red potatoes, unpeeled, halved
    1 teaspoon table salt, divided
    ½ teaspoon plus ⅛ teaspoon pepper, divided
    4 ears corn, husks and silk removed, cut into thirds
   12 ounces andouille sausage, sliced 1 inch thick
    4 (6- to 8-ounce) skinless halibut fillets,
       1 to 1½ inches thick
    1 tablespoon minced fresh parsley

1. Adjust oven rack to lowest position and heat oven to 500 degrees. Mash butter, Old Bay, and lemon juice together in bowl; set aside for serving.

2. Brush rimmed baking sheet with 1 tablespoon oil. Toss potatoes with 2 tablespoons oil, ¼ teaspoon salt, and ¼ teaspoon pepper in bowl, then place cut side down on half of sheet. Toss corn in now-empty bowl with remaining 1 tablespoon oil, ¼ teaspoon salt, and ⅛ teaspoon pepper, then place on empty side of sheet. Nestle andouille onto sheet around corn. Roast until potatoes and andouille are lightly browned and corn kernels are plump, 20 to 25 minutes, rotating sheet halfway through roasting.

3. Remove sheet from oven and reduce oven temperature to 425 degrees. Transfer corn to clean bowl, leaving andouille and potatoes on sheet. Add 2 tablespoons Old Bay butter to corn, toss to coat, and cover bowl tightly with aluminum foil to keep warm; set aside for serving.

4. Pat halibut dry with paper towels and sprinkle with remaining ½ teaspoon salt and remaining ¼ teaspoon pepper. Slide andouille to side of sheet with potatoes, then place halibut skinned side up on now-empty side of sheet. Continue to roast potatoes, andouille, and halibut until fish flakes apart when gently prodded with paring knife and registers 140 degrees, 8 to 10 minutes, rotating sheet halfway through roasting.

5. Remove sheet from oven. Transfer potatoes, andouille, and halibut, browned side up, to serving platter. Dot remaining Old Bay butter over halibut, cover platter with foil, and let rest for 5 minutes. Add corn to platter, sprinkle with parsley, and serve.

Halibut with Warm Bean Salad
SLOW COOKER
Serves 4
Cook Time 1 to 2 hours on low

Why This Recipe Works Here, the slow cooker offers a hands-off, gentle cooking method to turn out meaty halibut fillets on a bed of creamy white beans. In the short time it took the fish to cook through perfectly, the beans absorbed the flavors of the cooking liquid. After removing the fish from the slow cooker, we drained the beans and tossed them with a zesty dressing and green beans (which we steamed in the microwave, leaving them tender). Briny kalamata olives and fresh tarragon intensified the overall flavor. Striped bass and swordfish are good substitutes for the halibut. To ensure that your fish cooks evenly, purchase fillets that are similarly shaped and uniformly thick. Check the halibut's temperature after 1 hour of cooking and continue to monitor until it registers 140 degrees. You will need an oval slow cooker for this recipe.

    1 (15-ounce) can small white beans, rinsed
    1 shallot, sliced thin
    2 (2-inch) strips lemon zest, plus 1 tablespoon
       juice, divided
    2 bay leaves
    4 (6- to 8-ounce) skinless halibut fillets,
       1 to 1½ inches thick
    3 tablespoons extra-virgin olive oil, divided
    ½ teaspoon table salt
    ¼ teaspoon pepper
    8 ounces green beans, trimmed and cut into
       1-inch lengths
    2 tablespoons minced fresh tarragon
    1 teaspoon Dijon mustard
    1 teaspoon honey
    2 tablespoons chopped pitted kalamata olives

1. Stir beans, ½ cup water, shallot, lemon zest, and bay leaves into slow cooker. Rub halibut with 1 tablespoon oil and sprinkle with salt and pepper. Nestle halibut into slow cooker. Cover and cook until halibut flakes apart when gently prodded with paring knife and registers 140 degrees, 1 to 2 hours on low.

2. Microwave green beans with 1 tablespoon water in covered bowl, stirring occasionally, until tender, 4 to 6 minutes. Drain green beans and return to now-empty bowl. Whisk remaining 2 tablespoons oil, lemon juice, tarragon, mustard, and honey together in separate bowl.

3. Transfer halibut to serving dish; discard lemon zest and bay leaves. Drain white bean mixture and transfer to bowl with green beans. Add dressing and olives and toss to combine. Season with salt and pepper to taste. Serve with halibut.

Cod with Warm Tabbouleh Salad

Cod with Warm Tabbouleh Salad

INSTANT POT

Serves 4

Total Time 45 minutes

Why This Recipe Works Adding accessories to the electric pressure cooker is an easy way to make recipes more one-pot friendly. Here, we used the pressure cooker's included trivet and a soufflé dish to first steam bulgur to the perfect tenderness; this allowed us to quickly remove the bulgur when it was done so we could reuse the then-empty pot. Flaky cod was the perfect pairing, and we used a foil sling to ensure it would be equally as easy to remove. We layered slices of lemon under the cod to infuse it with citrusy flavor. To season the bulgur, we created a tabbouleh salad featuring a lemony dressing and fresh herbs. Although it's often served at room temperature, we found this salad to be surprisingly elegant warm (this also cut down on waiting time). We stirred together our still-warm bulgur with some sweet cherry tomatoes, a generous helping of parsley and mint, and the lemon vinaigrette. Haddock and striped bass are good substitutes for the cod. Thin tail-end fillets can be folded to achieve proper thickness. The cod should

register about 135 degrees after cooking; if it doesn't, partially cover the pot with the lid and continue to cook using the highest sauté or browning function until the desired temperature is achieved. You will need a 1½-quart round soufflé dish or ceramic dish of similar size for this recipe. If your electric pressure cooker didn't come with a trivet, you can make your own (see page 365).

- 1 cup medium-grind bulgur, rinsed
- 1 teaspoon table salt, divided
- 1 lemon, sliced ¼ inch thick, plus 2 tablespoons juice, divided
- 4 (6- to 8-ounce) skinless cod fillets, 1½ inches thick
- 3 tablespoons extra-virgin olive oil, divided, plus extra for drizzling
- ¼ teaspoon pepper
- 1 small shallot, minced
- 10 ounces cherry tomatoes, halved
- 1 cup chopped fresh parsley
- ½ cup chopped fresh mint

1. Arrange trivet included with electric pressure cooker in base of insert and add 1 cup water. Fold sheet of aluminum foil into 16 by 6-inch sling, then rest 1½-quart round soufflé dish in center of sling. Combine 1 cup water, bulgur, and ½ teaspoon salt in dish. Using sling, lower soufflé dish into pot and onto trivet; allow narrow edges of sling to rest along sides of insert.

2. Lock lid in place and close pressure release valve. Select high pressure cook function and cook for 3 minutes. Turn off pressure cooker and quick-release pressure. Carefully remove lid, allowing steam to escape away from you. Using sling, transfer soufflé dish to wire rack; set aside to cool. Remove trivet; do not discard sling or water in pot.

3. Arrange lemon slices widthwise in 2 rows across center of sling. Brush cod with 1 tablespoon oil and sprinkle with remaining ½ teaspoon salt and pepper. Arrange cod skinned side down in even layer on top of lemon slices. Using sling, lower cod into pressure cooker; allow narrow edges of sling to rest along sides of insert. Lock lid in place and close pressure release valve. Select high pressure cook function and cook for 3 minutes.

4. Meanwhile, whisk remaining 2 tablespoons oil, lemon juice, and shallot together in large bowl. Add bulgur, tomatoes, parsley, and mint, and gently toss to combine. Season with salt and pepper to taste.

5. Turn off pressure cooker and quick-release pressure. Carefully remove lid, allowing steam to escape away from you. Using sling, transfer cod to large plate. Gently lift and tilt fillets with spatula to remove lemon slices. Serve cod with salad, drizzling individual portions with extra oil.

Braised Halibut with Leeks and Mustard

SKILLET

Serves 4
Total Time 35 minutes

Why This Recipe Works When it comes to methods for cooking fish, skillet braising, which involves cooking the fish in a small amount of liquid so that it gently simmers and steams, has a lot going for it. As a moist-heat cooking method, braising is gentle and thus forgiving, all but guaranteeing tender fish. Plus, it allows for a great one-pan meal: It's easy to add vegetables to the skillet to cook at the same time, and the cooking liquid becomes a sauce. We chose halibut for its sweet, delicate flavor and its firm texture, which made for easier handling, and paired it with classic French flavors of leeks, white wine, and Dijon mustard. Because the portion of the fillets submerged in liquid cooks more quickly than the upper half that cooks in the steam, we cooked the fillets for a few minutes in the pan on just one side and then braised them parcooked side up to even out the cooking. For the liquid component, wine supplemented by the juices released by the fish and leeks during cooking delivered a sauce with balanced flavor and just the right amount of brightness. Striped bass and swordfish are good substitutes for the halibut. To ensure that your fish cooks evenly, purchase fillets that are similarly shaped and uniformly thick. You will need a 12-inch skillet with a tight-fitting lid for this recipe.

- 4 (6- to 8-ounce) skinless halibut fillets, ¾ to 1 inch thick
- 1 teaspoon table salt, divided
- 6 tablespoons unsalted butter
- 1 pound leeks, white and light green parts only, halved lengthwise, sliced thin, and washed thoroughly
- 1 teaspoon Dijon mustard
- ¾ cup dry white wine
- 1 teaspoon lemon juice, plus lemon wedges for serving
- 1 tablespoon minced fresh parsley

1. Pat halibut dry with paper towels and sprinkle with ½ teaspoon salt. Melt butter in 12-inch skillet over low heat. Place halibut skinned side up in skillet, increase heat to medium, and cook, shaking skillet occasionally, until butter begins to brown (fish should not brown), 3 to 4 minutes. Using spatula, carefully transfer halibut to large plate, raw side down.

2. Add leeks, mustard, and remaining ½ teaspoon salt to fat left in skillet and cook, stirring frequently, until leeks begin to soften, 2 to 4 minutes. Stir in wine and bring to gentle simmer. Place halibut, raw side down, on top of leeks. Cover

skillet and cook, adjusting heat to maintain gentle simmer, until halibut flakes apart when gently prodded with paring knife and registers 140 degrees, 10 to 14 minutes. Remove skillet from heat and, using 2 spatulas, transfer halibut and leeks to serving platter or individual plates. Tent with aluminum foil.

3. Return skillet to high heat and simmer briskly until sauce is thickened, 2 to 3 minutes. Off heat, stir in lemon juice and season with salt and pepper to taste. Spoon sauce over halibut and sprinkle with parsley. Serve immediately with lemon wedges.

VARIATION

Braised Halibut with Carrots and Coriander for Two

SKILLET

Serves 2
Total Time 35 minutes

Striped bass and swordfish are good substitutes for the halibut. To ensure that your fish cooks evenly, purchase fillets that are similarly shaped and uniformly thick. You will need an 8-inch skillet with a tight-fitting lid for this recipe.

- 2 (6- to 8-ounce) skinless halibut fillets, ¾ to 1 inch thick
- ½ teaspoon table salt, divided
- 3 tablespoons unsalted butter
- 3 carrots, peeled and shaved with vegetable peeler lengthwise into ribbons
- 2 shallots, halved and sliced thin
- ¼ teaspoon ground coriander
- ⅓ cup dry white wine
- ¾ teaspoon lemon juice, plus lemon wedges for serving
- 1½ teaspoons minced fresh cilantro

1. Sprinkle halibut with ¼ teaspoon salt. Melt butter in 8-inch skillet over low heat. Place halibut skinned side up in skillet, increase heat to medium, and cook, shaking skillet occasionally, until butter begins to brown (fish should not brown), 2 to 3 minutes. Using spatula, carefully transfer halibut to large plate, raw side down.

2. Add carrots, shallots, coriander, and remaining ¼ teaspoon salt to fat left in skillet and cook, stirring frequently, until vegetables begin to soften, 1 to 2 minutes. Stir in wine and bring to gentle simmer. Place halibut, raw side down, on top of vegetables. Cover skillet and cook, adjusting heat to maintain gentle simmer, until halibut flakes apart when gently prodded with paring knife and registers 140 degrees, 10 to 14 minutes. Remove skillet from heat and, using 2 spatulas, transfer halibut and vegetables to serving platter or individual plates. Tent with aluminum foil.

3. Cook liquid left in skillet over high heat until sauce is thickened, 1 to 2 minutes. Off heat, stir in lemon juice and season with salt and pepper to taste. Spoon sauce over halibut and sprinkle with cilantro. Serve immediately with lemon wedges.

Braised Striped Bass with Zucchini and Tomatoes

INSTANT POT
Serves 4
Total Time 1 hour

Why This Recipe Works One of the most appealing attributes of an electric pressure cooker for one-pot meals is the ease with which you can switch between cooking functions to create the best environment for each element of a meal. We started by using the sauté function to cook zucchini, which we then set aside to avoid overcooking. Next we sautéed onion and other aromatics and added canned tomatoes, which would serve as a braising liquid for flaky-yet-meaty striped bass. Once the bass was in the pot, we switched to pressure cooking—the fish needed just long enough for the pot to come up to pressure. While the fish rested we added the zucchini back to the pot with the warm tomatoes and finished our stewed vegetables with briny olives. Halibut and swordfish are good substitutes for the striped bass here. To prevent the striped bass from overcooking, be sure to turn off the pressure cooker as soon as it reaches pressure. The striped bass should register about 135 degrees after cooking; if it doesn't, partially cover the pot with the lid and continue to cook using the highest sauté or browning function until the desired temperature is achieved.

- 2 tablespoons extra-virgin olive oil, divided, plus extra for drizzling
- 3 zucchini (8 ounces each), halved lengthwise and sliced ¼ inch thick
- 1 onion, chopped
- ¾ teaspoon table salt, divided
- 3 garlic cloves, minced
- 1 teaspoon minced fresh oregano or ¼ teaspoon dried
- ¼ teaspoon red pepper flakes
- 1 (28-ounce) can whole peeled tomatoes, drained with juice reserved, halved
- 1½ pounds skinless striped bass, 1 to 1½ inches thick, cut into 2-inch pieces
- ¼ teaspoon pepper
- 2 tablespoons chopped pitted kalamata olives
- 2 tablespoons shredded fresh mint

Braised Halibut with Leeks and Mustard

Braised Striped Bass with Zucchini and Tomatoes

**Braised Cod
with Peperonata**

1. Using highest sauté or browning function, heat 1 table-spoon oil in electric pressure cooker until just smoking. Add zucchini and cook until tender, about 5 minutes; transfer to bowl and set aside.

2. Add remaining 1 tablespoon oil, onion, and ¼ teaspoon salt to now-empty pressure cooker and cook, using highest sauté or browning function, until onion is softened, 3 to 5 minutes. Stir in garlic, oregano, and pepper flakes and cook until fragrant, about 30 seconds. Stir in tomatoes and reserved juice.

3. Sprinkle bass with remaining ½ teaspoon salt and pepper. Nestle bass into tomato mixture and spoon some of cooking liquid on top of pieces. Lock lid in place and close pressure release valve. Select high pressure cook function and set cook time for 0 minutes. Once pressure cooker has reached pressure, immediately turn off pot and quick-release pressure. Carefully remove lid, allowing steam to escape away from you.

4. Transfer bass to plate, tent with aluminum foil, and let rest while finishing vegetables. Stir zucchini into pot and let sit until heated through, about 5 minutes. Stir in olives and season with salt and pepper to taste. Serve bass with vegetables, sprinkling individual portions with mint and drizzling with extra oil.

Braised Cod with Peperonata
SKILLET
Serves 4
Total Time 45 minutes

Why This Recipe Works For this braised cod recipe, we cooked the fish with peperonata, a side dish that highlights sweet sautéed bell peppers. We laid down a base of sautéed onion, bell pepper, garlic, and paprika in a skillet, to which we added tomatoes, fresh thyme, and wine. Once our peperonata was prepared, we simply nestled the pieces of fish into the sauce, lowered the heat, covered the skillet, and let the fish cook in the steamy environment. We served the tender, moist cod topped with the peperonata. Haddock and striped bass are good substitutes for the cod. Thin tail-end fillets can be folded to achieve proper thickness. You will need a 12-inch nonstick skillet with a tight-fitting lid for this recipe.

- 2 tablespoons extra-virgin olive oil, plus extra for serving
- 1 onion, halved and sliced thin
- 2 red bell peppers, stemmed, seeded, and cut into ½-inch-wide strips
- 1 teaspoon table salt, divided
- 4 garlic cloves, minced
- 2 teaspoons paprika
- 1 (14.5-ounce) can diced tomatoes, drained
- ½ cup dry white wine
- 1 teaspoon minced fresh thyme or ¼ teaspoon dried
- 4 (6- to 8-ounce) skinless cod fillets, 1 to 1½ inches thick
- ¼ teaspoon pepper
- 2 tablespoons chopped fresh basil
  Balsamic or sherry vinegar

1. Heat oil in 12-inch nonstick skillet over medium-high heat until shimmering. Add onion, bell peppers, and ½ tea-spoon salt and cook until vegetables are softened, about 5 minutes. Stir in garlic and paprika and cook until fragrant, about 30 seconds. Stir in tomatoes, wine, and thyme and bring to simmer.

2. Sprinkle cod with remaining ½ teaspoon salt and pepper. Nestle cod skinned side down into skillet and spoon some of sauce over top. Bring to simmer. Reduce heat to medium-low, cover, and cook until cod flakes apart when gently prodded with paring knife and registers 140 degrees, about 10 minutes.

3. Transfer fish to individual plates. Stir basil into sauce and season with salt and pepper to taste. Spoon sauce over fish, drizzle with extra oil, and sprinkle lightly with vinegar before serving.

Thai Curry Rice with Cod

SKILLET
Serves 4
Total Time 45 minutes

Why This Recipe Works Cod's mild flavor makes it the perfect fish to infuse with the zesty, aromatic flavors of Thai curry. Though this dish could easily involve lots of prep and multiple pans, we layered the fish and a rice-and-vegetable side all in one skillet and timed everything just right for a minimalist but boldly flavored meal. To start, we enhanced our rice with meaty mushrooms and crunchy bamboo shoots; sautéing them all in a gingery scallion oil built lots of flavor quickly. After simmering the rice for 10 minutes, we laid fresh cod fillets on top, ensuring the fish and rice would finish at the same time. We prepared a simple coconut–red curry sauce and drizzled some over the cod to infuse the fish while it cooked. The cod exuded juices as it simmered, flavoring the rice from above and marrying all the elements. Sprinkled with scallions and served with extra sauce and a squeeze of lime, our cod was ready to serve. Haddock and striped bass are good substitutes for the cod. Thin tail-end fillets can be folded to achieve proper thickness. You will need a 12-inch nonstick skillet with a tight-fitting lid for this recipe.

Thai Curry Rice with Cod

- 1 tablespoon vegetable oil
- 1½ cups long-grain white rice
- 8 ounces white mushrooms, trimmed and sliced thin
- 1 (8-ounce) can bamboo shoots, rinsed
- 2 teaspoons grated fresh ginger
- 3 scallions, white and green parts separated and sliced thin
- 2¼ cups water
- 1 teaspoon table salt, divided
- ¾ cup canned coconut milk
- 3 tablespoons red curry paste
- 4 (6- to 8-ounce) skinless cod fillets, 1 to 1½ inches thick
- ¼ teaspoon pepper
- Lime wedges

1. Heat oil in 12-inch nonstick skillet over medium heat until shimmering. Add rice, mushrooms, bamboo shoots, ginger, and scallion whites. Cook, stirring often, until edges of rice begin to turn translucent, about 2 minutes. Stir in water and ½ teaspoon salt and bring to boil. Reduce heat to medium-low, cover, and simmer for 10 minutes.

2. Whisk coconut milk and curry paste together in bowl. Pat cod dry with paper towels and sprinkle with remaining ½ teaspoon salt and pepper. Lay cod skinned side down on top of rice mixture and drizzle with one-third of

Hake in Saffron Broth with Chorizo and Potatoes

coconut-curry sauce. Cover and cook until liquid is absorbed and cod flakes apart when gently prodded with paring knife and registers 140 degrees, 10 to 12 minutes.

3. Meanwhile, microwave remaining coconut-curry sauce mixture until warm, about 1 minute. Sprinkle scallion greens over fish and rice mixture. Serve with remaining coconut-curry sauce and lime wedges.

Hake in Saffron Broth with Chorizo and Potatoes

SKILLET
Serves 4
Total Time 1 hour

Why This Recipe Works Saffron's distinctive aroma and bright yellow-orange color pair particularly well with delicate fish; we wanted to create a Spanish-inspired seafood dish that cooked all in one skillet so every element was infused with this exquisite spice. Versatile, mild hake, a favorite white fish in Spain, was an ideal choice for the seafood. We created a saffron broth with aromatics, white wine, and clam juice in which we braised the fish; we also used some of this flavorful broth to ladle over the fillets before serving. Adding some spicy Spanish-style chorizo to the pan with the onion and sautéing it until browned added a pleasant smokiness. Waxy red potatoes, sliced into coins to mirror the slices of chorizo, brought in creaminess to soak up the flavorful broth. A hit of lemon added brightness to the broth at the end of cooking, and a sprinkle of parsley and drizzle of olive oil brought it all together. Haddock and cod are good substitutes for the hake. Use small red potatoes measuring 1 to 2 inches in diameter. You will need a 12-inch skillet with a tight-fitting lid for this recipe. Serve with crusty bread to dip into the broth.

- 1 tablespoon extra-virgin olive oil, plus extra for serving
- 1 onion, chopped fine
- 3 ounces Spanish-style chorizo sausage, sliced ¼ inch thick
- 4 garlic cloves, minced
- ¼ teaspoon saffron threads, crumbled
- 1 (8-ounce) bottle clam juice
- ¾ cup water
- ½ cup dry white wine
- 8 ounces small red potatoes, unpeeled, sliced ¼ inch thick
- 1 bay leaf
- 4 (6- to 8-ounce) skinless hake fillets, 1 to 1½ inches thick

Fish Tagine with Artichoke Hearts

½ teaspoon table salt
¼ teaspoon pepper
1 teaspoon lemon juice
2 tablespoons minced fresh parsley

1. Heat oil in 12-inch skillet over medium heat until shimmering. Add onion and chorizo and cook until onion is softened and lightly browned, 5 to 7 minutes. Stir in garlic and saffron and cook until fragrant, about 30 seconds. Stir in clam juice, water, wine, potatoes, and bay leaf and bring to simmer. Reduce heat to medium-low, cover, and cook until potatoes are almost tender, about 10 minutes.

2. Pat hake dry with paper towels and sprinkle with salt and pepper. Nestle hake skinned side down into skillet and spoon some broth over top. Bring to simmer, cover, and cook until potatoes are fully tender and hake flakes apart when gently prodded with paring knife and registers 140 degrees, 10 to 12 minutes.

3. Carefully transfer hake to individual shallow bowls. Using slotted spoon, divide potatoes and chorizo evenly among bowls. Discard bay leaf. Stir lemon juice into broth and season with salt and pepper to taste. Spoon broth over hake, sprinkle with parsley, and drizzle with extra oil. Serve.

Fish Tagine with Artichoke Hearts

SLOW COOKER

Serves 4 to 6

Cook Time 7 to 8 hours on low or 4 to 5 hours on high, plus 30 minutes on high

Why This Recipe Works Although we typically cook tagines in a Dutch oven, the slow cooker offers a similar hands-off environment. To create a fish tagine, we built a brothy base and let the vegetables simmer for several hours before adding the delicate fish at the end of the cooking time to absorb the tagine's flavors and poach gently. The broth started with white wine, diced tomatoes, and chicken broth. Microwaving onions and garlic with tomato paste and warm spices developed a complex flavor base for our tagine. We simmered this mixture with artichoke hearts until the broth was deeply flavorful and the artichokes were tender. Next we added the cod and allowed it to cook gently in the savory liquid for 30 minutes. Stirring in olives with the cod gave them time to warm through and lightly flavor the broth. All the tagine needed was a sprinkle of fresh parsley to finish. Haddock and striped bass are good substitutes for the cod. While we prefer the flavor and texture of jarred whole baby artichokes, you can substitute 18 ounces frozen artichoke hearts, thawed and patted dry, for the jarred. You will need an oval slow cooker for this recipe.

NOTES FROM THE TEST KITCHEN

BUYING AND STORING FISH

What to Look For Always buy fish from a trusted source (preferably one with high volume to help ensure freshness). The store, and the fish in it, should smell like the sea, not fishy or sour. All the fish should be on ice or properly refrigerated. Fillets and steaks should look bright, shiny, and firm, not dull or mushy. Whole fish should have moist, taut skin, clear eyes, and bright red gills.

What to Ask For It is always better to have your fishmonger slice steaks and fillets to order rather than buying precut pieces that may have been sitting around. Don't be afraid to be picky at the seafood counter; a ragged piece of fish will be difficult to cook properly. It is important to keep your fish cold, so if you have a long ride home, ask for a bag of ice.

Buying Frozen Fish Firm fillets such as halibut, snapper, tilapia, and salmon are acceptable to buy frozen if cooked beyond medium-rare, but at lower degrees of doneness they will have a dry, stringy texture. Make sure frozen fish is frozen solid, with no signs of freezer burn or excessive crystallization around the edges and no blood in the packaging. The ingredients should include only the name of the fish.

Defrosting Fish To defrost fish in the refrigerator overnight, remove the fish from its packaging, place it in a single layer on a rimmed plate or dish (to catch any water), and cover it with plastic wrap. You can also do a "quick thaw" by leaving the vacuum-sealed bags under cool running tap water for 30 minutes. Do not use a microwave to defrost fish; it will alter the texture of the fish or, worse, partially cook it. Dry the fish thoroughly with paper towels before seasoning and cooking it.

How to Store It If you're not using fish the same day you buy it, it's important to store it properly: Unwrap the fish, pat it dry, put it in a zipper-lock bag, press out the air, and seal the bag. Set the fish on a bed of ice in a bowl or container (to hold the water once the ice melts), and place it in the back of the fridge, where it' s coldest. If the ice melts before you use the fish, replenish it. The fish should keep for one day.

Bouillabaisse

2. Stir cod and olives into tagine, cover, and cook on high until cod flakes apart when gently prodded with paring knife, 30 to 40 minutes. Gently stir in parsley and season with salt and pepper to taste. Serve.

Bouillabaisse

DUTCH OVEN
Serves 6 to 8
Total Time 1 hour

Why This Recipe Works Bouillabaisse is a classic Provençal dish with humble origins, a fisherman's cost-effective family meal turned upscale seafood stew. It typically features a wide variety of fish and shellfish poached in a homemade broth that simmers for hours. Our goal was to create a streamlined adaptation that was still authentic in flavor. We limited our seafood to a diverse yet widely available combination of shrimp, scallops, and halibut. Wishing to have at least one shell-on mollusk in the mix, we added mussels for their delicate flavor and shorter cooking time. Rather than prepare a time-consuming home-made fish broth, we used bottled clam juice; fortified with sautéed aromatics, fennel, white wine, and a generous amount of garlic, it created a solidly flavorful broth. We added diced tomatoes and just enough saffron to perfume the broth, and then added fresh thyme and bay leaves. Striped bass and swordfish are good substitutes for the halibut. Serve with Rouille (page 253) and crusty bread, if desired.

- 2 onions, chopped fine
- 2 tablespoons tomato paste
- 4 garlic cloves, minced
- 1 tablespoon vegetable oil
- 2 teaspoons garam masala
- 1½ teaspoons paprika
- ¼ teaspoon cayenne pepper
- 3 cups jarred whole baby artichokes packed in water, halved, rinsed, and patted dry
- 2 cups chicken or vegetable broth
- 1 (14.5-ounce) can diced tomatoes, drained
- ¼ cup dry white wine
- ½ teaspoon table salt
- 1½ pounds skinless cod fillets, 1 to 1½ inches thick, cut into 2-inch pieces
- ½ cup pitted kalamata olives, chopped coarse
- 2 tablespoons minced fresh parsley

1. Microwave onions, tomato paste, garlic, oil, garam masala, paprika, and cayenne in bowl, stirring occasionally, until onions are softened, about 5 minutes; transfer to slow cooker. Stir in artichokes, broth, tomatoes, wine, and salt. Cover and cook until flavors meld, 7 to 8 hours on low or 4 to 5 hours on high.

- ¼ cup extra-virgin olive oil
- 1 small fennel bulb, stalks discarded, bulb halved, cored, and chopped fine
- 1 onion, chopped fine
- ½ teaspoon table salt
- 8 garlic cloves, minced
- 1 teaspoon minced fresh thyme or ¼ teaspoon dried
- ¼ teaspoon saffron threads, crumbled
- ⅛ teaspoon red pepper flakes
- ¾ cup dry white wine or dry vermouth
- 2 (8-ounce) bottles clam juice
- 1 (14.5-ounce) can whole peeled tomatoes, drained with juice reserved, chopped
- 2 bay leaves
- 1 pound skinless halibut fillets, ¾ to 1 inch thick, cut into 3- to 4-inch pieces
- 12 ounces mussels, scrubbed and debearded
- 1 pound large sea scallops, tendons removed
- 8 ounces medium-large shrimp (31 to 40 per pound), peeled and deveined
- 2 tablespoons minced fresh tarragon

1. Heat oil in Dutch oven over medium-high heat until shimmering. Add fennel, onion, and salt and cook until softened, about 5 minutes. Stir in garlic, thyme, saffron, and pepper flakes and cook until fragrant, about 30 seconds. Stir in wine and cook until slightly reduced, about 30 seconds.

2. Stir in clam juice, tomatoes and their juice, and bay leaves. Bring to simmer and cook until liquid has reduced by about half, 7 to 9 minutes.

3. Nestle halibut into pot, spoon some cooking liquid over top, and bring to simmer. Reduce heat to medium-low, cover, and simmer gently for 2 minutes. Nestle mussels and scallops into pot, cover, and continue to cook until halibut is almost cooked through, about 3 minutes.

4. Arrange shrimp evenly over stew, cover, and continue to cook until halibut flakes apart when gently prodded with paring knife, shrimp and scallops are firm and opaque in center, and mussels have opened, about 2 minutes.

5. Off heat, discard bay leaves and any mussels that refuse to open. Gently stir in tarragon and season with salt and pepper to taste. Serve in wide, shallow bowls.

Rouille

Makes about 1 cup

Rouille can be used as a sauce for fish and vegetables; leftover rouille can be refrigerated for up to 1 week.

- 3 tablespoons boiling water
- ¼ teaspoon saffron threads, crumbled
- 1 (3-inch) piece baguette, crusts removed, torn into 1-inch pieces (1 cup)
- 4 teaspoons lemon juice
- 1 large egg yolk
- 2 teaspoons Dijon mustard
- 2 small garlic cloves, minced
- ¼ teaspoon cayenne pepper
- ½ cup vegetable oil
- ½ cup extra-virgin olive oil

Combine boiling water and saffron in medium bowl and let steep for 5 minutes. Stir bread pieces and lemon juice into saffron-infused water and let soak for 5 minutes. Using whisk, mash soaked bread mixture until uniform paste forms, 1 to 2 minutes. Whisk in egg yolk, mustard, garlic, and cayenne until smooth, about 15 seconds. Whisking constantly, slowly drizzle in vegetable oil until smooth mayonnaise-like consistency is reached, scraping down bowl as necessary. Slowly whisk in olive oil in steady stream until smooth. Season with salt and pepper to taste.

California-Style Fish Tacos
SLOW COOKER
Serves 4
Cook Time 1 to 2 hours on low

Why This Recipe Works The best fish tacos are simple and fresh with a combination of tender fish, crisp sliced cabbage, and a tangy sauce. We wanted a hands-off recipe for fish tacos that we could prepare in our slow cooker without compromising flavor or texture. To start, we chose mild but sturdy halibut fillets and coated them with a spice rub that we bloomed in the microwave. We placed the fillets on a bed of sliced limes and added just enough water to steam the fish, ensuring that it would be moist and flaky. After trying a variety of dairy products for our sauce, we settled on a combination of two—mayonnaise and sour cream—for tangy flavor and richness. Lime juice and chipotle chiles gave the sauce citrusy tartness and a subtle, smoky heat. Mixing cabbage with fresh cilantro, scallions, and lime juice created a salad with nice crunch and was the perfect finishing touch. Striped bass and swordfish are good substitutes for the halibut. To ensure that your fish cooks evenly, purchase fillets that are similarly shaped and uniformly thick. Check the halibut's temperature after 1 hour of cooking and continue to monitor until it registers 140 degrees. For more information on warming tortillas, see page 116. You will need an oval slow cooker for this recipe.

- 1 lime, sliced ¼ inch thick, plus 3 tablespoons lime juice (2 limes), divided, plus lime wedges for serving
- 6 tablespoons minced fresh cilantro, divided, stems reserved
- ¼ cup dry white wine
- 2 tablespoons extra-virgin olive oil, divided
- 1 tablespoon minced canned chipotle chile in adobo sauce, divided
- ½ teaspoon ground coriander
- ¼ teaspoon ground cumin
- ¾ teaspoon table salt, divided
- ¼ teaspoon pepper
- 4 (6- to 8-ounce) skinless halibut fillets, 1 to 1½ inches thick
- 4 cups shredded green cabbage
- 3 scallions, sliced thin
- ¼ cup mayonnaise
- ¼ cup sour cream
- 2 garlic cloves, minced
- 12 (6-inch) corn tortillas, warmed

1. Fold sheet of aluminum foil into 12 by 9-inch sling and press widthwise into slow cooker. Arrange lime slices in single layer in bottom of prepared slow cooker. Scatter cilantro stems over lime slices. Add wine to slow cooker, then add water until liquid level is even with lime slices (about ¼ cup).

2. Microwave 1 tablespoon oil, 2 teaspoons chipotle, coriander, cumin, ½ teaspoon salt, and pepper in bowl until fragrant, about 30 seconds; let cool slightly. Rub halibut with spice mixture, then arrange in even layer on top of cilantro stems. Cover and cook until halibut flakes apart when gently prodded with paring knife and registers 140 degrees, 1 to 2 hours on low.

3. Combine cabbage, scallions, 2 tablespoons lime juice, ¼ cup cilantro, remaining ¼ teaspoon salt, and remaining 1 tablespoon oil in bowl. In separate bowl, combine mayonnaise, sour cream, garlic, remaining 1 tablespoon lime juice, remaining 2 tablespoons cilantro, and remaining 1 teaspoon chipotle. Season with salt and pepper to taste.

4. Using sling, transfer halibut to cutting board. Gently lift and tilt fillets with spatula to remove cilantro stems and lime slices; discard poaching liquid and remove any white albumin from halibut. Cut each fillet into 3 equal pieces. Spread sauce evenly onto warm tortillas, top with fish and cabbage mixture, and serve with lime wedges.

Shrimp Fajitas

Shrimp Fajitas

SKILLET

Serves 4
Total Time 1¼ hours

Why This Recipe Works While chicken or beef are the more common choices for fajitas, simply seasoned shrimp shines when draped with onions and peppers and wrapped in warm flour tortillas. But shrimp is also easy to overcook, so we wanted to develop a method that would guarantee perfectly tender, not rubbery, shrimp fajitas. The filling for fajitas is often grilled, but for a more foolproof approach we decided to bring the shrimp indoors and use a skillet; cooked this way, we could closely monitor their progress. To infuse our shrimp with flavor, we marinated them briefly in an aromatic mixture of garlic, lime, cumin seeds, and a small amount of chipotle in adobo sauce for some smoky spice. While the shrimp marinated, we cooked our pepper and onion topping in the skillet; after setting the vegetables aside we seared the shrimp until golden brown and succulent. A sprinkling of cilantro and a squeeze of lime juice brightened up the shrimp and vegetables and brought all the flavors together perfectly. If your shrimp are treated with salt, omit the salt in step 1.

6 tablespoons extra-virgin olive oil, divided
2 tablespoons lime juice, plus lime wedges for serving
4 garlic cloves, peeled and smashed
1 teaspoon minced canned chipotle chile in adobo sauce
1 teaspoon sugar
1 teaspoon cumin seeds, divided
1½ teaspoons table salt, divided
½ teaspoon pepper
⅛ teaspoon cayenne pepper
1½ pounds large shrimp (26 to 30 per pound), peeled, deveined, and tails removed
2 red bell peppers, stemmed, seeded, and sliced thin
1 large red onion, halved and sliced thin
¼ cup minced fresh cilantro
8–12 (6-inch) flour tortillas, warmed

1. Whisk 3 tablespoons oil, lime juice, garlic, chipotle, sugar, ½ teaspoon cumin seeds, 1 teaspoon salt, pepper, and cayenne together in large bowl. Add shrimp and toss to coat. Cover and refrigerate for 30 minutes.

2. Heat 1 tablespoon oil in 12-inch nonstick skillet over medium-high heat until shimmering. Add bell peppers, onion, remaining ½ teaspoon cumin seeds, and remaining ½ teaspoon salt and cook until peppers are soft and onion is browned, about 8 minutes. Transfer to serving bowl and season with salt and pepper to taste.

3. Wipe skillet clean with paper towels. Remove garlic from shrimp marinade and discard. Heat 1 tablespoon oil in now-empty skillet over high heat until just smoking. Add half of shrimp to skillet in single layer and cook until spotty brown and edges turn pink, 1 to 2 minutes. Remove skillet from heat and flip each shrimp over using tongs. Cover and let shrimp sit off heat until just cooked through, 1 to 2 minutes; transfer to separate bowl and cover to keep warm.

4. Repeat with remaining 1 tablespoon oil and remaining shrimp. Toss shrimp with cilantro and serve with vegetables, warm tortillas, and lime wedges.

Mediterranean Shrimp

SHEET PAN

Serves 4 to 6
Total Time 1 hour

Why This Recipe Works Bold spices infuse quick-cooking shrimp with big flavor, and adding a vegetable side easily turns this dish into a simple weeknight meal with little fuss and lots of flavor. Rather than searing, grilling, or frying—all common methods for cooking shrimp—we opted to roast our shrimp on a sheet pan; not only was this method simple, but the sheet pan's ample surface area allowed us to cook our vegetables at the same time. Inspired by the flavors of the Mediterranean, we seasoned the shrimp with oregano and lemon zest along with a little oil, salt, and pepper. Since shrimp cook so quickly, we jump-started our vegetables—potatoes and fennel—before scattering the shellfish over the top to finish in the oven. Briny kalamata olives and salty feta cheese gave this simple dish a savory finish, and lemon juice brought it all to life. Don't core the fennel before cutting it into wedges; the core helps hold the wedges together during cooking.

1½ pounds Yukon Gold potatoes, peeled and sliced ½ inch thick
2 fennel bulbs, stalks discarded, bulbs halved and cut into 1-inch-thick wedges
3 tablespoons extra-virgin olive oil, divided, plus extra for drizzling
1½ teaspoons table salt, divided
½ teaspoon pepper, divided

2 pounds jumbo shrimp (16 to 20 per pound), peeled, deveined, and tails removed
2 teaspoons dried oregano
1 teaspoon grated lemon zest, plus lemon wedges for serving
4 ounces feta cheese, crumbled (1 cup)
½ cup pitted kalamata olives, halved
2 tablespoons chopped fresh parsley

1. Adjust oven rack to lower-middle position and heat oven to 450 degrees. Toss potatoes and fennel with 2 tablespoons oil, 1 teaspoon salt, and ¼ teaspoon pepper in bowl. Spread vegetables in single layer on rimmed baking sheet and roast until just tender, about 25 minutes.

2. Pat shrimp dry with paper towels. Toss shrimp with oregano, lemon zest, remaining 1 tablespoon oil, remaining ½ teaspoon salt, and remaining ¼ teaspoon pepper in now-empty bowl.

3. Using spatula, flip potatoes and fennel so browned sides are facing up. Scatter shrimp and feta over top. Return to oven and roast until shrimp are cooked through, 6 to 8 minutes. Sprinkle olives and parsley over top and drizzle with extra oil. Serve with lemon wedges.

VARIATION

Mediterranean Shrimp for Two

SHEET PAN

Serves 2
Total Time 1 hour

Don't core the fennel before cutting it into wedges; the core helps hold the wedges together during cooking.

12 ounces Yukon Gold potatoes, peeled and sliced ½ inch thick
1 fennel bulb, stalks discarded, bulb halved and cut into 1-inch-thick wedges
2 tablespoons extra-virgin olive oil, divided, plus extra for drizzling
¾ teaspoon table salt, divided
¼ teaspoon pepper, divided
1 pound jumbo shrimp (16 to 20 per pound), peeled, deveined, and tails removed
1 teaspoon dried oregano
½ teaspoon grated lemon zest, plus lemon wedges for serving
2 ounces feta cheese, crumbled (½ cup)
¼ cup pitted kalamata olives, halved
1 tablespoon chopped fresh parsley

1. Adjust oven rack to lower-middle position and heat oven to 450 degrees. Toss potatoes and fennel with 1 tablespoon oil,

½ teaspoon salt, and ⅛ teaspoon pepper in bowl. Spread vegetables in single layer on rimmed baking sheet and roast until just tender, about 25 minutes.

2. Pat shrimp dry with paper towels. Toss shrimp with oregano, lemon zest, remaining 1 tablespoon oil, remaining ¼ teaspoon salt, and remaining ⅛ teaspoon pepper in now-empty bowl.

3. Using spatula, flip potatoes and fennel so browned sides are facing up. Scatter shrimp and feta over top. Return to oven and roast until shrimp are cooked through, 6 to 8 minutes. Sprinkle olives and parsley over top and drizzle with extra oil. Serve with lemon wedges.

Shrimp with Spiced Quinoa and Corn Salad

SLOW COOKER

Serves 4

Cook Time 3 to 4 hours on low or 2 to 3 hours on high, plus 30 minutes on high

Why This Recipe Works To create a main course featuring both quinoa and quick-cooking shrimp, we turned to the slow cooker, which would allow us to cook both together in the same pot by staggering the cooking times. Jalapeños, scallions, and chili powder gave the quinoa a hit of spicy heat. To keep the quinoa grains separate and fluffy during cooking, we quickly toasted them in the microwave before adding them to the slow cooker. The heat of the slow cooker further toasted our grains, giving a nicely caramelized flavor to our salad. We then added in the shrimp, along with some corn to round out our salad's Southwestern flavor profile. A fresh salsa made with tomatoes, cilantro, scallions, and lime juice and a sprinkling of Cotija cheese perfectly complemented our salad. We like the convenience of prewashed quinoa; rinsing removes the quinoa's bitter protective coating (called saponin). If you buy unwashed quinoa, rinse it and then spread it out on a clean dish towel to dry for 15 minutes. Do not substitute larger shrimp here; they will not cook through in time. You will need an oval slow cooker for this recipe.

- 1 cup prewashed white quinoa
- 2 scallions, white parts minced, green parts cut into ½-inch pieces, divided
- 2 jalapeño chiles, stemmed, seeded, and minced
- 2 tablespoons extra-virgin olive oil, divided
- 1 teaspoon chili powder
- 1⅓ cups water
- ¾ teaspoon table salt, divided

- 1 pound large shrimp (26 to 30 per pound), peeled, deveined, and tails removed
- ¾ cup frozen corn, thawed
- 3 tomatoes, cored and chopped
- ⅓ cup minced fresh cilantro
- 1 tablespoon lime juice
- ¼ teaspoon pepper
- 2 ounces Cotija cheese, crumbled (½ cup)

1. Lightly coat slow cooker with vegetable oil spray. Microwave quinoa, scallion whites, jalapeños, 1 tablespoon oil, and chili powder in bowl, stirring occasionally, until vegetables are softened, about 2 minutes; transfer to prepared slow cooker. Stir in water and ½ teaspoon salt. Cover and cook until water is absorbed and quinoa is tender, 3 to 4 hours on low or 2 to 3 hours on high.

2. Fluff quinoa with fork, then nestle shrimp into quinoa and sprinkle with corn. Cover and cook on high until shrimp are opaque throughout, 30 to 40 minutes.

3. Combine tomatoes, cilantro, lime juice, scallion greens, remaining 1 tablespoon oil, remaining ¼ teaspoon salt, and pepper in bowl. Sprinkle quinoa and shrimp with Cotija and serve, passing salsa separately.

Shrimp and Asparagus Risotto

INSTANT POT

Serves 4

Total Time 1 hour

Why This Recipe Works Labor-intensive risotto is often relegated to special-occasion menus, but the pressure cooker's concentrated, moist heat and closed cooking environment make luxurious shrimp and asparagus risotto attainable any day of the week. We used the sauté function to cook the asparagus and then set it aside to ensure it stayed al dente. After toasting the rice, we added wine and broth and cooked it under pressure. Stirring the asparagus and shrimp into the cooked rice allowed the shrimp to steam gently, achieving flawlessly tender results. Parmesan added to the velvety texture. Arborio rice, which is high in starch, gives risotto its characteristic creaminess; do not substitute other types of rice. Do not substitute larger shrimp here; they will not cook through in time.

- ¼ cup extra-virgin olive oil, divided
- 8 ounces asparagus, trimmed and cut on bias into 1-inch lengths
- ½ onion, chopped fine
- ¼ teaspoon table salt

1½ cups Arborio rice

3 garlic cloves, minced

½ cup dry white wine

3 cups chicken or vegetable broth, plus extra as needed

1 pound large shrimp (26 to 30 per pound), peeled and deveined

2 ounces Parmesan cheese, grated (1 cup)

1 tablespoon lemon juice

1 tablespoon minced fresh chives

1. Using highest sauté or browning function, heat 1 tablespoon oil in electric pressure cooker until shimmering. Add asparagus, partially cover, and cook until just crisp-tender, about 4 minutes. Using slotted spoon, transfer asparagus to bowl; set aside.

2. Add onion, 2 tablespoons oil, and salt to now-empty pressure cooker and cook, using highest sauté or browning function, until onion is softened, 3 to 5 minutes. Stir in rice and garlic and cook until grains are translucent around edges, about 3 minutes. Stir in wine and cook until nearly evaporated, about 1 minute.

3. Stir in broth, scraping up any rice that sticks to bottom of pressure cooker. Lock lid in place and close pressure release valve. Select high pressure cook function and cook for 7 minutes.

4. Turn off pressure cooker and quick-release pressure. Carefully remove lid, allowing steam to escape away from you. Stir shrimp and asparagus into risotto, cover, and let sit until shrimp are opaque throughout, 5 to 7 minutes. Add Parmesan and remaining 1 tablespoon oil, and stir vigorously until risotto becomes creamy. Adjust consistency with extra hot broth as needed. Stir in lemon juice and season with salt and pepper to taste. Sprinkle individual portions with chives before serving.

PEELING AND DEVEINING SHRIMP

1. Break shell under swimming legs, which will come off as shell is removed. Leave tail intact if desired, or tug tail to remove shell.

2. Use paring knife to make shallow cut along back of shrimp to expose vein. Use tip of knife to lift out vein. Discard vein by wiping blade against paper towel.

Shrimp with Spiced Quinoa and Corn Salad

Shrimp and Asparagus Risotto

Cajun-Style Rice with
Andouille, Shrimp, and Okra

Indoor Paella

Cajun-Style Rice with Andouille, Shrimp, and Okra

CASSEROLE DISH
Serves 4
Total Time 1¼ hours

Why This Recipe Works Jambalaya is a Cajun favorite that can require a lot of standing at the stove. We decided to take jambalaya's spicy, bold flavors and apply them to a dish that could be baked in the oven. Blooming Cajun seasoning in the microwave with onion, garlic, and celery brought the flavors to life before we combined the mixture with rice. Using chicken broth as our cooking liquid promised rice with rich flavor, and adding canned diced tomatoes delivered juicy brightness. Once everything was combined in the casserole dish, we covered it tightly with aluminum foil to ensure gently steamed grains. We added andouille sausage, shrimp, and okra to cook in the last 10 minutes of baking. Spiciness will vary between the different brands of Cajun seasoning; start with the lesser amount and add more to taste. If andouille is not available, Portuguese linguiça or Polish kielbasa can be substituted.

 2 celery ribs, chopped fine
 1 onion, chopped fine
 3 garlic cloves, minced
 1 tablespoon extra-virgin olive oil
2–3 teaspoons Cajun seasoning
 1 teaspoon table salt
 ¼ teaspoon pepper
1⅓ cups long-grain white rice
 1 (14.5-ounce) can diced tomatoes, drained
2¾ cups chicken broth
 12 ounces large shrimp (26 to 30 per pound), peeled and deveined
 12 ounces andouille sausage, sliced ¼ inch thick on bias
1½ cups frozen sliced okra, thawed
 2 scallions, sliced thin
  Hot sauce

1. Adjust oven rack to middle position and heat oven to 450 degrees. Combine celery, onion, garlic, oil, Cajun seasoning, salt, and pepper in bowl and microwave, stirring occasionally, until vegetables are softened, about 5 minutes. Transfer vegetables to 13 by 9-inch baking dish and stir in rice and tomatoes.

2. Microwave broth in covered bowl until steaming, about 3 minutes, then pour over mixture in dish. Cover dish tightly with aluminum foil and bake until rice is nearly tender, 25 to 30 minutes.

3. Remove foil, fluff rice with fork, and gently stir in shrimp, andouille, and okra. Cover tightly with foil and continue to bake until rice is tender, sausage and okra are warmed through, and shrimp is opaque throughout, 10 to 15 minutes.

4. Remove dish from oven and let cool for 10 minutes. Fluff rice gently with fork, sprinkle with scallions, and serve with hot sauce.

Indoor Paella

DUTCH OVEN
Serves 6
Total Time 1¾ hours

Why This Recipe Works Traditional paella cooks in a wide, shallow pan over an open fire, but we wanted a simplified version that stayed true to this Spanish rice dish's heritage without relying on specialty equipment or ingredients. First, we substituted a Dutch oven for the traditional paella pan. Paring down the sometimes lengthy ingredient list was next; chorizo, chicken thighs, tomatoes (canned rather than fresh), shrimp, and mussels made the cut. Bomba rice is traditional, but we opted for Arborio instead. Chicken broth, white wine, saffron, and a bay leaf added liquid and flavor. Dry-cured Spanish chorizo is the sausage of choice for paella, but fresh chorizo or linguiça sausage will work. Socarrat, a layer of browned rice, is a traditional part of paella. Here, socarrat does not develop because most of the cooking is done in the oven; if desired, there are socarrat directions in step 7. Use a Dutch oven that holds 6 quarts or more for this recipe.

- 1 pound extra-large shrimp (21 to 25 per pound), peeled and deveined
- 2 tablespoons extra-virgin olive oil, divided, plus extra as needed
- 8 garlic cloves, minced, divided
- 1 teaspoon table salt, divided
- ½ teaspoon pepper, divided
- 1 pound boneless, skinless chicken thighs, trimmed and halved crosswise
- 1 red bell pepper, stemmed, seeded, and cut into ½-inch-wide strips
- 8 ounces Spanish-style chorizo sausage, sliced on bias ½ inch thick
- 1 onion, chopped fine
- 1 (14.5-ounce) can diced tomatoes, drained, minced, and drained again
- 2 cups Arborio rice
- 3 cups chicken broth
- ⅓ cup dry white wine
- ½ teaspoon saffron threads, crumbled
- 1 bay leaf
- 12 mussels, scrubbed and debearded
- ½ cup frozen peas, thawed
- 2 teaspoons chopped fresh parsley
  Lemon wedges

1. Adjust oven rack to lower-middle position and heat oven to 350 degrees. Toss shrimp with 1 tablespoon oil, 1 teaspoon garlic, ¼ teaspoon salt, and ¼ teaspoon pepper in bowl until evenly coated. Cover and refrigerate until needed. Pat chicken dry with paper towels and sprinkle with ¼ teaspoon salt and remaining ¼ teaspoon pepper.

2. Heat 2 teaspoons oil in large Dutch oven over medium-high heat until shimmering. Add bell pepper and cook, stirring occasionally, until skin begins to blister and turn spotty black, about 4 minutes; transfer to bowl.

3. Heat remaining 1 teaspoon oil in now-empty pot until shimmering. Add chicken in single layer and cook, without moving, until browned, about 3 minutes. Turn pieces and cook until browned on second side, about 3 minutes; transfer to separate bowl. Reduce heat to medium and add chorizo to now-empty pot. Cook, stirring frequently, until deeply browned and fat begins to render, about 5 minutes; transfer to bowl with chicken.

4. Add extra oil to fat left in pot to equal 2 tablespoons and heat over medium heat until shimmering. Add onion and cook until softened, about 3 minutes. Stir in remaining garlic and cook until fragrant, about 1 minute. Stir in tomatoes and cook until mixture begins to darken and thicken slightly, about 3 minutes. Stir in rice and cook until grains are well coated with tomato mixture, about 2 minutes.

5. Stir in broth, wine, saffron, bay leaf, and remaining ½ teaspoon salt. Return chicken and chorizo to pot, increase heat to medium-high, and bring to boil, stirring occasionally. Cover, transfer pot to oven, and bake until almost all liquid is absorbed, 15 to 20 minutes.

6. Remove pot from oven. Scatter shrimp and mussels evenly over rice and push hinge side of mussels into rice so they stand up. Cover, return pot to oven, and bake until shrimp are opaque throughout and mussels have opened, 10 to 15 minutes.

7. For optional socarrat, transfer pot to stovetop and remove lid. Cook over medium-high heat for about 5 minutes, rotating pot as needed, until bottom layer of rice is well browned and crisp.

8. Discard any mussels that refuse to open and bay leaf, if it can be easily removed. Arrange bell pepper strips in pinwheel pattern over rice and sprinkle peas over top. Cover and let paella sit for 5 minutes. Sprinkle with parsley and serve with lemon wedges.

Indoor Paella for Two

SAUCEPAN

Serves 2

Total Time 1¾ hours

Dry-cured Spanish chorizo is the sausage of choice for paella, but fresh chorizo or linguiça sausage will work. Socarrat, a layer of browned rice, is a traditional part of paella. Here, socarrat does not develop because most of the cooking is done in the oven; if desired, there are socarrat directions in step 7.

- 8 ounces extra-large shrimp (21 to 25 per pound), peeled and deveined
- 2 tablespoons extra-virgin olive oil, divided
- 3 garlic cloves, minced, divided
- ½ teaspoon table salt, divided
- ¼ teaspoon pepper, divided
- 1 (3- to 5-ounce) boneless, skinless chicken thigh, trimmed and halved crosswise
- 1 small red bell pepper, stemmed, seeded, and cut into ½-inch-wide strips
- 4 ounces Spanish-style chorizo sausage, sliced ½ inch thick on bias
- 1 shallot, chopped fine
- 1 tablespoon tomato paste
- ⅔ cup Arborio rice
- 1 cup chicken broth
- 1 tablespoon lemon juice, plus lemon wedges for serving
- ⅛ teaspoon saffron threads, crumbled
- 1 bay leaf
- 6 mussels, scrubbed and debearded (optional)
- 2 tablespoons frozen peas, thawed
- 1 teaspoon chopped fresh parsley

1. Adjust oven rack to lower-middle position and heat oven to 350 degrees. Toss shrimp with 2 teaspoons oil, ½ teaspoon garlic, ⅛ teaspoon salt, and ⅛ teaspoon pepper in bowl until evenly coated. Cover and refrigerate until needed. Pat chicken dry with paper towels and sprinkle with ⅛ teaspoon salt and remaining ⅛ teaspoon pepper.

2. Heat 2 teaspoons oil in large saucepan over medium heat until shimmering. Add bell pepper and cook, stirring occasionally, until skin begins to blister and turn spotty black, 4 to 6 minutes; transfer to bowl.

3. Heat remaining 2 teaspoons oil in now-empty saucepan until shimmering. Add chicken and cook, without moving, until browned, about 3 minutes. Turn pieces and cook until browned on second side, about 3 minutes; transfer to separate bowl. Reduce heat to medium-low and add chorizo to now-empty saucepan. Cook, stirring frequently, until deeply browned and fat begins to render, 3 to 5 minutes; transfer to bowl with chicken.

4. Pour off all but 1 tablespoon fat from saucepan. Add shallot and cook over medium heat until softened, about 2 minutes. Stir in remaining garlic and tomato paste and cook until fragrant, about 30 seconds. Stir in rice and cook until grains are well coated with tomato mixture, about 1 minute.

5. Stir in broth, lemon juice, saffron, bay leaf, and remaining ¼ teaspoon salt. Return chicken and chorizo to saucepan, increase heat to medium-high, and bring to boil, stirring occasionally. Cover, transfer saucepan to oven, and bake until almost all liquid is absorbed, 15 to 20 minutes.

6. Remove saucepan from oven. Scatter shrimp and mussels, if using, evenly over rice and push hinge side of mussels into rice so they stand up at an angle. Cover, return saucepan to oven, and bake until shrimp are opaque throughout and mussels have opened, 10 to 15 minutes.

7. For optional socarrat, transfer saucepan to stovetop and remove lid. Cook over medium heat for about 5 minutes, rotating saucepan as needed, until bottom layer of rice is well browned and crisp.

8. Discard any mussels that refuse to open and bay leaf, if it can be easily removed. Arrange bell pepper strips in pinwheel pattern over rice and sprinkle peas over top. Cover and let paella sit for 5 minutes. Sprinkle with parsley and serve with lemon wedges.

NOTES FROM THE TEST KITCHEN

BUYING SHRIMP

Virtually all of the shrimp sold in supermarkets today have been previously frozen, either in large blocks of ice or by a method called "individually quick-frozen," or IQF for short. Supermarkets simply defrost the shrimp before displaying them on ice at the fish counter. We highly recommend purchasing bags of still-frozen shrimp and defrosting them as needed at home, since there is no telling how long "fresh" shrimp may have been kept on ice at the market. IQF shrimp have a better flavor and texture than shrimp frozen in blocks, and they are convenient because it's easy to defrost just the amount you need. Shrimp are sold both with and without their shells, but we find shell-on shrimp to be firmer and sweeter. Also, shrimp should be the only ingredient listed on the bag; some packagers add preservatives, but we find treated shrimp to have an unpleasant, rubbery texture.

Shrimp Skewers with Cheesy Grits

Shrimp Skewers with Cheesy Grits

CASEROLE DISH

Serves 4 to 6
Total Time 1½ hours

Why This Recipe Works The much-loved combination of Lowcountry-style shrimp and creamy grits doesn't immediately conjure up images of a casserole dish, but we thought this vessel had the potential to turn out a hands-off version of this comfort classic. A baking dish was certainly big enough to cook grits for four to six people, and across its low sides we could perch rows of seasoned shrimp suspended on skewers. We started by combining the dry grits with bold flavorings, chicken broth, and milk right in our casserole dish, covering it, and baking until the grits were tender. Adding cheddar cheese at this point (rather than at the start of baking) kept it from breaking down into an oily mess. Meanwhile, we tossed the shrimp with melted butter and chili powder, threaded them on skewers, and balanced them on the casserole. After 10 more minutes, the shrimp emerged tender and spicy above the now-thickened grits. Since we hadn't sautéed the shrimp in a sauce, we created a simple, fragrant mixture of butter, chili

powder, and smoky chipotle chile powder to drizzle over our meal and tie the whole thing together. Chopped scallions and lime wedges finished the dish with a burst of fresh brightness. The grits' cooking time in step 1 will depend on the brand of grits. You will need eight 12-inch metal or bamboo skewers for this recipe.

4½ cups chicken or vegetable broth
1½ cups old-fashioned grits
¾ cup whole milk
3 scallions, white parts minced, green parts sliced thin on bias, divided
2 garlic cloves, minced
½ teaspoon plus ⅛ teaspoon table salt, divided
1½ pounds jumbo shrimp (16 to 20 per pound), peeled and deveined
4 tablespoons unsalted butter, melted, divided
2 teaspoons chili powder, divided
¼ teaspoon pepper
6 ounces sharp cheddar cheese, shredded (1½ cups)
1 teaspoon chipotle chile powder
Lime wedges

1. Adjust oven rack to middle position and heat oven to 350 degrees. Spray 13 by 9-inch baking dish with vegetable oil spray. Combine broth, grits, milk, scallion whites, garlic, and ¼ teaspoon salt in prepared dish, cover tightly with aluminum foil, and bake until grits are tender, 50 to 75 minutes.

2. Toss shrimp with 1 tablespoon melted butter, 1 teaspoon chili powder, pepper, and ¼ teaspoon salt. Working with 1 shrimp at a time, thread tail onto one 12-inch skewer, and head onto second 12-inch skewer. Repeat with remaining shrimp, alternating direction of heads and tails, packing 6 to 8 shrimp tightly onto each pair of skewers.

3. Remove grits from oven, uncover, and increase oven temperature to 450 degrees. Stir cheddar into grits and season with salt and pepper to taste. Lay shrimp skewers widthwise across baking dish so that shrimp hover over grits. Continue to bake grits and shrimp until shrimp are opaque throughout and grits have thickened slightly, about 10 minutes.

4. Meanwhile, microwave remaining 3 tablespoons melted butter, remaining 1 teaspoon chili powder, remaining ⅛ teaspoon salt, and chipotle chile powder until fragrant, about 20 seconds.

5. Carefully remove dish from oven and transfer shrimp skewers to plate. Stir grits thoroughly, then portion into serving bowls. Remove shrimp from skewers and place on top of grits. Drizzle with spiced butter, sprinkle with scallion greens, and serve with lime wedges.

South Carolina Shrimp Boil

Crab Cakes with Roasted Corn and Old Bay Fries

South Carolina Shrimp Boil

DUTCH OVEN

Serves 8
Total Time 1 hour

Why This Recipe Works South Carolina is famous for its shrimp boil, made by simmering shell-on shrimp, smoked sausage, corn on the cob, and potatoes in a broth seasoned with Old Bay. While the simple, one-pot aspect of this dish is part of its charm, it can also be its biggest downfall; throwing all the ingredients in together yields blown-out potatoes, mealy corn, and rubbery shrimp. For foolproof results, we staggered the cooking, first browning the smoky sausage in a Dutch oven to render the fat before setting it aside to avoid overcooking. We added just enough water to cover the potatoes and corn and simmered them along with tomatoes, clam juice, the requisite Old Bay, and a bay leaf. Finally, we added the sausage back to the pot and elevated the shrimp in a steamer basket so it cooked gently. If andouille is not available, Portuguese linguiça or Polish kielbasa can be substituted. This dish is always made with shell-on shrimp, and we think peeling them is half the fun of eating this. Use small red potatoes measuring 1 to 2 inches in diameter; if your potatoes are larger, cut them into 1-inch pieces to ensure that they cook through properly. You will need a collapsible steamer basket for this recipe.

2 teaspoons vegetable oil
1½ pounds andouille sausage, cut into 2-inch lengths
4 cups water
1½ pounds small red potatoes, unpeeled, halved
4 ears corn, husks and silks removed, cut into 2-inch lengths
1 (14.5-ounce) can diced tomatoes, drained
1 (8-ounce) bottle clam juice
5 teaspoons Old Bay seasoning, divided
1 bay leaf
2 pounds extra-large shrimp (21 to 25 per pound)

1. Heat oil in Dutch oven over medium-high heat until just smoking. Brown sausage on all sides, about 5 minutes; transfer to plate.

2. Add water, potatoes, corn, tomatoes, clam juice, 1 tablespoon Old Bay, and bay leaf to now-empty pot and bring to boil. Reduce heat to medium-low, cover, and simmer until potatoes are just tender, about 10 minutes.

3. Nestle sausage into pot and place steamer basket over top. Toss shrimp with remaining 2 teaspoons Old Bay and transfer to steamer basket. Cook, covered, stirring shrimp occasionally, until opaque throughout, about 10 minutes. Transfer shrimp to serving platter. Drain stew, discarding bay leaf and liquid, and transfer to platter with shrimp. Serve.

Crab Cakes with Roasted Corn and Old Bay Fries

SHEET PAN

Serves 4
Total Time 1¼ hours

Why This Recipe Works Crab cakes are prone to falling apart, so many recipes call for lots of flavor-obscuring binders before pan-frying to keep them together. Looking for a way to make Maryland-style crab cakes with just a little binder and a lot of tender crabmeat, we used a sheet pan to cook the delicate cakes, which also allowed us to roast a couple of side dishes simultaneously. Starting with fresh crabmeat and blotting away the excess moisture ensured that the cakes weren't wet and dense. Mayonnaise added richness, Dijon mustard and a pinch of cayenne added tanginess and heat, and minced scallions added fresh flavor. A little panko and an egg bound the cakes together without overpowering the delicate crab flavor. We gave our vegetables a head start, roasting potato wedges seasoned with Old Bay and a mixture of fresh corn kernels, bell pepper, and onion. We then pushed the softened vegetables to the sides and added the crab cakes to the middle to cook. Buy crabmeat (either fresh or pasteurized) packed in plastic containers in the refrigerated section of your grocer's fish department. We do not recommend canned crabmeat.

Crab Cakes

- 1 pound fresh crabmeat, picked over for shells
- ¼ cup panko bread crumbs
- 3 scallions, minced
- 1 large egg
- 2 tablespoons mayonnaise
- 1 tablespoon Dijon mustard
- ⅛ teaspoon cayenne pepper
- 1 tablespoon unsalted butter

Corn and Potatoes

- 4 ears corn, kernels cut from cobs
- 1 onion, chopped
- 1 red bell pepper, stemmed, seeded, and cut into ½-inch pieces
- ¼ cup extra-virgin olive oil, divided
- 2 garlic cloves, sliced thin
- ½ teaspoon table salt
- ¼ teaspoon pepper
- 2 russet potatoes, unpeeled, each cut lengthwise into 8 equal wedges
- 1½ teaspoons Old Bay seasoning
- 2 tablespoons chopped fresh basil
- 2 teaspoons lemon juice

1. For the crab cakes Line plate with triple layer of paper towels. Transfer crabmeat to prepared plate and pat dry with additional paper towels. Combine panko, scallions, egg, mayonnaise, mustard, and cayenne in bowl. Using rubber spatula, gently stir in crabmeat until combined. Discard paper towels. Divide mixture into 4 equal portions (about ½ cup each). Shape portions into tight balls, then shape balls into cakes measuring about 1 inch thick and 3 inches wide (cakes will be delicate). Transfer cakes to now-empty plate and refrigerate until ready to use.

2. For the corn and potatoes Adjust oven rack to lower-middle position and heat oven to 475 degrees. Toss corn, onion, bell pepper, 2 tablespoons oil, garlic, salt, and pepper together in bowl. Transfer corn mixture to one half of rimmed baking sheet.

3. In now-empty bowl, toss potatoes, Old Bay, and remaining 2 tablespoons oil together. Arrange potatoes cut side down in single layer on empty half of sheet. Bake until corn mixture is just softened and potatoes are lightly browned on bottom, about 15 minutes.

4. Remove sheet from oven. Using metal spatula, clear section in middle of sheet by pushing potatoes into pile at 1 end of sheet and corn mixture into another pile at opposite end of sheet. Place butter on now-empty middle section of sheet and use metal spatula to evenly distribute. Using spatula, gently place crab cakes on middle section of sheet. Return sheet to oven and bake until crab cakes are golden on bottom and potatoes are tender, about 20 minutes.

5. Transfer sheet to wire rack. Stir basil and lemon juice into corn mixture and season with salt and pepper to taste. Flip crab cakes browned side up. Serve.

Seared Scallops with Warm Barley Salad

DUTCH OVEN

Serves 4
Total Time 1 hour

Why This Recipe Works Perfectly cooked scallops can be difficult to achieve at home, but the appeal of their delicate, almost creamy centers encased in golden, nutty exteriors is undeniable. We wanted to bring this luxury to our weeknight dinner table, and while we were at it we also wanted to make our scallops into a complete meal. First, we cooked hearty, nutty barley in a Dutch oven in plenty of water for an easy salad base. The keys to perfect scallops are speed and heat—the quicker a good sear develops, the less likely the centers are to overcook. Since moisture prevents browning, we blotted the scallops with dish towels so they were as dry as possible. Meanwhile, we crisped a few slices of chopped bacon in the same pot we had used to cook the barley; using the rendered fat to cook the scallops produced gorgeously browned crusts. We finished our barley salad with sweet apple, crunchy fennel, bitter frisée, and a bright cider vinegar–based dressing. We recommend buying "dry" scallops, which don't have chemical additives and taste better than "wet." Dry scallops will look ivory or pinkish; wet scallops are bright white. Do not substitute hulled, hull-less, quick-cooking, or presteamed barley (read the ingredient list on the package to determine this).

1	cup pearl barley
¾	teaspoon table salt, divided, plus salt for cooking barley
6	slices bacon, cut into ½-inch pieces
1½	pounds large sea scallops, tendons removed
¼	teaspoon pepper
3	tablespoons extra-virgin olive oil
2	tablespoons cider vinegar
1	fennel bulb, 3 tablespoons fronds chopped coarse, stalks discarded, bulb halved, cored, and sliced thin
1	Fuji or Honeycrisp apple, cored and cut into ½-inch pieces
1	head frisée (6 ounces), torn into bite-size pieces Lemon wedges

1. Bring 4 quarts water to boil in Dutch oven. Add barley and 1 tablespoon salt, return to boil, and cook until barley is tender, 20 to 40 minutes. Drain barley and set aside. Wipe pot clean with paper towels.

2. Cook bacon in now-empty pot over medium-high heat until crisp, about 5 minutes. Using slotted spoon, transfer bacon to paper towel–lined plate; set aside for serving.

3. Meanwhile, place scallops in rimmed baking sheet lined with clean dish towel. Place second clean dish towel on top of scallops and press gently on towel to blot liquid. Let scallops sit at room temperature, covered with towel, for 10 minutes.

4. Sprinkle scallops with ½ teaspoon salt and pepper. Heat fat left in pot over high heat until just smoking. Add half of scallops in single layer and cook, undisturbed, until well browned on first side, about 2 minutes. Flip scallops and continue to cook, undisturbed, until well browned on second side, about 2 minutes. Transfer scallops to serving platter and tent with aluminum foil. Repeat with remaining scallops; transfer to platter.

5. Whisk oil, vinegar, and remaining ¼ teaspoon salt together in large bowl. Add barley, fennel and fennel fronds, apple, and frisée and gently toss to combine. Season with salt and pepper to taste and sprinkle with reserved bacon. Serve scallops with salad and lemon wedges.

Baked Scallops with Couscous, Leeks and Tarragon-Orange Vinaigrette

Baked Scallops with Couscous, Leeks, and Tarragon-Orange Vinaigrette

CASSEROLE DISH
Serves 4
Total Time 1 hour

Why This Recipe Works For a simple, hands-off way to prepare scallops that would guarantee tender results and would infuse the scallops with sophisticated flavors, we opted for a casserole dish. Cooking the scallops on a bed of Israeli couscous, leeks, and white wine allowed the pearls of pasta to absorb the scallops' briny liquid. To ensure our scallops finished cooking at the same time as the rest of the dish, we jump-started the leeks and couscous in the microwave, adding garlic and a pinch of saffron to subtly perfume the dish. We stirred in the wine along with some boiling water; starting the dish off hot shortened the cooking time. Using a very hot oven and sealing the pan with foil promised perfectly (and efficiently) cooked scallops that steamed atop the couscous. Finally, a quick tarragon-orange vinaigrette drizzled over the finished dish provided an appealing accent that complemented the scallops and leeks without overpowering them. We recommend buying "dry" scallops, which don't have chemical additives and taste better than "wet." For an accurate measurement of boiling water, bring a full kettle of water to a boil and then measure out the desired amount.

- 1 pound leeks, white and light green parts only, halved lengthwise, sliced thin, and washed thoroughly
- 1 cup Israeli couscous
- 5 tablespoons extra-virgin olive oil, divided, plus extra for serving
- 4 garlic cloves, minced
- 1 teaspoon plus ⅛ teaspoon table salt, divided
- ½ teaspoon pepper, divided
  Pinch saffron threads (optional)
- ¾ cup boiling water
- ¼ cup dry white wine
- 1½ pounds large sea scallops, tendons removed
- ¼ teaspoon pepper
- 2 tablespoons minced fresh tarragon
- 1 tablespoon white wine vinegar
- ½ teaspoon Dijon mustard
- ½ teaspoon grated orange zest plus 1 tablespoon juice

1. Adjust oven rack to middle position and heat oven to 450 degrees. Combine leeks, couscous, 2 tablespoons oil, garlic, ½ teaspoon salt, ¼ teaspoon pepper, and saffron, if using, in bowl. Cover and microwave, stirring occasionally, until leeks are softened, about 6 minutes. Stir in boiling water and wine, then transfer mixture to 13 by 9-inch baking dish.

2. Season scallops with ½ teaspoon salt and remaining ¼ teaspoon pepper. Nestle scallops into couscous mixture and cover dish tightly with aluminum foil. Bake until couscous is tender, sides of scallops are firm, and centers are opaque, 20 to 25 minutes.

3. Meanwhile, whisk remaining 3 tablespoons oil, remaining ⅛ teaspoon salt, tarragon, vinegar, mustard, and orange zest and juice together in bowl. Remove dish from oven. Drizzle vinaigrette over scallops and serve, passing extra oil separately.

PREPPING SCALLOPS

Use your fingers to peel away the small, crescent-shaped muscle that is sometimes attached to scallops, as this tendon becomes incredibly tough when cooked.

Roasted Mussels with Tomato and Chorizo

ROASTING PAN
Serves 2 to 4
Total Time 45 minutes

Why This Recipe Works Ask almost anyone how to prepare mussels and they will likely recite the standard stovetop steaming steps. But here in the test kitchen, we learned that roasting them is far better. Mussels come in a range of sizes, making it a challenge to cook them evenly, so rather than piling them into a Dutch oven (where the mussels closest to the stove's burner will overcook), we roasted them in the generous space afforded by a roasting pan. After browning chorizo, oil, and garlic in the pan for richness and flavor, we added canned tomatoes and their liquid, a couple bay leaves, and the mussels and sealed them under a sheet of aluminum foil. The all-encompassing heat of a 500-degree oven heated the shellfish so the majority of the mussels, both big and small, yawned open in about 15 minutes, their liquid mingling with the reduced wine for an irresistible briny-sweet broth. A hit of butter melted into the concentrated cooking liquid before serving offered a rich complement to the mussels. Discard any mussel with an unpleasant odor or with a cracked shell or a shell that won't close. Serve with crusty bread.

- 3 tablespoons extra-virgin olive oil
- 12 ounces Spanish-style chorizo sausage, cut into ½-inch pieces
- 3 garlic cloves, minced
- 1 (28-ounce) can diced tomatoes
- 2 bay leaves
- 4 pounds mussels, scrubbed and debearded
- ¼ teaspoon table salt
- 2 tablespoons unsalted butter, cut into 4 pieces
- 2 tablespoons minced fresh parsley

1. Adjust oven rack to lowest position and heat oven to 500 degrees. Cook oil, chorizo, and garlic in 16 by 12-inch roasting pan over medium heat (over 2 burners, if possible), stirring constantly, until chorizo starts to brown, about 5 minutes. Stir in tomatoes and their juice and bay leaves and boil until tomatoes are slightly reduced, about 1 minute.

2. Stir in mussels and salt. Cover pan tightly with aluminum foil and transfer to oven. Roast until most mussels have opened (a few may remain closed), 15 to 18 minutes.

3. Remove pan from oven. Push mussels to sides of pan. Being careful of hot pan handles, add butter to center and whisk until melted. Discard any mussels that refuse to open and bay leaves. Stir in parsley and serve.

VEGETARIAN

Shakshuka

* All slow cooker recipes work in a 4- to 7-quart traditional slow cooker unless noted.
** All Instant Pot recipes work in a 6- to 8-quart Instant Pot or other electric pressure cooker.

Pot-Roasted Cauliflower with Tomatoes and Olives

Stuffed Spiced Eggplants with Tomatoes and Pine Nuts

Pot-Roasted Cauliflower with Tomatoes and Olives

DUTCH OVEN
Serves 4
Total Time 1¼ hours

Why This Recipe Works Tender cauliflower braised in an aromatic tomato sauce has made its way into blogs, magazines, and restaurant menus alike. The recipes we came across all started by searing the cumbersome cauliflower in hopes of browning the exterior. But even in a large Dutch oven we found this task unwieldy. The browning was spotty at best, and once the cauliflower was coated in a piquant sauce of chunky tomatoes, golden raisins, and salty capers and olives, we couldn't taste or see the difference between browned and unbrowned cauliflower. So we skipped the hassle. To ensure the rich flavors penetrated the dense vegetable, we started by cooking the cauliflower upside down in the Dutch oven and spooned some of the sauce into the crevices between the stalk and florets. We then flipped it right side up, spooned more sauce on top, and left the pot uncovered to finish. The sauce thickened, the flavors intensified, and the cauliflower reached the ideal tender texture.

2 (28-ounce) cans whole peeled tomatoes
2 tablespoons extra-virgin olive oil, plus extra for serving
6 garlic cloves, minced
¼ teaspoon red pepper flakes
¼ teaspoon table salt
1 head cauliflower (2 pounds)
¼ cup golden raisins
¼ cup pitted kalamata olives, chopped coarse
3 tablespoons capers, rinsed
1 ounce Parmesan cheese, grated (½ cup)
¼ cup minced fresh parsley

1. Adjust oven rack to middle position and heat oven to 450 degrees. Pulse tomatoes and their juice in food processor until coarsely chopped, 6 to 8 pulses.

2. Cook oil, garlic, and pepper flakes in Dutch oven over medium heat, stirring constantly, until fragrant, about 2 minutes. Stir in tomatoes and salt, bring to simmer, and cook until slightly thickened, about 10 minutes.

3. Meanwhile, trim outer leaves of cauliflower and cut stem flush with bottom florets. Stir raisins, olives, and capers into tomatoes in pot, then nestle cauliflower, stem side up, into sauce. Spoon some of sauce over cauliflower, cover, transfer pot to oven, and roast until cauliflower is just tender (paring knife slips in and out of core with some resistance), 30 to 35 minutes.

4. Uncover pot and, using tongs, flip cauliflower stem side down. Spoon some of sauce over cauliflower, then scrape down sides of pot. Continue to roast, uncovered, until cauliflower is tender, 10 to 15 minutes.

5. Remove pot from oven. Sprinkle cauliflower with Parmesan and parsley and drizzle with extra oil. Cut cauliflower into wedges and serve, spooning sauce over individual portions.

Stuffed Spiced Eggplants with Tomatoes and Pine Nuts

SLOW COOKER

Serves 4

Cook Time 5 to 6 hours on low or 3 to 4 hours on high

Why This Recipe Works Inspired by the flavors of Turkey, where stuffed eggplant is a staple meal, we wanted to create a streamlined stuffed eggplant with a filling that wouldn't require extra pots and pans. The slow cooker turns eggplant rich and creamy and offered the opportunity to cook the filling underneath the eggplant. Precooking the onion, garlic, and spices (oregano, cinnamon, and cayenne) in the microwave softened the onion and bloomed the spices. We added canned diced tomatoes, Pecorino Romano, pine nuts, and vinegar and nestled the halved eggplants cut side down so they could absorb the flavors. Once the eggplants had softened, we gently pushed the flesh to the sides to create a cavity, which we filled with the aromatic tomato mixture. To finish, we sprinkled on a topping of extra cheese and fresh minced parsley. Be sure to buy eggplants that are no more than 10 ounces; larger eggplants will not fit properly in your slow cooker. You may need to trim off the eggplant stems to help them fit. You will need a 5- to 7-quart oval slow cooker for this recipe.

- 1 onion, chopped fine
- 2 tablespoons extra-virgin olive oil, divided
- 3 garlic cloves, minced
- 2 teaspoons minced fresh oregano or ½ teaspoon dried
- ¼ teaspoon ground cinnamon
- ¾ teaspoon table salt, divided
- ⅛ teaspoon cayenne pepper
- 1 (14.5-ounce) can diced tomatoes, drained
- 2 ounces Pecorino Romano cheese, grated (1 cup), divided
- ¼ cup pine nuts, toasted
- 1 tablespoon red wine vinegar
- ¼ teaspoon pepper
- 2 (10-ounce) Italian eggplants, halved lengthwise
- 2 tablespoons minced fresh parsley

1. Microwave onion, 1 tablespoon oil, garlic, oregano, cinnamon, ¼ teaspoon salt, and cayenne in bowl, stirring occasionally, until onion is softened, about 5 minutes; transfer to slow cooker. Stir in tomatoes, ¾ cup Pecorino, pine nuts, and vinegar. Sprinkle eggplant halves with remaining ½ teaspoon salt and pepper and nestle cut side down into slow cooker (eggplants may overlap slightly). Cover and cook until eggplants are tender, 5 to 6 hours on low or 3 to 4 hours on high.

2. Transfer eggplant halves cut side up to serving platter. Using 2 forks, gently push eggplant flesh to sides of each half to make room for filling. Stir remaining 1 tablespoon oil into tomato mixture and season with salt and pepper to taste. Mound tomato mixture evenly into eggplants and sprinkle with parsley and remaining ¼ cup Pecorino. Serve.

PREPARING EGGPLANT FOR STUFFING

Using 2 forks, gently push flesh to sides of each eggplant half to make room in center for filling.

Stir-Fried Eggplant

SKILLET

Serves 4

Total Time 45 minutes

Why This Recipe Works Eggplant is something of a blank canvas, as its mild flesh readily absorbs whatever flavors you cook it with. That quality makes eggplant ideal for a vegetable-forward stir-fry. Cooking the eggplant over high heat in a shallow skillet allowed its excess moisture to evaporate quickly, leaving the eggplant browned and tender. For our sauce, we opted for classic stir-fry flavors: soy sauce, Chinese rice wine, and, for umami depth, hoisin sauce. Just a teaspoon of cornstarch was enough to thicken our sauce to a glossy consistency. Scallions and fresh cilantro lent the dish some herbaceous notes that played nicely off the savory sauce, and a sprinkling of toasted sesame seeds provided a bit of crunch to finish. This recipe works with Italian or globe eggplants, too. Stir-fries cook quickly, so have everything prepped before you begin cooking. You will need a 12-inch nonstick skillet with a tight-fitting lid for this recipe; a 14-inch flat-bottomed wok with a tight-fitting lid can be used instead.

Spaghetti Squash with Fresh Tomato Sauce

½ cup vegetable broth
¼ cup Shaoxing wine or dry sherry
3 tablespoons hoisin sauce
1 tablespoon soy sauce
1 teaspoon cornstarch
1 teaspoon toasted sesame oil
6 garlic cloves, minced
3 tablespoons vegetable oil, divided
1 tablespoon grated fresh ginger
1½ pounds Japanese eggplant, cut into ¾-inch pieces
1 red bell pepper, stemmed, seeded, and cut into ¼-inch-wide strips
2 scallions, sliced thin on bias
½ cup fresh cilantro sprigs, cut into 2-inch pieces
1 tablespoon sesame seeds, toasted

1. Whisk broth, Shaoxing wine, hoisin, soy sauce, cornstarch, and sesame oil together in bowl. Combine garlic, 1 tablespoon vegetable oil, and ginger in second bowl.

2. Heat 1 tablespoon vegetable oil in 12-inch nonstick skillet over medium-high heat until just smoking. Increase heat to high and add half of eggplant and half of bell pepper. Cook, tossing slowly but constantly, until browned and tender,

8 to 10 minutes; transfer to bowl. Repeat with remaining 1 tablespoon vegetable oil, eggplant, and bell pepper.

3. Return first batch of vegetables and any accumulated juices to skillet and push to sides. Reduce heat to medium. Add garlic mixture to center and cook, mashing mixture into skillet, until fragrant, about 30 seconds. Stir garlic mixture into eggplant.

4. Whisk sauce to recombine, then add to skillet. Increase heat to high and cook, tossing constantly, until vegetables are well coated and sauce is thickened, about 30 seconds. Off heat, stir in scallions and cilantro and sprinkle with sesame seeds. Serve.

VARIATION

Sesame-Basil Stir-Fried Eggplant for Two

SKILLET

Serves 2

Total Time 30 minutes

This recipe works with Italian or globe eggplants, too. Stir-fries cook quickly, so have everything prepped before you begin cooking. You will need a 12-inch nonstick skillet with a tight-fitting lid for this recipe; a 14-inch flat-bottomed wok with a tight-fitting lid can be used instead.

¼ cup vegetable broth
2 tablespoons Shaoxing wine or dry sherry
1 tablespoon liquid aminos
1 tablespoon packed brown sugar
1½ teaspoons rice wine vinegar
1½ teaspoons soy sauce
1 teaspoon toasted sesame oil
½ teaspoon cornstarch
3 garlic cloves, minced
2 tablespoons vegetable oil, divided
1 teaspoon grated fresh ginger
12 ounces Japanese eggplant, cut into ¾-inch pieces
½ red bell pepper, cut into ¼-inch-wide strips
½ cup fresh basil leaves, torn
2 teaspoons sesame seeds, toasted

1. Whisk broth, Shaoxing wine, liquid aminos, sugar, vinegar, soy sauce, sesame oil, and cornstarch together in bowl. Combine garlic, 1 tablespoon vegetable oil, and ginger in second bowl.

2. Heat remaining 1 tablespoon vegetable oil in 12-inch nonstick skillet over medium-high heat until just smoking. Increase heat to high and add eggplant and bell pepper. Cook, tossing slowly but constantly, until browned and tender, 8 to 10 minutes.

3. Push vegetables to sides of skillet and reduce heat to medium. Add garlic mixture to center and cook, mashing mixture into skillet, until fragrant, about 30 seconds. Stir garlic mixture into eggplant.

4. Whisk sauce to recombine, then add to skillet. Increase heat to high and cook, tossing constantly, until vegetables are well coated and sauce is thickened, about 30 seconds. Off heat, stir in basil and sprinkle with sesame seeds. Serve.

Spaghetti Squash with Fresh Tomato Sauce

INSTANT POT
Serves 4
Total Time 45 minutes

Why This Recipe Works Spaghetti squash makes an ideal vegetarian base for a variety of sauces, but often the squash must be roasted in the oven while a sauce is cooked separately on the stove. In the pressure cooker, however, we could make a simple tomato sauce and cook a large spaghetti squash together. For the tomatoes themselves we opted for the plum variety, which didn't require seeding or peeling and saved us time. Finally, we added the squash, halved and seeded, to the pot and cooked it until it was tender. Draining the shredded squash in a strainer eliminated excess moisture and using the sauté function of our pressure cooker allowed us to reduce the sauce further for concentrated tomato flavor.

- 3 tablespoons extra-virgin olive oil
- 3 garlic cloves, minced
- 1 tablespoon tomato paste
- 1 teaspoon minced fresh oregano or ½ teaspoon dried
    Pinch red pepper flakes
- 1 teaspoon table salt, divided
- 2 pounds plum tomatoes, cored and cut into
    1-inch pieces
- 1 (4-pound) spaghetti squash, halved lengthwise
    and seeded
- ¼ teaspoon pepper
- 2 tablespoons chopped fresh basil
    Shaved Parmesan cheese

1. Using highest sauté or browning function, heat oil in electric pressure cooker until shimmering. Add garlic, tomato paste, oregano, pepper flakes, and ½ teaspoon salt and cook, stirring frequently, until fragrant, about 30 seconds. Stir in tomatoes. Sprinkle squash halves with remaining ½ teaspoon salt and pepper and nestle cut side down into pot.

2. Lock lid in place and close pressure release valve. Select high pressure cook function and cook for 10 minutes. Turn off pressure cooker and quick-release pressure. Carefully remove lid, allowing steam to escape away from you.

3. Transfer squash to cutting board, let cool slightly, then shred flesh into strands using 2 forks; discard skins. Transfer squash to fine-mesh strainer and let drain while finishing sauce.

4. Cook sauce using highest sauté or browning function until tomatoes are completely broken down and sauce is thickened, 15 to 20 minutes. Transfer squash to serving platter, spoon sauce over top, and sprinkle with basil and Parmesan. Serve.

Spaghetti Squash and Black Bean Casserole

CASSEROLE DISH
Serves 4
Total Time 2 hours

Why This Recipe Works To make a vegetarian casserole featuring spaghetti squash using only one pan, we first roasted the spaghetti squash and then reused the casserole dish to assemble the rest of the components. While the squash roasted, we built a flavorful base by blooming minced garlic, smoked paprika, and cumin in the microwave. Incorporating black beans, corn, and tomatoes turned the spiced squash into a true meal and gave it a Southwestern flavor profile. Once we shredded the cooled squash, we mixed it with the other vegetables and baked the whole thing in the oven until it had just warmed through; covering it with aluminum foil helped trap steam and prevented the top of the casserole from drying out. Scallions lent a subtle flavor, minced jalapeño brought gentle heat, a squeeze of lime lent tartness, and creamy avocado and queso fresco balanced the textures. Crumbled feta can be substituted for the queso fresco. To make this dish spicier, reserve and add the chile seeds to the filling.

- 1 (2½- to 3-pound) spaghetti squash, halved lengthwise
    and seeded
- 3 tablespoons extra-virgin olive oil, divided
- 1¼ teaspoons table salt, divided
- ¼ teaspoon pepper
- 2 garlic cloves, minced
- ½ teaspoon smoked paprika
- ½ teaspoon ground cumin
- 1 (15-ounce) can black beans, rinsed
- 1 cup frozen corn
- 6 ounces cherry tomatoes, halved
- 6 scallions (4 minced, 2 sliced thin), divided
- 1 jalapeño chile, stemmed, seeded, and minced
- 1 avocado, halved, pitted, and cut into ½-inch pieces
- 2 ounces queso fresco, crumbled (½ cup)
    Lime wedges

Spiced Winter Squash with Halloumi and Shaved Brussels Sprouts

Spiced Winter Squash with Halloumi and Shaved Brussels Sprouts

INSTANT POT

Serves 4

Total Time 1 hour

Why This Recipe Works The pairing of golden-crusted, salty halloumi with velvety, sweet squash creates a marriage of contrasting textures and flavors. To cook both in the same pot we looked to the pressure cooker, where we could sauté the halloumi (a brined cheese with a semifirm, springy texture) and pressure cook the squash. Using the sauté function to cook the halloumi slices yielded crispy exteriors and creamy interiors; we used the rendered fat to quickly cook some scallion whites and bloom warm spices to create the flavor base for the squash. Raw, hard cubes of squash were transformed into meltingly tender chunks when cooked under pressure, and we quickly coaxed the pieces into a smooth puree with a masher. A lemony Brussels sprouts salad provided acidity to offset the squash's sweetness as well as crunch against its silky texture. A little drizzle of honey accentuated the salty cheese, and chewy dried cherries and roasted pepitas brought textural contrast. Use Brussels sprouts no bigger than golf balls, as larger ones are often tough and woody.

3 tablespoons extra-virgin olive oil, divided
2 tablespoons lemon juice
2 garlic cloves, minced, divided
⅛ teaspoon plus ½ teaspoon table salt, divided
8 ounces Brussels sprouts, trimmed, halved, and sliced very thin
1 (8-ounce) block halloumi cheese, sliced crosswise into ¾-inch-thick slabs
4 scallions, white parts minced, green parts sliced thin on bias, divided
½ teaspoon ground cardamom
¼ teaspoon ground cumin
⅛ teaspoon cayenne pepper
2 pounds butternut squash, peeled, seeded, and cut into 1-inch pieces (5 cups)
½ cup chicken or vegetable broth
2 teaspoons honey
¼ cup dried cherries
2 tablespoons roasted pepitas

1. Whisk 1 tablespoon oil, lemon juice, ¼ teaspoon garlic, and ⅛ teaspoon salt together in bowl. Add Brussels sprouts and toss to coat; let sit until ready to serve.

1. Adjust oven rack to middle position and heat oven to 375 degrees. Spray 8-inch square baking dish with vegetable oil spray. Brush cut sides of squash with 1 tablespoon oil and sprinkle with ½ teaspoon salt and pepper. Place squash cut side down in prepared dish (squash will not sit flat in dish) and roast until just tender, 40 to 45 minutes. Flip squash cut side up and let sit until cool enough to handle, about 20 minutes.

2. Meanwhile, combine remaining 2 tablespoons oil, remaining ¾ teaspoon salt, garlic, paprika, and cumin in large bowl and microwave until fragrant, about 30 seconds. Stir in beans, corn, tomatoes, minced scallions, and jalapeño until well combined.

3. Transfer squash to cutting board, let cool slightly, then shred flesh into strands using 2 forks; discard skins. Stir squash into bean mixture, then spread mixture evenly in dish and cover tightly with aluminum foil. Bake until warmed through, 20 to 25 minutes. Sprinkle with avocado, queso fresco, and sliced scallions. Serve with lime wedges.

2. Using highest sauté or browning function, heat remaining 2 tablespoons oil in electric pressure cooker until shimmering. Arrange halloumi around edges of pot and cook until browned, about 3 minutes per side; transfer to plate. Add scallion whites to fat left in pot and cook until softened, about 2 minutes. Stir in remaining garlic, cardamom, cumin, and cayenne and cook until fragrant, about 30 seconds. Stir in squash, broth, and remaining ½ teaspoon salt. Lock lid in place and close pressure release valve. Select high pressure cook function and cook for 6 minutes.

3. Turn off pressure cooker and quick-release pressure. Carefully remove lid, allowing steam to escape away from you. Using highest sauté or browning function, continue to cook squash mixture, stirring occasionally until liquid is almost completely evaporated, about 5 minutes. Turn off pressure cooker. Using potato masher, mash squash until mostly smooth. Season with salt and pepper to taste.

4. Spread portion of squash over bottom of individual serving plates. Top with Brussels sprouts and halloumi. Drizzle with honey and sprinkle with cherries, pepitas, and scallion greens. Serve.

Beet and Wheat Berry Salad with Arugula and Apples

SLOW COOKER

Serves 4 to 6
Cook Time 6 to 8 hours on low or 4 to 5 hours on high

Why This Recipe Works The slow cooker offers an exceptional hands-off option for all the elements of this hearty, nutty wheat berry salad. Typically, cooking wheat berries on the stovetop can take over an hour, and roasting beets in the oven requires just as long (and a separate pan). But in the slow cooker we found that the wheat berries could slowly simmer right alongside the beets, which we wrapped in foil to ensure even cooking and prevent the deep color from bleeding into the grain. Minced garlic and thyme provided an aromatic backbone. Once the wheat berries were tender, we drained them and dressed them with a simple cider vinaigrette. Baby arugula and Granny Smith apples rounded out our salad with their respective bitter and sweet-tart notes, and crumbled goat cheese provided a creamy, tangy counterpoint to the wheat berries and beets. To ensure even cooking, we recommend using beets that are similar in size—roughly 3 inches in diameter. If using quick-cooking or presteamed wheat berries (the ingredient list on the package specifies the type), you will need to decrease the cooking time. The wheat berries will retain a chewy texture once fully cooked.

Beet and Wheat
Berry Salad with
Arugula and Apples

1 cup wheat berries
2 garlic cloves, minced
2 teaspoons minced fresh thyme or ½ teaspoon dried
½ teaspoon table salt, plus salt for cooking wheat berries
1 pound beets, trimmed
1 Granny Smith apple, cored, halved, and sliced ¼ inch thick
4 ounces (4 cups) baby arugula
3 tablespoons extra-virgin olive oil
3 tablespoons apple cider vinegar
⅛ teaspoon pepper
⅛ teaspoon sugar
4 ounces goat cheese, crumbled (1 cup)

1. Combine 5 cups water, wheat berries, garlic, thyme, and ½ teaspoon salt in slow cooker. Wrap beets individually in aluminum foil and place in slow cooker. Cover and cook until wheat berries and beets are tender, 6 to 8 hours on low or 4 to 5 hours on high.

2. Transfer beets to cutting board, open foil, and let sit until cool enough to handle. Rub off beet skins with paper towels and cut beets into ½-inch-thick wedges.

3. Drain wheat berries, transfer to large serving bowl, and let cool slightly. Add beets, apple, arugula, oil, vinegar, salt, pepper, and sugar and toss to combine. Season with salt and pepper to taste. Sprinkle with goat cheese and serve.

VARIATION

Beet and Wheat Berry Salad with Kale and Pear for Two

SLOW COOKER

Serves 2

Cook Time 6 to 8 hours on low or 4 to 5 hours on high
To ensure even cooking, we recommend using beets that are similar in size—roughly 3 inches in diameter. If using quick-cooking or presteamed wheat berries (the ingredient list on the package specifies the type), you will need to decrease the cooking time. The wheat berries will retain a chewy texture once fully cooked.

½ cup wheat berries
2 garlic cloves, minced
2 teaspoons minced fresh thyme or ½ teaspoon dried
¼ teaspoon table salt, plus salt for cooking wheat berries
8 ounces beets, trimmed
½ ripe but firm pear, cored and sliced ¼ inch thick
2 ounces (2 cups) baby kale
2 tablespoons extra-virgin olive oil
1 tablespoon red wine vinegar
Pinch pepper
Pinch sugar
2 ounces Parmesan cheese, shaved

1. Combine 5 cups water, wheat berries, garlic, thyme, and ½ teaspoon salt in slow cooker. Wrap beets individually in aluminum foil and place in slow cooker. Cover and cook until wheat berries and beets are tender, 6 to 8 hours on low or 4 to 5 hours on high.

2. Transfer beets to cutting board, open foil, and let sit until cool enough to handle. Rub off beet skins with paper towels and cut beets into ½-inch-thick wedges.

3. Drain wheat berries, transfer to large serving bowl, and let cool slightly. Add beets, pear, kale, oil, vinegar, salt, pepper, and sugar and toss to combine. Season with salt and pepper to taste. Sprinkle with Parmesan and serve.

HOW TO PEEL BEETS

Peel slow-cooked (or roasted) beets by rubbing them with paper towels. The skins should slide right off. For easy cleanup, do this over the foil used for roasting the beets.

Vegetable Curry with Potatoes and Cauliflower

DUTCH OVEN

Serves 4 to 6

Total Time 1 hour

Why This Recipe Works Vegetable curry brings together a variety of perfectly cooked vegetables and a deeply flavorful (but weeknight-friendly) curry sauce assembled in one Dutch oven. Toasting store-bought curry powder turned it into a flavor powerhouse, and garam masala added even more spiced complexity. We also used a generous amount of sautéed onion, garlic, ginger, and fresh chile, as well as tomato paste for a touch of sweetness. For the vegetables, we chose potatoes, cauliflower, and peas, plus convenient canned chickpeas. Adding the vegetables right to the sauce base in the pot enhanced and melded the flavors. Finally, we rounded out the sauce with pureed canned tomatoes, water, and a splash of creamy coconut milk. For more heat, include the chile seeds and ribs when mincing. We prefer the richer flavor of regular coconut milk here; however, light coconut milk can be substituted.

1 (14.5-ounce) can diced tomatoes
3 tablespoons vegetable oil
1 tablespoon plus 1 teaspoon curry powder
1½ teaspoons garam masala
2 onions, chopped fine
12 ounces red potatoes, unpeeled, cut into ½-inch pieces
¼ teaspoon table salt
3 garlic cloves, minced
1 serrano chile, stemmed, seeded, and minced
1 tablespoon grated fresh ginger
1 tablespoon tomato paste
½ head cauliflower (1 pound), cut into 1-inch florets
1½ cups vegetable broth

Vegetable Curry with Potatoes and Cauliflower

1 (15-ounce) can chickpeas, rinsed
1½ cups frozen peas
½ cup canned coconut milk
¼ cup minced fresh cilantro

1. Pulse diced tomatoes with their juice in food processor until nearly smooth, with some ¼-inch pieces visible, about 3 pulses.

2. Heat oil in Dutch oven over medium-high heat until shimmering. Add curry powder and garam masala and cook until fragrant, about 10 seconds. Add onions, potatoes, and salt and cook, stirring occasionally, until onions are browned and potatoes are golden at edges, about 10 minutes.

3. Reduce heat to medium. Stir in garlic, serrano, ginger, and tomato paste and cook until fragrant, about 30 seconds. Add cauliflower florets and cook, stirring constantly, until florets are coated with spices, about 2 minutes.

4. Gradually stir in broth, scraping up any browned bits. Stir in chickpeas and processed tomatoes and bring to simmer. Cover, reduce heat to medium-low, and gently simmer until vegetables are tender, 20 to 25 minutes.

5. Uncover, stir in frozen peas and coconut milk, and continue to cook until peas are heated through, 1 to 2 minutes. Off heat, stir in cilantro and season with salt and pepper to taste. Serve.

VARIATION

Vegetable Curry with Sweet Potato and Eggplant For Two

SAUCEPAN
Serves 2
Total Time 45 minutes

Do not peel the eggplant as the skin helps hold it together during cooking. We prefer the richer flavor of regular coconut milk here; however, light coconut milk can be substituted.

1 tablespoon vegetable oil
1 tablespoon curry powder
½ teaspoon garam masala
1 small onion, chopped fine
⅛ teaspoon table salt
2 teaspoons grated fresh ginger
2 teaspoons tomato paste
2 garlic cloves, minced
½ eggplant (8 ounces), cut into 1-inch pieces
½ sweet potato (6 ounces), peeled and cut into ½-inch pieces
3 ounces green beans, trimmed and cut into 1-inch lengths
1½ cups vegetable broth
½ cup canned coconut milk
2 tablespoons minced fresh cilantro

1. Heat oil in large saucepan over medium-high heat until shimmering. Add curry powder and garam masala and cook until fragrant, about 10 seconds. Add onion and salt and cook, stirring occasionally, until onion is softened and lightly browned, 5 to 7 minutes.

2. Reduce heat to medium. Stir in ginger, tomato paste, and garlic and cook until fragrant, about 30 seconds. Stir in eggplant, potato, and green beans. Reduce heat to medium-low, cover, and cook until vegetables are softened, about 10 minutes. Stir in broth, scraping up any browned bits. Bring to simmer, cover, and cook until vegetables are tender, about 10 minutes.

3. Stir in coconut milk and cook until heated through, about 1 minute. Off heat, stir in cilantro and season with salt and pepper to taste. Serve.

Thai Vegetable Green Curry
with Jasmine Rice Cakes

Spanakopita

Thai Vegetable Green Curry with Jasmine Rice Cakes

SKILLET
Serves 4
Total Time 45 minutes

Why This Recipe Works When making our Thai Green Curry with Shrimp, Snow Peas, and Shiitakes (page 263), we realized just how easy and versatile store-bought green curry paste can be. Here, we used the boldly flavored paste to make an elegant vegetable-based green curry with green beans and bamboo shoots. To soak up all the extra sauce and turn this dish into a meal, we made jasmine rice cakes to go along with our curry. Pulsing some of the cooked rice in a food processor created a sticky base, and an egg and some flour ensured the cakes wouldn't crumble apart. We cooked the rice cakes to a crisp golden brown in a skillet, set them aside, and added the green beans to the pan. Just a few tablespoons of green curry paste provided a vibrant base for the sauce while a whole can of coconut milk added richness. The bamboo shoots needed to spend time in the skillet just long enough to warm through. Chopped radishes and fresh cilantro brought color and fresh flavor. You can use store-bought precooked jasmine rice. Basmati or long-grain white rice can be substituted for the jasmine rice; however, the cakes will be slightly less flavorful.

- 4 cups cooked jasmine rice
- 1 large egg, lightly beaten
- 2 tablespoons all-purpose flour
- ¾ teaspoon table salt
- ½ teaspoon pepper
- 3 tablespoons vegetable oil, divided
- 1 (14-ounce) can coconut milk
- 3 tablespoons Thai green curry paste
- 2 tablespoons liquid aminos
- 1 tablespoon packed brown sugar
- 12 ounces green beans, trimmed and cut into 2-inch lengths
- 1 (8-ounce) can sliced bamboo shoots, rinsed
- 1 tablespoon lime juice
- 2 radishes, trimmed and chopped fine
- 2 tablespoons minced fresh cilantro

1. Adjust oven rack to middle position and heat oven to 200 degrees. Microwave rice in covered bowl until hot, about 90 seconds. Pulse half of rice in food processor until coarsely ground, about 10 pulses. Return processed rice to bowl with unprocessed rice, let cool, then stir in egg, flour, salt, and pepper. Using your wet hands, pack rice mixture into eight 3-inch-wide cakes.

2. Line ovensafe platter with triple layer of paper towels. Heat 1 tablespoon oil in 12-inch nonstick skillet over medium-high heat until shimmering. Gently lay cakes in skillet and cook until golden brown and crisp on both sides, about 6 minutes, turning gently halfway through cooking. Transfer cakes to prepared platter and keep warm in oven.

3. Whisk coconut milk, curry paste, liquid aminos, and sugar together in bowl. Wipe out now-empty skillet with paper towels, add remaining 2 tablespoons oil, and heat over medium-high heat until shimmering. Add green beans and cook, stirring occasionally, until tender, about 5 minutes.

4. Stir in coconut milk mixture and bamboo shoots and simmer until sauce is slightly thickened, about 4 minutes. Off heat, stir in lime juice and season with salt and pepper to taste. Sprinkle with radishes and cilantro and serve with rice cakes.

NOTES FROM THE TEST KITCHEN

VEGETARIAN FISH SAUCE SUBSTITUTES
Traditional fish sauce is a salty, amber-colored liquid made from fermented fish. It's rich in glutamates, taste bud stimulators that give food the meaty, savory flavor known as umami. Many recipes in Asian cuisines rely on fish sauce to provide a distinctive rich, salty, fermented flavor.

In search of a vegetarian alternative, we found a variety of brands that offered a "vegetarian fish sauce." These sauces varied drastically in consistency (some were thick, some were thin), ingredients (some were fruit-flavored, others were mushroom based), and flavor (some were simply funky, some almost cheese-flavored). Overall, the products were inconsistent, and none of them were similar enough to traditional fish sauce to make a reliable substitute.

Luckily, with a little more research, we discovered Bragg Liquid Aminos. Made from 16 amino acids derived from soybeans (amino acids are the structural units that make up proteins), it is advertised as a healthy alternative to soy sauce. Tasters found it to be surprisingly similar to fish sauce, offering a great saltiness and a bit of fermented flavor.

Spanakopita

SKILLET
Serves 4
Total Time 1½ hours

Why This Recipe Works Making spanakopita, a Greek spinach-and-cheese pie with a crisp phyllo shell, typically requires buttering or oiling and stacking endless sheets of phyllo dough. Although this method results in flaky layers, we wondered if we could create a version of spanakopita that was less labor-intensive. Rather than cooking the filling and the crust separately, we used a skillet to make the spinach and cheese filling and put the crust on top. For the filling, we quickly cooked the thawed spinach to drive off any moisture so our crust wouldn't steam in the oven. A mix of feta and ricotta cheeses added briny flavor and creamy texture, while scallions, mint, and dill delivered an herbal backbone. We simplified the pastry component by spraying sheets of phyllo with oil spray, crumpling each into a ball, and placing them on the filling before we put the skillet in the oven to crisp up the dough. Phyllo dough is also available in larger 18 by 14-inch sheets; if using these, cut them in half to make 14 by 9-inch sheets. Don't thaw the phyllo in the microwave; let it sit in the refrigerator overnight or on the counter for 4 to 5 hours. You will need a 10-inch ovensafe nonstick skillet for this recipe.

 1 tablespoon unsalted butter
20 ounces frozen chopped spinach, thawed and squeezed dry
 ¼ teaspoon table salt
 ¼ teaspoon pepper
 3 garlic cloves, minced
 ⅛ teaspoon ground nutmeg
 ⅛ teaspoon cayenne pepper
 8 ounces feta cheese, crumbled (2 cups)
 6 ounces (¾ cup) whole-milk ricotta cheese
 4 scallions, sliced thin
 2 large eggs, lightly beaten
 ¼ cup minced fresh mint
 2 tablespoons minced fresh dill
20 (14 by 9-inch) phyllo sheets, thawed
   Olive oil spray

1. Adjust oven rack to lower-middle position and heat oven to 375 degrees. Melt butter in 10-inch ovensafe nonstick skillet over medium heat. Add spinach, salt, and pepper and cook until mixture is dry, about 4 minutes. Stir in garlic, nutmeg, and cayenne and cook until fragrant, about 30 seconds. Transfer mixture to large bowl and let cool slightly, about 5 minutes.

2. Stir feta, ricotta, scallions, eggs, mint, and dill into cooled spinach mixture until well combined. Spread mixture evenly into now-empty skillet.

3. Working with 1 sheet phyllo at a time, lay flat on clean counter and spray liberally with oil spray. Crumple oiled phyllo into 2-inch ball and place on top of spinach mixture in skillet.

4. Transfer skillet to oven and bake until phyllo is golden brown and crisp, about 25 minutes, rotating skillet halfway through baking. Remove skillet from oven (skillet handle will be hot). Let cool for 10 minutes before serving.

Shakshuka

SKILLET

Serves 4
Total Time 1 hour

Why This Recipe Works The classic Tunisian dish shakshuka is a simple yet satisfying one-pot meal consisting of eggs cooked in a long-simmered, spiced tomato and pepper sauce. For the sauce, we blended whole peeled tomatoes and jarred roasted red peppers for a mix of sweetness, smokiness, and acidity. Adding pita bread helped prevent the silky-smooth sauce from weeping. A combination of garlic, tomato paste, and ground spices created the distinct flavor profile. We poured the sauce into a skillet and simmered it until thickened; after removing the pan from the heat we used the back of a spoon to make indentations in the sauce, cracked the eggs right into the wells, and covered the whites with sauce to ensure even cooking. Covering the skillet after bringing everything back to a simmer created a steamy environment that quickly cooked the eggs from both above and below. Chopped cilantro, crumbled feta, and sliced kalamata olives on top provided brightness, texture, and flavor. The shallow indentations made in the sauce in step 3 cradle the yolks and ensure even placement of the eggs. Don't be concerned if the whites run together. Use a glass lid for your skillet, if possible. If not, check the eggs frequently.

- 4 (8-inch) pita breads, divided
- 1 (28-ounce) can whole peeled tomatoes, drained
- 3 cups jarred roasted red peppers, divided
- ¼ cup extra-virgin olive oil
- 4 garlic cloves, sliced thin
- 1 tablespoon tomato paste
- 2 teaspoons ground coriander
- 2 teaspoons smoked paprika
- 1 teaspoon ground cumin

Shakshuka

- ½ teaspoon table salt
- ¼ teaspoon pepper
- ¼ teaspoon cayenne pepper
- 8 large eggs
- ½ cup coarsely chopped fresh cilantro leaves and stems
- 1 ounce feta cheese, crumbled (¼ cup)
- ¼ cup pitted kalamata olives, sliced

1. Cut enough pita bread into ½-inch pieces to equal ½ cup (about one-third of 1 pita bread). Cut remaining pita breads into wedges for serving. Process pita pieces, tomatoes, and half of red peppers in blender until smooth, 1 to 2 minutes, scraping down sides of blender jar as needed. Cut remaining red peppers into ¼-inch pieces and set aside.

2. Heat oil in 12-inch skillet over medium heat until shimmering. Add garlic and cook, stirring occasionally, until golden, 1 to 2 minutes. Add tomato paste, coriander, paprika, cumin, salt, pepper, and cayenne and cook, stirring constantly, until rust-colored and fragrant, 1 to 2 minutes. Stir in tomato–red pepper puree and reserved red peppers (mixture may sputter) and bring to simmer. Reduce heat to maintain simmer; cook, stirring occasionally, until slightly thickened (spatula will leave trail that slowly fills in behind it, but sauce will still slosh when skillet is shaken), 10 to 12 minutes.

3. Remove skillet from heat. Using back of spoon, make 8 shallow dime-size indentations in sauce (7 around perimeter and 1 in center). Crack 1 egg into small bowl and pour into 1 indentation (it will hold yolk in place but not fully contain egg). Repeat with remaining 7 eggs. Spoon sauce over edges of egg whites so that whites are partially covered and yolks are exposed.

4. Bring to simmer over medium heat (there should be small bubbles across entire surface). Reduce heat to maintain simmer. Cover and cook until yolks film over, 4 to 5 minutes. Continue to cook, covered, until whites are softly but uniformly set (if skillet is shaken lightly, each egg should jiggle as a single unit), 1 to 2 minutes. Off heat, sprinkle with cilantro, feta, and olives. Serve immediately, passing pita wedges separately.

VARIATION

Shakshuka for Two

SKILLET

Serves 2

Total Time 1 hour

The shallow indentations made in the sauce in step 3 cradle the yolks and ensure even placement of the eggs. Don't be concerned if the whites run together. Use a glass lid for your skillet, if possible. If not, check the eggs frequently.

- 2 (8-inch) pita breads, divided
- 1 (14-ounce) can whole peeled tomatoes, drained
- 1½ cups jarred roasted red peppers, divided
- 2 tablespoons extra-virgin olive oil
- 2 garlic cloves, sliced thin
- 1½ teaspoons tomato paste
- 1 teaspoon ground coriander
- 1 teaspoon smoked paprika
- ½ teaspoon ground cumin
- ¼ teaspoon table salt
- ⅛ teaspoon pepper
- ⅛ teaspoon cayenne pepper
- 4 large eggs
- ¼ cup coarsely chopped fresh cilantro leaves and stems
- 2 tablespoons crumbled feta cheese
- 2 tablespoons pitted kalamata olives, sliced

1. Cut enough pita bread into ½-inch pieces to make ¼ cup (about one-eighth of 1 pita bread). Cut remaining pita breads into wedges for serving. Process pita pieces, tomatoes, and half of red peppers in blender until smooth, 1 to 2 minutes, scraping down sides of blender jar as needed. Cut remaining red peppers into ¼-inch pieces and set aside.

2. Heat oil in 10-inch skillet over medium heat until shimmering. Add garlic and cook, stirring occasionally, until golden, about 1 minute. Add tomato paste, coriander, paprika, cumin, salt, pepper, and cayenne and cook, stirring constantly, until rust-colored and fragrant, about 1 minute. Stir in tomato–red pepper puree and reserved red peppers (mixture may sputter) and bring to simmer. Reduce heat to maintain simmer; cook, stirring occasionally, until slightly thickened (spatula will leave trail that slowly fills in behind it, but sauce will still slosh when skillet is shaken), 6 to 8 minutes.

3. Remove skillet from heat. Using back of spoon, make 4 shallow dime-size indentations in sauce. Crack 1 egg into small bowl and pour into 1 indentation (it will hold yolk in place but not fully contain egg). Repeat with remaining 3 eggs. Spoon sauce over edges of egg whites so that whites are partially covered and yolks are exposed.

4. Bring to simmer over medium heat (there should be small bubbles across entire surface). Reduce heat to maintain simmer. Cover and cook until yolks film over, 3 to 4 minutes. Continue to cook, covered, until whites are softly but uniformly set (if skillet is shaken lightly, each egg should jiggle as a single unit), 1 to 2 minutes. Off heat, sprinkle with cilantro, feta, and olives. Serve immediately, passing pita wedges separately.

Green Shakshuka

DUTCH OVEN

Serves 4

Total Time 1 hour

Why This Recipe Works This version of shakshuka swaps out the simmered red sauce for a fresh, vibrant mix of greens. For the greens, we settled on savory Swiss chard and easy-to-prep baby spinach. We cooked a cup of the sliced chard stems (any more and their vegetal flavor overwhelmed the dish) with onion to create an aromatic base. We eschewed the traditional strong flavors of cumin and paprika in favor of coriander and mild Aleppo pepper—their citrusy notes allowed the greens' flavors to stay center stage. Rather than use a skillet we opted for a roomy Dutch oven, which allowed us to wilt a large volume of raw greens easily. We blended a cup of the greens mixture with broth to give the sauce a creamy, cohesive texture, and added frozen peas for contrasting pops of sweetness. To finish, we poached eight eggs directly in the sauce, covering the pot to contain the heat for efficient, even cooking. If you can't find Aleppo pepper, you can substitute ⅛ teaspoon paprika and ⅛ teaspoon finely chopped red pepper flakes. The Dutch oven will seem crowded when you first add the greens, but they will quickly wilt down. Avoid removing the lid during the first 5 minutes of cooking in step 3; it will increase the total cooking time of the eggs.

Green Shakshuka

2. Add chard leaves and spinach. Increase heat to medium-high, cover, and cook, stirring occasionally, until wilted but still bright green, 3 to 5 minutes. Off heat, transfer 1 cup chard mixture to blender. Add broth and process until smooth, about 45 seconds, scraping down sides of blender jar as needed. Stir chard mixture, peas, and lemon juice into pot.

3. Using back of spoon, make 4 shallow indentations (about 2 inches wide) in surface of greens. Crack 2 eggs into each indentation, sprinkle with Aleppo pepper, and season with salt to taste. Cover and cook over medium-low heat until edges of egg whites are just set, 5 to 10 minutes. Off heat, let sit, covered, until whites are fully set and yolks are still runny, 2 to 4 minutes. Sprinkle with feta, dill, and mint and drizzle with remaining 2 tablespoons oil. Serve immediately.

Huevos Rancheros
SHEET PAN
Serves 4
Total Time 1¼ hours

Why This Recipe Works To make huevos rancheros more manageable, we prepared them on a sheet pan. We built a robust tomato sauce by roasting diced tomatoes, onion, and chiles on the pan. Stirring in tomato juice created a saucy bed for our eggs. After sprinkling on pepper Jack cheese, we created eight wells with a spoon and cracked in our eggs. The key to oven-poached eggs was adding a second baking sheet for insulation so the eggs could cook gently—but was it still a one-pan meal? Since the second pan didn't need washing, we decided that this still qualified. We like our eggs slightly runny; if you prefer well-done eggs, cook them to the end of the time range in step 4. Serve with hot sauce.

- 2 pounds Swiss chard, stems removed and reserved, leaves chopped, divided
- ¼ cup extra-virgin olive oil, divided
- 1 large onion, chopped fine
- ¾ teaspoon table salt
- 4 garlic cloves, minced
- 2 teaspoons ground coriander
- 11 ounces (11 cups) baby spinach, chopped
- ½ cup vegetable broth
- 1 cup frozen peas
- 1½ tablespoons lemon juice
- 8 large eggs
- ½ teaspoon ground dried Aleppo pepper
- 2 ounces feta cheese, crumbled (½ cup)
- 2 tablespoons chopped fresh dill
- 2 tablespoons chopped fresh mint

1. Slice chard stems thin to yield 1 cup; discard remaining stems or reserve for another use. Heat 2 tablespoons oil in Dutch oven over medium heat until shimmering. Add chard stems, onion, and salt and cook until vegetables are softened and lightly browned, 5 to 7 minutes. Stir in garlic and coriander and cook until fragrant, about 1 minute.

- 2 (28-ounce) cans diced tomatoes
- 1 tablespoon packed brown sugar
- 1 tablespoon lime juice
- 1 onion, chopped
- ½ cup canned chopped green chiles
- ¼ cup extra-virgin olive oil
- 3 tablespoons chili powder
- 4 garlic cloves, sliced thin
- 1 teaspoon table salt, divided
- 8 (6-inch) corn tortillas
- 4 ounces pepper Jack cheese, shredded (1 cup)
- 8 large eggs
- ¼ teaspoon pepper
- 1 avocado, halved, pitted, and diced
- 2 scallions, sliced thin
- ¼ cup minced fresh cilantro

1. Adjust oven racks to lowest and middle positions and heat oven to 500 degrees. Drain tomatoes in fine-mesh strainer set over bowl, pressing with rubber spatula to extract as much juice as possible. Combine 1¾ cups drained tomato juice, sugar, and lime juice in bowl and set aside; discard extra drained juice.

2. Combine tomatoes, onion, chiles, oil, chili powder, garlic, and ½ teaspoon salt in bowl, then spread mixture out evenly on rimmed baking sheet. Wrap tortillas in aluminum foil and place on lower rack. Place sheet with tomato mixture on upper rack and roast until charred in spots, 35 to 40 minutes, stirring and redistributing into even layer halfway through roasting.

3. Remove sheet from oven and place inside second rimmed baking sheet. Carefully stir reserved tomato juice mixture into roasted vegetables, season with salt and pepper to taste, and spread into even layer. Sprinkle pepper Jack over top and, using back of spoon, hollow out eight 3-inch-wide holes in mixture. Crack 1 egg into each hole and sprinkle with remaining ½ teaspoon salt and pepper.

4. Bake until whites are just beginning to set but still have some movement when sheet is shaken, 7 to 8 minutes for slightly runny yolks or 9 to 10 minutes for soft-cooked yolks, rotating sheet halfway through baking.

5. Remove sheet from oven and top with avocado, scallions, and cilantro. To serve, slide spatula underneath eggs and sauce and gently transfer to warm tortillas.

Huevos Rancheros

Fried Eggs with Parmesan and Potato Roesti

SKILLET
Serves 4
Total Time 1¼ hours

Why This Recipe Works Swedish roesti—a crisp, golden cake of seasoned grated potatoes fried in butter—is both elegant and decadent topped with a layer of fried eggs. Producing a golden-brown crust wasn't a problem using a skillet, but to avoid a gluey interior we rinsed excess starch from the shredded potatoes before wringing them in a dish towel to eliminate moisture. Tossing the dry potatoes with cornstarch helped hold the cake together. We set the roesti aside and used the skillet to quickly fry the eggs; covering the skillet trapped in steam, cooking the eggs from above as well as below. Use the large holes of a box grater to shred the potatoes; for the best texture, shred the potatoes lengthwise into long shreds. Squeeze the potatoes as dry as possible. You will need a 12-inch nonstick skillet with a tight-fitting lid for this recipe.

2½ pounds Yukon Gold potatoes, peeled and shredded
1½ teaspoons cornstarch
1¼ teaspoons table salt, divided
⅛ teaspoon plus ¼ teaspoon pepper, divided
5 tablespoons unsalted butter, plus 1 tablespoon cut into 4 pieces and chilled, divided
8 large eggs
2 teaspoons vegetable oil
1 ounce Parmesan cheese, grated (½ cup)

1. Place potatoes in large bowl and fill with cold water. Using hands, swirl to remove excess starch, then drain, leaving potatoes in colander.

2. Wipe bowl dry. Place one-third of potatoes in center of dish towel. Gather towel ends together and twist tightly to squeeze out moisture. Transfer potatoes to now-empty bowl and repeat process with remaining potatoes in 2 batches. Sprinkle cornstarch, ¾ teaspoon salt, and ⅛ teaspoon pepper over potatoes. Using hands or fork, toss ingredients together until well blended.

3. Melt 2½ tablespoons butter in 12-inch nonstick skillet over medium heat. Add potato mixture and spread into even layer. Cover and cook for 6 minutes. Uncover and, using spatula, gently press potatoes down to form round cake. Cook, occasionally pressing on potatoes to shape into uniform round cake, until bottom is deep golden brown, 8 to 10 minutes.

4. Shake skillet to loosen roesti and slide onto large plate. Add 2½ tablespoons butter to skillet and swirl to coat skillet. Invert roesti onto second plate and slide roesti, browned side up, back into skillet. Cook, occasionally pressing down on roesti, until bottom is well browned, 8 to 10 minutes. Transfer roesti to cutting board and let cool slightly while making eggs. Wipe skillet clean with paper towels.

5. Crack eggs into 2 small bowls (4 eggs per bowl) and sprinkle with remaining ½ teaspoon salt and remaining ¼ teaspoon pepper. Heat oil in now-empty skillet over medium heat until shimmering. Add remaining 1 tablespoon chilled butter to skillet and quickly swirl to coat skillet. Working quickly, pour 1 bowl of eggs in 1 side of pan and second bowl of eggs in other side. Cover and cook for 2 minutes.

6. Remove skillet from heat and let sit, covered, about 2 minutes for runny yolks (white around edge of yolk will be barely opaque), about 3 minutes for soft but set yolks, and about 4 minutes for medium-set yolks. Slide eggs onto roesti, sprinkle with Parmesan cheese, and season with salt to taste. Cut into wedges and serve.

Shiitake Mushroom Frittata with Pecorino Romano

Shiitake Mushroom Frittata with Pecorino Romano

SKILLET

Serves 4
Total Time 45 minutes

Why This Recipe Works Frittata needn't be limited to just breakfast; a well-seasoned filling made with bold ingredients and a dozen eggs can make a substantial dinner. For a cohesive frittata, we chopped savory shiitake mushrooms small so that they could be surrounded and held in place by the eggs. Giving the mushrooms a head start in the skillet guaranteed they would be cooked through at the same time as the eggs, which we added to the skillet to thicken on the stovetop before we transferred the skillet to the oven to gently finish cooking through. To help the eggs stay tender even when cooked to a relatively high temperature, we added milk (which prevented a rubbery texture) and salt (which produced a softer curd). While the shiitake mushrooms needn't be cut into exact ½-inch pieces, make sure that no pieces are much larger than ¾ inch to ensure a cohesive frittata. You will need a 12-inch ovensafe nonstick skillet for this recipe. This frittata can be served warm or at room temperature. Serve with an Easy Green Salad (see page 17).

12 large eggs
⅓ cup whole milk
¾ teaspoon table salt, divided
1 tablespoon extra-virgin olive oil
1 pound shiitake mushrooms, stemmed and cut into ½-inch pieces
¼ teaspoon pepper
2 scallions, white parts minced, green parts sliced thin, divided
1 tablespoon sherry vinegar
1½ teaspoons minced fresh thyme
2¼ ounces Pecorino Romano, shredded (¾ cup)

1. Adjust oven rack to middle position and heat oven to 350 degrees. Whisk eggs, milk, and ½ teaspoon salt in bowl until well combined.

2. Heat oil in 12-inch ovensafe nonstick skillet over medium-high heat until shimmering. Add mushrooms, pepper, and remaining ¼ teaspoon salt and cook, stirring frequently, until mushrooms are tender and spotty brown, 7 to 9 minutes. Add 2 tablespoons water, scallion whites, vinegar, and thyme and cook, stirring constantly, until no water remains in skillet, about 1 minute.

3. Add Pecorino, scallion greens, and egg mixture and cook, using rubber spatula to stir and scrape bottom of skillet until large curds form and spatula leaves trail through eggs but eggs are still very wet, about 30 seconds. Smooth curds into even layer and cook, without stirring, for 30 seconds. Transfer skillet to oven and bake until frittata is slightly puffy and surface bounces back when lightly pressed, 6 to 9 minutes. Using rubber spatula, loosen frittata from skillet and transfer to cutting board. Let sit for 5 minutes before slicing and serving.

VARIATION
Broccoli and Feta Frittata for Two
SKILLET

Serves 2

Total Time 45 minutes

You will need an 8-inch ovensafe nonstick skillet for this recipe. This frittata can also be served warm or at room temperature. Serve with an Easy Green Salad (see page 17).

6 large eggs
2 tablespoons whole milk
¼ teaspoon plus ⅛ teaspoon table salt, divided
1½ teaspoons extra-virgin olive oil
6 ounces broccoli florets, cut into ½-inch pieces (2 cups)
Pinch red pepper flakes
¼ teaspoon grated lemon zest plus ¼ teaspoon juice
2 ounces feta cheese, crumbled into ½-inch pieces (½ cup)

1. Adjust oven rack to middle position and heat oven to 350 degrees. Whisk eggs, milk, and ¼ teaspoon salt in bowl until well combined.

2. Heat oil in 8-inch ovensafe nonstick skillet over medium-high heat until shimmering. Add broccoli, pepper flakes, and remaining ⅛ teaspoon salt and cook, stirring frequently, until broccoli is crisp-tender and spotty brown, 4 to 6 minutes. Add 1½ tablespoons water and lemon zest and juice and cook, stirring constantly, until broccoli is just tender and no water remains in skillet, about 30 seconds.

3. Add feta and egg mixture and cook, using rubber spatula to stir and scrape bottom of skillet until large curds form and spatula leaves trail through eggs but eggs are still very wet, about 30 seconds. Smooth curds into even layer and cook, without stirring, for 30 seconds. Transfer skillet to oven and bake until frittata is slightly puffy and surface bounces back when lightly pressed, 6 to 9 minutes. Using rubber spatula, loosen frittata from skillet and transfer to cutting board. Let sit for 5 minutes before slicing and serving.

Philly-Style Broccoli Rabe, Portobello, and Cheese Sandwiches
SKILLET

Serves 4

Total Time 45 minutes

Why This Recipe Works Philadelphia's roast pork sandwich with broccoli rabe (see our version on page 198), a lesser-known cousin to Philly's mighty cheesesteak, features a meaty filling, slightly bitter broccoli rabe, and melty cheese. For a vegetarian version of this sandwich filling that we could make in one skillet, we swapped out the meat for umami-rich portobellos. We sautéed the broccoli rabe with some garlic and pepper flakes for heat and then tossed it with vinegar and set it aside to cook the mushrooms. Cutting the mushrooms into thin slices gave us nicely browned pieces. Once the mushrooms were cooked, we stirred in the broccoli rabe. To bind it all together, we let slices of American cheese melt into the vegetables for a rich, cohesive filling we could pile high on toasted sub rolls.

3 tablespoons extra-virgin olive oil, divided
2 garlic cloves, sliced thin
⅛ teaspoon red pepper flakes
¾ pound broccoli rabe, trimmed and cut into ½-inch pieces
½ teaspoon table salt
2 tablespoons balsamic vinegar
6 portobello mushroom caps, gills removed, halved, and sliced thin
10 slices (10 ounces) deli American cheese
4 (8-inch) Italian sub rolls, split lengthwise and toasted

1. Heat 1 tablespoon oil in 12-inch nonstick skillet over medium heat until shimmering. Add garlic and pepper flakes and cook for 1 minute. Stir in broccoli rabe, 2 tablespoons water, and salt. Cover and cook until broccoli rabe is bright green and crisp-tender, 3 to 4 minutes. Off heat, stir in vinegar, then transfer to bowl.

2. Heat remaining 2 tablespoons oil in now-empty skillet over medium-high heat until shimmering. Add mushrooms (skillet will be very full), cover, and cook, stirring occasionally, until mushrooms release their liquid, 6 to 8 minutes. Uncover and continue to cook until moisture has evaporated and mushrooms begin to brown, 6 to 8 minutes.

3. Stir broccoli rabe back into skillet and season with salt and pepper to taste. Reduce heat to low and shingle cheese over vegetables. Cook until cheese is melted, about 2 minutes. Fold melted cheese thoroughly into mushroom mixture. Divide mixture evenly among toasted rolls. Serve.

Tofu, Thai Chile, and Basil Lettuce Cups

Crispy Tofu with Warm Cabbage Salad

Tofu, Thai Chile, and Basil Lettuce Cups

SKILLET
Serves 4
Total Time 45 minutes

Why This Recipe Works Tofu has a unique ability to absorb flavors, making it the perfect one-skillet filling for a vegetarian lettuce wrap. Draining the tofu, pulsing it in the food processor, and patting the pieces dry ensured that it would be well browned, not soggy. We also turned to the food processor to chop basil, garlic, and Thai chiles. We combined a portion of this fragrant mixture with liquid aminos, vegetarian oyster sauce, sugar, and vinegar to make a sauce. We added oil, aromatics, shallot, and tofu to a cold skillet and browned the tofu and shallots. Then we stirred in the sauce and another cup of basil leaves, along with crunchy peanuts. You can use either firm or extra-firm tofu in this recipe. If fresh Thai chiles are unavailable, substitute two serranos or one jalapeño. For a milder dish, remove the seeds and ribs from the chiles.

14 ounces extra-firm tofu, cut into 2-inch pieces
½ teaspoon table salt
¼ teaspoon pepper
2 cups fresh basil leaves, divided
3 garlic cloves, peeled
6 green or red Thai chiles, stemmed
2 tablespoons liquid aminos, plus extra for serving
1 tablespoon vegetarian oyster sauce
1 tablespoon sugar
1 teaspoon distilled white vinegar, plus extra for serving
3 shallots, halved and sliced thin
2 tablespoons vegetable oil
¼ cup dry-roasted peanuts, chopped
2 heads Bibb lettuce (1 pound), leaves separated
   Red pepper flakes

1. Spread tofu over paper towel–lined platter, let drain for 20 minutes, then gently press dry with paper towels. Sprinkle with salt and pepper.

2. Meanwhile, pulse 1 cup basil, garlic, and chiles in food processor until finely chopped, 6 to 10 pulses, scraping down sides of bowl as needed. Transfer 1 tablespoon basil mixture to small bowl and stir in liquid aminos, oyster sauce, sugar, and vinegar. Transfer remaining basil mixture to 12-inch nonstick skillet.

3. Pulse tofu in now-empty food processor until coarsely chopped, 3 to 4 pulses. Line baking sheet with clean paper towels. Spread processed tofu over prepared baking sheet and press gently with paper towels to dry.

4. Stir dried tofu, shallots, and oil into skillet with basil mixture and cook over medium heat, stirring occasionally, until tofu and shallots are browned, 10 to 15 minutes. (Mixture should start to sizzle after about 1½ minutes; adjust heat as needed.)

5. Add reserved basil mixture and continue to cook, stirring constantly, until well coated, about 1 minute. Stir in remaining 1 cup basil and cook, stirring constantly, until wilted, 30 to 60 seconds. Off heat, stir in peanuts. Transfer mixture to platter and serve with lettuce leaves, pepper flakes, extra liquid aminos, and extra vinegar.

Crispy Tofu with Warm Cabbage Salad

SKILLET

Serves 4 to 6
Total Time 45 minutes

Why This Recipe Works Pan-frying tofu in a skillet gives it a crisped, golden exterior to contrast the creamy interior. Paired with an easy salad made from bagged coleslaw mix and a zesty dressing, this meal is simple and speedy. For a dressing with some punch, we mixed together oil, vinegar, soy sauce, sugar, and Asian chili-garlic sauce and heated it in the microwave; we then tossed the warm dressing with the coleslaw mix, peanuts, scallions, cilantro, and mint. For the tofu, draining it and dredging it in a mixture of cornmeal and cornstarch before pan-frying it created the perfect light, crispy crust. Working in batches ensured we didn't overcrowd the skillet. We prefer the texture of soft tofu here. Firm or extra-firm tofu will also work, but they will taste drier. For a spicier dish use the greater amount of chili-garlic sauce.

28 ounces soft tofu, halved lengthwise and sliced crosswise into 3-inch-long by ½-inch-thick planks
½ teaspoon table salt
¼ teaspoon pepper
3 tablespoons vegetable oil
5 tablespoons unseasoned rice vinegar
2 tablespoons soy sauce
2 tablespoons sugar
1–2 teaspoons Asian chili-garlic sauce
6 cups (15 ounces) green coleslaw mix
¾ cup unsalted dry-roasted peanuts, chopped
4 scallions, sliced thin
½ cup fresh cilantro leaves
½ cup chopped fresh mint
¾ cup cornstarch
¼ cup cornmeal
¾ cup vegetable oil for frying

ALL ABOUT TOFU

Tofu is the result of a process that is similar to cheese making: Curds, the result of coagulating soy milk, are set in a mold and pressed to extract as much, or as little, of the liquid whey as desired. Depending on how long the tofu is pressed and how much coagulant is used, the amount of whey released will vary, creating a range of textures from soft to firm.

Choosing the Right Tofu Tofu is available in a variety of textures: extra-firm, firm, medium-firm, soft, and silken. Reaching for the right variety can be key to the success of any given recipe. In general, firmer varieties hold their shape when cooking, while softer varieties do not, so it follows that each type of tofu is best when used in specific ways.

Extra-Firm and Firm Tofu We prefer extra-firm or firm tofu for stir-fries and noodle dishes as they hold their shape in high heat cooking applications or when tossed with pasta. These two varieties of tofu are also great marinated (they absorb marinade better than softer varieties) or tossed raw into salads.

Medium and Soft Tofu Medium and soft tofu boast a creamy texture; we love to pan-fry these kinds of tofu, as in our Crispy Tofu with Warm Cabbage Salad to achieve a crisp outside, which makes a nice textural contrast to the silky interior.

Silken Tofu Silken tofu has a soft, ultracreamy texture and is often used as a base for smoothies and dips, in desserts such as puddings, or as an egg replacement in vegan baked goods.

Storing Tofu Tofu is highly perishable, so look for a package with the latest expiration date possible. To store an opened package, cover the tofu with water and store, refrigerated, in a covered container, changing the water daily.

Butternut Squash, Poblano, and Corn Tacos

Butternut Squash, Poblano, and Corn Tacos

SHEET PAN

Serves 4

Total Time 1 hour

Why This Recipe Works Tacos are usually focused on the meat, but we wanted a great-tasting taco that was all about the vegetables. Selecting the right vegetables was the first step, and our favorite combination turned out to be butternut squash (sweet potatoes for our version for two), poblano peppers, and corn. Roasting them on a sheet pan allowed us to cook them all at once and was a surefire way to bring out their sweetness. To balance the flavors, we seasoned them with plenty of garlic, cumin, coriander, and oregano; we then spread all of the vegetables out on a baking sheet and roasted for crunchy, caramelized exteriors and tender interiors. Finally, we topped the tacos with crumbled queso fresco, tangy pickled onions, and cool sour cream. Crumbled feta can be substituted for the queso fresco. For more information on warming tortillas, see page 116.

> 3 tablespoons extra-virgin olive oil
> 3 garlic cloves, minced
> 1½ teaspoons ground cumin
> 1½ teaspoons ground coriander
> 1 teaspoon minced fresh oregano or ¼ teaspoon dried
> 1 teaspoon table salt
> ½ teaspoon pepper
> 1½ pounds butternut squash, peeled, seeded, and cut into ½-inch pieces (4 cups)
> 4 poblano chiles, stemmed, seeded, and cut into ½-inch-wide strips
> 3 ears corn, kernels cut from cobs
> 1 large onion, halved and sliced ½ inch thick
> ¼ cup minced fresh cilantro
> 8–12 (6-inch) corn tortillas, warmed
> 2 ounces queso fresco, crumbled (½ cup)
> 1 recipe Quick Pickled Onions (page 223)
> Sour cream

1. Adjust oven rack to middle position and heat oven to 450 degrees. Whisk oil, garlic, cumin, coriander, oregano, salt, and pepper together in large bowl. Add squash, poblanos, corn, and onion and toss to coat.

1. Spread tofu over paper towel–lined platter, let drain for 20 minutes, then gently press dry with paper towels. Sprinkle with salt and pepper.

2. Meanwhile, whisk 3 tablespoons oil, vinegar, soy sauce, sugar, and chili-garlic sauce together in bowl, cover, and microwave until simmering, 1 to 2 minutes. Measure out and reserve 2 tablespoons dressing separately for drizzling over tofu. Toss remaining dressing with coleslaw mix, peanuts, scallions, cilantro, and mint; set aside.

3. Combine cornstarch and cornmeal in shallow dish. Working with several tofu pieces at a time, coat thoroughly with cornstarch mixture, pressing gently to adhere; transfer to wire rack set in rimmed baking sheet.

4. Line large plate with triple layer of paper towels. Heat ¾ cup oil in 12-inch nonstick skillet over medium-high heat until shimmering. Working in 2 batches, cook tofu until crisp and golden on all sides, about 4 minutes. Gently lift tofu from oil, letting excess oil drip back into skillet, and transfer to prepared plate. Drizzle tofu with reserved dressing and serve with cabbage salad.

2. Spread vegetable mixture in even layer over rimmed baking sheet. Roast vegetables until tender and golden brown, about 30 minutes, stirring vegetables halfway through roasting.

3. Return vegetables to now-empty bowl, add cilantro, and toss to combine. Divide vegetables evenly among tortillas and top with queso fresco and pickled onions. Serve with sour cream.

VARIATION

Sweet Potato, Poblano, and Corn Tacos for Two
SHEET PAN
Serves 2
Total Time 1 hour

Crumbled feta can be substituted for the queso fresco. For more information on warming tortillas, see page 116.

- 1½ tablespoons extra-virgin olive oil
- 1 garlic clove, minced
- ¾ teaspoon ground cumin
- ¾ teaspoon ground coriander
- ½ teaspoon minced fresh oregano or ⅛ teaspoon dried
- ½ teaspoon table salt
- ¼ teaspoon pepper
- 8 ounces sweet potatoes, peeled and cut into ½-inch pieces
- 3 poblano chiles, stemmed, seeded, and cut into ½-inch-wide strips
- 1 ear corn, kernels cut from cobs
- 1 small onion, halved and sliced ½ inch thick
- 2 tablespoons minced fresh cilantro
- 4–6 (6-inch) corn tortillas, warmed
- 1 ounce queso fresco, crumbled (¼ cup)
- ½ cup Quick Pickled Onions (page 223)
  Sour cream

1. Adjust oven rack to middle position and heat oven to 450 degrees. Whisk oil, garlic, cumin, coriander, oregano, salt, and pepper together in large bowl. Add potatoes, poblanos, corn, and onion and toss to coat.

2. Spread vegetable mixture in even layer over rimmed baking sheet. Roast vegetables until tender and golden brown, about 30 minutes, stirring vegetables halfway through roasting.

3. Return vegetables to now-empty bowl, add cilantro, and toss to combine. Divide vegetables evenly among tortillas and top with queso fresco and pickled onions. Serve with sour cream.

Baja-Style Cauliflower Tacos with Mango Cabbage Slaw

Baja-Style Cauliflower Tacos with Mango Cabbage Slaw
SHEET PAN
Serves 4
Total Time 45 minutes

Why This Recipe Works Preparing Baja California tacos is usually a messy affair that requires frying fish, and although this method is undeniably tasty, it's far from weeknight-friendly. For a simplified, vegetarian take on Baja-style tacos at home, we opted to use battered, roasted cauliflower as a stand-in for the fried fish. We cut the cauliflower into large florets and roasted them on a sheet pan after dunking the pieces in coconut milk seasoned with garlic and spices and then rolling them in a mixture of panko bread crumbs and shredded coconut. Not only did this add richness and flavor, but it also mimicked the crisp crust of batter-fried fish. A crunchy slaw with juicy mango and spicy jalapeño provided a balance of sweetness and heat. For a creamy topping, we blended equal parts mayonnaise and sour cream, plus cilantro. For a spicier slaw, add the jalapeño ribs and seeds. For more information on warming tortillas, see page 116.

SPICED LENTIL AND RICE PILAF

The hearty combination of lentils and rice appears in dishes across the globe. The humble ingredients come together to create a dish that's satisfying and complex, and this versatile base can take on a variety of substitution and add-in options. Lentils and rice cook at different rates, so we knew that making a one-pot recipe would require staggering the cooking. We started by precooking brown lentils, which needed longer to cook through than the rice. For the pot, a saucepan was big enough for a recipe to serve two or four, but for a version to serve eight we switched to a Dutch oven. After setting the lentils aside, we added onion (or smaller shallot in the version for two) to the pot to soften along with a fragrant mix of garlic, turmeric, coriander, and cayenne to bloom. Adding the rice and cooked lentils to this aromatic base gave them a flavorful backbone as they cooked. A sprinkle of toasted pistachios provided much-needed textural contrast, cilantro leaves added freshness, and cooling yogurt provided the perfect finishing touch.

CLASSIC

SAUCEPAN
Serves 4
Total Time 1½ hours
Allow the rice to cook for the full 12 minutes before lifting the lid to check it.

  1 cup brown lentils, picked over and rinsed
  ½ teaspoon table salt, plus salt for cooking lentils
  3 tablespoons extra-virgin olive oil
  1 small onion, chopped fine
  2 garlic cloves, minced
1½ teaspoons ground turmeric
  1 teaspoon ground coriander
  ⅛ teaspoon cayenne pepper
1½ cups long-grain white rice, rinsed
2¼ cups vegetable broth
  ¼ cup shelled toasted pistachios, chopped
  ¼ cup fresh cilantro leaves
  ½ cup plain Greek yogurt

1. Bring lentils, 4 cups water, and 1 teaspoon salt to boil in large saucepan over high heat. Reduce heat to low and cook until lentils are tender, 12 to 15 minutes. Drain and set aside. Wipe saucepan clean with paper towels.

2. Heat oil in now-empty saucepan over medium heat until shimmering. Add onion and ½ teaspoon salt and cook until softened, 3 to 5 minutes. Stir in garlic, turmeric, coriander, and cayenne and cook until fragrant, about 30 seconds. Add rice and cook, stirring frequently, until edges begin to turn translucent, about 2 minutes. Stir in broth and lentils and bring to boil. Reduce heat to low, cover, and cook until rice is tender and water is absorbed, 12 to 18 minutes.

3. Let sit off heat for 10 minutes. Fluff rice and lentils with fork. Transfer to serving platter and sprinkle with pistachios and cilantro. Serve with yogurt.

MAKE IT YOUR WAY →

> **Use What You've Got** Substitute green lentils or French green lentils (lentilles du Puy) for brown lentils; do not substitute red or yellow lentils. Substitute jasmine or basmati rice for long-grain rice; chicken broth for vegetable broth; walnuts, pecans, or pine nuts for pistachios; and/or parsley, dill, or tarragon for cilantro.

COOK IT FOR TWO

SAUCEPAN
Serves 2
Total Time 1½ hours
Allow the rice to cook for the full 12 minutes before lifting the lid to check it.

- ½ cup brown lentils, picked over and rinsed
- ⅛ teaspoon table salt, plus salt for cooking lentils
- 1 tablespoon extra-virgin olive oil
- 1 shallot, minced
- 1 garlic clove, minced
- ¾ teaspoon ground turmeric
- ½ teaspoon ground coriander
  Pinch cayenne pepper
- ¾ cup long-grain white rice, rinsed
- 1¼ cups vegetable broth
- 2 tablespoons chopped toasted pistachios
- 2 tablespoons fresh cilantro leaves
- ¼ cup plain Greek yogurt

1. Bring lentils, 2 cups water, and ½ teaspoon salt to boil in small saucepan over high heat. Reduce heat to low and cook until lentils are tender, 12 to 15 minutes. Drain and set aside. Wipe saucepan clean with paper towels.

2. Heat oil in now-empty saucepan over medium heat until shimmering. Add shallot and ⅛ teaspoon salt and cook until softened, about 3 minutes. Stir in garlic, turmeric, coriander, and cayenne and cook until fragrant, about 30 seconds. Add rice and cook, stirring frequently, until edges begin to turn translucent, about 2 minutes. Stir in broth and lentils and bring to boil. Reduce heat to low, cover, and cook until rice is tender and water is absorbed, 12 to 15 minutes.

3. Let sit off heat for 10 minutes. Fluff rice and lentils with fork. Transfer to serving platter and sprinkle with pistachios and cilantro. Serve with yogurt.

COOK IT FOR A CROWD

DUTCH OVEN
Serves 8
Total Time 1½ hours
Allow the rice to cook for the full 18 minutes before lifting the lid to check it.

- 14 ounces (2 cups) brown lentils, picked over and rinsed
- ¾ teaspoon table salt, plus salt for cooking lentils
- ¼ cup extra-virgin olive oil
- 1 onion, chopped fine
- 4 garlic cloves, minced
- 2 teaspoons ground turmeric
- 2 teaspoons ground coriander
- ¼ teaspoon cayenne pepper
- 3 cups long-grain white rice, rinsed
- 6 cups vegetable broth
- ½ cup shelled toasted pistachios, chopped
- ½ cup fresh cilantro leaves
- 1 cup plain Greek yogurt

1. Bring lentils, 8 cups water, and 1 teaspoon salt to boil in Dutch oven over high heat. Reduce heat to low and cook until lentils are tender, 12 to 15 minutes. Drain and set aside. Wipe pot clean with paper towels.

2. Heat oil in now-empty pot over medium heat until shimmering. Add onion and ¾ teaspoon salt and cook until softened, about 5 minutes. Stir in garlic, turmeric, coriander, and cayenne and cook until fragrant, about 30 seconds. Add rice and cook, stirring frequently, until edges begin to turn translucent, about 2 minutes. Stir in broth and lentils and bring to boil. Reduce heat to low, cover, and cook until rice is tender and water is absorbed, 18 to 22 minutes.

3. Let sit off heat for 10 minutes. Fluff rice and lentils with fork. Transfer to serving platter and sprinkle with pistachios and cilantro. Serve with yogurt.

> **Bulk it Up** Stir thawed frozen vegetables (lima beans, cut green beans, peas) and/or chopped dried fruit (apricots, figs, raisins) into cooked lentil and rice mixture.

> **Add an Upgrade** Extra-virgin olive oil and pomegranate seeds make great finishing touches. Serve with Tzatziki Sauce (page 225) instead of yogurt.

Pearl Couscous with Tomatoes and Chickpeas

DUTCH OVEN
Serves 4
Total Time 45 minutes

Why This Recipe Works Couscous has a mild flavor on its own, but by simmering it in a tomatoey broth in a Dutch oven we were able to easily imbue it with plenty of flavor. As a bonus, we could build the sauce right in the pot before adding the couscous—no need to use separate pots to precook the sauce or cook the couscous. We opted for large-grain pearl couscous rather than traditional small-grain couscous, as its bigger size allowed it to soak up lots of tomatoey flavor. Softening some onion and then adding garlic and red pepper flakes gave the sauce an aromatic backbone; vegetable broth and canned tomatoes rounded out the sauce. Starting with crushed tomatoes allowed them to break down, further thickening the sauce around the fluffy pearls of couscous. Canned chickpeas added bulk and needed just a few minutes to heat through once added to the pot, and a sprinkling of fresh oregano before serving brightened everything up. Serve with shaved Parmesan or Pecorino Romano cheese.

- 3 tablespoons extra-virgin olive oil, plus extra for drizzling
- 1 small onion, chopped fine
- 3 garlic cloves, minced
- ¾ teaspoon table salt
- ½ teaspoon pepper
- ½ teaspoon red pepper flakes
- 4 cups vegetable broth
- 1 (28-ounce) can crushed tomatoes
- 1½ cups pearl couscous
- 1 (15-ounce) can chickpeas, rinsed
- 2 tablespoons fresh oregano leaves, chopped coarse

1. Heat oil in Dutch oven over medium heat until shimmering. Add onion and cook until softened, about 5 minutes. Stir in garlic, salt, pepper, and pepper flakes and cook until fragrant, about 30 seconds. Stir in broth, tomatoes, and couscous. Bring to simmer and cook, stirring often, until couscous is tender and sauce has thickened, about 15 minutes.

2. Stir in chickpeas and let sit until heated through, about 2 minutes. Divide evenly among 4 individual bowls. Sprinkle with oregano, drizzle with extra oil, and serve.

Vegetable and Orzo Tian

CASSEROLE DISH
Serves 4
Total Time 1 hour

Why This Recipe Works This Mediterranean-inspired vegetable casserole features striking layers of zucchini, summer squash, and tomatoes over a bed of creamy orzo. The challenge with this theoretically hands-off dish was finishing the pasta and vegetables simultaneously. Rather than cook the orzo separately in a pot, we achieved perfectly cooked pasta by tightly shingling the vegetables over the orzo, trapping moisture in the casserole dish. Vegetable broth reinforced the vegetables' flavor, and shallots and garlic mixed into the orzo provided depth. Parmesan gave the orzo a creamy texture, and a combination of oregano and red pepper flakes contributed floral, spicy notes. A few minutes under the broiler and a sprinkle of basil made for an appealing presentation. Look for squash, zucchini, and tomatoes with similar-size circumferences so that they are easy to shingle into the dish. You will need a broiler-safe 13 by 9-inch baking dish for this recipe.

- 3 ounces Parmesan cheese, grated (1½ cups), divided
- 1 cup orzo
- 2 shallots, minced
- 3 tablespoons minced fresh oregano or 1 teaspoon dried
- 3 garlic cloves, minced
- ¼ teaspoon table salt
- ⅛ teaspoon red pepper flakes
- 1 zucchini, sliced ¼ inch thick
- 1 yellow summer squash, sliced ¼ inch thick
- 1 pound plum tomatoes, cored and sliced ¼ inch thick
- 1¾ cups vegetable broth
- 1 tablespoon extra-virgin olive oil
- 2 tablespoons chopped fresh basil

1. Adjust oven rack to middle position and heat oven to 425 degrees. Combine ½ cup Parmesan, orzo, shallots, oregano, garlic, salt, and pepper flakes in bowl. Spread mixture evenly into broiler-safe 13 by 9-inch baking dish. Alternately shingle zucchini, squash, and tomatoes in tidy rows on top of orzo.

2. Carefully pour broth over top of vegetables. Bake until orzo is just tender and most of broth is absorbed, about 20 minutes.

3. Remove dish from oven, adjust oven rack 9 inches from broiler element, and heat broiler. Drizzle vegetables with oil, season with salt and pepper to taste, and sprinkle with remaining 1 cup Parmesan. Broil until spotty brown and bubbling around edges, about 5 minutes.

4. Remove dish from oven and let rest for 10 minutes. Sprinkle with basil and serve.

Brown Rice and Black Beans with Corn and Tomatoes

SKILLET
Serves 4 to 6
Total Time 1½ hours

Why This Recipe Works Rice and beans are usually relegated to side dish status, but here a few additions transform them into a satisfying vegetarian meal—and instead of cooking the rice and beans separately, we set out to make our meal in one skillet. We liked the hearty texture and robust flavor of brown rice. Because a skillet has a greater surface area than a saucepan, we had to adjust our usual liquid-to-rice ratio: We needed 4 cups of broth to cook 1 cup of rice. For more heft we added corn, sautéing it briefly to give it toasty flavor before adding garlic, cumin, and cayenne. Stirring in convenient canned black beans partway through cooking allowed them just enough time to warm through without breaking down. For a fresh, bright finish, we created a quick salsa. You will need a 12-inch nonstick skillet with a tight-fitting lid for this recipe.

- 2 tablespoons extra-virgin olive oil, divided
- 1 onion, chopped fine
- ¼ teaspoon table salt
- 1½ cups frozen corn, thawed and patted dry
- 1 cup long-grain brown rice
- 4 garlic cloves, minced
- 1 teaspoon ground cumin
  Pinch cayenne pepper
- 4 cups vegetable broth
- 2 (15-ounce) cans black beans, rinsed
- 12 ounces cherry tomatoes, quartered
- 5 scallions, sliced thin
- ¼ cup minced fresh cilantro
- 1 tablespoon lime juice

1. Heat 1 tablespoon oil in 12-inch nonstick skillet over medium-high heat until shimmering. Add onion and salt and cook until onion is softened and beginning to brown, 5 to 7 minutes. Stir in corn and cook until lightly browned, about 4 minutes. Stir in rice, garlic, cumin, and cayenne and cook until fragrant, about 30 seconds.

2. Stir in broth and bring to simmer. Reduce heat to medium-low, cover, and simmer gently, stirring occasionally, for 25 minutes.

3. Stir in beans. Cover and simmer gently, stirring occasionally, until liquid is absorbed and rice is tender, about 30 minutes. Season with salt and pepper to taste.

4. Combine remaining 1 tablespoon oil, tomatoes, scallions, cilantro, and lime juice in bowl and season with salt and pepper to taste. Spoon tomato mixture over rice and beans and serve.

Vegetable and Orzo Tian

Brown Rice and Black Beans with Corn and Tomatoes

Wild Mushroom Farrotto

and cook until softened, about 2 minutes. Stir in rice and cook, stirring often, until grain edges begin to turn translucent, about 1 minute.

3. Stir in wine and cook, stirring constantly, until fully absorbed, 2 to 3 minutes. Stir in hot broth. Reduce heat to medium-low, cover, and simmer until almost all liquid has been absorbed and rice is just al dente, about 12 minutes, stirring twice during cooking.

4. Stir in asparagus, cover, and cook for 2 minutes. Add remaining ¾ cup broth and stir gently and constantly until risotto becomes creamy, about 3 minutes. Stir in mushrooms, peas, and Parmesan. Remove saucepan from heat, cover, and let sit for 5 minutes. Stir in basil, lemon juice, and remaining 1 tablespoon butter. Season with salt and pepper to taste. Before serving, stir in extra hot broth as needed to loosen consistency of risotto.

Wild Mushroom Farrotto

INSTANT POT

Serves 4 to 6
Total Time 1 hour

Why This Recipe Works Farrotto is a robust risotto-style dish swapping in farro for the traditional Arborio rice. For a streamlined recipe, we turned to the pressure cooker. Once we decided to cook the farro under pressure, we simply added a measured amount of liquid up front; with no stirring, no adding broth in stages, and no standing by the stove, the cooking was completely hands-off. Achieving a velvety texture with farro can be a challenge, since much of farro's starch is trapped inside the outer bran. Cracking the farro in a blender freed up enough starch to create the appropriate risotto-like consistency. We used the pressure cooker's sauté function to jump-start some meaty mushrooms before adding the cracked farro along with garlic, dried porcinis, thyme, and some white wine for an aromatic backbone. A healthy heaping of Parmesan cheese at the end made the finished farrotto luxuriously creamy. Do not use quick-cooking, presteamed, or pearl farro (read the ingredient list on the package to determine this) in this recipe. Be sure to use a blender in step 1; the farro will not pulse properly in a food processor.

NOTES FROM THE TEST KITCHEN

ALL ABOUT FARRO

Farro is a whole-grain form of wheat that has been enjoyed for centuries in Tuscany and central Italy. Thanks to praise for farro from scores of culinary magazines and top chefs, it is gaining favor with home cooks and has become more widely available in supermarkets. We love it for its slightly sweet, nutty flavor and chewy texture, not to mention its health benefits (it is high in fiber and protein). Like many other grains, farro is available in multiple quicker-cooking varieties, including pearl, quick-cooking, and presteamed. While the quicker-cooking varieties are convenient in other applications, we prefer the taste and texture of traditional whole farro in our Wild Mushroom Farrotto.

1½ cups whole farro
 3 tablespoons extra-virgin olive oil, divided, plus extra for drizzling
12 ounces cremini or white mushrooms, trimmed and sliced thin
½ onion, chopped fine
½ teaspoon table salt
¼ teaspoon pepper
 1 garlic clove, minced
¼ ounce dried porcini mushrooms, rinsed and chopped fine
 2 teaspoons minced fresh thyme or ½ teaspoon dried
¼ cup dry white wine
2½ cups vegetable broth, plus extra as needed
 2 ounces Parmesan cheese, grated (1 cup), plus extra for serving
 2 teaspoons lemon juice
½ cup chopped fresh parsley

1. Pulse farro in blender until about half of grains are broken into smaller pieces, about 6 pulses.

2. Using highest sauté or browning function, heat 2 tablespoons oil in electric pressure cooker until shimmering. Add cremini mushrooms, onion, salt, and pepper, partially cover, and cook until mushrooms are softened and have released their liquid, about 5 minutes. Stir in farro, garlic, porcini mushrooms, and thyme and cook until fragrant, about 1 minute. Stir in wine and cook until nearly evaporated, about 30 seconds. Stir in broth.

3. Lock lid in place and close pressure release valve. Select high pressure cook function and cook for 12 minutes. Turn off pressure cooker and quick-release pressure. Carefully remove lid, allowing steam to escape away from you.

4. If necessary, adjust consistency with extra hot broth, or continue to cook farrotto, using highest sauté or browning function, stirring frequently, until proper consistency is achieved. (Farrotto should be slightly thickened, and spoon dragged along bottom of pressure cooker should leave trail that quickly fills in.) Add Parmesan and remaining 1 tablespoon oil and stir vigorously until farrotto becomes creamy. Stir in lemon juice and season with salt and pepper to taste. Sprinkle individual portions with parsley and extra Parmesan, and drizzle with extra oil before serving.

Parmesan Polenta with Broccoli Rabe, Sun-Dried Tomatoes, and Pine Nuts

SKILLET
Serves 4
Total Time 45 minutes

Why This Recipe Works Broccoli rabe, sun-dried tomatoes, garlic, and red pepper flakes combine to make a savory, intensely flavored topping for sweet, nutty polenta in this simple vegetarian dinner. Cooking the broccoli rabe first and then reusing the pan to make the polenta allowed us to use only one skillet. We reduced polenta's typical lengthy cooking time by using instant polenta, which had a creamy consistency and soft texture in just a few minutes with minimal stirring. Parmesan cheese and butter added richness, and toasted pine nuts sprinkled on top offered a bit of crunch. Shopping for polenta can be confusing—instant polenta can look just like traditional polenta and is often identifiable only by the word "instant" in its title, which in our experience can be slightly hidden. Be sure to use instant polenta here; traditional polenta requires a slightly different cooking method. You will need a 12-inch nonstick skillet with a tight-fitting lid for this recipe.

Topping
 3 tablespoons extra-virgin olive oil
½ cup oil-packed sun-dried tomatoes, chopped coarse
 6 garlic cloves, minced
½ teaspoon red pepper flakes
½ teaspoon table salt
 1 pound broccoli rabe, trimmed and cut into 1½-inch pieces
¼ cup vegetable broth
 3 tablespoons pine nuts, toasted

Polenta
 4 cups water
 1 cup instant polenta
½ teaspoon table salt
 2 ounces Parmesan cheese, grated (1 cup), plus extra for serving
 4 tablespoons unsalted butter

1. For the topping Cook oil, tomatoes, garlic, pepper flakes, and salt in 12-inch nonstick skillet over medium-high heat until garlic is fragrant and slightly toasted, about 1½ minutes. Add broccoli rabe and broth, cover, and cook until broccoli rabe turns bright green, about 2 minutes. Uncover and continue to cook, stirring frequently, until most of broth has evaporated and broccoli rabe is just tender, about 2 minutes. Season with salt to taste. Transfer to bowl and cover to keep warm. Wipe skillet clean with paper towels.

2. For the polenta Bring water to boil in now-empty skillet. Gradually whisk in polenta and salt. Cook over medium heat, whisking constantly, until very thick, about 5 minutes. Off heat, stir in Parmesan and butter and season with salt and pepper to taste.

3. Portion polenta into 4 individual serving bowls, top with broccoli rabe mixture, and sprinkle with pine nuts. Serve with extra Parmesan.

Baked Quinoa with Kale and Chickpeas

CASSEROLE DISH
Serves 4
Total Time 45 minutes

Why This Recipe Works Quinoa makes a stellar side dish, but we wanted this healthy grain to be the center of attention in a robust vegetarian casserole with layers of flavor and a creamy goat cheese topping. We started with a combination of quinoa and chickpeas, pouring lemon-infused water over the mixture and baking it until the quinoa had absorbed the liquid. Roasted kale seemed a surefire way to bulk up the dish, but we found the extra step of roasting the leaves too fussy; instead, we used the microwave to steam the kale and tenderize its leaves. Our quinoa bake was taking on a distinctly Mediterranean flavor profile, so we added some chopped fresh tomatoes and a lemony vinaigrette, which also ensured our dish was bright-tasting and colorful. A generous sprinkling of goat cheese finished this simple casserole with perfect tangy complexity. We like the convenience of prewashed quinoa; rinsing removes the quinoa's bitter protective coating (called saponin). If you buy unwashed quinoa, rinse it and then spread it out on a clean dish towel to dry for 15 minutes.

5   ounces (5 cups) baby kale
1   cup prewashed white quinoa
1   (15-ounce) can chickpeas, rinsed
1   teaspoon table salt, divided
½   teaspoon pepper, divided
2   teaspoons grated lemon zest plus 1 tablespoon
      juice, divided
2   tablespoons extra-virgin olive oil
2   plum tomatoes, cored and finely chopped
6   ounces goat cheese, crumbled (1½ cups)

1. Adjust oven rack to middle position and heat oven to 450 degrees. Combine kale and 1 tablespoon water in bowl, cover, and microwave until slightly wilted, 1 to 2 minutes. Transfer to colander and let drain, pressing with back of spoon to remove as much moisture as possible.

2. Combine wilted kale, quinoa, chickpeas, ½ teaspoon salt, and ¼ teaspoon pepper in 8-inch square baking dish. Combine ½ cup water and 1 teaspoon lemon zest in bowl, cover, and microwave until just steaming, about 1 minute. Pour water mixture evenly into dish and cover tightly with aluminum foil. Bake until quinoa is tender and no liquid remains, 20 to 30 minutes.

3. Meanwhile, whisk oil, lemon juice, remaining 1 teaspoon lemon zest, remaining ½ teaspoon salt, and remaining ¼ teaspoon pepper together in bowl.

4. Remove dish from oven and fluff quinoa with fork. Gently fold in tomatoes and lemon vinaigrette. Sprinkle with goat cheese and continue to bake, uncovered, until cheese is heated through, 3 to 5 minutes. Serve.

Quinoa and Vegetable Lettuce Cups with Feta and Mint

SLOW COOKER
Serves 4
Cook Time 3 to 4 hours on low or 2 to 3 hours on high

Why This Recipe Works The slow cooker offers a hands-off environment to cook quinoa to the perfect consistency, and this tender grain makes an ideal vegetarian filling for lettuce cups when paired with fresh vegetables and an herbaceous yogurt dressing. Since we wanted a quinoa mixture that would be easy to scoop into the cups, we skipped the step of toasting the quinoa in the microwave. Putting the quinoa into the slow cooker raw gave it a softer, more cohesive texture. Our creamy dressing, flavored with tangy feta cheese and fresh mint, also helped to bind the quinoa. Tomatoes and cucumber made our filling more substantial and also added welcome color and crunch; shallot offered a pleasant bite. We tossed the quinoa and vegetables with a portion of the bold dressing and reserved the rest to drizzle on once we scooped our salad into the lettuce cups. We like the convenience of prewashed quinoa; rinsing removes the quinoa's bitter protective coating (called saponin). If you buy unwashed quinoa, rinse it and then spread it out on a clean dish towel to dry for 15 minutes. You will need an oval slow cooker for this recipe.

2   tablespoons extra-virgin olive oil, divided
1   tablespoon minced fresh oregano or 1 teaspoon dried

2   garlic cloves, minced

1½ cups vegetable broth

1   cup prewashed white quinoa

⅔   cup plain yogurt

2   ounces feta cheese, crumbled (½ cup)

¼   cup minced fresh mint, divided

2   tablespoons red wine vinegar

½   teaspoon table salt

¼   teaspoon pepper

2   tomatoes, cored, seeded, and chopped

1   cucumber, peeled, halved lengthwise, seeded, and cut into ¼-inch pieces

1   small shallot, halved and sliced thin

2   heads Bibb lettuce (8 ounces each), leaves separated

1. Lightly coat slow cooker with vegetable oil spray. Microwave 1 tablespoon oil, oregano, and garlic in bowl until fragrant, about 1 minute; transfer to prepared slow cooker. Stir in broth and quinoa, cover, and cook until quinoa is tender and all broth is absorbed, 3 to 4 hours on low or 2 to 3 hours on high.

2. Fluff quinoa with fork, transfer to large serving bowl, and let cool slightly. Combine yogurt, feta, 2 tablespoons mint, vinegar, salt, pepper, and remaining 1 tablespoon oil in separate bowl. Add half of dressing, tomatoes, cucumber, shallot, and remaining 2 tablespoons mint to quinoa and gently toss to combine. Season with salt and pepper to taste. Serve quinoa salad with lettuce leaves, passing remaining dressing separately.

Bulgur with Chickpeas, Spinach, and Za'atar

INSTANT POT
Serves 4 to 6
Total Time 45 minutes

Why This Recipe Works Hearty bulgur, nutty chickpeas, and fresh spinach come together in the pressure cooker to create a unique meld of textures. Za'atar, the aromatic eastern Mediterranean spice blend, gives the whole dish a boost with its fragrant wild herbs, toasted sesame seeds, and tangy sumac. Fluffing the bulgur right after cooking and then letting it sit was crucial to achieving perfectly cooked grains that weren't soggy: Agitating the grains and putting a towel under the lid allowed excess moisture in the pot to be absorbed. We used the residual heat from the bulgur to wilt baby spinach gently without turning it gummy. When shopping, don't confuse bulgur with cracked wheat, which has a much longer cooking time and will not work in this recipe.

Baked Quinoa with Kale and Chickpeas

Quinoa and Vegetable Lettuce Cups with Feta and Mint

3 tablespoons extra-virgin olive oil, divided
1 onion, chopped fine
½ teaspoon table salt
3 garlic cloves, minced
2 tablespoons za'atar, divided
1 cup medium-grind bulgur, rinsed
1 (15-ounce) can chickpeas, rinsed
1½ cups water
5 ounces (5 cups) baby spinach, chopped
1 tablespoon lemon juice, plus lemon wedges
   for serving

1. Using highest sauté or browning function, heat 2 tablespoons oil in electric pressure cooker until shimmering. Add onion and salt and cook until onion is softened, about 5 minutes. Stir in garlic and 1 tablespoon za'atar and cook until fragrant, about 30 seconds. Stir in bulgur, chickpeas, and water.

2. Lock lid in place and close pressure release valve. Select high pressure cook function and cook for 1 minute. Turn off pressure cooker and quick-release pressure. Carefully remove lid, allowing steam to escape away from you.

3. Gently fluff bulgur with fork. Lay clean dish towel over pot, replace lid, and let sit for 5 minutes. Add spinach, lemon juice, remaining 1 tablespoon za'atar, and remaining 1 tablespoon oil and gently toss to combine. Season with salt and pepper to taste. Serve with lemon wedges.

Bulgur with Chickpeas, Spinach, and Za'atar

Lentil Salad with Radishes, Cilantro, and Pepitas for Two

Lentil Salad with Dill, Orange, and Spinach

SLOW COOKER
Serves 4
Cook Time 3 to 4 hours on low or 2 to 3 hours on high

Why This Recipe Works Lentil salad can be a hearty, impressive, and easy main course. But all too often the lentils overcook and break down, resembling more of a porridge than a salad. The slow, even heat of the slow cooker guaranteed great lentils every time. Cooking the lentils with plenty of liquid ensured even cooking. Adding a little salt and vinegar to the liquid (we preferred water as it didn't compete with the flavor of the lentils) produced lentils that were firm yet creamy. Some garlic, orange zest, and a bay leaf provided a flavorful foundation. Once the lentils were cooked and drained, we added fresh, bright ingredients that offered big flavor and turned this dish into a hearty main vegetarian course. We prefer French green lentils (lentilles du Puy) for this recipe, but it will work with any type of lentil except red or yellow.

1 cup French green lentils, picked over and rinsed
2½ tablespoons red wine vinegar, divided
3 garlic cloves, minced
3 (2-inch) strips orange zest, plus 2 oranges, divided
1 bay leaf
¼ teaspoon table salt, plus salt for cooking lentils
4 ounces (4 cups) baby spinach, chopped coarse
¼ cup extra-virgin olive oil
1 shallot, minced
2 tablespoons chopped fresh dill
2 tablespoons chopped toasted pecans

1. Combine 4 cups water, lentils, 1 tablespoon vinegar, garlic, orange zest, bay leaf, and ¾ teaspoon salt in slow cooker. Cover and cook until lentils are tender, 3 to 4 hours on low or 2 to 3 hours on high.

2. Cut away peel and pith from oranges. Cut oranges into 8 wedges, then slice wedges crosswise into ¼-inch-thick pieces.

3. Drain lentils, discarding orange zest and bay leaf, and transfer to large serving bowl; let cool slightly. Add oranges, along with any accumulated juices, spinach, oil, shallot, dill, ¼ teaspoon salt, and remaining 1½ tablespoons vinegar; gently toss to combine. Season with salt and pepper to taste. Sprinkle with pecans. Serve.

VARIATION

Lentil Salad with Radishes, Cilantro, and Pepitas for Two
SLOW COOKER
Serves 2
Cook Time 3 to 4 hours on low or 2 to 3 hours on high
We prefer French green lentils (lentilles du Puy) for this recipe, but it will work with any type of lentil except red or yellow. Crumbled feta can be substituted for the queso fresco.

½ cup French green lentils, picked over and rinsed
3 tablespoons lime juice, divided
3 garlic cloves, minced
1 tablespoon ground cumin
1½ teaspoons dried oregano
⅛ teaspoon table salt, plus salt for cooking lentils
3 radishes, trimmed, halved, and sliced thin
½ red bell pepper, cut into ½-inch pieces
2 tablespoons fresh cilantro leaves
2 tablespoons extra-virgin olive oil
½ jalapeño chile, stemmed, seeded, and minced
1 small shallot, minced
¼ cup crumbled queso fresco
2 tablespoons roasted pepitas

1. Combine 4 cups water, lentils, 1 tablespoon lime juice, garlic, cumin, oregano, and ¾ teaspoon salt in slow cooker. Cover and cook until lentils are tender, 3 to 4 hours on low or 2 to 3 hours on high.

2. Drain lentils and transfer to large serving bowl; let cool slightly. Add radishes, bell pepper, cilantro, oil, jalapeño, shallot, ⅛ teaspoon salt, and remaining 2 tablespoons lime juice; gently toss to combine. Season with salt and pepper to taste. Sprinkle with queso fresco and pepitas. Serve.

RINSING RICE AND GRAINS

Place rice or grains in fine-mesh strainer and rinse under cool water until water runs clear, occasionally stirring lightly with your hand. Let drain briefly.

NOTES FROM THE TEST KITCHEN

GETTING TO KNOW LENTILS
Lentils come in dozens of sizes and colors, and the variations in flavor and color are considerable.

Brown and Green Lentils These larger lentils are what you'll find in every supermarket. They are a uniform drab brown or green. They have a mild yet light and earthy flavor and creamy texture. They hold their shape well when cooked and have tender insides. These are all-purpose lentils, great in soups and salads or tossed with olive oil and herbs.

Lentilles du Puy These French lentils are smaller than the common brown and green varieties. They are a dark olive-green, almost black. We love them for their rich, earthy, complex flavor and firm yet tender texture. They keep their shape and look beautiful on the plate when cooked, so they're perfect for salads and dishes where the lentils take center stage.

Red and Yellow Lentils These small, split orange-red or golden-yellow lentils completely disintegrate when cooked. If you are looking for a lentil that will quickly break down into a thick puree, this is the one to use.

PASTA AND NOODLES

Hands-Off Spaghetti and Meatballs

* All slow cooker recipes work in a 4- to 7-quart traditional slow cooker unless noted.
** All Instant Pot recipes work in a 6- to 8-quart Instant Pot or other electric pressure cooker.

Penne with Fresh Tomato Sauce

Penne with Fresh Tomato Sauce

DUTCH OVEN

Serves 4 to 6

Total Time 45 minutes

Why This Recipe Works The best tomato sauce recipes have a short ingredient list, consisting of nothing more than garlic, olive oil, tomatoes, salt, a bit of sugar, and pepper. To capitalize on this simplicity, we cooked the pasta right in the sauce for a fresh, one-pot weeknight meal. Cooking the garlic in oil for just a minute kept it from burning. We minimized tomato prep by coring and chopping—but not peeling or seeding—our tomatoes, and we simmered them briefly until they started to break down and exude their juice. With the addition of a few cups of water to the sauce, there was enough liquid in the Dutch oven to cook the pasta; and by covering the pot, we ensured that the sauce didn't dry out. Starch released from the pasta thickened the sauce, helping it cling nicely. The tubular shape of penne allowed for the sauce to be perfectly trapped inside and helped give this rustic dish an even more comforting appeal. Other pasta shapes such as ziti, farfalle, and campanelle can be substituted for the penne.

3 tablespoons extra-virgin olive oil
2 garlic cloves, minced
2 pounds plum tomatoes, cored and cut into ½-inch pieces
¾ teaspoon table salt
½ teaspoon pepper
½ teaspoon sugar
5 cups water, plus extra as needed
1 pound penne
2 tablespoons chopped fresh basil

1. Cook oil and garlic in Dutch oven over medium heat until fragrant, 1 to 2 minutes. Stir in tomatoes, salt, pepper, and sugar. Increase heat to medium-high and cook until tomatoes are broken down and sauce is slightly thickened, about 10 minutes.

2. Stir in water and pasta and bring to vigorous simmer. Reduce heat to medium, cover, and cook, stirring gently and often, until pasta is nearly tender, about 12 minutes. (If sauce becomes too thick, add extra water as needed.)

3. Uncover and continue to simmer, stirring often, until pasta is tender and sauce has thickened, 3 to 5 minutes. Off heat, stir in basil and season with salt and pepper to taste. Serve.

VARIATION

Penne with Fresh Tomato Sauce for Two

SAUCEPAN

Serves 2

Total Time 45 minutes

Other pasta shapes such as ziti, farfalle, and campanelle can be substituted for the penne; however, the cup measurements will vary.

1 tablespoon extra-virgin olive oil
1 garlic clove, minced
1 pound plum tomatoes, cored and cut into ½-inch pieces
¼ teaspoon table salt
¼ teaspoon pepper
¼ teaspoon sugar
2 cups water, plus extra as needed
6 ounces (2 cups) penne
1 tablespoon chopped fresh basil

1. Cook oil and garlic in large saucepan over medium heat until fragrant, 1 to 2 minutes. Stir in tomatoes, salt, pepper, and sugar. Increase heat to medium-high and cook until tomatoes are broken down and sauce is slightly thickened, about 10 minutes.

2. Stir in water and pasta and bring to vigorous simmer. Reduce heat to medium, cover, and cook, stirring gently and often, until pasta is nearly tender, about 12 minutes. (If sauce becomes too thick, add extra water as needed.)

3. Uncover and continue to simmer, stirring often, until pasta is tender and sauce has thickened, 3 to 5 minutes. Off heat, stir in basil and season with salt and pepper to taste. Serve.

Pasta Puttanesca

DUTCH OVEN

Serves 4 to 6
Total Time 45 minutes

Why This Recipe Works Pasta alla puttanesca, a classic Italian dish featuring tomatoes, garlic, capers, and olives, offers bold flavor and comes together fairly quickly. We streamlined our recipe even more by cooking the fresh tomato sauce in a Dutch oven before adding the pasta to the pot so that the pasta and sauce finished cooking together. We started by using the same method as our Penne with Fresh Tomato Sauce (page 310), cooking garlic in the Dutch oven before adding plum tomatoes (which required minimal preparation), salt, pepper, and sugar. Extra water added to the pot along with the pasta provided enough liquid to cook the pasta through. Stirring in the olives and capers at the end of cooking preserved their bright brininess, and a final sprinkle of basil brought the flavors together. Other pasta shapes such as ziti, farfalle, and campanelle can be substituted for the penne.

- 3 tablespoon extra-virgin olive oil
- 2 garlic cloves, minced
- 2 pounds plum tomatoes, cored and cut into ½-inch pieces
- ½ teaspoon table salt
- ½ teaspoon pepper
- ½ teaspoon sugar
- 5 cups water, plus extra as needed
- 1 pound penne
- ¼ cup coarsely chopped pitted kalamata olives
- ¼ cup capers, rinsed
- 2 tablespoons chopped fresh basil

1. Cook oil and garlic in Dutch oven over medium heat until fragrant, 1 to 2 minutes. Stir in tomatoes, salt, pepper, and sugar. Increase heat to medium-high and cook until tomatoes are broken down and sauce is slightly thickened, about 10 minutes.

2. Stir in water and pasta and bring to vigorous simmer. Reduce heat to medium, cover, and cook, stirring gently and often, until pasta is nearly tender, about 12 minutes. (If sauce becomes too thick, add extra water as needed.)

3. Uncover, add olives and capers, and simmer, stirring often, until pasta is tender and sauce has thickened, 3 to 5 minutes. Off heat, stir in basil and season with salt and pepper to taste. Serve.

NOTES FROM THE TEST KITCHEN

MEASURING PASTA SHAPES
In our one-pot pasta recipes, the ratio of pasta to cooking liquid is critical to success. As the pasta cooks at a vigorous simmer, it absorbs the majority of the liquid and the rest reduces to a saucy consistency. Therefore, if you use more pasta than called for, there won't be enough liquid to cook it through. Conversely, if you use less, the resulting sauce will be too thin or soupy. Also, pay close attention to the shape of pasta called for in each recipe; different pasta shapes and sizes have slightly different cooking times and, therefore, not all shapes are interchangeable. The best method for measuring pasta is to weigh it using a scale. However, if you do not own a scale, we have provided the equivalent cup measurements for various shapes. Use dry measuring cups for the most accurate measurements, and pack them full.

PASTA TYPE	8 OUNCES	12 OUNCES
Penne	2½ cups	3¾ cups
Ziti	2½ cups	3¾ cups
Orecchiette	2½ cups	3½ cups
Campanelle	3 cups	4½ cups
Farfalle (Bow Ties)	3 cups	4½ cups
Medium Shells	3 cups	4½ cups
Elbow Macaroni	2 cups	3 cups

Penne with Chicken, Broccoli, and Bell Pepper

DUTCH OVEN

Serves 4

Total Time 1 hour

Why This Recipe Works Once we had established a basic one-pot technique for simmering pasta in a Dutch oven in homemade tomato sauce, we wanted to translate the same idea to a dish with a light, brothy sauce. Chicken (cut into strips to speed up cooking), broccoli, and bell pepper bulked up the pasta and a light sauce brought together this hearty meal. Cooking the broccoli first and then the chicken in a Dutch oven and setting both aside ensured they wouldn't overcook. Bell pepper, onion, and some aromatics went into the pot next, and deglazing the pot with white wine provided a balanced acidic note. Chicken broth added savoriness to the sauce, and water guaranteed enough liquid to cook the pasta. Tubular penne paired beautifully with the brothy sauce, which clung to the starchy surface of the pasta both inside and out. Adding Parmesan at the end along with the cooked chicken and broccoli deepened the flavor of the sauce. Other pasta shapes such as ziti, farfalle, and campanelle can be substituted for the penne; however, the cup measurements will vary.

- ¼ cup extra-virgin olive oil, divided
- 1½ pounds broccoli florets, stems discarded, florets cut into 1-inch pieces
- 2 cups water, divided, plus extra as needed Pinch plus 1 teaspoon table salt, divided
- 1 pound boneless, skinless chicken breasts, trimmed and sliced ¼ inch thick
- ½ teaspoon pepper
- 1 onion, chopped fine
- 1 red bell pepper, stemmed, seeded, and cut into ½-inch pieces
- 6 garlic cloves, minced
- 1 teaspoon minced fresh oregano or ¼ teaspoon dried
- ⅛ teaspoon red pepper flakes
- ½ cup dry white wine
- 2 cups chicken broth
- 8 ounces (2½ cups) penne
- 2 ounces Parmesan cheese, grated (1 cup), plus extra for serving

1. Heat 1 tablespoon oil in large Dutch oven over medium heat until shimmering. Add broccoli, ¼ cup water, and pinch salt. Cover and cook until broccoli is crisp-tender, 3 to 4 minutes. Uncover and continue to cook until broccoli is just tender and liquid has evaporated, 1 to 2 minutes; transfer to bowl.

2. Pat chicken dry with paper towels and sprinkle with ½ teaspoon salt and pepper. Heat 2 tablespoons oil in now-empty pot over medium-high heat until just smoking. Add chicken, break up any clumps, and cook, without stirring, until beginning to brown, about 1 minute. Stir chicken and continue to cook until just cooked through, about 2 minutes; transfer chicken to bowl with broccoli.

3. Add remaining 1 tablespoon oil, onion, and bell pepper to again-empty pot and cook over medium heat until vegetables are softened, 5 to 7 minutes. Stir in garlic, oregano, and pepper flakes and cook until fragrant, about 30 seconds. Stir in wine, scraping up any browned bits, and cook until nearly evaporated, about 1 minute.

4. Stir in remaining 1¾ cups water, broth, pasta, and remaining ½ teaspoon salt and bring to vigorous simmer. Reduce heat to medium, cover, and cook, stirring gently and often, until pasta is tender and sauce has thickened, 15 to 18 minutes. (If sauce becomes too thick, add extra water as needed.)

5. Reduce heat to low and stir in broccoli, chicken with any accumulated juice, and Parmesan. Cook, uncovered, stirring often, until pasta is well coated, 1 to 2 minutes. Season with salt and pepper to taste. Serve with extra Parmesan.

VARIATION

Penne with Chicken, Mushrooms, and Gorgonzola for Two

SKILLET

Serves 2

Total Time 45 minutes

Other pasta shapes such as ziti, farfalle, and campanelle can be substituted for the penne; however, the cup measurements will vary.

- 8 ounces boneless, skinless chicken breasts, trimmed and sliced ¼ inch thick
- ⅛ plus ¼ teaspoon table salt, divided
- ⅛ teaspoon pepper
- 2 tablespoons extra-virgin olive oil, divided
- 4 ounces white mushrooms, trimmed and quartered
- 3 garlic cloves, minced
- 1 teaspoon minced fresh oregano or ¼ teaspoon dried Pinch red pepper flakes
- ½ cup dry white wine
- 6 ounces (2 cups) penne
- 1½ cups chicken broth
- 1 cup water, plus extra as needed
- 1 ounce Gorgonzola cheese, crumbled (¼ cup), plus extra for serving
- 1 tablespoon unsalted butter
- 1 tablespoon minced fresh parsley

1. Pat chicken dry with paper towels and sprinkle with ⅛ teaspoon salt and pepper. Heat 1 tablespoon oil in 10-inch nonstick skillet over medium-high heat until just smoking. Add chicken, break up any clumps, and cook, without stirring, until beginning to brown, about 1 minute. Stir chicken and continue to cook until just cooked through, about 2 minutes; transfer to bowl.

2. Add remaining 1 tablespoon oil and mushrooms to now-empty skillet and cook over medium heat, stirring occasionally, until mushrooms have released their liquid and are golden brown, 7 to 10 minutes. Stir in garlic, oregano, and pepper flakes and cook until fragrant, about 30 seconds. Stir in wine, bring to simmer, and cook until nearly evaporated, about 2 minutes.

3. Stir in pasta, broth, water, and remaining ¼ teaspoon salt and bring to vigorous simmer. Reduce heat to medium, cover, and cook, stirring gently and often, until pasta is tender and sauce has thickened, 12 to 15 minutes. (If sauce becomes too thick, add extra water as needed.)

4. Reduce heat to low and stir in chicken with any accumulated juices, Gorgonzola, and butter. Cook, uncovered, stirring often, until pasta is well coated with sauce, 1 to 2 minutes. Stir in parsley and season with salt and pepper to taste. Serve with extra Gorgonzola.

Orecchiette with Broccoli Rabe and Sausage

Orecchiette with Broccoli Rabe and Sausage

INSTANT POT
Serves 4 to 6
Total Time 45 minutes

Why This Recipe Works The pressure cooker works exceptionally well for turning out perfect al dente pasta. Inspired by a dinner found on many tables in southern Italy, we paired "little ear" orecchiette pasta with slightly bitter broccoli rabe and fennel seed–scented sausage. To keep the broccoli rabe from overcooking and losing its vibrant green color, we sautéed it briefly in the pressure cooker and set it aside to stir into the pasta right before serving. We then browned Italian sausage and aromatics in the pot before adding our pasta and chicken broth. Cooked at pressure, the orecchiette readily absorbed most of the flavorful broth. The small amount of broth left in the pot transformed into a smooth sauce once some Parmesan was stirred in, and the orecchiette's curved shape scooped up the sauce, nestling against the bits of savory sausage and crisp-tender broccoli rabe. Do not substitute other pasta shapes in this dish, as they require different liquid amounts and will not work in this recipe.

2 tablespoons extra-virgin olive oil, divided
1 pound broccoli rabe, trimmed and cut into 1½-inch pieces
¼ teaspoon table salt
8 ounces hot or sweet Italian sausage, casings removed
6 garlic cloves, minced
¼ teaspoon red pepper flakes
¼ cup dry white wine
4½ cups chicken broth
1 pound orecchiette
2 ounces Parmesan cheese, grated (1 cup), plus extra for serving

1. Using highest sauté or browning function, heat 1 tablespoon oil in electric pressure cooker until shimmering. Add broccoli rabe and salt, cover, and cook, stirring occasionally, until softened, 3 to 5 minutes. Using slotted spoon, transfer broccoli rabe to bowl; set aside.

2. Add sausage and remaining 1 tablespoon oil to now-empty pressure cooker and cook, breaking up meat with wooden spoon, until lightly browned, about 5 minutes. Stir in garlic and pepper flakes and cook until fragrant, about 30 seconds. Stir in wine, scraping up any browned bits, then stir in broth and pasta.

3. Lock lid in place and close pressure release valve. Select high pressure cook function and cook for 4 minutes. Turn off pressure cooker and quick-release pressure. Carefully remove lid, allowing steam to escape away from you.

4. Stir broccoli rabe and any accumulated juices and Parmesan into pasta. Season with salt and pepper to taste. Serve, passing extra Parmesan separately.

Weeknight Bolognese
DUTCH OVEN

Serves 4 to 6
Total Time 1½ hours

Why This Recipe Works Making Bolognese is often an all-day affair, but the complexity and richness of this hearty sauce can't be beat. We wanted a one-pot version that wouldn't sacrifice flavor. We first used our Dutch oven to deeply brown the aromatics and some pancetta to develop a flavorful fond. We skipped browning the ground beef, which would dry out and toughen if seared, and treated it with a baking soda solution to ensure it stayed tender. Tomato paste and red wine added brightness. Grated Parmesan thickened the sauce and offered depth. We cooked the pasta right in the pot by thinning the sauce with some broth and water before stirring in the pappardelle. You can substitute fettucine for the pappardelle, if desired; break the pasta in half before adding it to the pot and increase the cooking time to 16 to 18 minutes in step 5.

    1 pound 93 percent lean ground beef
    2 tablespoons plus 1½ cups water, divided,
         plus extra as needed
    ¼ teaspoon baking soda
    ½ teaspoon pepper, divided
    6 ounces pancetta, chopped coarse
    1 onion, chopped coarse
    1 large carrot, peeled and chopped coarse
    1 celery rib, chopped coarse
    1 tablespoon unsalted butter
    1 tablespoon extra-virgin olive oil
    3 tablespoons tomato paste
    1 cup dry red wine
    4 cups beef broth
    1 ounce Parmesan cheese, grated (½ cup),
         plus extra for serving
    1 pound dried pappardelle

1. Toss beef with 2 tablespoons water, baking soda, and ¼ teaspoon pepper in bowl until thoroughly combined; set aside.

2. Pulse pancetta in food processor until finely chopped, 15 to 20 pulses. Add onion, carrot, and celery and pulse until vegetables are finely chopped and mixture has paste-like consistency, 12 to 15 pulses, scraping down sides of bowl as needed.

3. Heat butter and oil in Dutch oven over medium-high heat until shimmering. Add pancetta-vegetable mixture and remaining ¼ teaspoon pepper and cook, stirring occasionally, until liquid has evaporated, about 8 minutes. Spread mixture in even layer in bottom of pot and continue to cook, stirring every couple of minutes, until very dark, browned bits form on bottom of pot, 7 to 12 minutes. Stir in tomato paste and cook until paste is rust-colored and bottom of pot is dark brown, 1 to 2 minutes.

4. Reduce heat to medium, add beef mixture, and cook, using wooden spoon to break meat into pieces no larger than ¼ inch, until beef has just lost its raw pink color, 4 to 7 minutes. Stir in wine, scraping up any browned bits, and bring to simmer. Cook until wine has evaporated and sauce has thickened, about 5 minutes. Stir in broth, Parmesan, and remaining 1½ cups water and bring to simmer. Reduce heat to low, cover, and cook for 20 minutes.

5. Increase heat to medium-high and bring sauce to vigorous simmer. Gently nestle pasta into sauce. Reduce heat to medium, cover, and cook, stirring gently and often, until pasta is tender, 10 to 12 minutes. (If sauce becomes too thick, add extra water as needed.) Season with salt and pepper to taste. Serve, passing extra Parmesan separately.

Slow-Cooked Pork Ragu with Ziti
DUTCH OVEN

Serves 4 to 6
Total Time 3 hours

Why This Recipe Works Italian pork ragu promises rich, rustic complexity: Pork is slow-cooked with tomatoes and wine until fall-apart tender, at which point it's shredded and returned to the sauce. Served atop a steaming bowl of al dente pasta and crowned with grated cheese, this sauce is an expressive example of Italy's deeply comforting food. Although it's a casual recipe at heart, not any cut of pork will do. We tried all manner of chops, but they turned dry during the long cooking time in the oven, so we turned to a fattier cut—country-style pork ribs—which turned meltingly tender and gave the sauce meaty flavor. Browning them in the Dutch oven first ensured there was rich fond left behind on the bottom of the pan. After setting the browned pork aside, we softened onions in the leftover fat and then stirred in garlic and anchovies for a savory backbone. We deglazed the pot with red wine and added canned tomatoes and chicken broth. The browned pork nestled right into the flavorful sauce to cook in the oven. After shredding the cooked pork and adding it back into the sauce, we brought the whole pot back to the stovetop to add our pasta, stirring it in along with some water so that everything finished cooking together. Other pasta shapes such as penne, farfalle, and campanelle can be substituted for the ziti.

2½ pounds bone-in country-style pork ribs, trimmed
1 teaspoon table salt, divided
½ teaspoon pepper
2 tablespoons extra-virgin olive oil, divided
1 onion, chopped fine
5 garlic cloves, minced
2 anchovy fillets, rinsed and minced
½ cup dry red wine
3 (14.5-ounce) cans diced tomatoes
1 cup chicken broth
2½ cups water
1 pound ziti
2 tablespoons minced fresh parsley
Grated Parmesan cheese

1. Adjust oven rack to lower-middle position and heat the oven to 300 degrees. Pat pork dry with paper towels and sprinkle with ½ teaspoon salt and pepper. Heat 1 tablespoon oil in Dutch oven over medium-high heat until just smoking. Brown half of pork, 8 to 10 minutes; transfer to large plate. Repeat with remaining 1 tablespoon oil and remaining pork; transfer to plate.

2. Add onion to fat left in pot and cook over medium heat until softened, about 5 minutes. Stir in garlic and anchovies and cook until fragrant, about 30 seconds. Stir in wine, scraping up any browned bits, and cook until nearly evaporated, 3 to 4 minutes. Stir in tomatoes and their juice and broth and bring to simmer.

3. Return pork and any accumulated juices to pot. Cover, transfer pot to oven, and cook until meat is very tender, about 1½ hours, flipping pork halfway through cooking.

4. Remove pot from oven and transfer pork to cutting board. Let pork cool slightly, then shred into bite-size pieces using 2 forks; discard fat and bones.

5. Stir water, pasta, and remaining ½ teaspoon salt into pot and bring to vigorous simmer. Reduce heat to medium, cover, and cook, stirring gently and often, until pasta is nearly tender and sauce is thickened, 15 to 18 minutes. (If sauce becomes too thick, add extra water as needed.)

6. Uncover, reduce heat to low and stir in shredded pork. Cook, stirring often, until pasta is well coated with sauce and pork is heated through, about 2 minutes. Season with salt and pepper to taste. Serve with Parmesan.

Weeknight Bolognese

Slow-Cooked Pork Ragu with Ziti

Hands-Off Spaghetti and Meatballs

CASSEROLE DISH

Serves 4

Total Time 1¼ hours

Why This Recipe Works An entirely hands-off dinner of spaghetti and meatballs sounds like a dream: no long wait for the water to boil, no tedious browning of the meatballs, no time-consuming sauce. For our super-simple version of one-pot spaghetti and meatballs, we pared it down to the basics to deliver the nostalgic, satisfying meal of our childhoods. An easy combination of ground beef, store-bought pesto, and panko bread crumbs yielded meatballs with plenty of flavor. We wanted the pasta to cook right in the sauce, so we spread spaghetti in a casserole dish and covered it with jarred marinara sauce; thinning the sauce with water ensured there would be enough moisture to properly cook the strands. We then nestled the meatballs into the sauce and let everything bake, covered, in a very hot oven for 30 minutes. These conditions simulated boiling on the stovetop, enabling our pasta to cook in the sauce and absorb the flavors surrounding it. Once our pasta was al dente, we uncovered it, gave it a stir, and let the meatballs brown and the sauce thicken for the last few minutes of baking. A sprinkling of nutty Parmesan and fresh basil was the perfect finishing touch. We developed this recipe using jarred marinara sauce, but you can also use our Quick Marinara Sauce (page 317). You can use our Classic Basil Pesto (page 45) or any fresh store-bought variety here.

Hands-Off Spaghetti and Meatballs

12 ounces spaghetti
3 cups jarred marinara sauce
2 cups water, plus extra as needed
¾ cup panko bread crumbs
6 tablespoons milk
1 pound 85 percent lean ground beef
⅓ cup basil pesto
1 teaspoon table salt
¼ teaspoon pepper
2 tablespoons chopped fresh basil

1. Adjust oven rack to middle position and heat oven to 475 degrees. Spray 13 by 9-inch baking dish with vegetable oil spray. Loosely wrap half of pasta in dish towel, then press bundle against corner of counter to break noodles into 6-inch lengths; repeat with remaining pasta. Spread pasta in prepared dish. Pour marinara sauce and water over pasta and toss gently with tongs to coat.

2. Using fork, mash panko and milk in large bowl until smooth paste forms. Add beef, pesto, salt, and pepper and knead mixture with your hands until well combined. Pinch off and roll mixture into 1½-inch meatballs (you should have about 16 meatballs). Place meatballs on top of pasta in dish. Cover dish tightly with aluminum foil and bake for 30 minutes.

3. Remove dish from oven and stir pasta thoroughly, scraping sides and bottom of dish. Return uncovered dish to oven and continue to bake until pasta is tender and sauce is thickened, 5 to 8 minutes.

4. Remove dish from oven. Toss to coat pasta and meatballs with sauce, adjusting sauce consistency with extra hot water as needed. Let cool for 10 minutes. Season with salt and pepper to taste. Sprinkle with basil and serve.

BREAKING PASTA

Loosely fold noodles in dish towel, then press bundle against counter to break pasta into desired lengths.

Hands-Off Spaghetti and Meatballs for Two
CASSEROLE DISH

Serves 2
Total Time 1¼ hours

We developed this recipe using jarred marinara sauce, but you can also use our Quick Marinara Sauce. You can use our Classic Basil Pesto (page 45) or any fresh store-bought variety here.

6	ounces spaghetti
1½	cup jarred marinara sauce
1	cups water, plus extra as needed
⅓	cup panko bread crumbs
3	tablespoons milk
8	ounces 85 percent lean ground beef
2	tablespoons basil pesto
½	teaspoon table salt
⅛	teaspoon pepper
1	tablespoon chopped fresh basil

1. Adjust oven rack to middle position and heat oven to 475 degrees. Spray 8-inch square baking dish with vegetable oil spray. Loosely wrap pasta in dish towel, then press bundle against corner of counter to break noodles into 6-inch lengths. Spread pasta in prepared dish. Pour marinara sauce and water over pasta and toss gently with tongs to coat.

2. Using fork, mash panko and milk in large bowl until smooth paste forms. Add beef, pesto, salt, and pepper and knead mixture with your hands until well combined. Pinch off and roll mixture into 1½-inch meatballs (you should have about 8 meatballs). Place meatballs on top of pasta in dish. Cover dish tightly with aluminum foil and bake for 30 minutes.

3. Remove dish from oven and stir pasta thoroughly, scraping sides and bottom of dish. Return uncovered dish to oven and continue to bake until pasta is tender and sauce is thickened, 5 to 8 minutes.

4. Remove dish from oven. Toss to coat pasta and meatballs with sauce, adjusting sauce consistency with extra hot water as needed. Let cool for 10 minutes. Season with salt and pepper to taste. Sprinkle with basil and serve.

INGREDIENT SPOTLIGHT

ALL ABOUT CANNED TOMATOES
Canned tomatoes are processed at the height of freshness, so they deliver more flavor than off-season fresh tomatoes.

Whole Tomatoes Whole tomatoes are peeled tomatoes packed in either their own juice or puree. Whole tomatoes are soft and break down quickly when cooked. Our favorite brand is **Muir Glen**.

Diced Tomatoes Diced tomatoes are peeled, machine-diced, and packed in either their own juice or puree. We favor diced tomatoes packed in juice for their fresh flavor; our favorite is **Hunt's**.

Crushed Tomatoes Crushed tomatoes are whole tomatoes ground finely and enriched with tomato puree. We like **Tuttorosso**; you can also make your own by crushing diced tomatoes in a food processor.

Tomato Puree Tomato puree is made from cooked tomatoes that have been strained to remove seeds and skins. Our favorite brand is **Muir Glen Organic**.

Tomato Paste Tomato paste is tomato puree that has been cooked to remove most moisture. Because it's naturally full of glutamates, tomato paste brings out savory notes. Our preferred brand is **Goya**.

Quick Marinara Sauce
Makes 3 cups

¼	cup extra-virgin olive oil
2	garlic cloves, minced
1	(28-ounce) can crushed tomatoes
2	tablespoons minced fresh basil
¼	teaspoon sugar

Cook oil and garlic in large saucepan over medium heat until fragrant but not browned, about 2 minutes. Stir in tomatoes, bring to simmer, and cook until slightly thickened, about 5 minutes. Off heat, stir in basil and sugar and season with salt to taste. (Sauce can be refrigerated for up to 1 week or frozen for up to 1 month.)

BAKED ZITI

There's a lot to love about baked ziti: tender pasta, vibrant tomato sauce, oozy pockets of mozzarella, and dollops of creamy, bubbling ricotta. We wanted a flexible recipe that could feed two or 12 (yes, 12!) using just one pot for every step. Our streamlined approach started with the sauce. First we cooked garlic in the base of our pot—a Dutch oven for our classic recipe, a smaller skillet for two, and a roomy roasting pan over two burners to serve a crowd. Next we added a combination of convenient canned tomato sauce and diced tomatoes, which offered the right consistency with zero preparation. Oregano, red pepper flakes, and a bit of sugar contributed complexity as well as some sweetness to temper the tomatoes' acidity. We added the pasta directly to our sauce along with some water to adequately cook the ziti, and we stirred in basil for freshness (we reserved some to sprinkle on before serving). Simmering the pasta until it was only partially cooked kept the ziti from turning mushy when we placed the pot under the broiler to brown the top. And since no baked ziti is complete without gooey cheese, we stirred in plenty of mozzarella and Parmesan off heat. Before moving the pot to the oven, we dolloped the surface with ricotta and gave it a final topping of even more mozzarella and Parmesan, which melted and browned into an exquisite crust.

CLASSIC

DUTCH OVEN
Serves 4 to 6
Total Time 1¼ hours

- 2 teaspoons extra-virgin olive oil
- 3 garlic cloves, minced
- 1 (28-ounce) can tomato sauce
- 1 (14.5-ounce) can diced tomatoes
- ¾ teaspoon table salt
- ½ teaspoon dried oregano
- ½ teaspoon sugar
- ⅛ teaspoon red pepper flakes
- 12 ounces (3¾ cups) ziti
- 2 cups water, plus extra as needed
- 6 tablespoons chopped fresh basil, divided
- 6 ounces whole-milk mozzarella cheese, cut into ¼-inch pieces (1½ cups), divided
- 2 ounces Parmesan cheese, grated (1 cup), divided
- 8 ounces (1 cup) whole-milk ricotta cheese

1. Cook oil and garlic in Dutch oven over medium heat until fragrant, about 1 minute. Stir in tomato sauce, tomatoes and their juice, salt, oregano, sugar, and pepper flakes. Bring to simmer and cook until thickened, about 10 minutes.

2. Stir in pasta, water, and ¼ cup basil and bring to vigorous simmer. Reduce heat to medium, cover, and cook, stirring gently and often, until pasta is almost tender, 6 to 8 minutes. (If sauce becomes too thick, add extra water as needed.) Off heat, stir in ¾ cup mozzarella and ½ cup Parmesan.

3. Meanwhile, adjust oven rack 10 inches from broiler element and heat broiler. Dollop surface of pasta evenly with ricotta. Top with remaining ¾ cup mozzarella and remaining ½ cup Parmesan. Broil until cheese is bubbling and beginning to brown, 5 to 7 minutes.

4. Transfer pot to wire rack and let cool for 10 minutes. Sprinkle with remaining 2 tablespoons basil. Serve.

MAKE IT YOUR WAY →

> **Use What You've Got** Substitute other pasta shapes (penne, farfalle, and campanelle); cup measurements will vary. Substitute fire-roasted tomatoes for canned diced tomatoes, part-skim mozzarella cheese for whole-milk mozzarella, and/or Pecorino Romano for Parmesan cheese.

COOK IT FOR TWO

SKILLET
Serves 2
Total Time 1 hour
You will need a 10-inch ovensafe skillet for this recipe.

- 1 teaspoon extra-virgin olive oil
- 1 garlic clove, minced
- 1 (15-ounce) can tomato sauce
- ½ (14.5-ounce) can diced tomatoes
- ¼ teaspoon table salt
- ¼ teaspoon dried oregano
- ¼ teaspoon sugar
-   Pinch red pepper flakes
- 6 ounces (2 cups) ziti
- 1 cup water, plus extra as needed
- 3 tablespoons chopped fresh basil, divided
- 3 ounces whole-milk mozzarella cheese, cut into ¼-inch pieces (¾ cup), divided
- 1 ounce Parmesan cheese, grated (½ cup), divided
- 4 ounces (½ cup) whole-milk ricotta cheese

1. Cook oil and garlic in 10-inch ovensafe skillet over medium heat until fragrant, about 1 minute. Stir in tomato sauce, tomatoes and their juice, salt, oregano, sugar, and pepper flakes. Bring to simmer and cook until thickened, about 8 minutes.

2. Stir in pasta, water, and 2 tablespoons basil and bring to vigorous simmer. Reduce heat to medium, cover, and cook, stirring gently and often, until pasta is almost tender, 6 to 8 minutes. (If sauce becomes too thick, add extra water as needed.) Off heat, stir in ½ cup mozzarella and ¼ cup Parmesan.

3. Meanwhile, adjust oven rack 10 inches from broiler element and heat broiler. Dollop surface of pasta evenly with ricotta. Top with remaining ¼ cup mozzarella and remaining ¼ cup Parmesan. Broil until cheese is bubbling and beginning to brown, 5 to 7 minutes.

4. Transfer skillet to wire rack and let cool for 10 minutes. Sprinkle with remaining 1 tablespoon basil. Serve.

COOK IT FOR A CROWD

ROASTING PAN
Serves 10 to 12
Total Time 1¼ hours

- 2 tablespoons extra-virgin olive oil
- 6 garlic cloves, minced
- 2 (28-ounce) cans tomato sauce
- 1 (28-ounce) can diced tomatoes
- 1½ teaspoons table salt
- 1 teaspoon dried oregano
- 1 teaspoon sugar
- ¼ teaspoon red pepper flakes
- 2 pounds ziti
- 6 cups water, plus extra as needed
- ¾ cup chopped fresh basil, divided
- 12 ounces whole-milk mozzarella cheese, cut into ¼-inch pieces (3 cups), divided
- 4 ounces Parmesan cheese, grated (2 cups), divided
- 1 pound (2 cups) whole-milk ricotta cheese

1. Cook oil and garlic in 16 by 12-inch roasting pan over medium heat (over 2 burners, if possible) until fragrant, about 1 minute. Stir in tomato sauce, tomatoes and their juice, salt, oregano, sugar, and pepper flakes. Bring to simmer and cook until thickened, 6 to 8 minutes.

2. Stir in pasta, water, and ½ cup basil and bring to vigorous simmer. Reduce heat to medium, cover with aluminum foil, and cook, stirring gently and often, until pasta is almost tender, 8 to 10 minutes. (If sauce becomes too thick, add extra water as needed.) Off heat, stir in 1½ cups mozzarella and 1 cup Parmesan.

3. Meanwhile, adjust oven rack 10 inches from broiler element and heat broiler. Dollop surface of pasta evenly with ricotta. Top with remaining 1½ cups mozzarella and remaining 1 cup Parmesan. Broil until cheese is bubbling and beginning to brown, 5 to 7 minutes.

4. Transfer pan to wire rack and let cool for 10 minutes. Sprinkle with remaining ¼ cup basil. Serve.

> **Bulk it Up** Add shredded cooked chicken, crumbled cooked Italian sausage, and/or roasted vegetable pieces (butternut squash, fennel, mushrooms) with ziti. Add roasted red peppers, baby spinach, and/or frozen peas during last 2 minutes of simmering.

> **Add an Upgrade** Add minced anchovies, rinsed and minced porcini mushrooms, and/or rinsed and minced capers in place of—or in addition to—the oregano. Crisp pancetta or bacon pieces, chopped olives, and extra-virgin olive oil all make great finishing touches.

Bucatini with Peas, Kale, and Pancetta

Lemony Spaghetti with Shrimp and Spinach

Bucatini with Peas, Kale, and Pancetta

DUTCH OVEN

Serves 4 to 6
Total Time 45 minutes

Why This Recipe Works Salty pancetta makes a great addition to a variety of pasta dishes, as the pasta eagerly soaks up the pancetta's rich flavors. Add in quick-cooking sweet peas and baby kale and you have a simple, fresh pasta dish with a meaty backbone. We first rendered the pancetta in a Dutch oven, reserving the crispy pieces for garnish and using the fat to bloom bright lemon zest and garlic. We added white wine, chicken broth, and water to build a savory cooking liquid. For our pasta, we opted for thick-stranded bucatini, which is similar to spaghetti but hollow; its unique shape allowed it to absorb plenty of flavorful sauce. Stirring in the peas and kale during the last few minutes ensured they didn't overcook, and a final addition of Parmesan bound the cooking liquid into a cohesive sauce. For crunch, we topped each serving with a mixture of panko and more Parmesan and lemon zest, plus the crisped pancetta. You can substitute spaghetti for the bucatini, if desired.

- ½ cup panko bread crumbs, toasted
- 1½ ounces Parmesan cheese, grated (¾ cup), divided
- 1 tablespoon extra-virgin olive oil
- 1 tablespoon grated lemon zest, divided
- ¼ teaspoon table salt
- ¼ teaspoon pepper
- 2 ounces pancetta, cut into ½-inch pieces
- 2 garlic cloves, minced
- ½ cup dry white wine
- 2½ cups water
- 2 cups chicken broth
- 1 pound bucatini
- 5 ounces (5 cups) baby kale
- 1 cup frozen peas

1. Combine panko, ¼ cup Parmesan, oil, 1 teaspoon lemon zest, salt, and pepper in bowl; set aside. Cook pancetta in Dutch oven over medium heat until rendered and crisp, 6 to 8 minutes. Using slotted spoon, transfer pancetta to paper towel–lined plate.

2. Add garlic and remaining 2 teaspoons lemon zest to fat left in pot and cook until fragrant, about 30 seconds. Stir in wine, scraping up any browned bits, and cook until nearly evaporated, about 3 minutes. Stir in water, broth, and pasta and bring to vigorous simmer. Reduce heat to medium, cover, and cook, stirring gently and often, until pasta is nearly tender, 8 to 10 minutes.

3. Uncover, stir in kale and peas and simmer until pasta and kale are tender, about 4 minutes. Add remaining ½ cup Parmesan and stir vigorously until pasta is creamy and well coated, about 30 seconds. Season with salt and pepper to taste. Serve, sprinkling individual portions with pancetta and panko mixture.

Lemony Spaghetti with Shrimp and Spinach

DUTCH OVEN
Serves 4 to 6
Total Time 1 hour

Why This Recipe Works Sweet shrimp, bright lemon, and tender spinach come together seamlessly in this one-pot interpretation of the Italian classic spaghetti al limone. We knew the key to making our pasta sing was to coax maximum flavor out of each ingredient. Thinking resourcefully, we saved the shrimp shells and made a quick shrimp broth by simmering them in our Dutch oven with white wine. We used this flavorful liquid to poach our shrimp and cook our pasta, which became infused with the shrimp's briny flavor as the liquid reduced. To add plenty of lemon flavor, we whisked up a lemon-Parmesan dressing and poured this over the still-hot pasta to maximize absorption and create a nutty, creamy sauce. Finally, we finished the dish with a healthy pat of butter and a sprinkling of fresh basil, which balanced the sauce and accented it with a hint of sweet, herbal flavor.

5 tablespoons extra-virgin olive oil, divided
2 teaspoons grated lemon zest plus ¼ cup juice (2 lemons)
1 garlic clove, minced
½ teaspoon table salt
1 ounce Parmesan cheese, grated (½ cup)
1 pound jumbo shrimp (16 to 20 per pound), peeled, deveined, and tails removed, shells reserved
2½ cups dry white wine
2½ cups water
1 (8-ounce) bottle clam juice
1 pound spaghetti
5 ounces (5 cups) baby spinach
¼ cup shredded fresh basil
2 tablespoons unsalted butter, softened

1. Whisk ¼ cup oil, lemon zest and juice, garlic, and salt together in bowl. Add Parmesan and stir until thick and creamy; set aside.

2. Heat remaining 1 tablespoon oil in Dutch oven over medium heat until shimmering. Add reserved shrimp shells and cook, stirring frequently, until beginning to turn spotty brown, 2 to 4 minutes. Stir in wine and simmer until slightly reduced, about 5 minutes. Strain wine mixture through fine-mesh strainer set over large bowl, pressing on solids to extract as much liquid as possible; discard shells.

3. Return wine mixture to now-empty pot, add water and clam juice, and bring to gentle simmer over medium heat. Stir in shrimp and cook until just opaque throughout, about 2 minutes. Using slotted spoon, transfer shrimp to second bowl.

4. Add pasta to liquid left in pot and bring to vigorous simmer over medium-high heat. Reduce heat to medium, cover, and cook, stirring gently and often, until pasta is tender, 12 to 14 minutes.

5. Off heat, stir in spinach and shrimp and let sit until spinach is wilted and shrimp are heated through, about 30 seconds. Stir in basil, butter, and lemon sauce until butter is melted and pasta is well coated. Season with salt and pepper to taste. Serve.

Mussels Marinara with Spaghetti

DUTCH OVEN
Serves 4 to 6
Total Time 1 hour

Why This Recipe Works Quick-cooking, flavorful, and relatively inexpensive mussels infuse everything in the pot with their briny liquid, providing the base for a great sauce. To turn these shellfish into a complete meal, we looked to an Italian classic, mussels marinara. Traditionally, the mussels are draped in a spicy tomato sauce and served over pasta; for our version we planned to cook everything in the same Dutch oven, preparing both the pasta and the mussels directly in the sauce. We pulsed whole canned tomatoes in the food processor, leaving them somewhat chunky, and then gave our sauce plenty of oomph by adding finely chopped onion, lots of garlic, minced anchovy, and red pepper flakes. Substituting clam juice for some of the water gave the sauce more seafood flavor. The pasta went right into the sauce to cook, and as the spaghetti was nearing doneness we added the mussels. Within minutes, the shells gently opened and released their liquid, bolstering the briny marinara sauce further. With a glug of olive oil and a sprinkling of parsley, our simple yet sensational mussels marinara was ready.

2 (28-ounce) cans whole peeled tomatoes
3 tablespoons extra-virgin olive oil, divided
1 onion, chopped fine
6 garlic cloves, minced
1 anchovy fillet, rinsed and minced
½ teaspoon red pepper flakes
2 cups water, plus extra as needed
1 (8-ounce) bottle clam juice
1 pound spaghetti
2 pounds mussels, scrubbed and debearded
¼ cup minced fresh parsley

1. Working in 2 batches, pulse tomatoes and their juice in food processor until coarsely chopped and no large pieces remain, 6 to 8 pulses; transfer to bowl.

2. Heat 2 tablespoons oil in Dutch oven over medium heat until shimmering. Add onion and cook until softened, about 5 minutes. Stir in garlic, anchovy, and pepper flakes and cook until fragrant, about 30 seconds. Stir in tomatoes, bring to simmer, and cook until flavors meld, about 10 minutes.

3. Stir in water, clam juice, and pasta and bring to vigorous simmer. Reduce heat to medium, cover, and cook, stirring gently and often, for 12 minutes. (If sauce becomes too thick, add extra water as needed.) Stir in mussels, cover, and cook until pasta is tender and mussels have opened, 2 to 4 minutes.

4. Uncover and discard any unopened mussels. Reduce heat to low and stir in parsley and remaining 1 tablespoon oil; if sauce becomes too thick, add extra water as needed. Cook, tossing pasta gently until well coated with sauce, 1 to 2 minutes. Season with salt and pepper to taste. Serve.

Mussels Marinara with Spaghetti for Two
DUTCH OVEN
Serves 2
Total Time 1 hour

1 (28-ounce) can whole peeled tomatoes
2 tablespoons extra-virgin olive oil, divided
1 small onion, chopped fine
3 garlic cloves, minced
½ anchovy fillet, rinsed and minced
¼ teaspoon red pepper flakes
1½ cups water, plus extra as needed
½ cup bottled clam juice
6 ounces spaghetti
1 pound mussels, scrubbed and debearded
2 tablespoons minced fresh parsley

1. Pulse tomatoes and their juice in food processor until coarsely chopped and no large pieces remain, 6 to 8 pulses; transfer to bowl.

2. Heat 1 tablespoon oil in Dutch oven over medium heat until shimmering. Add onion and cook until softened, about 5 minutes. Stir in garlic, anchovy, and pepper flakes and cook until fragrant, about 30 seconds. Stir in tomatoes, bring to simmer, and cook until flavors meld, about 10 minutes.

3. Stir in water, clam juice, and pasta and bring to vigorous simmer. Reduce heat to medium, cover, and cook, stirring gently and often, for 12 minutes. (If sauce becomes too thick, add extra water as needed.) Stir in mussels, cover, and cook until pasta is tender and mussels have opened, 2 to 4 minutes.

4. Uncover and discard any unopened mussels. Reduce heat to low and stir in parsley and remaining 1 tablespoon oil; if sauce becomes too thick, add extra water as needed. Cook, tossing pasta gently until well coated with sauce, 1 to 2 minutes. Season with salt and pepper to taste. Serve.

Creamy Spring Vegetable Linguine
INSTANT POT
Serves 4 to 6
Total Time 45 minutes

Why This Recipe Works This uncomplicated pasta dish combines perfectly cooked al dente noodles with a silky sauce and a vibrant mix of vegetables and flavors—but without multiple pots, boiling water, or draining thanks to the pressure cooker. Linguine was our favored shape, as the thicker strands retained their bite in the ultrahigh heat of the pressure cooker. After cooking the pasta, we stirred in convenient jarred baby artichokes and frozen peas. By using just the right amount of water, we didn't need to drain the pasta; instead we could capture all of the starch that it released, which made it a cinch to emulsify grated Pecorino and the residual cooking liquid into a luscious sauce. Lemon zest and fresh tarragon brightened the dish. Do not substitute other pasta shapes in this dish, as they require different liquid amounts and will not work in this recipe. While we prefer the flavor and texture of jarred whole baby artichoke hearts in this recipe, you can substitute 6 ounces frozen artichoke hearts, thawed and patted dry, for the jarred.

1 pound linguine
5 cups water, plus extra as needed
1 tablespoon extra-virgin olive oil
1 teaspoon table salt
1 cup jarred whole baby artichokes packed in water, drained and quartered

Creamy Spring Vegetable Linguine

Tortellini with Fennel, Peas, and Spinach

DUTCH OVEN
Serves 4
Total Time 45 minutes

Why This Recipe Works Tender tortellini, spring vegetables, and a luxurious (but not overly rich) sauce—it's hard to believe this elegant meal uses just one pot and cooks in under an hour. Fennel, peas, and spinach proved the perfect trio of vegetables, providing sweetness, freshness, and texture. Slicing the fennel thin and browning it in butter in a Dutch oven before adding the cooking liquid (chicken broth alone worked well here) and pasta deepened its flavor. Once the tortellini were tender and the sauce was nicely thickened we added the spinach and peas, along with some cream for richness and body. Parmesan helped thicken the sauce and contributed nutty flavor, while a splash of lemon juice added brightness. To top it all off, we added a garnish of crisped prosciutto, which we cooked first before setting it aside—this enabled us to incorporate its rendered fat into the dish, adding another layer of flavor. For the best flavor and texture, be sure to buy fresh tortellini sold in the refrigerator case at the supermarket. Do not substitute frozen or dried tortellini, as they require different liquid amounts and will not work in this recipe.

1 cup frozen peas, thawed
4 ounces grated Pecorino Romano (2 cups), plus extra for serving
½ teaspoon pepper
2 teaspoons grated lemon zest
2 tablespoons chopped fresh tarragon

1. Loosely wrap half of pasta in dish towel, then press bundle against corner of counter to break noodles into 6-inch lengths; repeat with remaining pasta.

2. Add pasta, water, oil, and salt to electric pressure cooker, making sure pasta is completely submerged. Lock lid in place and close pressure release valve. Select high pressure cook function and cook for 4 minutes. Turn off pressure cooker and quick-release pressure. Carefully remove lid, allowing steam to escape away from you.

3. Stir artichokes and peas into pasta, cover, and let sit until heated through, about 3 minutes. Gently stir in Pecorino and pepper until cheese is melted and fully combined, 1 to 2 minutes. Adjust consistency with extra water as needed. Stir in lemon zest and tarragon, and season with salt and pepper to taste. Serve, passing extra Pecorino separately.

2 ounces thinly sliced prosciutto, cut into ¼-inch pieces
1 tablespoon unsalted butter
1 fennel bulb, stalks discarded, bulb halved, cored, and cut into ½-inch pieces
3 garlic cloves, minced
2¾ cups chicken broth
2 (9-ounce) packages fresh cheese tortellini
½ cup heavy cream
5 ounces (5 cups) baby spinach
1 cup frozen peas
1 ounce Parmesan cheese, grated (½ cup), plus extra for serving
1 tablespoon lemon juice

1. Cook prosciutto in Dutch oven over medium heat, stirring often, until browned and crisp, 5 to 7 minutes. Using slotted spoon, transfer prosciutto to paper towel–lined plate.

2. Melt butter in now-empty pot over medium heat. Add fennel and cook until softened and lightly browned, 6 to 9 minutes. Stir in garlic and cook until fragrant, about 30 seconds. Stir in broth and tortellini and bring to vigorous simmer. Reduce heat to medium, cover, and cook, stirring gently and often, until tortellini is tender and sauce is thickened, 6 to 9 minutes.

3. Uncover, reduce heat to low, and stir in cream, spinach, and peas. Cook, stirring gently, until spinach is wilted and tortellini is coated in sauce, 2 to 3 minutes.

4. Off heat, stir in Parmesan and lemon juice and season with salt and pepper to taste. Adjust consistency with extra water as needed. Serve, sprinkling individual portions with prosciutto and extra Parmesan.

Easiest-Ever Tomato and Cheese Lasagna

CASSEROLE DISH

Serves 4
Total Time 1¼ hours

Why This Recipe Works A prep-free (no chopping required), one-pot lasagna with rich flavor and a bubbling, cheesy topping? No problem. We developed a satisfying, simplified version of this comfort food classic so that it doesn't have to be relegated to Sunday-only status. Convenient jarred marinara sauce took the place of simmered-all-day sauce. Instead of the traditional time-consuming layering method, we shortened the process by combining the cheeses for a more streamlined assembly. We added the mixture to an 8-inch baking dish, which was just the right size for four servings, alternating it with the sauce and no-boil noodles. Leaving some clumps of ricotta cheese in the mixture ensured creamy bites throughout, and a sprinkling of extra mozzarella on top gave the lasagna a picture-perfect cheesy blanket. Cooking the lasagna first covered with foil and then uncovered guaranteed the lasagna was cooked all the way through and the top was browned. We developed this recipe using jarred marinara sauce, but you can also use our Quick Marinara Sauce (page 317).

- 8 ounces mozzarella cheese, shredded (2 cups), divided
- 1 ounce Parmesan cheese, grated (½ cup)
- 8 ounces (1 cup) whole-milk ricotta cheese
- 3 cups jarred marinara sauce, divided
- 6 no-boil lasagna noodles, divided

1. Adjust oven rack to middle position and heat oven to 375 degrees. Combine 1½ cups mozzarella and Parmesan in large bowl. Gently fold in ricotta, leaving some clumps.

2. Spread ½ cup marinara sauce into greased 8-inch square baking dish. Lay 2 noodles in dish (noodles may overlap slightly) and top with 1 cup sauce. Dollop half of ricotta mixture over top. Repeat layering of noodles and sauce one more time, followed by remaining ricotta mixture. Top with

Easiest-Ever Tomato and Cheese Lasagna

remaining 2 noodles, remaining ½ cup sauce, and remaining ½ cup mozzarella (in that order). (Assembled lasagna can be refrigerated for up to 24 hours; increase covered baking time in step 3 to 45 minutes.)

3. Cover dish tightly with greased aluminum foil and bake until bubbling around edges, about 20 minutes. Remove foil and continue to bake until cheese is spotty brown, 15 to 20 minutes. Let cool for 15 minutes before serving.

VARIATION

Easiest-Ever Tomato and Cheese Lasagna for Two
LOAF PAN

Serves 2
Total Time 1¼ hours
We developed this recipe using jarred marinara sauce, but you can also use our Quick Marinara Sauce (page 317). A 9 by 5-inch loaf pan also works here.

- 4 ounces mozzarella cheese, shredded (1 cup), divided
- ¼ cup grated Parmesan cheese
- 4 ounces (½ cup) whole-milk ricotta cheese
- 1½ cups jarred marinara sauce
- 3 no-boil lasagna noodles, divided

1. Adjust oven rack to middle position and heat oven to 375 degrees. Combine ¾ cup mozzarella and Parmesan in large bowl. Gently fold in ricotta, leaving some clumps.

2. Spread ¼ cup marinara sauce into greased 8½ by 4½-inch loaf pan. Lay 1 noodle in dish and top with ½ cup sauce. Dollop half of ricotta mixture over top. Repeat layering of noodle and sauce one more time, followed by remaining ricotta mixture. Top with remaining 1 noodle, remaining ¼ cup sauce, and remaining ¼ cup mozzarella (in that order). (Assembled lasagna can be refrigerated for up to 24 hours; increase covered baking time in step 3 to 45 minutes.)

3. Cover dish tightly with greased aluminum foil and bake until bubbling around edges, about 20 minutes. Remove foil and continue to bake until cheese is spotty brown, 15 to 20 minutes. Let cool for 10 minutes before serving.

Sausage Lasagna with Spinach and Mushrooms

CASSEROLE DISH
Serves 4
Total Time 1½ hours

Why This Recipe Works Once we had mastered our Easiest-Ever Tomato and Cheese Lasagna (page 324), we wanted to create an upgraded—but still streamlined—lasagna featuring meat and vegetables. Instead of making laborious béchamel and tomato sauces on the stovetop, we opted for a quick and flavorful no-cook cheese sauce and a jar of our favorite marinara. For the cheese sauce, we chose cottage cheese as our base, as it proved more flavorful than ricotta and turned creamy (instead of grainy) when cooked. To bump up the cheese flavor without adding excess moisture, we mixed in Parmesan. For the filling, we chose a supersavory combination of Italian sausage, cremini mushrooms, and baby spinach. To precook the filling without requiring an extra pot, we microwaved it; this allowed the sausage to cook through, the spinach to wilt, and the mushrooms to shed their moisture. After pressing out the filling's excess moisture, we began layering. Working in an 8-inch square baking dish, we layered no-boil noodles with the marinara, cheese sauce, sausage filling, and some shredded mozzarella. We repeated these layers once more and topped the lasagna with plenty of mozzarella. After cooking under foil for 30 minutes, we finished the lasagna uncovered for a bubbly, cheesy crust. We prefer the flavor of whole-milk cottage cheese here, but low-fat cottage cheese can be substituted; do not use nonfat cottage cheese. We developed this recipe using jarred marinara sauce, but you can also use our Quick Marinara Sauce (page 317).

4 ounces (½ cup) whole-milk cottage cheese
2 ounces Parmesan cheese, grated (1 cup)
1 garlic clove, minced
½ teaspoon pepper, divided
12 ounces hot or sweet Italian sausage, casings removed
8 ounces cremini mushrooms, trimmed and sliced thin
¼ teaspoon table salt
5 ounces (5 cups) baby spinach
3 cups jarred marinara sauce, divided
6 no-boil lasagna noodles, divided
8 ounces whole-milk mozzarella cheese, shredded (2 cups), divided

1. Adjust oven rack to middle position and heat oven to 425 degrees. Combine cottage cheese, Parmesan, garlic, and ¼ teaspoon pepper in bowl.

2. Pinch sausage into ½-inch pieces and combine with mushrooms, salt, and remaining ¼ teaspoon pepper in bowl. Cover and microwave, stirring occasionally, until sausage is no longer pink and mushrooms have released their liquid, about 9 minutes. Stir in spinach, cover, and microwave until wilted, about 1 minute. Transfer mixture to colander and let drain for 5 minutes, pressing on mixture with back of spoon to remove as much moisture as possible.

3. Spread ½ cup marinara sauce into greased 8-inch square baking dish. Lay 2 noodles in dish (noodles may overlap slightly) and top with 1 cup sauce. Dollop half of cottage cheese mixture over top and sprinkle with half of sausage and ½ cup mozzarella. Repeat layering of noodles and sauce one more time, followed by remaining cottage cheese, remaining sausage, and ½ cup mozzarella. Top with remaining 2 noodles, remaining ½ cup sauce, and remaining 1 cup mozzarella (in that order). (Assembled lasagna can be refrigerated for up to 24 hours; increase covered baking time in step 4 to 45 minutes.)

4. Cover dish tightly with greased aluminum foil and bake until bubbling around edges, about 30 minutes. Remove foil and continue to bake until cheese is spotty brown, 10 to 15 minutes. Let cool for 15 minutes before serving.

REMOVING MEAT FROM ITS CASING

To remove sausage meat from its casing before cooking, hold sausage firmly at one end and squeeze meat out through opposite end.

Cheesy Butternut Squash and Swiss Chard Lasagna

CASSEROLE DISH

Serves 4
Total Time 1¾ hours

Why This Recipe Works It's a shame how often vegetable lasagnas end up a flavorless mass of mushy vegetables and limp noodles. To create the ideal vegetarian lasagna—with a crisp, browned crust, tender noodles, and perfectly cooked vegetables bathed in a rich sauce—we started from the bottom up. We began with a creamy no-cook sauce (creamier than ricotta, way less effort than béchamel) by combining cottage cheese, Parmesan, cream, and cornstarch, plus fresh sage for its savory notes. To keep this a one-pot meal, we chose no-boil noodles. For our vegetables, butternut squash and Swiss chard paired well, and adding lemon zest, garlic, and nutmeg gave the veggies a refined flavor profile. Microwaving the vegetables helped them release excess liquid and prevented a waterlogged lasagna. To assemble, we layered the sauce, noodles, and vegetables in our 8-inch square casserole dish and topped it all off with shredded mozzarella. After 30 minutes of baking under an aluminum foil cover, we finished it uncovered for a bubbly, browned top. We prefer the flavor of whole-milk cottage cheese here, but low-fat cottage cheese can be substituted; do not use nonfat cottage cheese.

- 10 ounces (1¼ cups) whole-milk cottage cheese
- 2 ounces Parmesan cheese, grated (1 cup)
- 1 cup heavy cream
- 1 tablespoon minced fresh sage or 1 teaspoon dried
- 1 teaspoon cornstarch
- ½ teaspoon table salt, divided
- ¼ teaspoon plus ⅛ teaspoon pepper, divided
- 1 pound butternut squash, peeled, seeded, and cut into ½-inch pieces (3 cups)
- 1 pound Swiss chard, stemmed and cut into 1-inch pieces
- 1 tablespoon extra-virgin olive oil
- 2 garlic cloves, minced
- 1 teaspoon grated lemon zest
- ⅛ teaspoon ground nutmeg
- 6 no-boil lasagna noodles, divided
- 4 ounces whole-milk mozzarella cheese, shredded (1 cup)

1. Adjust oven rack to middle position and heat oven to 425 degrees. Whisk cottage cheese, Parmesan, cream, sage, cornstarch, ¼ teaspoon salt, and ¼ teaspoon pepper together in bowl.

2. Combine squash, chard, oil, garlic, lemon zest, nutmeg, remaining ¼ teaspoon salt, and remaining ⅛ teaspoon pepper in bowl, cover, and microwave until chard is wilted and butternut squash is just tender, about 7 minutes. Transfer mixture to colander and let drain for 5 minutes.

3. Spread 1 cup cheese sauce into greased 8-inch square baking dish. Lay 2 noodles in dish (noodles may overlap slightly) and top with half of squash mixture and half of cheese sauce. Repeat layering with 2 noodles, remaining squash mixture, and ½ cup cheese sauce. Lay remaining 2 noodles on top, cover with remaining cheese sauce, and sprinkle with mozzarella. (Assembled lasagna can be refrigerated for up to 24 hours; increase covered baking time in step 4 to 45 minutes.)

4. Cover dish tightly with greased aluminum foil and bake until bubbling around edges, about 30 minutes. Remove foil and continue to bake until cheese is spotty brown, 10 to 15 minutes, rotating dish halfway through baking. Let cool for 15 minutes before serving.

Baked Macaroni and Cheese

CASSEROLE DISH

Serves 4
Total Time 1 hour

Why This Recipe Works The test kitchen has no shortage of baked macaroni and cheese recipes, but could we create a one-pan version—one that skipped the pot of boiling water but didn't compromise on flavor? For our streamlined approach, we added the pasta to a casserole dish along with dry mustard (to enhance the cheesy flavor) and a mixture of water and evaporated milk, which helped establish a creamy base for the cheese sauce. Cooking the pasta in the oven under a foil cover guaranteed the perfect texture, and stirring in a meltable blend of shredded cheddar and American cheeses at the end of baking ensured a lush, smooth sauce. Finally, panko bread crumbs, browned in the microwave and sprinkled on before serving, provided an irresistible crunchy topping.

- 12 ounces (3 cups) elbow macaroni
- 2½ cups water, divided
- 1 (12-ounce) can evaporated milk
- ½ teaspoon dry mustard
- 1 teaspoon table salt
- ½ teaspoon pepper
- 6 ounces sharp cheddar cheese, shredded (1½ cups)
- 6 ounces American cheese, shredded (1½ cups)
- ½ cup panko bread crumbs, toasted

1 tablespoon extra-virgin olive oil
¼ cup grated Parmesan cheese
1 tablespoon minced fresh parsley, basil, or chives

1. Adjust oven rack to middle position and heat oven to 375 degrees. Spread macaroni into greased 13 by 9-inch baking dish. Whisk 2 cups water, evaporated milk, dry mustard, salt, and pepper together in bowl. Pour into baking dish and stir gently to combine.

2. Cover dish tightly with greased aluminum foil and bake, stirring occasionally, until macaroni is nearly tender and most liquid has been absorbed, about 30 minutes.

3. Remove dish from oven and stir macaroni thoroughly, scraping sides and bottom of dish. Stir in remaining ½ cup water, cheddar, and American cheese. Cover dish with foil and bake until macaroni is tender and cheese is melted, 5 to 8 minutes.

4. Remove dish from oven. Stir to coat pasta evenly in sauce and let cool while preparing topping. Toss panko with oil in bowl and microwave, stirring occasionally, until deep golden brown, 2 to 4 minutes. Let cool for 5 minutes, then stir in Parmesan and parsley. Sprinkle casserole with panko mixture and serve.

Pastitsio

SKILLET
Serves 4
Total Time 1 hour

Why This Recipe Works Translated from Greek as "made from pasta," pastitsio is a layered baked casserole of pasta, creamy béchamel sauce, ground meat and tomato sauce, and cheese. For this streamlined one-pan approach, we ditched the layering and cooked the pasta, meat, and sauce in one skillet on the stovetop. Ground lamb lent a grassy depth, and we used its flavorful rendered fat to cook our aromatics as well as to bloom some oregano and cinnamon, which offered fragrant and warm complexity. The liquid from canned diced tomatoes and a couple of cups of water served two purposes: They created a sauce and provided enough moisture to cook the pasta (lasagna noodles broken into pieces). And in place of the usual béchamel sauce, we simply added heavy cream to the meat sauce and topped the finished dish with feta for a similar richness. While lamb is traditional here, 85 percent lean ground beef can be substituted, if desired.

Cheesy Butternut Squash and Swiss Chard Lasagna

Baked Macaroni and Cheese

**Unstuffed Shells
with Butternut
Squash and Leeks**

2. Scatter noodles over meat but do not stir. Pour tomatoes and their juice over noodles and bring to vigorous simmer. Reduce heat to medium, cover, and cook, stirring gently and often, until noodles are tender, about 18 minutes.

3. Stir in cream and simmer until slightly thickened, about 3 minutes. Season with salt and pepper to taste. Sprinkle with feta and serve.

Unstuffed Shells with Butternut Squash and Leeks

SKILLET

Serves 4
Total Time 1¼ hours

Why This Recipe Works Cheesy jumbo stuffed shells have undeniable appeal, but preboiling and stuffing individual shells can be an ordeal. We set out to develop an easy unstuffed version in which the pasta cooked directly in the sauce. We quickly determined the right ratio of liquid to shells to ensure perfectly cooked noodles, but finding the ideal amount of vegetables proved trickier. Cooking butternut squash and leeks in a creamy sauce promised a hearty vegetarian meal, but if we used too much of either vegetable, the skillet was prone to overflowing; too little, however, and the servings looked meager. We settled on 1½ pounds of butternut squash and 1 pound of leeks. Cooking the squash and leeks briefly before adding the pasta and liquid deepened the vegetables' flavors and ensured that the pasta and squash would finish cooking at the same time. Instead of stuffing the shells with cheese, we sprinkled some Parmesan on top and dolloped a rich lemon-ricotta mixture over everything. We then slid the skillet into the oven to brown and melt the cheesy toppings. You can substitute large or medium shells, ziti, farfalle, campanelle, or orecchiette for the jumbo shells here. The skillet will be very full when you add the shells in step 3 (stir gently to start) but will become more manageable as the liquid evaporates and the shells become more malleable. You will need a 12-inch ovensafe nonstick skillet for this recipe.

1 pound ground lamb
1 onion, chopped fine
½ teaspoon table salt
4 garlic cloves, minced
1 teaspoon dried oregano
¼ teaspoon ground cinnamon
2 cups water
10 curly-edged lasagna noodles, broken into 2-inch lengths
1 (28-ounce) can diced tomatoes
¾ cup heavy cream
3 ounces feta cheese, crumbled (¾ cup)

1. Cook lamb in 12-inch skillet over medium-high heat, breaking up meat with wooden spoon, until lamb is no longer pink, about 5 minutes. Using slotted spoon, transfer lamb to paper towel–lined plate and pour off all but 1 tablespoon fat from skillet. Add onion and salt to fat left in skillet and cook until softened, about 5 minutes. Stir in garlic, oregano, and cinnamon and cook until fragrant, about 30 seconds. Stir in water and lamb and bring to simmer, scraping up any browned bits.

8 ounces (1 cup) whole-milk ricotta cheese
2 ounces Parmesan cheese, grated (1 cup), divided
1 teaspoon grated lemon zest
¾ teaspoon table salt, divided
¼ teaspoon pepper
1 tablespoon extra-virgin olive oil
1½ pounds butternut squash, peeled, seeded, and cut into ½-inch pieces (5 cups)

1 pound leeks, white and light green parts only, halved lengthwise, sliced thin, and washed thoroughly

2 garlic cloves, minced

Pinch cayenne pepper

¼ cup dry white wine

4 cups water

1 cup heavy cream

12 ounces jumbo pasta shells

2 tablespoons chopped fresh basil

1. Adjust oven rack to middle position and heat oven to 375 degrees. Combine ricotta, ½ cup Parmesan, lemon zest, ¼ teaspoon salt, and pepper in bowl; cover and refrigerate until needed.

2. Heat oil in 12-inch ovensafe nonstick skillet over medium heat until shimmering. Add squash, leeks, and remaining ½ teaspoon salt and cook until leeks are softened, about 5 minutes. Stir in garlic and cayenne and cook until fragrant, about 30 seconds. Stir in wine and cook until almost completely evaporated, about 1 minute.

3. Stir in water and cream, then add pasta and bring to vigorous simmer. Reduce heat to medium, cover, and cook, stirring gently and often, until pasta is tender and liquid has thickened, about 15 minutes.

4. Season with salt and pepper to taste. Sprinkle remaining ½ cup Parmesan over top, then dollop evenly with ricotta mixture. Transfer skillet to oven and bake until Parmesan is melted and spotty brown, about 5 minutes. Let cool for 10 minutes, then sprinkle with basil and serve.

Fideos with Chickpeas and Fennel

INSTANT POT

Serves 4

Total Time 45 minutes

Why This Recipe Works One of the biggest stars of traditional Spanish cooking is fideos, a richly flavored dish in which thin noodles are toasted until nut-brown and then cooked in a garlicky, tomatoey stock. Traditional recipes often include a homemade stock, a flavorful sofrito base of slowly reduced fresh tomatoes with aromatics and seasonings, and time in the oven. The complex flavors are undeniably delicious, but the preparation is far from weeknight-friendly. For a one-pot version that cut down on time without skimping on flavor, we turned to the pressure cooker. Toasting vermicelli in the microwave was simple and allowed us to start browning the sofrito in the meantime. We streamlined the sofrito base by finely chopping the onion (so it softened and browned quickly) and using canned tomatoes instead of fresh. Fennel added

brightness. The sauté function of the pressure cooker handled the vegetables in no time. Garlic, paprika, wine, and the juice from our canned tomatoes added even more depth to the broth. Some recipes use chorizo or shellfish, but for a prep-free (and vegetarian) version we opted for hearty, creamy canned chickpeas. Adding the right amount of broth (there is no evaporation) was key; we needed enough liquid for tender pasta, which we cooked under pressure with the sauce and vegetables for just two minutes, while still leaving a little sauciness. Any remaining liquid left in the pot after cooking will be absorbed by the pasta before serving. Serve with Garlic Aioli (page 73).

8 ounces vermicelli or thin spaghetti

2 teaspoons plus 2 tablespoons extra-virgin olive oil, divided

1 onion, chopped fine

1 fennel bulb, 1 tablespoon fronds minced, stalks discarded, bulb halved, cored, and sliced thin, divided

½ teaspoon table salt, divided

1 (14.5-ounce) can diced tomatoes, drained and chopped fine, juice reserved

3 garlic cloves, minced

1½ teaspoons smoked paprika

1½ cups vegetable or chicken broth

1 (15-ounce) can chickpeas, rinsed

¼ cup dry white wine

¼ teaspoon pepper

¼ cup sliced almonds, toasted

Lemon wedges

1. Loosely wrap pasta in dish towel, then press bundle against corner of counter to break noodles into 1- to 2-inch lengths. Toss pasta and 2 teaspoons oil in bowl and microwave at 50 percent power, stirring occasionally, until some pieces look toasted and blistered, 3 to 5 minutes.

2. Using highest sauté or browning function, heat remaining 2 tablespoons oil in electric pressure cooker until shimmering. Add onion, fennel, and ¼ teaspoon salt and cook until vegetables are softened, about 5 minutes. Stir in tomatoes and cook until mixture has thickened and darkened in color, 4 to 6 minutes.

3. Stir in garlic and paprika and cook until fragrant, about 30 seconds. Stir in pasta, broth, chickpeas, wine, reserved tomato juice, remaining ¼ teaspoon salt, and pepper.

4. Lock lid in place and close pressure release valve. Select high pressure cook function and cook for 2 minutes. Turn off pressure cooker and quick-release pressure. Carefully remove lid, allowing steam to escape away from you. Season with salt and pepper to taste. Sprinkle with fennel fronds and almonds. Serve with lemon wedges.

Fideos with Chickpeas and Fennel for Two

INSTANT POT

Serves 2

Total Time 45 minutes

Any canned small white bean will work here. Any remaining liquid left in the pot after cooking will be absorbed by the pasta before serving. Serve with Garlic Aioli (page 73).

- 4 ounces vermicelli or thin spaghetti
- 4 teaspoons extra-virgin olive oil, divided
- 1 small fennel bulb, 1½ teaspoons fronds minced, stalks discarded, bulb halved, cored, and sliced thin, divided
- ¼ teaspoon table salt, divided
- ½ (14.5-ounce) can diced tomatoes, drained with ½ juice reserved
- 1 garlic clove, minced
- ¾ teaspoon smoked paprika
- ¾ cup vegetable or chicken broth
- 1 cup canned chickpeas, rinsed
- ⅛ teaspoon pepper
- 2 tablespoons sliced almonds, toasted
  Lemon wedges

1. Loosely wrap pasta in dish towel, then press bundle against corner of counter to break noodles into 1- to 2-inch lengths. Toss pasta and 1 teaspoon oil in bowl and microwave at 50 percent power, stirring occasionally, until some pieces look toasted and blistered, 3 to 5 minutes.

2. Using highest sauté or browning function, heat remaining 1 tablespoon oil in electric pressure cooker until shimmering. Add fennel and ⅛ teaspoon salt and cook until softened, about 5 minutes. Stir in tomatoes and cook until mixture has thickened and darkened in color, 3 to 5 minutes.

3. Stir in garlic and paprika and cook until fragrant, about 30 seconds. Stir in pasta, broth, chickpeas, reserved tomato juice, remaining ⅛ teaspoon salt, and pepper.

4. Lock lid in place and close pressure release valve. Select high pressure cook function and cook for 2 minutes. Turn off pressure cooker and quick-release pressure. Carefully remove lid, allowing steam to escape away from you. Season with salt and pepper to taste. Sprinkle with fennel fronds and almonds. Serve with lemon wedges.

Sopa Seca with Chorizo and Black Beans

SKILLET

Serves 4

Total Time 45 minutes

Why This Recipe Works Its name might mean "dry soup," but sopa seca is really a saucy pasta dish. In this enticing Mexican specialty, fideos—thin strands of pasta toasted until golden—are baked in a flavorful broth studded with tomatoes and capped with melted cheese. Pretoasted fideos are hard to find, so we used vermicelli, broken into pieces, and toasted them to golden-brown in a skillet. Most sopa seca recipes call for a variety of dried chiles that must be rehydrated before being used; to keep things streamlined, we reached for canned, smoky chipotle chiles, which delivered serious flavor and ample heat with minimum work. Chicken broth provided the "soupy" portion of the dish and offered a savory backbone. To make our skillet sopa seca a complete meal, we added chorizo and black beans, which stayed true to the dish's Mexican roots. Serve with sour cream, diced avocado, and thinly sliced scallions.

- 8 ounces vermicelli or thin spaghetti
- 2 tablespoons vegetable oil, divided
- 1 onion, chopped fine
- 4 ounces chorizo, halved lengthwise and sliced ¼ inch thick
- 2 garlic cloves, minced
- 2 teaspoons minced canned chipotle chile in adobo sauce
- 2 cups chicken broth
- 1 (15-ounce) can black beans, rinsed
- 1 (14.5-ounce) can diced tomatoes
- 2 ounces Monterey Jack cheese, shredded (½ cup)
- ¼ cup minced fresh cilantro

1. Loosely wrap pasta in dish towel, then press bundle against corner of counter to break noodles into 6-inch lengths. Toast pasta in 1 tablespoon oil in 12-inch nonstick skillet over medium-high heat, tossing frequently with tongs, until golden, about 4 minutes; transfer to paper towel–lined plate.

2. Add remaining 1 tablespoon oil and onion to now-empty skillet and cook over medium heat until softened, 5 to 7 minutes. Stir in chorizo, garlic, and chipotle and cook until fragrant, about 30 seconds. Stir in broth, beans, tomatoes, and toasted pasta and bring to vigorous simmer. Reduce heat to medium, cover, and cook, stirring gently and often, until pasta is tender, about 10 minutes.

3. Off heat, season with salt and pepper to taste and sprinkle with Monterey Jack. Cover and let sit until cheese melts, 2 to 4 minutes. Sprinkle with cilantro and serve.

Drunken Noodles with Chicken

SKILLET

Serves 4

Total Time 45 minutes

Why This Recipe Works Despite the name, there's no alcohol in drunken noodles—originally translated from Thai as drunkard noodles. This renowned dish does feature wide rice noodles in a spicy, potent sauce flavored with lots of basil, and it's a surprisingly quick-cooking one-pan meal. For our version, we soaked the rice noodles in boiling water until they were just pliable so that we could finish cooking them in the sauce and infuse them with flavor. Chicken and napa cabbage, which we quickly stir-fried one after the other, made it a filling entrée. We found that tossing the chicken with soy sauce and letting it sit before cooking boosted its flavor and helped to keep it moist. After cooking the chicken and vegetables, we added the noodles to the skillet along with a mixture of soy sauce (for savory depth), lime juice (for its sweet-tart notes), brown sugar (preferred over white sugar for its richer flavor), and Thai chiles (which developed that spicy flavor). Waiting to add the basil until the last minute ensured its flavor and color stayed fresh. If fresh Thai chiles are unavailable, substitute one serrano or one-half jalapeño. For a milder version of this dish, remove the seeds and ribs from the chile. To make the chicken easier to slice, freeze it for 15 minutes. We developed this recipe for a 12-inch nonstick skillet, but a 14-inch flat-bottomed wok can be used instead.

- 8 ounces (⅜-inch-wide) flat rice noodles
- 2 tablespoons vegetable oil, divided
- ⅛ teaspoon baking soda
- 12 ounces boneless, skinless chicken breasts, trimmed and sliced thin crosswise
- 2 teaspoons plus ¼ cup soy sauce, divided
- ½ teaspoon cornstarch
- ½ cup packed brown sugar
- 3 tablespoons lime juice (2 limes), plus lime wedges for serving
- 2 tablespoons fish sauce
- 3 Thai chiles, stemmed and sliced into thin rings
- ½ head napa cabbage, cored and cut into 1-inch pieces (6 cups)
- 1½ cups coarsely chopped fresh Thai or Italian basil

Drunken Noodles with Chicken

1. Place noodles in large bowl and cover with boiling water. Let sit, stirring occasionally, until soft and pliable but not fully tender. Drain noodles and rinse under cold running water until chilled. Drain noodles well again and toss with 2 teaspoons oil; set aside.

2. Combine 2 teaspoons water and baking soda in medium bowl. Add chicken and toss to coat; let sit for 5 minutes. Add 2 teaspoons soy sauce and cornstarch and toss until well combined. Whisk remaining ¼ cup soy sauce, sugar, lime juice, fish sauce, 2 tablespoons water, and Thai chiles in small bowl until sugar has dissolved; set aside.

3. Heat 2 teaspoons oil in 12-inch nonstick skillet over medium-high heat until just smoking. Add chicken and increase heat to high. Cook, tossing chicken slowly but constantly, until no longer pink, 2 to 6 minutes; transfer to clean bowl.

4. Heat remaining 2 teaspoons oil in again-empty skillet over high heat until just smoking. Add cabbage and cook, tossing slowly but constantly, until crisp-tender, about 3 minutes. Add noodles, sauce, and chicken and cook, tossing slowly but constantly, until mixture is thoroughly combined and noodles are well coated and tender, 2 to 4 minutes. Off heat, fold in basil. Serve with lime wedges.

Drunken Noodles with Chicken for Two

SKILLET

Serves 2

Total Time 45 minutes

For a milder version of this dish, remove the seeds and ribs from the chile. To make the chicken easier to slice, freeze it for 15 minutes. We developed this recipe for a 12-inch nonstick skillet, but a 14-inch flat-bottomed wok can be used instead.

- 4 ounces (⅜-inch-wide) flat rice noodles
- 2 tablespoons vegetable oil, divided
- ⅛ teaspoon baking soda
- 6 ounces boneless, skinless chicken breasts, trimmed and sliced thin crosswise
- 2 tablespoons soy sauce, divided
- ¼ teaspoon cornstarch
- ¼ cup packed brown sugar
- 1½ tablespoons lime juice, plus lime wedges for serving
- 1 tablespoon fish sauce
- ½ serrano chile, sliced into thin rings
- 3 cups shredded napa cabbage
- ¾ cup coarsely chopped fresh Thai or Italian basil

1. Place noodles in large bowl and cover with boiling water. Let sit, stirring occasionally, until soft and pliable, but not fully tender. Drain noodles and rinse under cold running water until chilled. Drain noodles well again and toss with 2 teaspoons oil; set aside.

2. Combine 1 teaspoon water and baking soda in medium bowl. Add chicken and toss to coat; let sit for 5 minutes. Add 1 teaspoon soy sauce and cornstarch and toss until well combined. Whisk remaining soy sauce, sugar, lime juice, fish sauce, 1 tablespoon water, and chile in small bowl until sugar has dissolved; set aside.

3. Heat 2 teaspoons oil in 12-inch nonstick skillet over medium-high heat until just smoking. Add chicken and increase heat to high. Cook, tossing chicken slowly but constantly, until no longer pink, 2 to 6 minutes; transfer to clean medium bowl.

4. Heat remaining 2 teaspoons oil in again-empty skillet over high heat until just smoking. Add cabbage and cook, tossing slowly but constantly, until crisp-tender, about 3 minutes. Add noodles, sauce, and chicken and cook, tossing slowly but constantly, until mixture is thoroughly combined and noodles are well coated and tender, 2 to 4 minutes. Off heat, fold in basil. Serve with lime wedges.

Thai-Style Stir-Fried Noodles with Chicken and Broccolini

Thai-Style Stir-Fried Noodles with Chicken and Broccolini

SKILLET

Serves 4

Total Time 1 hour

Why This Recipe Works We wanted a streamlined, one-pan version of pad see ew—a traditional Thai dish of chewy, lightly charred rice noodles with chicken, crisp broccolini, and moist egg, bound with a sweet-and-salty soy-based sauce. Using a skillet or wok over high heat worked best, and we cooked our chicken (coated in savory sauce), eggs, and broccolini in batches. We added, everything back to the pan with more sauce and presoaked rice noodles to cook together and develop the perfect char. A quick chile vinegar rounded out the flavors. If fresh Thai chiles are unavailable, substitute one serrano or one-half jalapeño. For a milder dish, remove the seeds and ribs from the chile. You can substitute an equal amount of conventional broccoli; trim and peel the stalks before cutting. To make the chicken easier to slice, freeze it for 15 minutes. We developed this recipe for a 12-inch nonstick skillet, but a 14-inch flat-bottomed wok can be used instead.

Chile Vinegar

⅓ cup distilled white vinegar

3 Thai chiles, stemmed and sliced into thin rings

Stir-Fry

8 ounces (¼-inch-wide) flat rice noodles

3 tablespoons vegetable oil, divided

⅛ teaspoon baking soda

12 ounces boneless, skinless chicken breasts, trimmed and sliced thin crosswise

1 tablespoon plus 2 teaspoons soy sauce, divided

½ teaspoon cornstarch

¼ cup oyster sauce

2 tablespoons packed dark brown sugar

1 tablespoon distilled white vinegar

1 teaspoon molasses

1 teaspoon fish sauce

3 garlic cloves, sliced thin

3 large eggs

10 ounces broccolini, trimmed, florets cut into 1-inch pieces, stalks cut ½ inch thick on bias

1. For the chile vinegar Combine vinegar and Thai chiles in bowl; set aside for serving. (Chile vinegar can be refrigerated for up to 24 hours; bring to room temperature before serving.)

2. For the stir-fry Place noodles in large bowl and cover with boiling water. Let sit, stirring occasionally, until soft and pliable, but not fully tender. Drain noodles and rinse under cold running water until chilled. Drain noodles well again and toss with 2 teaspoons oil; set aside.

3. Combine 2 teaspoons water and baking soda in medium bowl. Add chicken and toss to coat; let sit for 5 minutes. Add 2 teaspoons soy sauce and cornstarch and toss until well combined. Whisk oyster sauce, sugar, vinegar, molasses, fish sauce, and remaining 1 tablespoon soy sauce in small bowl until sugar dissolves; set aside.

4. Cook 2 teaspoons oil and garlic in 12-inch nonstick skillet over medium-low heat until garlic is deep golden brown, 1 to 2 minutes. Add chicken and increase heat to high. Cook, tossing chicken slowly but constantly, until no longer pink, 2 to 6 minutes; transfer to large bowl.

5. Heat 1 tablespoon oil in now-empty skillet over high heat until shimmering. Add eggs and scramble quickly using rubber spatula. Continue to cook, scraping slowly but constantly along bottom and sides of pan until eggs just form cohesive mass, 15 to 30 seconds (eggs will not be completely dry). Transfer to bowl with chicken and break up any large egg curds.

6. Heat remaining 2 teaspoons oil in now-empty skillet over high heat until just smoking. Add broccolini and ¼ cup water (water will sputter) and cover immediately. Cook,

without stirring, until broccolini is bright green, about 2 minutes. Uncover, and continue to cook, tossing slowly but constantly, until all water has evaporated and broccolini is crisp-tender and spotty-brown, 1 to 3 minutes. Add noodles, oyster sauce mixture, and chicken-egg mixture and cook, tossing slowly but constantly, until mixture is thoroughly combined and noodles are well coated and tender, 2 to 4 minutes. Serve, passing chile vinegar separately.

Ramen with Beef, Shiitakes, and Spinach

DUTCH OVEN

Serves 4 to 6

Total Time 1 hour

Why This Recipe Works Instant ramen might come with microwave instructions, but the quick preparation doesn't do these Japanese noodles justice. For our recipe we'd keep the instant noodles but ditch the salty seasoning packet in favor of building our own sauce. We started by stir-frying marinated flank steak strips in a Dutch oven, which was big enough to hold the beef, vegetables, and noodles. Next we browned some shiitake mushrooms before adding garlic and ginger. Chicken broth, soy sauce, rice wine, and a bit of sugar created a sauce with savory, sweet flavor in which we simmered the ramen until it was tender and the sauce was thickened. Spinach, stirred in at the end, added freshness. It doesn't matter which flavor of ramen noodles you buy since you won't be using the seasoning packets sold with the noodles. The sauce in this dish will seem a bit brothy when finished, but the liquid will be absorbed quickly by the noodles when serving. To make the beef easier to slice, freeze it for 15 minutes.

1 pound flank steak, trimmed

1 tablespoon water

¼ teaspoon baking soda

8 teaspoons soy sauce, divided

¾ teaspoon cornstarch

2 tablespoons vegetable oil, divided

8 ounces shiitake mushrooms, stemmed and sliced thin

3 garlic cloves, minced

1 tablespoon grated fresh ginger

3½ cups chicken broth

3 tablespoons Shaoxing wine or dry sherry

2 teaspoons sugar

4 (3-ounce) packages ramen noodles, seasoning packets discarded

6 ounces (6 cups) baby spinach

1. Cut steak with grain into 2½- to 3-inch-wide strips, then cut strips crosswise against grain into ⅛-inch-thick slices. Combine water and baking soda in medium bowl. Add beef and toss to coat; let sit for 5 minutes. Add 2 teaspoons soy sauce and cornstarch and toss until well combined.

2. Heat 1 tablespoon oil in Dutch oven over medium-high heat until just smoking. Add beef in single layer, breaking up any clumps, and cook, without stirring, until browned on bottom, about 1 minute. Stir and continue to cook until beef is no longer pink, about 1 minute; transfer to clean bowl.

3. Wipe pot clean with paper towels. Heat remaining 1 tablespoon oil in now-empty pot over medium-high heat until shimmering. Add mushrooms and cook until softened and lightly browned, about 4 minutes. Stir in garlic and ginger and cook until fragrant, about 30 seconds. Stir in broth, Shaoxing wine, sugar, and remaining 2 tablespoons soy sauce and bring to boil. Arrange noodles in pot in even layer; you may need to break noodles to fit. Cover, reduce heat to medium, and simmer until noodles have softened on bottoms (tops will still be dry), about 3 minutes.

4. Uncover pot and, using tongs, flip noodles and stir to separate. Stir in spinach, 1 handful at a time, and cook until noodles are tender and spinach has wilted, about 2 minutes. Stir in beef and any accumulated juices and cook until heated through, about 30 seconds. Serve.

VARIATION

Ramen with Pork and Cabbage for Two
SKILLET
Serves 2
Total Time 1 hour

It doesn't matter which flavor of ramen noodles you buy since you won't be using the seasoning packets sold with the noodles. To make the pork easier to slice, freeze it for 15 minutes. The sauce in this dish will seem a bit brothy when finished, but the liquid will be absorbed quickly by the noodles when serving.

1½ teaspoons water
⅛ teaspoon baking soda
8 ounces boneless country-style pork ribs, trimmed and sliced thin crosswise
4 teaspoons soy sauce, divided
¼ teaspoon cornstarch
1 tablespoon vegetable oil, divided
6 scallions, white and green parts separated, sliced thin on bias
3 garlic cloves, minced
1 teaspoon grated fresh ginger
Pinch red pepper flakes
1¾ cups chicken broth

1 tablespoon oyster sauce
1 teaspoon toasted sesame oil
2 (3-ounce) packages ramen noodles, seasoning packets discarded
1½ cups shredded green cabbage

1. Combine water and baking soda in medium bowl. Add pork and toss to coat; let sit for 5 minutes. Add 1 teaspoon soy sauce and cornstarch and toss until well combined.

2. Heat 1½ teaspoons vegetable oil in 12-inch nonstick skillet over medium-high heat until just smoking. Add pork in single layer, breaking up any clumps, and cook, without stirring, until browned on bottom, about 1 minute. Stir and continue to cook until pork is no longer pink, about 1 minute; transfer to clean bowl.

3. Heat remaining 1½ teaspoons vegetable oil in now-empty skillet over medium-high heat until shimmering. Add scallion whites and cook until softened, about 2 minutes. Stir in garlic, ginger, and pepper flakes and cook until fragrant, about 30 seconds. Stir in broth, oyster sauce, sesame oil, and remaining 1 tablespoon soy sauce and bring to boil. Arrange noodles in skillet in even layer; you may need to break noodles to fit. Cover, reduce heat to medium, and simmer until noodles have softened on bottoms (tops will still be dry), about 3 minutes.

4. Uncover pot and, using tongs, flip noodles and stir to separate. Stir in cabbage and scallion greens and cook until noodles are tender and cabbage is wilted, about 2 minutes. Stir in pork and any accumulated juices and cook until heated through, about 30 seconds. Serve.

Pork Pad Thai
SLOW COOKER
Serves 4 to 6
Total Time 6 to 7 hours on low or 4 to 5 hours on high, plus 20 minutes on high

Why This Recipe Works Great pad thai should feature clean, fresh, not-too-sweet flavors; perfectly cooked noodles; and plenty of tender protein—not exactly a dish you would expect to come out of the slow cooker. But this hands-off recipe achieves just that, using the slow cooker to create a unique blend of perfectly cooked noodles and moist meat. Most recipes include shrimp and egg, but we sidestepped tradition in favor of boneless country-style pork ribs, which yielded tender, flavorful meat after a slow cook. Braising the pork in a combination of chicken broth, fish sauce, sugar, and tamarind juice created a distinct pad thai flavor profile. Blooming the aromatics (scallion whites, garlic, and a chile) in toasted sesame oil in the microwave before adding them to the slow cooker elevated their flavors. After removing the pork from the slow cooker, we placed the noodles in the remaining braising liquid and let them rehydrate for 20 minutes. To complete the dish, we returned the shredded pork to the slow cooker along with bean sprouts, scallion greens, cilantro, and peanuts for added freshness and crunch. Look for tamarind juice concentrate manufactured in Thailand, which is thinner and tastes brighter than the paste concentrate produced in other countries. If you can't find it, substitute 1½ tablespoons lime juice and 1½ tablespoons water, and omit the lime wedges. Look for country-style pork ribs with lots of fat and dark meat, and stay away from ribs that look overly lean with pale meat, as they will taste very dry after the extended cooking time.

Pork Pad Thai

3 tablespoons toasted sesame oil
4 scallions, white parts minced, green parts cut into 1-inch pieces, divided
4 garlic cloves, minced
1 serrano chile, stemmed and sliced into thin rings
1¾ cups chicken broth
¼ cup sugar
3 tablespoons tamarind juice concentrate
3 tablespoons fish sauce, divided
1½ pounds boneless country-style pork ribs, trimmed
½ teaspoon table salt
½ teaspoon pepper
8 ounces (¼-inch-wide) rice noodles
4 ounces (2 cups) bean sprouts
2 tablespoons rice vinegar
¼ cup fresh cilantro leaves
¼ cup dry-roasted peanuts, chopped coarse
Lime wedges

1. Microwave oil, scallion whites, garlic, and serrano in bowl, stirring occasionally, until fragrant, about 1 minute; transfer to slow cooker. Whisk in broth, sugar, tamarind juice, and 2 tablespoons fish sauce.

2. Sprinkle pork with salt and pepper and nestle into slow cooker. Cover and cook until pork is tender and fork slips easily in and out of meat, 6 to 7 hours on low or 4 to 5 hours on high.

3. Transfer pork to cutting board, let cool slightly, then pull apart into large chunks using 2 forks. Nestle noodles into cooking liquid left in slow cooker, cover, and cook on high until tender, 20 to 30 minutes.

4. Add pork to noodles and gently toss to combine. Let sit until heated through, about 5 minutes. Add bean sprouts, scallion greens, vinegar, and remaining 1 tablespoon fish sauce and toss to combine. Sprinkle with cilantro and peanuts. Serve with lime wedges.

INGREDIENT SPOTLIGHT

BUYING FISH SAUCE
Fish sauce is a salty, amber-colored liquid made from salted, fermented fish. It is used as both an ingredient and a condiment in Southeast Asia and can be found in the international aisle of most American supermarkets. Fish sauce has a very concentrated flavor. Like anchovy paste, it lends a salty complexity to dishes when used judiciously that is nearly impossible to replicate. We gathered five sauces from grocery stores and Asian markets and sampled them over white rice, mixed into a simple Thai dipping sauce, and cooked into a chicken dish. Our favorite is **Red Boat 40° N Fish Sauce**. Tasters detected earthy, slightly "sweet" notes for a flavor that was "complex, not just fishy."

Pork Lo Mein

1 tablespoon water plus 3 cups water, divided
¼ teaspoon baking soda
1 pound boneless country-style pork ribs, trimmed and sliced thin crosswise
3 tablespoons soy sauce, plus extra as needed
2 tablespoons oyster sauce
2 tablespoons hoisin sauce
1 tablespoon toasted sesame oil
2 tablespoons vegetable oil, divided
2 tablespoons Shaoxing wine or dry sherry
8 ounces shiitake mushrooms, stemmed, halved if large
6 scallions, white and green parts separated, whites sliced thin and greens cut into 1-inch lengths
2 garlic cloves, minced
2 teaspoons grated fresh ginger
8 ounces dried lo mein noodles
1 small head napa cabbage, quartered, cored, and sliced crosswise into ½-inch strips (8 cups)
1–3 teaspoons Asian chili-garlic sauce

1. Combine 1 tablespoon water and baking soda in medium bowl. Add pork and toss to coat; let sit for 5 minutes. Whisk soy sauce, oyster sauce, hoisin sauce, and sesame oil together in medium bowl. Toss pork with 3 tablespoons soy sauce mixture.

2. Heat 1 tablespoon vegetable oil in Dutch oven over medium-high heat until just smoking. Add pork in single layer, breaking up any clumps, and cook, without stirring, until browned on bottom, about 1 minute. Stir and continue to cook until pork is no longer pink, about 1 minute. Add Shaoxing wine and cook until nearly evaporated, 30 to 60 seconds; transfer to clean bowl.

3. Heat remaining 1 tablespoon vegetable oil in now-empty pot over medium-high heat until shimmering. Add mushrooms and cook until softened and light golden brown, about 5 minutes. Stir in scallion whites, garlic, and ginger and cook until fragrant, about 30 seconds.

4. Stir in 3 cups water and lo mein and bring to vigorous simmer. Reduce heat to medium, cover, and cook, stirring gently and often, until noodles are tender, 12 to 16 minutes. Stir in cabbage and cook until cabbage is wilted and sauce is thickened, about 2 minutes.

5. Reduce heat to low and stir in pork and any accumulated juice, remaining soy sauce mixture, chili-garlic sauce, and scallion greens. Cook, tossing gently, until noodles are well coated with sauce, 1 to 2 minutes. Season with soy sauce to taste. Serve.

Pork Lo Mein

DUTCH OVEN

Serves 4
Total Time 1 hour

Why This Recipe Works Pork lo mein features chewy noodles tossed in a salty-sweet sauce and accented with bits of tender pork and still-crisp cabbage. Country-style ribs were an ideal choice for the pork, as they have a rich, meaty flavor but don't need to be cooked for hours since they're naturally tender. To avoid an overly greasy dish, we trimmed the fat and cut the meat into thin strips that would allow our marinade (soy sauce, oyster sauce, hoisin sauce, and sesame oil) to penetrate effectively. We cooked the pork over high heat in a Dutch oven and then set it aside before adding umami-rich shiitakes and aromatics to the pot. Stirring the lo mein noodles and some water into the pot with the mushroom mixture allowed them to cook through perfectly before we added the pork, cabbage (adding it at the end ensured it was just wilted), and some reserved marinade, which served as a sauce. Linguini, broken into 6-inch lengths, can be substituted for the lo mein noodles. To make the pork easier to slice, freeze it for 15 minutes. For a spicier dish, use the greater amount of chili-garlic sauce.

Singapore Noodles

SKILLET

Serves 4

Total Time 1 hour

Why This Recipe Works This light stir-fry of thin rice noodles, vegetables, and shrimp is native to Hong Kong (not Singapore as the name suggests). Along with the traditional Chinese flavorings of garlic, ginger, and soy, this dish prominently features curry powder. The heady spice mixture lends an inviting aroma and a pleasant heat. But because this dish is not saucy, the dry powder doesn't distribute evenly, leading to patchy curry flavor (and color), not to mention gritty texture. We set out to find a foolproof spice distribution method, and also to up the traditional amount of vegetables and protein to make a satisfying one-dish meal. Blooming the curry in hot oil in a skillet not only released its complex flavor, it also combated grittiness and helped the spice coat the noodles evenly. A spoonful of sugar dispelled lingering bitter notes. We wanted plenty of protein and vegetables, so we added shrimp—cut into ½-inch pieces to disperse nicely throughout the noodles—as well as eggs, scallions, bell pepper, and plenty of bean sprouts. Stir-frying in batches guaranteed everything was perfectly cooked, and presoaking the noodles ensured they were tender. We developed this recipe for a 12-inch nonstick skillet, but a 14-inch flat-bottomed wok can be used instead.

Singapore Noodles

8 ounces rice vermicelli

¼ cup plus 4 teaspoons vegetable oil, divided

2 tablespoons curry powder

3 garlic cloves, minced

1 teaspoon grated fresh ginger

⅛ teaspoon cayenne pepper

2 tablespoons soy sauce

1 teaspoon sugar

12 ounces extra-large shrimp (21 to 25 per pound), peeled, deveined, tails removed, and cut crosswise into thirds

4 large eggs

1 red bell pepper, stemmed, seeded, and cut into 2-inch-long matchsticks

2 large shallots, sliced thin

⅔ cup chicken broth

4 ounces (2 cups) bean sprouts

4 scallions, cut into ½-inch pieces

2 teaspoons lime juice, plus lime wedges for serving

1. Place noodles in large bowl and cover with boiling water. Let sit, stirring occasionally, until soft and pliable, but not fully tender. Drain noodles and rinse under cold running water until chilled. Drain noodles again and transfer to large bowl.

2. Meanwhile, cook 3 tablespoons oil, curry powder, garlic, ginger, and cayenne in 12-inch nonstick skillet over medium-low heat, stirring occasionally, until fragrant, about 4 minutes. Add curry mixture, soy sauce, and sugar to bowl with noodles and toss until well combined; set aside.

3. Wipe skillet clean with paper towels. Heat 2 teaspoons oil in now-empty skillet over medium-high heat until just smoking. Add shrimp and increase heat to high. Cook, tossing shrimp slowly but constantly, until just opaque, about 2 minutes; transfer to medium bowl.

4. Heat 1 tablespoon oil in again-empty skillet over high heat until shimmering. Add eggs and scramble quickly using rubber spatula. Continue to cook, scraping slowly but constantly along bottom and sides of skillet until eggs just form cohesive mass, 15 to 30 seconds (eggs will not be completely dry). Transfer to bowl with shrimp and break up any large egg curds.

5. Heat remaining 2 teaspoons oil in again-empty skillet over high heat until just smoking. Add bell pepper and shallots and cook, tossing slowly but constantly, until vegetables are crisp-tender, about 2 minutes. Push vegetables to one side of skillet and reduce heat to medium. Add garlic mixture to clearing and cook, mashing mixture into skillet, until fragrant, about 30 seconds. Stir garlic mixture into vegetables; transfer to bowl with shrimp and eggs.

6. Return skillet to high heat, add broth, and bring to simmer. Add noodles and cook, tossing slowly but constantly, until liquid is absorbed, about 2 minutes. Add shrimp mixture, bean sprouts, and scallions and cook, tossing slowly but constantly, until mixture is thoroughly combined and heated through, about 2 minutes. Off heat, add lime juice and toss to combine. Serve, passing lime wedges separately.

Udon Noodles with Mustard Greens and Shiitake-Ginger Sauce

DUTCH OVEN
Serves 4 to 6
Total Time 1¼ hours

Why This Recipe Works Noodles and greens are a common pairing in many Asian cuisines. We thought this partnership was a great way to create a delicate yet filling noodle dish, and we set out to develop a recipe that married the spicy bite of mustard greens with rustic udon noodles. Udon are plump, chewy noodles made of wheat flour; because they're starchy and a bit sweet, they stand up well to savory sauces. We made a highly aromatic broth from Asian pantry staples, first browning meaty shiitake mushrooms in a Dutch oven for flavor and then adding water, mirin, rice vinegar, soy sauce, cloves of garlic, and a chunk of fresh ginger. Dried shiitake mushrooms, sesame oil, and chili-garlic sauce rounded out the flavors. After this mixture reduced, we had a sauce that was light and brothy yet supersavory—and we could use the pot again to cook our noodles and greens together. Because fresh noodles cook so quickly, we made sure to add the greens to the pot before the noodles. Do not substitute other types of noodles for the fresh udon noodles here.

- 1 tablespoon vegetable oil
- 8 ounces fresh shiitake mushrooms, stemmed and sliced thin
- ¼ cup mirin
- 3 tablespoons unseasoned rice vinegar
- 3 tablespoons soy sauce
- 2 garlic cloves, peeled and smashed
- 1 (1-inch) piece ginger, peeled, halved, and smashed
- ½ ounce dried shiitake mushrooms, rinsed and minced
- 1 teaspoon toasted sesame oil
- 1 teaspoon Asian chili-garlic sauce
- 1 pound mustard greens, stemmed and cut into 2-inch pieces
- 1 pound fresh udon noodles

1. Heat vegetable oil in Dutch oven over medium-high heat until shimmering. Add fresh mushrooms and cook, stirring occasionally, until softened and lightly browned, about 5 minutes. Stir in 2 cups water, mirin, vinegar, soy sauce, garlic, ginger, dried mushrooms, sesame oil, and chili-garlic sauce and bring to simmer. Reduce heat to medium-low and simmer until liquid has reduced by half, 8 to 10 minutes. Off heat, discard garlic and ginger. Transfer mixture to bowl and cover to keep warm.

2. Bring 4 quarts water to boil in now-empty pot. Add mustard greens and cook until greens are nearly tender, about 5 minutes. Add noodles and cook until greens and noodles are tender, about 2 minutes. Reserve ⅓ cup cooking water, drain noodles and greens, and return them to pot. Add sauce and reserved cooking water and toss to combine. Cook over medium-low heat, tossing constantly, until sauce clings to noodles, about 1 minute. Season with salt and pepper to taste, and serve.

NOTES FROM THE TEST KITCHEN

BUYING ASIAN NOODLES
Like Italian pasta, Asian pasta can come in a variety of shapes and sizes.

Chinese Noodles Chinese noodles can be fresh or dried. Fresh Chinese noodles cook quickly, usually in no more than three to four minutes in boiling water.

Rice Noodles Rice noodles are made from rice powder and water. They come in several widths. They can overcook quickly; we often soften them off the heat in hot water an add them at the end of cooking.

Soba Noodles Soba noodles get their unusual flavor from buckwheat flour. Buckwheat flour contains no gluten, so a binder, usually wheat, is added to give the noodles structure and hold them together.

Udon Noodles These Japanese noodles can be fresh or dried, are made from wheat, and are available in varying thicknesses. They can contain quite a bit of salt; because of that, we don't add salt to the cooking water when boiling them.

Ramen Noodles Ramen noodles can come fresh or dried. If using "instant" ramen noodles we usually discard the flavor packet.

Chilled Soba Noodles with Cucumbers, Snow Peas, and Radishes

DUTCH OVEN

Serves 4

Total Time 45 minutes

Why This Recipe Works Soba noodles have a chewy texture and nutty flavor, and are as enjoyable chilled as they are hot. For a refreshing cold noodle salad, we cooked soba noodles in unsalted boiling water in a Dutch oven until tender but still resilient and rinsed them under cold running water to remove excess starch and prevent sticking. We then tossed the soba with a miso-based dressing, which clung to and flavored the noodles. We also cut a mix of raw vegetables into varying sizes so they'd incorporate nicely into the noodles while adding crunch and color. Sprinkling strips of toasted nori over the top added texture and a subtle briny taste. Yellow, red, or brown miso can be substituted for the white miso, if desired. We prefer the subtle flavor and crisp texture that freshly toasted nori brings to this dish; however, plain pretoasted seaweed snacks can be substituted. For a spicier dish, use the greater amount of arbol chiles. If dried arbol chiles are unavailable, you can substitute ¼ to ½ teaspoon red pepper flakes.

- 3 tablespoons white miso
- 3 tablespoons mirin
- 2 tablespoons toasted sesame oil
- 1 tablespoon sesame seeds
- 1 teaspoon grated fresh ginger
- 1–2 dried arbol chiles (each about 2 inches long), stemmed and minced
- 8 ounces dried soba noodles
- ⅓ English cucumber, quartered lengthwise, seeded, and sliced thin on bias
- 4 ounces snow peas, strings removed, cut lengthwise into matchsticks
- 4 radishes, trimmed, halved, and sliced thin
- 3 scallions, sliced thin on bias
- 1 (8-inch-square) sheet nori, toasted and cut into 2-inch-long matchsticks (optional)

1. Whisk miso, mirin, oil, sesame seeds, 1 tablespoon water, ginger, and arbol chiles in large bowl until smooth.

2. Meanwhile, bring 4 quarts water to boil in large pot. Add noodles and cook, stirring occasionally, until cooked through but still retain some chew. Drain noodles and rinse under cold water until chilled. Drain well and transfer to bowl with dressing. Add cucumber, snow peas, radishes, scallions, and nori, if using, and toss to combine. Season with salt to taste. Serve.

Udon Noodles with Mustard Greens and Shiitake-Ginger Sauce

Chilled Soba Noodles with Cucumbers, Snow Peas, and Radishes

DESSERTS

Cherry Cobbler

* All slow cooker recipes work in a 4- to 7-quart traditional slow cooker unless noted.
** All Instant Pot recipes work in a 6- to 8-quart Instant Pot or other electric pressure cooker.

Honey-Glazed Roasted Peaches

SKILLET

Serves 6

Total Time 45 minutes

Why This Recipe Works It might seem impossible to improve on perfect summer peaches, but roasting them in a skillet and coating them with a honey glaze amplifies their flavor, and reducing the juices left in the pan makes a sweet syrup to enhance the roasted peaches even more. Tossing peeled, halved peaches with a little sugar, salt, and lemon juice seasoned the fruit and helped extract some juice. We broiled the peach halves cut side up in a skillet, adding water to prevent sticking. Once the peaches had begun to brown, we took them out and brushed them with a mixture of honey and butter (which we microwaved first to melt the butter), and then slid them back under the broiler to caramelize the glaze and produce beautifully browned peaches. Lastly, we reduced the juices that had accumulated in the skillet into a thick, intensely peachy syrup to drizzle over the warm peaches and topped them with some toasted hazelnuts. Select peaches that yield slightly when pressed. You will need a 12-inch ovensafe skillet for this recipe. Use a serrated peeler to peel the peaches. These peaches are best served warm and with vanilla ice cream or plain Greek yogurt, if desired.

- 2 tablespoons lemon juice
- 1 tablespoon sugar
- ¼ teaspoon table salt
- 6 firm, ripe peaches, peeled, halved, and pitted
- ⅓ cup water
- ¼ cup honey
- 2 tablespoons unsalted butter
- ¼ cup hazelnuts, toasted, skinned, and chopped coarse

1. Adjust oven rack 6 inches from broiler element and heat broiler. Combine lemon juice, sugar, and salt in large bowl. Add peaches and toss to combine, making sure to coat all sides with sugar mixture.

2. Transfer peaches cut side up to 12-inch ovensafe skillet. Pour any remaining sugar mixture into peach cavities. Pour water around peaches in skillet. Broil until peaches are just beginning to brown, 11 to 15 minutes.

3. Combine honey and butter in bowl and microwave until melted, about 30 seconds, then stir to combine. Using potholder, remove peaches from oven and brush half of honey mixture over peaches. Return peaches to oven and continue to broil until spotty brown, 5 to 7 minutes.

4. Remove skillet from oven, brush peaches with remaining honey mixture, and transfer peaches to serving platter, leaving juices behind. Being careful of hot skillet handle, bring accumulated juices in skillet to simmer over medium heat and cook until syrupy, about 1 minute. Pour syrup over peaches. Sprinkle with hazelnuts and serve.

VARIATION

Raspberry-Glazed Peaches with Walnuts for Two

SKILLET

Serves 2

Total Time 45 minutes

Select peaches that yield slightly when pressed. You will need a 10-inch ovensafe skillet for this recipe. Use a serrated peeler to peel the peaches. Any fruit jelly or nut will work well here. These peaches are best served warm and with vanilla ice cream or plain Greek yogurt, if desired.

- 2 teaspoons lemon juice
- 1 teaspoon sugar
  Pinch table salt
- 2 firm, ripe peaches, peeled, halved, and pitted
- 2 tablespoons water
- 1½ tablespoons seedless raspberry jelly
- 1 tablespoon unsalted butter
- 1 tablespoon coarsely chopped toasted walnuts

1. Adjust oven rack 6 inches from broiler element and heat broiler. Combine lemon juice, sugar, and salt in large bowl. Add peaches and toss to combine, making sure to coat all sides with sugar mixture.

2. Transfer peaches cut side up to 10-inch ovensafe skillet. Pour any remaining sugar mixture into peach cavities. Pour water around peaches in skillet. Broil until peaches are just beginning to brown, 11 to 15 minutes.

3. Combine jelly and butter in bowl and microwave until melted, about 30 seconds, then stir to combine. Using potholder, remove peaches from oven and brush half of jelly mixture over peaches. Return peaches to oven and continue to broil until spotty brown, 5 to 7 minutes.

4. Remove skillet from oven, brush peaches with remaining jelly mixture, and transfer peaches to serving platter, leaving juices behind. Whisk juices to combine, then pour over peaches. Sprinkle with walnuts and serve.

Roasted Pears with Dried Apricots and Pistachios

2½ tablespoons unsalted butter, divided
4 ripe but firm Bosc pears (6 to 7 ounces each), peeled, halved, and cored
1¼ cups dry white wine
½ cup dried apricots, quartered
⅓ cup (2⅓ ounces) sugar
¼ teaspoon ground cardamom
⅛ teaspoon table salt
1 teaspoon lemon juice
⅓ cup shelled pistachios, toasted and chopped

1. Adjust oven rack to middle position and heat oven to 450 degrees. Melt 1½ tablespoons butter in 12-inch ovensafe skillet over medium-high heat. Place pear halves cut side down in skillet. Cook, without moving, until pears are just beginning to brown, 3 to 5 minutes.

2. Transfer skillet to oven and roast for 15 minutes. Flip pears and continue to roast until fork easily pierces fruit, 10 to 15 minutes.

3. Using potholder, remove skillet from oven and transfer pears to serving platter. Being careful of hot skillet handle, return skillet to medium-high heat and add wine, apricots, sugar, cardamom, salt, and remaining 1 tablespoon butter. Bring to vigorous simmer, whisking to scrape up any browned bits. Cook until sauce is reduced and has consistency of maple syrup, 7 to 10 minutes. Off heat, stir in lemon juice. Pour sauce over pears and sprinkle with pistachios. Serve.

Roasted Pears with Dried Apricots and Pistachios

SKILLET
Serves 4
Total Time 1 hour

Why This Recipe Works Much like peaches, pears are well-suited to roasting since their shape and texture hold up well. After peeling and halving the pears, we cooked them in butter in a skillet on the stovetop to evaporate some of their juices and concentrate their flavor; this also jump-started caramelization. Next we moved the pears to the oven to turn their flesh tender and brown. Once the pears were cooked we set them aside and put the exuded juices to use in a quick pan sauce, deglazing the pan with dry white wine and adding the complementary flavors of dried apricots and cardamom plus a little lemon for a burst of citrus. Select pears that yield slightly when pressed. We prefer Bosc pears in this recipe, but Comice and Bartlett pears will also work. You will need a 12-inch ovensafe skillet for this recipe. The pears can be served as is or with vanilla ice cream or plain Greek yogurt.

> **NOTES FROM THE TEST KITCHEN**
>
> **STORING NUTS**
> Since nuts are high in oil, they can become rancid fairly quickly if not properly stored. In the test kitchen, we store all nuts in the freezer in sealed freezer-safe zipper-lock bags. Frozen nuts will keep for months, and there's no need to defrost them before chopping or toasting. If you use toasted nuts often, you can toast them in large batches and, when the nuts are cool, transfer them to a zipper-lock bag, then freeze them. Do not use pretoasted frozen nuts for recipes in which a crisp texture is desired, such as salads.

Roasted Pears with Golden Raisins and Hazelnuts for Two

SKILLET

Serves 2

Total Time 1 hour

Select pears that yield slightly when pressed. We prefer Bosc pears in this recipe, but Comice and Bartlett pears will also work. You will need a 10-inch ovensafe skillet for this recipe. The pears can be served as is or with vanilla ice cream or plain Greek yogurt.

1½ tablespoons unsalted butter, divided
 2 ripe but firm Bosc pears (6 to 7 ounces each), peeled, halved, and cored
 ½ cup dry white wine
 ¼ cup dried golden raisins
 3 tablespoons sugar
 Pinch table salt
 ½ teaspoon lemon juice
 ½ teaspoon grated fresh ginger
 3 tablespoons coarsely chopped toasted and skinned hazelnuts

1. Adjust oven rack to middle position and heat oven to 450 degrees. Melt 1 tablespoon butter in 10-inch ovensafe skillet over medium-high heat. Place pear halves cut side down in skillet. Cook, without moving, until pears are just beginning to brown, 3 to 5 minutes.

2. Transfer skillet to oven and roast for 15 minutes. Flip pears and continue to roast until fork easily pierces fruit, 10 to 15 minutes.

3. Using potholder, remove skillet from oven and transfer pears to serving platter. Being careful of hot skillet handle, return skillet to medium-high heat and add wine, raisins,

sugar, salt, and remaining ½ tablespoon butter. Bring to vigorous simmer, whisking to scrape up any browned bits. Cook until sauce is reduced and has consistency of maple syrup, about 5 minutes. Off heat, stir in lemon juice and ginger. Pour sauce over pears and sprinkle with hazelnuts. Serve.

Roasted Figs with Balsamic Glaze and Mascarpone

SKILLET

Serves 6

Total Time 40 minutes

Why This Recipe Works Fresh figs are a treat in their own right, but they turn wonderfully tender and rich when roasted. To take things a step further, we infused them with complex glaze of balsamic vinegar and honey. Reducing the vinegar in a skillet on the stovetop turned it viscous and syrupy (much like the texture of high-end drizzling balsamics), and adding honey to it banished any harshness. We then added the halved figs to the pan, tossed them with the glaze so they were nicely coated, and moved the skillet to the oven. As the figs quickly roasted, they grew increasingly tender and lent their natural sweetness to the surrounding syrup. While the glazed figs were delicious on their own, we created an easy, creamy topping of honeyed mascarpone cheese flavored with lemon zest. A final sprinkle of toasted pistachios added a pleasant crunch. You will need a 12-inch ovensafe skillet for this recipe.

½ cup balsamic vinegar
 ¼ cup honey, divided
 1 tablespoon unsalted butter
1½ pounds fresh figs, stemmed and halved
 4 ounces (½ cup) mascarpone cheese
 ½ teaspoon grated lemon zest
 ⅓ cup shelled pistachios, toasted and chopped

1. Adjust oven rack to middle position and heat oven to 450 degrees. Bring vinegar, 3 tablespoons honey, and butter to simmer in 12-inch ovensafe skillet over medium-high heat and cook until reduced to ⅓ cup, about 3 minutes. Off heat, add figs and toss to coat. Transfer skillet to oven and roast until figs are tender, 8 to 10 minutes.

2. Remove skillet from oven and let figs rest for 5 minutes. Combine mascarpone, lemon zest, and remaining 1 tablespoon honey in bowl. Divide figs among individual bowls. Dollop with mascarpone mixture, drizzle with balsamic syrup, and sprinkle with pistachios. Serve.

CORING PEARS

1. Peel pear (if directed) and cut in half through core.

2. Guide melon baller in circular motion to cut around central core. Draw melon baller to top of pear, then remove blossom end.

Stuffed Apples with Dried Cherries and Hazelnuts

SLOW COOKER
Serves 6
Cooking Time 4 to 5 hours on low

Why This Recipe Works Baked apples are an old-fashioned dessert, but that doesn't mean they need to taste frumpy. To freshen up this fruit dessert, we stuffed them with a complex filling and cooked them in the slow cooker, which guaranteed evenly cooked, but not mushy, apples. Granny Smith was the best apple for the job with its firm flesh and tart, fruity flavor. To ensure our fruit wouldn't collapse, we peeled the apples after cutting off their tops. The skin on top trapped steam, while removing the rest of the skin allowed the steam to escape and the apple to retain its firm texture. For the filling, we opted for a bold mix of dried cherries, brown sugar, and hazelnuts with black pepper, orange zest, and a few pats of butter. Chewy rolled oats and diced apple made our filling more substantial. A drizzle of maple syrup commingled with the cooking juices, which, when emulsified with more butter at the end, turned into a complex sauce. A melon baller helps to create a cavity that allows for plenty of filling. You will need a 5- to 7-quart oval slow cooker for this recipe.

- 7 large Granny Smith apples
- 8 tablespoons unsalted butter, softened, divided
- ¼ cup packed (1¾ ounces) brown sugar
- ⅓ cup dried cherries, chopped
- ⅓ cup hazelnuts, toasted, skinned, and chopped
- 3 tablespoons old-fashioned rolled oats
- 1 teaspoon grated orange zest
- ½ teaspoon pepper
  Pinch table salt
- ⅓ cup maple syrup

1. Peel and core 1 apple and cut into ¼-inch pieces. Combine apple, 5 tablespoons butter, sugar, cherries, hazelnuts, oats, orange zest, pepper, and salt in bowl; set aside.

2. Shave thin slice off bottom (blossom end) of remaining 6 apples to allow them to sit flat. Cut top ½ inch off stem end of apples and reserve. Peel apples and use melon baller or small measuring spoon to cut 1½-inch diameter opening from core, being careful not to cut through bottom of apple. Spoon filling inside apples, mounding excess filling over cavities; top with reserved apple caps.

3. Lightly coat slow cooker with vegetable oil spray. Arrange stuffed apples in prepared slow cooker. Drizzle with maple syrup, cover, and cook until skewer inserted into apples meets little resistance, 4 to 5 hours on low.

Roasted Figs with Balsamic Glaze and Mascarpone

Stuffed Apples with Dried Cherries and Hazelnuts

White Wine–Poached Pears with Lemon and Herbs for Two

Bananas Foster

4. Using tongs and sturdy spatula, transfer apples to serving dish. Whisk remaining 3 tablespoons butter into cooking liquid, 1 tablespoon at a time, until incorporated. Spoon sauce over apples and serve.

PREPARING APPLES FOR STUFFING

After peeling apples, use melon baller or small measuring spoon to remove 1½-inch diameter opening from core, being careful not to cut through bottom of apples.

Red Wine–Poached Pears with Black Pepper and Cloves

DUTCH OVEN

Serves 6 to 8
Total Time 45 minutes, plus 2 hours chilling

Why This Recipe Works Poached pears are a classic French dessert that is surprisingly simple to make at home. We wanted a recipe for meltingly tender pears that we could serve chilled, and planned to reuse the poaching liquid as an aromatic sauce to keep the preparation contained to just one pot. We discovered that not all varieties of pears worked equally well; Bartlett and Bosc won tasters over with their honeyed sweetness and clean appearance. Cutting the pears in half ensured that they cooked evenly. Poaching the fruit in red wine offered a nuanced flavor that tasters loved, especially when enhanced with warm spices such as cinnamon, black pepper, and cloves. To poach six pears at once, we found it was necessary to use a Dutch oven and a full bottle of wine. After turning the pears several times as they cooked, we removed them from the pot and reduced the cooking liquid to a syrupy consistency. Letting the pears cool in the syrup prevented them from drying out; it also allowed them to absorb some of the syrup, giving them a candied translucency and making them plump, sweet, and pleasantly spiced. Select pears that yield slightly when pressed. Use a dry medium-bodied red, such as a Côtes du Rhône, Pinot Noir, or Merlot. The fruit can be served as is or with crème fraîche.

1 vanilla bean
1 (750-ml) bottle dry red wine
¾ cup (5¼ ounces) sugar

5 sprigs fresh mint
3 sprigs fresh thyme
½ cinnamon stick
½ teaspoon peppercorns
3 whole cloves
⅛ teaspoon table salt
6 ripe but firm Bosc or Bartlett pears (8 ounces each),
    peeled, halved, and cored

1. Cut vanilla bean in half lengthwise. Using tip of paring knife, scrape out seeds. Bring wine, sugar, mint sprigs, thyme sprigs, cinnamon stick, peppercorns, cloves, salt, and vanilla seeds and pod to boil in Dutch oven over high heat and cook, stirring occasionally, until sugar has dissolved, about 5 minutes.

2. Add pears and return to boil. Reduce heat to medium-low, cover, and simmer until pears are tender and toothpick slips easily in and out of pears, 10 to 20 minutes, gently turning pears over every 5 minutes.

3. Using slotted spoon, transfer pears to plate; discard solids. Bring syrup to simmer over medium heat and cook, stirring occasionally, until slightly thickened and measures 1¼ to 1½ cups, about 15 minutes. Return pears and any accumulated juices to syrup and let cool to room temperature. Cover and refrigerate until well chilled, at least 2 hours or up to 3 days. Serve.

VARIATION

White Wine–Poached Pears with Lemon and Herbs for Two

SAUCEPAN

Serves 2

Total Time 45 minutes, plus 2 hours chilling

Select pears that yield slightly when pressed. Use a medium-bodied dry white wine such as Sauvignon Blanc or Chardonnay here. The fruit can be served as is or with crème fraîche.

½ vanilla bean
2 cups dry white wine
⅓ cup (2⅓ ounces) sugar
5 (2-inch) strips lemon zest
4 sprigs fresh mint
3 sprigs fresh thyme
  Pinch table salt
2 ripe but firm Bosc or Bartlett pears (8 ounces each),
    peeled, halved, and cored

1. Cut vanilla bean in half lengthwise. Using tip of paring knife, scrape out seeds. Bring wine, sugar, lemon zest, mint sprigs, thyme sprigs, salt, and vanilla seeds and pod to boil in medium saucepan over high heat and cook, stirring occasionally, until sugar has dissolved, about 5 minutes.

2. Add pears and return to boil. Reduce heat to medium-low, cover, and simmer until pears are tender and toothpick slips easily in and out of pears, 10 to 20 minutes, gently turning pears over every 5 minutes.

3. Using slotted spoon, transfer pears to plate; discard solids. Bring syrup to simmer over medium heat and cook, stirring occasionally, until slightly thickened and measures ½ cup, about 15 minutes. Return pears and any accumulated juices to syrup and let cool to room temperature. Cover and refrigerate until well chilled, at least 2 hours or up to 3 days. Serve.

Bananas Foster

SKILLET

Serves 4

Total Time 30 minutes

Why This Recipe Works Although the classic New Orleans dessert bananas Foster requires few ingredients (butter, brown sugar, rum, and bananas), the traditional technique of flambéing can be tricky and intimidating. We wanted to develop a foolproof way to make a quick, reliable version of this dessert featuring tender bananas and a flavorful—and flameless—sauce. We started with the sauce, which we prepared in a skillet before adding the bananas to cook right in the sauce until they were soft, flipping them halfway through cooking so they turned out perfectly tender, not mushy. We struck just the right balance of sweetness from brown sugar, rich depth of flavor from a small amount of golden rum, spiced notes from one cinnamon stick, and a splash of acidity from lemon juice for a sophisticated dish that made fussy flambéing entirely unnecessary. Sticking with tradition, we served the bananas and sauce with ice cream. Look for yellow bananas or those with very few spots; overly ripe bananas will fall apart during cooking. We prefer the flavor of aged rum, but you can substitute white rum, if desired.

½ cup packed (3½ ounces) dark brown sugar
¼ cup plus 2 teaspoons aged rum, divided
2 tablespoons water
1 cinnamon stick
¼ teaspoon table salt
3 ripe bananas, peeled, halved crosswise,
    then halved lengthwise
1 pint vanilla ice cream
4 tablespoons unsalted butter, cut into 4 pieces
1 teaspoon lemon juice

1. Bring sugar, ¼ cup rum, water, cinnamon stick, and salt to simmer in 12-inch skillet over medium heat. Cook, whisking frequently, until sugar is completely dissolved, about 2 minutes.

2. Add bananas to skillet, cut sides down, and cook until sauce is glossy and cut sides of bananas are golden brown, 2 to 4 minutes. Flip bananas and continue to cook until soft but not mushy, 2 to 3 minutes longer. Using tongs, divide bananas among 4 bowls and top with ice cream.

3. Off heat, discard cinnamon stick. Whisk butter into sauce, 1 piece at a time, until incorporated. Whisk in lemon juice and remaining 2 teaspoons rum. Spoon sauce over bananas and ice cream. Serve.

Warm Peach-Raspberry Compote

SLOW COOKER

Serves 6

Cooking Time 3 to 4 hours on low or 2 to 3 hours on high

Why This Recipe Works This effortless yet brightly flavored fruit compote takes a simple bowl of vanilla ice cream from ordinary to extraordinary. The slow cooker provided a gentle cooking environment that released the fruit's juices without breaking it down into jam. Frozen sliced peaches offered consistent quality, guaranteeing a compote that thickened to just the right texture with the help of a little tapioca. Raspberries, stirred in at the end, provided a lively, tart punch, and chopped mint added freshness. This compote can top more than just ice cream; it's also good on frozen yogurt, Greek yogurt, or ricotta cheese. You do not need to thaw the peaches for this recipe.

   2 pounds frozen sliced peaches, cut into 1-inch pieces
  ⅓ cup (2⅓ ounces) sugar
   2 tablespoons instant tapioca
   1 teaspoon lemon juice
   1 teaspoon vanilla extract
  ⅛ teaspoon table salt
  10 ounces (2 cups) raspberries
  ¼ cup chopped fresh mint
   2 pints vanilla ice cream

1. Combine peaches, sugar, tapioca, lemon juice, vanilla, and salt in slow cooker. Cover and cook until peaches are tender and sauce is thickened, 3 to 4 hours on low or 2 to 3 hours on high. (Compote can be held on warm or low setting for up to 2 hours.)

2. Stir raspberries into compote and let sit until heated through, about 5 minutes. Stir in mint. Portion ice cream into individual bowls and spoon compote over top. Serve.

Blueberry Grunt

DUTCH OVEN

Serves 12

Total Time 1 hour

Why This Recipe Works This old-fashioned fruit dessert boasts sweetened stewed berries covered with drop biscuits. It is traditionally steamed on the stovetop, so we knew a Dutch oven would be the perfect vessel; the heavy bottom prevented the fruit from burning, and the heavy lid held in steam nicely. To ensure a bright-tasting filling, we cooked down only half of the berries until jammy and then stirred in the remaining berries at the end so they retained their fresh fruit flavor. A little bit of cornstarch helped thicken the filling. For a fluffy biscuit topping, we placed a dish towel under the lid during cooking to absorb condensation that would turn the biscuits soggy. You will need a clean dish towel for this recipe.

Filling

  2½ pounds (8 cups) blueberries, divided
  ½ cup (3½ ounces) sugar
  ½ teaspoon ground cinnamon
   2 tablespoons water
   1 teaspoon grated lemon zest plus 1 tablespoon juice, divided
   1 teaspoon cornstarch

Topping

  ¾ cup buttermilk
   6 tablespoons unsalted butter, melted and cooled slightly
   1 teaspoon vanilla extract
  2¼ cups (11¼ ounces) all-purpose flour
  1½ teaspoons baking powder
  ½ teaspoon baking soda
  ½ teaspoon table salt
  ½ cup (3½ ounces) sugar, divided
  ½ teaspoon ground cinnamon

1. For the filling Cook 4 cups blueberries, sugar, cinnamon, water, and lemon zest in Dutch oven over medium-high heat, stirring occasionally, until mixture is thick and jamlike, 10 to 12 minutes. Whisk lemon juice and cornstarch in small bowl, then stir into blueberry mixture. Add remaining 4 cups blueberries and cook until heated through, about 1 minute; remove pot from heat, cover, and keep warm.

2. For the topping Combine buttermilk, butter, and vanilla in 2-cup liquid measuring cup. Whisk flour, baking powder, baking soda, salt, and 6 tablespoons sugar in large bowl. Slowly stir buttermilk mixture into flour mixture until dough forms.

3. Using small ice cream scoop or 2 large spoons, spoon golf-ball size dough pieces on top of warm berry mixture (you should have 14 pieces). Wrap lid of Dutch oven with clean dish towel (keeping towel away from heat source) and cover pot. Simmer gently until biscuits have doubled in size and toothpick inserted in center comes out clean, 16 to 22 minutes.

4. Combine remaining 2 tablespoons sugar and cinnamon in small bowl. Remove lid and sprinkle biscuit topping with cinnamon sugar. Serve immediately.

Blueberry Grunt

Cherry Cobbler
SKILLET
Serves 6 to 8
Total Time 1½ hours

Why This Recipe Works For an easy, rustic dessert, you can't beat a cobbler. With a fleet of tender biscuits floating on a sea of sweet fruit, a good cobbler can hold its own against any fancy cake or pastry. Sour cherries have sufficient acidity to cook up well and become truly flavorful with a touch of sugar and some heat, and using jarred cherries meant we could skip the tedious step of pitting them. Cooking a portion of the cherry syrup—thickened with cornstarch and seasoned with allspice, nutmeg, and vanilla—in a skillet before adding the cherries enriched our filling to just the right consistency. For the topping, we wanted fluffy but sturdy biscuits that didn't need to be baked separately from the cherries. To accomplish this, we incorporated a combination of baking powder and baking soda into the biscuit dough; and because baking soda is activated by an acidic ingredient we also added buttermilk, which lent our biscuits great flavor. We spaced our biscuits ½ inch apart on top of the filling to give them room to grow and moved the skillet to the oven to bake the topping and meld the two components. We prefer the crunchy texture of turbinado sugar sprinkled on the biscuits before baking, but regular granulated sugar can be substituted. You will need a 12-inch ovensafe skillet for this recipe. For best results, serve within 15 minutes and transfer any leftovers to an airtight container.

Cherry Cobbler

Filling
- 6 cups jarred sour cherries in light syrup, drained with 2 cups syrup reserved
- ½ cup (3½ ounces) granulated sugar
- 3 tablespoons cornstarch
- ½ teaspoon vanilla extract
- ¼ teaspoon ground allspice
  Pinch ground nutmeg
  Pinch table salt

Topping
1½ cups (7½ ounces) all-purpose flour
5 tablespoons (2¼ ounces) granulated sugar
1½ teaspoons baking powder
¼ teaspoon baking soda
¼ teaspoon table salt
¾ cup buttermilk
4 tablespoons unsalted butter, melted
2 tablespoons turbinado sugar

1. For the filling Adjust oven rack to middle position and heat oven to 400 degrees. Whisk cherry syrup, sugar, cornstarch, vanilla, allspice, nutmeg, and salt in 12-inch ovensafe skillet until well combined. Bring to simmer over medium-high heat and cook, whisking frequently, until slightly thickened, 5 to 7 minutes. Off heat, stir in cherries.

2. For the topping Whisk flour, granulated sugar, baking powder, baking soda, and salt together in medium bowl. Stir in buttermilk and melted butter until just combined. Using small ice cream scoop or 2 large spoons, scoop out and drop 1-inch pieces of dough onto filling, spaced about ½ inch apart. Sprinkle biscuits with turbinado sugar.

3. Transfer skillet to oven and bake until biscuits are golden brown and filling is thick and glossy, 30 to 35 minutes, rotating skillet halfway through baking. Let cobbler cool for 15 minutes before serving.

`VARIATION`

Cherry Cobbler for Two
SKILLET
Serves 2
Total Time 1¼ hours
We prefer the crunchy texture of turbinado sugar sprinkled on the biscuits before baking, but regular granulated sugar can be substituted. You will need an 8-inch ovensafe skillet for this recipe. For best results, serve within 15 minutes.

Filling
1½ cups jarred sour cherries in light syrup, drained with ½ cup syrup reserved
¼ cup (1¾ ounces) granulated sugar
1 tablespoon cornstarch
¼ teaspoon vanilla extract
Pinch ground allspice
Pinch ground nutmeg
Pinch table salt

Topping
½ cup (2½ ounces) all-purpose flour
3 tablespoons granulated sugar
½ teaspoon baking powder

⅛ teaspoon baking soda
⅛ teaspoon table salt
¼ cup buttermilk
2 tablespoons unsalted butter, melted
1 teaspoon turbinado sugar

1. For the filling Adjust oven rack to middle position and heat oven to 400 degrees. Whisk cherry syrup, sugar, cornstarch, vanilla, allspice, nutmeg, and salt in 8-inch ovensafe skillet until well combined. Bring to simmer over medium-high heat and cook, whisking frequently, until slightly thickened, 1 to 3 minutes. Off heat, stir in cherries.

2. For the topping Whisk flour, granulated sugar, baking powder, baking soda, and salt together in medium bowl. Stir in buttermilk and melted butter until just combined. Using small ice cream scoop or 2 large spoons, scoop out and drop 1-inch pieces of dough onto filling, spaced about ½ inch apart. Sprinkle biscuits with turbinado sugar.

3. Transfer skillet to oven and bake until biscuits are golden brown and filling is thick and glossy, 20 to 25 minutes, rotating skillet halfway through baking. Let cobbler cool for 10 minutes before serving.

NOTES FROM THE TEST KITCHEN

ALL ABOUT SUGAR
Sugar not only adds sweetness to baked goods; it affects texture, too.

White Granulated Sugar Made either from sugar cane or sugar beets, this type of sugar has a clean flavor, and an evenly ground, loose texture.

Brown Sugar Brown sugar is simply granulated white sugar that has been combined with molasses. (When necessary, our ingredient list will indicate "light" or "dark" brown sugar. If either can be used, we simply list "brown sugar.") Store brown sugar in an airtight container to prevent it from drying out.

Confectioners' Sugar Also called powdered sugar, this is the most finely ground sugar. To prevent clumping, confectioners' sugar contains a small amount of cornstarch.

Turbinado and Demerara Sugar These "raw" sugars have large crystals that do not readily dissolve—a reason to avoid them in dough. Instead, we like to sprinkle them on baked goods to create crunch.

Pear-Ginger Crisp

DUTCH OVEN

Serves 6 to 8
Total Time 1¼ hours

Why This Recipe Works We wanted a simple pear crisp that would allow the fruit's subtle floral flavor to shine against the sweet, lightly spiced topping. Using a spacious Dutch oven allowed us to easily increase the amount of pears (we preferred Bartlett pears here since their sweet, flowery flavor intensifies when baked) from the usual 3 pounds to a generous 5 pounds for a more fruit-forward crisp. To keep the pears' ample moisture in check, we added some cornstarch to the filling. For the topping, we first prepared a standard streusel but found that the juicy pears made this loose mixture too soggy. The solution was to replace the cold butter with melted, which soaked up the flour for a more cohesive streusel that stayed crunchy atop the pear filling. Adding almonds to the topping provided more texture and a richness that tasters liked. To give the crisp more character, we traded the typical warm spices for a triple hit of ginger—using fresh ginger in the pear filling and a mix of ground and crystallized in the topping. After sprinkling on the topping we transferred the whole pot to the oven and baked our crisp uncovered, allowing the top to brown nicely. After baking, we let the crisp rest for a generous 20 minutes so that the filling could set. We prefer a crisp made with Bartlett pears, but Bosc pears can also be used. Select pears that yield slightly when pressed. Serve with ice cream.

Topping
- ¾ cup slivered almonds
- ½ cup (2½ ounces) all-purpose flour
- ¼ cup packed (1¾ ounces) light brown sugar
- 2 tablespoons chopped crystallized ginger
- 2 tablespoons granulated sugar
- ¾ teaspoon ground ginger
- ⅛ teaspoon table salt
- 5 tablespoons unsalted butter, melted and cooled

Filling
- 4 tablespoons unsalted butter
- 3 tablespoons granulated sugar
- 1½ teaspoons cornstarch
- 1½ teaspoons lemon juice
- 1 teaspoon grated fresh ginger
  Pinch table salt
- 5 pounds ripe but firm Bartlett pears, peeled, halved, cored, and cut into 1½-inch pieces

Pear-Ginger Crisp

1. For the topping Adjust oven rack to lower-middle position and heat oven to 425 degrees. Pulse almonds, flour, brown sugar, crystallized ginger, granulated sugar, ground ginger, and salt in food processor until nuts are finely chopped, about 10 pulses. Drizzle melted butter over flour mixture and pulse until mixture resembles wet sand, about 5 pulses, scraping down sides of bowl as needed.

2. For the filling Melt butter in Dutch oven over medium heat. Off heat, whisk in sugar, cornstarch, lemon juice, ginger, and salt. Add pears and toss to coat.

3. Sprinkle topping evenly over fruit, breaking up any large chunks. Scrape down exposed sides of pot, then transfer to oven. Bake, uncovered, until pears are bubbling around edges and topping is deep golden brown, 25 to 30 minutes, rotating pot halfway through baking.

4. Remove pot from oven and transfer to wire rack. Let crisp cool for 20 minutes before serving.

BREAD PUDDING

Bread pudding started as a frugal way to transform stale, old loaves of bread into an appetizing dish. We wanted a version that was as simple as its humble origins. Good bread pudding starts with the bread, so we chose challah for its rich flavor. We cut it into cubes, staled them overnight, and soaked the cubes in custard, which we made using just egg yolks to avoid the "eggy" taste that the sulfur compounds in egg whites cause. A combination of cream and milk, along with some sugar, vanilla, and salt, guaranteed a rich, creamy custard. Once the cubes were saturated, it was time to cook. For our casserole dish version, we added melted butter and sugar to the top for a browned crust. A slow cooker offered an alternative environment to turn out a creamy custard, but we skipped the sugar topping since it wouldn't brown and lined the slow cooker with foil to prevent sticking. Finally, while we knew the pudding would cook well in the pressure cooker, we also knew it would be a challenge to remove, so we used a soufflé dish elevated on a trivet. Challah is an egg-enriched bread that can be found in most bakeries and supermarkets. Using staled, day-old bread in our bread pudding allows us to assemble these dishes quickly. However, if you don't have this on hand, you can also dry out fresh bread pieces by baking them in a rimmed baking sheet in a 225-degree oven for about 35 minutes.

CLASSIC

CASEROLE

CASSEROLE
Serves 8 to 10
Total Time 2¼ hours

- 1 pound challah, cut into 1-inch pieces (12 cups), staled overnight
- 9 large egg yolks
- ¾ cup (5¼ ounces) plus 1 tablespoon granulated sugar, divided
- 4 teaspoons vanilla extract
- ¾ teaspoon table salt
- 2½ cups heavy cream
- 2½ cups milk
- 2 tablespoons packed light brown sugar
- 2 tablespoons unsalted butter, melted

1. Adjust oven rack to middle position and heat oven to 325 degrees. Measure out 2 cups challah and set aside for topping. Whisk egg yolks, ¾ cup granulated sugar, vanilla, and salt together in large bowl. Whisk in cream and milk until combined. Add remaining challah and toss to combine. Transfer mixture to 13 by 9-inch baking dish and let sit, occasionally pressing on challah to submerge, until bread is well saturated, about 30 minutes.

2. Combine brown sugar and remaining 1 tablespoon granulated sugar in bowl. Sprinkle reserved challah evenly over top of bread pudding and press gently into custard. Brush with melted butter and sprinkle with sugar mixture. Bake until custard is just set and center of pudding registers 170 degrees, 45 to 50 minutes, rotating dish halfway through baking.

3. Transfer bread pudding to wire rack and let cool until pudding is set, about 15 minutes. Serve.

MAKE IT YOUR WAY →

> **Use What You've Got** Substitute half-and-half for the combination of heavy cream and milk. Substitute French or Italian bread, brioche rolls, or hearty sandwich bread for the challah.

SLOW COOK IT

SLOW COOKER

Serves 8 to 10
Cooking Time 3 to 4 hours on low
You will need a 5- to 7-quart oval slow cooker for this recipe.

- 9 large egg yolks
- ¾ cup (5¼ ounces) sugar
- 4 teaspoons vanilla extract
- ¾ teaspoon table salt
- 2½ cups heavy cream
- 2½ cups milk
- 1 pound challah, cut into 1-inch pieces (12 cups), staled overnight

1. Whisk egg yolks, sugar, vanilla, and salt together in large bowl. Whisk in cream and milk until combined. Add challah and toss to combine. Let sit, occasionally pressing on challah to submerge, until bread is well saturated, about 30 minutes.

2. Line slow cooker with aluminum foil collar and lightly coat with vegetable oil spray. Transfer challah mixture to prepared slow cooker and spread into even layer. Cover and cook until center of bread pudding is set, 3 to 4 hours on low.

3. Turn off slow cooker and let bread pudding sit, covered, until pudding is set, about 15 minute. Discard foil collar. Serve.

PRESSURE COOK IT

INSTANT POT

Serves 4 to 6
Total Time 1¾ hours
You will need a 1½-quart round soufflé dish or ceramic dish of similar size for this recipe. If your pressure cooker didn't come with a trivet, you can make your own (see page 365).

- 5 large egg yolks
- 6 tablespoons (2⅔ ounces) sugar
- 2 teaspoons vanilla extract
- ¼ teaspoon table salt
- 1¼ cups heavy cream
- 1¼ cups milk
- 8 ounces challah, cut into 1-inch pieces (6 cups), staled overnight

1. Whisk egg yolks, sugar, vanilla, and salt together in large bowl. Whisk in cream and milk until combined. Add challah and toss to combine. Let sit, occasionally pressing on challah to submerge, until bread is well saturated, about 20 minutes.

2. Arrange trivet included with pressure cooker in base of insert and add 1½ cups water. Fold sheet of aluminum foil into 16 by 6-inch sling, then rest 1½-quart round soufflé dish in center of sling. Transfer challah mixture to prepared soufflé dish and spread into even layer. Using sling, lower soufflé dish into pot and onto trivet; allow narrow edges of sling to rest along sides of insert.

3. Lock lid in place and close pressure release valve. Select high pressure cook function and cook for 45 minutes.

4. Turn off pressure cooker and quick-release pressure. Carefully remove lid, allowing steam to escape away from you. Using sling, transfer soufflé dish to wire rack and let sit until pudding is set, about 10 minutes. Serve.

> **Bulk it Up** Add dried fruit (cherries, cranberries, raisins, chopped figs) and/or chocolate chips to the custard with the challah.

> **Add an Upgrade** Add ¼ cup whiskey, aged rum, or brandy (2 tablespoons for pressure cooker version), warm spices (cinnamon, cardamom, nutmeg, ginger), and/or grated citrus zest in place of—or in addition to—the vanilla. Chopped, toasted nuts (walnuts, pecans, almonds, pistachios, hazelnuts) make a great finishing touch.

Blueberry Pie

Blueberry Pie
CAST-IRON SKILLET
Serves 8
Total Time 1½ hours, plus 4 hours cooling

Why This Recipe Works We wanted a blueberry pie with a browned, tender crust and a filling full of fresh flavor and plump berries. A traditional pie plate was out of the question since we would need to precook the filling and our goal was to use only one pan. But a cast-iron skillet's heat retention was perfect for creating a crisp, flaky bottom crust that could stand up to a wet fruit filling. Plus, its deep sides gave the pie plenty of space to bake without bubbling over. We first cooked the filling and then set it aside to place the crust in the skillet before moving the pie to the oven. To thicken the filling, we used tapioca plus a shredded Granny Smith apple; the pectin in the apple allowed us to use less tapioca, which meant the bright blueberry flavor could shine through. To vent the steam from the berries, we cut out circles in the top dough. This recipe was developed using fresh blueberries, but unthawed frozen blueberries will work. In step 1, cook half the frozen blueberries, without mashing, for 12 to 15 minutes, until reduced to 1¼ cups. Grind the tapioca to a powder in a spice

grinder or mini food processor. We developed this recipe using a 10-inch cast-iron skillet. If using an ovensafe traditional or nonstick skillet, or enameled cast-iron skillet, place a baking sheet underneath to catch any juices that might bubble over. We prefer to use homemade pie dough here; however, store-bought pie dough can be substituted.

30 ounces (6 cups) fresh blueberries, divided
1 Granny Smith apple, peeled and shredded
¾ cup (5¼ ounces) sugar
2 tablespoons instant tapioca, ground
2 teaspoons grated lemon zest plus 2 teaspoons juice
Pinch table salt
1 recipe Classic Double-Crust Pie Dough, rolled into 12-inch rounds (page 355)
2 tablespoons unsalted butter, cut into ¼-inch pieces
1 large egg, lightly beaten with 2 tablespoons water

1. Adjust oven rack to lowest position and heat oven to 400 degrees. Cook 3 cups blueberries in 10-inch cast-iron skillet over medium heat, mashing occasionally with potato masher, until blueberries are broken down and mixture is thickened and measures about 1½ cups, 6 to 8 minutes; transfer to large bowl. Let cool slightly.

2. Wring apple in clean dish towel to squeeze out as much liquid as possible; transfer apple to bowl with cooked blueberries. Stir in sugar, tapioca, lemon zest and juice, salt, and remaining 3 cups blueberries.

3. Grease clean, dry, cooled skillet. Loosely roll 1 dough round around rolling pin and gently unroll it onto prepared skillet. Ease dough into skillet by gently lifting and supporting edge of dough with your hand while pressing into skillet bottom and corners with your other hand.

4. Transfer blueberry mixture to dough-lined skillet and scatter butter on top. Using 1¼-inch round cookie cutter, cut circle from center of remaining dough round. Cut 6 more circles from dough round, 1½ inches from edge of center hole and equally spaced around center hole. Loosely roll dough round around rolling pin and gently unroll it onto filling.

5. Trim overhang to ½ inch beyond lip of skillet, then ease edge of dough into skillet until flush with bottom crust. Gently press top and bottom crusts together to seal. Roll in edge of crust; then, using your index finger, press rolled edge against sides of skillet to create attractive fluted rim. Brush crust liberally with egg wash.

6. Bake until crust is golden brown, about 25 minutes. Reduce oven temperature to 350 degrees, rotate skillet, and continue to bake until crust is deep golden brown and filling is bubbling, 25 to 35 minutes longer. Transfer skillet to wire rack and let pie cool completely, about 4 hours. Serve.

Using 1¼-inch round cookie cutter, cut round from center of dough. Cut 6 more rounds from dough, 1½ inches from edge of center hole and equally spaced around center hole.

Classic Double-Crust Pie Dough

Makes enough for one 10-inch pie

2½ cups (12½ ounces) all-purpose flour
2 tablespoons sugar
1 teaspoon table salt
8 tablespoons vegetable shortening, cut into ½-inch pieces and chilled
12 tablespoons unsalted butter, cut into ¼-inch pieces and chilled
6 tablespoons ice water, plus extra as needed

1. Process flour, sugar, and salt in food processor until combined, about 5 seconds. Scatter shortening over top and process until mixture resembles coarse cornmeal, about 10 seconds. Scatter butter over top and pulse until mixture resembles coarse crumbs, about 10 pulses.

2. Transfer mixture to large bowl. Sprinkle ice water over mixture. Stir and press dough with spatula until dough sticks together. If dough does not come together, stir in up to 2 tablespoons ice water, 1 tablespoon at a time, until it does.

3. Using spatula, divide dough into 2 equal portions. Transfer each portion to sheet of plastic wrap and form each into 4-inch disk. Wrap each piece tightly in plastic and refrigerate for at least 1 hour or up to 2 days. Let chilled dough sit on counter to soften slightly, about 10 minutes, before rolling. (Wrapped dough can be frozen for up to 1 month. If frozen, let dough thaw completely on counter before rolling.)

Easy Apple Galettes

SHEET PAN
Serves 4
Total Time 1½ hours

Why This Recipe Works An apple galette is a free-form dessert with a crust boasting the buttery flakiness of a croissant topped by a generous layer of apples. We bypassed labor-intensive, time-consuming homemade pastry and reached for store-bought frozen puff pastry instead, cutting the pastry in half to make two small galettes (the perfect amount to serve 4 people) on a baking sheet. Forming an attractive crust was as easy as folding over the edges of the pastry. Granny Smith apples worked best; the slices stayed moist in the oven and maintained their shape. Sprinkling a little sugar on the apples prevented them from drying out and also helped them brown nicely. A simple glaze made from apple jelly and a small amount of water was the perfect finishing touch, contributing an attractive sheen and fruity tartness. Be sure to let the puff pastry thaw completely before using; otherwise, it can crack and break apart. To thaw frozen puff pastry, let it sit either in the refrigerator for 24 hours or on the counter for 30 minutes to 1 hour.

1 (9½ by 9-inch) sheet puff pastry, thawed and halved
1 pound Granny Smith apples, peeled, cored, halved, and sliced ⅛ inch thick, divided
1 tablespoon unsalted butter, cut into ¼-inch pieces, divided
4 teaspoons sugar, divided
2 tablespoons apple jelly
2 teaspoons water

1. Adjust oven rack to middle position and heat oven to 400 degrees. Arrange puff pastry halves spaced evenly apart on parchment paper–lined rimmed baking sheet. Fold edges of each pastry over by ¼ inch; crimp to create ¼-inch-thick border.

2. Starting in 1 corner of 1 tart, shingle half of apple slices into crust in tidy diagonal rows, overlapping them by about half, until surface is completely covered. Dot apples with half of butter pieces and sprinkle evenly with 2 teaspoons sugar. Repeat with remaining tart, remaining apples, remaining butter, and remaining 2 teaspoons sugar. Bake until bottoms of tarts are deep golden brown and apples have caramelized, 40 to 45 minutes, rotating sheet halfway through baking.

3. Combine apple jelly and water in bowl and microwave until mixture begins to bubble, about 30 seconds. Brush glaze over apples and let tarts cool slightly on sheet for 15 minutes. Slice and serve warm or at room temperature.

VARIATION

Easy Apple Galette for Two
SHEET PAN
Serves 2
Total Time 1½ hours

Be sure to let the puff pastry thaw completely before using; otherwise, it can crack and break apart. To thaw frozen puff pastry, let it sit either in the refrigerator for 24 hours or on the counter for 30 minutes to 1 hour. The remaining half sheet of puff pastry can be refrigerated for up to 1 week; we like to use it for our Potato, Artichoke, and Sun-Dried Tomato Tart for Two (page 295).

½ (9½ by 9-inch) sheet puff pastry, thawed
1 large Granny Smith apple (8 ounces), peeled, cored, halved, and sliced ⅛ inch thick
½ tablespoon unsalted butter, cut into ¼-inch pieces
2 teaspoons sugar
1 tablespoon apple jelly
1 teaspoon water

1. Adjust oven rack to middle position and heat oven to 400 degrees. Arrange puff pastry on parchment paper–lined rimmed baking sheet. Fold edges of pastry over by ¼ inch; crimp to create ¼-inch-thick border.

2. Starting in 1 corner of tart, shingle apple slices into crust in tidy diagonal rows, overlapping them by about half, until surface is completely covered. Dot apple with butter pieces and sprinkle evenly with sugar. Bake until bottom of tart is deep golden brown and apple has caramelized, 40 to 45 minutes, rotating sheet halfway through baking.

3. Combine apple jelly and water in bowl and microwave until mixture begins to bubble, about 30 seconds. Brush glaze over apples and let tart cool slightly on sheet for 15 minutes. Slice and serve warm or at room temperature.

MAKING EASY APPLE GALETTES

1. Fold edges of pastry over by ¼ inch and crimp to create ¼-inch-thick border.

2. Starting in 1 corner, shingle sliced apples to form even rows across dough, overlapping each slice by about half.

Apple Strudel
SHEET PAN
Serves 6
Total Time 1½ hours

Why This Recipe Works Apple strudel is a marriage of flaky pastry and just-sweet-enough raisin-studded apples. Starting with frozen phyllo dough kept our recipe simple, and two small strudels fit easily on a baking sheet. For the filling, we first warmed our apples in the microwave; this step activated an enzyme that allowed the apples to bake until tender without collapsing. Bread crumbs are a common addition to prevent leaking, so we stirred in panko bread crumbs to soak up some of the liquid. To avoid a compressed, tough underside, we changed the typical wrapping technique so the seam was on the top instead of on the bottom. Sprinkling confectioners' sugar between the phyllo layers allowed them to fuse together in the oven. Gala apples can be substituted for Golden Delicious. Phyllo dough is also available in larger 18 by 14-inch sheets; if using, cut them in half to make 14 by 9-inch sheets. Thaw phyllo in the refrigerator overnight or on the counter for 4 to 5 hours; don't thaw it in the microwave.

1¾ pounds Golden Delicious apples, peeled, cored, and cut into ½-inch pieces
3 tablespoons granulated sugar
½ teaspoon grated lemon zest plus 1½ teaspoons juice
¼ teaspoon ground cinnamon
¼ teaspoon ground ginger
¼ teaspoon table salt, divided
3 tablespoons golden raisins
1½ tablespoons panko bread crumbs
7 tablespoons unsalted butter, melted
1 tablespoon confectioners' sugar, plus extra for serving
14 (14 by 9-inch) phyllo sheets, thawed

1. Toss apples, granulated sugar, lemon zest and juice, cinnamon, ginger, and ⅛ teaspoon salt together in large bowl. Cover and microwave until apples are warm to touch, about 2 minutes, stirring once halfway through microwaving. Let apples sit, covered, for 5 minutes. Transfer apples to colander set in second large bowl and let drain, reserving liquid. Return apples to bowl; stir in raisins and panko.

2. Adjust oven rack to upper-middle position and heat oven to 375 degrees. Spray rimmed baking sheet with vegetable oil spray. Stir remaining ⅛ teaspoon salt into melted butter.

3. Place 16½ by 12-inch sheet of parchment paper on counter with long side parallel to edge of counter. Place 1 phyllo sheet on parchment with long side parallel to edge of counter. Place 1½ teaspoons confectioners' sugar in fine-mesh strainer (rest strainer in bowl to prevent making mess). Lightly

Apple Strudel

ASSEMBLING APPLE STRUDEL

1. Mound filling along bottom third of 7 layered phyllo sheets on parchment paper, leaving 2-inch border at bottom edge and sides of phyllo.

2. Using parchment, fold sides of phyllo over filling, then fold over bottom edge of phyllo. Brush folded portions with apple liquid.

3. Fold top edge of phyllo over mounded filling, which should overlap the bottom edge by about 1 inch. Press to seal.

brush sheet with melted butter and dust sparingly with confectioners' sugar. Repeat with 6 more phyllo sheets, melted butter, and confectioners' sugar, stacking sheets one on top of other as you go.

4. Arrange half of apple mixture in 2½ by 10-inch rectangle 2 inches from bottom of phyllo and about 2 inches from each side. Using parchment, fold sides of phyllo over filling, then fold bottom edge of phyllo over filling. Brush folded portions of phyllo with reserved apple liquid. Fold top edge over filling, making sure top and bottom edges overlap by about 1 inch. (If they do not overlap, unfold, rearrange filling into slightly narrower strip, and refold.) Press firmly to seal. Using thin metal spatula, transfer strudel to 1 side of prepared baking sheet, facing seam toward center of sheet. Lightly brush top and sides of strudel with half of remaining apple liquid. Repeat process with remaining phyllo, melted butter, confectioners' sugar, filling, and apple liquid. Place second strudel on other side of prepared sheet, with seam facing center of sheet.

5. Bake strudels until golden brown, 27 to 35 minutes, rotating sheet halfway through baking. Using thin metal spatula, immediately transfer strudels to cutting board. Let cool for 3 minutes. Slice each strudel into thirds and let cool for at least 20 minutes. Serve warm or at room temperature, dusting with extra confectioners' sugar before serving.

VARIATION

Apple Strudel for Two

SHEET PAN

Serves 2

Total Time 1½ hours

Gala apples can be substituted for Golden Delicious. Phyllo dough is also available in larger 18 by 14-inch sheets; if using, cut them in half to make 14 by 9-inch sheets. Thaw phyllo in the refrigerator overnight or on the counter for 4 to 5 hours; don't thaw it in the microwave.

- 2 Golden Delicious apples (7 ounces each), peeled, cored, and cut into ½-inch pieces
- 1½ tablespoons granulated sugar
- ¼ teaspoon grated lemon zest plus ¾ teaspoon juice
- ⅛ teaspoon ground cinnamon
- ⅛ teaspoon ground ginger
- ⅛ teaspoon table salt, divided
- 1½ tablespoons golden raisins
- 2¼ teaspoons panko bread crumbs
- 3½ tablespoons unsalted butter, melted
- 1½ teaspoons confectioners' sugar, plus extra for serving
- 7 (14 by 9-inch) phyllo sheets, thawed

Crepes with Chocolate and Orange

making sure top and bottom edges overlap by about 1 inch. (If they do not overlap, unfold, rearrange filling into slightly narrower strip, and refold.) Press firmly to seal. Using thin metal spatula, transfer strudel to prepared sheet. Lightly brush top and sides of strudel with remaining apple liquid.

5. Bake until golden brown, 25 to 30 minutes, rotating sheet halfway through baking. Using thin metal spatula, immediately transfer strudel to cutting board. Let cool for 3 minutes. Slice strudel into quarters and let cool for at least 20 minutes. Serve warm or at room temperature, dusting with extra confectioners' sugar before serving.

Crepes with Chocolate and Orange
SKILLET
Serves 4
Total Time 45 minutes

Why This Recipe Works Crepes have a reputation for being difficult, but we were determined to make a foolproof version that required just a 12-inch nonstick skillet (rather than a specialized pan). Heating the pan properly was essential. If too hot, the batter set up before it evenly coated the surface. If too cool, the crepe was pale (read: bland) and too flimsy to flip without tearing. Using just enough of our crepe batter to coat the bottom of the pan was also important, as was the tilt-and-shake method that we employed to distribute it. To avoid singed fingertips, we loosened the crepe with a rubber spatula before grasping its edge and nimbly turning it to the flip side to cook until spotty brown. Heating the stack of finished crepes in the microwave briefly guaranteed that they were all warm when served. A dusting of sugar with orange zest and grated chocolate melted into the warmed crepes to make a citrusy-sweet filling. Crepes will give off steam as they cook, but if at any point the skillet begins to smoke, remove it from the heat immediately and turn down the heat. Stacking the crepes on a wire rack allows excess steam to escape so they won't stick together. To allow for practice, the recipe yields 10 crepes; only 8 are needed for the filling.

½ teaspoon vegetable oil
¼ cup (1¾ ounces) plus 1 teaspoon sugar, divided
1 teaspoon finely grated orange zest
2 ounces bittersweet chocolate, finely grated
1 cup (5 ounces) all-purpose flour
¼ teaspoon table salt
1½ cups whole milk
3 large eggs
2 tablespoons unsalted butter, melted and cooled

1. Toss apples, granulated sugar, lemon zest and juice, cinnamon, ginger, and pinch salt together in large bowl. Cover and microwave until apples are warm to touch, 60 to 75 seconds, stirring once halfway through microwaving. Let apples sit, covered, for 5 minutes. Transfer apples to colander set in second large bowl and let drain, reserving liquid. Return apples to bowl; stir in raisins and panko.

2. Adjust oven rack to upper-middle position and heat oven to 375 degrees. Spray rimmed baking sheet with vegetable oil spray. Stir remaining pinch salt into melted butter.

3. Place 16½ by 12-inch sheet of parchment paper on counter with long side parallel to edge of counter. Place 1 phyllo sheet on parchment with long side parallel to edge of counter. Place confectioners' sugar in fine-mesh strainer (rest strainer in bowl to prevent making mess). Lightly brush sheet with melted butter and dust sparingly with confectioners' sugar. Repeat with 6 more phyllo sheets, melted butter, and confectioners' sugar, stacking sheets one on top of other as you go.

4. Arrange apple mixture in 2½ by 10-inch rectangle 2 inches from bottom of phyllo and about 2 inches from each side. Using parchment, fold sides of phyllo over filling, then fold bottom edge of phyllo over filling. Brush folded portions of phyllo with reserved apple liquid. Fold top edge over filling,

1. Heat oil in 12-inch nonstick skillet over low heat for at least 10 minutes.

2. While oil is heating, rub ¼ cup sugar and orange zest together in small bowl until fragrant. Stir in chocolate; set aside. Whisk flour, salt, and remaining 1 teaspoon sugar together in medium bowl. Whisk milk and eggs together in second bowl. Add half of milk mixture to dry ingredients and whisk until smooth. Add melted butter and whisk until incorporated. Whisk in remaining milk mixture until smooth.

3. Wipe out skillet with paper towels, leaving thin film of oil on bottom and sides of pan. Increase heat to medium and let skillet heat for 1 minute. After 1 minute, test heat of skillet by placing 1 teaspoon batter in center of pan and cooking for 20 seconds. If mini crepe is golden brown on bottom, skillet is properly heated; if it is too light or too dark, adjust heat accordingly and retest.

4. Pour ¼ cup batter into far side of skillet and tilt and shake gently until batter evenly covers bottom of pan. Cook crepe without moving it until top surface is dry and edges are starting to brown, about 25 seconds. Using heat-resistant rubber spatula, loosen crepe from side of skillet. Gently slide spatula underneath edge of crepe, grasp edge with your finger-tips, and flip crepe. Cook until second side is lightly spotted, about 20 seconds. Transfer cooked crepe, spotted side up, to wire rack. Return skillet to heat and heat for 10 seconds before repeating with remaining batter. As crepes are done, stack on wire rack.

5. Transfer stack of crepes to large plate and invert second plate over crepes. Microwave until crepes are warm, 30 to 45 seconds (45 to 60 seconds if crepes have cooled completely). Remove top plate and wipe dry with paper towel. Sprinkle half of top crepe with 1½ tablespoons sugar mixture. Fold unsugared bottom half over sugared half, then fold in half again. Transfer sugared crepe to second plate. Repeat with remaining crepes. Serve immediately.

VARIATION

Crepes with Honey and Toasted Almonds for Two
SKILLET

Serves 2

Total Time 30 minutes

Crepes will give off steam as they cook, but if at any point the skillet begins to smoke, remove it from the heat immediately and turn down the heat. Stacking the crepes on a wire rack allows excess steam to escape so they won't stick together. To allow for practice, the recipe yields 5 crepes; only 4 are needed for the filling.

½ teaspoon vegetable oil
½ cup (2½ ounces) all-purpose flour
½ teaspoon sugar
⅛ teaspoon plus ¼ teaspoon table salt, divided
¾ cup whole milk
1 large egg
1 tablespoon unsalted butter, melted and cooled
4 teaspoons honey, divided
2 teaspoons finely chopped toasted sliced almonds, divided

1. Heat oil in 12-inch nonstick skillet over low heat for at least 10 minutes.

2. Whisk flour, sugar, and ⅛ teaspoon salt together in medium bowl. Whisk milk and egg together in second bowl. Add half of milk mixture to dry ingredients and whisk until smooth. Add melted butter and whisk until incorporated. Whisk in remaining milk mixture until smooth.

3. Wipe out skillet with paper towels, leaving thin film of oil on bottom and sides of pan. Increase heat to medium and let skillet heat for 1 minute. After 1 minute, test heat of skillet by placing 1 teaspoon batter in center of pan and cooking for 20 seconds. If mini crepe is golden brown on bottom, skillet is properly heated; if it is too light or too dark, adjust heat accordingly and retest.

4. Pour ¼ cup batter into far side of skillet and tilt and shake gently until batter evenly covers bottom of pan. Cook crepe without moving it until top surface is dry and edges are starting to brown, about 25 seconds. Using heat-resistant rubber spatula, loosen crepe from side of skillet. Gently slide spatula underneath edge of crepe, grasp edge with your finger-tips, and flip crepe. Cook until second side is lightly spotted, about 20 seconds. Transfer cooked crepe, spotted side up, to wire rack. Return skillet to heat and heat for 10 seconds before repeating with remaining batter. As crepes are done, stack on wire rack.

5. Transfer stack of crepes to large plate and invert second plate over crepes. Microwave until crepes are warm, 30 to 45 seconds (45 to 60 seconds if crepes have cooled completely). Remove top plate and wipe dry with paper towel. Drizzle half of top crepe with 1 teaspoon honey and sprinkle with ¼ teaspoon almonds and pinch salt. Fold uncoated bottom half over covered half, then fold in half again. Transfer filled crepe to second plate. Repeat with remaining crepes. Serve immediately.

German Pancake

Chocolate Chip Skillet Cookie

German Pancake

SKILLET

Serves 4
Total Time 45 minutes

Why This Recipe Works The German pancake, sometimes called a Dutch baby, makes for an excellent brunch dish or dessert: The edge of this skillet-size specialty puffs to form a tall, crispy rim with a texture similar to that of a popover while the base remains flat, custardy, and tender, like a thick crepe. We enhanced a simple batter of eggs, flour, and milk with a little sugar for sweetness and lemon zest, salt, nutmeg, and vanilla for more complex flavor. To produce a tall, puffy rim and an even, substantial center, we started the pancake in a skillet in a cold oven and then turned the oven to 375 degrees. This allowed the center of the pancake to begin to set up before the rim got hot enough to puff up delicately and uniformly. A final sprinkle of sugar and a squeeze of lemon juice were the finishing touches for this simple skillet treat. You will need a 12-inch ovensafe nonstick skillet for this recipe. A traditional 12-inch skillet may be used in place of the nonstick skillet; coat it lightly with vegetable oil spray before using. As an alternative to sugar and lemon juice, serve the pancake with maple syrup.

1¾ cups (8¾ ounces) all-purpose flour
¼ cup (1¾ ounces) sugar, divided
1 tablespoon grated lemon zest plus 1 tablespoon juice, divided
½ teaspoon table salt
⅛ teaspoon ground nutmeg
1½ cups milk
6 large eggs
1½ teaspoons vanilla extract
3 tablespoons unsalted butter

1. Whisk flour, 3 tablespoons sugar, lemon zest, salt, and nutmeg together in large bowl. Whisk milk, eggs, and vanilla together in second bowl. Whisk two-thirds of milk mixture into flour mixture until no lumps remain, then slowly whisk in remaining milk mixture until smooth.

2. Adjust oven rack to lower-middle position. Melt butter in 12-inch ovensafe nonstick skillet over medium-low heat. Add batter to skillet, immediately transfer to oven, and set oven to 375 degrees. Bake until edges are deep golden brown and center is beginning to brown, 30 to 35 minutes.

3. Using potholder, transfer skillet to wire rack and sprinkle pancake with lemon juice and remaining 1 tablespoon sugar. Being careful of hot skillet handle, cut pancake into wedges and serve.

Chocolate Chip Skillet Cookie

CAST-IRON SKILLET

Serves 8
Total Time 1½ hours

Why This Recipe Works A cookie in a skillet? Unlike a traditional batch of cookies, this treatment doesn't require scooping, baking, and cooling multiple sheets of treats; instead, the whole thing bakes at once in a skillet. Plus, the hot bottom and tall sides of a cast-iron pan create a great crust. We cut back on the butter and chocolate chips in our usual cookie dough to ensure that the skillet cookie was crisp at the edges, baked through in the middle, and perfectly chewy. We increased the baking time to accommodate the giant size, but otherwise our skillet recipe was simpler and faster than baking regular cookies. We developed this recipe using a 12-inch cast-iron skillet; an ovensafe traditional or nonstick skillet can also be used. Top with ice cream, if desired.

12 tablespoons unsalted butter, divided
¾ cup packed (5¼ ounces) dark brown sugar
½ cup (3½ ounces) granulated sugar
2 teaspoons vanilla extract
1 teaspoon table salt
1 large egg plus 1 large yolk
1¾ cups (8¾ ounces) all-purpose flour
½ teaspoon baking soda
1 cup (6 ounces) semisweet chocolate chips

1. Adjust oven rack to upper-middle position and heat oven to 375 degrees. Melt 9 tablespoons butter in 12-inch cast-iron skillet over medium heat. Continue to cook, stirring constantly, until butter is dark golden brown and has nutty aroma and bubbling subsides, about 5 minutes; transfer to large bowl. Stir remaining 3 tablespoons butter into hot butter until completely melted.

2. Whisk brown sugar, granulated sugar, vanilla, and salt into melted butter until smooth. Whisk in egg and yolk until smooth, about 30 seconds. Let mixture sit for 3 minutes, then whisk for 30 seconds. Repeat process of resting and whisking 2 more times until mixture is thick, smooth, and shiny.

3. Whisk flour and baking soda together in separate bowl, then stir flour mixture into butter mixture until just combined, about 1 minute. Stir in chocolate chips, making sure no flour pockets remain.

4. Wipe skillet clean with paper towels. Transfer dough to now-empty skillet and press into even layer with spatula. Transfer skillet to oven and bake until cookie is golden brown and edges are set, about 20 minutes, rotating skillet halfway through baking. Using potholders, transfer skillet to wire rack and let cookie cool for 30 minutes. Being careful of hot skillet handle, slice cookie into wedges and serve.

Easy Chocolate Chunk Brownies

CASSEROLE DISH

Serves 8 to 10
Total Time 1 hour, plus 2½ hours cooling

Why This Recipe Works Box mixes may seem to be the easiest route to chewy, moist brownies, but we wanted better-than-boxed brownies that wouldn't require much more effort (or more dishes). For chewiness, we used a combination of butter and oil. Using both cocoa powder and unsweetened chocolate ensured chocolaty richness, and folding bittersweet chunks into the batter gave our chewy brownies gooey pockets of melted chocolate. By being strategic with the addition of ingredients, we saved dishes and combined the batter all in one large bowl. Baked on the lowest rack in the oven in a 13 by 9-inch baking dish, the brownies cooked nicely on the bottom and edges without drying out. For an accurate measurement of boiling water, bring a full kettle to a boil and then measure out the desired amount.

½ cup plus 2 tablespoons boiling water
2 ounces unsweetened chocolate, chopped fine
⅓ cup (1 ounce) Dutch-processed cocoa powder
2½ cups (17½ ounces) sugar
½ cup plus 2 tablespoons vegetable oil
2 large eggs plus 2 large yolks
4 tablespoons unsalted butter, melted
2 teaspoons vanilla extract
1¾ cups (8¾ ounces) all-purpose flour
¾ teaspoon table salt
6 ounces bittersweet chocolate, cut into ½-inch pieces

1. Adjust oven rack to lowest position and heat oven to 350 degrees. Make foil sling for 13 by 9-inch baking pan by folding 2 long sheets of aluminum foil; first sheet should be 13 inches wide and second sheet should be 9 inches wide. Lay sheets of foil in pan perpendicular to each other, with extra foil hanging over edges of pan. Push foil into corners and up sides of pan, smoothing foil flush to pan. Spray foil with vegetable oil spray.

2. Whisk boiling water, unsweetened chocolate, and cocoa in large bowl until chocolate is melted. Whisk in sugar, oil, eggs and yolks, melted butter, and vanilla until combined. Gently whisk in flour and salt until just incorporated. Stir in bittersweet chocolate.

3. Transfer batter to prepared pan. Bake until toothpick inserted in center comes out with few moist crumbs attached, 30 to 35 minutes, rotating pan halfway through baking. Transfer pan to wire rack and let cool for 1½ hours.

4. Using foil overhang, lift brownies out of pan. Return brownies to wire rack and let cool completely, about 1 hour. Cut into 2-inch squares and serve.

Chocolate Lava Cake

DUTCH OVEN

Serves 12
Total Time 2 hours

Why This Recipe Works Individual-size chocolate lava cakes are a restaurant classic: Moist chocolate cake surrounds a fudgy, molten center that serves as a sauce when the cake is cut open. But this chocolaty dessert can be fussy to make at home, especially when serving a crowd—individual servings guarantee lots of dishes and cleanup. We wondered if we could use our Dutch oven to make a large-scale lava cake that would maintain the magic without the mess. We started by mixing the batter right in the pot, and then we sprinkled it with a mixture of granulated sugar, brown sugar, and cocoa powder and finished the assembly by pouring boiling water over the top. During baking, the sugar-cocoa mixture sank to the bottom and the cake rose to the top, creating the fudgy layers we were looking for. After removing the cake from the oven we let it cool slightly; the Dutch oven's heat-retaining walls effectively kept the cake's center gooey and warm even as we went back for seconds. For an accurate measurement of boiling water, bring a full kettle to a boil and then measure out the desired amount. Serve with whipped cream.

 12 tablespoons unsalted butter, cut into 12 pieces
  4 ounces bittersweet chocolate, chopped coarse
1⅓ cups (4 ounces) unsweetened cocoa powder, divided
 ⅔ cup packed (4⅔ ounces) light brown sugar
  2 cups (14 ounces) granulated sugar, divided
 ⅔ cup whole milk
  2 tablespoons vanilla extract
  2 large egg yolks
  4 teaspoons baking powder
 ½ teaspoon table salt
1½ cups (7½ ounces) all-purpose flour
  3 cups boiling water

1. Adjust oven rack to middle position and heat oven to 325 degrees. Melt butter, chocolate, and ⅔ cup cocoa in Dutch oven over low heat, stirring frequently, until smooth, 2 to 4 minutes. Remove pot from heat and let cool slightly.

2. Whisk brown sugar, ⅔ cup granulated sugar, and remaining ⅔ cup cocoa together in bowl, breaking up any large clumps of brown sugar with your fingers.

3. Whisk milk, vanilla, egg yolks, baking powder, salt, and remaining 1⅓ cups granulated sugar into cooled chocolate mixture. Whisk in flour until just combined. Sprinkle brown sugar mixture evenly over top, covering entire surface of batter. Pour boiling water gently over brown sugar mixture.

4. Scrape down exposed sides of pot, then transfer to oven. Bake, uncovered, until cake begins to pull away from sides of pot and top is just firm to touch, 1¼ to 1½ hours, rotating pot halfway through baking. Remove pot from oven and transfer to wire rack. Let cake cool for 15 minutes before serving.

VARIATION

Chocolate Lava Cake for Two

SKILLET

Serves 2
Total Time 1 hour

You will need an 8-inch ovensafe skillet for this recipe. For an accurate measurement of boiling water, bring a full kettle to a boil and then measure out the desired amount. Serve with whipped cream.

  2 tablespoons unsalted butter
  1 ounce bittersweet chocolate, chopped coarse
  3 tablespoons unsweetened cocoa powder, divided
  5 tablespoons (2¼ ounces) granulated sugar, divided
  2 tablespoons packed light brown sugar
  2 tablespoons whole milk
  1 large egg yolk
  1 teaspoon vanilla extract
 ½ teaspoon baking powder
    Pinch table salt
 ¼ cup (1¼ ounces) all-purpose flour
 ½ cup boiling water

1. Adjust oven rack to middle position and heat oven to 325 degrees. Melt butter, chocolate, and 1 tablespoon cocoa in 8-inch skillet over low heat, stirring frequently, until smooth, about 2 minutes. Remove skillet from heat and let cool slightly.

2. Whisk 1 tablespoon granulated sugar, brown sugar, and remaining 2 tablespoons cocoa together in bowl, breaking up any large clumps of brown sugar with your fingers.

3. Whisk milk, egg yolk, vanilla, baking powder, salt, and remaining ¼ cup granulated sugar into cooled chocolate mixture. Whisk in flour until just combined. Sprinkle brown sugar mixture evenly over top, covering entire surface of batter. Pour boiling water over brown sugar mixture.

4. Scrape down exposed sides of skillet, then transfer to oven. Bake, uncovered, until cake begins to pull away from sides of skillet and top is just firm to touch, about 25 minutes, rotating skillet halfway through baking. Remove skillet from oven and transfer to wire rack. Let cake cool for 10 minutes before serving.

Pour-Over Peach Cake

SKILLET
Serves 8
Total Time 1¼ hours, plus 1 hour cooling

Why This Recipe Works Skillet upside-down cake is a simple affair: Sauté the fruit, top with batter, and pop the skillet in the oven—and then flip to reveal beautifully caramelized fruit atop a rustic cake. But too often the result is a soggy mess. We added toasted cornmeal to the cake batter for flavor and texture and nestled the peaches in a sauce of sugar and butter before baking, for a top layer of perfect peaches. You can substitute 12 ounces frozen sliced peaches; thaw and drain them before using. Use a serrated peeler to peel the peaches.

- ½ cup (2½ ounces) cornmeal
- 2 tablespoons unsalted butter plus 6 tablespoons melted and cooled, divided
- ⅓ cup (2⅓ ounces) sugar, plus ¾ cup (5¼ ounces), divided
- Pinch plus ½ teaspoon table salt, divided
- 1 pound peaches, peeled, halved, pitted, and cut into ¾-inch wedges
- 1 cup (5 ounces) all-purpose flour
- 1 teaspoon baking powder
- ⅛ teaspoon baking soda
- ½ cup whole milk
- 2 teaspoons grated orange zest plus ¼ cup juice
- 1 large egg plus 1 large yolk

1. Adjust oven rack to middle position and heat oven to 350 degrees. Toast cornmeal in 10-inch ovensafe nonstick skillet over medium heat until fragrant, 2 to 3 minutes, stirring frequently. Transfer to large bowl and let cool slightly.

2. Wipe skillet clean with paper towels. Melt 2 tablespoons butter in now-empty skillet over medium heat. Add ⅓ cup sugar and pinch salt and cook, whisking constantly, until sugar is melted, smooth, and deep golden brown, 3 to 5 minutes. (Mixture may look broken but will come together.) Off heat, carefully arrange peaches cut side down in tight pinwheel around edge of skillet. Arrange remaining peaches in center of skillet.

3. Whisk flour, baking powder, baking soda, and remaining ½ teaspoon salt into cornmeal. In separate bowl, whisk milk, orange zest and juice, egg and yolk, remaining melted butter, and remaining ¾ cup sugar until smooth. Stir milk mixture into flour mixture until just combined.

4. Pour batter over peaches and spread into even layer. Bake until cake is golden brown and toothpick inserted in center comes out clean, 28 to 33 minutes, rotating skillet halfway through baking.

Chocolate Lava Cake

Pour-Over Peach Cake

5. Let cake cool in skillet on wire rack for 15 minutes. Run knife around edge of skillet to loosen cake. Place large, flat serving platter over skillet. Using potholders and holding platter tightly, invert skillet and platter together; lift off skillet (if any peaches stick to skillet, remove and position on top of cake). Let cake cool completely, about 1 hour. Serve.

New York–Style Cheesecake

INSTANT POT

Serves 8

Total Time 2 hours, plus 4 hours cooling

Why This Recipe Works Cheesecake may not be the first thing you think of making in your pressure cooker, but the moist cooking environment produces a rich, creamy cake that doesn't crack. A simple graham cracker crust and a lump-free filling came together quickly in our food processor. We covered the cheesecake with foil and created a steamy environment by adding water to the bottom of the pot, using a trivet to elevate our springform pan. This recipe was developed using an 8-quart pressure cooker. If using a 6-quart pressure cooker, increase cooking time to 50 minutes (if using a brand of electric pressure cooker other than Instant Pot, increase cooking time to 40 minutes). You will need a 6-inch springform pan for this recipe. If your pressure cooker didn't come with a trivet, you can make your own (see page 365). Serve with Strawberry Topping (page 365) if desired.

- 6 whole graham crackers, broken into 1-inch pieces
- 2 tablespoons unsalted butter, melted and cooled
- 1 tablespoon plus ⅔ cup (4⅔ ounces) sugar, divided
- ½ teaspoon ground cinnamon
  Pinch plus ¼ teaspoon table salt, divided
- 18 ounces cream cheese, softened
- 1 teaspoon vanilla extract
- ¼ cup sour cream
- 2 large eggs, room temperature

1. Pulse cracker pieces in food processor to fine crumbs, about 20 pulses. Add butter, 1 tablespoon sugar, cinnamon, and pinch salt and pulse to combine, about 4 pulses. Sprinkle crumbs into 6-inch springform pan and press into even layer using bottom of dry measuring cup. Wipe out processor bowl.

2. Process cream cheese, vanilla, remaining ⅔ cup sugar, and remaining ¼ teaspoon salt in now-empty processor until combined, about 15 seconds, scraping down sides of bowl as needed. Add sour cream and eggs and process until just incorporated, about 15 seconds; do not overmix. Pour filling over crust in pan, smooth top, and cover with aluminum foil.

New York–Style Cheesecake

3. Add water to electric pressure cooker until it reaches about ½ inch up sides of insert (about 2 cups). Arrange trivet included with pressure cooker in base of insert and add ½ cup water. Fold sheet of aluminum foil into 16 by 6-inch sling, then rest pan in center of sling. Using sling, lower pan into pot and onto trivet; allow narrow edges of sling to rest along sides of insert.

4. Lock lid in place and close pressure release valve. Select low pressure cook function and cook for 25 minutes. (If using using a brand of electric pressure cooker other than Instant Pot, increase cooking time to 30 minutes.) Turn off pressure cooker and let pressure release naturally for 30 minutes. Quick-release any remaining pressure, then carefully remove lid, allowing steam to escape away from you.

5. Using sling, transfer cheesecake to wire rack and discard foil cover. Run small knife around edge of cake and gently blot away condensation using paper towels. Let cheesecake cool in pan to room temperature, about 1 hour. Cover with plastic wrap and refrigerate until well chilled, at least 3 hours or up to 3 days.

6. About 30 minutes before serving, run small knife around edge of cheesecake, then remove sides of pan. Invert cheesecake onto sheet of parchment paper, then turn cheesecake right side up onto serving dish. Serve.

Strawberry Topping

Makes about 2 cups
This topping is best the day it's made. Do not use frozen strawberries in this recipe.

1¼ pounds strawberries, hulled and
      sliced thin (3 cups), divided
   3 tablespoons sugar

Using potato masher, mash 8 ounces strawberries in bowl into paste. Stir in remaining 12 ounces strawberries and sugar and let sit at room temperature until sugar has dissolved and berries are juicy, at least 30 minutes or up to 2 hours.

Spiced Pumpkin Cheesecake

SLOW COOKER

Serves 8
Cooking Time 1½ to 2½ hours on high, plus 4 hours cooling

Why This Recipe Works As with our pressure cooker method for cheesecake (see page 364), using a slow cooker to prepare this luxurious dessert ensures that it "bakes" through perfectly every time—no need to worry about cracks on the top. For a supremely creamy texture, we turned off the slow cooker once the cake registered 150 degrees on an instant-read thermometer and let the cheesecake sit in the slow cooker for an hour so it could gently finish cooking. The food processor made it a breeze to prepare a simple crust as well as a balanced, smooth filling. For an autumnal take, we substituted a little pumpkin puree for some of the cream cheese. Thoroughly drying the puree before mixing ensured the filling remained indulgently creamy and dense. We eschewed store-bought pumpkin spice for a judicious custom blend so that the flavor of the pumpkin would shine through. You will need a 5- to 7-quart oval slow cooker and a 6-inch springform pan for this recipe. Check the temperature of the cheesecake after 1½ hours of cooking and continue to monitor until it registers 150 degrees.

   6 whole graham crackers, broken into 1-inch pieces
   2 tablespoons unsalted butter, melted and cooled
   1 tablespoon plus ⅔ cup (4⅔ ounces) sugar, divided
1½ teaspoons ground cinnamon, divided
      Pinch plus ¼ teaspoon table salt, divided
   1 cup canned unsweetened pumpkin puree
12 ounces cream cheese, softened
½ teaspoon ground ginger
⅛ teaspoon ground cloves
¼ cup sour cream
   2 large eggs, room temperature

1. Pulse cracker pieces in food processor to fine crumbs, about 20 pulses. Add melted butter, 1 tablespoon sugar, ½ teaspoon cinnamon, and pinch salt and pulse to combine, about 4 pulses. Sprinkle crumbs into 6-inch springform pan and press into even layer using bottom of dry measuring cup. Wipe out processor bowl.

2. Spread pumpkin puree over large plate lined with several layers of paper towels and press dry with additional towels. Transfer puree to now-empty processor bowl (puree will separate easily from towels). Add cream cheese, ginger, cloves, remaining ⅔ cup sugar, remaining ¼ teaspoon salt, and remaining 1 teaspoon cinnamon and process until combined, about 15 seconds, scraping down sides of bowl as needed. Add sour cream and eggs and process until just incorporated, about 15 seconds; do not overmix. Pour filling over crust in pan, smooth top, and cover with aluminum foil.

3. Arrange foil trivet in base of slow cooker and add water until it reaches ½ inch up (about 2 cups). Set pan on trivet, cover, and cook until cheesecake registers 150 degrees, 1½ to 2½ hours on high. Turn off slow cooker and let cheesecake sit, covered, for 1 hour.

4. Transfer cheesecake to wire rack. Run small knife around edge of cake and gently blot away condensation using paper towels. Let cheesecake cool in pan to room temperature, about 1 hour. Cover with plastic wrap and refrigerate until well chilled, at least 3 hours or up to 3 days.

5. About 30 minutes before serving, run small knife around edge of cheesecake, then remove sides of pan. Invert cheesecake onto sheet of parchment paper, then turn cheesecake right side up onto serving dish. Serve.

MAKING A FOIL TRIVET

Loosely roll 24 by 12-inch piece of foil into 1-inch cylinder, then bend sides in to form oval ring that measures 8 inches long by 5 inches wide (for slow cooker) or 5-inch ring (for pressure cooker).

NUTRITIONAL INFORMATION FOR OUR RECIPES

We calculate the nutritional values of our recipes per serving; if there is a range in the serving size, we used the highest number of servings to calculate the nutritional values. We entered all the ingredients, using weights for important ingredients such as most vegetables. We also used our preferred brands in these analyses. We did not include additional salt or pepper for food that's "seasoned to taste."

	Cal	Total Fat (g)	Sat Fat (g)	Chol (mg)	Sodium (mg)	Total Carbs (g)	Fiber (g)	Total Sugar (g)	Protein (g)
SOUPS									
Weeknight Chicken Noodle Soup	220	6	1	75	740	19	1	4	21
Weeknight Chicken Noodle Soup for Two	*340*	*10*	*1.5*	*110*	*1110*	*29*	*2*	*6*	*32*
Tortilla Soup	380	24	8	70	1290	18	2	3	23
Spiced Chicken Soup with Squash and Chickpeas	290	14	3.5	65	710	16	4	3	24
Chicken Soup with Parmesan Dumplings	390	22	6	105	1560	18	3	5	27
Chicken and Vegetable Soup									
Dutch Oven	*100*	*1.5*	*0*	*40*	*140*	*5*	*1*	*2*	*15*
Slow Cooker	*100*	*1.5*	*0*	*40*	*140*	*5*	*1*	*2*	*15*
Instant Pot	*100*	*1.5*	*0*	*40*	*140*	*5*	*1*	*2*	*15*
Thai Curry and Coconut Soup with Chicken	430	33	26	55	850	14	1	5	23
Greek Chicken and Rice Soup	230	5	1.5	155	1140	21	0	1	25
Turkey Meatball Soup with Kale	170	5	2.5	25	810	10	2	4	18
Beef and Vegetable Soup	330	12	4.5	0.5	1410	25	4	7	29
Mexican Beef and Vegetable Soup	210	9	2.5	35	630	18	3	5	15
Beef and Barley Soup	300	11	3.5	80	1400	21	5	5	29
Beef and Barley Soup with Wild Mushrooms for Two	*400*	*15*	*3.5*	*80*	*1410*	*32*	*5*	*6*	*34*
Beef Pho	300	4	1	30	530	46	0	0	19
Pork Ramen	820	43	17	115	3640	62	2	5	45
Meatball and Escarole Soup	260	16	5	45	720	13	4	3	16
Spicy Lamb and Lentil Soup	260	8	2	35	1110	24	6	5	20
New England Clam Chowder	270	17	9	60	620	20	2	3	11
New England Clam Chowder with Parsnips and Corn for Two	*510*	*33*	*18*	*120*	*1120*	*34*	*4*	*7*	*21*
Hearty Seafood and Saffron Soup	200	6	1	120	820	13	1	6	22
Cioppino	420	20	7	105	990	15	2	5	35
Creamy Carrot Soup with Warm Spices	180	11	2.5	5	460	19	5	10	4
Fresh Corn Chowder	380	23	11	55	790	37	4	12	11
Tuscan Tomato and Bread Soup	280	16	2	0	1040	31	4	11	6

	Cal	Total Fat (g)	Sat Fat (g)	Chol (mg)	Sodium (mg)	Total Carbs (g)	Fiber (g)	Total Sugar (g)	Protein (g)
SOUPS (CONTINUED)									
Summer Vegetable Soup	100	2	0	0	310	18	4	3	5
Miso Soup with Shiitakes and Sweet Potatoes	180	6	0	0	930	23	2	9	10
Kimchi and Tofu Soup	130	6	0	0	1260	10	1	2	8
Portuguese Potato, Sausage, and Greens Soup	380	24	7	35	1190	26	3	1	15
Spiced Wild Rice and Coconut Soup	350	25	19	0	330	29	3	3	7
Curried Wild Rice and Coconut Soup for Two	*720*	*50*	*38*	*0*	*620*	*61*	*5*	*7*	*16*
Easy Tortellini Minestrone	380	24	5	25	920	30	3	8	12
Tomato, Bulgur, and Red Pepper Soup	140	4	0.05	0	730	19	4	6	4
Farro and Leek Soup	180	6	1.5	10	800	25	1	4	7
Red Lentil Soup with North African Spices	230	6	0.05	0	800	34	8	3	12
Lentil and Chorizo Soup	400	18	4.5	25	950	41	11	4	22
White Bean Soup with Pancetta and Rosemary	310	10	2.5	15	1260	37	10	5	19
White Bean Soup with Sun-dried Tomatoes and Kale for Two	*380*	*17*	*4.5*	*20*	*1360*	*40*	*11*	*5*	*19*
Black Bean Soup	360	10	2.5	35	570	42	2	8	23
15-Bean Soup with Sausage and Spinach	250	6	1.5	25	1180	30	1	6	17
Italian Pasta and Bean Soup	210	4.5	1	5	910	32	6	5	11
STEWS AND CHILIS									
Daube Provençal	910	63	23	220	1280	19	3	6	48
Greek Beef Stew	500	31	12	140	895	10	1	5	41
Easy Beef Stew with Mushrooms and Bacon	620	44	18	145	1100	17	1	8	40
Beef Goulash	580	18	5	195	1340	29	7	14	71
Classic Beef Stew									
Dutch Oven	*500*	*15*	*4*	*145*	*1140*	*28*	*4*	*6*	*54*
Roasting Pan	*520*	*14*	*4*	*145*	*910*	*35*	*6*	*9*	*55*
Saucepan	*640*	*31*	*10*	*135*	*1250*	*34*	*5*	*8*	*49*
Pork Stew with Sausage, Potatoes, and Cabbage	420	25	8	40	1110	30	5	4	18
Chipotle Pork and Hominy Stew	520	30	10	120	1310	21	3	4	35
Chipotle Pork and Bean Stew For Two	*520*	*30*	*10*	*120*	*1310*	*21*	*3*	*4*	*35*
Spicy Pork and Black Bean Stew	830	45	15	235	1190	28	7	6	68
Lamb Stew with Green Beans, Tomatoes, and Basil	570	22	7	120	930	43	4	6	43
Spiced Lamb Stew with White Beans	450	19	8	50	530	41	13	4	27
Easy Chicken Stew	590	21	3.5	215	1620	41	6	9	51
Easy Chicken Stew with Fennel and Olives for Two	*590*	*21*	*3.5*	*215*	*1620*	*41*	*6*	*9*	*51*
Chicken Stew with Cheddar Biscuits	700	40	19	160	800	44	3	7	38
Chicken Stew with Winter Vegetables	480	17	3	215	1010	27	5	7	48
Chicken and Sausage Gumbo	510	31	5	140	970	22	3	5	36
Chicken Bouillabaisse	320	12	2.5	105	790	20	2	4	26
Fisherman's Stew	380	16	6	120	1000	19	3	4	36
Sicilian Fish Stew	480	24	4	115	1370	24	3	15	38
Spanish Shellfish Stew	350	13	2	70	870	21	3	6	23
Spanish Shellfish Stew For Two	*500*	*20*	*2.5*	*90*	*1330*	*30*	*4*	*9*	*28*
Hearty Ten-Vegetable Stew	140	4	0.5	0	280	21	4	6	4

	Cal	Total Fat (g)	Sat Fat (g)	Chol (mg)	Sodium (mg)	Total Carbs (g)	Fiber (g)	Total Sugar (g)	Protein (g)
STEWS AND CHILIS (CONTINUED)									
Quinoa and Vegetable Stew	320	15	5	25	310	37	7	6	11
Wheat Berry and Wild Mushroom Stew	230	6	0.5	0	200	33	5	4	8
Hearty Tuscan White Bean Stew	300	7	2	10	710	43	22	5	17
Hearty White Bean Stew with Sausage and Mustard Greens for Two	*420*	*18*	*4.5*	*35*	*1530*	*36*	*10*	*6*	*30*
Vegetable and Chickpea Stew	190	8	1	0	500	25	4	5	5
Classic Ground Beef Chili	400	21	7	75	1300	26	8	6	28
Classic Ground Beef Chili for Two	*630*	*35*	*11*	*115*	*1430*	*39*	*12*	*10*	*43*
Beef and Three-Bean Chili	490	24	7	80	1340	43	4	9	33
Hearty Beef and Vegetable Chili	730	43	15	175	1200	38	5	9	45
Chili con Carne	630	44	15	175	790	18	3	6	41
New Mexican Red Pork Chili	550	35	12	140	1110	18	2	11	39
Classic Turkey Chili	350	6	2.5	45	1210	40	12	14	38
White Chicken Chili	360	15	4	85	760	20	6	5	35
White Chicken Chili for Two	*490*	*21*	*4*	*85*	*1390*	*36*	*10*	*9*	*40*
Black Bean Chili	410	8	0.5	0	420	66	5	17	20
CHICKEN									
Sautéed Chicken with Cherry Tomatoes, Olives, and Feta	390	17	3.5	130	260	15	1	3	42
Sautéed Chicken with Cherry Tomatoes, Toasted Corn, and Avocado for Two	*530*	*26*	*4*	*125*	*230*	*30*	*5*	*4*	*43*
Chicken Fricassee with Apples	480	24	13	180	380	23	2	13	41
Crispy Parmesan Chicken with Warm Fennel, Radicchio, and Arugula Salad	830	55	9	230	1310	26	3	6	55
Prosciutto-Wrapped Chicken with Asparagus	600	37	10	180	1110	11	4	4	58
Chicken Baked in Foil with Fennel and Sun-Dried Tomatoes	490	24	3.5	125	600	26	3	4	42
Unstuffed Ham & Cheese Chicken with Roasted Broccoli	540	24	8	165	1130	20	0	4	56
Chicken and Rice with Carrots and Peas	580	12	1.5	125	920	68	4	7	47
Chicken Kebabs with Potatoes and Green Beans	630	29	8	135	1140	42	3	6	49
Three-Cup Chicken	400	21	3	160	1720	12	1	5	36
Three-Cup Chicken for Two	*390*	*20*	*2.5*	*135*	*1900*	*12*	*1*	*6*	*38*
Stir-Fried Chicken with Bok Choy and Crispy Noodle Cake	640	36	3.5	90	2100	44	2	4	35
Massaman Chicken Curry with Potatoes and Peanuts	420	26	14	60	730	29	3	4	23
Chicken and Arugula Salad with Warm Fig Dressing	670	34	4.5	125	680	47	9	30	46
Chicken Sausages with Braised Red Cabbage and Potatoes	490	25	6	75	990	40	4	11	26
Braised Chicken Sausages with White Beans and Spinach	620	30	10	120	2110	33	7	5	47
Braised Chicken Sausages with Chickpeas and Kale for Two	*560*	*29*	*8*	*110*	*1750*	*26*	*6*	*3*	*39*
Italian Braised Chicken Sausages with Potatoes and Peppers	480	23	8	110	1370	28	3	6	36

	Cal	Total Fat (g)	Sat Fat (g)	Chol (mg)	Sodium (mg)	Total Carbs (g)	Fiber (g)	Total Sugar (g)	Protein (g)
CHICKEN (CONTINUED)									
Turkey Meatballs with Coconut Rice, Bell Peppers, and Peas	580	23	11	90	1430	56	4	7	40
Crispy Skillet Turkey Burgers with Tomato-Feta Salad	690	40	11	80	1140	44	2	8	41
Pan-Roasted Chicken Breasts with Root Vegetables	460	10	1.5	160	750	39	6	8	54
Pan-Roasted Chicken Breasts with Sweet Potatoes and Fennel for Two	*500*	*11*	*1.5*	*160*	*830*	*46*	*9*	*15*	*55*
Roasted Chicken Parts with Brussels Sprouts and Shallots	610	35	11	195	1090	31	6	7	47
Roasted Chicken Breasts with Ratatouille	470	18	3	195	890	12	3	6	62
Lemon–Goat Cheese Stuffed Chicken Breasts with Carrots	510	23	7	175	910	18	4	10	57
Roasted Chicken Breasts with Butternut Squash and Kale	810	36	6	165	730	67	8	28	59
Crispy Chicken with Spiced Carrot, Orange, and Chickpea Salad	510	17	4.5	170	1230	28	7	12	58
Chicken with Spiced Freekeh, Cilantro, and Preserved Lemon	610	16	2	160	720	54	12	2	60
Lemon-Oregano Chicken with Warm Tabbouleh Salad	570	21	6	185	860	32	5	3	63
Pulled Chicken Sandwiches with Sweet and Tangy Coleslaw	430	9	1.5	90	1410	57	1	33	28
Shredded Chicken Tacos	600	21	9	145	1000	53	0	6	48
Easy Tomatillo Chicken Soft Tacos	580	16	4.5	180	1470	52	1	5	56
Easy Tomatillo Chicken Soft Tacos for Two	*590*	*16*	*4.5*	*180*	*1670*	*54*	*2*	*6*	*56*
Teriyaki Chicken Thighs with Sesame Vegetables	490	19	3	160	1920	35	4	21	39
Chicken Leg Quarters with Cauliflower and Shallots	810	49	12	365	1940	26	5	7	73
Peruvian Roast Chicken Leg Quarters with Swiss Chard and Sweet Potatoes	890	44	11	365	2620	51	11	16	75
Chicken Thighs with Lentils and Butternut Squash	510	14	3	160	1050	50	10	8	47
Braised Chicken Thighs with Tomatoes and Mushrooms									
Dutch Oven	*700*	*44*	*11*	*235*	*1730*	*30*	*7*	*14*	*47*
Instant Pot	*700*	*44*	*11*	*235*	*1730*	*30*	*7*	*14*	*47*
Slow Cooker	*700*	*44*	*11*	*235*	*1730*	*30*	*7*	*14*	*47*
Lemony Chicken Thighs with Fingerling Potatoes and Olives	700	43	11	235	620	33	4	1	44
Chicken Tagine with Fennel, Chickpeas, and Apricots	930	54	12	235	1680	56	12	25	50
Chicken and Rice with Caramelized Onions, Cardamom, and Raisins	660	29	8	155	740	63	1	10	35
Chicken with Spiced Couscous and Carrots	850	46	11	235	1400	57	9	7	50
Arroz Con Pollo	1010	50	12	250	1410	86	3	4	51
Arroz Con Pollo for Two	*930*	*44*	*10*	*190*	*1300*	*89*	*3*	*5*	*42*
Roasted Chicken with Potatoes	900	56	14	225	1680	35	1	0	60
Herbed Chicken with Warm Spring Vegetable Salad	950	70	17	230	930	16	5	9	60
Roast Chicken with Warm Bread Salad	1040	71	17	225	1590	34	1	5	62
Spice-Rubbed Roasted Turkey Breast with Green Beans	370	7	2.5	160	870	9	3	4	66

	Cal	Total Fat (g)	Sat Fat (g)	Chol (mg)	Sodium (mg)	Total Carbs (g)	Fiber (g)	Total Sugar (g)	Protein (g)
CHICKEN (CONTINUED)									
Roast Turkey Breast with Herb Stuffing and Cranberry Sauce	820	30	10	220	1300	59	4	33	73
Easy Chicken Enchiladas	460	22	8	95	780	35	3	7	34
Easy Chicken Enchiladas for Two	*1430*	*73*	*24*	*280*	*2280*	*103*	*7*	*22*	*103*
Easy Chicken, Spinach, and Artichoke Pot Pie	710	45	25	180	1280	45	6	7	36
Chicken Pot Pie with Spring Vegetables	570	28	14	205	1040	44	5	8	41
BEEF									
Steak Tips with Spicy Cauliflower	630	40	11	155	920	15	5	6	52
Steak Tips with Wilted Spinach, Goat Cheese, and Pear Salad	600	38	12	160	650	12	3	6	52
Steak Tips with Wilted Spinach, Gorgonzola, and Apple Salad for Two	*660*	*43*	*13*	*165*	*780*	*16*	*3*	*10*	*52*
Steak Tips with Horseradish Potato Salad	690	38	11	165	1010	34	5	3	51
Steak Tips with Spiced Couscous and Spinach	680	27	8	155	1500	52	6	15	55
Steak Tips with Tomatillo Salsa and Refried Black Beans	560	23	8	155	930	36	3	7	56
Spice-Rubbed Flank Steak with Toasted Corn and Black Bean Salad	640	32	9	155	700	34	2	6	55
Strip Steaks with Mushrooms, Asparagus, and Potatoes	600	28	14	165	1050	29	2	5	59
Hibachi-Style Steaks with Zucchini and Shiitakes	500	24	10	145	1190	15	3	8	56
Coffee-Chili–Rubbed Steaks with Sweet Potatoes and Scallions	580	19	5	120	1100	46	9	19	57
Seared Steaks with Crispy Potatoes and Herb Sauce	830	54	10	120	1190	30	4	3	56
Seared Steak with Crispy Potatoes and Herb Sauce for Two	*830*	*54*	*10*	*120*	*890*	*30*	*4*	*3*	*56*
Tuscan-Style Steak with Garlicky Spinach	640	41	11	190	570	7	4	0	57
Tuscan-Style Steak with Garlicky Spinach for Two	*660*	*43*	*11*	*190*	*570*	*8*	*4*	*0*	*57*
Teriyaki Stir-Fried Beef with Green Beans and Shiitakes	460	25	7	115	940	17	3	11	40
Teriyaki Stir-Fried Beef with Green Beans and Shiitakes for Two	*490*	*29*	*7*	*115*	*1020*	*18*	*3*	*11*	*40*
Stir-Fried Thai-Style Beef with Chiles and Shallots	480	28	7	115	770	14	2	6	41
Steak Fajitas	680	26	9	115	2800	61	4	10	47
Shredded Beef Lettuce Wraps with Pickled Cucumber and Bean Sprouts	340	18	7	90	470	14	1	8	31
Shredded Beef Tacos with Cabbage-Carrot Slaw	470	20	7	90	540	39	3	8	34
Classic Ground Beef Tacos	350	15	5	65	590	32	1	5	22
Wild Mushroom Burgers with Bistro Salad	890	60	23	170	1030	31	2	7	49
Meatball Subs with Roasted Broccoli	1030	46	16	210	2220	103	5	23	57
Zucchini Noodles with Pesto Meatballs	540	36	11	95	1030	21	2	8	32
Glazed Meatloaf with Potatoes and Brussels Sprouts	990	54	18	260	2420	61	6	13	62
Glazed Meatloaf with Carrots and Turnips for Two	*700*	*43*	*14*	*220*	*1480*	*32*	*4*	*12*	*44*
Braised Blade Steaks with Mushrooms, Vidalias, and Steamed Asparagus	480	25	7	125	850	19	4	8	41
Braised Steaks with Garlicky Smashed Potatoes	550	28	13	155	560	37	4	7	40
Braised Steaks with Herbed Smashed Potatoes for Two	*600*	*34*	*15*	*165*	*560*	*36*	*4*	*7*	*40*

	Cal	Total Fat (g)	Sat Fat (g)	Chol (mg)	Sodium (mg)	Total Carbs (g)	Fiber (g)	Total Sugar (g)	Protein (g)
BEEF (CONTINUED)									
Cuban Braised Shredded Beef	380	20	3	100	970	11	2	5	35
Wine-Braised Short Ribs with Potatoes	420	18	7	80	1070	28	3	6	31
Braised Beef Short Ribs with Daikon and Shiitakes	500	19	7	90	1600	38	4	19	35
Classic Pot Roast									
Dutch Oven	*690*	*43*	*15*	*175*	*650*	*32*	*5*	*8*	*42*
Instant Pot	*690*	*43*	*15*	*175*	*650*	*32*	*5*	*8*	*42*
Slow Cooker	*680*	*41*	*15*	*175*	*660*	*33*	*5*	*8*	*42*
Braised Short Ribs with Fennel and Pickled Grapes	470	27	10	135	770	16	4	9	45
Braised Short Ribs with Tomatoes, Olives, and Orange for Two	*540*	*31*	*11*	*135*	*1340*	*17*	*3*	*8*	*46*
Osso Buco with Sweet and Spicy Peperonata	400	16	3.5	130	830	17	3	11	41
Corned Beef and Cabbage Dinner	490	31	12	105	2140	23	5	6	28
Modern Beef Pot Pie	490	24	8	95	730	26	3	6	37
Modern Beef Pot Pie with Mushrooms and Sherry for Two	*740*	*43*	*14*	*150*	*1000*	*289*	*2*	*5*	*56*
Shepherd's Pie	480	19	9	125	750	46	4	6	31
Beef Taco Bake	550	30	13	85	1320	40	4	3	32
Reuben Strata	420	19	11	170	1720	33	4	6	32
Top Sirloin Roast with Caramelized Potatoes and Carrots	410	14	3	115	650	29	5	7	42
Beef en Cocotte with Creamy Mushroom Barley	680	30	6	160	900	38	8	2	61
Chuck Roast in Foil	780	49	20	235	1300	27	4	6	54
Boneless Rib Roast with Yorkshire Pudding	650	44	18	185	990	22	0	4	38
Prime Rib and Roasted Vegetables	730	52	21	150	980	21	6	8	43
Roast Beef Tenderloin with Smoky Potatoes and Persillade Relish	760	41	9	145	1260	41	5	4	56
PORK AND LAMB									
Pan-Seared Pork Cutlets with Horseradish-Herb Green Beans	440	23	9	175	580	7	3	3	49
Pan-Seared Pork Cutlets with Lemon-Caper Green Beans for Two	*480*	*28*	*13*	*185*	*720*	*7*	*3*	*3*	*47*
Sesame Pork Cutlets with Wilted Napa Cabbage Salad	650	30	3.5	235	830	28	6	5	59
Crunchy Parmesan-Crusted Pork Chops with Glazed Winter Squash	1050	40	13	230	1340	111	7	62	60
Barbecued Pork Chops with Succotash Salad	600	18	3.5	95	1300	69	9	30	44
Maple-Glazed Pork Chops with Sweet Potato–Bacon Hash	670	27	9	140	830	53	4	32	52
Roasted Pork Chops and Vegetables with Parsley Vinaigrette	810	36	8	190	1470	39	5	8	80
Roasted Pork Chops and Vegetables with Basil Vinaigrette for Two	*700*	*38*	*9*	*190*	*950*	*9*	*2*	*6*	*77*
Smothered Pork Chops with Broccoli	550	31	8	140	1010	12	3	3	55
Smothered Pork Chops with Leeks and Mustard	550	22	7	145	850	23	3	6	54
Deviled Pork Chops with Scalloped Potatoes	850	47	21	175	1240	55	3	3	55
Pork Chops with Chile Rice and Peanuts	840	40	11	130	1100	66	2	7	55

	Cal	Total Fat (g)	Sat Fat (g)	Chol (mg)	Sodium (mg)	Total Carbs (g)	Fiber (g)	Total Sugar (g)	Protein (g)
PORK AND LAMB (CONTINUED)									
Stir-Fried Pork, Eggplant, and Onions with Garlic and Black Pepper	320	15	2	60	660	22	4	12	26
Stir-Fried Pork, Asparagus, and Red Bell Pepper with Gingery Oyster Sauce for Two	*450*	*25*	*3.5*	*125*	*930*	*8*	*2*	*3*	*47*
Pulled Pork Tacos with Radish-Apple Slaw	900	43	11	155	2320	75	10	28	54
Pulled Pork Tacos with Radish-Apple Slaw for Two	*1050*	*65*	*17*	*150*	*1910*	*76*	*13*	*34*	*47*
Vietnamese Pork Banh Mi	440	25	4.5	230	610	27	2	7	27
Philadelphia Roast Pork Sandwiches with Broccoli Rabe	580	35	11	30	680	46	5	8	22
Skillet Sausage and Cheese Pizza	760	41	15	65	1820	62	1	12	36
Skillet Fontina, Arugula, and Prosciutto Pizza for Two	*770*	*44*	*15*	*75*	*1940*	*65*	*2*	*13*	*30*
Pork Sausage with Polenta	680	40	17g	100	2320	41	3	9	40
Pork Sausage with White Beans and Mustard Greens	590	30	12g	75	1470	34	7	3	44
Bratwurst Sandwiches with Red Potato and Kale Salad	1140	78	21	125	2620	69	3	7	35
Italian Stuffed Bell Peppers	410	20	8	45	1340	35	4	8	24
Milk-Can Supper	690	44	14	105	1570	45	7	9	25
Chorizo, Corn, and Tomato Tostadas with Lime Crema	840	45	17	80	1420	29	7	9	29
Braised Country-Style Ribs with Black-Eyed Peas and Collard Greens	340	14	4.5	95	580	20	5	2	33
Spiced Pork Loin with Butternut Squash and Brussels Sprouts									
Sheet Pan	*460*	*18*	*3.5*	*120*	*990*	*29*	*6*	*9*	*46*
Skillet	*410*	*19*	*3.5*	*90*	*1160*	*24*	*7*	*5*	*38*
Roasting Pan	*490*	*19*	*4*	*115*	*1160*	*35*	*7*	*11*	*45*
Braised Pork with Broccoli Rabe and Sage	410	27	9	105	790	6	3	1	31
Caraway-Crusted Pork Tenderloin with Sauerkraut and Apples	340	11	1.5	110	1300	24	5	16	36
Pork Tenderloin with Fennel, Tomatoes, Artichokes, and Olives	390	16	3	110	790	21	5	9	41
Spiced Pork Tenderloin with Raisin-Almond Couscous	600	35	5	110	540	29	1	15	40
Spiced Pork Tenderloin with Cherry-Pepita Couscous for Two	*670*	*37*	*6*	*150*	*650*	*27*	*1*	*9*	*53*
Pork Tenderloin and Panzanella Salad	590	33	5	110	1040	28	3	10	40
Pork Loin en Cocotte with Kale, Shallots, and Mustard	370	16	3.5	100	370	18	5	8	38
Pork Loin en Cocotte with Barley, Butternut Squash, and Swiss Chard	460	15	3	100	970	38	7	4	41
Roasted Pork Loin with Sweet Potatoes and Cilantro Sauce	610	32g	5g	95	640	42	8	13	38
Bacon-Wrapped Pork Loin with Roasted Red Potatoes and Peach Sauce	570	25	8	130	1120	38g	4	11	45
Pork Loin with Warm Spiced Chickpea Salad	380	14	3	100	750	22	6	5	41
Spicy Pork Tinga and Rice	480	20	6	90	850	43	2	4	31
Spiced Pork and Orzo Casserole	260	8	3	15	280	33	1	4	10
Green Chile–Chorizo Enchiladas	680	44	17	90	1350	46	5	12	29
Mustard-Thyme Lamb Chops with Roasted Carrots	510	24	6	125	880	31	7	19	41
Mustard-Rosemary Lamb Chops with Roasted Parsnips for Two	*640*	*30*	*7*	*125*	*750*	*50*	*11*	*19*	*42*

	Cal	Total Fat (g)	Sat Fat (g)	Chol (mg)	Sodium (mg)	Total Carbs (g)	Fiber (g)	Total Sugar (g)	Protein (g)
PORK AND LAMB (CONTINUED)									
Lamb Chops with Shaved Zucchini Salad	390	20	7	110	720	14	2	9	38
Herbed Leg of Lamb with Fingerling Potatoes and Asparagus	390	14	4.5	110	510	25	5	3	39
Lamb Meatballs with Couscous and Pickled Onions	640	36	13	85	790	51	4	8	29
Lamb Meatballs with Couscous and Pickled Onions for Two	*640*	*32*	*13*	*85*	*980*	*59*	*7*	*15*	*31*
Lamb Meatballs with Orzo and Tomatoes	880	51	23	190	1610	55	2	8	45
Lamb Pita Sandwiches	580	32	15	105	1010	43	1	7	30
SEAFOOD									
Roasted Salmon with Broccoli, Red Potatoes, and Mustard Sauce	780	52	10	125	1100	26	5	5	52
Pan-Seared Paprika Salmon with Spicy Green Beans	580	38	8	125	880	10	3	3	49
Sweet and Sour Salmon with Bok Choy	690	44	8	125	860	23	1	20	48
Sweet and Sour Salmon with Bok Choy for Two	*700*	*44*	*8*	*125*	*860*	*26*	*1*	*22*	*48*
Glazed Salmon with Black-Eyed Peas, Walnuts, and Pomegranate	830	50	9	125	990	39	7	13	56
Salmon with Lemon-Garlic Mashed Cauliflower	590	39	8	125	680	9	3	3	50
Salmon with Mediterranean Rice Salad	850	53	12	135	860	40	2	6	51
Salmon with Spiced Chickpea, Cucumber, and Tomato Salad									
Dutch Oven	*610*	*32*	*5*	*105*	*1000*	*25*	*8*	*3*	*55*
Slow Cooker	*610*	*32*	*5*	*105*	*1000*	*25*	*8*	*3*	*55*
Instant Pot	*610*	*32*	*5*	*105*	*1000*	*25*	*8*	*3*	*55*
Salmon Burgers with Asparagus and Lemon-Herb Sauce	550	34	7	70	870	31	2	6	30
Salmon Burgers with Charred Cabbage and Wasabi Mayonnaise for Two	*880*	*53*	*10*	*135*	*1110*	*44*	*7*	*10*	*56*
Salmon Tacos with Collards and Radish Slaw	510	26	4	95	530	33	3	4	38
Seared Trout with Brussels Sprouts and Bacon	470	29	5	105	960	10	4	2	42
Roasted Cod with Artichokes, Olives, and Sun-Dried Tomatoes	380	19	1.5	75	1070	16	1	1	35
Cod Baked in Foil with Leeks and Carrots	300	12	7	105	710	11	2	4	32
Cod Baked in Foil with Zucchini and Tomatoes for Two	*240*	*9*	*1.5*	*75*	*830*	*8*	*2*	*5*	*33*
Cod with Warm Beet and Arugula Salad	340	16	2.5	75	430	14	4	9	33
Lemon-Herb Cod Fillets with Crispy Garlic Potatoes	400	15	9	110	680	32	2	1	34
Halibut with Red Potatoes, Corn, and Andouille	750	41	13	165	1740	46	5	8	54
Halibut with Warm Bean Salad	340	13	2	85	640	17	5	5	37
Cod with Warm Tabbouleh Salad	380	12	2	75	690	32	7	2	36
Braised Halibut with Leeks and Mustard	370	19	11	130	740	8	1	2	32
Braised Halibut with Carrots and Coriander for Two	*400*	*19*	*11*	*130*	*770*	*15*	*4*	*7*	*33*
Braised Striped Bass with Zucchini and Tomatoes	310	12	2	135	1010	17	4	10	34
Braised Cod with Peperonata	280	9	1.5	75	860	12	2	6	32
Thai Curry Rice with Cod	540	14	9	75	1120	63	1	2	38
Hake in Saffron Broth with Chorizo and Potatoes	370	16	4	60	860	14	2	2	38
Fish Tagine with Artichoke Hearts	210	4	0	50	1030	16	1	5	25

	Cal	Total Fat (g)	Sat Fat (g)	Chol (mg)	Sodium (mg)	Total Carbs (g)	Fiber (g)	Total Sugar (g)	Protein (g)
SEAFOOD (CONTINUED)									
Bouillabaisse	110	7	1	0	360	6	1	3	1
California-Style Fish Tacos	580	25	5	100	730	49	3	7	39
Shrimp Fajitas	560	28	5	215	1710	44	2	7	31
Mediterranean Shrimp	350	13	4.5	205	1700	28	3	4	27
Mediterranean Shrimp for Two	*550*	*24*	*7*	*310*	*2540*	*43*	*4*	*6*	*40*
Shrimp with Spiced Quinoa and Corn Salad	400	16	4	155	830	40	5	5	26
Shrimp and Asparagus Risotto	620	21	4.5	155	950	71	3	2	35
Cajun-Style Rice with Andouille, Shrimp, and Okra	530	16	4.5	155	2020	62	2	6	37
Indoor Paella	660	25	7	210	1510	58	3	4	48
Indoor Paella for Two	*830*	*41*	*11*	*245*	*1950*	*61*	*3*	*5*	*54*
Shrimp Skewers with Cheesy Grits	430	20	12	195	1070	33	3	2	28
Stir-Fried Shrimp and Broccoli	220	9	1	145	1030	12	3	4	19
Stir-Fried Shrimp and Asparagus in Garlic Sauce for Two	*220*	*9*	*1*	*145*	*1070*	*14*	*4*	*5*	*21*
Thai Green Curry with Shrimp, Snow Peas, and Shiitakes	660	51	39	215	810	24	2	11	30
South Carolina Shrimp Boil	380	15	4.5	195	1420	29	3	6	35
Crab Cakes with Roasted Corn and Old Bay Fries	550	27	5	135	1110	47	5	9	33
Seared Scallops with Warm Barley Salad	510	17	3.5	55	164	57	11	9	31
Baked Scallops with Couscous, Leeks and Tarragon-Orange Vinaigrette	490	19	2.5	40	1350	50	1	3	28
Roasted Mussels with Tomato and Chorizo	970	59	19	215	3000	29	0	5	76
VEGETARIAN									
Pot-Roasted Cauliflower with Tomatoes and Olives	190	7	1.5	5	910	25	5	14	8
Stuffed Spiced Eggplants with Tomatoes and Pine Nuts	240	17	4	10	560	17	5	9	7
Stir-Fried Eggplant	240	13	1	0	440	21	5	11	4
Sesame-Basil Stir-Fried Eggplant For Two	*290*	*18*	*1.5*	*0*	*720*	*23*	*5*	*14*	*5*
Spaghetti Squash with Fresh Tomato Sauce	240	13	2	0	680	33	8	15	4
Spaghetti Squash and Black Bean Casserole	400	24	4.5	10	960	41	11	9	11
Spiced Winter Squash with Halloumi and Shaved Brussels Sprouts	470	28	12	45	1070	40	7	13	18
Beet and Wheat Berry Salad with Arugula and Apples	260	12	4	10	420	33	6	7	9
Beet and Wheat Berry Salad with Kale and Pear for Two	*640*	*35*	*14*	*45*	*1280*	*52*	*11*	*10*	*31*
Vegetable Curry with Potatoes and Cauliflower	270	12	4.5	0	480	33	9	7	8
Vegetable Curry with Sweet Potato and Eggplant for Two	*110*	*7*	*4*	*0*	*95*	*12*	*4*	*4*	*2*
Thai Vegetable Green Curry with Jasmine Rice Cakes	640	33	21	45	1230	79	3	9	13
Spanakopita	160	8	5	55	370	14	1	1	7
Shakshuka	550	28	6	380	1610	50	2	11	23
Shakshuka for Two	*560*	*28*	*6*	*380*	*1630*	*50*	*2*	*11*	*24*
Green Shakshuka	410	27	7	385	1260	22	8	6	23
Huevos Rancheros	720	43	11	395	1870	59	12	17	27
Fried Eggs with Parmesan and Potato Roesti	580	30	15	420	1010	52	0	0	22
Shiitake Mushroom Frittata with Pecorino Romano	360	24	9	575	760	11	3	5	26
Broccoli and Feta Frittata for Two	*360*	*25*	*10*	*585*	*940*	*9*	*2*	*4*	*26*

	Cal	Total Fat (g)	Sat Fat (g)	Chol (mg)	Sodium (mg)	Total Carbs (g)	Fiber (g)	Total Sugar (g)	Protein (g)
VEGETARIAN (CONTINUED)									
Philly-Style Broccoli Rabe, Portobello, and Cheese Sandwiches	490	27	10	35	1200	43	3	8	14
Tofu, Thai Chile, and Basil Lettuce Cups	270	17	2.5	0	760	15	3	7	16
Crispy Tofu with Warm Cabbage Salad	480	31	2.5	0	540	35	4	8	16
Butternut Squash, Poblano, and Corn Tacos	500	16	2.5	5	700	84	7	30	11
Sweet Potato, Poblano, and Corn Tacos for Two	*510*	*15*	*2.5*	*5*	*760*	*85*	*8*	*33*	*10*
Baja-Style Cauliflower Tacos with Mango Cabbage Slaw	630	40	26	10	790	66	7	13	11
Mushroom and Swiss Chard Quesadillas with Avocado Salad	780	64	17	50	1290	37	10	7	21
Sheet Pan Veggie Pizza	810	38	14	50	1630	86	2	15	33
Skillet Veggie Pizza for Two	*840*	*48*	*15*	*50*	*1610*	*71*	*3*	*15*	*31*
Pizza al Taglio with Arugula and Fresh Mozzarella	450	19	3.5	5	1030	54	3	2	14
Fennel, Olive, and Goat Cheese Tarts	450	32	13	15	440	37	4	5	11
Potato, Artichoke, and Sun-Dried Tomato Tart for Two	*570*	*35*	*14*	*15*	*560*	*58*	*4*	*4*	*15*
Pearl Couscous with Tomatoes and Chickpeas	480	13	1.5	0	1040	79	7	10	16
Vegetable and Orzo Tian	360	11	4	15	560	48	3	8	19
Brown Rice and Black Beans with Corn and Tomatoes	280	7	0.5	0	480	54	4	4	9
Spiced Lentil and Rice Pilaf									
Saucepan	*560*	*15*	*4*	*5*	*260*	*88*	*9*	*4*	*21*
Saucepan	*590*	*19*	*4.5*	*5*	*370*	*87*	*9*	*3*	*20*
Dutch Oven	*550*	*15*	*4*	*5*	*280*	*87*	*9*	*3*	*20*
Mushroom Biryani	320	11	2	5	440	47	2	10	8
Risotto with Fava Beans, Peas, and Arugula	450	12	6	25	520	66	8	9	18
Risotto with Mushrooms, Asparagus, and Peas for Two	*440*	*22*	*1*	*3*	*880*	*45*	*3*	*4*	*14*
Wild Mushroom Farrotto	280	10	2.5	5	41	35	4	2	12
Parmesan Polenta with Broccoli Rabe, Sun-Dried Tomatoes, and Pine Nuts	450	33	11	40	920	29	6	1	14
Baked Quinoa with Kale and Chickpeas	290	11	1.5	0	800	39	8	1	11
Quinoa and Vegetable Lettuce Cups with Feta and Mint	320	14	4	15	470	37	5	8	12
Bulgur with Chickpeas, Spinach, and Za'atar	200	8	1	0	350	28	6	1	6
Lentil Salad with Dill, Orange, and Spinach	350	18	2	0	340	40	11	8	13
Lentil Salad with Radishes, Cilantro, and Pepitas for Two	*410*	*23*	*4.5*	*10*	*450*	*37*	*10*	*4*	*17*
PASTA AND NOODLES									
Penne with Fresh Tomato Sauce	360	9	1	0	300	61	2	5	11
Penne with Fresh Tomato Sauce for Two	*410*	*9*	*1*	*0*	*310*	*71*	*3*	*7*	*12*
Pasta Puttanesca	360	9	1	0	360	61	2	5	11
Penne with Chicken, Broccoli, and Bell Pepper	630	23	4.5	95	1300	57	5	7	45
Penne with Chicken, Mushrooms, and Gorgonzola for Two	*740*	*29*	*9*	*110*	*1410*	*68*	*0*	*4*	*41*
Orecchiette with Broccoli Rabe and Sausage	450	13	3.5	20	930	60	2	2	23
Weeknight Bolognese	600	20	7	75	1120	59	0	3	36
Slow-Cooked Pork Ragu with Ziti	550	13	3	85	1090	68	4	8	35
Hands-Off Spaghetti and Meatballs	800	34	10	80	1470	87	0	11	38
Hands-Off Spaghetti and Meatballs for Two	*780*	*32*	*10*	*80*	*1410*	*86*	*0*	*11*	*37*

	Cal	Total Fat (g)	Sat Fat (g)	Chol (mg)	Sodium (mg)	Total Carbs (g)	Fiber (g)	Total Sugar (g)	Protein (g)
PASTA AND NOODLES (CONTINUED)									
Baked Ziti									
Dutch Oven	*680*	*24*	*13*	*65*	*2190*	*81*	*5*	*14*	*37*
Skillet	*680*	*24*	*13*	*65*	*2190*	*81*	*5*	*14*	*37*
Roasting Pan	*520*	*17*	*9*	*40*	*1510*	*67*	*3*	*9*	*27*
Bucatini with Peas, Kale, and Pancetta	420	9	2.5	10	630	66	2	3	17
Lemony Spaghetti with Shrimp and Spinach	570	19	5	110	500	60	1	2	23
Mussels Marinara with Spaghetti	530	12	1.5	45	1110	74	3	9	30
Mussels Marinara with Spaghetti for Two	*690*	*16*	*2.5*	*65*	*1660*	*91*	*4*	*13*	*42*
Creamy Spring Vegetable Linguine	380	9	3.5	15	720	60	1	3	17
Tortellini with Fennel, Peas, and Spinach	650	28	14	105	1520	68	4	9	31
Easiest-Ever Tomato and Cheese Lasagna	490	27	15	70	1190	35	0	11	29
Easiest-Ever Tomato and Cheese Lasagna for Two	*520*	*29*	*16*	*75*	*1320*	*35*	*0*	*11*	*32*
Sausage Lasagna with Spinach and Mushrooms	540	26	14	80	2440	39	4	12	43
Cheesy Butternut Squash and Swiss Chard Lasagna	610	39	22	110	1240	42	4	9	28
Baked Macaroni and Cheese	770	31	17	95	1660	80	0	11	40
Pastitsio	740	45	25	155	1050	50	4	10	32
Unstuffed Shells with Butternut Squash and Leeks	800	37	21	100	820	88	4	8	28
Fideos with Chickpeas and Fennel	460	15	1.5	0	970	66	8	8	14
Fideos with Chickpeas and Fennel for Two	*490*	*16*	*1*	*0*	*1120*	*71*	*11*	*8*	*17*
Sopa Seca with Chorizo and Black Beans	550	24	7	40	1230	63	2	6	23
Drunken Noodles with Chicken	520	10	1	60	1540	78	2	29	28
Drunken Noodles with Chicken for Two	*540*	*13*	*1*	*60*	*1420*	*78*	*2*	*29*	*27*
Thai-Style Stir-Fried Noodles with Chicken and Broccolini	530	17	2.5	200	1280	60	1	9	31
Ramen with Beef, Shitakes, and Spinach	390	12	3	50	1070	44	1	4	24
Ramen with Pork and Cabbage for Two	*570*	*17*	*3*	*85*	*1940*	*67*	*3*	*6*	*36*
Pork Pad Thai	450	17	4	85	800	45	1	11	29
Pork Lo Mein	430	19	3.5	100	1390	29	4	20	32
Singapore Noodles	540	26	3	265	750	58	4	6	22
Udon Noodles with Mustard Greens and Shiitake-Ginger Sauce	150	3.5	0	0	610	36	4	5	8
Chilled Soba Noodles with Cucumbers, Snow Peas, and Radishes	350	10	1	0	500	52	1	11	11
DESSERTS									
Honey-Glazed Roasted Peaches	170	7	2.5	10	100	29	3	25	2
Raspberry-Glazed Peaches with Walnuts for Two	*180*	*8*	*4*	*15*	*75*	*27*	*2*	*23*	*2*
Roasted Pears with Dried Apricots and Pistachios	400	12	5	20	80	60	8	44	3
Roasted Pears with Golden Raisins and Hazelnuts for Two	*450*	*15*	*6*	*25*	*85*	*67*	*7*	*53*	*3*
Roasted Figs with Balsamic Glaze and Mascarpone	300	14	6	30	10	42	4	36	4
Stuffed Apples with Dried Cherries and Hazelnuts	430	19	10	40	30	61	8	46	3

	Cal	Total Fat (g)	Sat Fat (g)	Chol (mg)	Sodium (mg)	Total Carbs (g)	Fiber (g)	Total Sugar (g)	Protein (g)
DESSERTS (CONTINUED)									
Red Wine–Poached Pears with Black Pepper and Cloves	240	0	0	0	45	43	4	33	1
White Wine–Poached Pears with Lemon and Herbs for Two	*450*	*0*	*0*	*0*	*85*	*69*	*6*	*54*	*1*
Bananas Foster	470	18	11	60	210	64	2	52	3
Warm Peach-Raspberry Compote	340	10	6	40	150	58	5	46	5
Blueberry Grunt	270	6	3.5	15	220	51	2	27	4
Cherry Cobbler	400	6	3.5	15	250	83	2	25	5
Cherry Cobbler for Two	*570*	*12*	*7*	*30*	*450*	*114*	*2*	*48*	*6*
Pear-Ginger Crisp	410	18	8	35	60	63	10	40	4
Bread Pudding									
Slow Cooker	*490*	*30*	*16*	*245*	*460*	*44*	*0*	*22*	*11*
Casserole	*520*	*32*	*18*	*250*	*460*	*48*	*0*	*26*	*11*
Instant Pot	*410*	*25*	*14*	*220*	*340*	*37*	*0*	*19*	*9*
Blueberry Pie	620	33	16	75	320	76	3	35	6
Easy Apple Galettes	230	9	5	10	125	36	2	20	3
Easy Apple Galette for Two	*240*	*9*	*5*	*10*	*125*	*36*	*3*	*20*	*3*
Apple Strudel	310	13	8	35	150	47	0	24	4
Apple Strudel for Two	*490*	*20*	*12*	*55*	*220*	*73*	*4*	*35*	*5*
Crepes with Chocolate and Orange	400	17	9	165	240	53	0	24	12
Crepes with Honey and Toasted Almonds for Two	*330*	*13*	*6*	*115*	*510*	*43*	*0*	*17*	*10*
German Pancake	510	18	9	310	440	63	0	18	19
Chocolate Chip Skillet Cookie	480	24	15	90	380	64	1	39	5
Easy Chocolate Chunk Brownies	580	29	9	85	190	81	1	57	7
Chocolate Lava Cake	420	17	10	60	250	68	1	45	4
Chocolate Lava Cake for Two	*470*	*20*	*11*	*125*	*200*	*71*	*1*	*46*	*5*
Pour Over Peach Cake	350	13	8	80	260	53	1	32	5
New York–Cheesecake	360	26	17	140	350	24	0	20	6
Spiced Pumpkin Cheesecake	300	19	12	110	290	25	1	20	5

CONVERSIONS AND EQUIVALENTS

Some say cooking is a science and an art. We would say that geography has a hand in it, too. Flours and sugars manufactured in the United Kingdom and elsewhere will feel and taste different from those manufactured in the United States. So we cannot promise that the loaf of bread you bake in Canada or England will taste the same as a loaf baked in the States, but we can offer guidelines for converting weights and measures. We also recommend that you rely on your instincts when making our recipes. Refer to the visual cues provided. If the dough hasn't "come together in a ball" as described, you may need to add more flour—even if the recipe doesn't tell you to. You be the judge.

The recipes in this book were developed using standard U.S. measures following U.S. government guidelines. The charts below offer equivalents for U.S. and metric measures. All conversions are approximate and have been rounded up or down to the nearest whole number.

EXAMPLE

1 teaspoon = 4.9292 milliliters, rounded up to 5 milliliters
1 ounce = 28.3495 grams, rounded down to 28 grams

VOLUME CONVERSIONS

U.S.	METRIC
1 teaspoon	5 milliliters
2 teaspoons	10 milliliters
1 tablespoon	15 milliliters
2 tablespoons	30 milliliters
¼ cup	59 milliliters
⅓ cup	79 milliliters
½ cup	118 milliliters
¾ cup	177 milliliters
1 cup	237 milliliters
1¼ cups	296 milliliters
1½ cups	355 milliliters
2 cups (1 pint)	473 milliliters
2½ cups	591 milliliters
3 cups	710 milliliters
4 cups (1 quart)	0.946 liter
1.06 quarts	1 liter
4 quarts (1 gallon)	3.8 liters

WEIGHT CONVERSIONS

OUNCES	GRAMS
½	14
¾	21
1	28
1½	43
2	57
2½	71
3	85
3½	99
4	113
4½	128
5	142
6	170
7	198
8	227
9	255
10	283
12	340
16 (1 pound)	454

CONVERSIONS FOR COMMON BAKING INGREDIENTS

Baking is an exacting science. Because measuring by weight is far more accurate than measuring by volume, and thus more likely to produce reliable results, in our recipes we provide ounce measures in addition to cup measures for many ingredients. Refer to the chart below to convert these measures into grams.

INGREDIENT	OUNCES	GRAMS
Flour		
1 cup all-purpose flour*	5	142
1 cup cake flour	4	113
1 cup whole-wheat flour	5½	156
Sugar		
1 cup granulated (white) sugar	7	198
1 cup packed brown sugar (light or dark)	7	198
1 cup confectioners' sugar	4	113
Cocoa Powder		
1 cup cocoa powder	3	85
Butter†		
4 tablespoons (½ stick or ¼ cup)	2	57
8 tablespoons (1 stick or ½ cup)	4	113
16 tablespoons (2 sticks or 1 cup)	8	227

* U.S. all-purpose flour, the most frequently used flour in this book, does not contain leaveners, as some European flours do. These leavened flours are called self-rising or self-raising. If you are using self-rising flour, take this into consideration before adding leaveners to a recipe.

† In the United States, butter is sold both salted and unsalted. We generally recommend unsalted butter. If you are using salted butter, take this into consideration before adding salt to a recipe.

OVEN TEMPERATURES

FAHRENHEIT	CELSIUS	GAS MARK
225	105	¼
250	120	½
275	135	1
300	150	2
325	165	3
350	180	4
375	190	5
400	200	6
425	220	7
450	230	8
475	245	9

CONVERTING TEMPERATURES FROM AN INSTANT-READ THERMOMETER

We include doneness temperatures in many of the recipes in this book. We recommend an instant-read thermometer for the job. Refer to the table above to convert Fahrenheit degrees to Celsius. Or, for temperatures not represented in the chart, use this simple formula:

Subtract 32 degrees from the Fahrenheit reading, then divide the result by 1.8 to find the Celsius reading.

EXAMPLE

"Roast chicken until thighs register 175 degrees."

To convert:
$$160°F - 32 = 128°$$
$$128° \div 1.8 = 71.11°C, \text{ rounded down to } 71°C$$

INDEX

Note: Page references in *italics* indicate photographs.